LEMON-AID
USED CARS
2002

LEMON-AID
USED CARS
2002

PHIL EDMONSTON

Published in 2001 by Stoddart Publishing Co. Limited
895 Don Mills Road, 400-2 Park Centre, Toronto, Canada M3C 1W3

Distributed by:
General Distribution Services Ltd.
325 Humber College Boulevard, Toronto, Canada M9W 7C3
Tel. (416) 213-1919   Fax (416) 213-1917

Email cservice@genpub.com

Canadian Cataloguing in Publication Data

The National Library of Canada has catalogued this publication as follows:

Edmonston, Louis-Philippe, 1944–
Lemon-Aid used cars

Annual.
1998–
ISSN 1485-1121
ISBN 0-7737-6182-9 (2002)
1. Used cars — Purchasing — Periodicals. I. Title.

TL162.E3398   629.222   C98-300799-3

Cover design: Bill Douglas @ The Bang
Typesetting and text design: Worldstyle Productions
Editing: Moira Bayne, Colborne Communications
Proofreading: Jennifer Sweetlove and Paula Krulicki,
Colborne Communications

THE CANADA COUNCIL | LE CONSEIL DES ARTS
FOR THE ARTS | DU CANADA
SINCE 1957 | DEPUIS 1957

We acknowledge for their financial support of our publishing program the Canada Council, the Ontario Arts Council, and the Government of Canada through the Book Publishing Industry Development Program (BPIDP).

Printed and bound in Canada

CONTENTS

Key Documents
ix

Introduction/STEALS AND DEALS
1

Part One/GET THE BEST FOR LESS
3

Part Two/FIGHTING BACK!
49

Part Three/VEHICLE RATINGS:
THE GOOD, THE BAD, AND THE UGLY!
118

SMALL CARS
125

MEDIUM CARS
180

LARGE CARS/WAGONS
273

LUXURY CARS
295

SPORTS CARS
372

MINIVANS
412

Key Documents

The following photos, charts, documents, memos, and service bulletins are included in this index so that you can easily find and photocopy whichever document will prove helpful in your dealings with automakers, government agencies, dealers, or service managers. Most of the service bulletins outline repairs or replacements that should be done for free.

Part One

Get the Best for Less

Part Two

Legal Rights and Wrongs

Part Three

Vehicle Ratings
Service Bulletins and Secret Warranties

Introduction
STEALS AND DEALS

The 29th edition of *Lemon-Aid Used Cars* is unlike any other auto book on the market. Its main objective, to inform and protect consumers in an industry known for its dishonesty and exaggerated claims, remains unchanged. However, this guide also focuses on secret warranties and confidential service bulletins that automakers swear don't exist. That's why you'll be interested in the "Key Documents" list found on the previous pages. There you'll find the exact bulletin, memo, or news clipping reproduced from the original so neither the dealer nor the automaker can weasel out of its obligations.

Lemon-Aid's information is culled mostly from Canadian and U.S. sources and is gathered throughout the year from owner complaints, whistleblowers, lawsuits, and judgments, as well as from confidential manufacturer service bulletins.

Each year, we target abusive auto industry practices and lobby for changes. For example, in last year's guide, we:
• blasted General Motors for ABS brakes that don't brake;
• exposed engine defects on 1991–97 Saturns;
• highlighted Chrysler's automatic transmission, engine head gasket, paint, and brake problems, and downgraded ratings on its minivans;
• kept pressure on Ford over its failure-prone Taurus, Sable, and Windstar 3.8L engine head gaskets, automatic transmissions, ACs, and brakes;
• blew the whistle on deadly airbags, using unpublicized U.S. and Canadian government studies that showed death and severe injuries are the prices women and seniors routinely pay for airbags that deploy during fender-bender accidents or inadvertently when the vehicle is started.

Following *Lemon-Aid*'s urging, Chrysler continues to use a special review committee (see Part Two) to compensate owners even if their warranty has expired or they have been refused a refund in the past. Ford extended its warranty to 7 years/160,000 km for engine gasket failures affecting 1994–95 Sables, Tauruses, and Windstars; and 1996–97 Thunderbirds, Cougars, and Mustangs; and 1997 F-Series trucks equipped with a 3.8L or 4.2L engine. Ford has also paid off owners with engine claims falling outside of the above parameters under its "after warranty adjustment" (AWA) programs and by empowering dealers to pay off claims through newly enacted P-05, P-06, and P-07 claims procedures. GM has also reacted by extending the warranty on 1994–96 Saturns and recalling millions of vehicles with faulty ABS brakes.

The above successes have come about because *Lemon-Aid* publishes *in toto* secret warranty memos, internal service bulletins, and bulletin summaries showing that many parts failures are factory related and are *not* the owner's responsibility. This year's guide expands its service bulletin listings and updates which vehicles are covered by "goodwill" programs long after the base warranty has expired.

This guide also makes a critical comparison of 1991–99 cars and minivans. Furthermore, comprehensive crash ratings, troubleshooting shortcuts taken from actual service bulletins, and sample complaint letters with jurisprudence are included.

Our goal for almost 29 years: to put you into a safe, reliable, and reasonably priced vehicle—with a minimum of fear and loathing.

Phil Edmonston
March 2001

Part One
GET THE BEST FOR LESS

How To Be a Millionaire

"Thirty-seven percent of millionaires buy used cars, which is one reason why they're so well off..."

Getting Rich in America
Dwight R. Lee and
Richard B. McKenzie

This woman's '96 Windstar needed a new $3,200 automatic transmission after only 62,000 km. Ford wanted her to pay $800. After she took her sign off, Ford paid over 90 percent of the bill.

Okay, so I may be a car curmudgeon, but I've earned the title over the past 30 years battling automakers that routinely cheat customers and treat their dealers as serfs. When I founded the Automobile Protection Association (APA) in Montreal in the fall of 1969, American Motors was giving out free television sets with the purchase of their problem-plagued Concorde and Hornet (actually, the television sets lasted longer than their cars); Volkswagen had a monopoly on hazardous, poorly heated, and sluggish Beetles and minivans; Ford was churning out biodegradable rustbuckets (and denying they had a secret "J-67" warranty to cover repairs); Firestone was dragged, kicking and screaming, into announcing an 11-million tire recall; and the Chrysler Valiant and Dart were the epitome of reliability (except for chronic stalling when it rained). Imagine, when the first guides were written a few years after the APA founding, a good, 3-year-old used vehicle could be had for less than $1,500; the average price now tops $7,500.

3

Garbage in, garbage out: 1970–90

Japanese and European cars imported into Canada during the early '70s were junk—as thousands of owners of rust-cankered Fiats, Hondas, Toyotas, and Nissans will confirm.

How did they get a toehold in the North American market? The Big Three's products were worse. Seizing the opportunity, foreign automakers smaretened up quickly. They started building reliable, durable cars and trucks and selling them fully loaded for reasonable prices.

Meanwhile, American automakers continued to pump out junk for another decade—small cars like GM's Chevy Vega, Firenza, and Fiero; Chrysler's Omni, Horizon, Dynasty, Imperial, and Concorde; and Ford's Pinto, Bobcat, Tempo, Topaz, and Merkur.

The Pinto was Ford's rolling Molotov cocktail, catching fire and trapping occupants when hit from the rear. Ford knew of the danger before the first Pinto rolled off the assembly line but bowed to its accountants, who figured it would cost less to stonewall each future death and burn injury than to recall and redesign the fuel tank. They projected losses based upon 180 people burned to death and another 180 people severely burned over the Pinto's life span. Ford executives concluded it would be more "cost effective" to let drivers and passengers burn.

Savvy Canadian car buyers, turned off by poor-quality American vehicles, bought the cheaper, more reliable, and feature-laden Japanese compacts or re-badged imports like the GM Firefly and Metro, Dodge Colt, and Ford Probe.

Consequently, throughout the '80s, the quality of imports improved dramatically (Hyundai, Audi, and VW excepted), with Toyota and Honda leading the pack. American quality, on the other hand, improved at a snail's pace over the same period. Today, American cars' quality control is about where Japanese cars' was in the mid-'80s. Where the gap hasn't narrowed (and a case can be made that it's actually gotten wider) is in engine, automatic transmission, airbag, and anti-lock brake reliability, and fit and finish.

For example, take a look at the following three confidential internal service bulletins depicting serious automatic transmission problems with Chrysler, Ford, and GM cars and minivans. Note how the Big Three automakers have allowed the same defect to be carried over year after year.

Ford's "Biodegradable" Aluminum Transmissions

SUBJECT: Forward Piston Change
APPLICATION: Ford
DATE: 1995
Forward Piston Change
• No forward or reverse engagement.
• Delayed forward and/or reverse engagement.
• Shifts out of gear when coming to a stop.

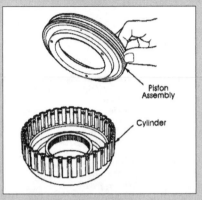

Piston
Assembly

Cylinder

All of these complaints can be attributed to a cracked or broken forward piston clutch. There have been three different versions of the aluminum piston in this location (the original plus two updates). Problems with cracking still persist.
A steel version of this part has been released that should prevent this from happening.
The Ford part number is F4DZ-7A262-A. The aluminum piston should always be replaced with the steel piston.

Failures with Ford's aluminum forward piston clutch affect most of the company's products made since 1986, though complaints on the most recent models target mainly the Taurus, Sable, and Windstar. In February 1999, Ford executives promised me that the company would give "goodwill" refunds on a case-by-case basis to new- or used-vehicle owners who had been previously denied compensation for this defect.

Chrysler's "Limping" Transmissions

NO: 18-24-95
GROUP: Veh. Performance
DATE: Jun. 23, 1995
SUBJECT:
Improved Transmission Shift Quality

MODELS:
1989-1995	(AA) Acclaim/Sprit/LeBaron Sedan
1989-1993	(AC) Dynasty/New Yorker/New Yorker Salon
1990-1993	(AG) Daytona
1990-1994	(AJ) LeBaron Coupe/LeBaron Convertible
1993-1994	(AP) Sundance/Shadow/Shadow Convertible
1990-1991	(AQ) Chrysler TC
1989-1995	(AS) Caravan/Voyager/Town & Country
1990-1992	(AY) Imperial/New Yorker Fifth Avenue
1993-1995	(ES) Chrysler Voyager (European Market)
**1995	(FJ) Sebring/Avenger/Talon**
1995	(JA) Cirrus/Stratus
1993-1995	(LH) Concorde/Intrepid/Vision/LHS/New Yorker

NOTE: THIS BULLETIN APPLIES TO VEHICLES EQUIPPED WITH THE 41TE OR 42LE TRANSAXLE.

SYMPTOM/CONDITION:

1992 AC. & AY VEHICLES BUILT AFTER FEB. 15, 1992 (MDH 02-15-XX). **1995 FJ VEHICLES** AND ALL OTHER 1993-1995 SUBJECT VEHICLES BUILT BEFORE OCT. 24, 1994, (MDH 10-24-XX) ARE VEHICLES EQUIPPED WITH AN ELECTRONICALLY MODU-LATED CONVERTOR CLUTCH (EMCC).

Vehicles that operate at speeds where EMCC usage is engaged (vehicle speeds 34 – 41 MPH) may experience early deteriora-tion of the transmission fluid (15,000 – 30,000 miles), exhibit a pronounced shudder during EMCC operation, harsh upshifts/downshifts, and/or harsh torque converter engagements. Performing REPAIR PROCEDURE # 2, which includes updates to the Transmission Control Module (TCM) calibration and eliminates EMCC, will resolve these symptoms/conditions. However, if an overheat condition is identified by the PCM or TCM, EMCC operation will be temporarily enabled.

ALL 1995 FJ VEHICLES AND ALL OTHER 1989-1995 SUBJECT VEHICLES BUILT BEFORE OCT. 24, 1994 (MDH 10-24-XX).

The TCM calibration used in the 1995 model year 41TE and 42LE TCM is being made available for all vehicles dating back to the 1989 model year. The shift quality improvements and default issues that will be corrected by the new TCM calibration are:

1. COASTDOWN TIP-IN BUMP: Vehicle is decelerated almost to a stop (less than 8 MPH), then the driver tips back into the throttle to accelerate, a noticeable bump may be felt.
2. COASTDOWN SHIFT HARSHNESS: Harsh coastdown shifts on some 4-3, 3-2, 2-1 downshifts.
3. 1995 LH WITH 42LE TRANSAXLE – SLUGGISHNESS/LACK OF RESPONSE: On some early 1995 LH vehicles built prior to Oct. 24, 1994, a perceived lack of power or transmission responsiveness may be encountered under normal operating conditions. The transmission may not release the converter clutch as desired with increased throttle. This occurs in 4th gear 35–50 MPH.
4. 1989-1994 WITH 41TE & 42LE TRANSAXLES: Harsh shifts and/or vehicle shudder during 3-2 or 2-1 kickdowns at speeds less than 25 MPH.
5. 1993 WITH 41TE TRANSAXLE: Harsh 3-4 upshifts may occur, especially at highway speeds, while using the speed control.
6. 1989-1994 WITH 41TE TRANSAXLE – HARSH/DELAYED GARAGE SHIFTS: Delay is less than 2 seconds and the shift is harsh after the brief delay. NOTE: Delays greater than 2 seconds are caused by transmission hardware malfunction, i.⑤., valve body, pump, failed lip seals, or malfunctioning PRNDL or neutral start switch.
7. EARLY 1993 WITH 41TE & 42LE TRANSAXLE – INTERMITTENT SPEED CONTROL DROP OUT: The new service calibration change corrects this condition (this condition was also covered in Technical Service Bulletin 08-09-93 dated Mar. 12, 1993).
8. 1989-1993 WITH 41TE & 42LE TRANSAXLES: New fault code 35 (failure to achieve pump prime) has been added for improved diagnostic capability, and fault codes 21, 22 and 24 are desensitized to reduce erroneous limp-in conditions.

Chrysler's problems are caused by both hardware and computer software glitches that affect almost its entire product line. Owners of 1991–97 vehicles should claim a "goodwill" repair refund from Chrysler. Hundreds of Chrysler claimants have received compensation up to 75 percent of the repair amount on vehicles not exceeding 100,000 miles (150,000 kilometres) when the transmission failed (see Part Two).

GM's "Neutral" Transmissions

Bulletin No.: 67-71-64
Date: February, 1997
Subject:
Intermittent Neutral or Loss of Drive at Highway Speeds or from Fourth Gear
(Replace Control Valve Body Assembly)
Models:
1995–96 Buick Skylark Regal, Century, Park Avenue, Riviera, LeSabre
1997 Buick Skylark, Regal, Century, LeSabre
1995 Cadillac DeVille
1995–96 Chevrolet Beretta, Corsica, Lumina APV, Lumina, Monte Carlo 1997 Chevrolet Lumina, Monte Carlo, Venture
1995–96 Oldsmobile Cutlass Ciera, Cutlass Cruiser, LSS, Ninety Eight, Ninety Eight Regency, Eighty Eight, Achieva, Silhouette, Cutlass Supreme
1997 Oldsmobile Eighty Eight, Achieva, Cutlass Supreme, LSS, Silhouette
1995–97 Pontiac Bonneville, Grand Am, Trans Sport, Grand Prix with HYDRA-MATIC 4T60-E Transaxle (RPO M13)
Condition
Some owners may comment about an intermittent, neutral condition while driving at highway speeds or intermittent neutral from fourth gear.
Cause
The 3–2 Manual Downshift valve may be sticking intermittently.

How's this for a scary scenario: you're cruising down the highway or in city traffic and the transmission of your 1995–97 GM front-wheel-drive car or minivan drops into "neutral." Another traffic fatality blamed on driver's error?

Good buys are out there

A year of record-breaking new-car sales has led to an unusually large number of reasonably priced, good-quality used cars and minivans coming on to the market. Most vehicles are now equipped with many of the essential safety features that were ignored by automakers two decades ago; overall reliability and durability have improved and are backed by longer warranties that are still in force; and millions of reasonably priced leased vehicles are now entering the used-car market. Right now, for example, Ford's popular Crown Victoria and Mercury Grand Marquis are coming off 2- and 3-year leases and are in abundant supply from both dealers and private parties.

J.D. Power and Associates says, "today's well-maintained, 2- to 4-year-old used cars are more reliable and less expensive to maintain than new cars were a decade ago." Furthermore, you can reduce your risk of buying a lemon by getting a recommended vehicle that has some of the original warranty in effect. This protects you from some of the costly defects that are bound to crop up shortly after your purchase. The warranty allows you to make one final inspection before it expires and requires both the dealer and the automaker to compensate you for all warrantable defects found at that time.

Five Reasons Canadians Buy Used

How popular are used cars in Canada? According to industry analyst Dennis DesRosiers, almost 3 million used vehicles change hands each year. Of that number, an estimated 70 percent are private sales. Why are people buying used? To save money. While the cost of cars in Canada has risen by an average of 4 percent since 1990, the Royal Bank of Canada says Canadians' take-home pay has grown by only 3.8 percent, meaning fewer and fewer people can afford a new car or minivan.

Following are the main reasons Canadians say they prefer buying used vehicles:

1. Less initial cash outlay, slower vehicle depreciation, and better and cheaper parts availability.
New-vehicle prices are going through the roof due to our declining dollar and the automakers' push for larger profits. The Automotive Industries Association of Canada (AIA) pegs the average cost for a new 1998 model vehicle at $26,139. Insurance for young drivers runs to about $4,000 a year—probably more than the monthly vehicle payment. And once you add GST, financing costs, maintenance, taxes, and a host of other expenses, the Canadian Automobile Association (CAA) calculates the yearly outlay at over $6,000, or 30.1¢/km for a compact car. Subcompact cars, like the Geo Metro, would cost about $5,476, or 24.3¢/km, a year; a standard-sized car would cost $8,252, or 36.7¢/km, per year. Operating expenses for minivans are a bit lower than for a standard-sized car due to their slower rate of depreciation, which is judged to be the biggest expense for most vehicles.

Be practical. When buying a used car or minivan, keep in mind you're simply buying transportation and function. You want no-surprise handling; a comfortable ride; reliable performance; and interior, cargo, and passenger capacity. Because you only need about one-half the cash or credit required for a new vehicle, it's easy to see that you won't have to invest as much money in a depreciating investment. You may even be fortunate enough to forgo a loan.

Depreciation savings
If someone were to ask you to invest in stocks or bonds guaranteed to be worth about half their initial purchase value after four or five years, you'd probably head for the door. But this is exactly the trap you're falling into when you buy a new vehicle that could depreciate 20 percent in the first year and 15 percent each year thereafter (minivans and other specialty vehicles like trucks and sport-utilities depreciate about 10 percent each subsequent year). Here's how a new car in Ontario adds up:

New-Car Cost

Purchase price	$20,000
Provincial tax (8%)	$1,600
Federal GST (7%)	$1,400
Total price	$23,000

Now, the motorist buying a new vehicle is certain that the warranty and status far outweigh any inconvenience. He or she happily forks over $23,000 and takes possession of a new car or minivan. If the motorist had a trade-in, its value would be subtracted from the negotiated price of the new vehicle, and sales tax would be paid on the reduced amount.

When you buy used, the situation is altogether different. That same vehicle can be purchased three years later, in good condition and with much of the manufacturer's warranty remaining, for about one-half to two-thirds of its original cost (in the truck and sport-utility market, depreciation may be a bit less). Look at what happens to the price:

Used-Car Cost

Manufacturer's Suggested Retail Price (MSRP)	($20,000)
Purchase price (three years old, 60,000 km)	$15,000
Provincial tax (8%)	$1,200
No GST (if sold privately)	—
Total price	$16,200

In this conservative example (some savings exceed 50 percent), the used-vehicle buyer saves $1,400 in federal taxes, $400 in provincial taxes, and gets a reliable, guaranteed set of wheels for about two-thirds of its original price. Furthermore, the depreciation "hit" will be much less in the ensuing years.

Parts
You don't want to put high-priced original equipment parts in your car or minivan. Studies carried out by the American Alliance of Independent Insurers show that the average car rebuilt with factory-supplied new parts would cost three times its initial selling price. For example, a 1999 Ford Taurus SE equipped with typical options would cost about $25,000 if purchased new in the States. Rebuilding it with factory parts would cost over $72,000 (U.S.); no wonder insurance companies prefer to scrap rather than repair.

Generally, a new gasoline-powered car or truck can be expected to run, relatively trouble-free, at least 200,000 km (125,000 miles) to 240,000 km (150,000 miles) in its lifetime, and a diesel-powered vehicle can easily triple those figures. Some repairs will crop up at regular intervals, and your yearly running costs, along with preventative maintenance, should average about $700–$800. Buttressing the argument that vehicles get cheaper to operate the longer you keep them, the U.S. Department of Transportation points out that the average vehicle requires one or more major repairs after every five years of use. However, once these repairs are done, it can then be run relatively trouble-free for another five years or more.

Time is on your side in other ways, too. Three years after a model's launching, the replacement-parts market catches up to consumer demand. Dealers stock larger inventories, and parts wholesalers and independent parts manufacturers expand their output. Used replacement parts are unquestionably easier to come by through bargaining with local garages or through a careful search of auto wreckers' yards. A reconditioned or used part usually costs one-third to one-half the cost of a new part. There's generally no difference in the quality of reconditioned mechanical components, and they're often guaranteed for as long as or longer than new ones. In fact, some savvy shoppers use the Part Three ratings in this guide to see which parts have a short life and then buy those parts from retailers that give lifetime warranties on their brakes, exhaust system, tires, batteries, etc.

Also, buying from discount outlets or independent garages or ordering through mail order houses can save you big bucks (30–35 percent) on the cost of new parts and another 15 percent on labour when compared with dealer charges. Price-Costco is another good example of savings realized through independent retailers. At Costco, you can buy replacement tires more cheaply than elsewhere and get free rotation, balancing, and other inspections during the life of the tire.

Body parts are a different story, however. Buyers would be wise to buy only original equipment manufacturer (OEM) parts supplied by automakers in order to get body panels that fit well, protect better in collisions, and have maximum rust resistance, says *Consumer Reports* in its February 1999 study. Although insurance appraisers often substitute cheaper, lower-quality aftermarket body parts in collision repairs, *Consumer Reports* found that 71 percent of those policyholders who requested OEM parts got them with little or no hassle. It suggests that consumers complain to their provincial Superintendent of Insurance if OEM parts aren't provided. If that doesn't produce the desired results, take out a small claims action or file a class action similar to the one recently won in the state of Illinois against State Farm (see page 117).

With many European imports, including those built in North America, you can count on a lot of aggravation and expense caused by the unacceptably slow distribution of parts and their high markup. Because these companies have a quasi-monopoly on replacement parts, there are few independent suppliers you can turn to for help. And auto wreckers, the last-chance repository for inexpensive car parts, are unlikely to carry foreign parts for vehicles more than three years old or manufactured in small numbers.

Finding parts for Japanese, South Korean, and domestic cars is hardly a problem, though, due to the large number of vehicles produced, the presence of hundreds of independent suppliers, the ease with which relatively simple parts can be interchanged from one model to another, and the large reservoir of used parts stocked by junkyards.

Auto clubs listed on the Internet are often helpful sources for parts that are otherwise unobtainable. Club members trade and sell specialty parts, keep a list of where rare parts can be found, and are usually well informed as to where independent parts suppliers are located. Most car enthusiast magazines will put you in touch with auto clubs and suppliers of hard-to-find parts.

2. There are lower insurance rates.

The difference in annual insurance costs between a new car or minivan and a used one may be only a few hundred dollars, but by carefully negotiating the deductible, the smart shopper can further reduce insurance premiums by another couple hundred dollars. For example, as an automobile gets older, the amount of the deductible should increase. It may reach a maximum of $500 per collision. As the deductible increases, the annual premium for collision coverage decreases.

The Vehicle Insurance Information Centre of Canada at *www.vice.com* lists which vehicles have the highest collision, comprehensive, and theft claim rates and cost the most to insure. The Centre can also be reached at 1-800-761-6703 or 416-445-5912.

3. There are fewer "hidden" defects.

Have your choice checked out by an independent mechanic (for $75–$100) before paying for a used vehicle. This examination before purchase protects you against any hidden defects the vehicle may have. It's also a tremendous negotiating tool since you can use the cost of any needed repairs to bargain down the purchase price.

It's easier to get permission to have the vehicle inspected if you promise to give the seller a copy of the inspection report should you decide not to buy it. If you still can't get permission to have the vehicle inspected elsewhere, walk away from the deal, no matter how tempting the selling price. The seller is obviously trying to put something over on you. Ignore the standard excuses that the vehicle isn't insured, the license plates have expired, or the vehicle has a dead battery.

4. You know the vehicle's history.

Smart customers will want to get answers to the following questions before paying a penny for any used vehicle: What did it first sell for and what is its present value? How much of the original warranty is left? How many times has the vehicle been recalled for safety-related defects? Are parts easily available? Does the vehicle have a history of costly performance-related defects that can be corrected under a secret warranty, through a safety recall campaign, or with an upgraded part? (See Part Three, "Secret Warranties/Service Tips.")

5. Litigation is quick, easy, and relatively inexpensive.

A multitude of federal and provincial consumer protection laws go far beyond whatever protection may be offered by the standard new-vehicle warranty. Furthermore, buyers of used vehicles don't usually have to conform to any arbitrary rules or service guidelines to get this protection.

Let's say you do get stuck with a lemon. Most small claims courts have a jurisdiction limit of $3,000–$10,000, which should cover the cost

of most used cars or minivans. Therefore, any dispute between buyer
and seller can be settled within a few months, without lawyers or excessive court costs. Furthermore, you're not likely to face a battery of
lawyers standing in for the automaker and dealer. Actually, you may not
have to face a judge since many cases are settled through court-
imposed mediators.

Safety Features

Before buying any used "bargain," determine what degree of active and
passive safety the vehicle provides. Passive safety assumes that you will be
involved in life-threatening situations and should be warned in time to
avoid injury. Daytime running lights and a third, centre-mounted brake
light are two passive safety features that do this job extremely well.

Passive safety features also assume some accidents aren't avoidable
and that when that accident occurs, the vehicle should provide as much
protection as possible to the driver, the vehicle's other occupants, and
other vehicles that may be struck—without depending on the driver's
reactions. Passive safety components that have consistently proven to
reduce vehicular deaths and injuries are safety belts and vehicle struc-
tures that enhance crashworthiness by absorbing or deflecting crash
forces away from the vehicle's occupants.

Advocates of active safety stress that accidents are caused by the
proverbial "nut behind the wheel" and believe that safe driving can best
be taught through schools or by private driving courses. Active safety
components are generally those mechanical systems, such as high-
performance tires and traction control, that may help avoid accidents
if the driver is skillful and mature.

The theory of active safety has several drawbacks. First, there's no
independent proof that safe driving can be taught successfully. Even if
a young driver learns how to master defensive-driving techniques,
there's still no assurance that this training will be of any use in an
emergency. Second, 40–50 percent of all fatal accidents are caused by
drivers who are under the influence of alcohol or drugs. Surely all the
high-performance options and specialized driving courses in the world
will not provide much protection from impaired drivers who draw a
bead on your vehicle. Finally, because active safety components get a lot
of use—you're likely to need anti-lock brakes 99 times more often than
an airbag—they have to be well maintained to remain effective.

Two safety features that may kill (ABS and airbags)
In the late '60s, Washington forced automakers to include essential
safety features like collapsing steering columns and safety windshields in
their cars. As the years have passed, the number of mandatory safety features has increased to include seatbelts, airbags, and crashworthy construction. These improvements met with public approval until five years
ago, when reports of deaths and injuries caused by ABS and airbag fail-

ures showed that defective components and poor engineering negated the potential life-saving benefits associated with these devices.

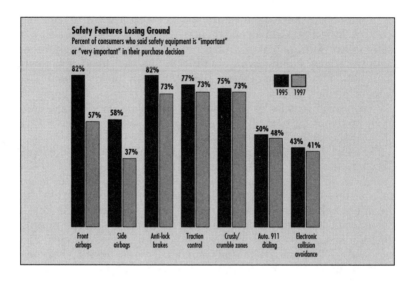

Safety Features Losing Ground
Percent of consumers who said safety equipment is "important" or "very important" in their purchase decision

Complicating matters further, owners of vehicles that have been recalled to correct dangerous airbags and anti-lock brakes are often forced to wait a year or longer until parts are available. GM has been particularly lackadaisical in correcting its safety defects. Although the company has sent out warning letters to owners advising them to leave their vehicle if the airbag or ABS light comes on, no quick relief is in sight. GM says repair parts won't be available before mid-2001!

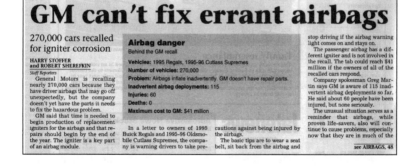

GM can't fix errant airbags

270,000 cars recalled for igniter corrosion

HARRY STOFFER
and ROBERT SHEREFKIN
Staff Reporters

General Motors is recalling nearly 270,000 cars because they have driver airbags that may go off unexpectedly, but the company doesn't yet have the parts it needs to fix the hazardous problem.

GM said that time is needed to begin production of replacement igniters for the airbags and that repairs should begin by the end of the year. The igniter is a key part of an airbag module.

Airbag danger
Behind the GM recall

Vehicles: 1995 Regals, 1995-96 Cutlass Supremes
Number of vehicles: 270,000
Problem: Airbags inflate inadvertently. GM doesn't have repair parts.
Inadvertent airbag deployments: 115
Injuries: 60
Deaths: 0
Maximum cost to GM: $41 million

In a letter to owners of 1995 Buick Regals and 1995-96 Oldsmobile Cutlass Supremes, the company is warning drivers to take precautions against being injured by the airbags.

The basic tips are to wear a seat belt, sit back from the airbag and

stop driving if the airbag warning light comes on and stays on.

The passenger airbag has a different igniter and is not involved in the recall. The tab could reach $41 million if the owners of all of the recalled cars respond.

Company spokesman Greg Martin says GM is aware of 115 inadvertent airbag deployments so far. He said about 60 people have been injured, but none seriously.

The unusual situation serves as a reminder that airbags, while proven life-savers, also will continue to cause problems, especially now that they are in much of the

see AIRBAGS, 48

Anti-lock brake system (ABS)
Essentially, ABS prevents a vehicle's wheels from locking when the brakes are applied in an emergency situation, thus reducing skidding and the loss of directional control. When braking on wet and dry roads,

your stopping distance will be about the same as with conventional braking systems. But in gravel, slush, or snow, your stopping distance will be greater.

A particularly important feature of ABS is that it preserves steering control. As you brake in an emergency, ABS will release the brakes if it senses wheel lockup. Braking distances will lengthen accordingly, but at least you'll have some steering control. On the other hand, if you start sliding on glare ice don't expect ABS to help you out very much. The laws of physics, particularly the coefficient of friction, still apply on ABS-equipped vehicles. You can decrease the stopping distance, however, by removing your all-season tires and installing four snow tires that are the same make and size.

Anti-lock brakes are impressive on the test track but not on the road. In fact, the Insurance Institute for Highway Safety (IIHS)—an American insurance research group that collects and analyzes insurance claims data—says that cars with anti-lock brakes are more likely to be in crashes where no other car is involved but a passenger is killed. Insurance claim statistics show that anti-lock brakes aren't producing the overall safety benefits that were predicted by the government and automakers. The latest IIHS study found that a passenger has a 45 percent greater chance of dying in a single-vehicle crash in a car with anti-lock brakes than in the same car with old-style brakes. On wet pavement, where ABS supposedly excels, that figure rises to a 65 percent greater chance of being killed. In multi-vehicle crashes, ABS-equipped vehicles have a passenger death rate 6 percent higher than vehicles not equipped with ABS.

The high cost of ABS maintenance is one disadvantage that few safety advocates mention, but consider the following: 1) original parts can cost five times more than regular braking components, and 2) many dealers prefer to replace the entire ABS unit rather than troubleshoot what is a very complex system.

Keep in mind that anti-lock brakes are notoriously unreliable. They often fail completely, resulting in no braking whatsoever, or they may extend stopping distance by 30 percent. While General Motors continued to blame drivers for ABS brake failures, *AutoWeek* magazine reported four years ago that NHTSA knew GM had secretly bought back hundreds of vehicles equipped with failure-prone Kelsey-Hayes anti-lock brakes the automaker couldn't fix.

Airbags (unsafe at any speed?)
Unlike anti-lock brakes, airbags are killers *when* they work properly. Granted, in high-speed collisions they save lives, particularly if you're an unbelted male. However, in fender-benders where no one would have been hurt if the airbag hadn't deployed, airbags often kill women, seniors, and children—or leave them horribly scarred, or deaf. And you can never be sure when an airbag will suddenly explode in your face. In fact, millions of vehicles have been recalled because their airbags go off when they shouldn't and don't go off when they should.

Plus, it doesn't matter when they were installed or where they are placed—recent injury stats show that even depowered and side airbags can also be deadly.

I have read the stats and they are *scary*.

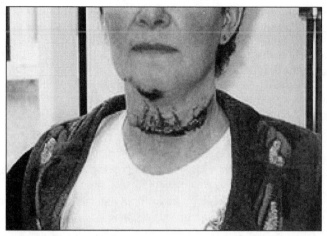

This woman had just negotiated a traffic circle on a busy, single-lane road when her airbag exploded. "I was doing about 60 km/h, no more. The road was straight and I hadn't hit anything."

If you want to know the truth about airbag dangers, you'll have to do a bit of digging (this guide's Appendix II, "Best Internet Gripe Sites", is a good starting point) and look at research done in other countries where researchers don't have an "airbag at all costs" agenda. You'll be surprised to find that the chance of airbag-induced injury increases if you are a woman, a senior, not an average size, have had upper torso surgery, use a tilt steering wheel, or are out of position when the airbag strikes.

What does it mean to be "out of position?"
If you are hit from the rear and thrown within 25 centimetres of the steering wheel, you are out of position. As the airbag deploys, you risk severe head, neck, or chest trauma, or death. If you are making a turn, with your arms crossing in front of the steering wheel, you are out of position and risk fractures to both arms. If you drive with your thumbs extended a bit into the steering hub area, as I often do, you risk losing both thumbs when the housing cover explodes.

But just being female is enough to get you killed
Two startling Transport Canada studies were uncovered last October as part of a CBC *Marketplace* investigation into airbag safety. The consumer TV show unearthed government-financed research that showed airbags

reduce the risk of injury by *only* 2 percent for adults who wear seatbelts.

Even more incredible, the studies confirm that airbags actually *increase* the risk of injury to women by 9 percent and the risk of death for children by 21 percent.

The research was completed in 1996 and 1998. Fearing the public disclosure of the findings, it took Transport Canada four months to release the studies to *Marketplace*. American government officials have refused to comment upon the Canadian research, despite the fact that it contradicts the basic premise of airbag use—they are safe at any speed, regardless of gender.

In fact, the danger to women is so great, an earlier 1996 Transport Canada and George Washington University study of 445 drivers and passengers concluded:

> While the initial findings of this study confirm that belted drivers are afforded added protection against head and facial injury in moderate to severe frontal collisions, the findings also suggest that these benefits are being negated by a high incidence of bag-induced injury. The incidence of bag-induced injury was greatest among female drivers. Furthermore, the intervention of the air bag can be expected to introduce a variety of new injury mechanisms such as facial injuries from "bag slap," upper extremity fractures, either directly from the deploying air bag module or from arm flailing, and thermal burns to the face and arms.

A frightening admission. Don't look for the above study on Transport Canada's website. It's not there. It can be found in its entirety on NHTSA's website at www.nhtsa.dot.gov/esv/16/98S5O07.PDF. *Incidentally, GM now claims competitors' side airbags on 1999 and year 2000 models are equally hazardous to children.*

Janet Garman, an Illinois registered nurse, says there are now over 90 cases cited in medical literature where hearing has been damaged by airbag deployment. "Physicians are finding the following damage: hearing loss, tinnitus (ear ringing or roaring), hypercusis and recruitment (sound sensitivities) vertigo, and eardrum perforation.... In many of these injuries, there was no crash, just inadvertent deployment.... Even though the National Highway Traffic Safety Administration (NHTSA) and the auto industry have known about this for years, they have chosen not to inform the public..."

A campaign of misinformation
One out of every five ongoing NHTSA investigations into possible defects in cars and light trucks concerns inadvertent airbag deployment, failure of the airbag to deploy, or injuries suffered when the bag did go off. In fact, airbags are the agency's single largest cause of current investigations, exceeding even the full range of brake problems, which runs second.

As I fit together all the recent accident reports and emergency-room studies, it's obvious that for over three decades engineers, automakers, and government bureaucrats have lied to us about airbag dangers. While head of NHTSA in the late 1970s, fellow "Nader Raider" Joan Claybrook told parents that airbags were safe for *unbelted* children, were safe for both adults and children *without* seatbelts, and were *preferable* to belts because they were hidden away and automatic. Claybrook also fought against strong airbag warning labels in the early 1990s because she feared they might discourage airbag installation in vehicles.

Yet, Claybrook and many government and industry safety researchers knew that, instead of the promised billowing protective cloud that would gently cushion us in an accident, the airbag's 330 km/h deployment is more like a Mike Tyson right cross. Since 1990, front airbags have killed 161 people, 92 of them children, in low-speed collisions or otherwise survivable accidents. All these deaths came from accidents with speeds as slow as 12–15 km/h, and three-quarters of the adults killed were women.

North America's safety "establishment," composed of government, automakers, and safety advocates, hasn't levelled with the public about airbag dangers inherent in the more than 75 million airbag-equipped vehicles on our highways. For example, the admonition that children under the age of 13 should sit in the rear is nonsense, since it's a question of size, not age (a small 18-year-old could be more vulnerable). Actually, no one who is of small stature, child or adult, should sit behind an airbag. The government also has yet to explain why airbags are of little benefit to seniors 70 and older, and why there have been 25,000+ injuries from airbag deployment between 1988 and 1991, according to NHTSA.

Most importantly, we have to stop blaming the victims of airbag deployment for sitting too close, not buckling up, or allowing their children to ride in the front seat. The studies and statistics clearly demonstrate that most of the belted drivers and passengers who were injured did nothing to put themselves at risk, except perhaps having a federal ministry of transport that blindly followed Washington's lead or "driving while female."

Inadvertent airbag deployment
Airbags frequently go off for no apparent reason. Ralph Hoar, an Arlington, Virginia, safety adviser to plaintiffs' attorneys, blames this on cheap sensors. Causes of sudden deployment include: passing over a bump in the road in your GM Cavalier or Sunfire; slamming the car door; having wet carpets in your Cadillac; or, in some Chrysler minivans, simply putting the key in the ignition. This happens more often than you might imagine, judging by the frequent recalls and thousands of complaints recorded on NHTSA's website at *www.nhtsa.dot.gov/cars/problems/complain/compmmy1.cfm*. Incidentally, insurers are refusing to pay for damage to the car or for airbag replacements unless there has been a

collision. Meanwhile, automakers deny responsibility on the grounds that the vehicle collided with something. In the end, the driver is faced with a hefty repair bill and no means of proving the automaker's liability.

Airbag deployment for no apparent reason is bad enough if the vehicle is parked; however, if the airbag explodes while the vehicle is being driven, it will likely cause an accident and then be of no use during the ensuing impact because it has already deflated. Says Michael Leshner, a U.S. forensic engineer, "The airbag knocks them silly—*then* they have an accident."

Protect yourself
Because not all airbags function, or malfunction, the same way, *Lemon-Aid* has done an exhaustive analysis of U.S. and Canadian recalls, crash data, and owner complaints to determine which vehicles and which model years use airbags that may seriously injure occupants or deploy inadvertently. That data can be found in Part Three's model ratings.

Additionally, you should take the following steps to reduce the dangers from airbag deployment:

- don't buy a vehicle with side airbags until the federal government comes up with standards;
- make sure that seatbelts are buckled and all head restraints are properly adjusted (about ear level);
- make sure the head restraints are rated "good" by IIHS;
- insist that passengers who are frail, short, or have recently had surgery sit in the back;
- make sure that the driver's seat can be adjusted for height and has tracks with sufficient rearward travel to allow short drivers to remain a safe distance away from the bag's deployment (at least 25 centimeters) and still reach the accelerator and brake (buy pedal extensions, if needed);
- try to have a retrofitted cut-off switch installed by a dealer, but don't be surprised to find Canadian dealers reluctant to install the devices due to their unfounded fear of lawsuits (see Appendix II for *Marketplace*'s website, which lists which automakers will install retrofitted devices);
- buy a vehicle that comes with manual passenger-side airbag disablers;
- buy a vehicle that uses sensors to detect the presence of an electronically tagged child safety seat in the passenger seat and disables the airbag for that seat;
- if you are short-statured, consider buying aftermarket pedal extensions from auto parts retailers or optional adjustable accelerator and brake pedals to keep you a safe distance away from a deploying airbag;
- pop the airbag housing covers to ensure the airbags haven't been removed.

Crashworthiness

It's ironic that crashworthiness, a safety feature not mandated by government, is the one safety improvement over the past thirty years that everyone agrees has paid off handsomely without presenting any additional risks to drivers or passengers. By surrounding occupants in a protective cocoon and deflecting crash forces away from the interior, auto engineers have successively created safer vehicles without increasing size or cost. Purchasing a vehicle with the idea that you'll be involved in an accident is not unreasonable. According to the Insurance Institute for Highway Safety (IIHS), the average car will likely have two accidents before ending up as scrap and is twice as likely to be in a severe front-impact crash as a side-impact crash.

Two Washington-based agencies monitor how vehicle design affects crash safety: NHTSA and IIHS. Crash information from these two groups doesn't always agree because while IIHS's results incorporate all kinds of accidents at higher speeds, NHTSA figures relate only to 57 km/h (35 mph) frontal and side collisions. The frontal tests are equivalent to two vehicles of equal weight hitting each other head-on while travelling at 57 km/h or to a car slamming into a parked car at 114 km/h (70 mph). Bear in mind that a car providing good injury protection often produces the highest damage claims because its structure, not the occupants, absorbs most of the force of the collision.

Also, remember that child safety seats reduce the risk of death significantly—as much as 71 percent for infants, says the U.S. Centers for Disease Control and Prevention. They should be replaced after all crashes because hidden damage can endanger kids. Be especially wary of hand-me-down car seats because you may not know the history of the seat.

Large vs. small

Occupants of large vehicles have fewer severe injury claims than do occupants of small vehicles. This was proven conclusively in a 1996 NHTSA study that showed collisions between light trucks or vans and small cars resulted in an 81 percent higher fatality rate for the occupants of the small cars than occupants in light trucks or vans.

Vehicle weight protects you, principally, in two-vehicle crashes. In a head-on crash, for example, the heavier vehicle drives the lighter one backward, which decreases forces inside the heavy vehicle and increases forces in the lighter one. All heavy vehicles, even poorly designed ones, offer this advantage in two-vehicle collisions but may not offer good protection in single-vehicle crashes or rollovers.

IIHS figures show that for every 1,000 pounds added to a vehicle's mass, the risk of injury to an unrestrained driver is lowered by 34 percent, and the risk of injury to a restrained driver is lowered by 25 percent. GM's recent two-car crash tests dramatically confirm this fact. Its engineers concluded that if two cars collide, and one weighs half as much as the other, the driver in the lighter car is 10 times more likely to be killed than the driver in the heavier one. This held true no matter how many crash stars the smaller car was awarded in government crash tests.

Interestingly, a vehicle's size doesn't *always* guarantee that you won't be injured in an accident. U.S. government crash tests show, for example, that a small car like the 1991 Ford Escort gives better full-front collision protection than a 1994 Mercury Villager or Nissan Quest, two large minivans that could have been easily engineered to crash safely at moderate speeds of 57 km/h. Some small vehicles are designed better than larger ones to absorb crash forces. VW's New Beetle is a good example. So far, it's the only small car to win a good crash rating from IIHS, while a handful of larger sport-utilities and even some Cadillacs rate poorly at protecting their occupants. Also, different years of the same model or size variation can produce startlingly different scores. For example, Chrysler's 1995 Caravan and Voyager minivans earned better driver crash protection scores than did the 1996 and 1997 Grand Caravan and Grand Voyager.

There are some factors that can skew crash scores, such as size, height, and frame rail placement. If your Ford Taurus (five-star crash rating) is clobbered by a Dodge Durango 4X4 (two-star crash rating), chances are you'll still fare much worse than the sport-utility's occupants simply because their car is so much heavier and will likely ride over the Taurus's protective frame. Other factors are whether or not occupants are wearing seatbelts, and airbag and head restraint design.

Unsafe designs
Although it sounds hard to believe, automakers will deliberately manufacture a vehicle that will kill or maim simply because, in the long run, it costs less to pay off victims than to make a safer vehicle. I learned this lesson after reading the court transcripts of *Grimshaw v. Ford* and listening to court testimony of GM engineers who deliberately placed fire-prone "side-saddle" gas tanks in millions of pickups to save $3 per vehicle.

More recent examples of corporate greed triumphing over public safety: airbag designs that maim or kill women, children, and seniors; anti-lock brake systems that don't brake (a major problem with GM minivans, trucks, and sport-utilities, and Chrysler sport-utilities and minivans); flimsy front seats; the absence of rear head restraints; fire-prone GM pickup fuel tanks and Ford ignition switches; and failure-prone Chrysler, Ford, and GM automatic transmissions that suddenly shift into Neutral or self-destruct (1991–99 front-drives). All are examples of hazardous engineering designs that put profit ahead of safety.

Top 20 safety defects reported by owners
The federal government's on-line safety complaints database contains well over 100,000 entries, going back to vehicles made in the late '70s. Although originally intended to record incidents of component failures

that only relate to safety, you will find every problem imaginable dutifully recorded by NHTSA clerks.

A perusal of the listed complaints shows that some safety-related failures occur more frequently than others and often affect one manufacturer more than another. Here is a summary of some of the more commonly reported failures in order of frequency:

1. airbags not deploying when they should; deploying when they shouldn't
2. ABS total brake failure; wheel lockup
3. tire tread separation
4. electrical or fuel system fires
5. sudden acceleration
6. sudden stalling
7. sudden electrical failure
8. transmission fails to engage or suddenly disengages
9. transmission jumps from Park to Reverse or Neutral; vehicle rolls away when parked
10. steering or suspension failure
11. seatbelt failures
12. collapsing seatbacks
13. defective sliding door, door locks, and latches
14. poor headlight illumination
15. dash reflects into windshield
16. hood flies up
17. wheel falls away
18. steering wheel lifts off
19. transmission lever pulls out
20. exploding windshields

Recalls

Vehicles are recalled for one of two reasons: they may be unsafe or they may not conform to federal and state pollution control regulations. Whatever the reason, though, recalls are a great way to get free repairs—if you know which ones apply to you.

More than 300 million unsafe vehicles have been recalled by automakers for the free correction of safety-related defects since American recall legislation was passed in 1966 (equivalent Canadian laws were enacted in 1971). During that time, about one-third of the recalled vehicles never made it back to the dealership for repairs. Auto Service Monitor, an American firm that tracks recalls, estimates this means there are close to 20 million vehicles, still on North American roads, that could suddenly careen out of control, catch fire, or fail to brake. Surprisingly, motorists aren't generally motivated to bring in their recalled vehicles—even when the result of the defect is as life-threatening as fire.

Choosing the Right Seller

Good months, bad months

Car sales are seasonal, depending where you live. In the northern and western regions, fewer vehicles are sold in the winter months of December through February than in the spring, summer, and fall. New-car dealers use this period to saturate the media with ads that hype the first wave of rebates and low-financing programs to off-set the winter sales doldrums.

Used-car dealers and private sellers are generally easier to deal with in the winter. Although they have fewer vehicles available, they usually offer lower prices and are less hard-nosed in bargaining because they see fewer customers, and used vehicles generally show their worst characteristics during the winter months. On the other hand, in fall and spring, dealer stocks of good quality trade-ins and off-lease returns are at their highest level and private sellers are more active. Prices will be higher, but there will be a greater choice of vehicles available.

Private sellers

Private sellers are your best source for a cheap and reliable used vehicle, because you're on an equal bargaining level with a vendor who isn't trying to profit from your inexperience. This translates into a golden opportunity to negotiate a fair price, which isn't common in many dealer transactions.

Apart from newspaper classified ads, you can track down deals and get a good idea of prices through the following:
• word of mouth;
• grocery store bulletin boards;
• specialty publications (e.g., *Auto Trader, Auto Mart,* or *Buy and Sell Bargain Hunter*);
• the *Canadian Red Book* or the Provincial Automobile Dealers Association *Black Book;*
• free Internet price guides (see Appendix II, "Best Internet Gripe Sites").

CHEVROLET 1997

Fact S.R.P./Whsl	Avg. Whsl	Mod. No.	Description		Avg. Retail
CORVETTE					
48895	34425	YY2	Coupe H/B	5.7L-E V8	38625
LUMINA					
22340	12875	WL5	Sedan	3.1L-E V6	14975
23810	13725	WL5	Sedan LS	3.1L-E V6	15825
25305	14225			3.4L-E V6	16325
25145	14275	WN5	Sedan LTZ	3.1L-E V6	16375
26640	14775			3.4L-E V6	16875
MALIBU					
19095	12550	ND5	Sedan		14550
23095	14450	NE5	Sedan LS		16450
MONTE CARLO					
24275	14800	WW1	Coupe LS	3.1L-E V6	17000
26500	15950	WX1	Coupe Z34	3.4L-E V6	18150

CHEVROLET 1996

NOTE: Model Numbers shown are the 4th, 5th & 6th Digits of the VIN No.

Fact S.R.P./Whsl	Avg. Whsl	Mod. No.	Description		Avg. Retail
BERETTA					
17275	7950	LV1	2dr Coupe	2.2L-E 4	9650
27939	8350			3.1L-E V6	10050
BERETTA Z26					
21140	10000	LW1	2dr Coupe	3.1L-E V6	11700
CAMARO					
20195	12350	FP2	2dr Coupe	3.8L-E V6	14150
28365	16350	FP3	Convt	3.8L-E V6	18450
CAMARO Z28					
25530	16050	FP2	Coupe Z28	5.7L-E V8	18050
32330	20050	FP3	Convt Z28	5.7L-E V8	22450
CAPRICE CLASSIC					
28345	14750	BN5	Sed Class	4.3L-E V8	16950
29720	15050			5.7L-E V8	17250
30980	16050	BL8	Wgn Class	5.7L-E V8	18350
CAVALIER					
13030	8250	JC1	2dr Coupe	2.2L-E 4	9850
13530	8550	JC5	4dr Sedan	2.2L-E 4	10150
16840	10425	JF5	4dr Sedan LS	2.2L-E 4	12025
17643	11400	JF1	2dr Cpe Z24	2.4L-E 4	13100
22925	13200	JF3	Convt LS	2.4L-E 4	15250
CORSICA					
17885	9900	LD5	4dr Sedan	2.2L-E 4	11600
18620	10400			3.1L-E V6	12100
CORVETTE					
48080	29325	YY2	Coupe H/B	5.7L-E V8	33425
56335	32925	YY3	Convertible	5.7L-E V8	37025
IMPALA SS					
30675	19375	BL5	Sedan SS	5.7L-E V8	21775
LUMINA					
21455	11075	WL5	Sedan	3.1L-E V6	13075
22706	11925	WN5	Sedan LS	3.1L-E V6	13925

CHEVROLET 1996

Fact S.R.P./Whsl	Avg. Whsl	Mod. No.	Description		Avg. Retail
LUMINA (Continued)					
24905	12425			3.4L-E V6	14425
MONTE CARLO					
23625	12525	WW1	Coupe LS	3.1L-E V6	14625
25826	13225			3.4L-E V6	15325
25850	13675	WX1	Coupe Z34	3.4L-E V6	15775

CHEVROLET 1995

NOTE: Model Numbers shown are the 4th, 5th & 6th Digits of the VIN No.

Fact S.R.P./Whsl	Avg. Whsl	Mod. No.	Description		Avg. Retail
BERETTA					
16950	6650	LV1	2dr Coupe	2.2L-E 4	8250
17621	7150			3.1L-E V6	8750
BERETTA Z26					
20815	8800	LW1	2dr Coupe	3.1L-E V6	10200
CAMARO					
18995	10250	FP2	2dr Coupe	3.4L-E V6	11950
20045	13975	FP3	Convt	3.4L-E V6	15975
CAMARO Z28					
23650	13950	FP2	Coupe Z28	5.7L-E V8	15850
30450	17475	FP3	Convt Z28	5.7L-E V8	19775
CAPRICE CLASSIC					
26455	12350	BN5	Sed Class	4.3L-E V8	14550
26145	12650			5.7L-E V8	14850
29120	13625	BL8	Wgn Class	5.7L-E V8	16025
CAVALIER					
12245	6650	JC1	2dr Coupe	2.2L-E 4	8150
12745	6950	JC5	4dr Sedan	2.2L-E 4	8450
15645	8825	JF5	4dr Sedan LS	2.2L-E 4	10325
16895	9350	JF1	2dr Cpe Z24	2.3L-E 4	10950
22185	11075	JF3	Convt LS	2.3L-E 4	13025
CORSICA					
17380	7975	LD5	4dr Sedan	2.2L-E 4	9575
18015	8475			3.1L-E V6	10075
CORVETTE					
47580	25150	YY2	Coupe H/B	5.7L-E V8	29150
55020	26550	YY3	Convertible	5.7L-E V8	32550
86765	40425	YZ2	Coupe ZR1	5.7L-E V8	45425
IMPALA SS					
29005	15800	BL5	Sedan SS	5.7L-E V8	18100
LUMINA					
20730	9375	WL5	Sedan	3.1L-E V6	11275
21950	10225	WN5	Sedan LS	3.1L-E V6	12125
23695	10725			3.4L-E V6	12625
MONTE CARLO					
22578	10400	WW1	Coupe LS	3.1L-E V6	12400
22579	10900			3.4L-E V6	12900
24678	11575	WX1	Coupe Z34	3.4L-E V6	13675

For Provincial Valuations - See Inside Back Cover
* Valuation does not include air conditioning

12

Both the Red Book *and the* Black Book *list three prices, from left to right: the MSRP, showing what the vehicle sold for new; the wholesale price negotiated between dealers; and the retail price charged by dealers to walk-in customers. Used vehicles purchased from dealers over the Internet or from private sellers will sell for somewhere between the wholesale and retail prices. When you compare dealer ads with the price guides, you'll see the dealers have added substantial markups that ensnare unsuspecting buyers. Take* Lemon-Aid *along and bargain down the markup as much as you can.*

The best way to determine the price range for a particular model is to read the publications or surf the websites listed in Appendix II before you buy the vehicle. This will give you a reasonably good idea of the top asking price. Remember, no seller expects to get his or her asking price, be it a dealer or private party. As with price reductions on home listings, a 10–20 percent reduction on the advertised price is common with private sellers. Dealers usually won't cut more than 10 percent off their advertised price.

Find out which published used-car guide is the accepted standard in your area of the country. The *Red Book* and *Black Book* serve Canadian dealers, while the *Kelley Blue Book* and *Edmund's Price Guide* are two of the most popular American guides offering comprehensive ratings and prices, gratis, through the Internet. You can visit the *Kelley Blue Book* at *www.kbb.com* or Edmund's at *www.edmunds.com*.

Don't be surprised to find that many national price guides have an eastern Ontario–Quebec price bias. They often list unrealistically low prices compared with what you'll actually see in the eastern and western provinces and in rural areas, where good used cars are often sold for outrageously high prices or simply passed down through the family.

Be wary

As a buyer, you should get a printed sales agreement, even if it's just handwritten, that includes a clause stating there are no outstanding traffic violations or liens against the vehicle. It doesn't make a great deal of difference whether the car will be purchased "as is" or as certified under provincial regulation. A vehicle sold as safety "certified" can still be dangerous to drive or turn into a lemon. The certification process can be sabotaged if a minimal number of components are checked, the mechanic is incompetent, or the instruments are poorly calibrated. "Certified" is not the same as having a warranty to protect you from engine seizure or transmission failure. Certified means only that the vehicle has met minimum safety standards on the day tested.

TELL-TALE SIGNS OF FLOOD DAMAGE

Car experts agree buying a flooded vehicle is a bad idea, even if the price seems right and the car looks like new. Used-car buyers should have their mechanics check for these warning signs of flooding.

Damp or musty odor inside the vehicle or trunk.

Newly shampooed or replaced carpet or upholstery in a vehicle that is old enough to show wear and tear.

Dampness under carpeting or between seat cushions.

Rusty brackets and/or screws under dash.

Watermarks under the hood.

Dried mud in cracks and crevices under the hood, behind trim panels inside the car, inside door joints or wheel wells, or under the dashboard.

Traces of water in engine, transmission or axle lubricants.

SOURCE: The American Automobile Association.

Make sure the vehicle is lien-free and has not been damaged in a flood or written off after an accident. Several years ago, Hurricane Floyd flooded about 75,000 cars throughout the United States. AAA says between 15,000 and 20,000 flooded vehicles have made it into the market nationally.

Flood damage can be hard to see. However, it impairs ABS, power steering, and airbag deployment (deploys ten-times slower).

Canada has become a haven for rebuilt U.S. wrecks. Write-offs are also shipped from provinces where there are stringent disclosure regulations to provinces where there are lax rules—if rules exist at all. Ron Giblin of the Canadian Insurance Crime Prevention Bureau (ICPB) told the *Toronto Sun* that ICPB members voluntarily reported 26,709 salvaged vehicles in 1996 in Ontario alone. He estimates the true figure is about double that number. *Consumer Reports* estimates that 50 percent of the cars declared a total loss by insurers are put back on the road—12,000 vehicles a month in the States.

If you suspect your vehicle is a rebuilt wreck from the States, use Carfax (*www.carfax.com*; tel.: 1-888-422-7329) to carry out a background check to see if the vehicle has been wrecked, had flood damage, is stolen, or shows incorrect mileage on the odometer. The $20 fee by telephone is cut to $14.95 (U.S.) if the order is placed via the Internet. A typical search takes only a few minutes and most Canadian provinces are included in the database. The search will also turn up which cars were trucked across the border as "parts" and then sold to resellers. A word of caution, though. When asking for a free Carfax trial search, you may be misled to believe there is some important info still available that can be accessed only by paying the regular Carfax fee. I was told there were six other important pieces of info available, paid the fee, and was given a list showing the six times my car was taken in for a mandatory emissions test. (See email below.)

> I came across Carfax online with it's BBB endorsement and decided to run the VIN for my car. The free lemon-check report indicated that "The Carfax database contains 1 important vehicle history record about this 1998 Ford Contour." Note the use of the word "important". So believing that Carfax was actually in possession of some "important" info regarding my car I purchased the "full report" for $15 U.S...or in other words close to $30 Canadian. Turns out the only info they had to offer for that amount was that registration was issued by the Quebec Motor Vehicle Dept. in Montreal, Quebec. What an earth shattering revelation that is!! Obviously I went after a refund, which they say they will eventually award. I'm not holding my breath.
>
> My point is, how many people are being ripped off by this outfit? They are preying on people's fears and cashing in by doling out useless information. I realize that you deal mainly with car manufacturers but this seems to be closely related since it is based on the used car industry. I think someone should be holding them accountable for their business practices....

In most provinces, you can do a lien and registration search yourself. If a lien does exist, you should contact the creditor(s) listed to find out whether any debts have been paid. If a debt is outstanding, you should arrange with the vendor to pay the creditor the outstanding balance. If the debt is larger than the purchase price of the car, it's up to you to decide whether or not you wish to complete the deal. If the seller agrees to clear the title personally, make sure that you receive a written relinquishment of title from the creditor before paying any money to the vendor. Make sure the title doesn't show an "R" for "restored" since this indicates the vehicle was written off as a total loss and may not have been properly repaired.

Even if all documents are in order, ask the seller to show you the vehicle's original sales contract and a few repair bills in order to ascertain how well it was maintained. The bills will show you if the odometer was turned back, and will also indicate which repairs are still guaranteed. If none of these can be found, run (don't walk!) away. If the contract shows that the car was financed, verify that the loan was paid. If you're still not sure that the vehicle is free of liens, ask your bank or credit union manager to check for you. If no clear answer is forthcoming, look for another car.

Repossessed vehicles

Repossessed vehicles are usually found at auctions, but they're sometimes sold by finance companies or banks. In these cases, the institutions (just like car dealers) are legally responsible for defects found in the vehicles they sell. The biggest problem with repossessed vans, sport-utilities, and pickups, in particular, is that they were likely abused or neglected by their financially troubled owners. A local dealer may be able to produce a vehicle maintenance history by running the VIN through its manufacturer's database.

Cross-border shopping

There's no ironclad guarantee that you'll save money if you purchase a used vehicle in the U.S. and bring it into Canada. But free trade in the other direction is booming. In fact, Dave Lawrence, Toronto Metro Credit Union's auto consultant, tells me that American dealers are drying up the Toronto-area supply of good used vehicles by overbidding for Canadian cars and selling them at a profit in the U.S.

Safety and pollution control regulations differ considerably between the two countries and it may be impossible to upgrade your used vehicle to Canadian standards. Transport Canada estimates that 15–20 percent of American vehicles can't meet Canadian standards, no matter how they're modified. To find out which ones pass muster, download Transport Canada's list of vehicles approved for import from its website *www.tc.gc.ca/roadsafety* or call the Registrar of Imported Vehicles at 1-800-511-7755.

Be aware that U.S. vehicles' odometers register in miles instead of kilometres and are likely to have the mileage rolled back. Furthermore, you won't benefit that much from the lower prices on American-sourced cars because of the higher cost of the American dollar and the substantial Canadian sales taxes (GST, provincial sales taxes, and a gas-guzzling surcharge) that you'll pay to bring your vehicle home. Servicing may be a problem as well, since dealers will put their own customers first and give them "goodwill" warranty coverage before you.

If you do decide to import a used vehicle from the U.S., check for liens, make sure the vehicle isn't stolen, and ask an independent dealer selling that make of vehicle to pull the automaker history on the car through its VIN. Unfortunately, there's little co-operation among provincial registrars and no link-up between U.S. and Canadian registrars, so your chances of getting the required information from government sources are pretty slim.

Finally, if you aren't convinced importing a used vehicle from the States is a daunting task, let Ted Harmon's experience give you a taste of what it entails:

> When buying from the States, the first thing to consider is costs. As you mentioned, the difference in the dollar quickly inflates the price of the car. Second is the consideration of import fees. According to Revenue Canada, a car manufactured in North America is subject to a 1.6% import surtax (I may be wrong on the figure), and cars manufactured outside of North America are subject to a 6.7% import surtax. I was trying to import a Mazda Precidia from my sister who lives in Indiana. She was sure that the car was manufactured in the U.S., but only after closer inspection did she realize that the car was actually manufactured in Japan.
>
> Other fees to consider: an air-conditioning "tax" of $100, an entrance fee of anywhere from $210 to $280 for bringing the car into Canada, and of course the dreaded GST or HST, which is determined by the Canadian book value price of the car. All of these fees must be paid for at the border when you import the car.
>
> After the car is home, you still have to ensure that the car is certified and modified to meet Canadian safety standards. This can be a relatively inexpensive job, but it depends on the specification of the car. For me, it would have involved installing day running lights, anchors for a child seat, bumpers that meet Canadian specs, and, if installed with airbags that expire, then the notice of expiry must be posted both in French and English. All in all, after consulting with my local dealer, the modifications wouldn't be too expensive, and many of the items they offered to do for free.
>
> In addition, as you mentioned, the car might not be eligible for import. This depends on Transport Canada's guidelines, and does not run in any chronological order. For example, a 1992 Precidia V6 might be okay, but a 1992 four-cylinder would not. The same goes for two- and four-door models of cars. It is important to check for this information *before* bringing the car to Canada, because if you get denied at the border, they won't let

you even bring the car into Canada. Furthermore, the car must meet all U.S. Transport safety regulations. Simply put, the previous owner must have brought the car in for all recalls and safety updates. Apparently, it is not simple to prove. My sister brought the car to the Mazda dealer, and they told her straight out that it complied, but after further consultation with the Registrar of Imported Vehicles (RIV), I was informed that they have to go first to the manufacturer for certification, and then to the dealer for certification (in writing) that all safety recalls have been installed.

As you can see from my narrative, the key to this transaction was planning. I spent about two months of telephone calls to Transport Canada, Revenue Canada, and my sister trying ensure that the car could be brought to Canada. The various offices of the government were helpful. The people at RIV and Revenue Canada were of great help, and they both send you smart little checklist packages to get you going, but even they did not offer full disclosure. That is why I recommend visiting the RIV website. For example, RIV told me that the entrance fee was between $210 and $280 depending on which customs office you use when crossing the border. It wasn't until I used their website that I found the official list of customs offices which detailed the services and the prices they charge, so I didn't have to throw the dice when I crossed the border....

Rental and leased vehicles

The second-best choice for getting a good used vehicle is a rental company or leasing agency. Budget, Hertz, Avis, and National sell cars, minivans, vans, and sport-utilities that have one to two years of service and approximately 80,000–100,000 km. These rental companies will gladly provide a vehicle's complete history and allow an independent inspection by a qualified mechanic of the buyer's choice, as well as arrange competitive financing without "boosting" the price.

Rental vehicles are generally well maintained, sell for a few thousand dollars more than a privately sold vehicle, and come with a strong guarantee, like Budget's 30-day money-back guarantee. Rental car companies also usually settle customer complaints without much hassle so as not to tarnish their image with rental customers.

Vehicles that have just come off a 3-year lease are much more competitively priced, generally have less mileage, and are usually as well maintained as rental vehicles. You're also likely to get a better price if you buy directly from the lessee rather than going through the dealership or an independent agency, but remember, you won't have the dealer's leverage to extract post-warranty "goodwill" repairs from the automaker.

New-car dealers

Most used-car buyers prefer to deal with private sellers. In fact, the Federation of Automobile Dealer Associations of Canada states that 20 years ago, 86 percent of used cars were sold by new-car dealers—today that number is less than 25 percent, due mainly to the GST, which has driven buyers into the arms of private sellers.

Nevertheless, new-car dealers aren't a bad place to pick up a good used car or minivan, if you don't mind paying top dollar (prices are 20–30 percent higher than those for vehicles sold privately). For example, dealers are insured against selling stolen vehicles or vehicles with finance owing or other liens. They also offer financing, occasionally allow prospective buyers to have a used vehicle inspected by an independent garage, offer a much wider choice of models, and usually have their own repair facilities to do warranty work. Additionally, if there's a possibility of getting post-warranty "goodwill" compensation from the manufacturer, your dealer can provide additional leverage, particularly if he's a franchisee for the model you have purchased. Plus, if things do go terribly wrong, dealers have "deeper pockets" than private sellers, so there's a better chance of getting paid should a court judgment be won against the firm.

"Certified" vehicles

Try to get a vehicle that the dealer has had certified by an auto association or an automaker, and that has had the required repairs carried out. In Alberta, the Alberta Motor Association (AMA) will perform a vehicle inspection at a dealer's request. On each occasion, the AMA gives the dealer a written report that identifies potential and actual problems, required repairs, and serious defects. Nevertheless, consumers shouldn't let down their guard, says John C. Orr, the Edmonton general manager for the AMA:

> It is up to each dealer to effect the repairs that the dealer deems appropriate. Accordingly, a dealer may
>
> 1) remedy all problems and effect all necessary repairs prior to selling a vehicle;
> 2) remedy some problems or effect some repairs prior to selling a vehicle;
> 3) remedy none of the problems and effect no repairs prior to selling a vehicle; or
> 4) dispose of a vehicle by "wholesaling" it.
>
> It is important for the public to understand that the AMA does not certify vehicles for dealers and that the AMA does not effect repairs. The buying public should ask the dealer to provide a copy of the AMA report, where the dealer has represented that the vehicle has been AMA inspected, and the buying public should inquire what, if any, repairs have been effected....

The Big Three American automakers and many importers have begun to refurbish and certify used vehicles sold by their dealers. They guarantee the vehicle's mechanical fitness and provide a warranty where length depends on the age of the vehicle. But these vehicles don't come cheap, mainly because automakers force their dealers to bring them up to better-than-average condition before certifying them.

Buying a vehicle that's been certified by an auto association or an automaker allows you to sue both the dealer and the certifier if things go wrong.

Automaker and dealer leasing

Leasing is costlier than an outright purchase. In most cases, if you can't afford a new car, buy used. And, if a used car breaks your budget, choose one that's a few model years older, but still rated as reliable. If you must lease, do it for the shortest time possible and make sure the lease is closed-ended (meaning that you walk away from the vehicle when the lease period ends). Also, make sure there's a maximum mileage allowance of at least 25,000 km a year and that the charge per excess kilometre is no higher than 8 cents.

Used-car dealers

Used-car dealers usually sell their vehicles for a bit less than what new-car dealers charge. However, their vehicles may be worth a lot less because they don't get the first pick of top-quality trade-ins. They're usually marginal operations that can't invest much money in reconditioning their vehicles, which are often collected from auctions and new-car dealers reluctant to sell the vehicles to their own customers. And used-car dealers don't always have repair facilities to honour what warranties they do provide. Often, their credit terms are easier (but more expensive) than those offered by franchised new-car dealers.

That said, used-car dealers operating in small towns are an entirely different breed. These small, often family-run businesses recondition and resell cars and trucks that usually come from within their community. Routine servicing is often done in-house and more complicated repairs are subcontracted out to specialized garages nearby. These small outlets survive by word-of-mouth advertising and would never last long if they didn't deal fairly with local townsfolk. On the other hand, their prices will likely be higher than elsewhere due to the better quality of used vehicles they offer and the cost of reconditioning and repairing under warranty what they sell.

Auctions

You need patience and smarts to pick up anything worthwhile at an auction. Government auctions—places where the mythical $50 Jeep is sold—are fun to attend but are risky ventures. You can't determine the condition of the vehicles put up for bid and government employees often pick over the stock before you ever see it.

To attend commercial auctions, however, is to swim with the piranhas. They are frequented by "ringers," who bid up the prices, and professional dealers, who pick up cheap, worn-out vehicles unloaded by new-car dealers and independents. There are no guarantees, cash is required, and quality is apt to be as low as the price. Remember, too, that auction purchases are subject to provincial and federal sales taxes, the auction's sales commission (3–5 percent), and in some cases, an administrative fee of $25–$50.

Say what? This Chicago Times *ad promises there's no need to purchase anything in order to win one of three $1,000 prizes—to be used* only *with the purchase of an auctioned vehicle. Watch out! Like phony carpet "Customs auction" scams, there are many false auto auctions run by used-car dealers and independent brokers. Make sure you're dealing with a legitimate auctioneer.*

If you are interested in shopping at a legitimate auto auction, remember that certain days are reserved for dealers only, so call ahead. You'll find the cars locked in a compound, but you should have ample opportunity to inspect them and, in some cases, take a short drive around the property before the auction begins.

Here are some auctioneers in the Toronto area and around Canada:

AB Toronto Auctions
14 Canso Rd, Rexdale
416-245-2277

GTA Auctions and
Liquidations Inc.
54 Murray Rd, Downsview
416-630-7253

Metro Auto Auction
23 Metropolitan Rd,
Scarborough
416-292-0909

Canadian Auction Group
3365 Highway 7 East,
Brampton (Head Office)
905-791-9800

- Edmonton
  780-465-4900

- Hamilton
  905-560-4851

M. Wilson & Co.
555 Denison St, Markham
905-479-2886

- Saskatoon
  306-242-8771

- St. John's
  709-364-3250

- Vancouver
  604-580-0011

- Winnipeg
  204-694-4944

Paying the Right Price

Get ready for "sticker shock" when pricing popular used cars, pickups, sport-utilities, and vans—most of these vehicles don't depreciate very much and it's easy to get stuck with a cheap one that's been abused through hard off-roading or lack of care. Furthermore, it's such a seller's market out there that even those vehicles with worse-than-average reliability ratings, like many GM front-drives; Ford's Taurus, Sable, and Windstar; and Chrysler minivans, still command ridiculously high resale prices for the simple reason that they're popular, though not as popular as they once were.

If you don't want to pay too much when buying used, you've got the following four alternatives.

- Buy an older vehicle. Choose one that's five years old or more and has a good reliability and durability record, and buy extra protection with an extended warranty. The money you save from the extra years' depreciation and lower insurance premiums will more than make up for the extra warranty cost.
- Look for off-lease vehicles sold privately by owners who want more than what their dealer is offering. If you can't find what you're looking for in the local classified ads, put in your own ad asking for lessees to contact you if they're not satisfied with their dealer's offer.
- Buy a vehicle that's depreciated more than average simply because of its bland styling, lack of high-performance features, or discontinuation. For example, many of the Japanese pickups cost less to own than their flashier American-made counterparts, yet are more reliable and equally functional for most driving chores. Of the discontinued vehicles, choose one with a twin still in production. Although Ford no longer carries the Mercury Sable, for example, parts and servicing will be readily available as long as its twin (the Ford Taurus) is around.
- Buy a twin or re-badged model, vehicles that are nearly identical but sold under other nameplates (see Part Three). They usually share the same basic design, appearance, dimensions, and mechanical components, but their resale values may differ considerably.

Prices will vary

There are several price guidelines, and dealers use the one that will make the most profit on each transaction. The most common price quoted is the *Red Book*, which shows the price the vehicle is worth when sold at full retail (similar to the Manufacturer's Suggested Retail Price, or MSRP). The wholesale price, thousands of dollars less, is more likely what the dealer paid. Never mind that few people ever pay the MSRP; the fact that it's there is sufficient reason for most dealers to charge the higher rate. Both price indicators leave considerable room for the dealer's profit margin and some extra padding—inflated preparation charges and administration fees that shouldn't exist for a used vehicle.

Just as with new cars, dealers know that last-minute add-on charges to used cars are the way to stick it to you just before the contract is signed. They therefore try to extort extra profits through so-called preparation and documentation fees and charge extra handling costs that give you nothing in return. These charges should have no place in a used-vehicle transaction—but wait until the opportune moment before objecting. Patiently await management's approval of the vehicle's bottom-line price and then reject these add-on charges; otherwise, the dealer may try to pad the price to get its normal add-on profit.

TRADE IN DESCRIPTION & LIEN DISCLOSURE			TERMS OF SETTLEMENT		
☐ G.S.T. REGISTRANT	G.S.T. REGISTRANT NO.		TOTAL CASH SALE PRICE	10800	00
YEAR	MI / KM	ODOMETER READING			
MAKE	MODEL				
SERIAL			SUBTOTAL	10800	0.
YEAR	MI / KM	ODOMETER READING	TRADE-IN ALLOWANCE		
MAKE	MODEL		SUBTOTAL		
SERIAL			G.S.T.	756	00
I HEREWITH TRANSFER TO DEALER ALL MY RIGHTS, TITLE AND OWNERSHIP IN THE ABOVE MOTOR VEHICLE, AND I DECLARE I AM THE SOLE OWNER AND POSSESSOR OF SAME AND THAT THERE IS NO MORTGAGE, LIEN, NOTE OR CLAIM OF ANY KIND OR NATURE ADVERSE TO MY RIGHTS OF, UPON, OR AGAINST SAID VEHICLE OTHER THAN AS STATED BELOW			SUBTOTAL	11556	00
I HEREBY STATE THAT TO THE BEST OF MY KNOWLEDGE THE ODOMETER READING AS STATED ABOVE INDICATES THE TOTAL DISTANCE ACTUALLY TRAVELLED BY THE VEHICLE.					
CUSTOMER SIGNATURE X			ADMINISTRATION FEE	99	00
LIEN PAYABLE TO			PAYOUT LIEN ON TRADE-IN		

Dealer greed knows no bounds. This buyer was charged a $99 "administration fee" for a used car!

Financing Choices

No one should spend more than 30 percent of his or her annual gross income on the purchase of a used vehicle. By keeping the initial cost of a used vehicle low, the purchaser may be able to pay in cash—a key bargaining tool to use with private individuals selling cars directly. Used-car dealers are not all that impressed by cash sales because they lose their kickback from the finance companies, which is based on the volume and amount of finance business they write up.

Credit unions

A credit union is the preferred place to borrow money at low interest rates and with easy repayment terms. You'll have to join the credit union or have an account with it before the loan is approved. You'll also probably have to come up with a larger down payment relative to what other lending institutions require.

In addition to giving you reasonable loan rates, credit unions help car buyers out in a number of other ways. Toronto's Metro Credit Union (*www.metrocu.com*), for example, has offered for many years a Car Facts Centre, which provides free, objective advice on car shopping, purchasing, financing, and leasing. Car Facts advisors provide free consultations in person or by phone. This includes:

- fact sheets on all aspects of buying new or used cars
- a circulating library of car buying and car maintenance books and magazines
- a computerized analysis of different buying, leasing, and borrowing options
- *Red Book* used-car price quotations
- dealer invoice price quotations on any make or model of new vehicle, at $20 each

Additionally, Metro has an AutoBuy program where members can hire an expert "car shopper" who will do the legwork—including the tedious and frustrating dickering with sales staff—and thus save themselves time and hassle. Plus, AutoBuy can get that new or used vehicle at a reduced (fleet) rate, arrange top-dollar prices for trade-ins, provide independent advice on options like rustproofing and extended warranties, carry out lien searches, and even negotiate the best settlement with insurance agents.

Rosemary Edwards, a Car Facts advisor, says Metro's Car Facts program has saved members hundreds of thousands of dollars since its inception. For information on how you can join Metro or start up a similar program with your credit union, contact Rosemary Edwards or Dave Lawrence at 1-800-777-8507 or 416-252-5621 (Dave Lawrence's direct line is 416-525-2214). Metro also holds regular car buying seminars throughout the year in the Greater Toronto Area.

Banks

Banks want to make small loans to consumers who have average incomes and appear to be financially responsible. Banks' interest rates are very attractive and can be negotiated downward if you have a good credit history or agree to give them other business. Auto club members can benefit from lower interest rates at banking institutions recommended by the association. Note that bank loans are seldom made for more than 36–48 months.

In your quest for a bank loan, keep in mind that the Internet offers help for people who need an auto loan and want quick approval but don't like to face a banker. The Bank of Montreal (*www.bmo.com*) was the first Canadian bank to allow car buyers to post loan applications on its website, and it promises to send a loan response within 20 seconds. The service is available to any web surfer, including those who aren't current Bank of Montreal customers.

Dealers

Dealers can finance the cost of a used vehicle at rates that compete with those of banks and finance companies. This is because they get substantial rebates from lenders and agree to take back the vehicle if the creditor defaults on the loan. Some dealers mislead their customers into thinking they can get financing at rates 3–4 percentage points below the prime rate. Actually, the dealer jacks up the base price of the vehicle to compensate for the lower interest charges.

Finance companies

With their excessive interest rates, finance companies should be the last place to go for a small, short-term loan, but the fact remains that these lenders fill a consumer need created by the restrictive policies of other institutions. The advantages of relaxed credit restrictions and quick loans appeal to many people who can't get financing elsewhere, or who may wish to extend their payments for up to 60 months.

Dealer Scams

Used vehicles are subject to the same deceptive sales practices deployed by dealers who sell new vehicles. One of the more common tricks is to not identify the previous owner, because the vehicle either was used commercially or had been written off as a total loss from an accident. It's also not uncommon to discover that the mileage has been turned back, particularly if the vehicle was part of a company's fleet. These scams can be thwarted if you demand the name of the vehicle's previous owner as a prerequisite to purchasing the vehicle.

Here are some of the more common fraudulent practices you're likely to encounter.

Failing to declare full purchase price

This tactic, used almost exclusively by small, independent dealers, involves the salesperson telling the buyer that he or she can save on sales tax by listing a lower selling price on the contract. But what if the vehicle turns out to be a lemon or the sales agent has falsified the model year or mileage? The hapless buyer will usually be offered a refund only on the fictitious purchase price indicated on the contract. If the buyer wanted to take the dealer to court, it's quite unlikely that he or she would get any more than the contract price. Moreover, both the buyer and dealer could be prosecuted for making a false declaration to avoid paying sales tax.

Sales agents posing as private parties ("curbsiders")

Individuals sell about three times as many used vehicles as dealers. Some crooked dealers, though, are using agents to pose as private sellers in order to get a better price for their cars and to avoid paying GST and giving a warranty. Once again, this scam is easy to detect if the seller can't produce the original sales contract or show some repair bills made out in his or her own name. You can usually identify a car dealer in the want ads section of the newspaper by checking to see if the same telephone number is repeated in many different ads. Sometimes you can trip up a curbsider by requesting information on the phone, without identifying the specific vehicle. If the seller asks you which car you are considering, you then know you're talking to a dealer.

Most new-car dealers get very angry when one of these scamming teams hits town. Unfortunately they don't get angry enough, because they continue to sell used cars at wholesale prices to curbsiders, who they know are stealing their business and cheating consumers and tax authorities.

Curbsiders are particularly active in the west, buying cars at wholesale prices from dealers, auto auctions, and junkyards (some of these cars have been written off as total losses). They then place private classified ads in B.C. and Alberta papers, sell their stock, and leave town.

If you get taken by one of these scam artists, don't hesitate to sue the publication carrying the ad through small claims court for allowing this rip-off artist to operate.

"Free-exchange" privilege

Dealers get a lot of sales mileage out of this deceptive offer. The dealer offers to exchange any defective vehicle for any other vehicle in stock. What really happens, though, is that the dealer won't have any other vehicles selling for the same price and thus will demand a cash bonus for the exchange, or he or she may have nothing but lemons in stock.

"Money-back" guarantee

Once again, the purchaser feels safe in buying a used car with this kind of guarantee, because what could be more honest than a money-back guarantee? Dealers using this technique often charge exorbitant handling charges, rental fees, or mechanical repair costs to the customer who's bought one of these vehicles and then returned it.

"50/50" guarantee

This means that the dealer will pay half the repair costs over a limited period of time. It's a fair offer if an independent garage may do the repairs. If not, the dealer is free to inflate the repair costs to double their actual worth and write up a bill for that amount. The buyer winds up paying the full price of repairs that would probably have been much cheaper at an independent garage. The best kind of used-vehicle warranty is 100 percent with full coverage for a fixed term.

"As is" cars

Buying a vehicle "as is" means that you're aware of mechanical defects, that you're prepared to accept the responsibility for any damage or injuries caused by the vehicle, and that all costs to fix it shall be paid by you. The courts have held that the "as is" clause is not a blank cheque to cheat buyers and therefore must be interpreted in light of the seller's true intent. That is, was there an attempt to deceive the buyer by including this clause? Did the buyer really know what the "as is" clause could do to his or her future legal rights? It's also been held that the courts may consider oral representations ("parole evidence") that were never written into the formal contract. So that if a seller makes a statement as to the fine quality of the used car, it may now be considered evidence. Courts generally ignore "as is" clauses when the vehicle has been misrepresented, when the dealer is the seller, or when the defects are so serious that the seller is presumed to have known of their existence.

Odometer tampering

It's often too dangerous for the dealer to turn back the mileage, so independent outfits are hired to pick up the car or visit the dealership and "fix" the odometer, a practice allowed under Canadian federal law. For more recent models, a computer chip that turns back the odometer reading can be inserted for less than $50.

Until federal and provincial statutes are toughened and convictions result in severe penalties to anyone engaging in this practice (American laws allow citizens to sue for triple damages plus lawyer and court costs), take steps to protect yourself. Demand that the dealer put the mileage figure on the contract and give you the name and address of the previous owner as well as all repair receipts. It would be smart to demand the same things of a private seller.

Misrepresentation

Used vehicles can be misrepresented in a variety of ways. A used airport commuter minivan may be represented as having been used by a Sunday school class. A mechanically defective pickup that's been rebuilt after several major accidents may have sawdust in its transmission to muffle the "clunks," heavy oil in the motor to stifle the "clanks," and cheap retread tires to eliminate the "thumps." These fraudulent practices may lead to the seller being charged with civil or criminal fraud. The best protection against these dirty tricks is to have the vehicle's quality completely verified by an independent mechanic before completing the sale.

Private Scams

A lot of space in this guide has been used to describe how used-car dealers and scam artists cheat uninformed buyers. Of course, private individuals can be dishonest too; so in either case protect yourself at the
outset by keeping your deposit small and getting as much information
as possible about the vehicle you're considering buying. Then, after a
test drive, you may sign a written agreement to purchase the vehicle
and give a deposit of sufficient value to cover the seller's advertising
costs, subject to cancellation if the automobile fails its inspection.

After you've taken these precautions, watch out for the following private sellers' tricks:

Used vehicles that are stolen or have finance owing

Many used vehicles are sold privately without free title because the original auto loan was never repaid. Here's where car dealers have a net
advantage over private parties. Dealers aren't easily fooled and they
have insurance to compensate buyers if they do inadvertently sell a
vehicle with finance owing or one that's stolen. Stolen cars are almost
always sold through private individuals.

In Ontario, the Used Vehicle Information Package (mandatory for
private sellers) will alert buyers to any problems with the title. In other
provinces, buyers don't have access to this information. Generally, you
have to contact the provincial office that registers property and pay a
small fee for a computer printout that may or may not be accurate.
You'll be asked for the current owner's name and the car's VIN, which
is usually found on the driver's side of the dashboard.

You can avoid buying vehicles that are stolen or have finance owing
by asking for proof of purchase and payment from any individual who
offers to sell a used car for an incredibly low price. Check the sales contract to determine who granted the original loan and call the lender to
see if it's been repaid. Place a call to the provincial Ministry of
Transport to ascertain whether the car is registered in the seller's
name. Find out if a finance company is named as beneficiary on the
auto insurance policy. Finally, call up the original dealer to determine
whether there are any outstanding claims.

There's another, high-tech, way to get the goods on the seller. Have
a "vehicle history" check done by a dealer of that particular model
through a computer link-up with the automaker's on-line network.
That check will tell you who the previous owners and dealers were, what
warranty and recall repairs were carried out at what mileage, and what
other free "goodwill" repairs may still apply.

Misrepresentation (wrong model year)

That bargain-priced car or truck you just bought may be a year older
than you think. That's why you should check its true age by looking at
the date-of-manufacture plate found on the driver's side door pillar. If

the date of manufacture reads 7/96, it was one of the last 1996 models made before the September changeover to the 1997 models. Exceptions to this rule are those vehicles that are redesigned or relatively new to the market, which arrive at dealerships in early spring or mid-summer. They're considered to be next year's models but depreciate more quickly due to their earlier launching (a difference that narrows over time).

Seller, protect thyself (!)

Now, one last word on protecting yourself from legal liability if you are selling a vehicle to a private individual. Normally, once you take the tags and give the buyer a bill of sale, you're no longer the registered owner. Unfortunately, though, if you don't personally go down to the registry office and make sure the title has changed, you could be sued by an insurance company for damages arising from an accident if you're still the owner of record. *Toronto Sun* columnist Maryanna Lewyckyj tells of one case where a driver sold his clunker for $250; six months later he was sued by Liberty Mutual Insurance for $30,000 in damages caused by the subsequent owner. Apparently, the new owner never changed the registration.

Choosing the Right Kind of Vehicle

Import or domestic model?

Forget the popular mythology about "North American–made" and "foreign-made." DaimlerChrysler has dramatically altered the rules of interpretation. Furthermore, the seesawing of foreign currency values has led to a rush of foreign automakers moving production facilities to the U.S., Canada, and Mexico, in addition to importing major components from offshore. Surprisingly, this has been accomplished without a corresponding drop in quality control. On the other hand, it has made it practically impossible to designate many vehicles as "American."

Whether you buy domestic or imported, overall vehicle quality has improved a great deal during the past decade. Premature rusting is less of a problem and factory-related defects aren't as numerous as they once were. But problems remain. Owners of vehicles made by GM, Ford, or Chrysler still report serious deficiencies, often during the first three years in service. These include electrical system failures caused by faulty computer modules, malfunctioning ABS, failure-prone air conditioning and automatic transmissions, as well as defective powertrains, fuel systems, suspensions, steering, and paint. Further evidence that American-built cars are more failure-prone than their Japanese-made counterparts can be seen in the service bulletins sent out each month by the automakers. For this guide, I've compared the bulletins of a 1996 Ford Taurus and Sable to those of a 1996 Toyota Camry and Honda Accord.

1996 Toyota Camry Sedan
Technical Service Bulletins

Number	Date	Name
BR003-98	Aug 98	Front Brake Noise
BO020-98	Jul 98	1999 Toyota Seat Belt Extenders
EL002-98	Apr 98	Cigarette Lighter Service
EG00597	May 97	Charcoal Canister Humming Noise
AC00297	May 97	Air Conditioning Evaporator Odor
BR00697	Mar 97	Rear Brake Squeak
AU00296	Oct 96	AM Static Noise on Vehicles With Power Antennas
BO008-96	Aug 96	Stain on Paint
BO00696	May 96	Rattle from Rear Window
BO00496	Apr 96	Moonroof Panel Wind Noise
BR00296	Mar 96	Front Brake Groan Noise
SU00196	Mar 96	Rear Suspension Squeak/Groan Noise

1996 Honda Accord Sedan
Technical Service Bulletins

Number	Date	Name
98-072	Oct 98	Recall: Accord Wire Harness Routing
98-081	Oct 98	Emissions Warranty Extension
98-061	Sep 98	Automatic Transmission In Warranty Exchange Program
98-058	Aug 98	Poor Radio Reception
98-042	May 98	Oil Seepage From The Engine Block
98-023	Mar 98	Leak From The Power Steering Pump
98-019	Feb 98	Audio Unit In Warranty Exchange/Out of Warranty Repair
98-009	Jan 98	Ticking Noise From the Valve Train
97-060	Sep 97	Front Door Glass Comes Out of Run Channel
95-057	Aug 97	Fifth Gear Grinds During Upshift.
97-031	Aug 97	A/C Does Not Blow Cold Air
97-016	Apr 97	Manually Adjustable Seats Hard to Release
97-018	Mar 97	Rear Wheel Bearing Noise
97-008	Feb 97	Static When Adjusting the Radio Volume
96-050	Nov 96	Brake Fluid Leak from the ABS Modulator
96-052	Oct 96	Fuel Gauge Stays At Empty
96-055	Oct 96	Clutch Judder At Cold Start
93033	Jun 96	Seat Belt Tongue Stopper Button
96025	Jun 96	Power Seat Does Not Move Forward or Backward
94041	May 96	Exhaust System Buzz
96022	Apr 96	Doors Lock When Lifting Handle
95025	Mar 96	Creaking from Clutch Pedal
91030	Jan 96	Seat Belt - Slow to Retract
93049	Oct 95	Instrument Panel Creak
95043	Oct 95	Poor Fit Of Wheel Center Cap
95041	Oct 95	Screeching Noise When Lowering The Drivers Window

1996 Ford Taurus
Technical Service Bulletins

Number	Date	Name
99-19-4	Sep 99	Brake Vibration/Inspection/Friction Material Replacement
99-19-5	Sep 99	A/C-Musty and Mildew Type Odors-Service Procedure
99-18-4	Sep 99	Harsh 3-2 Downshift/Shudder When Accelerating-Turning
99-18-3	Sep 99	Engine Oil Leak From Oil Pan Gasket – Previous Repair
99-13-9	Jun 99	Inadvertent Disabling Of Brake Shift Interlock
99-12-10	Jun 99	Industrial Fallout/Acid Rain Etching Neutralization
99-12-9	Jun 99	Whining/Buzzing Noise In Speakers Caused By Fuel Pump
99-12-7	Jun 99	Long Crank/Slow Start/MIL Lamp On/Trouble Codes
99-11-1	Jun 99	Noise/Vibration/Harshness-TSB Special
99-7-1	Apr 99	A/T-High Idle Harsh Engage/Surge or Power Shuffle
99-6-5	Apr 99	Windnoise Around Side Doors-Service Tips
99-5-7	Mar 99	Anti-Lock Brake System (ABS) Lamp On, Codes C1165, C1175
99-2-3	Feb 99	Windshield Sealing For Water Leaks-Service Tip
99-2-6	Feb 99	Fuel Gauge Concerns-Service Tip
99-1-5	Jan 99	MIL Illuminated/Trouble Codes Stored/Spark Knock
99-1-4	Jan 99	A/T-Harsh 3-2 Downshifts During Braking/High Engine RPM
98-26-2	Jan 99	Tips To Resolve Volatility Related Driveability Concerns
98-25-13	Dec 98	Power Windows May Not Operate
98-25-1	Dec 98	No Start/Fuel Pump Inoperative/Fuel Pump Wire Chafing
98-23-10	Nov 98	Mass Air Flow Sensor Contamination-Service Tip
98-21-12	Oct 98	Hard Start/Long Crank Time, 3.0L, 3.4L
98-20-10	Oct 98	Buzz/Rattle Noise-Loose Catalyst Or Muffler Heat Shield
98-19-2	Sep 98	No Start/No Crank-Battery Discharged/Current Drain
98-18-13	Sep 98	Steering Wheel Nibble Felt When Driving At 45 And 75 MPH
98-13-7	Jul 98	Power Shuffle And/Or Surge Between 45-60 MPH, 3.0L 2V
98-10-7	May 98	A/T-No 4th Gear And Trouble Codes Stored, AX4N
98-9-4	May 98	Front End Accessory Drive Belt Noise/Slipping
98-9-9	May 98	Fuel Injectors, Non-Warranty Reimbursement Testing
98-7-4	Apr 98	Oil Leaks-New Silicone Gasket And Sealant
98-6-5	Mar 98	A/T-Torque Converter Clutch Not Engaging/Codes Stored
98-5A-6	Mar 98	Anti-Lock Brakes Cycling On Rough Roads
98-5A-13	Mar 98	Brakes-New Application-Silicone Compound/Grease
98-5A-11	Mar 98	Brakes-Elimination Of Sanding Rotors And Drums
98-5A-4	Mar 98	Preventing Brake Vibration, Lug Nut Torque Procedures
98-3-7	Feb 98	Intermittent Neutral Condition, No Forward/Reverse, AX4N
98-3-8	Feb 98	AX4S/AX4N New Transaxle Fluid
98-2-7	Feb 98	Air Conditioning Musty And Mildew Type Odors
97-26-11	Dec 97	Rattling Noise During Acceleration, 3.0L
97-25-2	Dec 97	Subframe-Front, Rear Retention Nuts Spin During Removal
97-25-5	Dec 97	Chirping/Squeaking From Blower Motor At Low Speeds
97-24-16	Nov 97	All Cooling System Concerns, 3.0L Engines
97-24-2	Nov 97	Water Leaking Onto Passenger Compartment Floor
97-23-7	Nov 97	AX4S/AX4N, Trouble Codes Stored After Transaxle Replaced
97-22-1	Oct 97	Revised Delta Pressure Feedback EGR (DPFE) Voltage Range
97-19-11	Sep 97	On-Vehicle Heater Core Pressure Test For Warranty Claim
97-18-4	Sep 97	Radio Am Band Static While Driving
97-17-9	Aug 97	Stall On Deceleration or Intermittent Stall Warm Weather
97-17-2	Aug 97	Rear View Mirror Reattachment
97-15-2	Jul 97	High Effort, Rough Feel When Operating Door Handles
97-13-3	Jun 97	Grunt or Honk Noise from Steering Wheel
97-11-9	May 97	Windshield Wiper Blade Element
97-11-5	May 97	Remote Anti-Theft Personality Transmitter Reprogramming
97-10-4	May 97	Engine Cooling Fan Module Service Information

97-9-12	Apr 97	Service Tip - Extended 2-3 Shift
97-9-8	Apr 97	Service Tip - Reprogramming the PCM
97-9-5	Apr 97	Hard Starting, Long Crank, Stalling
9788	Apr 97	Service Tips - Electronic Automatic Temperature Control
9786	Apr 97	MIL ON, Any DTCs From P0300 to P0308 in Memory
9763	Mar 97	Service Tip - Air Bag Sliding Contact Service
9723	Jan 97	Clunk on Heavy Accel or Decel
9725	Jan 97	Clunking Noise from Front Suspension
96263	Dec 96	Rear Tire Inner Edge Wear
96255	Dec 96	Reduction in Power Steering Assist While in Gear
962515	Dec 96	Creaking Noise in A-Pillar
96241	Nov 96	Headliner Sag in Rear
96221	Oct 96	Fog/Film on Windshield/Interior Glass
96S51	Sep 96	Recall 96S51 AX4N Transaxle Park Mechanism Inspection
96S50	Sep 96	Recall 96S50 AX4S and AX4N Transaxle Park Mechanism
96156	Jul 96	A/C System Service TSB List
96141	Jul 96	Windnoise at A-Pillar at Highway Speeds
96131	Jun 96	Thump, Clunk, or Chuckle from Front End
96S39	Jun 96	Recall 96S39 Park Mechanism Malfunction
96B90	Jun 96	Program 96B90 – Tailgate Applique Inspection/Replacement
96109	May 96	Malfunction Indicator Lamp On, Codes P0300 - P0306
96106	May 96	NGS Tester - Incorrect Display During Diagnostics
9687	Apr 96	Transaxle - AX4S/AX4N Driveline Noises
9676	Mar 96	Malfunction Indicator Lamp Illuminated
9678	Mar 96	Cooling System - Drain Plug on Block is Oversized
9659	Feb 96	Noise - Click from Transaxle during Reverse Engagement
9649	Feb 96	Transaxle - AX4S- Revised Thrust Washer tabs
96S34	Feb 96	Recall 96S34 Brake Fluid Indicator Light Malfunction
96315	Jan 96	PDI - Transaxle Engagement and Shift Concerns
9631	Jan 96	Windnoise at A-Pillar or Windshield
9636	Jan 96	No Start or Stall
9635	Jan 96	Cold Engine Hesistation/Stumble
9633	Jan 96	Front Suspension Squeak or Groan

It doesn't take a genius to see that Ford's Taurus, like most American front-drives, is poorly engineered, and unreliable. Is it any wonder most buyers prefer Asian cars?

Japanese vehicles hold up fairly well, until their fifth year. Then the front brake calipers and rotors will need replacing and the rack-and-pinion steering system will likely have to be overhauled. Furthermore, the front-wheel-drive constant-velocity joints will probably need replacing—at a cost of about $350 each. These routine repairs pale in comparison to what the average Big Three vehicle will cost to maintain over the same period. Hence, a reputation for requiring fewer repairs than the competition and an incredibly slow rate of depreciation are two powerful reasons why shoppers willingly pay inflated prices (plus, they know they'll recoup much of what they paid come trade-in time).

Japanese automakers redesign their vehicles every three to four years, while American automakers often wait a decade or longer. The Big Three American automobile manufacturers know that the Japanese and their dealers build, market, and service vehicles to a higher standard than the Americans do. That's why the Big Three gave up much of the small-car market to Asian producers in the late '80s; it was easier and more profitable for them to buy high-quality Asian products and market them as homegrown. Today, the small, compact, and luxury car markets have been virtually conquered by Japanese imports.

Don't buy the myth that parts for imports aren't easily found. It's actually easier to locate parts for Japanese vehicles than for domestic vehicles. This is due to the large number of units produced, the presence of hundreds of independent suppliers, the ease with which relatively simple parts can be interchanged from one model to another, and the large reservoir of used parts stocked by junkyards. Incidentally, when a part is hard to find, the *Mitchell Manual* is a useful guide to substituting parts that can be used for many different models. It's available in some libraries, most auto parts stores, and practically all junkyards.

In my *Lemon-Aid New Cars*, the vehicles singled out as the most reliable and durable are Japanese makes, some European imports, and American co-ventures (such as the Chevrolet Metro, which is actually a re-badged Suzuki). But where used vehicles are concerned, the following American-made rear-drive cars are better choices than many imports: Ford's Mustang, T-Bird, Cougar, Crown Victoria, Mercury Grand Marquis, and Lincoln Town Car; and GM's Camaro, Caprice, and Cadillac Fleetwood. Their depreciated prices are more competitive than the inflated values of Asian and European imports, they're cheap and easy to service almost anywhere, they support lots of power-hungry accessories, and they sustain high mileage with fewer major breakdowns. The only problem is that American rear-drives have become an endangered species, with Ford being the only automaker still churning them out in large numbers. Interestingly, after changing over to front-drive for almost the past two decades, GM says it will soon return to rear-drive in its future luxury cars. One can only wonder what's next: perhaps, the return of the side-vent window?

Forget Lexus, Infiniti, and Cadillac. Ford's rear-drive Crown Victoria and Grand Marquis are two of the best large luxury cars money can buy (ask any cop).

Are South Korean cars and SUVs the bargains they pretend to be? Hyundai, perhaps. Daewoo and Kia, definitely not! Generally, South Korean vehicles are poor imitations of their Japanese counterparts. They start to fall apart after their third year due to poor-quality body construction, cheap and unreliable electrical components, and parts suppliers who put low prices ahead of reliability and durability. This has been particularly evident with Hyundai's Excel and early Sonatas. During the past several years, though, Hyundai's product lineup has improved and its base warranty is now sufficiently comprehensive to protect owners from most of the more expensive breakdowns.

Sales are soaring for both Daewoo and Kia, mainly because they offer inexpensive, fuel-efficient small cars (Kia also has a moderately priced SUV, the Sportage) that also come with comprehensive warranties. But, unlike Hyundai, both automakers lead a precarious existence; Hyundai recently bought Kia out of bankruptcy and Daewoo is up for sale. Furthermore, both automakers have very weak dealer networks, which makes for spotty servicing and a lower resale value.

European cars and minivans aren't as reliable as their Japanese counterparts. Instead, they offer first-class handling, extraordinary comfort, and a slow rate of depreciation that rivals all competitors. There are some exceptions to this rule, however, like the early VW EuroVan, Audi's Fox, and the Yugo.

VW's Camper minivan: all the comforts of home during those long roadside waits for Helmut and Franz to come along with a tow truck.

Now that we've pointed out what's good about European vehicles, let's look at their dark side. First and foremost, they are complicated and expensive to service, requiring frequent trips to the dealer. Secondly, parts aren't easily found outside of the dealer network. With some European models, you can count on lots of aggravation and expense due to the unacceptably slow distribution of parts and their high markup. Because these companies have a quasi-monopoly on replacement parts, there are few independent suppliers you can turn to for help. And auto wreckers, the last-chance repository for inexpensive car parts, are unlikely to carry European parts for vehicles older than three years or manufactured in small numbers.

These vehicles also age badly. Weakest areas remain the electronic control modules, electrical and fuel system, brakes, accessories (sound system, AC, etc.), and body components.

Other Buying Considerations

Front-wheel drive

Front-wheel drives direct engine power to the front wheels, which *pull* the vehicle forward, while the rear wheels simply support the rear. The biggest benefit of front-wheel drive (FWD) is foul-weather traction. With the engine and transmission up front, there's lots of extra weight pressing down on the front-drive wheels, increasing tire grip in snow and on wet pavement. However, when driving up a steep hill or towing a boat or trailer, the weight shifts and there's no longer a traction advantage.

Although I recommend a number of FWD vehicles in this guide, I don't like them. Granted, front-wheel drives give a bit more interior room (no transmission hump), provide more carlike handling, and offer better fuel economy than rear-drives. But damage from potholes and fender-benders is usually more extensive, and maintenance costs (premature front tire and brake wear, in particular) are much higher than with rear-wheel drives.

Servicing front-wheel drives can be a real nightmare. Entire steering, suspension, and drivetrain assemblies must be replaced when just one component is defective. Downtime is considerable, the cost of parts is far too high, and the drivetrain and its components are not designed for the do-it-yourself mechanic. A new FWD transmission assembly, called a transaxle, can cost about $3,000 to repair, compared to $1,000 for a rear-wheel-drive transmission.

I also feel front-wheel drives are unsafe because braking requires a whole new set of reflexes than what we've developed over the years with rear-wheel-drive vehicles. You remember the routine from driving school: *When in a skid, pump the brakes lightly and turn into the direction of the skid.* Well, if you pump the brakes of a FWD in a skid, you've bought the farm, because the front (steering) wheels will lock up, and you will lose steering control. The car will continue in a straight line, so if you skid on a right-hand curve, you will cross the path of oncoming traffic before you run off the road. On a left-hand curve, you will skid off the right hand side of the road before you stop. What should you do in a skid? Apply light brake and gas, while remembering that the front-drive wheels are trying to get enough traction to pull the front end to where they're pointed.

Rear-wheel drive

Rear-wheel drives direct engine power to the rear wheels, which *push* the vehicle forward. The front wheels steer and support the front of the vehicle. With the engine up front, the transmission in the middle, and the drive axle in the rear, there's plenty of room for larger and more durable drivetrain components. This makes for less crash damage, lower maintenance costs, and higher towing capacities than front-wheel drives.

On the other hand, rear-drives don't have as much weight over the rear wheels as front-drives do (and putting cement blocks in the bed or trunk will only void your transmission warranty). As such, they can't provide as much traction on wet and icy roads unless equipped with an expensive traction-control system.

Four-wheel drive

Four-wheel drives (4X4) direct engine power through a transfer case to all four wheels, which *pull and push* the vehicle forward, giving you twice as much traction. On most models, when four-wheel drive isn't engaged, the vehicle reverts to front- or rear-drive. Keep in mind that extended driving over dry pavement with four-wheel drive engaged will cause the driveline to bind and result in serious damage.

Many four-wheel-drive customers have been turned off by the typically rough and noisy driveline; vague, trucklike handling; high repair costs; and poor fuel economy. Also, extended driving over dry pavement with four-wheel-drive engaged will cause the driveline to bind and result in serious damage. No wonder car-based SUVs like the Toyota RAV4 and the Honda CR-V are so popular: buyers want versality without sacrificing fuel economy, comfort, or handling.

All-wheel drive

Essentially, this is four-wheel drive *all the time.* Used mostly in sedans and minivans, all-wheel drive (AWD) never needs to be deactivated when running over dry pavement and doesn't require the heavy transfer case (although some sport-utilities and pickups do use a special transfer case) that raises ground clearance and cuts fuel economy. AWD-equipped vehicles aren't recommended for off-roading because of their lower ground clearance and fragile driveline parts, which aren't as rugged as four-wheel-drive components.

Diesels

Diesel engines become more efficient as the engine load increases, whereas gasoline engines become less so. This is the main reason diesels are best used where the driving cycle includes a lot of city driving, with slow speeds, frequent stops, and long idling times. At full throttle, both engines are essentially equal from a fuel-efficiency standpoint. The gasoline engine, however, leaves the diesel in the dust when it comes to high-speed performance. Many owners of diesel-equipped vehicles are frustrated by excessive repair costs and poor road performance on vehicles that lack turbo. Bear in mind that before the fuel savings can outweigh the high cost of a diesel purchase, the average owner would have to drive 40,000–50,000 kilometres per year.

Diesel engines aren't all equally reliable, either. For passenger cars, Mercedes-Benz and Volkswagen diesels perform extraordinarily well and are quite durable. Chrysler trucks equipped with Cummins diesels are also good all-around performers. But, when it comes to Ford and GM diesels, owners report sub-par performance, frequent breakdowns, and poor dealer servicing. *Lemon-Aid Used 4X4s, Vans, and Trucks* gives a detailed analysis of the pros and cons of diesel performance and an evaluation of diesel-equipped vehicles.

GM says it will equip future trucks with an Isuzu diesel that's well-regarded by truckers in Europe and Japan and well-known to American boaters (it powers some of the larger Bayliner cruisers).

Rustproofing

First off, remember that the best rustproofing protection is to keep your vehicle in a dry, unheated garage or outside. Never bring your car in and out of a heated garage during the winter months. The months when temperatures are just a bit above freezing are the worst for rust promotion; especially during that time, keep your vehicle clean and dry.

If you live in an area where roads are heavily salted in winter, or in a coastal region, make sure you regularly have undercoating sprayed on the rocker panels (door bottoms), the rear hatch's bottom edge, and the wheelwells. This annual treatment costs less than $100. It will protect vital suspension and chassis components, make the vehicle ride more quietly, and allow you to ask a higher price at trade-in time. The only downside, which can be checked by asking for references: the undercoating may give off an unpleasant odour for months and it may drip, soiling your driveway.

A full rustproofing job doesn't offer that much protection—no matter how long the guarantee. In fact, you have a greater chance of seeing your rustproofer go belly-up before he makes good on your warranty than of having your untreated vehicle ravaged by premature rusting. Even if the rustproofer stays in business, you're likely to get a song-and-dance about why the warranty won't cover so-called "internal" rusting or why repairs will be delayed until the sheet metal is actually rusted through.

Collectibles?

If you're seriously interested in collecting cars, remember that most vehicles jump in value after their 20th birthday. So you probably won't lose money if you buy a car of this vintage, especially if it's a convertible (trucks, sport-utilities, and vans are riskier investments). Shop the Internet and auto shows—they're also good places to contact wholesalers and restorers. Car clubs also offer a wealth of information, and are regularly listed in major auto magazines like *AutoWeek, Car and Driver, Motor Trend,* and *Road & Track. Hemmings' Motor News* and *Old Cars Weekly* out of Iola, Wisconsin, are two other excellent sources of collector news.

Summary to Saving Money and Keeping Safe

You can get a good used vehicle at a reasonable price—it just takes lots of patience and homework. You can further protect yourself by becoming thoroughly familiar with your legal rights as outlined in Part Two and buying a vehicle recommended in Part Three. Here is a summary of the steps to take to keep your risk to a minimum:

1. Keep your vehicle for at least 10 years.
2. Trade in your vehicle if the dealer's sales tax reduction is more than the potential profit of selling privately.
3. Sell to a private party (10 percent premium).
4. Buy from a private party (10 percent savings).
5. Use an auto broker to save time and money.
6. Buy a *Lemon-Aid*-recommended vehicle for depreciation, parts, and service savings.
7. Buy a 3- or 4-year-old vehicle with lots of original warranty that can be transferred (35–50 percent savings over a new vehicle).
8. Choose a vehicle that's crashworthy and cheap to insure.
9. Carefully inspect Japanese-built vehicles that have reached their fifth year (CV joints, steering box, and front brakes).
10. Don't buy an extended warranty ($500–$1,000 savings) unless it's recommended in this guide.
11. Have non-warranty repairs done by independent garages offering lifetime brake and exhaust repairs (50 percent savings).
12. Install used or reconditioned mechanical parts (30–50 percent savings).
13. Keep all the previous owners' repair bills to facilitate warranty claims and help mechanics know what's already been replaced or repaired.
14. Upon delivery, adjust mirrors to eliminate blind spots and adjust head restraints to prevent your head from snapping back in the event of a collision. On airbag-equipped vehicles, move the seat backwards more than half its travel distance and sit at least 25 centimetres away from the airbag housing. Make sure the spare tire and tire jack haven't been removed from the trunk. Get shoulder/lapbelts for the rear seats; lapbelts alone can be deadly.
15. Make sure the dealer and automaker have your name in their computers as the new owner of record. Ask for a copy of your vehicle's history, stored in the same computers.

Part Two
FIGHTING BACK!

Dumb and Dumber

"Following our conversation this afternoon, I am submitting herewith a formal request that your company stop treating Canadian Firestone tire owners as second-class customers by denying them refunds if they wish to replace tires targeted in NHTSA's September 1st advisory.

As you know, your company in the United States has "done the right thing" by announcing that American owners of the affected tires would get up to $140 per replacement tire, if the owner wished to have the tire replaced. I applaud this decision benefiting your American customers.

On the other hand, I cannot accept that you won't give any refunds to Canadians. Why would you go out of your way to create a situation where you dictate a Scrooge-like Canadian policy that's inconsistent, unfair, and guaranteed to create distrust and anger between your Canadian customers and retailers?"

*October 27, 2000, email I sent to Jerry Priddle,
Bridgestone/Firestone Canada Administrator*

Chrysler's Armpit-solution for Paint Problems

"Paint-line workers at Chrysler Corp.'s Jeep plant were asked to stop using antiperspirant after the company discovered that falling flakes left costly blemishes on the new Jeep...General Motors officials contacted late yesterday said they didn't believe they had a similar problem....

One woman filed a grievance last year after her supervisor asked to check her armpits...."

Newsday, 1991

Protests Work

Chicago social activist Saul Alinsky was right: business leaders and politicians *do* hear better through their rears than their ears. If a Houston, Texas, TV station hadn't blown the whistle on Firestone "killer" tires this year, the tiremaker and Ford, its co-conspirator, would never have publicly recalled the tires. Plus, thanks to organized consumer protests, the Firestone recall took six months to complete, instead of the originally projected two years.

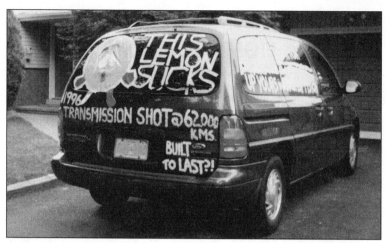

Ford customer relations has awesome, uncanny powers. It turned the owner of this Windstar from a dutiful wife and mother into a sign-carrying, service manager–chasing, letter-writing consumer activist in just a few weeks.

Automobile owners are angry and they're organizing. They're fed up with unreliable and expensive-to-maintain cars and trucks built by Chrysler, Ford, and General Motors. I'm not surprised that quality is so bad. DaimlerChrysler, having faced bankruptcy twice in the past three decades, uses suppliers that offer the cheapest, not the most reliable or durable, brake, AC, powertrain, and body components. Ford's continued use of a cheaper, failure-prone aluminum forward clutch piston in automatic transmissions for over a decade of production doesn't come as any great shock either. This is the same company that continued to make fire-prone Pintos and Bobcats in the '70s because its accountants projected greater savings in stonewalling burn victims than in changing a $10 part. And GM's switch to poor-quality front-drives almost two decades ago has made a dramatic impact upon its market share—down to almost 28 percent from a high of 50 percent.

Don't expect government to protect you or business to regulate itself effectively; there aren't any incentives for politicians or business leaders to give consumers first-class goods and services. This is why automobile owners are taking the initiative and organizing successful protests—on the Internet, in the streets, and through the courts—against unsafe, poor-quality cars and tires, secret warranties, and misrepresentation.

The British Columbia Dead Ford site (see Appendix II) mixed satire with effective consumer tips for dissatisfied Ford owners. Ford has failed to close down these kinds of sites because courts have ruled they have a right to be heard.

Few people like to complain, and even fewer are willing to make their dissatisfaction public. Automakers count on this apathy, and set up customer call centres to dissuade owners from pursuing their claims. Only complaints threatening legal action and sent to a manufacturer's product liability or legal affairs division are given serious consideration. With 10 percent of cars estimated by Runzheimer International to be "lemons" and automakers promising more quality than they deliver, buyers have discovered that they must either "act up" or get shut out. Is it any wonder that Canadian consumers, such as Sally (owner of the Windstar featured on the previous page), are banding together into protest groups and slapping lemon signs on their vehicles to get a fair shake?

Now before you take to the streets or set up your protest website, let's look at the laws you can use to your advantage without hiring a lawyer and the little-known warranties you can used to get your money back.

Getting Your Money Back

When letter writing and public protests fail to elicit a satisfactory response, your only recourse is to sue, or at least threaten to sue. Yet we all know that you can win in court and still end up losing your shirt. That's why this section of the book is dedicated to helping you get your money back—without going to court or getting frazzled by the broken promises or "benign neglect" of the seller. But if going to court is your only recourse, you'll find here the jurisprudence you need to get an out-of-court settlement or to win your case without spending a fortune on lawyers or research.

First of all, forget about the seller's claim that "there's no warranty" or "because it was sold 'as is' you can't claim a refund." This is all hogwash. Any sales contract for a used vehicle can be cancelled for one or more of the following reasons:
• The vehicle was misrepresented.
• The vehicle was unfit for the purpose for which it was purchased.
• The vehicle was not reasonably durable, considering its selling price, how well it was maintained, the mileage driven, and the type of driving.
• The vehicle was seriously defective at the time of purchase.

For example, if the seller claims that a minivan can pull a 900 kg (2,000 lb.) trailer and you discover that it can barely tow half that weight, you can cancel the contract for misrepresentation. The same principle applies to a seller's exaggerated claims concerning a vehicle's off-road capability, fuel economy, and reliability, as well as to "demonstrators" that are in fact used cars with false (rolled-back) odometer readings.

It's essential that printed evidence and/or witnesses (relatives are not excluded) be available to confirm that the false representation actually occurred. These misrepresentations must also concern an important fact that substantially affects the vehicle's performance, reliability, or value.

Some vehicles, like sports cars and full-sized trucks, are meant to be driven hard, but when they fail to live up to the advertised hype, sellers often blame the owner for having pushed the vehicle beyond its limits. Therefore, when you attempt to set aside the contract, the testimony of an independent mechanic is essential to prove that the vehicle's poor performance isn't caused by negligent maintenance or abusive driving.

Another hurdle to overcome is the "reasonable diligence" rule that requires one to file suit within a reasonable time after purchase or after the defect is discovered. The delay for filing a lawsuit can be extended if there's a secret warranty that extended the parameters of the original warranty, or if the seller has been promising to correct the defects for some time or has done some minor repairs while negotiating a final settlement. In cases of this sort, most courts will accept a four- to six-year delay, particularly with paint delamination claims.

Warranties

Unscrupulous dealers and con artists won't tell you this, but it's true: *every vehicle sold has some kind of warranty that can be enforced in court.* In fact, every new or used vehicle sold in Canada is covered by both provincial and federal warranties that protect you from misrepresentation and a host of other evils. Furthermore, Canadian law and jurisprudence presume that car dealers, unlike private sellers, are aware of the defects present in the vehicles they sell. That's why they're paid a commission. The vehicles they sell are expected to be reasonably durable and merchantable. What is reasonably durable depends on the price paid, kilometres driven, the purchaser's driving habits, and how well the vehicle was maintained by the owner. Judges carefully weigh all these factors in awarding compensation or cancelling a sale.

There is no standard warranty period; however, some provinces require that dealers provide minimal warranty coverage. Safety restraints, like airbags and seatbelts, often have coverage extended for the lifetime of the vehicle. On the other hand, you can lose warranty coverage through abusive driving or inadequate maintenance, or by purchasing aftermarket products and services, such as gas-saving gadgets, rustproofing, paint protectors, air conditioning, and van conversions.

The manufacturer's or dealer's warranty is a legal promise that the product sold will perform in the normal and customary manner for which it was designed. This promise remains in force regardless of the number of subsequent owners, as long as the warranty's original time/mileage limits haven't expired.

Sometimes dealers will do all sorts of minor repairs that don't correct the problem, and then after the warranty runs out they'll tell you that major repairs are needed. You can avoid this nasty surprise by repeatedly bringing in your vehicle to the dealership before the warranty ends. During each visit insist that a written work order include the specific nature of the problem, as *you* see it, and that it carries the notation that this is the second, third, or fourth time the same problem has been brought to the dealer's attention. Write it down yourself, if need be. This allows you to show a pattern of non-performance by the dealer during the warranty period and establishes that it's a serious and chronic problem. When the warranty expires, you have the legal right to demand that it be extended on those items consistently reappearing on your handful of work orders. *Lowe v. Chrysler,* found in "Key Court Decisions" (see page 101), is an excellent judgment that reinforces this important principle.

A retired GM service manager gave me another effective tactic to use when you're not sure a dealer's warranty "repairs" will actually correct the problem for a reasonable period of time after the warranty expires. Here's what he says you should do:

> When you pick up the vehicle after the warranty repair has been done, hand the service manager a note to be put in your file that says you appreciate the warranty repair; however, you intend to return and ask for further warranty coverage if the problem reappears before a reasonable amount of time has elapsed—even if the original warranty has expired. A copy of the same note should be sent to the automaker.... Keep your copy of the note in the glove compartment as cheap insurance against paying for a repair that wasn't fixed correctly the first time....

Emissions control warranties

These little-publicized warranties come with all new vehicles and are automatically transferred to subsequent owners. They cover the emissions control system for up to 8 years/130,000 km. Unfortunately, although owner manuals vaguely mention the emissions warranty, most don't specify which parts are guaranteed.

EPA investigators had waged a longstanding battle with Ford over the company's charging its customers for repairs covered by the emissions warranty. Each time customers complained to the EPA, Ford refunded the money or agreed to repair the vehicle—but not to change its warranty practice.

In 1989, the U.S. EPA sued Chrysler and Ford for billing customers for emissions-related repairs that should have been done for free. Chrysler was fined $660,000 for denying warranty coverage to 66 car owners for replacement of and repairs and adjustments to carburetors, fuel injectors, and turbochargers. These owners paid from $22 to $645 to have their cars fixed, even though the repairs fell under warranty. Ford was fined $92,000 for charging for similar repairs. The government had proposed a $230,000 fine for denying the warranty to 23 owners, but reduced the amount when Ford agreed to repay over 500 consumers.

EMISSIONS COVERAGE

Under the Emissions Control Systems coverage of this warranty, Ford Motor Company of Canada Limited warrants that your vehicle:

1) is designed, built and equipped to conform, at the time it was manufactured, with the Emissions Regulations under the Canada Motor Vehicle Safety Act. and

2) is free from defects in factory-supplied materials or workmanship which would cause it to fail to conform to those regulations for a period of five years or 80,000 kilometres, whichever occurs first.

Your Ford of Canada dealer will not charge you to adjust, repair, or replace (including labour and diagnosis) an emissions-related part. If the diagnosis reveals no emissions-related defect, the Emissions Control Systems coverage of this warranty does not apply.

The following list of parts is covered under the Emissions Control Systems coverage of this warranty for 5 years/80,000 kilometres.

• Air/Fuel Feedback Control System and Sensors
• Altitude Compensation System
• Catalytic Converter
• Controls for Deceleration
• Electronic Engine Control Processor
• Electronic Engine Control Sensors and Switches

• Electronic Ignition System
• Exhaust Gas Recirculating (EGR) Valve, Spacer, Plate, and Associated Parts
• Exhaust Manifold
• Exhaust Pipe (Manifold to Catalyst)
• Fuel Filler Cap and Neck Restrictor
• Fuel Injection System
• Fuel Tank
• Fuel Vapor Storage Canister, Liquid Separator, and Associated Controls
• Ignition Coil and/or Control Module
• Intake Air Flow Meter/Temperature Sensor Assembly
• Intake Manifold
• Malfunction Indicator Light System (MIL)
• PCV System and Oil Filler Cap
• Spark Control Components
• Spark Plugs and Ignition Wires
• Throttle Air Control Bypass Valve
• Throttle Body Assembly (MFI)
• TWC Air Control Valve

The emissions-related bulbs, hoses, clamps, brackets, tubes, gaskets, seals, belts, connectors, gasoline fuel lines, and wiring harnesses that are used with the components listed above are also covered by the Emissions Control Systems coverage of this warranty.

The above chart was prepared by Ford Canada to give consumers an idea as to which parts can be charged back to the company. American Ford owners have much longer extended warranties that cover essentially the same components.

The dealer service bulletins listed in Part Three, "Secret Warranties/Service Tips," show some parts failures that are covered under the emissions warranty. If you've paid for repairs that should have been covered by this warranty (Ford 3.8L and 4.2L engine gaskets and Villager, Quest, Maxima, and Pathfinder exhaust manifold bolts, for example), contact the automaker and your dealer and ask for a refund. (Don't be shy about mentioning the EPA lawsuit.)

Before leaving the subject of emission warranties, here's one last suggestion: make sure you get your emissions system checked out thoroughly by a dealer or independent garage before the emissions warranty expires and prior to having the vehicle inspected by provincial emissions inspectors. In addition to ensuring you pass provincial tests, this precaution could save you over $1,000 if both your catalytic converter and your other emissions components are faulty.

After-warranty Assistance

Chrysler

Unlike Ford and GM, Chrysler executives abhor putting anything in writing that customers can use to obtain post-warranty repair refunds—even when the defect, like faulty engines, transmissions, and paint, is inescapably evident. Consequently, the automaker has been dragged, kicking and screaming, into the public arena, through lawsuits and mass demonstrations, and forced to acknowledge that "goodwill" refunds are available for the above defects. Still, the details relating to these refund programs are sketchy and often contradictory.

⸱ ADDENDUM TO BASIC WARRANTY

The following applies to 1993 through 1997 New Yorker, LHS, Concorde, Intrepid, Vision and Grand Cherokee vehicles equipped with factory-installed air conditioning:

> *The Basic Warranty coverage for the air conditioner evaporator has been extended to 7 years or 115,000 kilometres, whichever occurs first, from the vehicle's warranty start date.*
>
> *This extended coverage applies to all owners of the vehicle. All of the other warranty terms apply to this extension.*

We suggest that you keep this addendum card in your warranty information booklet.

AD9502-B

This is a rare piece of written evidence, showing Chrysler will pay for an AC failure—long after the original warranty has elapsed. A Chrysler Canada official gave me this document following a settlement meeting; Chrysler U.S. officials swear it doesn't exist.

Nevertheless, Chrysler Canada has been much more successful in handling customer complaints than its U.S. counterpart. This is probably due to the sustained media and legal pressure the company has felt from well-organized, angry Canadian consumers who have organized themselves into provincial CLOGs (Chrysler Lemon Owners Group) in BC, Alberta, Saskatchewan, and New Brunswick. In response, Chrysler Canada energized and empowered its best service advisers and set up an easily accessible, efficient, owner-assistance structure that handles appeals for post-warranty "goodwill" adjustments. (Ford calls this AWA, for "After Warranty Assistance.")

Unfortunately, the post-warranty assistance guidelines are vague and unevenly applied. Overall, Chrysler's customer complaint handling is mediocre. Chrysler insiders tell me the company's low morale caused by the Daimler takeover has contributed to a cost-cutting obsession, where customer claims that were once accepted, are now routinely rejected. For example, Chrysler customer service administrators promised me that no claim would be automatically rejected because the vehicle owner had repairs done by an independent repair facility, yet, *Lemon-Aid* reader feedback indicates just the opposite.

Chrysler paint complaints have declined dramatically, though engine head gasket, automatic transmission, and AC failures are on the rise. Owners seeking assistance in the future should initially work through their dealer service manager, request help from a Chrysler regional team representative, or call the Chrysler customer assistance toll-free number, 1-800-387-9983. Only if these attempts prove unsatisfactory should owners make use of Chrysler's Review Committee; that number is 519-973-2300.

Ford

Like Chrysler's warranty performance, Ford's after-warranty assistance is more generously applied in Canada than in the U.S., where American Ford owners frequently relate how dealers deny "goodwill" programs exist, or refuse engine head gasket and other extended warranty repairs because the vehicle was bought used or from a rival dealer. Ford USA insiders tell me the company prefers to stonewall post-warranty complaints, unless small claims action is threatened. Then claims are quickly paid off.

In Canada, Ford's toll-free customer assistance centre has improved considerably since last year. This has come about because Ford Canada purchased the call centre company it formerly hired and made staffers Ford employees. In testing the centre recently over the Firestone flap, I was pleased to see how knowledgeable and efficient the staffers were.

This is a far cry from what I discovered in researching last year's *Lemon-Aid*, when rude, incompetent staffers wouldn't identify themselves, seldom returned calls, and didn't know their butts from a balljoint. Actually this shouldn't surprise anyone who knows how these centres work. They are set up by companies that sell their customer assistance services to a variety of other companies. Thus, the employee handling your call is simply reading from a computer databank that contains general guidelines for everything from Ford to Fruit Loops, but not necessarily the answer to your car inquiry. This led to dissatisfied customers becoming irritated, then angry, then *crazed* (only in extreme cases, though, because crazed Canadians are still relatively rare).

Lemon-Aid Used Cars 1999 and *2000* targeted Ford Canada for its denial of claims by owners of 1992–96 Tauruses, Sables, and Windstars who had experienced 3.8L V6 engine head gasket and automatic transmission failures. Subsequently, Ford formally extended the warranty on head gasket claims to up to 7 years/160,000 km or 100,000 miles (letters were sent out under the company's Owner Notification Program) for 1994–95 Tauruses, Sables, and Windstars. Ford also pledged to review on a case-by-case basis all engine head gasket and automatic transmission claims (principally, forward clutch piston failures) not fitting the above parameters.

When I met with Ford executives in February 1999, they flatly refused my request to formally extend the warranty relating to forward clutch piston defects, inadequate automatic transmission planetary gear lubrication, and clutch slave cylinder and Villager engine exhaust manifold stud failures, preferring to treat post-warranty claims on an individual basis. At that same meeting, they were very forthcoming in providing me with information on a number of free fixes available under a variety of Owner Notification Programs. These free fixes cover automatic transmission downshifts, front coil springs, engine head gaskets, engine intake manifolds, engine mount bolts, engine knocking, engine block heaters, seatbelt buckles, fuel tank stops, fuel hose replacement, cooling fans, GEM modules, cooling system by-pass kits, rear brake shields, and air cleaners (see following charts).

"M" EXTENDED WARRANTY PROGRAMS (AS OF 2/23/99)			
PROGRAM #	**AFFECTED COMPONENT**	**VEHICLE LINE**	**PARAMETERS**
98M04	Front Coil Springs	All 1995–1997 4cyl. Contour/Mystique	Through December 31, 2004
98M02	Front Coil Springs	Certain 1993 Taurus/Sable	December 31, 2001, regardless of distance
98M01	Headgasket 3.8L Engine	Certain 1994–1995 Taurus/Sable 3.8L engine	5 years or 100,000 km, whichever occurs first
		*1994 Continental	*6 years or 120,000 km,
		1995 Windstar	whichever occurs first
97M91	Intake Manifold	Certain 1996–1997 Crown Victoria (taxi), Thunderbird, Cougar, Mustang 4.6L Engine	7 years unlimited distance
97M90	Seat Belt Buckles	Certain 1989–1990 Continental	12 years, regardless of distance travelled
		Certain 1989 Taurus/Sable	
96M89	Engine Knock	Certain 1995–1996 Villager	7 years or 160,000 km, whichever occurs first

Owners seeking assistance or compensation for any of the above problems should call the Ford assistance toll-free number at 1-800-565-3673 (FORD). Since Ford has designated specific members of its staff to deal with engine head gasket and transmission forward clutch piston problems, it would be helpful if owners identify one of the above as their problem, or mention they were referred by Phil Edmonston, at the beginning of their call.

"B"			
EXTENDED WARRANTY PROGRAMS (AS OF 2/23/99)			
PROGRAM #	**AFFECTED COMPONENT**	**VEHICLE LINE**	**PARAMETERS**
98B37	Transmission Downshift	Certain 1999 Windstar 3.8L	Through July 31, 1999
98B36	Engine Mount Bolts	Certain 1999 Windstar 3.8L	Through July 31, 1999
98B35	Fuel Tank Stop	Certain 1999 F-800 (33KGVW)	Through July 31, 1999
98B32	Rear Brake Shields	Certain 1999 F250-550 SuperDuty 4x4 Trucks	April 30, 1999, regardless of distance
98B31	Fuel Hose Replacement	Certain 1992–1998 B-series chassis 5.9L	November 30, 1999, regardless of distance
98B30	Cooling Fan	Certain 1998 Contour/Mystique	April 30, 1999, regardless of distance
98B29	GEM Module	1999 F250/350 Super Duty 4x4	Through July 31, 1999
98B26	Cooling System By-pass	Certain 1996–1997 3.0L Taurus Methanol Engine	Through February 28, 1999, regardless of distance
98B23	Cooling System By-pass Kit	Certain 1996–1997 3.0L Taurus/Sable Gas/Ethanol	Through February 28, 1999, regardless of distance
98B21	Engine Block Heater	Certain 1995–1998 Contour/Mystique 1998 ZX2	Through February 28, 1999, regardless of distance
97B16	Air Cleaners	1994–1997 H.D. F-series with 7.3 DIT	Through February 28, 1999, or 160,000 km whichever occurs first

Although some of these warranty extensions have expired, they are still useful as benchmarks for other vehicles with similar deficiencies, or for demanding partial, pro-rated compensation if your vehicle is no longer eligible.

Since that last meeting, Ford issued an Owner Notification Program (extended warranty) for 1999 Taurus, Sable, and Windstar transmission defects, but denied my request for a 1994–99 automatic transmission extended warranty. In response, I sent the following October 26, 2000 email to Ford's Canadian and American CEOs, Bobbie Gaunt and Jac Nasser:

Sudden automatic transmission failures in 1994–99 Taurus and Sables and 1995–99 Windstars—I brought this safety- and performance-related defect to your attention several years ago, and at a meeting you kindly arranged with me and your key executives last March, I was assured that Ford would consider setting up an owner notification program (ONP) refunding repair costs up to 7 years/160,000 kilometres or 100,000 miles, as is the case with your six-cylinder engines under a recent ONP. As stated before, this defect concerns, among other parts, the failure of the forward clutch piston, planetary gears, and rear lube tube and bracket.

I note with a certain irony that just last week your dealers were given an advisory from A.R. O'Neill that an ONP (#00B51) is being prepared to refund repair costs on the 1999 Taurus, Sable, and Windstar for rear lube tube and bracket replacement until September 30, 2001. Obviously, that's insufficient coverage, inasmuch as this defect should be covered for the same period as your engines (7/160), and earlier years (1994–99) must be included....

The failure to bring forth a transmission ONP is particularly disappointing. During the conference call, I got the impression Ford of Canada made the case for an ONP but was over-ruled by Detroit bean-counters, who figure they can save millions by stonewalling complaints in the States and doling out dollops of "goodwill" refunds in Canada.

The company is doing the same thing with its defective automatic transmissions. Costing about $3,000 to repair, the tranny problem makes Ford's ($1,000 retail) engine ONP pale in comparison. Nevertheless, I believe that with sufficient pressure brought to bear against Ford and its dealers, we can get a formal 7-year/160,000 km (100,000 mile) ONP out of the automaker in the near future.

Ford automatic transmission complaints continue to pour in and a half-dozen websites that inform and mobilize owners have been set up (see Appendix II, "Best Internet Gripe Sites"). For my part, I am calling for a Taurus, Sable, and Windstar boycott, until the claims are settled. I also intend to continue lobbying Ford, NHTSA, the U.S. Congress, and different Nader groups for their support. Additionally, I'll help owners set up Ford Lemon Owners Groups (FLOG) in Canada and the U.S. with the avowed purpose of getting case-by-case refunds for FLOG members and an extended warranty for all owners.

General Motors

Gosh, I never though I'd say this, but General Motors' after-warranty assistance is the best of a bad lot, when compared with Chrysler and Ford. I believe this is due mainly to the company's successful dealer empowerment programs, which allow dealers to make substantial warranty and post-warranty refunds, without head office approval. GM quality control has also improved, particularly for its full-sized pickups, though most of GM's front-drive lineup is, like Ford and Chrysler, mediocre at best. Unfortunately, the automaker's out-sourced customer service staffers aren't very knowledgeable or helpful as far as warranty disputes are concerned, preferring to refer customers back to the dealer.

Like Ford, GM has a codified system of archiving post-warranty payout programs included in its monthly service bulletins. (As I said earlier, Chrysler doesn't leave much of a paper trail.) Overall, GM's "goodwill" programs are just as generous as Ford's and more comprehensive and detailed than Chrysler's, although, as you can see in the following GM service bulletin and the company's reply to my inquiry, safety-related transmission failures are routinely ignored.

Bulletin No.: 67-71-64
Date: February, 1997
Subject:
Intermittent Neutral or Loss of Drive at Highway Speeds or from Fourth Gear
(Replace Control Valve Body Assembly)
Models:
1995-96 Buick Skylark, Regal, Century, Park Avenue, Riviera, LeSabre
1997 Buick Skylark, Regal, Century, LeSabre
1995 Cedillac DeVille
1995-96 Chevrolet Beretta, Corsica, Lumina APV, Lumina, Monte Carlo 1997
Chevrolet Lumina, Monte Carlo, Venture
1995-96 Olddsmobile Cutlass Ciera, Cutlass Cruiser, LSS, Ninety Eight, Ninety Eight
Regency, Eighty Eight, Achieva, Silhouette, Cutlass Supreme
1997 Oldsmobile Eighty Eight, Achieva, Cutlass Supreme, LSS, Silhouette
1995-97 Pontiac Bonneville, Grand Am, Trans Sport, Grand Prix with HYDRA-MATIC
4T60-E Transaxle (RPO M13)
Condition
Some owners may comment about an intermittent, neutral condition while driving at
highway speeds or intermittent neutral from fourth gear.
Cause
The 3-2 Manual Downshift valve may be sticking intermittently. When the 3-2 downshift valve sticks, this allows the 2-3 shift valve to float in its bore either exhausting
2ND, 3RD and 4TH clutch oil or sending D-4 oil into the AUX input clutch feed.
Exhausting the 3RD and 4TH clutch oil could cause an intermittent loss of drive.
Sending D-4 oil into the input circuit could cause a potential tie up condition by
engaging the input clutch and 4TH clutch.

*This GM service bulletin clearly outlines the cause and correction for hun-
dreds of thousands of front-drive cars and minivans that can suddenly
lose automatic transmission power. Nowhere does GM propose to recall
these vehicles or refund the $3,000 repair cost.*

Asian and European automakers

Asian automakers have few written policies regarding after-warranty
assistance. Toyota and Honda have issued a few (Toyota engine head
gasket refunds; free engine tune-ups for Honda owners) but they are
rare. Interestingly, many of Honda's service bulletins indicate that corrective repairs are subject to "goodwill" refunds, if the service manager
so requests, while Toyota's bulletins indicate that the customer must
ask for the free repair. It doesn't appear that dealers are empowered to
make many post-warranty assistance calls. To the contrary, the Japanese
automakers' warranty process appears to be particularly bureaucratic.
Nevertheless, neither company gets as many complaints (units sold
considered) as Chrysler, Ford, and GM. I suspect it's because their vehicles are better built. Incidentally, Honda and Nissan are particularly
vehement in dismissing service bulletins as documents that have no
bearing on vehicles' factory-related defects or warranty policies. All of
the other Asian automakers are generally quite receptive to customer
complaints, whether or not the warranty has expired.

European automakers are a strange breed. Their service bulletins
are loaded with engineering jargon. I get the distinct impression that

their mindset hinges on the theory that less-than-perfect customers drive and maintain their perfect cars. I cannot recall a single written warranty extension. Apparently, dealers are given quite a lot of latitude (and attitude) to make on-the-spot after-warranty decisions.

Extended (supplementary) warranties

Supplementary warranties that provide extended coverage may be sold by the manufacturer, dealer, or an independent third party, and are automatically transferred when the vehicle is sold. They cost between $500 and $1,500, and should be purchased only if the vehicle you're buying is off its original warranty, has a poor repair history (see Part Three), or if you're reluctant to use the small claims courts when trouble arises that is factory related. Don't let the dealer pressure you into deciding right away. Generally, you can purchase an extended warranty anytime during the period the manufacturer's warranty is still in effect. Although dealers have a quasi-monopoly on selling these warranties, it still pays to shop around. One B.C. reader wrote that Global sells extended warranties at a competitive price.

Dealers love to sell extended warranties because about one-third to one-half of the warranty's cost represents dealer markup. Out of the remainder comes the sponsor's administration costs and profit margin, calculated at another 25 percent. What's left is a minuscule 25 percent of the original amount, also paid to the dealer, for the repairs done to your vehicle—if any actually need to be done. It's estimated that of the car buyers who purchase an extended service contract, fewer than half actually use it.

It's often difficult to collect on supplementary warranties because independent companies not tied to the automakers frequently go out of business. When this happens, and the company's insurance policy won't cover your claim, take the dealer to small claims court and ask for the repair cost and a refund of the extended warranty payment. Your argument for holding the dealer responsible is a simple one: by accepting a commission for acting as an agent of the defunct company, the selling dealer took on the obligations of the company as well.

"Goodwill" hunting: Tracking secret warranties

Few car owners know secret car warranties exist. Automakers are reluctant to make these free repair programs public because they feel it would weaken confidence in their product and increase their legal liability. The closest they come to an admission is sending a "goodwill policy," "product improvement program," or "special policy" service bulletin to dealers or first owners of record. Consequently, the only motorists who find out about these policies are the original owners who haven't moved or leased their vehicle. The other motorists who get compensated for repairs are the ones who read *Lemon-Aid* each year, yell the loudest, and produce automaker service bulletins. (See

Appendix II, "Best Internet Gripe Sites," for an address as to where you can order bulletins.)

This year's *Lemon-Aid* guides shine a light on all of these secret warranties, including reprints of confidential technical service bulletins (TSBs) and automaker memoranda, so car owners can stand toe-to-toe with automakers and service managers. An up-to-date listing of service bulletins for free repairs under secret warranties and assorted other service programs can be found in Part Three under the heading "Secret Warranties/Service Tips." They have gone through the various stages enumerated below, so some may be less a secret than others.

Secret warranties go through four stages:

1st Stage—Service advisories are posted on an automaker's internal computer network. They offer troubleshooting tips and allow the dealer to bill the manufacturer for the repair. This info is never shared with the customer.

2nd Stage—If the defect grows in scope and a more involved solution is needed (for example, one requiring upgraded parts), automakers then draw up a formal technical service bulletin (TSB), also called a dealer service bulletin (DSB). This is distributed to dealers and to the U.S. government agency, NHTSA. The service bulletin is only issued after the manufacturer thinks it has a solution for the defect. TSBs issued by Chrysler, Ford, and GM will usually spell out clearly which base warranty will cover the repair (emissions warranty, bumper-to-bumper, etc.). Interestingly, Asian and European automakers are vague in describing their warranty obligations. Honda, for example, uses the term "goodwill" as a euphemism to describe its warranty extensions.

3rd Stage—More and more customers hear through *Lemon-Aid*, ALL-DATA, friends, and relatives that some TSBs recognize that a common factory-related defect exists, and find that the base warranty is clearly inadequate to deal with the scope of the problem. Dealers and customers exert pressure for additional after-warranty assistance. This, in turn, results in a second TSB, sent only to dealers, extending the warranty coverage to correct the defect and leaving the amount of the customer's refund to the dealer's discretion.

Now, customer dissatisfaction builds to a crescendo. The dealers and automakers keep the extended guidelines to themselves and customers get widely divergent refunds. This only angers the owners more, brings in the media, and leads to a proliferation of Internet gripe sites and lawsuits (small claims and class actions).

4th Stage—Finally, the aggravation is too great and the automaker decides to make a press release, followed by an owner notification letter (sent to first owners only, at their last known address) that clearly spells out what all owners will get and which vehicles are involved. A special bulletin or letter is also sent out to dealers to ensure they follow the guidelines 100 percent. Ford calls these Owner Notification Policies, GM calls them Special Policies, and Chrysler calls them Owner Satisfaction Notifications. No matter the euphemism, they are all an extension of the original warranty and apply to vehicles purchased new or used.

Remember, second owners and repairs done by independent garages are included in these secret warranty programs. Large, costly repairs, such as blown engines, burnt transmissions, and peeling paint are often covered. Even mundane little repairs, which can still cost you a hundred bucks or more, are frequently included in these programs. Take, for example, the elimination of foul, musty, or mildew odours emitted by your air conditioning unit. Despite what the dealer may say, it's covered by the base warranty.

If you have a TSB but you're still refused compensation, keep in mind that secret warranties are an admission of manufacturing negligence. Try to compromise with a pro rata adjustment from the manufacturer. If polite negotiations fail, challenge the refusal in court on the grounds that you should not be penalized for failing to make a reimbursement claim under a secret warranty you never knew existed!

Here are a few examples of the latest and most comprehensive secret warranties that have come across my desk in the last several years.

Acura/Honda

1994–97 Acura CL, Honda Accord, Prelude, and Odyssey models equipped with 4-cylinder engines

Problem: Defective engine oil seals can slip, causing the engine to drain of oil and eventually seize.

Warranty coverage: Although Honda maintains this isn't a safety recall (hmm, sudden engine seizure on the highway certainly sounds scary to me), the company will inspect and replace the seal and install a clip to ensure the seal cannot move. There are about 1.4 million vehicles involved in this worldwide program. Repairs had been delayed due to poor parts availability.

Acura/Honda/Passport

1995 Accord V6, Acura NSX, Acura 2.5 TL; all 1996–97 Hondas and Acuras, except for the Acura Integra Type R and the Isuzu-built Acura and Honda Passport

Problem: Engine malfunctions cause emissions to exceed the federal norm.

Warranty coverage: In a settlement with the U.S. Environmental Protection Agency (EPA), Honda extended its emissions warranty to 14 years or 150,000 miles. The automaker has agreed to the EPA's demand that it provide a full engine check and emissions-related repairs at 50,000 to 75,000 miles and give free tune-ups at 75,000 to 150,000 miles. This means that costly engine components and exhaust system parts like catalytic converters will be replaced free of charge. It is estimated the free check-ups, repairs, and tune-ups for U.S. customers will cost Honda over $250 million (U.S.). The story of the settlement was first reported in the June 15, 1998, edition of *Automotive News*.

If your engine is malfunctioning, get the original EPA agreement from the ALLDATA website (see Appendix II) and quote it in when you ask Honda and the dealer to fix the problem. If this gets you nowhere, go to small claims court (with the EPA agreement in hand) and ask for the same benefit since the cars sold in Canada and the U.S. are identical.

Chrysler

1995–99 Breeze, Cirrus, Neon, Sebring convertible, Stratus, and minivans
Problem: Engine head gasket failure.
Warranty coverage: Chrysler is quietly paying off owners after the warranty has expired up to 5 years/115,000 km if they threaten small claims action. Unfortunately, there is no *written* proof of this extended warranty. All we have is owner feedback confirming the free repairs. Nevertheless, Chrysler bulletin number 09–05–98 shows that 1995–99 models equipped with 2.0L and 2.4L engines have weak head gaskets that should be replaced with more durable ones. It's as close as you'll get to "smoking gun" proof the head gaskets are faulty and so it can be useful in negotiating an out-of-court settlement.

I suggest you fight any payout of less than 100 percent with a small claims action reinforced by Ford's 7-year/160,000 km extended warranty benchmark and Chrysler's 7-year AC warranty. (Is it fair the engine won't last as long as Ford's or Chrysler's own ACs?)

NO: 09-05-98
GROUP: Engine
EFFECTIVE DATE: Nov. 6, 1998
SUBJECT:
Multi-Layer Steel (MLS)
Head Gasket installation
Procedures
MODELS:

1995–1999	(JA)	Cirrus/Stratus/Breeze
1996–1999	(JX)	Sebring Convertible
1996–1999	(NS)	Town & Country/Caravan/Voyager
1995–1999	(PL)	Neon
1997–1999	(GS)	Chrysler Voyager (International Market)

NOTE:
THIS INFORMATION APPLIES TO MODELS WITH A 2.0L SOHC/DOHC OR 2.4L
ENGINE.
DISCUSSION:
A new Multi-Layer Steel (MLS) head gasket has been developed and is being implemented
into production vehicles. Additionally, it has been approved for service applications.
This new gasket will provide superior sealing characteristics, but will require extra care
in its installation where a composite gasket was previously in place.

1	5014127AA	Package, Head Gasket 1995-1999 2.0L SOHC (Includes Head Gasket & Instruction Sheet)
1	5014131AA	Package, Head Gasket 1995-1999 2.0L DOHC (Includes Head Gasket & Instruction Sheet)
1	5014173AA	Package. Head Gasket 2.4L (Includes Head Gasket & Instruction Sheet)
1	5014132AA	Package, Upper Gasket 1995 2.0L SOHC (Includes following seals/gaskets: cam sensor, cam front, head, valve cover, spark plug tube, EGR - cover/tube/flange, intake manifold, throttle body & instruction sheet)

Premature engine head gasket failures affect Chrysler's entire product line; this bulletin is an admission that the previous component was inferior.

1991–99 models with A604, 41TE, 42LE, and later automatic transmissions

Problem: Faulty automatic transmissions that shift erratically, gear down to "limp mode," are slow to shift in or out of Reverse, and self-destruct. This is a software and hardware problem in the A604 and its spin-offs that has bedeviled Chrysler owners for over a decade. Dozens of service bulletins address the problem and can be useful in small claims court. However, it's likely your filing won't to beyond the pretrial mediation stage, inasmuch as Chrysler reps are loath to defend the cases in front of independent garage testimony.

Warranty coverage: Without a court threat, Chrysler usually denies any problem or refund program exists. If you have the assistance of your dealer's service manager, expect an offer of 50 percent (about $1,500). A court filing will sweeten the offer considerably.

Chrysler, Ford, and General Motors
All years/models

Problem: Faulty paint jobs that cause paint to turn white and peel off horizontal panels. Ford and GM internal memos and service bulletins admit this is a factory defect.

Warranty coverage: Automakers will offer a free paint job up to 6 years/no mileage limitation. Thereafter, all three manufacturers offer 50–75 percent refunds on the small claims courthouse steps. Out-of-court settlements proffered by all three automakers also confirm the 6-year benchmark, although Chrysler confirmation is anecdotal, not written. Three small claims judgments that nailed GM to the wall, however, have extended the benchmark to seven years, second owners, and pickups.

BULLETIN NO.: 23-10-54
DATE: June 1995
SUBJECT:
Service Procedures for the Repair of Paint Colorcoat Delamination from ELPO Primer (Repair Surfaces Above the Body Side Moldings)
MODELS:
1988-91 Buick Century (Plant Code 6)
1988-92 Buick LeSabre (Plant Code H), Skylark
1988-90 Chevrolet Celebrity
1988-92 Chevrolet Beretta, Corsica, Skylark
1988-90 Oldsmobile Cutlass Supreme
1988-91 Oldsmobile Calais, Ciera (Plant Code 6)
1988-92 Oldsmobile Achieva, Eighty Eight (Plant Code H)
1988-90 Pontiac Grand Prix
1988-91 Pontiac 6000 (Plant Code 6)
1988-92 Pontiac Firebird, Grand Am, Tempest
1988-92 Chevrolet and GMC Truck C/K, R/V, S/T M/L, G Models
1991-92 Oldsmobile Bravada
CONDITION:
This bulletin is being issued to assure that the correct procedure is followed to repair a condition known as delamination. Some of the listed passenger cars, light duty trucks, and vans may have DELAMINATION (peeling) of the paint colorcoat from the ELPO primer depending upon variable factors including prolonged exposure to sunlight and humidity.
Blues, Grays, Silvers and Black Metallics are the colors that have the highest potential for this condition. On rare occasions, other colors may be involved.
CAUSE:
*This condition may occur on vehicles produced in plants where the paint process did not call for application of a primer surfacer. Under certain conditions, ultraviolet light can penetrate the colorcoat, sometimes causing a reaction and separation of portions of the colorcoat from the ELPO (electrocoat) primer.
PROBLEM IDENTIFICATION:
On a clean surface, at or above room temperature, firmly apply a 2" wide piece of masking tape and pull upward quickly. DO NOT USE duct tape, cloth backed tape or other aggressive tapes. If the colorcoat flakes or peels away from the ELPO (leaving the ELPO intact) the colorcoat is delaminating and the vehicle should be repaired.

Judging by the GM models listed above, paint delamination can occur within the first three years that the vehicle is on the road.

Article No. 93-8-4
April 14, 1993
PAINT - EXTERIOR CLEARCOAT "MICROCHECKING," HAZING OR PEELING

FORD:

	LINCOLN-MERCURY
1983-93 THUNDERBIRD	1983-93 COUGAR
1984-93 TEMPO	1984-92 MARK VII
1985-93 ESCORT	1984-93 TOPAZ
1986 LTD	1985-89 TRACER
1986-93 TAURUS	1986 MARQUIS
1989-93 CROWN VICTORIA, MUSTANG, PROBE	1986-93 SABLE
	1988-93 CONTINENTAL, TOWN CAR
LIGHT TRUCK:	1989-93 GRAND MARQUIS
1983-93 RANGER	1991-93 TRACER
1986-93 AEROSTAR	1993 MARK VIII
1987-90 BRONCO II	
1988-93 F SUPER DUTY, F-47	
1991-93 ECONOLINE, EXPLORER	
1992-93 F-150-350 SERIES	
1993 VILLAGER	

ISSUE: The clearcoat layer of the basecoat/clearcoat paint system may "microcheck" (crack and erode), turn white, flake or peel off vehicle. This condition is noticeable on the horizontal surfaces only.
ACTION: Inspect the vehicle and if repair is necessary, refer to the following procedure for service details. This is a wet on wet procedure. Sanding is not required after the seal coat is applied.

Paint delamination afflicts Ford's entire lineup going back to the 1983 model year, according to Ford TSB 93-8-4.

Bulletin No.: 331708
Date: November, 1993
SUBJECT:
CLEARCOAT DEGRADATION - CHALKING AND WHITENING
MODELS:
PASSENGER CARS WITH BASECOAT/CLEARCOAT
CONDITION:
The vehicle exterior surface may show large chalky or white patches in the clearcoat, usually but not limited to the horizontal surfaces.
Blacks, Dark Blues, Reds, may have potential for this condition. On rare occasions, other colors may be involved.
CAUSE:
The clearcoat (with sunlight and heat) may degrade and turn white or chalky.
IDENTIFICATION:
On a clean surface, at or above room temperature, firmly apply a 2" wide piece of masking tape to the chalky or white area of the clearcoat and pull upward quickly. The adhesive side of the tape WILL NOT HAVE THE PAINT COLOR ON IT. A light shine or reduced tackiness may be noticed on the tape adhesive surface, indicating clearcoat transfer to the tape.
CORRECTION:
Refinish all horizontal surfaces using the following procedure.
- Remove the clearcoat layer from all horizontal surfaces and the top surfaces of fenders and quarter panels.
NOTE:
In some cases, it will be necessary to remove the clearcoat from the upper vertical surfaces of fenders, doors and quarters (approximately 3"), and the top areas directly above the front and rear wheelhouse openings.

This General Motors service bulletin not only is an admission of GM's paint delamination problem, it also gives a simple test for identifying the defect on any vehicle—not just '92 and earlier models.

Paint Should Last Six Years, Says GM!

 PONTIAC

PONTIAC DIVISION
General Motors Corporation
One Pontiac Plaza
Pontiac, Michigan 48340-2952

October 16, 1992

TO: All Pontiac Dealers

SUBJECT: Partners in Satisfaction (PICS)
           Dealer Authorization

Pontiac continually reviews the Warranty Management System to ensure that
Warranty Administration achieves its purposes, including high levels of customer satisfaction with after sale treatment.

Following a recent review, Pontiac has decided to provide dealers authorization for cases involving <u>paint repairs</u> for vehicles up to six (6) years from the
date of delivery, without regard for mileage. This is a change from the current PICS dealer self-authorization which allows paint repair goodwill
adjustments to be made up to 6 years/60,000 miles. Dealers who have a
deductible override capabilities may also waive deductibles as they see
appropriate on this type of repair.

Paint repairs are only to be authorized beyond the warranty period by the
Dealership <u>Service Manager</u> on a case-by-case basis as with any other goodwill policy adjustment.

Assistance should only be considered for cases involving evidence of a
defect in materials or workmanship by the manufacturer. Assistance should
not be considered for conditions related to wear and tear and/or lack of maintenance (such as fading, stone chips, scratches, environmental damage, etc.).

Please contact your Zone representative if you have specific questions.

Perry S. White

Perry S. White
Director of Service/
Customer Satisfaction

*This confidential memo to Pontiac dealers applies to all of GM's vehicles,
and can be used as a benchmark for what the automaker considers its obli-
gation when faced with paint claims. Note GM doesn't use any "weasel"
words, like "acid rain" or "UV ray deterioration," to avoid its responsibility.
Plus, GM says owners don't have to pay any deductible. Show your dealer
or service manager this memo when seeking a refund.*

Chrysler/Jeep
1990–93 Dynasty, New Yorker, Fifth Avenue, and Imperial; 1991–92 Eagle Premier; 1991–93 minivans; 1989–93 Cherokee and Wagoneer
Problem: ABS brakes that fail or malfunction.
Warranty coverage: Piggy-backing a service campaign onto a recall, Chrysler extended the warranty to 10 years/160,000 km on a number of costly ABS components. Owners will also be reimbursed for previous ABS repairs—not applicable to calipers, pads/shoe linings, or other maintenance items. Two other ABS components, piston seals (excessive wear) and the pump motor (deterioration), will be repaired free of charge at any time during the life of the vehicle. (See the recall notice on the following page.)

1993–99 Concorde, Intrepid, New Yorker, LHS, Vision, and Grand Cherokee
Problem: AC evaporator failure or malfunction.
Warranty coverage: 7 years/115,000 km. (See page 55 for a copy of the Chrysler warranty addendum). Chrysler is free to limit this program to the evaporator and to the vehicles listed above, after all, they are simply modifying their *expressed* warranty. But you are just as free to plead the *implied* warranty (in your letter to Chrysler and small claims filing). Argue that this extension sets a benchmark for the warranty repairs on the entire AC as to what Chrysler considers reasonable durability under consumer protection statutes. Also, make the point that Chrysler is unfairly excluding other models using the same system with the same AC failures. (C'mon, what's applicable to a Concorde should be applicable to a Caravan, n'est-ce-pas?)

Ford
1996 and 1997 Mustang, Cougar, and Thunderbird; 1997 F-Series trucks equipped with 3.8L or 4.2L engines
Problem: The above-listed vehicles may experience engine coolant leaks at the front cover gasket; this could cause severe engine damage from overheating if not corrected.
Warranty coverage: At no charge to the owner, the dealer will replace the engine front cover gasket with a redesigned gasket and—now get this—*replace the engine oil and filter!* This is a generous special warranty extension because: 1) it also covers lower intake side gaskets; 2) the free repair is still applicable even if there is a repeat failure; 3) there is no engine test required to get the new, more durable components installed; 4) costs for previous repairs will be paid in full; 5) the program will run until March 21, 2001, without any mileage limitation; 6) it includes vehicles purchased used.

Consumers whose cars already have been repaired should take their original receipt to a Ford or Lincoln-Mercury dealer. However, Ford has acknowledged that some of those consumers may have had their gaskets replaced with the older, troublesome gasket. That gasket could leak, too, and those consumers are eligible not only for the reimbursement but for a new repair, say Ford spokespeople.

The easiest way to tell if a new, improved gasket was used is to check the part number on the receipt or to call the dealer who did the work. An "early upgraded" gasket had this part number: F8ZZ-6020-AA. However, since the middle of 1999, an even newer design was used. Its part number is YF2Z-6020-AA. Ford engineers believe that the "early upgraded" gasket will be fine, but consumers who worry that it is not good enough are eligible for a second repair.

My only gripe about this warranty extension is that it leaves out the 1996–98 Windstar and the Econoline E-150 and E-250, the 1998 Mustang, and 1998 F-Series trucks, which are all included in service bulletin #99-20-7 detailing the failure that Ford is correcting. If you are the owner of one of these excluded vehicles, send the dealer and Ford a claim letter. If refused compensation, bring Ford's bulletin and owner letter to court as proof that you should have been included.

| A.R. O'Neill
Director
Vehicle Services and Programs
Ford Customer Service Division | *Ford* | Ford Motor Company
P.O. Box 1904
Dearborn, MI 48121-1904 |

January, 2000

Ford Motor Company is providing a no-charge Service Program, Number 99B29, to owners of certain 1996 and 1997 model year Mustang, Thunderbird, Cougar, and 1997 F-Series vehicles equipped with 3.8L or 4.2L engines.

What Is The Reason For This Program?	The affected vehicles may experience engine coolant leaks at the engine front cover gasket; this could cause severe engine damage if not corrected. To avoid engine damage, you should make an appointment to have this service performed on your vehicle at your Ford or Lincoln Mercury Dealer as soon as possible.
No Charge Service:	At no charge to you, your dealer will replace the engine from cover gasket with a redesigned gasket and change the engine oil and filter. This service will reduce the likelihood of coolant leaks at the engine front cover, and will help avoid the potential inconvenience of breakdowns and costly engine repairs.
	Your vehicle is eligible for this program until March 31, 2001, regardless of mileage.
How Long Will It Take?	The time needed for this repair is less than one day. However, due to service scheduling issues, your dealer may need your vehicle for a longer period of time. To avoid engine damage, inconvenience, and costly repairs please schedule a service date as soon as possible.
Call Your Dealer:	Call your dealer without delay. Ask for a service date and whether parts are in stock for Owner Notification Program 99B29.
	If your dealer does not have the parts in stock, they can be ordered before scheduling your service date. Parts would be expected to arrive within a week after the order is placed.
	When you bring your vehicle in, show the dealer this letter. If you misplace this letter, your dealer will still do the work, free of charge.
Refund:	If you paid for engine repairs caused by a front cover gasket leak on this vehicle *before* the date of this letter, Ford is offering a refund. For the refund, please give your paid original receipt to your Ford or Lincoln Mercury dealer. To avoid delays, do not send receipts to Ford Motor Company.

1994–99 models equipped with automatic transmissions; particlarly, Tauruses, Sables, and Windstars

Problem: Forward clutch piston, planetary gear, and clutch slave cylinder may fail prematurely. This problem is usually indicated by erratic shifting, delayed shifting, harsh engagement, and a tendency for the transmission to "hunt" for the proper gear. Barely noticeable at first, it will worsen progressively, until the transmission breaks down completely.

Warranty coverage: Ford will repair or replace the transmission at no charge up to 5 years/100,000 km, no matter if the vehicle was bought new or used. The company's initial offer is about 50 percent of the estimated $3,000 repair cost. Vehicles that have exceeded the above limitations will receive pro-rated refunds.

Affected owners should still claim 100 percent refunds for 7 years/160,000 km in conformity with Ford's engine ONP guidelines. The transmission is simply the other end of the powertrain and it's idiotic to maintain that the engine should last two years and 60,000 km longer than the automatic transmission, particularly since the original powertrain warranty doesn't differentiate between the two components.

Article No
94-24-7
11/28/94
TRANSAXLE - AXOD, AXOD-E, AX4S - FORWARD/REVERSE ENGAGEMENT CONCERN - REVISED FORWARD CLUTCH PISTON
FORD:
1986-95 TAURUS
1993-95 TAURUS SHO
LINCOLN-MERCURY:
1986-95 SABLE
1988-94 CONTINENTAL
LIGHT TRUCK:
1995 WINDSTAR
ISSUE:
The forward clutch piston may crack on its outside diameter, seal groove or apply wall (bottom of piston). This condition could allow internal clutch leakage resulting in engagement concerns.
STEEL CLUTCH PISTON PART APPLICATIONS
F4DZ-7A262-A   F4DZ-7A262-B
3.0L TAURUS
3.0L SABLE
3.8L TAURUS
3.8L SABLE
3.8L CONTINENTAL
3.8L WINDSTAR   3.2L TAURUS SHO
ACTION:
Use the chart for proper application if replacement of the forward clutch piston is necessary.
NOTE:
PREVIOUS TSB ARTICLES 91-5-7, 92-1-4, 92-26A-6 AND 93-9-11 SHOULD NOT BE USED DUE TO REVISED PARTS LISTED IN THIS ISSUE.
Use a magnet to verify the forward clutch piston being installed is the new steel piston. The magnet will adhere to the steel piston and not to the aluminum piston.
Do not use any service stock of aluminum forward clutch pistons. Return stock to parts depot for credit.

PART NUMBER	PART NAME	CLASS
F4DZ-7A262-A	Forward Clutch Piston	A
F4DZ-7A262-B	Forward Clutch Piston (SHO)	C

SUPERCEDES: 91-5-7, 92-1-4, 92-26A-6, 93-9-11

This first bulletin updates others going back several years and lists 1986–95 as the model years affected. Note how Ford clearly blames the aluminum piston as the culprit causing what the automaker understates as "engagement concerns."

Article No.
98-3-7
02/16/98
TRANSAXLE - AX4N - INTERMITTENT NEUTRAL CONDITION - NO FORWARD OR REVERSE MOVEMENT - VEHICLES BUILT
THROUGH 2/1/98
FORD:
1994-98 TAURUS
LINCOLN-MERCURY:
1994-98 SABLE
1995-98 CONTINENTAL

ISSUE:
Some vehicles may experience an intermittent Neutral condition after driving and coming to a stop. This may be caused by
the bonded seal on the forward clutch piston intermittently not sealing during the 3-2 downshift.
ACTION:
Replace the forward clutch piston with a revised Forward Clutch Piston (F8DZ-7A262-AB). Refer to the following Service
Procedure for details.
SERVICE PROCEDURE
Clean and reseal the transaxle completely including replacement of the forward clutch piston with revised forward clutch pis-
ton and replace the forward clutch plates if darkened or discolored from heat. Refer to the appropriate Continental Service
Manual, Section 07-01, or the appropriate Taurus/Sable Service Manual, Section 07-01B, for details.
Be sure to check end clearance on all three (3) select fit thrust washers (# 16, # 8, 1.02-1.50 mm (0.040-0.059")). Be sure
to clean and inspect the main control (pump and valve body) and servos. Prior to returning vehicle to customer recheck fluid
level at operating temperature.

PART NUMBER	PART NAME
F5DZJ153-AA	Seal And Gasket kit
F8DZ-7A262-AB	Forward Clutch Piston
F8DZ-7B164-AC	Forward Clutch Plates - Friction (4)
F2DZ-7B442-A	Forward Clutch Plates - Steel (4)

*Apparently, the move to a steel piston didn't make Ford's transmissions
more reliable or durable, as the above bulletin clearly demonstrates. Hence,
my ratings downgrade Ford's latest models.*

1999 Tauruses, Sables, and Windstars with defective rear lube tubes
and brackets are covered 100 percent by Ford's ONP 00B51 until
September 30, 2001, regardless of mileage. This defect results in the
vehicle being unable to move in either Drive or Reverse. If the vehicle
is moving when the malfunction occurs, there will be no forward power
and the vehicle will coast to a stop with the engine running.

General Motors
1992–94 Cavalier/Sunbird with 4-cylinder engines
Problem: Faulty head gaskets may cause loss of engine coolant, engine
overheating, or destruction of the engine. GM letter shows problem is
a factory defect, but only mentions the Cavalier's 2.2L engine, and
apparently only applies to Canada. Owner feedback, however, tells me
the Sunbird's 2.0L engine repairs are covered on a case-by-case basis
and that after-warranty consideration is given to owners on both sides
of the border.
Warranty coverage: GM will replace the faulty head gasket or repair the
engine damage caused by head gasket failure at no charge up to 7 years/
160,000 km. As for the '94 model engine, Chris Jensen, automotive

columnist for the *Cleveland Plain Dealer* disclosed in a June 3, 2000 article that GM spokesman Greg Martin confirmed that the '94s were also part of the "special policy" to repair this defect.

1995–1996 Cavalier/Sunfire and the two-wheel-drive models of the 1996 Chevrolet S-10 and GMC Sonoma pickups with 2.2L four-cylinder engines
Problem: Engine head gasket failures that include overheating, loss of coolant, the smell of coolant, coolant leaks around the cylinder head, and white smoke from the exhaust. Sometimes the heater won't work or a film (from the coolant) will be deposited on the inside glass surfaces. If the coolant leaks inside the engine it can cause severe engine damage from overheating.
Warranty coverage: The 1995 and 1996 vehicles are now covered for head gasket problems for seven years or 160,000 km, whichever comes first. Anyone who has paid for repairs at a dealership should contact the dealership to be reimbursed. Owners who did not have a GM dealership do the work aren't excluded from the refund program and should contact the toll-free customer assistance number in the owner's manual. Future repairs, however, must take place at a GM dealership. The program is not a recall, and owners should take their vehicles to a dealership only if it appears they have a problem.

Remember, if you have an engine head gasket failure on a GM vehicle or engine not included in the above-noted programs, don't despair. Simply use the same benchmarks for your own vehicle and threaten small claims action on those grounds.

GM/Saturn
1994–96 models
Problem: Faulty head gaskets may cause loss of engine coolant, engine overheating, or destruction of the engine.
Warranty coverage: GM will replace the faulty head gasket or repair the engine damage caused by head gasket failure at no charge up to 6 years/ 160,000 km, as set out in its June 7, 1999, statement to *Automotive News*. Second owners and repairs done by independent garages are included in this program. This warranty extension can be used in claims against all other GM models/years with similar engine problems and against other automakers. Apparently, this Saturn defect has existed since 1991, according to the GM bulletin reprinted on the following page.

BULLETIN NO.: 96-T-65A
ISSUE DATE: February 1997
GROUP/SEQ. NO. Engine-15
CORPORATION NO.: 686204R
SUBJECT:
Engine Runs Hot and Engine Oil Mixed with Engine Coolant in Engine Coolant Recovery Reservoir (Replace Cylinder Head Assembly)
This bulletin is revised to replace an incorrect part number for the one gallon container of DEX-COOL(TM) and supersedes bulletin 96-T-65, which should be discarded.
MODELS AFFECTED:
1991–1997 Saturns equipped with SOHC (LKO-1991-1994, L24-1995-1997) engines
CONDITION:
Engine may run hot and/or have engine oil mixed with engine coolant. This condition may be noticeable when checking coolant recovery reservoir level.
CAUSE:
Some 1991–1997 SOHC engines may develop a crack on or near the camshaft journals and surrounding casting areas allowing engine oil to mix with engine coolant. These cracks may be caused by "folds" in the aluminum that occur during the head casting process.
CLAIM INFORMATION

Case Type	Description	Labor Operation Code	Time
VW	Replace Cylinder Head Assembly	T9715	11.2 hrs
Add:	with A/C		0.8 hrs
	with power steering		0.3 hrs

To receive credit for this repair during the warranty coverage period, submit a claim through the Saturn Dealer System as shown.

Don't kid yourself. This is a major engine defect that'll take 11-plus hours to correct. GM will pay, if you refuse to go away.

ABS brakes
1991–1996 S/T-series four-wheel drive Blazers and pickups; 1992–1995 Astro/Safari minivans; 1993–1996 full-size vans equipped with 3-sensor EBC4 ABS brakes
Problem: Complete or partial brake failure.
Warranty coverage: GM initially recalled 1.1 million 1991–96 S/T-series four-wheel drive Blazers and pickups equipped with EBC4 ABS to change a sensor switch. Additionally, GM has a "special policy" set up to reprogram, at no charge, the software controlling the ABS system on 2.4 million 1994–1996 S/T-series Blazers and pickups; 1992–1995 Astro and Safari minivans; and 1993–1996 full-size vans.

Tires
Bridgestone/Firestone—all of the tires found in the chart below
Problem: Sudden tread separation.
Warranty coverage: In Canada, Bridgestone/Firestone has just confirmed to me that the company will replace for free any of the tires listed in the chart below, if requested to do so. Incidentally, many of these non-recalled tires have been linked to fatalities and injuries due to tread separation. So, if you've got them, take them off!

Tire Line	Size	Plant Code	Original Installation
Wilderness AT	P235/70R16	W2	1996-98 Ford F150
Wilderness AT	33X12.50R16.5LT	VD	
Wilderness HT	P255/70R15	VD	

Affinity brand tires
Problem: Sudden blowout, premature tread wear, and gradual loss of air.
Warranty coverage: Consumers (particularly GM Malibu owners) report their tires have been replaced free of charge up to 3 years/60,000 km.

Goodyear 16-inch load-range E tires used by DaimlerChrysler and Ford full-sized vans, 2-ton or larger pickups, and commercial vehicles like school vans and large SUVs, including the Chevy Suburban. Brand names include: Wrangler AT, Wrangler HT, Workhorse, Kelly-Springfield Trailbuster, and Kelly-Springfield Power King. 15-inch load-range D tires sold under the Marathon name.
Problem: Premature tread wear, bulges in the tires, and sudden tread separation. Problems are presently under investigation by NHTSA.
Warranty coverage: According to the *Los Angeles Times,* Goodyear has received more than 3,000 claims about its light-truck tires fitted on vans, light trucks, sport-utility vehicles and RVs since 1995. A majority of those claims have been quietly settled, with consumers receiving replacement tires and reimbursements if their vehicles were damaged. Goodyear also has been replacing its 15-inch load-range D tires, fitted mainly on recreational vehicles, after RV owners and manufacturers reported widespread Marathon brand tire failures. Some RV owners said it was only after they had experienced tread separation several times that they learned Goodyear would replace them for free. A class-action suit filed in Massachusetts accuses Goodyear of failing to warn consumers that its 15-inch Marathon tires are unsafe and unsuitable for campers.

Goodyear denies that it is conducting a silent recall. It says it is providing "customer satisfaction" replacements on a case-by-case basis. Interestingly, Goodyear's problems and PR campaign is quite similar to Firestone's early stonewalling of customer complaints. For example, the number of complaints received by Goodyear is nearly as high as the 3,700 complaints NHTSA has received about Firestone tires, and, while pledging "total disclosure," Goodyear is fighting desperately to keep the courts from disclosing the documents, which were heretofore kept secret.

Confidential service bulletins
The above special warranties are confirmed by technical service bulletins (confidential, for the most part) sent to dealers by automakers to advise them of special warranties and to help them quickly diagnose and correct factory defects. These bulletins also disclose how much of the repair the dealer can charge back to the manufacturer and which parts are available free of charge. Armed with these bulletins, motorists can use less expensive, independent garages to diagnose and repair

their vehicles or negotiate compensation for defects that the bulletins point out are the manufacturer's fault.

The major problem with these bulletins is that they're difficult to get. Dealers and automakers are reluctant to provide this kind of detailed technical information because it allows customers to second-guess a mechanic's work or to buttress the owners' demands for compensation. However, as long as their involvement isn't disclosed, some dealers will discreetly provide copies of service bulletins to help their customers fight for compensation from the auto manufacturer.

For just a summary of bulletins applicable to 1982–2000 vehicles, you have two sources: free summaries from the ALLDATA or the NHTSA sites on the Internet (listed in Appendix II, "Best Internet Gripe Sites"). Summaries of automotive recalls and technical service bulletins are listed by year, make, model, and engine option. Like the NHTSA summaries, though, ALLDATA's summaries are so short and cryptic, they're of limited usefulness. You *can* see the contents of individual bulletins if you purchase, for about $30 (U.S.), a CD-ROM disc that holds all the bulletins that pertain to your vehicle (BMW and Honda excluded). Considering that many vehicles have over three hundred bulletins, the ALLDATA fee is a real bargain.

How long should parts/repairs last?
Let's say you can't find a service bulletin that says your problem is factory related or covered by a special compensation program; or a part lasts just a little longer than its guarantee, but not as long as is generally expected. Can you get a refund if the same problem reappears shortly after it has been repaired? The answer is yes, if you can prove the part failed prematurely.

Automakers, mechanics, and the courts have their own benchmarks as to what's a reasonable period of time or amount of mileage one should expect a part or adjustment to last. The following table shows what most automakers consider is reasonable durability as expressed by their original warranties and secret warranties that are often called "goodwill" or "special policy" programs.

Estimated Part Durability

ACCESSORIES

Air conditioner	7 years	
Cellular phone	5 years	
Cruise control	5 years/	
	100,000 km	
Power antenna	5 years	
Power doors, windows	5 years	
Radio	5 years	

BODY

Paint (peeling)	7 years
Rust (perforations)	7 years
Rust (surface)	5 years
Vinyl roof	5 years
Water/wind/air leaks	5 years

BRAKE SYSTEM

Brake drum	120,000 km
Brake drum, turn	40,000 km
Brake drum linings	35,000 km
Disc brake calipers	30,000 km
Disc brake pads	30,000 km
Master cylinder, rebuild	100,000 km
Wheel cylinder, rebuild	80,000 km

ENGINE AND DRIVETRAIN

Constant velocity joint	5 years/100,000 km
Differential	7 years/150,000 km
Engine (gas)	7 years/160,000 km
Radiator	4 years/80,000 km
Transfer case	7 years/150,000 km
Transmission (auto.)	7 years/160,000 km
Transmission (man.)	7 years/200,000 km
Transmission oil cooler	5 years/100,000 km
Universal joint	5 years/100,000 km

EXHAUST SYSTEM

Catalytic converter	5 years/100,000 km or more
Muffler	2 years/40,000 km
Tailpipe	3 years/60,000 km

FUEL SYSTEM

Carburetor	5 years/120,000 km
Fuel filter	2 years/40,000 km
Fuel pump	5 years/80,000 km
Injectors	5 years/80,000 km

IGNITION SYSTEM

Cable set	60,000 km
Electronic module	5 years/80,000 km
Retiming	20,000 km
Spark plugs	20,000 km
Tune-up	20,000 km

SAFETY COMPONENTS

Airbags	life of vehicle
ABS brakes	7 years/150,000 km
ABS computer	10 years/160,000 km
Seatbelts	life of vehicle

STEERING AND SUSPENSION

Alignment	1 year 20,000 km
Ball joints	80,000 km
Power steering	5 years/80,000 km
Shock absorber	2 years/40,000 km
Struts	5 years/80,000 km
Tires (radial)	5 years/80,000 km
Wheel bearing	3 years/60,000 km

VISIBILITY

Aim headlights	20,000 km
Halogen/fog lights	3 years/60,000 km
Sealed beam	2 years/40,000 km
Windshield wiper motor	5 years/80,000 km

Much of the preceding guidelines were extrapolated from Chrysler and Ford payouts to thousands of dissatisfied customers over the past decade, in addition to Chrysler's original 7-year powertrain warranty applicable from 1991–95. Other sources for this chart were the Ford and GM transmission warranties outlined in their secret warranties; Ford, GM, and Toyota engine "special policy" programs laid out in their internal service bulletins; and court judgments where judges have given their own guidelines as to what is reasonable durability.

Safety features generally have a lifetime warranty, with the exception of ABS, which are a wear item. Nevertheless, the Chrysler 10-year "free service program" portion of its ABS recall announced five years ago can serve as a handy benchmark as to how long one can expect these components to last.

Airbags are a different matter. Those that are deployed in an accident, and the personal injury and interior damage their deployment will likely have caused, are covered by your accident insurance policy. However, if there is a sudden deployment for no apparent reason, the automaker and dealer should be held jointly responsible for all injuries and damages caused by the airbag. This will likely lead to a more generous settlement from the two parties and prevent your insurance premiums from being jacked up. Inadvertent deployment may occur after passing over a bump in the road, slamming the car door, having wet carpets in your Cadillac (no kidding), or, in some Chrysler minivans, simply putting the key in the ignition. This happens more often than you might imagine, judging by the hundreds of recalls and thousands of complaints recorded on the U.S. National Highway Traffic Safety Administration's (NHTSA) website (*www.nhtsa.dot.gov/cars/problems/complain/compmmy1.cfm*).

Finally, the manufacturer's emissions warranty serves as the primary guideline governing how long a vast array of electronic and mechanical components should last. Look first at your owner's manual for an indication of which parts on your vehicle are covered. If you come up with few specifics, use the provincial government's guidelines in provinces where emissions testing is mandatory. Keep in mind that these durability benchmarks, secret warranties, and emissions warranties all apply to subsequent owners.

Recall repairs

Let the automaker know who and where you are. If you've bought a used vehicle or moved, it's a smart idea to pay a visit to your local dealer and get a "report card" on which recalls, free-service campaigns, and warranties apply to it. Simply give the service advisor your vehicle identification number (VIN)—found on the dash just below the windshield on the driver's side, or on your insurance card—and have the number run through the automaker's computer system ("Function 70" for Chrysler, "OASIS" for Ford, and "CRIS" for GM). Ask for a computer printout of the vehicle's history (have it faxed to you, if you're so equipped) and make sure you're listed in the automaker's computer as the new owner. This ensures that you'll receive notices of warranty extensions and emissions and safety recalls.

Still, don't expect to be welcomed with open arms when your vehicle develops a safety- or emissions-related problem that's not yet part of a recall campaign. Automakers and dealers generally take a restrictive view of what constitutes a safety or emissions defect and frequently charge for repairs which should be free under federal safety or emissions legislation. To counter this tendency, look at the following list of typical defects that are clearly safety related, and if you experience similar problems, tell the dealer you expect your repair to be paid for by the manufacturer:

- airbag malfunctions;
- corrosion affecting safe operation;
- disconnected or stuck accelerators;
- electrical shorts;
- faulty windshield wipers;
- fuel leaks;
- problems with original axles, drive shafts, seats, seat recliners, or defrosters;

- seatbelt problems;
- stalling or sudden acceleration;
- sudden steering or brake loss;
- suspension failures;
- trailer coupling failures.

In the U.S., recall campaigns force automakers to pay the entire cost of fixing a vehicle's safety-related defect. This includes used vehicles, and has no cut-off limitation. Recalls may be voluntary or ordered by the U.S. Department of Transportation. Canadian regulation has an added twist: Transport Canada can only order automakers to notify owners that their vehicles may be unsafe; it can't force them to correct the problem. Fortunately, most U.S.-ordered recalls are carried out in Canada, and when Transport Canada makes a defect determination on its own, automakers generally comply with an owner notification letter.

Voluntary recall campaigns are a real problem, though. They aren't as rigorously monitored as government-ordered recalls, and dealers, automakers and tire manufacturers routinely deny there's a recall. Also, the company's so-called "fix" often leaves out many of the affected models or unreasonably excludes certain owners. Take, as an example, Bridgestone/Firestone's voluntary replacement program that targets 1.4 million tires found to be "hazardous" by the NHTSA (see page 75). Bridgestone/Firestone is replacing the tires free of charge in the States, while denying Canadians the same benefits.

Safety defect information
If you wish to report a safety defect or want recall info, you may access Transport Canada's website on the Internet. You'll get recall information in French or English as well as general information relating to road safety and importing a vehicle into Canada. The web page can be accessed by typing *www.tc.gc.ca/roadsafety/Recalls/search_e.asp*. Cyber-surfers can now access the recall database for 1970–2000 model vehicles, but, unlike NHTSA's website, owner complaints aren't listed, defect investigations aren't disclosed, and service bulletin summaries aren't provided. You can also call Transport Canada at 1-800-333-0510 (toll-free within Canada) or 613-993-9851 (within the Ottawa region or outside Canada) to get additional information.

Unfortunately, there are some problems with Ottawa's database, and attitude. First, when calling Ottawa through the toll-free line, Transport Canada bureaucrats insist that the dealer must already have refused you the recall info before they will give it to you. You won't be told if others have reported similar safety problems affecting your vehicle. And more often than not, if you suspect your car has a safety defect, you'll be asked to take it to the dealer for a safety exam (where there's a good chance the problem will be covered up or you'll be blamed for the malfunction).

If you're not happy with Ottawa's treatment of your recall inquiry, try the U.S. government's NHTSA website. It's more complete than

Transport Canada's site. (NHTSA's database is updated daily and covers vehicles built since 1952.) You can search the database for specific vehicle information and be thoroughly briefed on recalls, crash ratings, safety and performance defects reported by other car owners, and a host of other safety-related items. The web address is *www.nhtsa.dot.gov/cars/problems/recalls/recmmy1.cfm* for recalls and *www.nhtsa.dot.gov/cars/problems/complain/compmmy1.cfm* for the complaint database. By accessing NHTSA from the "Gripe Sites" pages of *lemonaidcars.com*, you'll automatically access NHTSA's complaint database, service bulletin summaries, recalls, and defect investigations.

NHTSA's fax-back service provides the same info through a local line that can be accessed from Canada—although long-distance charges will apply. (Most calls take 5–10 minutes to complete.) The following local numbers get you into the automatic response service quickly, and can be reached 24 hours a day: 202-366-0123 (202-366-7800 for the hearing impaired).

   People Saving People
   http://www.nhtsa.dot.gov

Office of Defects
Investigation
Complaints Database

Call the Auto Safety Hotline toll free at (888) 327-4236 to report safety defects or to obtain information on cars, trucks, child seats, highway or traffic safety.

Report Date: April 21, 1999 01:25:12 PM
ODI ID: 528567
Make: DODGE TRUCK
Model: CARAVAN
Year: 1998
Date of Failure: Tuesday, December 23, 1997
Incident: No
Fire: No
Number of Injuries: 3
Component: ELECTRICAL SYSTEM
Summary: TOTAL ELECTRICAL SYSTEM FAILURE, CAUSING ACCIDENT/INJURIES.

ODI ID: 528567
Make: DODGE TRUCK
Model: CARAVAN
Year: 1998
Date of Failure: Tuesday, December 23, 1997
Incident: No
Fire: No
Number of Injuries: 3
Component: INTERIOR SYSTEMS:PASSIVE RESTRAINT:AIR BAG
Summary: VIOLENT DEPLOYMENT OF AIR BAG DURING COLLISION, CAUSING BURNS AND INJURIES TO FACE, NECK AND CHEST.

ODI ID: 532607
Make: DODGE TRUCK
Model: CARAVAN
Year: 1998
Date of Failure: Tuesday, January 20, 1998
Incident: No
Fire: No
Number of Injuries: 0
Component: ENGINE:OTHER PARTS
Summary: ROCKER ARM GASKET FAILURE

By showing hundreds of similar owner complaints registered by the U.S. government, you strengthen your own claim's merits. The above report was quickly downloaded from NHTSA's website.

Three Steps to a Settlement

Step 1: Informal negotiations

If your vehicle was misrepresented, has major defects, or wasn't properly repaired under warranty, the first thing you should do is give the seller (the dealer and automaker or a private party) a written summary (by registered mail or fax) of the outstanding problems and stipulate a time period in which they will need to be corrected or your money will be refunded. Keep a copy for yourself along with all your repair records. Be sure to check all of the sales and warranty documents you were given to see if they conform to provincial laws. Any errors, omissions, or violations can be used to get a settlement with the dealer in lieu of making a formal complaint.

At the beginning, try to work things out informally and, in your attempt to reach a settlement, keep in mind the cardinal rule: ask only for what is fair and don't try to make anyone look bad.

• Listen. The really tough part of negotiating is listening. Listen to the automaker's representative or the dealership principal and try to understand their problem while thinking of a cooperative solution. This means frequently restating the other side's position so they realize you understand their offer.

• Line up evidence and allies. Be sure to line up your proof (like work orders, service bulletins, and independent garage reports) before making your claim.

• Be reasonable and give as well as take. Consumers are frequently given a "Let's Make a Deal" spiel where the initial offer of 50 percent is often boosted to 75 percent compensation if the customer will agree—at that very moment—to pay 25 percent of the repair.

• Keep your demands reasonable but add a request for consequential damages (frustration, inconvenience, rental cars, missed work/vacation, etc.) and keep it as a throwaway claim to be used at a critical juncture in the talks.

• Know when to shut up.

• Don't set up an unrealistic timetable.

Finally, when negotiating, speak in a calm, polite manner and try to avoid polarizing the issue. Talk about how "we can work together" on the problem. Let a compromise slowly emerge—don't come in with a hardline set of demands. Don't demand the settlement offer in writing, but make sure that you're accompanied by a friend who can confirm the offer in court if it isn't honoured. (Relatives may testify in court.) Be prepared to act upon the offer without delay so that you won't be blamed for its withdrawal.

Dealer/service manager

If you bought a used vehicle from a dealer who sells the same make new, you stand a good chance of getting free repairs, particularly if the vehicle is still under warranty or is covered by a "goodwill" or "special policy" program, or if you intend to plead premature failure of a specific part based upon the parameters listed in the Estimated Part Durability chart found on pages 76–77.

Service managers are directly responsible to the dealers and manufacturers and make the first determination of what work is covered under warranty. They are paid to save the dealers and automakers money and to mollify irate clients—almost an impossible balancing act, wherein my sympathies are more with the dealers than with the automakers. When service managers agree to warranty coverage, it's because you've convinced them that they must do so. This can be done by getting them to access the vehicle's history from the manufacturer's computer and by you presenting the facts of your case in a confident, forthright manner with as many dealer service bulletins and NHTSA owner complaint printouts as you can find for support.

Don't use your salesperson as a runner, since the sales staff are generally quite distant from the service staff and usually have less pull than you do. If the service manager can't or won't set things right, your next step is to convene a mini-summit with the service manager, the dealership principal, and the automaker's rep. By getting the automaker involved, you run less risk of having the dealer fob you off on the manufacturer and you can often get an agreement where the seller and automaker pay two-thirds of the repair cost.

Independent dealers and dealers who sell a brand of used vehicle that they don't sell new give you less latitude. You have to make the case that the vehicle's defects were present at the time of purchase or should have been known to the seller, or that the vehicle doesn't conform to the representations made when it was purchased. Emphasize that you intend to use the courts if necessary to obtain a refund—most independent sellers would rather settle than risk a lawsuit with all the attendant publicity. An independent estimate of the vehicle's defects and cost of repairs is essential if you want to convince the seller that you're serious in your claim and stand a good chance of winning your case in court. The estimated cost of repairs is also useful in challenging a dealer who agrees to pay half the repair costs and then jacks up the costs 100 percent so that you wind up paying the whole shot.

Step 2: Sending a registered letter or fax
This is the next step to take if your claim is refused. Send the dealer and manufacturer a polite registered letter or fax that asks for compensation for repairs that have been done or need to be done, insurance costs while the vehicle is being repaired, towing charges, supplementary transportation costs like taxis and rented cars, and damages for inconvenience.

Specify 5 days (but allow 10 days) for either party to respond. If no satisfactory offer is made, file suit in small claims court. Make the manufacturer a party to the lawsuit, especially if the emissions warranty, a secret warranty extension, a safety recall campaign, or extensive chassis rusting is involved. The two sample claim letters that follow can be useful in getting compensation for a defective used vehicle or for unsatisfactory repairs. Include a reference in your letter to any court decisions you find in this section of the book that support your claim.

Used-Car Complaint Letter/Fax

Without Prejudice

Date: _____
Name: _____

Please be advised that I am dissatisfied with my used vehicle, a (state model), for the following reasons:

1. _____
2. _____
3. _____
4. _____
5. _____

In compliance with the provincial consumer protection laws and the "implied warranty" set down by the Supreme Court of Canada in *Donoghue v. Stevenson* and *Longpré v. St-Jacques Automobile*, I hereby request that these defects be repaired without charge.

This vehicle has not been reasonably durable and is, therefore, not as represented to me.

Should you fail to repair these defects in a satisfactory manner and within a reasonable period of time, I shall get an estimate of the repairs from an independent source and claim them in court, without further delay.

I have dealt with your company because of its honesty, competence, and sincere regard for its clients. I am sure that my case is the exception and not the rule.

A response within the next five (5) days would be appreciated.

Sincerely,

_____
(signed with telephone or fax number)

Secret Warranty Claim Letter/Fax

Without Prejudice

Date: _____
Name: _____

Please be advised that I am dissatisfied with my vehicle, a
_____, bought from you on _____.

It has had the following recurring problems that I believe are factory-related defects, as confirmed by internal service bulletins sent to dealers, and are covered by your "goodwill" policies:

1. _____
2. _____
3. _____

If your "goodwill" program has ended, I ask that my claim be accepted nevertheless, inasmuch as I was never informed of your policy while it was in effect and should not be penalized for not knowing it existed.

I hereby formally put you on notice under federal and provincial consumer protection statutes that your refusal to apply this extended warranty coverage in my case would be an unfair warranty practice within the purview of the above-cited laws.

I have enclosed several estimates (my bill) showing that this problem is factory related and will (has) cost $_____ to correct. I would appreciate your refunding me the estimated (paid) amount, failing which, I reserve the right to have the repair done elsewhere and claim reimbursement, plus consequential and punitive damages from you in court, without further delay.

A response within the next five (5) days would be appreciated.

Sincerely,

_____
(signed with telephone or fax number)

Step 3: Mediation and arbitration

If the formality of a courtroom puts you off or you're not sure that your claim is all that solid and you don't want to pay legal costs to find out, consider using mediation or arbitration. These services are sponsored by the Better Business Bureau, Automobile Protection Association, Canadian Automobile Association, Canadian Automobile Manufacturers Vehicle Arbitration Program (CAMVAP), small claims court (usually a prerequisite to going to trial), and provincial and territorial governments.

Safety and Performance Defects: Step-by-Step Resolution

Sudden acceleration, chronic stalling, ABS and airbag failures, and powertrain glitches

Incidents of sudden acceleration or chronic stalling are difficult to diagnose and are treated quite differently by federal safety agencies. Whereas sudden acceleration is considered a safety-related problem, stalling isn't. Never mind that a vehicle's sudden loss of power on a busy highway puts everyone's life a risk. The same problem exists with engine and transmission powertrain failures, which are only occasionally considered to be safety-related. ABS and airbag failures are universally considered to be life-threatening defects. If your vehicle manifests any of these conditions, here's what you need to do:

1. Get independent witnesses that the problem exists (mechanic or passengers) and notify the dealer/manufacturer by fax, email, or registered letter that you consider the problem to be a factory-induced, safety-related defect. Make sure you address your correspondence to the manufacturer's "product liability" or legal affairs department. At the dealership's service bay, make sure that every work order clearly states the problem as well as the number of previous attempts to fix it. (This should result in you having a few complaint letters and a handful of work orders, confirming that this is an on-going deficiency.) If the dealer won't give you a copy of the work order because the work is a warranty claim, ask for a copy of the order number, in case your estate wishes to file a claim, pursuant to an accident. (This will get the service manager's attention.) Leaving this kind of "paper trail" is crucial for any claim you may have later on because it shows your fear and persistence and clearly indicates that the dealer and manufacturer had ample time to correct the defect. In California, for example, the state's recently revamped Lemon Law requires that car owners clearly show they made two attempts to have a safety defect corrected (other states require three or four attempts) before the court will grant a refund, order the car taken back, or impose punitive damages.

2. Note on the work order that you expect the problem to be diagnosed and corrected under the emissions warranty or a "goodwill" program. It also wouldn't hurt to add the phrase on the work order or in your claim letters that any deaths, injuries, or damage caused by the defect will be the dealer's and manufacturer's responsibility since this work order or letter, fax, or email constitutes you putting them on "formal notice."

3. If the dealer does the necessary repairs at little or no cost to you, send a follow-up confirmation that you appreciate the assistance.

Also, emphasize that you'll be back if the problem reappears, even if the warranty has expired, because the repair renews your warranty rights applicable to that defect. In other words, the warranty clock is set back to its original position. Understand that you won't likely get a copy of the repair bill, either, because dealers don't like to admit that there was a serious defect present. Keep in mind, however, that you can get your complete vehicle file from the dealer and manufacturer by issuing a subpoena (cost: about $25), if the case goes to small-claims or a higher court. This request has produced many out-of-court settlements when the internal documents show extensive work was carried out to correct the problem.

4. If the problem persists, send a letter, fax, or email to the dealer and manufacturer saying so, look for ALLDATA service bulletins to confirm your vehicle's defects are factory related and call Transport Canada and NHTSA or log onto NHTSA's website to report the failure. Also, call the Nader-founded Center for Auto Safety in Washington, D. C. (202-328-7700) for a lawyer referral and an information sheet covering the problem. For tire complaints, Strategic Safety should also be copied.

5. Now come two crucial questions: repair the defect now, or later; use the dealer or an independent? Generally it's smart to use an independent garage if: 1) you know the dealer isn't pushing for free corrective repairs from the manufacturer; 2) weeks or months have passed without any resolution of your claim; 3) the dealer keeps repeating it's a maintenance item; and 4) you know an independent mechanic who will give you a detailed work order showing the defect is factory related and not due to poor maintenance. Don't mention that a court case may ensue, since this will scare the dickens out of your only independent witness. An added bonus is that the repair charges will be about half of what a dealer would demand. Incidentally, if the automaker later denies warranty "goodwill" because you used an independent repairer, use the argument that the defect's safety implications required emergency repairs, carried out by whomever could see you first.

6. Dashboard-mounted warning lights usually come on prior to airbags suddenly deploying, ABS brakes failing, or engine glitches causing the vehicle to stall out. (Sudden acceleration usually occurs without warning.) Automakers consider these lights to be critical safety warnings and generally advise drivers to *immediately* have the vehicle serviced to correct the problem (advice found in the owner's manual) when any of the above lights are lit. This bolsters the argument that your life was threatened, emergency repairs were required, and your request for another vehicle or a complete refund isn't out of line.

7. Sudden acceleration can have multiple causes, isn't easy to duplicate, and is often blamed on the driver mistaking the accelerator for the brakes or failing to perform proper maintenance. Yet NHTSA data shows that with the 1992–2000 Explorer, for example,

a faulty cruise control or PCV valve, and poorly mounted pedals are the most likely causes of the Explorer's sudden acceleration. So how do you satisfy the burden of proof, showing the problem exists and is the automaker's responsibility? Use the legal doctrine called "the balance of probabilities" by eliminating all of the possible dodges the dealer or manufacturer may trot out. Show that proper maintenance has been carried out, you're a safe driver, and the incident occurs frequently and without warning.

8. If any of the above defects causes an accident, the airbag fails to deploy, or you're injured by its deployment, ask your insurance company to have the vehicle towed to a neutral location and clearly state that neither the dealer nor automaker should touch the vehicle until your insurance company and NHTSA have completed their investigation. Also, get as many witnesses as possible and immediately go to the hospital for a checkup, even if you're feeling okay. You may be injured and not know it because the adrenaline coursing through your veins is masking your injuries. Plus, a hospital exam will easily confirm that your injuries are accident-related, which is essential in court or for future settlement negotiations.

9. Peruse NHTSA's online accident database to find reports of other accidents caused by the same failure.

10. Don't let your insurance company settle the case if you're sure the accident was caused by a mechanical failure. Even if an engineering analysis fails to directly implicate the manufacturer or dealer, you can always plead the aforementioned balance of probabilities. If the insurance company settles, your insurance premiums will probably be increased.

Treacherous tires

Tire companies are far easier to deal with than automobile manufacturers because under the legal doctrine of *res ipsa loquitor* (liability is shown by the failure), tires aren't supposed to fail. It's for this reason that tire companies try to avoid liability by imputing blame to someone or something else, like punctures, impact damage, overloading, over-inflating, or under-inflating. If you have a premature tire failure, consider the ten steps outlined previously, plus include the following:

1. Access the NHTSA and Strategic Safety on the Internet (see Appendix II) for current data on which tires are failure prone and which companies are under investigation, conducting recalls, or carrying out "silent recalls."

2. Keep the tire. If the tiremaker says an analysis must be done, permit only a portion of the tire to be taken away.

3. Plead the balance of probabilities, using friends and family to refute the tire company's contention that you caused the failure.

4. Ask for damages that are adequate for the replacement of all the tires on your vehicle, including mounting costs.

5. Include in your damage claim any repairs needed to fix body damage caused by the tire's failure.

Paint and body defects

The following settlement advice applies mainly to paint defects, but you can use these tips for any other vehicle defect that you believe is the automaker's/dealer's responsibility. If you're not sure that the problem is a factory-related deficiency or a maintenance item, have it checked out by an independent garage or get a dealer service bulletin summary for your vehicle. The summary may include specific bulletins relating to the diagnosis, correction, and ordering of upgraded parts needed to fix your problem.

1. If you know your vehicle's paint problem is factory related, take your vehicle to the dealer and ask for a written, signed estimate. When you're handed the estimate, ask that the paint job be done for free under the manufacturer's "goodwill" program. (Ford's euphemism for this secret warranty is "Owner Dialogue Program," GM's term is "special policy," and Chrysler just calls it "goodwill." Don't use the term "secret warranty" yet; you'll just make the dealer and automaker angry and evasive.)

2. Your request will probably be met with a refusal, an offer to repaint the vehicle for half the cost, or, if you're lucky, an agreement to repaint the vehicle free of charge. If you accept half-cost, make sure that it's based on the original estimate you have in hand, since some dealers jack up their estimates so that your 50 percent is really 100 percent of the true cost.

3. If the dealer/automaker has already refused your claim and the repair hasn't been done yet, get an additional estimate from an independent garage that shows the problem is factory related.

4. Again, if the repair has yet to be done, mail or fax a registered claim to the automaker (send a copy to the dealer), claiming the average of both estimates. If the repair has been done at your expense, mail or fax a registered claim with a copy of your bill. A sample letter/fax can be found on page 83.

5. If you don't receive a satisfactory response within a week, deposit a copy of the estimate or paid bill and claim letter/fax before the small claims court and await a trial date. This means that the automaker/dealer will have to appear, no lawyer is required, costs should be minimal (under $100), and a mediation hearing or trial will be scheduled in a few months followed by a judgment a few weeks later (the time varies among different regions).

Things that you can do to help your case: collect photographs, maintenance work orders, previous work orders dealing with your problem, technical service bulletins, and an independent expert (the garage or body shop that did the estimate or repair is best, but you can also use a local teacher who teaches automotive repair).

Other situations

- If the vehicle has just been repainted but the dealer says that "good-will" coverage was denied by the automaker, pay for the repair with a certified check and write "under protest" on the check. Remember, though, if the dealer does the repair, you won't have an independent expert who can affirm that the problem was factory related or that it was a result of premature wearout. Plus, the dealer can say that you or the environment caused the paint problem. In these cases, internal service bulletins can make or break your case.
- If the dealer/automaker offers a partial repair or refund, take it. Then sue for the rest. Remember, if a partial repair has been done under warranty, it counts as an admission of responsibility, no matter what "goodwill" euphemism is used. Also, the repaired component/ body panel should be just as durable as if it were new. Hence, the clock starts ticking from the beginning until you reach the original warranty parameter—again, no matter what the dealer's repair warranty limit says.
- It's a lot easier to get the automaker to pay to replace a defective part than it is to be compensated for a missed day of work or a ruined vacation. Manufacturers hate to pay for consequential expenses apart from towing bills because they can't control the amount of the refund. Fortunately, Canadian courts have taken the position that all expenses (damages) flowing from a problem covered by a warranty or service bulletin are the manufacturer's/dealer's responsibility under negligence and product liability provisions found in provincial consumer protection statutes, common law jurisprudence, Quebec civil law, and federal consumer protection legislation. Nevertheless, don't risk a fair settlement for some outlandish claim of "emotional distress," "pain and suffering," etc. If you have invoices to prove actual consequential damages, then use them. If not, don't be greedy.

Very seldom do automakers contest these paint claims before small claims court, opting instead to settle once the court claim is bounced from their customer relations people to their legal affairs department. At that time, you'll probably be offered an out-of-court settlement for 50–75 percent of your claim.

Stand fast and make reference to the service bulletins you intend to subpoena in order to publicly contest in court the unfair nature of this "secret warranty" program. (Automaker lawyers cringe at the idea of trying to explain why consumers aren't made aware of these bulletins.) One hundred percent restitution will probably follow.

A good example is the *Shields v. General Motors of Canada* judgment rendered January 6, 1998.

Shields v. General Motors of Canada, No. 1398/96, Ontario Court (General Division), Oshawa Small Claims Court, 33 King Street West, Oshawa, Ontario L1H 1A1, July 24, 1997, Robert Zochodne, Deputy Judge. The owner of a 1991 Pontiac Grand Prix purchased the vehicle used with over 100,000 km on its odometer. Commencing in 1995, the paint began to bubble and then flake and eventually peel off. Deputy Judge Robert Zochodne awarded the plaintiff $1,205.72 and struck down every one of GM's environmental/acid rain/UV-rays arguments. Other important aspects of this 12-page judgment that GM did not appeal:

1. The judge admitted many of the service bulletins referred to in *Lemon-Aid* as proof of GM's negligence.
2. Although the vehicle had 156,000 km when the case went to court, GM still offered to pay 50 percent of the paint repairs if the plaintiff dropped his suit.
3. Deputy Judge Zochodne ruled that the failure to protect the paint from the damaging effects of UV rays is akin to engineering a car that won't start in cold weather. In essence, vehicles must be built to withstand the rigors of the environment.
4. Here's an interesting twist: the original warranty covered defects that were present at the time it was in effect. The judge, taking statements found in the GM bulletins, ruled the UV problem was factory related, and therefore, *it existed during the warranty period and thereby represented a latent defect* that appeared once the warranty expired.
5. The subsequent purchaser was not prevented from making the warranty claim, even though the warranty had long since expired from a time and mileage standpoint and he was the second owner.

Bentley v. Dave Wheaton Pontiac Buick GMC Ltd and General Motors of Canada, Victoria Registry No. 24779, British Columbia Small Claims Court, December 1, 1998, Judge Higinbotham. This is the third, and most recent, small claims judgment against GM. It builds upon the Ontario *Shields v. General Motors of Canada* decision and cites other jurisprudence as to how long paint should last on a house. If you're wondering why Ford and Chrysler haven't been hit by similar judgments, remember that they usually settle.

Reasons for Judgment

...In this case the claimant purchased a vehicle, a pickup truck, from a dealership, Dave Wheaton Pontiac Buick G.M.C. Ltd., a new vehicle, in 1991. There was an admitted defect in the paint which did not become apparent until later. General Motors is also a defendant in this action and discovered in a general sense this problem of delamination in the paint on some vehicles in 1992, about one year after the claimant purchased the vehicle in question.

The specific problem with this vehicle was observed early in 1994. It was brought to the attention of Wheaton when the vehicle was brought in for other maintenance two weeks after the warranty expired. At that time the problem was relatively minor. I say relatively in the sense that compared to what later occurred it was minor.

Mr. Palfry, who is the manager of the paint and body shop for the retailer Wheaton, was made aware of the problem. There is no dispute about that, and he sold the claimant a tub of touch-up paint.

The paint continued to deteriorate and in late 1996 was severely peeled.

In January of 1997, the claimant became aware that this problem was general to certain GM vehicles, vehicles of certain colours produced at a certain time by the defendant company.

The claimant took the vehicle back in but was told that it was too late. The warranty had expired and even the discretionary goodwill warranty was over. I do not think the claimant was told about the discretionary goodwill warranty, but in fact it was a policy of GM to extend the warranty for this sort of claim in certain circumstances, but it was discretionary. In any case, the claimant was told that it was too late for it to be fixed under warranty. Neither the dealership nor the manufacturer would accept responsibility at that time. As a result, this action was commenced.

I make the following findings: There was a latent defect in the vehicle relating to the paint, which revealed itself over time and in far less time than a good paint job would be expected to last.

The dealer or the manufacturer, had the manufacturer been informed by the dealer, ought to have advised the claimant in May of 1994 that they were aware of this general delamination problem and ought to have advised as to what warranty extension might be available. I will say more about this in a moment. In any event, the dealer and the manufacturer, if the dealer had notified the manufacturer of the problem, would have known that the delamination commenced within the three year period and ought to have honoured the warranty.

Despite my findings, as I said earlier that the dealer and manufacturer ought to have given guidance to the claimant in May of 1994 as to a possible warranty claim, I do not find any cause of action arising directly from this finding. It would simply have been good business practice for them to have advised the claimant.

If liability is to be found against General Motors, it must be for a breach of the warranty. On the other hand, if liability is to be found against Dave Wheaton, it must be because as a seller the dealership breached an implied condition of the Sale of Goods Act.

On the issue of the warranty supplied by General Motors, I note that it covers "repairs, or adjustments to correct any vehicle defect related to material or workmanship occurring during the warranty period." It appears from the evidence that General Motors' major concern with this particular case was that the problem with this specific vehicle was not brought to their attention during the warranty period, not that the problem with the paint did not actually arise within the warranty period.

I find the claimant has established that the paint problem was brought to the attention of the dealer in mid-May of 1994.

The warranty had expired two weeks earlier. I accept that the defect occurred during the warranty period on two bases. First, as submitted by the claimant, Ms. Bentley, the defect occurred at the time of manufacture and continues to this day.

Similar finding was made in *Shields v. General Motors of Canada,* a decision of the Ontario Court, General Division, number 1398 of 1996.

Secondly, in any event, based on the condition of the paint in mid-May 1994, the defect likely became apparent during the three year warranty period. I therefore find that General Motors has breached the warranty and the claimant is entitled to damages.

As for the dealership, defendant's counsel argues that there has been no breach of the Sale of Goods Act in that the vehicle when sold was of merchantable quality and reasonably fit for the purpose for which it was intended.

I agree as to merchantable quality. And as to the other implied condition, I also agree if what is meant by "reasonably fit for the purpose" is that it was a truck that operated and was capable of hauling cargo and passengers, but I am of the view that every seller of new vehicles knows that the purchaser expects the vehicle to be reasonably fit for the purpose of resale at some future time, depending upon the age and quality of the vehicle. This vehicle was not and is not reasonably fit for resale given those factors. It is not reasonably fit due to the latent defect in its quality, a defect which existed in incipient form at the time of sale.

I note that in *McCready Products v. Sherwin-Williams,* (1984) 53 A.R. 304, a decision of the Alberta Queen's Bench, referred to in the article by Fridman submitted by counsel, in that case paint that weathered and faded in less than three years was found unfit for its purpose. That was house paint. The same is true here. Even though the paint in question here was only a component of the item purchased, it was a very important component having a great deal to do with the value of the vehicle.

I therefore find the defendant Dave Wheaton Pontiac Buick G.M.C. Ltd. also liable for damages. The liability of both defendants is joint and several.

I turn now to the question of damages. The claimants have averaged three estimates they have placed before the court and claim the amount of twenty-three hundred seventy-three dollars and sixty-one cents.

The defendant says damages are lower as a different allowance to dealers are made under the warranty. The defendants cannot now get the benefit of this, in my opinion, as responsibility under the warranty was denied by them.

I prefer to assess damages by taking the defendant's estimate or figure of fifteen hundred eighty-eight dollars twenty-six cents, a sum which the dealer could charge under the warranty to GM, and multiply that figure by a factor admitted to by the defendant as to what another body shop would—the number of hours another body shop would employ in order to obtain a realistic assessment.

It was stated in evidence that twenty-two to twenty-five hours is required to repair this damage, of which two hours are the actual painting.

The defendant's estimate is based on sixteen point one hours, because that's all they can claim under the warranty. There is therefore a difference of approximately nine hours in the estimates based on the upper level of twenty-five hours required by another body shop. I accept the proportion of paint to labour as stated by the witness and therefore accept that the defendant's estimate is based on fourteen point one hours of labour.

I also accept that the acceptable labour rate is fifty dollars and fifty-five cents and the painting rate is twenty-three dollars and seventy-one cents. It is the nine hours of labour that is in issue here in the assessment of damages.

The costs of the paint and materials I accept is two hundred and sixty-two dollars and forty-two cents.

I am therefore going to base damages on the defendant's estimate of one thousand eight hundred and ten dollars and sixty-two cents, which includes taxes, plus an additional nine hours labour at fifty dollars and fifty-five cents per hour, plus taxes, or an additional five hundred eighteen dollars eighty-four cents, bringing the total to two thousand three hundred and twenty-nine dollars and forty-six cents, very close to the estimate given by the claimant.

I am making no adjustment for betterment as it is known because, in my opinion, this is offset by the fact that for seven and a half years, or at least most of those seven and a half years, the vehicle was essentially unmarketable, unsaleable without substantial loss.

The claimant will therefore have judgment against both defendants, joint and several, in the amount of two thousand three hundred twenty-nine dollars forty-six cents, plus costs. No interest is awarded as it is inapplicable to this type of claim.

Getting outside help
Remember, it's not the mediator or arbitrator's fault if you lose your case due to poor preparation. Ask government and independent consumer protection agencies, like the one listed below, to evaluate how well you're prepared before going to your first hearing.

Automobile Protection Association
292 St-Joseph Blvd West, Montreal, Quebec H2V 2N7
–and–
2 Carlton St., Suite 1319, Toronto, Ontario M5B 1S3
Tel.: 416-204-1444; Fax: 416-204-1985; Website: *www.apa.ca*

A non-profit Canadian motorist protection organization, the Automobile Protection Association (APA) mediates thousands of complaints yearly, mostly for its own members.

Government consumer affairs
Investigation, mediation, and some litigation are the primary areas in which consumer affairs offices can be helpful. Despite severe budget restraints to these offices, consumer protection legislation has been left standing in most of the provinces, and resourceful consumers can use these laws along with media coverage to prod provincial consumer affairs offices into action. Furthermore, provincial bureaucrats aren't as well shielded from criticism as are their federal counterparts. A call to your MPP, MLA, or the minister's executive assistant can often get things rolling.

Federal consumer protection is a crock. Although the revised Competition Act has some bite when challenging misleading advertising and a number of other nefarious business practices, reorganized Consumer and Corporate Affairs departments have been de-fanged and de-gummed.

On-line services/Internet/websites
America Online and CompuServe are two on-line service providers with active consumer forums that use experts to answer consumer queries, and to provide legal and technical advice. The Internet offers the same information using a worldwide database. If you or someone you know is able to create a website, you might consider using this site to attract attention to your plight and arm yourself for arbitration or court. You may wish to follow the example of some existing websites I've listed in Appendix II. A few of my favourites are: Chrysler Paint Peeling, Neon Enthusiasts Page (engine head gaskets), British Columbia Dead Ford Owner's Page, Ford Transmission Victims, Fordsuckz, Saturn Exposed, and Do Not Buy a Kia! I don't know why, but Ford seems to attract the most Web-savvy complainers. (Betcha they won't use that fact in their ads.)

 **DO NOT BUY A KIA!!!!!**
Note: In an effort to get this website highly ranked on search engines (and save people from buying a lemon), I have replaced Kia with K--, Sportage by Sport--- and Sephia by Seph---. This is because too many occurences of the same keyword is considered spamming

and can hurt your website ranking. You can avoid these replacements by clicking here to visit my mirror site.

Acura was one of the first targets of a successful consumer protest using the Internet. Michael Hos, a dissatisfied Acura owner from the United States, became fed up with what he felt was Acura's stonewalling of his complaints. Rather than getting angry, he got organized and set up a website called "Acura 1997 CL 3.0L: My Lemon" to collect other owners' comments and list some of the most common Acura problem areas. Within six months, Acura settled. Here's what Hos wrote me:

...As far as my website goes, I think it was a major part of them settling early. I had a counter placed on it that showed them how many people had visited the site. Anyone can set up a web page like mine pretty easily. I have web space on my university's computer, so it was free for me to use. Folks without space should expect to spend about $20 a month for space, or if they have their own e-mail account, web space is usually provided for free. If they don't know how to set up their web page, paying someone to do it will be kinda pricey, a few hundred bucks should cover it. The main thing it needs to have is the counter, and it also needs to be slander free. I had only facts on my web page as I didn't want to get involved in a slander suit. They also need to register the site with all the major search engines so it comes up when looking for the manufacturer. *Submitit.com* offers such services for free. Putting in a <Meta> tag into the page also helps move it up the search engines' list of hits. Posting to newsgroups also is helpful. I also wrote to J.D. Power, NHTSA, *Consumer Reports,* and any other consumer-oriented agency I could think of.

When we settled for $4,000 before going to court, I had to sign the settlement papers saying I would pull down my site. They would not settle with me until I did that. This shows how much power the site can have. I also put the manufacturer's phone number and address on it so viewers of the site could contact the manufacturer....

PROJECTS AND CAUSES

A BAD FIRE occured in our 1994 Jeep Cherokee because of driving with a compact spare tire while in 4WD (could not get out of 4WD). Compact spare is standard equipment but appropriate warning not in Owners Manual. No appropriate answers from Chrysler Canada yet. Seeking others with similar experience.

From the Globe and Mail.

Classified ads
Use your local paper's "Personals" column to pressure the seller and gather data from others who may have experienced a problem similar to your own. This alerts others to the potential problem, helps build a core base for a class action or group meeting with the automaker, and puts pressure on the dealer or manufacturer to settle. Sometimes it also leads to the newspaper doing a story on your plight.

Going to Court

When to sue

If the seller you've been negotiating with agrees to make things right, give him or her a deadline and then have an independent garage check the repairs. If no offer is made within 10 working days, file suit in court. Make the manufacturer a party to the lawsuit only if the original, unexpired warranty was transferred to you; your claim falls under the emissions warranty or a secret warranty extension; a safety recall campaign exists; or extensive chassis rusting is involved.

Choosing the right court

You must decide what remedy to pursue; that is, whether you want a partial refund or a cancellation of the sale. To determine the refund amount, add the estimated cost of repairing existing mechanical defects to the cost of prior repairs. Don't exaggerate your losses or claim for repairs that are considered routine maintenance.

A suit for cancellation of sale involves practical problems. The court requires that the vehicle be "tendered" back to the seller at the time the lawsuit is filed. This means you are without transportation for as long as the case continues, unless you purchase another car in the interim. If you lose the case, you must then take back the old car and pay storage fees. You could go from having no car to having two, one of which is a clunker.

Generally, if the cost of repairs or the sales contract amount falls within the small claims court limit (limits vary from province to province), the case should be filed there to keep costs to a minimum and to obtain a speedy hearing. Small claims court judgments aren't easily appealed, lawyers aren't necessary, filing fees are minimal (about $125), and cases are usually heard within a few months.

If the damages exceed the small claims court limit and there's no way to reduce them, you'll have to go to a higher court—where costs quickly add up and lengthy delays (a few years or more) are commonplace.

Small courts, big victories

There are small claims courts in most counties of every province, and you can make a claim in the county where the problem happened or where the defendant lives and conducts business. The first step is to make sure that your claim doesn't exceed the dollar limit of the court. (The limits differ from province to province.) Then, you should go to the small claims court office and ask for a claim form. Instructions on how to fill it out accompany the form. Remember, you must identify the defendant correctly. It's a practice of some dishonest firms to change a company's name to escape liability; for example, it would be impossible to sue Joe's Garage (1999) if your contract is with Joe's Garage Inc. (1984).

At this point, it would be a smart idea to hire a lawyer or a paralegal for a brief walk-through of small claims procedures to ensure that you've prepared your case properly and that you know what objections will likely be raised by the other side. If you'd like a lawyer to do all the work for you, there are a number of inexpensive law firms around the country that are experienced in small claims litigation. In Toronto, some law offices charge a flat fee of $750 for the basic small claims lawsuit and trial.

Remember that you're entitled to bring to court any evidence relevant to your case, including written documents, such as a bill of sale or receipt, contract, or letter. If your car has developed severe rust problems, bring a photograph (signed and dated by the photographer) to court. You may also have witnesses testify in court. It's important to discuss a witness's testimony prior to the court date. If a witness can't attend the court date, he or she can write a report and sign it for representation in court. This situation usually applies to an expert witness, such as an independent mechanic who has evaluated your car's problems.

If you lose your case in spite of all your preparation and research, some small claims court statutes allow cases to be retried, at a nominal cost, in exceptional circumstances. If a new witness has come forward, additional evidence has been discovered, or key documents (that were previously not available) have become accessible, apply for a retrial. In Ontario, this little-known provision is Rule 18.4 (1).B.

Presenting your case

As plaintiff, you will get the first opportunity to rise and state your case to the judge. You should ask for the exclusion of witnesses from the courtroom (this increases the chance that the other side will give contradictory testimony) and then proceed to lay out your proof, concluding within 5 to 10 minutes. Hang your narrative on the documents you produce (you can call them "P-1," "P-2," for "Proof 1," "Proof 2," and so on) and let them serve as note cards.

The first three documents should be the sales contract, all work orders relating to the problems you've had, and your registered complaint letter or fax. After that, you may wish to produce the dealer's or automaker's response, a report or work orders from an independent garage supporting your position, and copies of your maintenance records and dealer service bulletins in order to show the problems are factory related and not maintenance items. Conclude your presentation by simply restating the claim as it's written on your court complaint.

On the day of the trial, bring in a mechanic to confirm the defects exist and to provide an estimate of repair costs. If the repairs have already been carried out, he or she can explain what caused the defects and justify the bill for repairing them. This should be done by presenting the defective parts, if possible. The mechanic must convince the judge that the defects were present at the time the car was sold and were not caused by poor maintenance or abusive driving habits.

When the dealer gets on the stand, ask for the exclusion of all witnesses and try to ferret out the following facts:
• When and from whom was the used car last purchased?
• For how much was it bought?

- What was done to recondition the car, and at what cost?
- What was the *Red Book* value of the car when first bought from the previous owner and when sold to the plaintiff?

This line of questioning should show the judge the considerable profits the dealer made by buying the car below the market value, not spending much to recondition it, and reselling it far above the *Red Book* value.

Before the dealer leaves the stand, get him to confirm whether he or his salespeople made any representations, either verbally or through a newspaper ad, extolling the vehicle's qualities. With witnesses excluded, it's quite likely that the dealer's witnesses will contradict him when it's their turn to testify.

Other witnesses who can help your case are the car's previous owner (who can testify as to its deficiencies when sold) and any of your coworkers or friends who can testify as to how well you maintained your vehicle, how you drove it, and the seriousness of the defects.

Settlements

You may be asked to sign a document, called a release, which proves that a final settlement has been made. Generally, once you sign the release you can't sue the other person for that particular debt or injury. If you're the debtor, it's very important that you make sure the other person signs the release when you pay him or her. If you're the creditor collecting on the debt, you must sign the release, but don't do so until you've received the money. Release the debtor from that particular debt, but don't release him or her from all future debts.

Sample Settlement Form

I, John Doe, hereby acknowledge the payment of $300 by Jane Smith to compensate me for the defects in the vehicle I bought from her on _____. In accepting this payment, I hereby drop all present and future claims against Ms. Smith arising from the purchase of this vehicle.

_____   _____

Date   **John Doe**

                                 _____

                                 Jane Smith

Deadbeat defendants

If you're dealing with a professional crook, the real work begins once you win your case. You may have to garnish (seize) part of the defendant's bank account or wages or ask the court to serve a writ of execution. This writ allows the plaintiff to demand full settlement plus court costs and, failing that, to seize the defendant's goods to cover the amount of the judgment. But here's the catch: property that's needed to earn a living (car, tools, machinery, etc.), household goods, and anything encumbered by a lien are exempt from seizure.

Professional deadbeats can tell the court that practically everything they own is exempt—and it will take another action, at the plaintiff's expense, before the regular courts have the defendant questioned under oath. If he's found to be lying, he can then be sent to jail for perjury or contempt of court, but the small claims court judgment will remain unpaid.

Key Court Decisions

The following Canadian lawsuits and judgments cover typical problems that are likely to arise. Put any relevant case in your claim letter as leverage when negotiating a settlement, or as a reference should your claim go to trial. Legal principles are similarly applicable to Canadian and American law. Quebec court decisions, however, may be based on legal principles that don't apply outside that province. Therefore, do what most lawyers do: present all the court judgments that may be helpful and let the presiding judge or the defendant's lawyer sort out those that they feel apply.

Additional court judgments can be found in the "Jurisprudence" section of *lemonaidcars.com*, the legal reference section of your city's main public library, or at a nearby university law library. Ask the librarian for help in choosing the legal phrases that best describe your claim.

Damages (Punitive)

Punitive damages (also known as exemplary damages) allow the plaintiff to get compensation that exceeds his or her losses. In Canada, judges sometimes award punitive damages as a deterrent to those who carry out dishonest or negligent practices; however, these kinds of judgments are more common in the U.S. For example, in 1998 and 1999, both Ford and GM were hit with huge punitive judgments: the GM plaintiffs were given $4.9 billion (U.S.) by a California jury as compensation for burns sustained when a speeding Mustang rear-ended their 1972 Malibu; and Ford plaintiffs were awarded $295 million (U.S.) for injuries sustained from a Bronco rollover.

Travis Eby v. J. S. Saville Holdings and Guelph City Imports Subaru/Lada, and Cory Tanguay, September 5, 1997, Ontario Court (General Division), No. 9358/96, Justice Clarke. The purchaser of a used 1989 Pontiac Sprint discovered the vehicle had 83,000 km and 12 previous owners, instead of 16,000 km and only one previous owner, as had been represented by the dealer. Judge Clarke awarded the plaintiff $4,000 in damages as the difference in what the buyer would have paid had the true facts been known. Interestingly, under the Ontario Business Practices Act, the plaintiff was awarded another $1,000 in exemplary damages (rarely given in Canadian courts) because the judge found the dealer's staff made

> false, misleading or deceptive consumer representations as to the quality of the vehicle...failed to state material facts, which they knew or ought to have known and/or employed exaggeration, innuendo, and ambiguity with respect to material facts. I also find that s.4 of the Act applies. I find such business practices were unfair and warrant the court awarding exemplary or punitive damages....

Vlchek v. Koshel (1988), 44 C.C.L.T. 314, B.C.S.C., No. B842974. The plaintiff was seriously injured when she was thrown from a Honda all-terrain cycle on which she had been riding as a passenger. The Court allowed for punitive damages because the manufacturer was well aware of the injuries likely to be caused by the cycle. Specifically, the Court ruled that there is no firm and inflexible principle of law stipulating that punitive or exemplary damages must be denied unless the defendant's acts are specifically directed against the plaintiff. The Court may apply punitive damages "where the defendant's conduct has been indiscriminate of focus, but reckless or malicious in its character. Intent to injure the plaintiff need not be present, so long as intent to do the injurious act can be shown."

See also:
* *Bolduc v. Racicot,* April 2, 1982, Quebec Provincial Court (Hantruie), No. 665-02—00364-817
* *Granek v. Reiter,* Ont. Ct. (Gen. Div.), No. 35/741
* *Morrison v. Sharp,* Ont. Ct. (Gen. Div.), No. 43/548
* *Schryvers v. Richport Ford Sales,* May 18, 1993, B.C.S.C., No. C917060, Judge Tysoe
* *Varleg v. Angeloni,* B.C.S.C., No. 41/301

Furthermore, a slew of cases cover specifics in damage claims. Provincial business practices acts cover false, misleading, or deceptive representations, and allow for punitive damages should the unfair practice toward the consumer amount to an unconscionable representation. (See C.E.D. (3d) s. 76, pp. 140–45.) "Unconscionable" is defined as "where the consumer is not reasonably able to protect his or her interest because of physical infirmity, ignorance, illiteracy, or inability to understand the language of an agreement or similar factors."
* Exemplary damages are justified where compensatory damages are insufficient to deter and punish. See *Walker et al. v. CFTO Ltd. et al.* (1978), 59 O.R. (2nd), No. 104 (Ont. C.A.).
* Exemplary damages can be awarded in cases where the defendant's conduct was "cavalier." See *Ronald Elwyn Lister Ltd. et al. v. Dayton Tire Canada Ltd.* (1985), 52 O.R. (2nd), No. 89 (Ont. C.A.).

- The primary purpose of exemplary damages is to prevent the defendant and all others from doing similar wrongs. See *Fleming v. Spracklin* (1921).
- Disregard of the public's interest, lack of preventive measures, and a callous attitude all merit exemplary damages. See *Coughlin v. Kuntz* (1989), 2 C.C.L.T. (2nd) (B.C.C.A.).
- Punitive damages can be awarded for mental distress. See *Ribeiro v. Canadian Imperial Bank of Commerce* (1992), Ontario Reports 13 (3rd) and *Brown v. Waterloo Regional Board of Commissioners of Police* (1992), 37 O.R. (2nd).

Defects (Body/Performance Related)

When a used vehicle no longer falls within the limits of the warranty expressed by the manufacturer or dealer, it doesn't necessarily mean that the manufacturer can't be held liable for damages caused by defective design. The manufacturer is always liable for the replacement or repair of defective parts if independent testimony can show that the part was incorrectly manufactured or designed. The existence of a secret warranty extension or service bulletins will usually help to prove that the part has a high failure rate. For example, internal service bulletins were instrumental in showing an Ontario small claims court judge that Chrysler had had a history of automatic transmission failures since 1989! See *Lowe v. Fairview Chrysler-Dodge Limited and Chrysler Canada Limited*, May 14, 1996, Ontario Court (General Division), Burlington Small Claims Court, Claim No. 1224/95.

In addition to replacing or repairing the part that failed, an automaker can also be held responsible for any damages arising from the part's failure. This means that loss of wages, supplementary transportation costs, and damages for personal inconvenience can be awarded.

Paint delamination/peeling

A defect that first appeared on Ford sport-utilities, vans, and pickups in the '80s, paint delamination occurs when the top coat of paint separates from the primer coat or turns a chalky colour, mostly along horizontal surfaces and often as a result of intense sunlight. When the paint peels, the entire vehicle must be repainted after a new primer resurfacer has been added. For some vehicles, the labour alone can run about 20 hours at a cost of $75 an hour.

The same paint problem affects mostly 1986–97 Chrysler, Ford, and GM vehicles equally; however, each company has responded differently to owners' requests for compensation. To help you prepare the best arguments for negotiations or court, each automaker is profiled separately, beginning with an analysis of the problem and a website reference, followed by copies of lawsuits, judgments, or technical service bulletins that will help your claim.

Chrysler

Chrysler's paint deficiencies include paint delamination, cracking, and fading between the third and fifth year of ownership. Check out *www.wam.umd.edu/~gluckman/Chrysler/* to see what other owners have to say about their vehicles' problems. A class action lawsuit, *Schurk, Chanes, Jansen, and Ricker v. Chrysler,* No. 97-2-04113-9-SEA, was filed in the Superior Court of King County, Washington on October 2, 1997. It seeks damages for all American Chrysler owners who have owned or leased paint-delaminated 1986–97 models.

The 29-page Statement of Claim uses many photos and internal bulletins and memos to show that Chrysler engaged in

> ...unlawful, unfair, and fraudulent business practices and unfair competition by treating different members of the class differently with respect to repairs it agrees to perform as "goodwill gestures," and by effecting partial repairs that do not address the true nature and extent of the delamination defect.

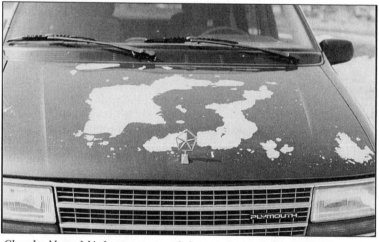

Chrysler blamed bird excrement and the sun for its paint problems.

Ford

Faced with an estimated 13 percent failure rate of its painting process, Ford repainted its delaminated 1983–93 cars, minivans, vans, F-Series trucks, Explorers, Rangers, and Broncos free of charge for five years under a secret "Owner Dialogue Program." Ford whistleblowers say the company discontinued the program in January 1995 because it was proving to be too costly. Nevertheless, owners of 6- to 7-year-old cars who cry foul and threaten small claims action are still routinely given initial offers of 50 percent compensation, and eventually complete refunds if they press further.

"...In 1998 my dad purchased a 1992 Mercury Grand Marquis (my retired company car) from my employer, it was in superb condition with 260,000 kms on the odometer with 80,000 kms on the new motor. Sadly within a little over a year the clear coat had turned cloudy in spots on the hood, roof and trunk of the car and began to peel off. After hearing you on several radio phone-in programs I purchased a "Lemon-Aid Guide" and persuaded Dad that we should go after Ford to repaint the car, he skeptically agreed.

On Dec. 10 1999 I contacted Ford on behalf of my dad, by the 23rd they notified us that the peeling clear coat was not a defect and this matter was closed. We then filed a Small Claims action against Ford of Canada, serving both the Oakville, Ontario, location and their legal representation in Saskatchewan with a summons and waited. The "mediation" hearing was set for early April, this is a procedure of having a judge meet with both parties and try to settle the matter before actually going to court.

After 3 hours and being totally disillusioned about the legal process we offered to take $1000 towards a new paint job. Dad told me outside, "After this BS I'm not going to court, cancel it."

On November 20th, Howard Thompson vs Ford of Canada with Judge Goldstein presiding was heard in Saskatchewan Small Claims Court.

This was a total turn around from mediation. Judge Goldstein assured Ford's Lead Counsel that he was not showing favoritism but he felt compelled to help us along with court procedures because he too would feel like a duck out of water if he had to be a mechanic or doctor for a day...

...Judge Goldstein retired to deliberate and returned in 20 minutes with this result. Based on a case in point from 1937 on "probability," in March the plaintiff purchased a car in perfect condition and within a year as shown in the photos and specifically described by Ford in the DSB and due to ultra violet rays as shown in the TSB, Judge Goldstein believed it to be a probable defect. He took into account the age of the car in awarding us $1518.80.

Once again, Phil thank you for your advice and encouragement, the court process can be intimidating but rewarding, feel free to pass on my e-mail address to anyone in Canada taking this route and needing support or a hand.
Barry Thompson
<barry.thompson@sk.sympatico.ca>

Many small claims courts are also routinely giving out 50 percent awards for bad paint up to eight years after the vehicle was built.

In your negotiations with Ford, be sure to refer to Ford's admission of the delamination problem found in Ford's service bulletin (see page 67). Ford prefers to settle before cases come to trial. You can get the latest information and internal documents relating to Ford's secret warranty for repainting by logging on to the following site set up by dissatisfied Ford owners: *www.ihs2000.com/~peel.*

General Motors
Confidential U.S. dealer service bulletins and memos confirm the 6-year/unlimited mileage benchmark that GM uses to accept or reject secret warranty paint claims. Of course, GM wants its customers to jump through hoops to benefit from its secret paint warranty.

The dealer service bulletin that GM put out several years ago (see page 66) guides dealers in determining whether paint delamination is a factory defect or is due to other external causes like acid rain, stone chips, etc. Pay particular attention to GM's explanation of the cause of the delamination problem. In effect, the automaker admits that it didn't apply sufficient primer to protect the clearcoat from ultraviolet light. Also, look at the masking-tape test GM recommends in its "Problem Identification" section to diagnose clearcoat delamination; it's the same test used by Ford and Chrysler. One helpful GM paint delamination site is *www.geocities.com/ihategm*.

Before settling your paint claim with GM or any other automaker, download the latest information from dissatisfied customers who've banded together and set up their own self-help websites. Follow the links at *www.lemonaidcars.com*.

Other defects

Fissel v. Ideal Auto Sales Ltd. (1991), 91 Sask. R. 266. Shortly after the vehicle was purchased, the car's motor seized and the dealer refused to replace it, even though the car was returned on several occasions. The court ruled that the dealer had breached the statutory warranties in s. 11 (4) and (7) of the Consumer Products Warranties Act. The purchasers were entitled to cancel the sale and recover the full purchase price.

Friskin v. Chevrolet Oldsmobile, 72 D.L.R. (3d), 289. A Manitoba used-car buyer asked that his contract be cancelled because of a chronic stalling problem. The garage owner did his best to correct it. Despite the seller's good intentions, the Manitoba Consumer Protection Act allowed for cancellation.

Graves v. C&R Motors Ltd., April 8, 1980, British Columbia County Court, Judge Skipp. The plaintiff bought a used car on the condition that certain deficiencies be remedied. They never were. He was promised a refund, but it never arrived. The plaintiff brought suit, claiming that the dealer's deceptive activities violated the provincial Trade Practices Act. The court agreed, concluding that a deceptive act that occurs before, during, or after the transaction can lead to the cancellation of the contract.

Green v. Holiday Motors (1975), 4 W.W.R., 445. The plaintiff was sold a used car that had been used for drag racing. The seller didn't make this fact known. The motor blew up. The judge ruled that the Manitoba Consumer Protection Act allowed damages of $1,000.

Hachey v. Galbraith Equipment Company (1991), 33 M.V.R. (2d) 242. The plaintiff bought a used truck from the dealer to use in hauling gravel. Shortly afterwards, the steering failed. The plaintiff's suit was successful because expert testimony showed that the truck wasn't roadworthy. The dealer was found liable for damages for being in breach of the implied condition of fitness for the purpose for which the truck was purchased, as set out in s. 15 (a) of the New Brunswick Sale of Goods Act.

Henzel v. Brussels Motors (1973), 1 O.R., 339 (C.C.). The dealer sold this used car while brandishing a copy of the mechanical fitness certificate as proof that the car was in good shape. The plaintiff was awarded his money back because the court held the certificate to be a warranty that was breached by the car's subsequent defects.

Johnston v. Bodasing Corporation Limited, February 23, 1983, Ontario County Court (Bruce), No. 15/11/83, Judge McKay. The plaintiff bought a used 1979 Buick Riviera, for $8,500, that was represented as being "reliable." Two weeks after the purchase, the motor self-destructed. Judge McKay awarded the plaintiff $2,318 as compensation to fix the Riviera's defects.

One feature of this particular decision is that the trial judge found that the Sale of Goods Act applied, notwithstanding the fact that the vendor used a standard contract that said there were no warranties or representations. The judge also accepted the decision in *Kendal v. Lillico* (1969), 2 Appeal Cases, 31, which indicates that the Sale of Goods Act covers not only defects that the seller ought to have detected, but also latent defects that even his utmost skill and judgment could not have detected. This places a very heavy onus on the vendor and it should prove useful in actions of this type in other common-law provinces where laws similar to Ontario's Sale of Goods Act are in force.

Kelly v. Mack Canada, 53 D.L.R. (4th), 476. Kelly bought two trucks from Mack Sales. The first, a used White Freightliner tractor and trailer, was purchased for $29,742. It cost him over $12,000 in repairs during the first five months, and another $9,000 was estimated for future engine repairs. Mack Sales convinced Kelly to trade in the old truck for a new Mack truck. Kelly did this, but shortly thereafter, the new truck had similar problems. Kelly sued for the return of all his money, arguing that the two transactions were really one.

The Ontario Court of Appeal agreed and awarded Kelly a complete refund. It stated: "There was such a congeries of defects that there had been a breach of the implied conditions set out in the Sale of Goods Act."

Although Mack Sales argued that the contract contained a clause excluding any implied warranties, the court determined that the breach was of such magnitude that the dealer could not rely upon that clause. The dealer then argued that since the client used the trucks, the depreciation of both should be taken into account in reducing the award. This was refused on the grounds that the plaintiff never had the product he bargained for and in no way did he profit from the trans- action. The court also awarded Kelly compensation for loss of income while the trucks were being repaired, as well as the interest on all of the money tied up in both transactions from the time of purchase until final judgment.

Mathieu v. Autos M.L., February 15, 1982, Quebec Small Claims Court (Levis), No. 230-32-000906-817, Judge Bosse. This consumer bought a 7-year-old car with 80,000 kilometres on it. Two months later, he spent $441 on motor repairs. Judge Bosse awarded him $441 because the vehicle "did not withstand normal usage over a reasonable period of time," as prescribed by Articles 37, 38, and 53 of Quebec's Consumer Protection Act.

Morrison v. Hillside Motors (1973) Ltd. (1981), 35 Nfld. & P.E.I.R. 361. A used car advertised to be in A-1 condition and carrying a 50/50 warranty developed a number of problems. The court decided that the purchaser should be partially compensated because of the ad's claim. In deciding how much compensation to award, the presiding judge considered the warranty's wording, the amount paid for the vehicle, the year of the vehicle, its average life, the type of defect that occurred, and how long the purchaser had use of the vehicle before its defects became evident. Although this judgment was rendered in Newfoundland, judges throughout Canada have used a similar approach for more than a decade.

Parent v. Le Grand Trianon and Ford Credit (1982), C.P., 194, Judge Bertrand Gagnon. Nineteen months after paying $3,300 for a used 1974 LTD, the plaintiff sued the Ford dealer for his money back because the car was prematurely rusted out. The dealer replied that rust was normal, there was no warranty, and the claim was too late. The court held that the garage was still responsible, for the following reasons:
• When purchased, the car had been repainted by the dealer to camouflage rust and perforations.
• During the 19 months, the plaintiff and the dealer continued to explore ways the rusting could be stopped.
• It wasn't until just before the lawsuit that the plaintiff found out how bad the rust was.
• Ford and its dealers admitted they knew that many of their 1970–74 cars had serious premature corrosion problems.

The plaintiff was awarded $1,500, representing the cost of rust repairs.

"As is" clauses
Since 1907, Canadian courts have ruled that a seller can't exclude the implied warranty as to fitness by including such phrases as "there are no other warranties or guarantees, promises or agreements, than those contained herein." See *Sawyer-Massey Co. v. Thibault* (1907), 5 W.L.R. 241.

Defects (Safety Related)

Airbags

National Highway Traffic Safety Administration (NTHSA) once claimed that airbags had saved 1,700 lives and reduced moderate and severe injuries in auto accidents by 25 percent. Unfortunately, says the *Wall Street Journal,* the government's figures are shaky and not based on real-world experiences.

There have been thousands of reports of airbags that have failed to deploy or have accidentally gone off and caused massive injuries. In fact, General Motors recalled almost a million Cadillacs, Cavaliers, and Sunfires because of accidental deployment—caused by wet carpeting in Cadillacs and passing over a bump in the road for the other vehicles.

Safety experts at NHTSA once estimated that 25,000 people were injured by airbags between 1988 and 1991. Additionally, recent NHTSA-run crash tests indicate that all of Chrysler's minivan airbags produced in 1997 and earlier deploy with such excessive force they may cause disabling or fatal injuries. In February 1999 crash tests, the deploying passenger-side airbag in a 1997 Caravan caused neck injuries to a small, belted, female dummy that, according to the agency, would have disabled or killed a person. The suspect airbags may be in as many as 1.9 million minivans.

Hundreds of lawsuits have been filed claiming airbags don't function as designed (not deploying when they should, or deploying when they shouldn't) and over 60 suits have been filed claiming the device caused or aggravated injuries after actually deploying as designed. Chrysler, the first automaker to install airbags as standard equipment, is the target of most of these lawsuits. So far, the successful suits against

Chrysler relate to poor design rather than malfunctions and fall into two categories: severe burns and premature deployment at low speeds.

Severe burns

Claimants have won substantial jury awards for first- or second-degree burns caused by the Thiokol-designed airbag directing hot gases at the driver's hands and wrists. Used on Chrysler's 1988–91 models, these airbags have vent holes that direct hot gases at the three o'clock and nine o'clock hand positions. In late 1990, the vent holes were relocated to the twelve o'clock position. A class action lawsuit asking for damages arising from the earlier Thiokol design was filed in Philadelphia County and ended with a verdict of $60 million in compensatory damages, and another $3.75 million in punitive damages, for 80,000 Pennsylvania Chrysler owners who purchased their vehicles between 1988 and 1990. The jury ruled that vehicles sold during that time came with airbags that, when deployed, could severely burn the hands and wrists of drivers. Martin D'Urso, from the law firm of Kohn, Swift & Graf, and Isaac Green, from Moody & Anderson, pleaded the case for the plaintiffs.

Collazo-Santiago v. Toyota, July 1998, 1st Circuit Court of Appeals. The driver of a 1994 Corolla suffered minor facial burns and abrasions when her airbag deployed as her car was rear-ended. The court concluded that the airbag's design caused the injuries. Toyota maintained that the airbag deployed as it should, and that it couldn't change the design without reducing the airbag's effectiveness. The plaintiff was awarded $30,000 compensation.

Premature airbag deployment

All automakers are worried they may face a slew of huge damage awards in the future following a $750,000 jury award for damages in the death of a five-year-old from a deploying airbag. In *Crespo v. Chrysler,* a New York jury concluded that the 1995 minivan's airbag design contributed to the child's death because it deployed too early (at a speed of between 13 and 15 km/h). Safety experts contend that the airbag should deploy within a range of 15–20 mph (24–32 km/h). Chrysler submitted, however, that there are no standards as to what speeds should trigger the airbag's deployment, and claimed most automakers program their airbags to deploy at crash speeds of 8–14 mph (13–23 km/h). The jury rejected Chrysler's argument and awarded half the damages sought by the child's family, despite the fact that the child was unbelted and not seated in a safety seat.

Failure to deploy

Taylor v. Ford, Wayne County Circuit Court. American courts are taking a harder look at the automakers' liability when airbags fail to deploy, following a recent Michigan Court of Appeals decision to uphold a lower court's $292,000 verdict against Ford. Although the 1990 Lincoln Continental's driver-side airbag failed to deploy during a frontal collision, the jury found no design defect, but awarded damages against Ford for breach of an implied warranty based on defective manufacturing.

Inadvertent deployment
Perez-Trujillo v. Volvo Car Corp. (*www.law.emory.edu/1circuit/mar98/97-1792.01a.html*). This lawsuit involves injuries suffered by a dockworker while parking a Volvo on the dock. The case has just been reinstated by a U.S. Appeals Court and provides an interesting, though lengthy, dissertation on the safety hazards that airbags pose and why automakers are ultimately responsible for the injuries and deaths caused by their deployment.

Axle
Fuller v. Ford of Canada Ltd. (1978), 2 O.R. (2d), 764. A new 1974 Econoline truck had an axle failure that caused an accident. The court held both the manufacturer and the seller responsible.

Battery
Marin v. Varta Batteries Ltd. (1983), 28 Sask. R. 173; 5 D.L.R. (4th) 427 (Q.B.). An exploding battery caused serious injuries to the plaintiff's face. The battery maker admitted liability and the court awarded the plaintiff $21,000 in damages.

Brakes
Chrysler and GM have both come under fire over the past several years for installing defective anti-lock brakes in their vehicles. GM has quietly bought back many of its vans and sport-utilities with ABS failures, while Chrysler has initiated a recall campaign and promised free servicing over a 10-year period.

Marton Properties v. Northbridge Chrysler Plymouth Ltd., March 2, 1979, British Columbia Supreme Court. The plaintiff's used Chrysler had serious brake defects that warranted cancellation of the sale contract. The court ordered the vehicle returned and the purchase price refunded.

Morschler v. Masser's Garage (1956), 2 D.L.R. (2d), 484. The plaintiff was awarded damages to a third party from a repairer who had failed to fix a car's brakes properly.

Phillips v. Ford of Canada and Elgin Motors (1970), 2 O.R., 714. Ford was held responsible for the injuries caused by power-brake defects that wouldn't be apparent to the plaintiff. The dealer and Ford had a duty to warn the plaintiff that if the power-brake unit failed, the back-up brakes would be inadequate.

Santos v. Chrysler Corporation, February 1996, Suffolk County Superior Court. The plaintiff's wife and three children were killed when his 1988 Caravan's rear brakes locked as he applied them to avoid rear-ending another vehicle. The jury award for $19.2 million followed Paul Santos's pleadings that Chrysler "knowingly built the vehicle with a deadly defect that caused the rear brakes to lock before the front brakes." Chrysler's defence was that Santos drove the Caravan 100 miles with a broken windshield wiper and steered directly into oncoming traffic.

Fires
Ford

Brown v. Ford of Canada Ltd. (1979), 27 N.B.R. (2d), 550. While under warranty, the plaintiff's 1977 van suddenly caught fire. The court held the manufacturer only partially negligent because the plaintiff's son, who was a mechanic, should have spotted the defect.

Chabot v. Ford Motor Company of Canada Ltd. (1983), 39 O.R. (2d) 162. This case contains an excellent and exhaustive review of a manufacturer's liability for defectively manufactured vehicles. It establishes liability for losses arising from a defect while the vehicle is being maintained by the dealer. Although the plaintiff could not prove that a defective part caused a fire, Judge Eberle's presumption that the 1979 F-250 truck ignited from some sort of manufacturing defect implied that the manufacturer was negligent (*re ipsa loquitur*).

The court also ruled that Ford breached a fundamental term of the sales contract by providing an unfit vehicle and that Ford also failed to meet its obligations as set by the Manitoba Sale of Goods Act (Ontario Sale of Goods Act R.S.O. 1980 c 462, 5-15).

In his decision, the judge made a number of interesting and critical observations about the motives and strategies of a large manufacturer like Ford when it prepares for a case and presents expert evidence. Most importantly, this decision confirms (from a common-law standpoint) that companies cannot avoid liability by invoking the limitations or exclusions expressed in their warranties. An earlier decision, *Kravitz v. General Motors,* had already struck down these exclusions under Quebec law.

See also:
- *CPR v. Kerr,* 49 S.C.R., 33 at 36
- *Gougeon v. Peugeot Canada,* July 20, 1973, Quebec Superior Court, No. 12736, Judge Kaufman
- *Lazanik v. Ford,* June 15, 1965, C.S.M., No. 623-664, Judge Challies
- *Parent v. Lapointe* (1952), I S.C.R., No. 381
- *Rioux v. General Motors,* March 9, 1970, C.S.M., No. 739-005, 6
- *Touchette v. Pizzagalli* (1938), S.C.R., No. 433
- *Zelezen v. Model Auto Sales Ltd.,* November 26, 1971, C.S.M., No. 722-487, Judge Nichols

Chrysler
La Paix v. Chrysler Canada, April 5, 1982, Quebec Provincial Court, No. 500-02-040677-796, Judge Prenouveau. A new 1976 Volaré suddenly caught fire when the owner tried to start the car. It had been in use for only 10 months. Chrysler Canada refused all liability, claiming the fire was probably due to poor starting technique. The court held Chrysler responsible for $4,039 in damages after it was proven that the fire was caused by unburned gasoline catching fire in the muffler.

General Motors
Racine v. Durand Pontiac-Buick and General Motors, December 15, 1977, Quebec Provincial Court, No. 02-015218-774, Judge Lacoste. The plaintiff claimed $700 for a catalytic converter that exploded. General Motors and the dealer claimed that the explosion was due to poor maintenance and that the 5-year/50,000 mile emissions warranty on the converter did not cover such maintenance-related defects. The judge disagreed, stating that the catalytic converter exploded due to a defective PCV valve for which General Motors and the dealer had to take responsibility. The fact that the converter could overheat and catch fire whenever the engine was badly tuned caused the judge to suggest that a warning be placed on all General Motors vehicles with the converter. The plaintiff was awarded $700.

Saab
Delage vs. Saab, November 1997, San Francisco Superior Court. A jury awarded Delage $1.4 million (U.S.) for damages caused by an electrical fire in his 1988 Saab 9000, even though the car was never examined. After hearing testimony from eight other Saab owners whose cars had caught on fire, the jury concluded that a defective fuse box caused the fire. Related to this, the *San Francisco Chronicle* published a Saab internal memo that indicated a main connection in the 9000 box (located behind the glove compartment) could loosen, overheat, and ignite the insulation.

Parking gear slippage
General Motors v. Colton, October 17, 1980, Quebec Court of Appeal, No. 500-09-000692-772. A 1970 Oldsmobile parked on the plaintiff's inclined driveway rolled back and injured the owner. Judgment was against General Motors for $29,000.

Rusting undercarriage
McGouey v. Lawson Motors Ltd. (1982), 42 N.B.R. (2d) 225. Seven weeks after McGouey bought a used Fiat, the frame collapsed from excessive corrosion. The purchaser was awarded a complete refund of the purchase price and damages.

R. v. Ford Motor Company of Canada. In this case, the federal Ministry of Transportation successfully pleaded that rusting of the undercarriage of Ford's 1965–74 midsize cars was a safety defect. Ford appealed the case for over a decade and agreed to notify owners of the defect (but not fix the vehicles) only after losing all its appeals.

Steering

Holley v. Ford of Canada, June 18, 1980, Nova Scotia Supreme Court, Judge Cowan. The plaintiff purchased a used 1976 Ford Custom 200 truck that was subsequently involved in an accident due to the failure of its steering assembly. The plaintiff was awarded $4,100 in damages.

White v. International Harvester (1969), W.W.R. 235 (Alta. T.D.). This new truck's steering assembly had problems and was adjusted by the dealer. However, 4,200 miles later, the truck suddenly veered out of control due to a defective steering component. The plaintiff was awarded both costs and damages.

Sudden acceleration

Willar v. Ford (1991), 118 N.B.R. (2d) 323. The owner sued Ford after his vehicle's throttle jammed open twice, causing several accidents. The court held that Ford, not the dealer, was responsible for the plaintiff's damages.

Tire iron placement adding to collision injuries

Gallant v. Beitz (1983), 42 O.R. (2d) 86. This judgment states clearly that automakers are presumed to know their vehicles will be involved in accidents and must take reasonable steps to minimize injuries caused by flaws inherent in the design of their vehicles.

Tires

Chase v. Goodyear Tire and Rubber Co. and Goodyear Canada Inc., April 12, 1991, New Brunswick Court of Queen's Bench, Trial Division, No. S/C/513/89. The plaintiff was injured when the tire he was inflating exploded. There was no evidence of a manufacturing defect on the original tire or on the retread. Goodyear was found negligent because it failed to warn its customers of the danger inherent in inflating a retreaded tire that had worn out and damaged radial cords, thereby breaching its duty to warn. The plaintiff was awarded $65,000 for his injuries.

Gagnon v. Canadian Tire (1979), C.P. 251, Quebec Provincial Court. The plaintiff was awarded $1,310 as compensation for a radial tire that exploded when he was rocking his car out of a snowbank.

Murphy v. D. & B. Holdings (1979), 31 N.S.R. (2d) 380; 52 A.P.R. 380 (S.C.). The court held that the manufacturer was liable for damages for permitting a customer to use its tires in a dangerous manner. (The tires were under-inflated and spun the wheels.)

Transmissions jump from "Park" to "Reverse"

McEvoy v. Ford Motor Company et al., September 6, 1989, Supreme Court of B.C., No. 3841989, Judge Hinds. McEvoy was killed when his new Ford pickup backed over him after the transmission jumped from "Park" to "Reverse." He had left the engine running and was unloading cargo when the right front wheel crushed his chest. Justice Hinds found Ford to be 65 percent negligent for the following reasons:

- The RCMP mechanic testified that the gearshift lever could easily be mispositioned into an "unstable Park" position.
- It was determined that Ford was aware of this defect as early as 1971, according to internal company documents presented during the trial.
- Ford had a duty to warn its customers of the hazard caused by the C-6 automatic transmission; the warning in the owner's manual was deemed insufficient to satisfy this duty.
- Ford and its Canadian distributor had breached their duty to the consumer.

Delay (in Bringing Lawsuit)

Bouchard v. Vaillancourt (1961), C.S., 171. If the seller has defrauded the consumer, delays for initiating a lawsuit are longer than in cases where fraud is not involved.

See also:
- *Ginn v. Canbec Auto* (1976), C.S., 1416
- *Lemire v. Pelchat* (1957), R.C.S., 823
- *Ennis v. Klassen,* 70 D.L.R. (4th), 325

False Advertising

Dealer posing as a private seller

A recent small claims judgment slams a practice called "curbsiding," whereby a professional sales agent posing as a private party sells cars from a residence. Frank Longstaff, the lawyer for the plaintiff, told me that a number of other New Brunswickers who fell for this scam have contacted his office after reading about the case in their local paper.

It was held that the defendant's practice of buying used cars wholesale from a dealer and then quickly advertising them for sale to consumers was sufficient to label him a distributor as defined in New Brunswick's Consumer Product Warranty and Liability Act. This made him subject to the act and, hence, required him to stand behind any warranty, either oral or written, he may have given the purchaser in his advertisement. It also meant that, pursuant to sections 10 (1) and 12 (1) of the act, he gave an implied warranty that the product was "fit for the purpose" and would be "durable for a reasonable period of time." Prior to this decision, private sellers (curbsiders) had not been subject to the act.

Van Wart v. MacDonald and MacDonald, July 25, 1994, the Court of
Queen's Bench, Trial Division, Judicial District of Saint John, New
Brunswick, Judge H.H. McLellan. Nineteen-year-old Van Wart bought
a 1987 Firefly for $2,000, with her parents' assistance, after responding
to a newspaper advertisement. MacDonald claimed that the car
belonged to his wife and sold it "as is, where is." At trial, it was learned
that MacDonald had bought the vehicle five days earlier from Brett
Chev-Olds for $1,200. Brett's sales manager said MacDonald had
bought eight cars from him the previous year and that the Firefly purchase was accompanied by a bill of sale stating, "This vehicle is junk.
There is no expectation of driving this vehicle."

Judge McLellan ordered the car be taken back and the $2,000 pur-
chase price and sales tax refunded, and made MacDonald responsible
for Van Wart's legal bills.

Misrepresentation

Belanger v. Fournier Chrysler Dodge Ltée. (1975), 25 N.B.R. (2d), 673. A
used car sold in New Brunswick carried an inspection sticker that stated
the body and mechanical components were in good condition.
Actually, the chassis was rusted through and the police ordered the
vehicle off the road. The plaintiff was awarded the purchase price.

Bellerose v. Bouvier (1955), B.R., 175. In this judgment, the court recog-
nized the right of a consumer to ask for a reduction or reimbursement
of part of the purchase price if there's a fraudulent representation of
part of the transaction. The plaintiff didn't have to ask for the contract
to be cancelled.

See also:
• *Nissan Automobile v. Pelletier* (1974) 503 (reaffirmed by the Supreme
  Court of Canada)
• *Bérubé v. Enright,* January 25, 1982, Quebec Provincial Court, No. 500-
  02-050980-791, Judge Filion

Bottcher v. Selig, 26 N.S.R. (2d) 347 (C.A.). A used car was represented
as needing only a quart of oil every 1,000 miles. The plaintiff was
awarded damages for serious oil leaks. In addition to misrepresenting
the condition of the vehicle, this Nova Scotia court held that the seller's
promise was an implied warranty.

Ennis v. Klassen, 70 D.L.R. (4th), 325. Ennis bought a $9,000 used BMW
that was represented as a 1980 733i. He learned two days later that it
was really a 1979 BMW 728—a model without fuel injection that wasn't
supposed to be allowed into Canada because of federal safety standards. It was also impossible to find parts for this vehicle. He kept the
car in his garage for two years thereafter.

Klassen, a private seller, maintained that the lawsuit was tardy, that Ennis had inspected the vehicle before purchase, and that the whole case revolved around innocent misrepresentation.

Manitoba's Court of Appeal disagreed on the grounds that "[t]he misrepresentation does go to the root of the contract. The plaintiff was led to believe that he was buying a BMW model 733 at a fair retail price for a second-hand vehicle of the advertised model, type and vintage. He received nothing of the kind, and so he may rescind [cancel] the sale."

As for the action being tardy, the Appeal Court also disagreed, stating: "The plaintiff no longer used the vehicle, and took immediate steps on the path to rescision." Ennis got a complete refund.

See also:
- *F&B Transport Ltd. v. White Truck Sales Manitoba Ltd.* (1975), 49 D.L.R. (2d) 670
- *Adams v. Canadian Co-Operative Implements Ltd.* (1980), 20 A.R. 533

Hanson and Campbell v. Cornell Chevrolet Oldsmobile Ltd. and Canadian Imperial Bank of Commerce and Weaver (1983), 4 W.W.R. 285. The purchaser of a used car in B.C. had it seized when he moved to Alberta. He then brought suit against the B.C. dealer that sold him the vehicle, which had a valid chattel mortgage registered against it. The court held that the British Columbia Sale of Goods Act, s. 16, protects consumers whether or not the goods remain in the province. The important element was that the contract was agreed to in B.C. As a result, the dealer had to compensate the client for his losses.

Henzel v. Brussels Motors Ltd. (1973), 1 O.R., 339 (C.C.). A used car sold with a mechanical fitness certificate had defective brakes. The court ordered the purchase price refunded.

Keilty v. East-Court Sales Limited, Ontario Court of Justice, 1996 C.J. Lexis 2247, June 14, 1996. The plaintiff purchased a used Lincoln Town Car that the dealer claimed was an "executive-driven car" from the Ford Motor Company for $20,000. When the car broke down, the owner ran a title check and found the vehicle had been a Budget rental prior to being sold to the defendant by Ford at an auction. The judge ruled that the seller was guilty of fraudulent misrepresentation and could not rely upon the sales contract's exclusionary clause to protect himself from the result of the fraud. The purchase price was refunded.

L.G. Wilson Motors v. Woods (1970), 2 N.B.R. (2d), 581 (S.C.). A safety certification carried out by a provincial inspector doesn't guarantee that a used vehicle is safe or that the inspector was competent. The buyer should have made his own inspection. The plaintiff's claim was rejected.

Presley v. MacDonald (1963), 1 O.R. (2d), 619. In this case, an Ontario judge ruled that, under s. 49 (1) of the Highway Traffic Act, the mechanical fitness certificate made the seller half liable for damages caused in a subsequent accident.

Sandilands v. Guelph Datsun 1980 Ltd. (1982), 35 O.R. (2d) 25. The dealer represented a used car as having "good" brakes. Four months after purchase, the vehicle was taken off the road by the provincial Ministry of Transportation because of defective brakes and rust perforations. The court held that the contract should be cancelled because the dealer's misrepresentation was an "unfair practice" according to Section 4(1)(a) of the Ontario Business Practices Act. The dealer was forced to take back the car and pay storage and transport costs.

Illegal/Unfair Insurance Company Practices

Inadequate compensation

The following two lawsuits may be helpful in any disputes you may have with an insurance company over its failure to pay a claim or use quality, original equipment manufacturer (OEM) replacement parts in repairs. Don't get the impression that this is just a State Farm problem. These abuses are widespread.

Campbell v. State Farm Mutual Insurance Automobile Insurance Co. This Utah case saw a $147.6 million jury award against State Farm cut to $26 million by the presiding judge who didn't want the case overturned on appeal because the original award may have been considered excessive.

In his verdict of December 19, 1997, Judge William B. Bohling called State Farm "greedy, callous, clandestine, fraudulent, and dishonest," after evidence showed the company refused to pay off a claim until the plaintiff sued it for bad-faith dealings. The Campbell attorneys successfully asserted that State Farm had a national plan to cheat policyholders, which included using inferior car parts in repairs, misleading consumers about policy benefits, and low-balling settlements. This evidence led the judge to conclude that State Farm "appeared to have preyed on the weakest of the herd" in cheating "the most vulnerable" policyholders with its "calculated and callous attitude towards settling valid claims." He concluded:

> ...It became a matter of plain evidence that State Farm has sold as its product, peace of mind, and has used as its advertising slogan, 'like a good neighbor.' State Farm's action amounts to betraying the trust that it invites its policyholders to place in it...

Poor-quality replacement parts

In a $2 billion (U.S.) Illinois class action, State Farm has been found guilty of breaching its promise to restore policyholders' autos to their "pre-loss condition," after it was found the company used aftermarket bumpers, door panels, and other parts that failed to meet automakers' specifications for fit, finish, corrosion protection, and safety. Over 20 million car owners whose vehicles were repaired since 1980 could be eligible for refunds or repairs. On the heels of this judgment, State Farm says it will only use original parts in collision repairs.

This is an important judgment in that it allows you to demand original equipment parts whenever you make an insurance company claim. If the insurer balks at your demand, complain to the provincial Superintendent of Insurance.

Part Three
Vehicle Ratings: The Good, the Bad, and the Ugly!

An Absurd Accusation?

"In your *Marketplace* report on Volvo's online advertising campaign, Sept. 25, you quote one Phil Bienert, who is identified as 'Volvo's manager of e-business,' as stating flatly that Volvo's purchase of advertising in Car and Driver magazine is 'sort of the price of entry to get your car reviewed.'

That is a painfully ignorant statement to be made by someone who works for Volvo, or any car company, for that matter. Mr. Bienert is more than 'sort of' clueless about how this car magazine operates. Fact is, it is the mission of the editorial staff of Car and Driver to evaluate every production car that is sold in this country, and that's what we do. It is absurd, not to mention libelous, to allege that a manufacturer has to buy an ad to get its car evaluated. Build a production vehicle, and we will road-test it and publish a report, period.

We would be delighted to see the evidence that Mr. Bienert must, no doubt, have in his possession to support such a brazen, mindless, and utterly false accusation."

Copy of an October 16, 2000, Letter to the Editor
Wall Street Journal
from Steve Spence, Managing Editor,
Car and Driver

A used car or minivan must first live up to the promises made by the manufacturer and dealer. Ideally, it should be crashworthy, reasonably durable (lasting at least 10 years), cost no more than $800 per year to maintain, and provide you with a fair resale value a few years down the road. Parts should be reasonably priced and easily available, and competent servicing shouldn't be hard to find. We also factor into the rating the relative availability of a particular vehicle, those models and years that are the best buys, the estimated annual maintenance and repair costs averaged over five years, and alternative vehicles that will give you as much, or more, for less money.

Models are rated on a scale from Recommended to Not Recommended. *Recommended* vehicles are those that are an excellent choice in their class and promise their owners relatively trouble-free service (like post-1991 Ford Escorts). Vehicles that are given an *Above Average* or *Average* rating are good second choices if a Recommended vehicle isn't your first choice or is too expensive. A *Below Average* vehicle will likely be troublesome; however, a low price and reasonably priced servicing may make it an acceptable buy. Vehicles given a *Not Recommended* rating are best avoided no matter how low the price. They may be attractively styled and loaded with convenience features (Chrysler minivans, for example), but they're likely to suffer from a variety of durability and performance problems that will make them expensive and frustrating to own. Sometimes, however, a Not Recommended model will improve over several model years and garner a better rating (as the Ford Aerostar and GM Astro and Safari minivans have done). Keep in mind, too, that the more complex and environmentally sensitive mechanical and electronic components of the newer vehicles are raising the reliability and quality averages, so that a newer vehicle rated Average is a far better buy than an older model with an Average rating.

Incidentally, for those owners who wonder how I can stop recommending model years I once recommended, let me be clear: as vehicles age, their ratings always change to reflect new information from owners, service bulletins, etc., relating to durability and the automaker's warranty performance. I warn shoppers of the changes in subsequent editions of *Lemon-Aid* or in updates to my website, *www.lemonaidcars.com.* But that's not enough. Throughout the year, I also lobby automakers to compensate out-of-warranty owners through formal "goodwill" programs or on an individual case-by-case basis. This way, I assist my readers in avoiding a bad purchase and provide an additional means to get compensation if that purchase has already been made.

Reliability data is compiled from a number of sources: confidential service bulletins; owner complaints sent to the author each year by over 5,000 *Lemon-Aid* readers; vehicle-owners' comments posted on the Internet; and survey reports and tests done by auto associations, consumer groups, and government organizations. Some auto columnists feel this isn't a scientific sampling, and they're quite right. Nevertheless, it seems to have been right on the mark over the past 29 years. Not all vehicles sold during the last decade are profiled; those that are newer to the market or relatively rare may receive only an abbreviated mention until sufficient owner or service bulletin information becomes available. Best and worst buys for each model category (e.g., "Small Cars" or "Medium Cars") are listed in a summary at the beginning of each rating section. Also, don't forget to look up the cheap "orphans" and "beaters" profiled in Appendix I.

Strengths and weaknesses

Unlike other auto guides, *Lemon-Aid* pinpoints potential parts failures and explains why those parts fail. We also give parts numbers for upgraded parts (why replace poor-quality brake pads with the same ones, for example?) and offer troubleshooting tips direct from the automakers' bulletins, so your mechanic won't replace parts unrelated to your troubles before coming upon the defective component that is actually responsible. To complement the "Secret Warranties/Service Tips" and vehicle "Profile" tables, we look at a vehicle's overall road performance and reliability, providing details as to which specific mechanical, electrical, or body parts fail repeatedly. This helps an independent mechanic check out the likely trouble spots before you make your purchase.

Safety summary/Recalls

Owner safety complaints, ongoing safety investigations, and insurance claims statistics make up the first part of this section, while recalls comprise the second. Both safety and emissions recalls are listed by model, in chronological order. If your vehicle is listed and hasn't been fixed, the dealer and manufacturer must pay for the inspection and correction of the defect regardless of the vehicle's mileage, model year, or number of previous owners. It's not the law, but it's general practice.

Keep in mind that only a sample of recalls are listed for each model and watch for the cut-off years. Even if your model year isn't listed, it may be currently under investigation or may have been recalled since this year's guide was published. Also, safety probes may be upgraded or dropped—download recalls and profiles from NHTSA's website at *www.nhtsa.dot.gov/cars/problems/recalls/recmmy1.cfm* for an update.

Secret warranties/Service tips

It's not enough to know which parts on your vehicle are likely to fail. You should also know which repairs will be done for free by the dealer and automaker even though you aren't the original owner and the manufacturer's warranty has long since expired.

Welcome to the hidden world of secret warranties found in confidential technical service bulletins (TSBs) or gleaned from owner feedback. A summary of all the important TSBs for each model year is listed, along with selected diagrams. These bulletins target defects—related to safety, emissions, and performance—that service managers would have you believe don't exist or are your responsibility. They also list the upgraded parts that will best repair the vehicle you plan to buy or have just bought.

Service bulletins cover repairs that may be eligible for warranty coverage in one or more of the following five categories:
• emissions warranty (five to eight years);
• safety component warranty (covers seatbelts and airbags and usually lasts the lifetime of the vehicle);
• body warranty (paint: six–eight years; rust perforations: seven years);
• secret warranty (coverage varies);
• factory defects (depends on mileage, use, and repair cost).

Use these bulletins to get free repairs—even if the vehicle has changed hands several times—and to alert an independent mechanic about which defects to look for. They're also great tools for getting compensation from automakers and dealer service managers after the warranty has expired, since they prove that a failure is factory related and, therefore, not part of routine maintenance or the result of an environmental anomaly (like bird droppings and acid rain).

Their diagnostic shortcuts and lists of upgraded parts make these bulletins invaluable in helping mechanics and do-it-yourselfers trouble-shoot problems inexpensively and replace the right part the first time. Auto owners can also use the TSBs listed here to verify that a repair was diagnosed correctly, the correct upgraded replacement part was used, and the labour costs were fair.

Getting your own bulletins
Summaries of service bulletins relating to 1982–2000 vehicles can be obtained for free from the ALLDATA or NHTSA sites on the Internet (listed in Appendix II).

Vehicle profiles
These tables cover the various aspects of vehicle ownership at a glance. Included for each model year are details on crashworthiness, as well as repair histories for major mechanical and body components (specific defective parts are listed in the "Strengths and weaknesses" section for each vehicle rated). The profiles also indicate which model years have secret warranties or should be bought with an extended warranty.

Prices
Dealer profit margins on used cars vary considerably—leaving lots of room to negotiate a fair price if you take the time to find out what the vehicle is really worth. Three prices are given for each model year: the vehicle's selling price when new as suggested by the manufacturer, its maximum price used (↑), and its lowest price used (↓).

Used prices are based on private sales figures current as of March 2001, and are for the lowest-priced standard model that is in good condition with a maximum of 20,000 km for each calendar year. Be watchful for price differences reflecting each model's equipment upgrades, which are designated by a numerical or alphabetical abbreviation. For example, L, LX, and LXT usually mean more standard features are included. Numerical progression, like the 2300 series of Mazda trucks or the Mercedes 300, usually relates to engine size.

The original selling price (Manufacturer's Suggested Retail Price, or MSRP) is given as a helpful reference point. Sellers usually overprice their vehicles (mostly Japanese imports, minivans, and sport-utilities) in order to get back some of the money *they* overpaid in the first place. This is particularly true in the Prairie provinces and B.C.

Prices reflect the auto markets in Quebec and Ontario, where the majority of used-vehicle transactions take place. Residents in eastern Canada should add 10 percent, and western Canadians should add

15–20 percent to the listed price. Why the higher cost? Less competition and inflated new-vehicle prices in these regions. Don't be too disheartened, though; some of what you overpay will be recouped when you resell the vehicle down the road.

Why are *Lemon-Aid*'s prices lower than the prices found in dealer guides? The answer is simple: dealer guides inflate their prices knowing that you will bargain the price down, so you'll be convinced you made a great deal even if you didn't.

I use newspaper classified ads from Quebec, Ontario, and B.C., as well as auction reports, for my used values. I then check these figures with the *Red Book* and *Black Book*; I don't start with the *Red Book*'s retail or wholesale figures. (Like real estate listings, vehicle prices are inflated about 10 percent for wholesale/private sales and almost 20 percent for retail/dealer sales—compare the two and you'll see what I mean.) I then project what the value will be by year's end, and that further lowers my prices. I almost always fall way under the *Red Book*'s value, but not far under the *Black Book*'s price. In the *Lemon-Aid* guide, I print a top and bottom price to give the buyer some margin for negotiation, as well as to account for regional differences in prices, the popularity of certain models or vehicle classes (sport-utilities, trucks, minivans, etc.), and the appreciated value of used cars generally.

Depreciation is the biggest (and often most ignored) expense new-car owners encounter when trading in a vehicle, but smart car shoppers who know which good-quality cars and minivans depreciate the most can save a bundle. Most new cars depreciate 30–40 percent during the first two years of ownership, despite the fact that good-quality used cars are in high demand. On the other hand, some minivans and most vans, pickups, and sport-utilities lose less of their value even after four years of ownership.

No evaluation method is foolproof: to come up with a fairly representative offer, check dealer prices against local private classified ads and add the option values listed below. Interestingly, the value of anti-lock brakes in trade-ins has plummeted in the last few years, undoubtedly as a result of insurance studies showing that ABS has failed to reduce collision fatalities and injuries.

Option	Model Year					
	1994	1995	1996	1997	1998	1999
Air conditioning	$300	$400	$500	$600	$700	$800
AM-FM-CD	100	100	150	175	200	350
Anti-lock brakes	100	100	125	150	175	300
Automatic transmission	200	250	275	300	400	600
Cruise control	50	50	75	100	125	225
Electric six-way seat	50	100	125	150	175	200
Leather upholstery	100	200	225	325	400	600
Level control (suspension)	50	75	100	125	150	250
Paint protector	0	0	0	0	0	0

Power antenna	0	25	50	50	75	125
Power door locks	50	100	125	150	175	250
Power windows	50	100	125	150	175	250
Rustproofing	0	0	0	25	50	75
Sunroof	50	50	75	125	150	300
T-top roof	200	300	400	500	700	750
Tilt steering	50	50	75	75	100	150
Tinted windows	0	0	0	25	50	50
Traction control	100	125	150	175	275	400
Wire wheels/locks	75	100	125	150	175	275

It will be easier for you to match the lower used prices if you buy privately. Dealers rarely sell much below the maximum prices. They inflate their prices to cover the costs of reconditioning and paying future warranty claims, and to make you feel better. If you can come within 5–10 percent of this guide's price, you'll have done well.

Extended warranties and secret warranties
Usually, but not always, an extended warranty is advised for those model years that aren't rated Recommended. In shopping for an extended warranty, don't be surprised to discover that dealers have the market practically sewn up. You can, however, bargain the price down by getting competing dealers to bid against each other, contacting them by fax or through their Internet sites. Be wary of extended-warranty companies that aren't backed by the major automakers. Model years for which we recommend an extended warranty are listed in the "Profile" section. A **Y** signifies that an extended warranty is needed. An **N** means that there's no need to buy an extended warranty.

Model years that are eligible for free repairs under a secret warranty are listed in the "Profile" section and further detailed in the "Secret Warranties/Service Tips" section. A **Y** signifies that one or more secret warranties exist. An **N** means that no secret warranty applies.

Reliability
The older a vehicle, the greater the chance that a major component like the engine or transmission will fail (due to high mileage and environmental wear and tear). Surprisingly, there's a host of other expensive-to-repair failures that are just as likely to occur in a new vehicle as in an older one. Air conditioners, electronic computer modules, electrical systems, and brakes are the most troublesome components, manifesting problems early in a vehicle's life. Other deficiencies that will appear early, due to sloppy manufacturing and a harsh environment, include failure-prone body hardware (trim, finish, locks, doors, and windows), water leaks, wind noise, and paint peeling/discoloration.

The following legend shows a vehicle's relative degree of overall reliability, as well as which mechanical and body parts are subject to premature failure. Note that the numbers change from dark to light as the rating becomes more positive, usually for younger vehicles.

❶	❷	③	④	⑤
Unacceptable	Below Average	Average	Above Average	Excellent

Crash safety

Vehicles are rated according to how well they performed in U.S. government 35 mph (57 km/h) frontal crash tests (the impact is the same as if two identical vehicles, each travelling at 35 mph, collided head-on) and in side-impact collisions. Information recorded during the crash tests measures the likelihood of serious injury, and vehicles are classified by the estimated chance of injury for the driver or passenger. For the past several years, vehicles have been given a one- to five-star rating by NHTSA, with five stars indicating the best protection. Cars and minivans that are identical but carry different nameplates from the same manufacturer can be expected to perform similarly in these crash tests. On the other hand, sometimes the same vehicle tested from one year to the next will post dramatically different results even though the model has remained relatively unchanged. Safety experts admit that this happens occasionally and that consumers should look at the trend established over several model years.

❶	❷	③	④	⑤
Multiple injuries	One injury	Average protection	Above average protection	Excellent protection

This guide's safety rating applies to the driver only, and if no tests were carried out that year, that fact will be indicated by a —. Readers who wish to read the complete crash test reports, which include passenger ratings, may do so by accessing *www.lemonaidcars.com* and following the NHTSA links.

SMALL CARS

The proverbial "econobox," this size of car is for city dwellers who want economy at any price. Small cars offer excellent gas economy, easy manoeuvrability in urban areas, and a low retail price.

One of the more alarming characteristics of a small car's highway performance is its extreme vulnerability to strong lateral winds, which may make the car difficult to keep on course. Most of these cars can carry only two passengers in comfort—rear seating is limited—and there is insufficient luggage capacity. As well, engine and road noise are fairly excessive.

Crash safety may be compromised by the small size and light weight of these vehicles. Nevertheless, engineering measures that direct crash forces away from occupants and the addition of airbags have made many small cars safer in collisions than some larger cars.

Recommended

Ford Escort, Tracer, ZX2 (1994–99)
Honda Civic, del Sol
  (1996–99)
Mazda 323, Protegé (1996–99)

Nissan Sentra (1995–99)
Subaru Impreza (1996–99)
Suzuki Esteem (1996–99)
Toyota Paseo (1994–99)
Toyota Tercel (1993–99)

Above Average

GM/Suzuki Firefly, Metro,
  Sprint/Swift (1995–99)
Honda Civic, del Sol (CRX)
  (1992–95)
Hyundai Accent (1995–99)
Hyundai Elantra (1996–99)
Mazda 323, Protegé (1991–95)

Nissan Sentra (1991–94)
Toyota Corolla (1991–99)
Toyota Paseo (1992–93)
Toyota Tercel (1991–92)
Volkswagen Cabrio, Golf,
  Jetta (1997–99)

Average

Ford Escort, Tracer (1992–93)
GM Cavalier, Sunfire (1996–99)
GM Saturn S-series (1997–99)
GM/Suzuki Firefly, Metro,
  Sprint/Swift (1990–94)
Honda Civic, CRX (1984–91)
Hyundai Elantra (1991–95)
Mazda 323, Protegé (1985–90)

Nissan Sentra (1988–90)
Subaru Impreza, Loyale
  (1993–95)
Toyota Corolla (1985–90)
Toyota Tercel (1987–90)
Volkswagen Cabrio, Golf,
  Jetta (1994–96)

Below Average

GM/Suzuki Firefly, Metro   Subaru Loyale (1984–92)
  Sprint/Swift (1987–89)   Volkswagen Cabrio, Golf,
                                    Jetta (1993)

Not Recommended

Chrysler Neon (1995–99)   GM Saturn S-series (1992–96)
Ford Escort, Tracer (1981–91)   Nissan Sentra (1983–87)
GM Cavalier, Sunfire (Sunbird)   Volkswagen Cabrio, Golf,
  (1984–95)   Jetta (1985–92)

CHRYSLER

Neon

Rating: Not Recommended (1995–99). A low-quality econobox that eats engine head gaskets for breakfast and wallets for lunch. Take note: A used '95 may be a year older than you think ('95s were sold in early '94). Choose a model with touring suspension for the best ride. The Highline and Sport versions are more feature laden. **Maintenance/ Repair costs:** Higher than average. **Parts:** Easily found and relatively inexpensive.

Strengths and weaknesses: A small, noisy car with big quality problems, the Neon does offer a spacious interior and responsive steering and handling. Nevertheless, it uses an antiquated 3-speed automatic gearbox, a DOHC 150-hp powerplant that has to be pushed hard to do as well as the SOHC 132-hp engine, and a mushy base suspension. A perusal of service bulletins and owner comments clearly shows that these cars have a plethora of serious factory-related defects, including a biodegradable 2.0L, 4-cylinder engine and engine head gasket (covered by a 7-year/160,000 km secret warranty, confirmed by anecdotal feedback from successful claimants), an abrupt-shifting and unreliable automatic transmission, an air conditioning system that often requires expensive servicing, a multitude of electrical glitches, lots of interior noise and leaks, uneven fit and finish, and poor-quality trim items that break or fall off easily. The finish is not as good as on most other subcompacts; Chrysler uses only two coats of paint versus the Japanese practice of applying three coats. Furthermore, the thickness of the coat varies considerably and can chip easily.

Except for the addition of a cast aluminum oil pan to reduce engine vibrations, redesigned wheel covers, improved sound system, and a centre console with armrest for 1997–98 models, the Neon has remained basically unchanged since it was first launched. '99 models got depowered airbags.

Technical service bulletins: All models: 1995—Engine sags, hesitates, shudders, and surges. • Rough idle especially bad during cold start-up. • Oil leaks at the cam position sensor. • Buzzy manual and automatic gearshift lever, and harsh-shifting, erratic automatic transmission. • Noisy clutch pedal and wheel cover. • Rear suspension bottoms out. • Steering wheel shakes and accelerator pedal vibrates. • Premature front brake-pad wear. • AC freeze-up, poor performance, and evaporator odours. • Inaccurate fuel gauge readings. • Instrument panel glare. • Water leaks into the passenger compartment on left-hand turns. • Flickering headlights. • Discharged battery. • Intermittent wiper operation. • Excessive engine noise in passenger compartment, exhaust noise/hiss, B-pillar wind noise, power-steering rattles, steering column and right engine-mount click, and chattering steering column tilt lever. • More noise: front seat rattle and front seatback squeak, hood prop-rod rattle, idle air control motor whistle, front brake moan, poorly fitted deck-lid rattle, and poor AM reception (static). **1996**—Cold-start hesitation, engine misfiring, and erratic idling. • Excessive engine vibration and exhaust noise. • Transmission slippage from second to third gear during light acceleration. • Speed control overshoots or undershoots. • Rear brake chirps or howls. • AC evaporator produces a high-pitched whistle. • Fuel tank won't fill or is slow to fill. • Interior window film buildup. • Water leaks at cowl cover seam. **1997**—Rear brake howl. • Front footwell creak/rattle. • Scratched door glass. • Improper AC compressor engagement. • Loss of power steering in heavy rain or when passing through puddles. • Poor radio reception. • Warning that premium fuel may cause stalling, long cold-start times, hesitation, and warm-up sags. • Front suspension popping/creaking noise. **1998**—Engine sag or hesitation. • AC compressor lockup at low mileage. • Harsh AC operation. • Headlight flickers. • Steering wheel/column rattles and clunks. • Cold-start power-steering noise. • Front brake squeal, creep, or groan. • Paint fogging. • Warning that premium fuel may cause stalling, long cold-start times, hesitation, and warm-up sags. • Popping noise when passing over bumps or making turns. • Remote keyless transmitter battery failure. • Sunroof shade rattles in open position. • Vehicle overheats or radiator fan runs continuously. **1999**—Oil leakage at cam position sensor. • Low mileage AC lockup. • Smooth road steering wheel vibration. • Sunroof ratcheting noise. • Steering wheel clunk/rattle. • Water leak at left side of trunk.

Safety summary/Recalls: All models: 1995–98—Poor performance in IIHS 40 mph crash tests. **1995**—Steering column fires. • 98 reports of "inappropriate" airbag deployment, causing 13 crashes and injuring 28 people. NHTSA officials have opened a formal investigation into reports of oversensitive airbag deployments on 1995 Neons. • Sudden steering loss. • Small horn buttons are hard to find in an emergency. • Headlight switch is a "hide and go seek" affair. • Axle shafts may suddenly fail, as the owner of a 1995 Neon discovered:

I was driving in traffic and the car just stopped. I couldn't move forward or backwards but the engine was still going. It turned out that the left front axle of the car had collapsed. I was just lucky that I wasn't driving on the highway when this occurred, because I would have been severely injured or killed. I had the car towed to the dealer, and they repaired the broken axle, but I just don't feel safe in the vehicle....

1995–96—Engine compartment fires. • Electrical short in dashboard. • Sudden acceleration. • ABS brake failures. • Inadvertent airbag deployment. • Failure of airbag to deploy. • Seatbelt failed to restrain driver. • Driver's seatbelt tightens uncomfortably. • Driver's side seatbelt pulled out from buckle during collision. • Premature front brake pad/rotor wearout. • Excessive wearout of brake rotors apparently caused by premature pitting of the rotors due to bubbles created during the casting process. • Front brake–caliper sticking. • Chronic engine head gasket failures. • Engine camshaft seal leaks oil • Engine motor mount and exhaust donut gasket failures. • Sticks in idle. • Chronic stalling. • Throttle system failures. • Faulty cruise control. • Chronic transmission failures. • Transmission suddenly downshifts to first gear when accelerating at 90 km/h. • Sudden steering loss. • Steering locks up every time it rains. • Trunk springs won't hold lid up. • Door hinge failures. • Premature wheel bearing and steering knuckle wear. • Chronic light and gauge failures. • Faulty Goodyear tires. • Fuel gauge failures. • Defective brake master cylinder. • Window rattles, goes off track, or shatters when door is closed. • AC condenser and compressor failures. • Water leaks in from dash on driver's side. • Poor door fit allows water to enter cabin. **1997**—Circuit board behind dash caught fire. • Sudden acceleration. • Cruise control won't disengage when braking. • Chronic stalling. • Airbag failure to deploy. • Gas tank leaks fuel. • O-ring in the fuel rail leaks fuel. • Chronic sudden brake failures. • Noisy brakes. • Brake rotor failures. • Steering belt failures. • Sudden steering lockup after passing over speed bump. • Engine head gasket failures. • Window seal failures. • Fuel pump failures. • Seatbelt failed to restrain occupant. • Catalytic converter failure. • Hood fell, injuring driver's arm. **1998**—Sudden acceleration. • Airbag failed to deploy. • Driver-side window exploded in warm weather. • Front right wheel bolt fell out, causing wheel to bend. • Trunk lid may fall. • Engine surging and stalling. • Engine loses speed rapidly when going uphill. • Excessive engine carbon buildup. • Timing belt broke, causing extensive engine damage. • Engine mounts break. • Head gaskets leaked. • Erratic automatic transmission performance. • Partial steering hang-up when making a right turn. **1999**—Ignition fire. • Automatic transmission suddenly self-destructed. • Vehicle suddenly "jumps" out of gear. • Airbags failed to deploy. • In rainy weather, vehicle makes loud noise, sometimes stalls, or loses steering power. • Engine mounts crack prematurely. • Defective ignition switch fuse causes sudden shutdown. **Recalls: All models: 1995**—Corroded fuel and rear brake tubes may fail. • Steering columns could snap loose from the car's frame. • Defective master cylinder piston. • Faulty PCM may cause chronic stalling. • Rear brake lines may be out of position. • Faulty rear ABS brake master cylinder seal. **1996**—Engine wiring harness may short, causing stalling. **1997**—Airbag module should be replaced to prevent airbags from deploying while vehicle is parked. **1997–98**—Faulty fan relay could cause engine overheating. **1998**—Rear suspension cross-member may be missing spot welds. • Emissions recall due to radiator fan malfunction.

Secret Warranties/Service Tips

All models: 1995–97—If water drips into the vehicle from the roof-rail weather-strip channel, Chrysler will provide, under warranty, a free anti-drip roof-rail retainer channel. **1995–99**—A new Multi-Layer Steel engine head gasket will provide superior sealing characteristics. Oil leakage at the cam position sensor is often mistaken for an engine head gasket failure. • Paint delamination, peeling, or fading (see Part Two). **1996**—Water could enter the air cleaner housing, be ingested into the engine, and cause serious engine damage. To prevent this from occurring, the dealer will drill a hole in the housing and seal the cowl-to-head weather stripping. This 30-minute correction is free of charge under Chrysler Customer Satisfaction Notice #660. It's not a safety recall, so you may have a hard time getting Chrysler to acknowledge the problem. **1998–99**—A water leak in the left side of the trunk below the body exhauster and/or water pooled in the spare tire well is caused by a gap between the wheel house outer panel and the left body side aperture panel (see illustration below).

Water Leak In Left Side Of Trunk
NO: 23-55-98
GROUP: Body
DATE: Nov. 13, 1998
SUBJECT:
Water Leak In Left
Side Of Trunk
MODELS:
1998-1999 (PL) Neon
SYMPTOM/CONDITION:
A water leak in the left side of the trunk below the body exhauster and/or water pooled in the spare tire well. This is caused by a gap between the wheel house outer panel and the left body side aperture panel where the fascia is bolted through the weld flanges.

Neon Profile

	1995	1996	1997	1998	1999
Cost Price ($)					
Base	11,866	12,835	14,750	15,350	15,215
Sport 4d	16,126	15,515	16,900	17,500	—
Used Values ($)					
Base ↑	4,000	6,500	8,000	10,000	12,000

Base ↓	3,500	5,000	6,000	8,000	10,000
Sport 4d ↑	5,500	7,500	9,000	11,000	—
Sport 4d ↓	4,500	6,500	8,000	10,000	—
Extended Warranty	Y	Y	Y	Y	Y
Secret Warranty	Y	Y	Y	Y	Y
Reliability	①	①	②	②	①
Air conditioning	①	①	②	③	②
Automatic transmission	②	②	③	③	②
Body integrity	②	②	②	②	①
Braking system	①	①	②	③	②
Electrical system	①	①	②	③	③
Engines	①	①	②	②	②
Exhaust/Converter	③	④	⑤	⑤	③
Fuel system	②	②	③	③	③
Ignition system	③	④	⑤	⑤	③
Rust/Paint	②	②	③	③	④
Steering	①	②	③	③	②
Suspension	⑤	⑤	⑤	⑤	②
Crash Safety	③	④	④	③	③
Side Impact	—	—	—	②	②

FORD

Escort, Tracer, ZX2

Rating: Recommended (1994–99); Average (1992–93); Not Recommended (1981–91). The LX became the base Escort during the 1994 model year. Lots of upgraded 1997 Escorts are coming off lease now; they represent an exceptionally good buy. The Escort was replaced by the Focus last year. **Maintenance/Repair costs:** Higher than average on pre-1991s; below average for later models. Repairs can be done by independents or Ford or Mazda dealers. **Parts:** Expensive, but easily found.

Strengths and weaknesses: These front-drive small cars are usually reasonably priced and economical to operate. They provide a comfortable though busy ride and adequate front seating for two adults. However, they have a "Dr. Jekyll and Mr. Hyde" disposition, depending on which model year you buy. From 1981 through 1991, these subcompacts were dull performers with uninspiring interiors. Worse, they had a nasty reputation for being unreliable and expensive to repair.

Be wary of early Escorts (1984–87) that use Mazda's 2.0L diesel 4-cylinder engine; it's weak, noisy, difficult to service, and prone to expensive cylinder head and gasket repairs. From 1987 until 1991, quality continued to go downhill. The 1.9L engine used from 1985 to 1990 gives respectable highway performance but its failure rate is still much higher than average. The radiator and other cooling components, including the fan switch and motor, are failure prone. Carburetors and fuel-injection systems are temperamental. Ignition modules are often defective. Power steering racks fail prematurely. Front and rear wheel alignment is difficult. Exhaust systems rust rapidly.

The 1991 model's changeover to mostly Mazda 323 components gave it a longer wheelbase, making for a more comfortable ride and a bit roomier interior. The 1.9L engine runs more smoothly as well. The Escort GT and Tracer LTS are equipped with Mazda's powerful 127-hp, 1.8L, 4-cylinder engine (premature timing belt replacement around 97,000 km), and their overall highway performance and fuel economy are far superior to what previous models offered. Wagon versions are particularly versatile and spacious. The front seats on the Tracer GS and LS are very comfortable and the cargo area is especially spacious in the wagon. Rear seat room is a bit cramped on all other models.

Quality control and reliability improved considerably over the following years but problems remain. Owner complaints relating to the 1991–96 model years concern primarily the automatic transmission and engine (premature timing belt replacement around 90,000 km), cooling system, brakes, electrical short circuits, air conditioning, fuel pump, and ignition-system failures.

The 1997 models were significantly improved quality-wise; are more attractively designed; ride and handle better; and feature improved comfort, a quieter interior, and more standard equipment. The car is four inches longer, mostly taken up by a larger trunk. New standard features include power steering; rear heat ducts; intermittent wipers; a battery-saver system; a 24-watt, four-speaker stereo unit that can be upgraded to an 80-watt system hooked to a trunk-mounted CD player; and solar glass. Three-door, five-door, and GT models were dropped and the ZX2—a revived, high-performance coupe—made its debut in late 1997 as a 1998 model. It's a peppier machine, with a less raucous engine, that sells in the U.S. for a $2,000 premium over the Escort. In Canada, it debuted for the 1999 model year. All '99 models were carried over unchanged.

Safety summary/Recalls: Recalls: Escort: 1995—Airbag mounting bolts may be missing or improperly torqued.

Secret Warranties/Service Tips

All models: 1993–99—Paint delamination, peeling, or fading (see Part Two). **Escort: 1983–94**—Hesitation, a rough idle, or poor heater output may all be caused by a faulty thermostat. **1990–99**—A radio speaker whining noise may be caused by fuel pump interference. **1991–93**—Metallic ticking heard after initial start-up or when returning to idle speed may be caused by a faulty lifter, low amount of oil in the crankcase, incorrect oil filter, or oil deterioration. **1991–94**—Under a recall and Service Program #94B55, Ford will install at no charge a fused jumper harness in the fuel pump electrical circuit. This will prevent short-circuit problems such as stalling, erratic instrument gauge readings, and extensive wiring damage, which are caused by water intrusion. • Fix a timing belt that's noisy during cold weather by installing an upgraded, more rigid belt tensioner. • A missing or loose front valance panel should be replaced or secured with longer bolts. **1992–93**—A high idle rpm after heavy use may be corrected by installing a new idle air control valve. **1994–98**—Tips on eliminating wind noise around doors are given in TSB #97-15-1. **1997–99**—PCV system may freeze, resulting in a serious oil leak through the dipstick tube (see following bulletin).

98-10-5
05/26/98
ENGINE - 2.0L SPI - PCV FREEZING AT COLD
AMBIENT TEMPERATURES - VEHICLES WITH
SOHC
LEAK - ENGINE OIL LEAK FROM OIL LEVEL
INDICATOR TUBE - PCV FREEZE - VEHICLES
BUILT WITH 2.0L SPI ENGINE
FORD:
1997–98 ESCORT
LINCOLN-MERCURY:
1997–98 TRACER
ISSUE
At cold ambient temperatures, the Positive Crankcase Ventilation (PCV) system may
freeze causing the engine to unseat the dipstick and vent crankcase gasses through the
dipstick tube. This may result in oil being discharged on some vehicles.
ACTION
Install PCV Service Kit (refer to Parts Block for correct service application) per this TSB.
WARRANTY STATUS: Eligible Under The Provisions Of Bumper To Bumper Warranty
Coverage And Emissions Warranty Coverage

*The above kit doesn't work any better than the original component; Ford
says it's still working on a solution to the problem. Remember all losses
caused by this defect are Ford's responsibility.*

• A front brake grinding noise, pulling or drag, and uneven brake pad wear
are all signs of corrosion affecting the caliper slide pins; Ford will correct
the problem under its bumper-to-bumper warranty, says TSB #00-6-9.
Excessive vibration at idle may be corrected by replacing the motor mount.
Tips on silencing a variety of squeaks and rattles. • No restart in cold
weather, the cooling fan won't shut off, or the battery goes dead all signal
the need to change the IRCM under the bumper-to-bumper warranty (see
following bulletin).

No Restart In –20 F/Cooling Fan Stays On, Engine Off
Article No.
98-13-8
07/06/98
NO START – AFTER SHORT DRIVE IN COLD AMBIENT TEMPERATURE (-29 DEGREES
CELSIUS (-20 DEGREES FAHRENHEIT))
BATTERY – DISCHARGED DUE TO COOLING FAN NOT TURNING OFF AFTER
SHUTDOWN
COOLING FAN – DOES NOT TURN OFF AFTER SHUTDOWN
FORD:
1997-98 ESCORT
LINCOLN MERCURY:
1997-98 TRACER
ISSUE
A no restart may occur after a short drive in cold ambient temperature of -29°C (-20°F),
or the cooling fan may not turn off with key out of the ignition on some vehicles. This
may result in a discharged battery. These concerns may be due to water or ice accumu-
lation in the Integrated Relay Control Module (IRCM).
ACTION
Replace the IRCM with a revised moisture resistant IRCM.

1998—An erratic transaxle shift may simply be caused by a pinched wire. • Erratic fuel gauge operation or slow fillups may be corrected by installing a slosh module fuel gauge kit. **1999**—Tips on reducing noise, vibration, and harshness.

Escort, Tracer, ZX2 Profile

	1992	1993	1994	1995	1996	1997	1998	1999
Cost Price ($)								
Escort Base/LX	11,195	10,795	12,195	12,995	13,595	14,595	14,895	14,895
GT	15,095	15,472	13,995	14,295	15,295	—	—	—
ZX2	—	—	—	—	—	—	—	15,895
Used Values ($)								
Base/LX ↑	2,500	3,500	4,500	5,500	7,000	8,500	10,000	11,000
Base/LX ↓	2,000	3,000	4,000	5,000	6,000	7,500	9,000	10,000
GT ↑	3,500	4,500	5,500	7,000	8,500	9,500	—	—
GT ↓	3,000	4,000	4,500	5,500	7,000	8,000	—	—
ZX2	—	—	—	—	—	—	—	11,500
ZX2	—	—	—	—	—	—	—	10,500

Note: Tracer prices are similar to those of the base Escort.

Extended Warranty	Y	Y	N	N	N	N	N	N
Secret Warranty	Y	Y	Y	Y	Y	Y	Y	Y
Reliability	②	③	③	④	④	④	⑤	⑤
Air conditioning	①	②	②	②	②	③	③	④
Auto. transmission	②	③	③	③	④	⑤	⑤	⑤
Body integrity	②	②	②	②	②	③	③	③
Braking system	①	①	①	②	③	③	④	④
Electrical system	①	②	②	②	②	②	③	④
Engines	②	③	③	③	③	③	④	④
Exhaust/Converter	③	③	③	③	③	④	④	⑤
Fuel system	③	③	③	③	③	④	⑤	⑤
Ignition system	②	③	③	③	④	⑤	⑤	⑤
Rust/Paint	①	②	②	③	③	③	③	④
Steering	③	⑤	⑤	⑤	⑤	⑤	⑤	⑤
Suspension	②	③	③	④	⑤	⑤	⑤	⑤
Crash Safety								
Escort	⑤	⑤	⑤	④	④	④	③	③
Tracer	—	—	—	④	④	④	③	③
Side Impact								
Escort	—	—	—	—	—	—	③	③
Tracer	—	—	—	—	—	—	③	③
Escort ZX2 2d	—	—	—	—	—	—	—	①

Note: Escort ZX2 2d crash rating is for the U.S. version.

GENERAL MOTORS

Cavalier/Sunfire (Sunbird)

Rating: Average (1996–99); Not Recommended (1984–95). Repair bills will run you bankrupt if you get a pre-1997 model or if maintenance schedules aren't followed to the letter. An incredibly slow depreciation rate means that recent models are no bargains. Still, I'd buy a Cavalier, Sunbird, or Sunfire over a Saturn any day. The base Sunbird became the LE in 1989, and then changed its name to the Sunfire in 1995. The Cavalier Z24 convertible was replaced by the LS in 1995. **Maintenance/Repair costs:** Average; repairs aren't dealer dependent; however, ABS troubleshooting is a real head-scratcher. **Parts:** Reasonably priced; often available for much less from independent suppliers.

Strengths and weaknesses: Snappy road performance (with the right engine and transmission hookup) has been marred by abysmally poor reliability up until the 1997–99 model years. The basic versions are lackluster performers. The 2.0L 4-cylinder engine gets overwhelmed by the demands of passing and merging. On top of that, major reliability weaknesses afflict all mechanical and body components. Engine, transmission, electronic module, and brake failures are common for all model years. 2.0L engine blocks crack, cylinder heads leak, and the turbocharged version frequently needs expensive repairs. Oil leakage from the rear crankshaft seal is common and oil filters on all model years tend to wear out quickly.

1986–89 model year improvements simply changed the nature, not the frequency, of engine and automatic transmission breakdowns. Power-steering rack and front suspension components aren't durable. Consider replacing the original components with front gas struts and rear cargo coil springs to improve handling and durability. Owners also report that a change to high-octane fuel can help improve engine performance and reduce knocking and engine run-on. The cooling, exhaust, ignition, and fuel systems have had more than the average number of problems. The manifold heat shield tends to be noisy. Front brakes wear out quickly, and rear brakes tend to lock the rear wheels in emergency stops (one cause being the seizure of the rear brake adjusters). The Cavalier's optional 2.8L V6 with 3-speed automatic transmission is the best highway performer, but intake manifold gasket failures, premature head gasket wear, and transmission malfunctions compromise driving pleasure.

For 1990–94 versions, the Cavalier's base 2.2L 4-cylinder and optional 3.1L engines replaced the failure-prone 2.0L and 2.8L power-plants. Unfortunately, the newer engines already have a checkered reputation, highlighted by reports of chronic head gasket failures causing coolant leakage, malfunctioning fuel pumps, overheating, engine seizure, hard starting, stalling, and surging—problems covered by a

secret warranty. Air conditioning and hood latch failures, seatbelt
defects, and a plethora of body deficiencies are also commonplace.
Door bottoms and wheel housings are particularly vulnerable to rust
perforation. Premature paint peeling and cracking, discoloration, and
surface rust have been regular problems through 1997.

The 1995 model is wider and taller. Although its wheelbase is a bit
longer, the body is about two inches shorter. Nevertheless, occupants
get two additional inches of rear leg room in the coupe and about an
inch and a half more in the sedan. The station wagon was dropped, but
a wagon and convertible were added. Standard dual airbags and ABS,
a stiffer structure, and an improved suspension were all part of the '95
redesign. In subsequent years, the '96 LS sedan and convertible got
standard traction control and the Z24 picked up a new dual-camshaft
2.2L engine. 1997 models were carried over with minor styling changes
for the Z24 and a new Rally Sport coupe. For 1998, the base engine
actually lost five horses.

Unfortunately, engine head gasket failures and chronic fuel pump
failures have apparently been carried over to the later models as well.
Brakes are still failure-prone, airbags continue to malfunction and
injure occupants, and stalling and transmission failures are common.

Technical service bulletins: All models: 1995—Engine failing to crank
and no-start. • Brake vibration and/or pedal pulsation. • Introduction
of longer-life front brake linings. • Low-voltage reading and dim lights
at idle. • Grinding/growling when in Park on an incline. • Knocking
noise when traversing rough roads. • Rear window panel squeaking. •
Rear quarter-panel road noise. • Loose door trim panel. • Poor paint
application and rust spots. **1996**—Excessive engine roll. • Low-speed
knocking noise when passing over rough roads. • Air conditioning
odours. • Radio frequency interference diagnosis tips. • Water leak
diagnostic guide. • Loose door trim panel. • Tips on silencing rear
quarter-panel road noise. • Condensation within exterior light housing.
• Rear edge of hood rubs windshield when opening. • Twisted seatbelt
webbing. **1997**—Axle seal leakage. • Scuffed interior quarter trim panels on convertibles. • Coolant odour or leakage. • Deck lid hard to open
or close. • Automatic transmission failure or delayed engagement. • Low
Engine Coolant light flashes. • Popping noise originating from the
engine compartment. • Rear seatback rattles/squeaks. • Rear shock
noise coming from the trunk area and door when the windows are lowered. • Engine cranks, but won't run. **1998**—Delayed, slow, or no
second-to-third-gear upshift. • Engine hesitation, sag, or stall when cold.
• Front bucket seatback bulge. • Measures to eliminate AC odours. •
Faulty rear trunk latch. • Convertible top water leaks and rear footwell
water leak. **1999**—Rough engine idle. • Engine running hot, and/or
loss of coolant. • No third and fourth gear. • Grinding or growling in
Park on incline. • Door rattles when closing. • Water leak at front heater.
Loose accessory power outlet housing. • Eliminating AC odours.

Safety summary/Recalls: All models: 1995—Steering locks up. • Faulty cruise control. • Windshield wipers fail in cold weather. • **1995–96**—ABS brake failure. • Airbags fail to deploy or deploy accidentally. • Inoperative horn. • Transmission slips out of Park. • Sudden acceleration, stalling. • Passenger-side seatbacks won't stay upright. **1996**—NHTSA has received 96 complaints of inadvertent airbag deployment, which include 10 crashes and injuries to 53 people. • Engine gaskets leak oil. • Mufflers fail frequently. **1997**—Engine fires. • Inadvertent airbag deployment. • Airbag failed to deploy. • During a collision, driver sustained serious leg injuries when the seat pushed her lower body under the instrument panel. • Sudden acceleration. • Chronic stalling and hesitation, particularly when it rains. • Premature engine cylinder failure; leaks oil. • Premature oil pump failure. • Faulty fuel pump relay provokes stalling. • Failure of the engine mounts and ignition switch. • Cruise control failure. • Restart after stalling causes engine to race. • Sudden loss of power. • Steering wheel locked up. • Transmission failures. • Noisy rear end due to faulty suspension struts. • Faulty master cylinder and modulator assembly led to brake failure. • Frequent front brake rotor warpage, premature pad wear, and excessive vibrations when braking. • ABS brake failure. • Horn failed. • Cracked water pump. • Dashboard cracking, rattling, and popping. • Defective instrument panel control module. • Low beam switch failure. • Inoperative lighting due to rotted-out wiring harness. • Door hinges don't hold door open. • Door came ajar while driving. • Windshield wiper failure. • When turned off, windshield wiper stops in the field of vision. • Lug nuts are easily broken when changing tire. **1998**—Fire in the trunk area. • Odour of burning wires when driving. • Sudden acceleration. • Chronic stalling at idle or highway speeds, when turning, or whenever the AC or defroster is engaged. • Brakes continue to be a common safety complaint. Owners report complete brake failure and lockup, extended stopping distances, ABS that self-activates, premature rotor warpage and pad wear, and a grinding and knocking noise when braking. • Other reports also target airbags that go off when they shouldn't and don't deploy when they should. • Airbag-induced burns and fractures are common. Loose or broken engine mounts. • Chronic engine overheating. • Many reports of automatic transmission failures, slippage, and failure to hold in Park. • Steering wheel locks up after a cold start. Steering shaft sheared off when turning. • Inaccurate fuel gauge. • One Saskatchewan *Lemon-Aid* reader reports that the rear bumper will crack extensively in cold weather if hit only slightly. • Windshield glare from the dash. • Driver seat lever interferes with entry/exit. **Recalls: All models: 1995**—Front suspension lower control arm assemblies may be defective. **1995–96**—Front or rear hazard warning lights could be faulty. **1996**—Accelerator cable may be kinked, requiring excessive pedal effort. • Interior lights may suddenly come on. **1996–97**—Airbag sensor is too sensitive. • Rear suspension trailing arm bolts can fatigue and break. **1997**—Airbags deploy with excessive force. • Compact tire may have incorrect rims. • Too-short wiper blades will be replaced for free.

Secret Warranties/Service Tips

All models: 1992–97—Excessive timing chain noise is likely due to lack of maintenance; inspect the timing chain and make sure the front oil passage plug isn't blocked by debris. **1993–94**—Excessive engine vibration at idle or a clunk upon acceleration is most likely due to a defective engine mount. **1993–99**—GM has a new kit that it says will eliminate AC odours. • A rotten-egg odour coming from the exhaust is probably caused by a malfunctioning catalytic converter; this repair is covered by GM's emissions warranty. • Paint delamination, peeling, or fading (see Part Two). **1994**—A squeaking noise heard when going over bumps, accelerating, or shifting can be stopped by replacing the exhaust manifold pipe seal. • Water leaks into the front footwell are discussed in depth in a December 1993 TSB. **1994–97**—An engine knock, rattle, or tap noise can be silenced by installing new pistons or rod assemblies. **Cavalier/Sunfire: 1995–96**—Engine head gasket failures that include overheating, loss of coolant, smell of coolant, coolant leaks around the cylinder head, and white smoke from the exhaust. Sometimes the heater won't work or a film (from the coolant) will be deposited on the inside glass surfaces. If the coolant leaks inside the engine it can cause severe engine damage from overheating. These vehicles are now covered for head gasket problems for 7 years or 100,000 miles (160,000 km), whichever comes first. Consumers who already paid for repairs at a dealership should contact the dealership to be reimbursed. Consumers who did not have a GM dealership do the work aren't excluded from the refund program and should contact the toll-free customer assistance number in the owner's manual. Future repairs, however, must take place at a GM dealership. The program is not a recall, and owners should take their vehicles to a dealership only if it appears they have a problem. Remember, if you have an engine head gasket failure on a GM vehicle or engine not included in the above-noted programs, don't despair. Simply use the same benchmarks for your own vehicle and threaten small claims action on those grounds. **1995–97**—Axle seal leakage may be caused by a pinched transaxle vent hose. • Delayed automatic transmission engagement after a cold soak signals the need to install a revised forward clutch housing assembly. • Rear brakes that heat up or drag may need the brake lamp switch adjusted or new parking brake cables. • Repair tips are offered for scuffed interior quarter-trim panels on convertibles. • A sticking deck lid may need an upgraded lid release cable. • A dome light that won't shut off probably has a corroded doorjamb switch. • The left-hand mirror may not adjust if the lever has become disengaged. • A popping noise originating from the engine compartment may mean that the torque strut-mount attaching bolts are loose. • Rear shock noise can be silenced by installing upgraded upper shock mounts. • Troubleshooting tips on silencing rear shock noise and rear seatback rattles and squeaks are available. • Door rattles when the window is lowered may be silenced by replacing the door glass downstop or front guides. **1995–98**—A bulge in the front bucket seatback requires additional bracing to correct. • Install a drain path in convertibles to prevent water from collecting in the rear footwell area. **1995–99**—A faulty rear lid (trunk) latch may only need a new cable. **1995–2000**—Instrument panel squeak or rattle, scratched right front door trim panel, or right side end of instrument panel contacting door trim panel can be fixed by removing the instrument panel assembly and realigning the tie bar. This two-hour repair will be covered under GM's base warranty or through its "goodwill" policy. • GM will install upgraded rear brake backing plates to prevent snow intrusion freezing the brake shoes to the drums. **1996–97**—Coolant odour or leakage may occur at the joint where the radiator outlet pipe is connected to the coolant pump cover or at the joint between the cooling system air-bleed pipe and the coolant outlet. • Coolant loss, leakage, coolant lamp on, or coolant odour can be corrected by installing a new thermostat gasket. **1997**—A Low Engine Coolant light may come on to signal that the cooling system surge tank is defective. **1998**—A delayed, slow, or no second-to-third-gear upshift may require a new transmission case cover or assembly. A 2.2L cold engine hesitation, sag, or stall may be corrected by recalibrating the power control module (PCM). **1999–2000**—No third and fourth gear may require a new direct clutch piston assembly (see following bulletin).

No Third and Fourth Gear
File In Section: 07 – Transmission/Transaxle
Bulletin No.: 99-07-30-031
Date: December, 1999
TECHNICAL
Subject:
No Third and Fourth Gear (Replace Direct Clutch Piston Assembly)
Models:
1999-2000 Chevrolet Cavalier, Malibu
1999 Oldsmobile Cutlass
1999-2000 Oldsmobile Alero
1999-2000 Pontiac Grand Am, Sunfire

Cavalier/Sunfire (Sunbird) Profile

	1992	1993	1994	1995	1996	1997	1998	1999
Cost Price ($)								
Cavalier	10,598	10,498	10,998	12,245	13,030	14,390	14,765	15,365
Z24	15,798	14,798	17,298	16,895	17,643	19,000	19,295	20,035
Z24 Conv./LS	18,400	18,098	20,298	22,185	22,925	24,285	25,880	26,450
Sunbird/LE	11,398	10,498	11,498	—	—	—	—	—
Sunbird GT	15,398	14,998	—	—	—	—	—	—
Sunfire	—	—	—	12,945	13,380	15,340	15,960	16,135
Used Values ($)								
Cavalier ↑	2,500	3,500	4,500	6,000	7,000	8,000	9,000	11,000
Cavalier ↓	2,000	3,000	4,000	5,000	6,000	7,000	8,000	10,000

Z24 ↑	4,000	5,500	6,500	7,500	8,500	10,000	11,000	12,500
Z24 ↓	3,500	4,500	6,000	6,500	8,000	9,000	10,000	11,500
Z24 Conv. /LS↑	—	7,000	8,000	9,500	11,000	12,000	16,000	18,000
Z24 Conv. /LS↓	—	6,000	7,500	8,500	10,000	11,000	14,000	17,000
Sunbird/LE ↑	3,000	3,500	4,000	5,000	—	—	—	—
Sunbird/LE ↓	2,500	3,000	3,500	4,000	—	—	—	—
Sunbird GT ↑	4,000	5,000	6,000	—	—	—	—	—
Sunbird GT ↓	3,500	4,500	5,000	—	—	—	—	—
Sunfire ↑	—	—	—	6,500	8,000	9,500	10,500	11,500
Sunfire ↓	—	—	—	5,000	7,000	8,500	9,000	10,000
Extended Warranty	Y	Y	Y	Y	Y	Y	Y	Y
Secret Warranty	N	N	Y	Y	Y	Y	Y	Y
Reliability	①	①	②	②	②	③	③	③
Air conditioning	②	②	②	②	③	③	④	④
Auto. transmission	①	①	①	②	②	②	③	③
Body integrity	①	①	①	②	②	②	②	②
Braking system	①	①	①	②	②	②	②	②
Electrical system	①	①	①	②	②	②	②	②
Engines	②	②	②	②	②	②	③	④
Exhaust/Converter	②	②	③	③	③	④	④	⑤
Fuel system	①	①	①	②	②	②	②	③
Ignition system	②	②	②	②	②	③	③	③
Rust/Paint	①	①	①	②	②	②	②	②
Steering	②	②	②	②	②	③	③	④
Suspension	①	①	①	②	③	③	③	④
Crash Safety								
Cavalier 2d	—	—	—	—	—	—	③	③
Cavalier 4d	④	④	④	④	④	④	④	④
Side Impact								
Cavalier 2d	—	—	—	—	—	—	①	①
Cavalier 4d	—	—	—	—	—	①	①	①

Note: NHTSA says the Sunbird and Sunfire safety ratings should be identical to the Cavalier's score.

Saturn S-series

Rating: Average (1997–99); Not Recommended (1992–96). The '91 model was only sold in the States. Don't go anywhere near a used Saturn unless you're armed to the teeth with a comprehensive extended warranty or have thoroughly perused this Saturn owners' website: *www.saturnexposed.com.* As bizarre as it may appear, the Saturn division has a better reputation than the car it sells. The automaker's poor quality control is masked by generous amounts of "goodwill" refunds that quickly dry up when the car changes hands. The Geo Storm, Honda Civic LX, and Toyota Corolla perform well and offer better quality. **Maintenance/Repair costs:** Average. Repairs aren't dealer dependent, unless you're seeking some Saturn "goodwill" refunds. **Parts:** Higher-than-average cost, but not hard to find through independent suppliers.

Strengths and weaknesses: Conceived as an all-American effort to beat the Japanese in the small-car market, the Saturn compact isn't any better built than the other GM home-grown compacts we've learned to dread over the past 30 years. The car is far from high-tech; it's remained virtually unchanged, except for a minor face-lift and a bit more leg room, since it was launched in 1991. (Canada got the car six months later as a '92 model.)

Saturns have exhibited a plethora of serious body and mechanical problems, which GM has masked by generously applying its base warranty. Second owners aren't treated as well, however, and complaints are frequent where owners of used Saturns report they had to pay dearly for GM's powertrain and body mistakes. Servicing quality is spotty. And if the rumors of GM merging Saturn with one of its other divisions are true, warranty claim servicing will become even more problematic and routine dealer servicing will likely deteriorate as well.

What's so great about Saturn? Its advertising agency.

Granted, these are competitively priced, roomy, and comfortable small cars. They handle nimbly in good weather where acceleration isn't a prime consideration. On the other hand, these lightweight vehicles are tricky to handle in snow or ice.

Powered by a 4-cylinder aluminum engine and a multi-valve variation of the same powerplant in the coupe, these cars are remarkably fuel-efficient, with the base engine hooked to a manual transmission. The rack-and-pinion steering is fairly precise and predictable, while the suspension gives a firm, but not harsh, ride.

The loud, coarse, standard single-cam engine gives barely adequate acceleration times with the manual transmission. This time is increased with the 4-speed automatic gearbox that robs the engine of what little power it produces. Other generic problems affecting all model years are stalling and hard starting. One Ontario owner of a 1994 Saturn plagued with chronic stalling problems had this to say:

After stalling in rush hour traffic, car was towed as hazard lights failed after ten minutes; unable to restart. Car was then towed. Cause indicated: bad fuel tank, pump, battery, ECM and ignition module. Replaced probe, module, pump, tank, valve, module, and battery.

Work order indicated that they performed various diagnostic checks, including: updated computer program, checked fuel pressure, checked ignition module circuit for proper operation, checked circuit from ignition switch to PCM for poor connection, and tried good ignition switch. Monitored voltage at back of ignition switch circuit for Fuse #1 PCM, replaced fuel tank and fuel pump as per tac, and replaced ECM. Car returned Feb. 27, 1998, but that evening car stalled again.

Car stalled Feb. 28, March 1, 2, and 3 and finally, after stalling a dozen or so times on my way to work and almost getting into an accident with a bus, I told the Customer Service in Toronto that they could come get the car from my work as I was not driving it home....

The 5-speed manual transmission sometimes has trouble going into Reverse. With the automatic, there's lots of gearbox shudder when the kickdown is engaged while passing.

Technical service bulletins indicate that four major quality problems are likely to crop up: self-destructing engines; chronically malfunctioning automatic transmissions ; myriad electrical short circuits; and a host of body defects, led by paint delamination, rattles, and wind and water leaks. On early models, the doors were poorly fitted, rear seats had to be lowered half an inch to give much-needed head room, engine mounts were changed to reduce vibrations, the shift mechanism on the manual transmission was unreliable, and the reclining front seats were recalled because they could suddenly slip backwards. Rear head room is a bit tight, and owners report that the headliner in the rear tends to sag. Despite the dent-resistant plastic body panels, Saturn owners complain that the fascia chips and discolours.

GM's minor refinements to the 1997–98 Saturns don't appear to justify their higher prices. The sedans and wagons got upgraded engine mounts to lessen noise and vibration, and the coupe was given the sedan's 102-inch wheelbase, providing additional leg room, particularly in the rear. More effective silencing materials were added forward of the dash, and the air inlet was redirected away from the passenger compartment. Upgraded seatbelts on all 1997 models are less likely to trip passengers trying to access the rear seat. 1998 models were carried over practically unchanged except for a quieter-running engine and new colours, hubcaps, and wheels. '99 model improvements: smoother-running engines and user-friendly front seatbelt latches.

Technical service bulletins: All models: 1995—Engine flares, loss of power, harsh shifts into Reverse. • Engine knock and/or rattle at normal temperature. • Engine stalls when cold, difficult to restart. • Excessive engine vibration at idle. • ATF leak at automatic transaxle oil pressure filter. • Guide to possible causes of brake pulsation. • More recent info on brake vibration and/or pedal pulsation. • Steering pull, torque steer and wander. • Squealing sound from front of engine during cold starts. • Buzzing noise at rear of vehicle. • Possible other causes of buzzing, rattling, and fluttering noises. • Hoot noise upon light deceleration. • Clicking, ticking noise from instrument cluster odometer. • Ignition noise heard through radio speakers. • Popping noise from front seatback frame. • Rattle or chatter coming from passenger side. • Rattle, pop, or click from front end whenever passing over rough roads. • Squeak/squawk noise from rear of vehicle. • Whistling produced by antenna mast. • Troubleshooting tips to silence wind noise at highway speeds. • Low-voltage reading or dim lights at idle. • Instrument panel centre air outlet closes. • Hard-to-operate sunroof sunshade. • Water drips onto seat/carpet with door open. • Water leaks into right front footwell from front of dash. • Water leak at front upper door frame. **1996**—Excessive engine vibration at idle. • Radio frequency interference diagnosis. **1997**—Automatic transmission malfunctions. • Failure-prone cylinder head. • Cruise control drops out intermittently or won't reset after dropout. • Faulty switch for front doorjamb causes the dome light to stay on and prevents the alarm from arming. • Ignition key can be removed when vehicle is in gear. • Defective ignition lock cylinders wreak havoc with accessories (radio, power windows, AC, etc.). • Ignition key may bind in the ignition's Run position. • Excessive front brake noise or pulsation. • Knocking/rattling from front of floor to front of dash area. • Loose rear exterior door panels. • Vehicle runs out of fuel while fuel gauge reads one-quarter full. • Automatic transmission whine. **1998**—Dozens of bulletins target a plethora of rattles, whistles, pops, clicks, knocking, and grinding noises. • Sunroof, footwell, and trunk water leaks are also common problems addressed in a variety of service bulletins. • Excessive vehicle vibration. • Noisy window regulator. • Premature corrosion near door weather strip. • Loss of AC vent airflow. • Reducing AC odours. • Power steering pump drive shaft seal leak. • Intermittent no-start. • Transaxle whine in second gear. • Rear brake noise and pulsation countermeasures. **1999**—Harsh shifting. • Excessive exhaust system noise. • Steering column popping. • Rattle, pop, or clicking noise from front of vehicle. • AC noise (hissing). • Clunking noise in front side door when windows are operated. • Troubleshooting chronic short circuits. • Water leak onto headliner and/or left footwell area and rear luggage compartment. • Excessive vibration at cruising speed.

Safety summary/Recalls: All models/years—Owners say horn isn't well positioned for emergency use and isn't sensitive enough. NHTSA probe of faulty seat recliners on 1994–95 models. **1995**—Reports of stuck accelerators. • Plastic fuel line leaks fuel. • Airbag failed to deploy. • Seatbelt failed to restrain driver in collision. • Gear lever slips out of gear and is hard to put into Reverse. • Manual transmission jumps out of third and fifth gear. • Brake rotor warpage and failures. • Steering wheel shakes uncontrollably at 65 km/h. • Sudden head gasket failure caused other engine components to self-destruct. • Prematurely worn engine timing chain. • AC fan knob broke in half. • Windshield wiper nut fell out, causing the wiper to fail. **1996**—Airbag failed to deploy. • Rack-and-pinion steering gear failure. • Frequent brake failures. • Firestone tire blowouts. • Inadequate defrosting. • Engine suddenly accelerates to 3500 rpm at idle or when driving. • Engine suddenly stalls and can't be restarted. • Car slips out of fifth gear. **1997**—Steering wheel came apart while car was being driven. • Several complaints of total loss of steering control. • Engine suddenly loses power while cruising on the highway. • In a rear-end collision, driver's seatback broke, causing serious injuries. **Recalls: All models: 1995**—In models with automatic transmissions, it is possible to shift from Park with key removed or to remove key when lever is in gear. **1996**—Some welds between roof and reinforcement panels on the wagon may not meet specifications. **1996–97**—Horn may not operate, may self activate, or can cause a fire; dealer will replace the horn assembly. • Manual steering could separate under load.

Secret Warranties/Service Tips

All models: 1991—Engine misses, surges, or backfires may be caused by a poor ground at the electronic distributorless ignition switch (DIS). Install another DIS module. • Headlights that stay on when the switch is turned off can be fixed by installing an upgraded switch. • Wind noise from the front and rear doors may be caused by insufficient sealing under the mirror patch gasket, missing sealer at certain locations (for example, the door frame to door assembly at the beltline), insufficient contact of the secondary seals to door openings, or the glass run channels not sealing to the glass at the upper corners. **1991–92**—Owners have reported excessive noise and vibration levels coming from the steering wheel, seat, and floor pan. Saturn officials say that the noise and vibration could be caused by the following: pre-loaded powertrain mounts (1991); a pre-loaded engine strut cradle bracket (1992); improperly positioned or worn exhaust system isolators and muffler band clamp/block (1991–92); lower cooling module grommets and improper positioning of wiring harnesses and upper cooling system module grommets (1991–92); improper routing of AC hoses or hood release cable and air inlet snorkel (1991–92); debris in accessory drive belt pulleys (1991); improper adjustment of hood stop(s) (1991–92); PCV or brake-booster check valve noise (1991); DOHC (LLO) automatic transaxle mount assembly replacement (1991); or a malfunctioning engine, electrical system, or fuel system (1991–92). **1991–94**—Rough running or surging after a cold start may signal the need to clean carbon or fuel deposits from the engine's intake valves. • The many causes of hard-to-crank windows are covered in TSB #94-T-19. • Inoperative electric door locks may have been shorted by water contamination. The design and positioning of the relay for the power door lock allows this to occur. • Whistling noises are also treated in two different bulletins published in June and October 1994. **1991–95**—Erratic cruise control operation can be corrected by replacing the cruise control module assembly. • If the engine stalls within five minutes of starting or when coming to a stop, or is difficult to restart, the oil viscosity or engine's hydraulic lifters may be at fault. • Engine squealing after a cold start can be corrected by installing an upgraded belt idler pulley assembly. **1991–97**—Engines that run hot or have coolant mixed in the engine oil probably have a defective engine cylinder—a factory-related goof, according to a GM service bulletin. As a partial response to angry Saturn owners, GM has set up a "goodwill" warranty to pay for head gasket repairs for 6 years/160,000 km on all 1994–96 models. Owners of model years not covered will get their refunds from small claims court.

Saturn Corporation
100 Saturn Parkway
PO Box 1000
Spring Hill, TN 37174-1500

June, 1999

Dear Saturn Owner,

We are writing to let you know of a Special Policy relating to 1994 through 1996 Saturn vehicles equipped with 1.9L Single Over Head Cam (SOHC) engines.

Certain Saturn Vehicles equipped with 1.9L SOHC engines may develop a crack internal to the cylinder head. Early evidence of this would be abnormal discoloration within the coolant reservoir, and/or the engine may run hot.

As a result, this Special Policy provides cylinder head coverage for a period of six years from the date the vehicle was originally placed in service, or 100,000 miles, whichever occurs first. The policy covers both the original owner, and any subsequent owners for the six-year/100,000 mile duration. Please keep this letter with your other important glovebox literature for further reference.

If your vehicle should develop a cylinder head crack within six-years/100,000 miles, whichever comes first, Saturn will repair your vehicle at no charge. A Saturn Retailer must perform repairs qualifying for this special coverage, and the time needed to replace a cylinder head is approximately ten (10) hours. Due to scheduling and processing time, your Retailer may need to keep your vehicle overnight.

You will be eligible for reimbursement if you have already paid for some or all of the cost to have the cylinder head replaced, and your vehicle was within the six-year/100,000 mile parameter at the time of repair.

Saturn Corporation
99P01

This letter sets the latest benchmark as to how long GM feels its engine head gaskets should last. Bring it to court with you, if polite negotiations fail.

• If your Saturn runs out of fuel while the fuel gauge reads one-quarter full, it's likely you have a plugged EVAP canister vent which should be repaired free of charge under the emissions warranty. • A whistle or groaning noise heard at highway speeds may be caused by the radio antenna mast. • Excessive front brake noise or pulsation requires the installation of upgraded brake pads, according to TSB #96-T-40A. **1991–98**—Excessive rear brake noise or pulsation requires the installation of upgraded rear brake pads, according to TSB #855001. • Water leaks into the front footwell and at the front upper door frame are treated in depth in TSB #481503R. **1992**—An engine that stalls, hesitates, or surges during light acceleration may require new PCM calibrations. • Harsh Reverse engagement can also be corrected with new PCM calibrations. • Engine rattling can be fixed by changing the motor mounts. **1993–94**—A popping noise coming from the base of the left-hand A-pillar, hinge pillar, and engine compartment is caused by a slight flexing in the area where the three are joined together. **1993–97**—Troubleshooting tips are available on diagnosing delayed or harsh automatic transmission shifting into Reverse. **1993–99**—A rotten-egg odour coming from the exhaust is likely the result of a malfunctioning catalytic converter, which you can have replaced free of charge under GM's emissions warranty. • Paint delamination, peeling, or fading (see Part Two). **1994**—White Saturns may have yellow stains or spotting along the fenders, fender extension, or quarter panel. • A Saturn equipped with a manual transmission may have the transaxle stuck in gear due to a defective shift control housing. • Excessive vibration between 77 and 87 km/h may be corrected by installing a powertrain damper kit. **1994–95**—Excessive engine knocking can be corrected by changing the clearance between the piston pin and connecting rod bushing. **1994–98**—Loss of airflow from the AC vents is likely due to the evaporator freezing; re-adjust the compressor. **1995–97**—Electrical accessories may lose power after the car is started or while it's on the road. GM blames the problem on a defective ignition lock cylinder. **1996–97**—If your security alarm won't work properly or your dome light won't go out, GM suggests you change the doorjamb switches. • Water leaks into the headliner on cars equipped with a sunroof require new drain hoses or better sealing. **1996–98**—A knock or rattle heard from the front of the vehicle when decelerating may be caused by a wiring harness short circuit. If the same noise is heard at all times, you may need to replace the clutch disc and the clutch cover. • A no-start condition accompanied by electrical malfunctions may be caused by a shorted instrument panel wire harness (see bulletin below).

Vehicle: All Technical Service Bulletins
Eng No Crnks, MIL/ABS Lght On, Prk Imp/Fuel Gge/Spkr inop
BULLETIN NO.: 98-T-22
ISSUE DATE: July, 1998
GROUP/SEQ. NO.: Electrical-03
CORPORATION NO.:887202
SUBJECT:
Engine will not Crank, MIL and ABS Light On, Park Lamps Inoperative, Fuel Gauge
Inoperative, and/or Radio Speaker Inoperative (Repair Wire Harness)
MODELS AFFECTED:
1996-1998 Saturns equipped with MP2/MP3 manual transaxles
CONDITION:
The customer may comment that on occasion, one or more of the following conditions
may have occurred:
• Engine will not crank
• Malfunction indicator lamp (MIL) (SERVICE ENGINE SOON lamp) On with or without
  inoperative fuel gauge
• Anti-Lock brake system (ABS) light on
• Park lamps inoperative
• One or more of the radio speakers inoperative
CAUSE
The cause of the above conditions may be the Instrument Panel wire harness coming into
contact with the clutch pedal pivot bolt/clip causing a short to ground.

1996–99—A noisy window regulator may need a new counter-balance spring. • Water leaks into the rear luggage compartment area need the body seam sealer gaps plugged. **1997–98**—A leaking automatic transaxle case assembly should be replaced with an upgraded assembly. **1996–2001 S-series sedans and 1997–2001 S-series coupes equipped with sunroofs**—Water leaks onto headliner are likely caused by a faulty sunroof or plugged drain hole grommets.

Saturn S-series Profile

	1992	1993	1994	1995	1996	1997	1998	1999
Cost Price ($)								
SL	9,895	10,995	11,595	12,395	12,998	13,948	14,188	13,488
SL1	11,080	12,350	12,825	13,795	14,398	14,948	15,118	14,398
SL2	13,865	15,095	14,510	15,495	16,148	16,758	17,128	17,183
SC	14,620	15,840	13,895	14,795	15,348	16,028	16,418	16,618
Used Values ($)								
SL ↑	3,000	3,500	4,500	5,000	6,000	7,000	8,000	9,000
SL ↓	2,500	3,000	4,000	4,500	5,000	6,000	7,000	8,000
SL1 ↑	3,500	4,000	4,500	5,500	6,500	7,500	9,000	10,500
SL1 ↓	3,000	3,500	4,000	5,000	5,500	6,500	8,000	9,500
SL2 ↑	4,500	5,000	6,000	7,000	8,500	10,000	11,000	12,500
SL2 ↓	3,500	4,500	5,000	6,000	7,500	8,500	9,500	11,000
SC ↑	4,500	5,000	6,000	7,000	9,000	10,000	11,500	13,000
SC ↓	4,000	4,500	5,500	6,000	8,000	8,500	10,000	11,500
Extended Warranty		Y	Y	Y	Y	Y	Y	Y
Secret Warranty		N	Y	Y	Y	Y	Y	Y

Reliability	②	②	②	②	②	③	④
Air conditioning	②	②	②	③	④	④	④
Auto. transmission	②	②	②	②	③	③	③
Body integrity	❶	❶	❶	❶	❶	❶	❶
Braking system	②	②	②	②	②	③	③
Electrical system	②	②	②	②	②	③	③
Engines	②	②	②	②	②	③	③
Exhaust/Converter	②	③	③	④	④	④	⑤
Fuel system	②	②	③	③	④	④	④
Ignition system	②	②	②	②	②	③	③
Rust/Paint	②	②	②	②	②	③	③
Steering	③	③	④	④	④	⑤	⑤
Suspension	③	③	④	④	④	④	④
Crash Safety							
SL2	④	④	④	④	④	④	⑤
Side Impact	—	—	—	—	—	③	③

GENERAL MOTORS/SUZUKI

Firefly, Metro, Sprint/Swift

Rating: Above Average (1995–99); Average (1990–94); Below Average (1987–89). Stay away from AC-equipped versions, unless you want to invest in an AC repair facility. Look at the redesigned 1995 version for better quality, a new body style, standard dual airbags, and a peppier 4-cylinder engine. The convertible version packs plenty of fun and performance into a reasonably priced subcompact body. **Maintenance/Repair costs:** Average. **Parts:** Expensive; sometimes drivetrain and body components are back-ordered several weeks.

Strengths and weaknesses: These tiny, economical 3- and 4-cylinder front-wheel-drive hatchback econoboxes, equipped with either a manual or an automatic transmission, offer acceptable performance and economy for urban dwellers. In fact, these little squirts should be considered primarily city vehicles due to their small size, small tires, low ground clearance, and average high-speed handling. Interior garnishing is decent but plain, and there's plenty of room for two passengers, with four fitting in without too much discomfort. The turbocharged convertible model is an excellent choice for high-performance thrills in an easy-to-handle ragtop.

Mechanically speaking, the GM/Suzuki partnership hasn't hurt quality control—though it hasn't helped either. Trouble spots on pre-'95 models: excessive oil consumption after the fourth year of service; automatic transmission and differential failures around 80,000 km; electrical system shorts; a faulty AC and cooling system (fogging of the side windows and windshield due to inadequate heat distribution is a common complaint); premature brake, clutch, and exhaust system wearout; and minor fuel-supply malfunctions. Body construction is the pits on early models.

Owners of 1990–94 models report that hatches vibrate when windows are open, the rear hatch seems to want to open on its own, pushing buttons for the lights causes wipers to fly off the dashboard, and fuel economy is often exaggerated by dealers. Front metallic brake pads are noisy and the front discs warp easily. Occasionally the third gear is hard to engage, and the fuel-injection system performs poorly. Owners also point out that the tiny radiator can't stand up to the rigours of northern climates. If it's not checked, the cooling system will eventually fail, causing great damage to the aluminum engine.

The cars were redesigned for the 1995 model year and were built with more care. Additionally, they gained more horsepower, and have improved road feel, a more comfortable ride, quieter operation, and more cabin space. Remaining problems on the 1995–98 models are premature front-brake wear; electrical system and AC malfunctions; and sub-par body assembly highlighted by paint peeling and discolouration, early rusting, and poorly fitted body panels, leading to rattles and air and water leaks.

Safety summary/Recalls: All models/years—Side window defogging is slow and sometimes inadequate. • Driver's window continually pops out of its mount. • A Maritime couple reported that their '91 Firefly suddenly careened out of control after the "control" bar broke. **1999**—Airbags failed to deploy. • Airbags deployed at very low collision speed. • Loose fuel hose caused fuel leak. • Premature wearout of front brake pads. • Tires aren't very durable. • Cracked engine head gasket. • Inaccurate speedometer; dealer says it can't be repaired. **Recalls: All models: 1989–91**—Takata seatbelts will be replaced. **1989–93**—Hood may fly up when car is in motion. **1995**—Faulty rear brake drums may lead to sudden wheel separation. **Metro: 1995**—In hatchbacks without ABS, faulty rear brake drums could cause wheel separation. **1997**—Dealers will replace the shifter assembly on the automatic transmission because the shift lever can move too easily out of Park.

Secret Warranties/Service Tips

All models: 1989–92—Stalling or loss of power shortly after starting may be due to high pressure in the hydraulic lifter assemblies. **1991–92**—Excessive vehicle vibration when the vehicle is in Reverse is most likely due to poor insulation between the engine/transaxle assembly and the vehicle's chassis. Install upgraded engine mounts. **1993–99**—Troubleshooting tips on correcting condensation in exterior lights. • Paint delamination, peeling, or fading (see Part Two). **1994**—Vehicles that won't start usually have defective oxygen sensors. • When the battery runs down in wintertime, it can set off the car alarm. Buy a heavy-duty battery. **1994–98**—GM outlines which conditions require new or refaced brake rotors. **1997–2000**—Reasons why speedometer gives inaccurate readings. **1999–2000**—Engine overheating and/or loss of coolant may be do to a faulty radiator filler neck or cap.

Firefly, Metro, Sprint/Swift Profile

	1992	1993	1994	1995	1996	1997	1998	1999
Cost Price ($)								
Firefly, Sprint	7,765	—	9,145	10,395	10,995	11,495	11,680	10,690
Metro	6,999	7,995	8,995	10,395	10,995	11,495	11,680	10,690
Swift	7,495	8,537	8,995	10,495	10,995	10,995	11,495	11,595
Used Values ($)								
Firefly, Sprint ↑	2,000	—	3,500	4,000	5,000	5,500	6,500	8,000
Firefly, Sprint ↓	1,500	—	3,000	3,500	4,500	5,000	6,000	7,000
Metro ↑	2,000	3,000	3,500	4,000	5,000	5,500	6,500	8,000
Metro ↓	1,500	2,500	3,000	3,500	4,500	5,000	6,000	7,000
Swift ↑	2,200	2,500	3,000	4,500	5,500	6,000	7,000	8,500
Swift ↓	1,800	2,000	2,500	4,000	5,000	5,000	5,500	7,500
Extended Warranty	Y	Y	N	N	N	N	N	N
Secret Warranty	N	Y	Y	Y	Y	Y	Y	N
Reliability	❷	❷	❷	❷	③	④	④	④
Air conditioning	❷	❷	❷	❷	❷	❷	❷	③
Auto. transmission	❶	❷	❷	❷	③	④	④	④
Body integrity	❶	❷	❷	❷	❷	❷	③	③
Braking system	❷	❷	❷	❷	❷	③	③	③
Electrical system	❷	❷	❷	❷	③	③	③	③
Engines	❷	❷	❷	❷	❷	④	⑤	⑤
Exhaust/Converter	❷	❷	❷	❷	③	④	⑤	⑤
Fuel system	❷	❷	③	③	④	④	⑤	⑤
Ignition system	③	④	④	③	④	④	④	④
Rust/Paint	❶	❷	❷	❷	❷	❷	③	④
Steering	④	④	⑤	⑤	⑤	⑤	⑤	⑤
Suspension	④	④	⑤	⑤	⑤	⑤	⑤	⑤
Crash Safety	③	③	③	④	④	④	—	—

HONDA

Civic, del Sol (CRX)

Rating: Recommended (1996–99); Above Average (1992–95); Average (1984–91). Depreciation is so minimal that, if you want to get a good buy at a fair price, the 1993–95s are your best bet. Keep in mind these well-made small cars may have serious safety defects that are not completely covered by recalls. These include airbags that fail to deploy or deploy with such force they cause severe injuries, ABS brake failures and constant rotor and pad maintenance, sudden acceleration, original equipment tire failures, and considerable instability on wet roads. **Maintenance/Repair costs:** Average. Repairs can be carried out by independent garages, but the 16-valve engine's complexity means that dealer servicing is a must. To avoid costly engine repairs, owners must check the engine timing belt every 3 years/60,000 km and replace it ($300) every 100,000 km. **Parts:** Parts are a bit more expensive than most other cars in this class, but they aren't hard to find.

Strengths and weaknesses: The quintessential econobox, Civics have distinguished themselves by providing sports-car acceleration and handling with excellent fuel economy and quality control that, despite its shortcomings, is far better than what American automakers can deliver. Other advantages: a roomy, practical trunk and simple maintenance.

Some Civic disadvantages: power steering isn't offered with the manual 5-speed transmission; there's no ABS available on many early models; you won't find much backseat head room; engine noise may seem excessive when under load; and the Civic's high resale value means bargains are rare, unless you go at least 3–4 years into the past where the best performance/price/reliability combination may be found.

Dropped after the '91 model year, the CRX is a sportier version of the Civic, equipped with a more refined 1.5L and 1.6L engine and stiffer suspension. It gives improved handling at the expense of fuel economy, interior space, and a comfortable ride, and requires valve adjustments every 30,000 km. The CRX's '93 del Sol replacement was a cheapened spin-off that carried over the CRX's disadvantages, without the high-performance thrills.

Si models are Honda's factory hot rods (the Acura 1.6 EL is an Si clone) that have been around for a decade and provide lots of high-performance thrills, without the bills. Equipped with four-wheel disc brakes, the Si's mediocre braking and its lack of low-end torque are the car's only flaws.

1984–91 Civics suffer from failing camshafts, crankshafts, and head gaskets, and prematurely worn piston rings. The 12-valve engine is prone to valve problems and is costly to repair. Early fuel-injection units were also problematic until the system was redesigned in 1988. Manual transmission shifter bushings need frequent replacement and the automatic version needs careful attention once the 5-year/150,000 km point has been reached.

What are minor body faults with recent models turn into major rust problems with older Civics, where simple surface rust rapidly turns into perforations. The underbody is also prone to corrosion, which leads to severe structural damage that compromises safety. The fuel tank, front suspension, and steering components, along with body attachment points, should be examined carefully in any Civic more than a decade old. Since 1988, Hondas have been much more resistant to rusting, and overall body construction has been vastly improved. All hatchbacks let in too much wind/road noise due to poor sound insulation. Owners complain of water leaking into the engine compartment and trunk area where suspension component mountings and trunk wheelwells quickly become rust-cankered.

The 1988 redesign improved handling and increased interior room, but engine head gasket failures on non-VTEC engines became a problem through 1999, although the following bulletin only includes 1988–95 models:

Head Gasket Leaks.
97-047
November 10, 1997
Applies To: 1988 - 95 Civic - All, except VTEC
Head Gasket Leaks
(Supercedes 97-047, dated September 29, 1997)
PROBLEM
The head gasket leaks oil externally or allows coolant into the combustion chambers.
CORRECTIVE ACTION
Install the new style cylinder head gasket and the new head bolts in the Cylinder Gasket Kit listed under PARTS INFORMATION. Use the cylinder head bolt torque sequence described in this bulletin.
Out of warranty:
Any repair performed after warranty expiration may be eligible for goodwill consideration by the District Service Manager or your Zone Office. You must request consideration, and get a decision, before starting work.

The repair is free, if the client squawks.

On 1988–91 models, there isn't a great deal of torque with the 1.6L engine below 3500 rpm, and serious powertrain, brake, electrical-system, and body problems (present since the car's debut) continue to appear. The front brakes continue to wear out quickly and are often noisy when applied, causing excessive steering wheel vibration. Premature constant-velocity-joint and boot wear on all cars is another problem area that needs careful inspection before purchasing. The rack-and-pinion steering assembly often needs replacement around the five-year mark.

The 1992 Civic redesign axed the wagon, added standard driver-side airbags, and offered upgraded engines to some models. As for performance and other features: EX and Si acceleration is smooth and sprightly, but CX and VX acceleration is painfully slow. The four-door models ride extremely well and all models exhibit nimble handling and good road holding under dry conditions. Unfortunately, the hatchback offers little rear-seat room, insufficient cargo space, and allows too much engine noise to intrude into the interior.

These models continued to be both more rugged and more reliable than the competition, yet they too have their faults. As an addendum to the safety problems mentioned earlier, owners report engine head gasket and crankshaft failures, transmission slippage, frequent and expensive brake repairs (rotor warpage, pad replacement, and defective master cylinder), AC failures, chronic water leaks, and early exhaust system rust-out.

1993 models returned practically unchanged, except for an optional passenger side airbag offered with the EX. The same airbag was added as a standard feature on all '94 models, in addition to 14-inch tires for the LX, and greater availability of optional ABS. The '95 models remained unchanged.

The '96 model redesign added standard dual airbags, standard ABS for EX sedans, additional length and soundproofing, and upgraded engines throughout the model lineup. Outward visibility is much improved through thinner roof pillars and a larger rear window. Cargo capacity was also expanded with split folding rear seatbacks. 1997–99 models have remained unchanged, except for larger 14-inch wheels, a slight restyling, and manual seat-height adjusters.

Quality control is still better than the competition; however, decade-old safety and performance problems continue to appear year after year. Owners complain of a constantly lit Check Engine light, faulty engine computer module and oxygen sensor, early replacement of the crankshaft pulley and timing belt, transmission and electrical failures, expensive front brake maintenance caused by warped rotors and prematurely worn pads, AC malfunctions, clogged AC drain pooling water on front passenger floor area, a clunky suspension, windshield air leaks and noise, hard-to-access horn buttons, windows that fall off their tracks, side mirrors that vibrate excessively, headlights that can't be focused properly and are prone to water leaks, gas-tank fumes that leak into the interior, and (are you ready for this?) premature rusting, uneven paint application, and *paint delamination.*

Yes, my little Civic *aficionados*, a few owners of '98 models have already reported that the paint on hood and roof areas turns a chalky white colour.

Safety summary/Recalls: All models: 1995–99—Spoiler restricts rear visibility and large rear view mirror restricts forward visibility for tall drivers. • Civic owners report numerous safety defects that include airbags that fail to deploy, deploy inadvertently, or deploy with such force they cause severe injuries. • Ball joints on these vehicles don't have a castilated nut to secure the ball in position; the nut can back off and the ball pulls out of the steering arm. • Other safety-related complaints: dangerous instability on wet roads, sudden acceleration or stalling, faulty cruise control, ABS brake failures, constant rotor and pad replacement, defective automatic transmission, transmission suddenly jumping into Reverse, original equipment tire failures, hood and trunk lids that come crashing down, inoperative door locks and headlights, cracked windshields, and interior lights that suddenly go out. **Recalls: All models: 1992–95**—Hood could fly up. **1994**—Passenger-side airbag module may carry a defective inflator. **1996**—Faulty brake-booster vacuum hose. **1996–98**—Passenger-side airbag may not deploy properly. **1997–98**—Floormat may prevent accelerator pedal from returning to the idle position.

Secret Warranties/Service Tips

All models: 1988–90—A clicking noise heard while making a left or right turn may be caused by a worn outboard drive shaft joint. **1988–2000**—A rear suspension clunk can be silenced by replacing the rear trailing arm bushing. **1991–99**—Most Honda TSBs allow for special warranty consideration on a "goodwill" basis even after the warranty has expired or the car has changed hands. Referring to this euphemism will increase your chances of getting some kind of refund for repairs that are obviously related to a factory defect. **1992**—A growling noise coming from the wheel area may mean that water has entered the wheel bearing through the hubcap and has damaged the bearing. • A steering wheel shake, or body vibration when braking, may indicate that the rear brake drum hub is crowned, causing excessive runout when the wheel nuts are torqued. Other factors could be a bent rear wheel, over-torqued wheel nuts, or excessive rust buildup on the brake rotors. **1992–95**—Power-steering pump fluid leakage requires a new O-ring, which may be eligible for "goodwill" consideration, says Honda. **1992–97**—An abnormally long crank time before the car starts may be caused by a leaking check valve inside the fuel pump. • Water leaking into the footwell from under the corner of the dash can be stopped by applying sealer to the seam where the side panel joins the bulkhead. **1994–97**—If the AC doesn't blow cold air, Honda will replace both the evaporator and the receiver/dryer free of charge or at a discount (see TSB #97-031 on page 242). • When operating a manual or power-assisted front window, the rear edge of the glass comes out of the channel (see TSB #97-060 on page 243). **1995–97**—A wind whistle at the top of the windshield can be silenced by applying additional sealer. **1996**—A clunking noise in the front suspension can be fixed by installing upgraded upper arm flange bolts. **1996–97**—In a settlement with the U.S. Environmental Protection Agency, Honda paid fines totaling $17.1 million and extended its emissions warranty on 1.6 million 1995–97 models to 14 years or 150,000 miles. This means that costly engine components and exhaust system parts like catalytic converters will be replaced free of charge, as long as the 14-year/150,000 mile limit hasn't been exceeded. Additionally, the automaker will provide a full engine check and emissions-related repairs at 50,000 to 75,000 miles and will give free tune-ups at 75,000 to 150,000 miles. Honda will spend an estimated $250 million (U.S.) on free checkups, repairs, and tune-ups. The story of the settlement was first reported on page 6 of the June 15, 1998, edition of *Automotive News*. Canadian owners may wish to use this settlement as leverage for free repairs in Canada, or use the full terms of the settlement when visiting the States. One thing is certain, neither Transport Canada nor Environment Canada are sufficiently enthused to render any assistance. **1996–98**—Windows that bind or fall out of their run channels need new run channels. • A poorly performing AC may need a new condenser fan motor and shroud. • An exhaust rattle or buzz can be silenced by replacing the heat shield or exhaust pipe. **1996–2000**—Fuse box cover may fall off. **1997–98**—Intermittent changes in the headlight and dash light intensity may be caused by a faulty voltage regulator. **1998**—Power door locks that intermittently lock themselves need a new control unit. **1998–2000**—Rear shelf rattling or buzzing. **1999–2000**—Coolant may leak from the reservoir cap outlet. Popping noise or vibration from driver's footrest.

Civic, del Sol (CRX) Profile

	1992	1993	1994	1995	1996	1997	1998	1999
Cost Price ($)								
Civic	9,112	10,395	10,595	11,495	12,995	13,495	14,000	14,200
Si	13,320	14,995	16,595	17,495	17,895	17,995	18,300	18,800
CRX/del Sol	—	16,795	18,595	20,295	20,495	20,995	—	—
Used Values ($)								
Civic ↑	3,500	4,500	5,500	6,500	8,000	9,500	10,500	12,000
Civic ↓	3,000	3,500	4,500	5,000	7,000	8,500	9,500	10,500
Si ↑	5,500	6,500	7,500	9,500	11,000	13,000	14,000	15,500
Si ↓	4,500	5,500	6,500	8,000	10,000	12,000	13,000	14,000
CRX/del Sol ↑	—	7,000	8,000	10,500	12,500	14,500	—	—
CRX/del Sol ↓	—	6,000	7,000	9,000	11,000	13,000	—	—
Extended Warranty	N	N	N	N	N	N	N	N
Secret Warranty	Y	Y	Y	Y	Y	Y	Y	Y
Reliability	③	③	③	③	③	④	④	④
Air conditioning	❷	❷	❷	❷	❷	③	③	④
Auto. transmission	③	③	③	③	③	③	③	③
Body integrity	❷	❷	③	③	③	③	④	④
Braking system	❷	❷	❷	❷	❷	③	③	④
Electrical system	③	③	③	③	③	③	③	③
Engines	③	③	③	③	③	③	④	⑤
Exhaust/Converter	❷	❷	③	③	④	⑤	⑤	⑤
Fuel system	③	③	④	④	④	④	⑤	⑤
Ignition system	③	③	④	④	④	④	⑤	⑤
Rust/Paint	❷	③	③	③	⑤	⑤	④	③
Steering	③	③	④	④	④	④	⑤	⑤
Suspension	③	③	④	④	④	④	⑤	⑤
Crash Safety								
Civic 2d	④	—	③	③	③	④	④	④
Civic 4d	④	—	③	③	③	④	④	④

Side Impact

Civic 2d	❷	—	—	—	—	—	—	❷
Civic 4d	③	—	—	—	—	—	③	③

HYUNDAI

Accent

Rating: Above Average (1995–99). Lots of standard features.
Maintenance/Repair costs: Average. Dealer servicing has been substandard in the past. Hyundai says that the timing chain should be replaced every 100,000 km. **Parts:** Reasonably priced and easily found.

Strengths and weaknesses: An upgraded Excel masquerading as a different car, this front-drive, 4-cylinder sedan retains most of the Excel's underpinnings, while dropping the Mitsubishi powerplant in favour of a new home-grown 1.5L 4-cylinder. It's built better than the old Excel, though: upgraded, smoother-shifting automatic transmission; stiffer, better-performing suspension; stronger and quieter-running engine; optional dual airbags; and ABS.

Excels have always had a checkered reliability history, so the Accent has a lot of bad karma to overcome, such as mediocre body assembly and poorly applied paint. Past problem areas include the engine cooling system and cylinder head gaskets (engine overheating); engine sputters, and Check Engine light constantly comes on; transmission, wheel bearings, fuel system, and electrical components; as well as premature front-brake wear and excessive noise when braking.

Safety summary/Recalls: All models/years—Horn controls may be hard to find in an emergency, rear head restraints appear to be too low to protect occupants, and rear seatbelt configuration complicates the installation of a child safety seat. **1995–97**—NHTSA believes airbags may deploy with too much force; seven children have been killed. **1998–99**—Airbags failed to deploy, or deploy inadvertently, headlights flicker when turning and high beam is inadequate. • Gearshift jumps out of Reverse. • Engine control monitor melted. • Fuel gauge failures. **Recalls: All models: 1995**—The ECM wiring harness may short on vehicles equipped with a manual transaxle. **1995–97**—Corroded coil spring may break. **1996–97**—Faulty wiper motor.

Secret Warranties/Service Tips

All models/years—Tips on troubleshooting excessive brake noise. • Apparent slow acceleration upon cold starts is dismissed as normal. • A new AC "refresher" will control AC odours. **All models: 1995–98**—Harsh shifting may be fixed by installing an upgraded Transaxle Control Module

(TCM). • Clutch drag may be caused by a restriction in the hydraulic line from grease used during the assembly of the clutch master assembly.

Accent Profile

	1995	1996	1997	1998	1999
Cost Price ($)					
L	9,295	10,495	10,995	11,295	11,565
GL 4d	10,995	12,195	12,695	12,995	12,995
Used Values ($)					
L ↑	3,500	4,500	5,500	7,000	8,000
L ↓	3,000	3,500	4,500	5,500	7,000
GL 4d ↑	4,500	5,500	7,000	8,000	9,000
GL 4d ↓	4,000	4,500	5,500	7,500	8,000
Extended Warranty	Y	Y	Y	Y	N
Secret Warranty	N	N	N	N	N
Reliability	④	④	④	⑤	⑤
Crash Safety	—	③	③	③	③

Elantra

Rating: Above Average (1996–99); Average (1991–95). Try to find a '98 with an unexpired comprehensive 5-year/100,000 km base warranty. There's a $1,000–$3,500 difference between the high-end and entry-level models. Frequent automatic transmission failures require an extended powertrain warranty. **Maintenance/Repair costs:** Average. Dealer servicing has been substandard in the past. Hyundai says that the timing chain should be replaced every 100,000 km. **Parts:** Reasonably priced and easily found.

Strengths and weaknesses: This conservatively styled "high-end" sedan is only marginally larger than the Excel, but its overall reliability is much better. It's a credible alternative to the Toyota Corolla, Nissan Sentra, and Saturn. In fact, the redesigned 1996–97 versions actually narrow the handling and performance gap with the Honda Civic. The 16-valve 1.6L 4-cylinder is smooth, efficient, and adequate when mated to the 5-speed manual transmission. It's not very quiet, however. The smooth ride causes excessive body lean when cornering, but overall handling is fairly good, due mainly to the Elantra's longer wheelbase and more sophisticated suspension.

The 4-speed automatic transmission robs the base engine of at least 10 horses. Brakes are adequate, though sometimes difficult to modulate. Conservative styling makes the Elantra look a bit like an underfed Accord, but there's plenty of room for four average-sized occupants. Tall drivers might find the driver's seat rearward travel insufficient, which makes head room a bit too tight.

1996–99 Elantras are the better buy due to their additional interior room, improved performance and handling, and quieter-running engine. Still, passing power with the automatic gearbox is perpetually unimpressive and the trunk's narrow opening makes for difficult loading.

Surprisingly for a Hyundai, owners report few serious defects. Nevertheless, be on the lookout for body deficiencies (fit, finish, and assembly), paint cracking, harsh shifting with both the manual (grinding) and the automatic transmission (slippage), engine misfire and oil leaks, hard starting, and brake pedal pulsation defects.

Technical service bulletins: All models: 1995—The exhaust system releases a rotten-egg odour. • Rear suspension squeaking noises. • An inaccurate fuel gauge. • Trunk water leaks and troubleshooting tips for locating and plugging other interior water leaks. **1996–97**—Automatic transmission won't engage Overdrive. • Clutch pedal squeaking. • Tapping noise coming from the passenger-side dash panel/engine compartment area. • Exhaust system buzz. • Improved shifting into all gears. • Improved shifting into Reverse. • Clutch drag. **1998–99**— Automatic transmission oil leakage.

Safety summary/Recalls: All models: 1998–99—Airbags failed to deploy. • Faulty speed sensor. • Passenger shoulder belt locks up and traps occupant. • Cracked transmission case. • Low beam headlights give poor illumination; weak. • Poorly designed jack. **Recalls: All models: 1992–95**—Defective rear suspension trailing arm bolts. **1994–95**—Driver-side airbag could be defective or the warning light could illuminate unnecessarily. **1996–97**—A faulty wiper motor will be replaced.

Secret Warranties/Service Tips

All models/years—Hyundai has a new brake pad kit (#58101-28A00) that the company says will eliminate squeaks and squeals during light brake application. Hyundai also suggests that you replace the oil pump assembly if the engine rpm increases as the automatic transmission engages abruptly during a cold start. • A harsh downshift when decelerating may require a free transmission replacement, says bulletin #98-40-001. • Bulletin #98-50-001 provides information regarding some brake noises and appropriate services for each condition. **All models: 1992**—A harsh shift when coming to a stop or upon acceleration could be due to an improperly adjusted accelerator switch TCU. • Oil leaking from between the oil filter and mounting bracket could be caused by an overly wide mounting surface on the bracket. Correct this by replacing the bracket. **1992–94**—Hyundai has a field fix for manual transaxle gear clash/grind (TSB #9440-004). • The difficult-to-engage Reverse gear needs an upgraded part. **1994**—Rear speaker whine can be stopped by installing an improved noise reduction filter. **1996**—A cold exhaust system buzz can be silenced by installing a sub-muffler resonator. • Improved shifting into all gears can be accomplished by installing an upgraded transaxle control module (TCM). **1996–97**—Tips on eliminating clutch drag and pedal squeaking are offered. **1996–98**—DOHC engine timing chain noise repair. **1996–99**—Transmission oil leakage likely caused by a defective oil pump housing seal.

Elantra Profile

	1992	1993	1994	1995	1996	1997	1998	1999
Cost Price ($)								
GL	10,795	11,295	11,795	12,295	13,495	13,995	14,295	14,595
GLS	11,995	12,795	13,695	14,195	16,745	17,245	17,545	17,695
Used Values ($)								
GL ↑	3,000	3,500	4,000	5,000	6,000	8,000	9,000	10,500
GL ↓	2,500	3,000	3,500	4,000	5,000	6,500	8,000	9,000
GLS ↑	4,000	4,500	5,500	7,000	9,000	10,500	11,500	12,500
GLS ↓	3,500	4,000	4,500	6,000	8,000	9,500	10,500	11,000
Extended Warranty	Y	Y	Y	N	N	N	N	N
Secret Warranty	N	N	N	Y	Y	Y	Y	Y
Reliability	③	③	③	③	④	④	④	④
Air conditioning	③	③	③	④	④	④	⑤	⑤
Auto. transmission	❷	❷	❷	❷	❷	❷	③	③
Body integrity	❷	❷	❷	❷	❷	③	③	③
Braking system	❷	❷	③	③	③	③	③	③
Electrical system	❷	❷	❷	❷	③	③	③	④
Engines	③	③	③	③	④	⑤	⑤	⑤
Exhaust/Converter	③	③	④	⑤	⑤	⑤	⑤	⑤
Fuel system	③	③	③	③	④	④	⑤	⑤
Ignition system	③	③	③	④	④	③	③	④
Rust/Paint	③	④	④	④	④	⑤	⑤	⑤
Steering	④	④	④	⑤	⑤	⑤	⑤	⑤
Suspension	③	③	③	③	④	④	④	④
Crash Safety	—	❶	❶	④	④	③	③	③
Side Impact	—	—	—	—	—	—	③	③

MAZDA

323, Protegé

Rating: Recommended (1996–99); Above Average (1991–95); Average (1985–90). If you can't find a reasonably priced 323 or Protegé, look for a Ford Escort or Tracer instead—they're basically Mazdas disguised as Fords. The redesigned 1995–96 Protegé offers fresh styling, a larger wheelbase, standard dual airbags, and a new 4-banger. Along with the 1997–98 versions, which were mostly carried over unchanged with a slightly restyled grille and headlights and interior refinements, they are good used-car buys. Plus, they should be plentiful at bargain prices as they come off their two- and three-year leases. The best buy of all, though, is the totally revamped 1999 model. Be wary of Firestone tires. **Maintenance/Repair costs:** Higher than average. Repairs are dealer dependent. To avoid costly engine repairs, check the engine timing belt every 2 years/40,000 km and replace it ($300) every 96,000 km. **Parts:** Expensive, but easily found.

Strengths and weaknesses: These Mazdas are peppy performers with a manual transmission hooked to the base engine. The automatic gearbox, however, produces lethargic acceleration that makes highway passing a bit chancy. Handling and fuel economy are fairly good for a car design this old. However, overall durability is not as good as that of more recent Mazda designs, beginning with the 1991 Mazda 323 and Protegé, both of which were also sold as Ford Escorts. Catalytic converters plug up easily and other pollution-control components have been troublesome. Automatic transmission defects, air conditioner breakdowns, and engine oil leaks are also commonplace. Oil leaks in the power-steering pump may also be a problem.

The fuel-injected 1.6L engine is a better performer than the 1.5L, but you also get excessive engine and exhaust noise. Stay away from the 3-speed automatic transmission. The car's small engine can't handle the extra burden without cutting fuel economy and performance. Both models are surprisingly roomy, but the Protegé's trunk is small for a sedan.

The 1985–90 models offer mediocre reliability. Owners report hard starting in cold weather, in addition to automatic transmission problems and electrical-system failures. The engine camshaft assembly and belt pulley often need replacing around 120,000 km. Clutch failure and exhaust-system rust-out are also common. Other areas of concern are constant velocity joint failures, rack-and-pinion steering wearout, and front-brake wear. The front brakes wear quickly due to poor-quality brake pads and seizure of the calipers in their housings. Check for disc scoring on the front brakes. Stay away from models equipped with a turbocharger—few mechanics want to bother repairing it or hunting for parts. Many owners report premature paint peeling.

The 1991–95 models are a bit more reliable and reasonably priced; however, the 1996–98 versions are the best of the lot. When the 323 was dropped at the end of 1994, the Protegé became Mazda's least costly model and underwent a major redesign the next year. It shares platforms with the Escort and Tracer, but keeps its own sheet metal, engine, and interior styling. Powered by a standard, fuel-efficient, 1.5L engine mated to a manual 5-speed transmission, the 1996 Protegé became one of the most responsive and roomiest small cars around. Three years later, though, the '99's more powerful engines, upgraded rear brakes and suspension, longer wheelbase, improved interior ergonomics, and more solid body made it *la crème de la crème* of Mazda's small cars.

Nevertheless, these cars aren't perfect and owners report problems with the front brakes (excessive noise and premature wear); weak rear defrosting; rough-shifting automatic transmissions; engine stalling; noisy suspension; AC failures; and body defects, including wind and water leaks into the interior, paint defects, and power mirror failures.

Technical service bulletins: All models: 1995–99—Poor engine performance; excessive engine vibrations; driveshaft noise; harsh, erratic shifting; shift lever hard to operate; musty AC odours; AC inoperative; ineffective heating; brake warning light always lit; brake popping noise; front console/dash noise; vibrating, cracked mirrors; rear suspension thump; and wind noise around doors.

Safety summary/Recalls: 1995–99—Airbags failed to deploy. • Cracked fuel line caused fire. • Sudden tire tread separation (Firestone). • Chronic stalling; excessive brake fade. • Harsh transmission shifts. • Metal rods in driver's seat could cause severe back injuries in a rear-end collision. • Driver's seatbelt buckle wouldn't unlatch. • Brake pedal pad is too narrow and should be coated with non-skid material. • Severe static electricity shock when exiting vehicle. **Recalls: Protegé: 1995**—The 1.5L engine valve springs are defective. • Tie-down hooks may cause inadvertent airbag deployment.

Secret Warranties/Service Tips

All models: 1995–96—A horn noise heard from the exhaust will be silenced with a special tailpipe tip furnished by Mazda. **1995–98**—Poor engine performance may require a new intake valve. • Excessive vibration in gear or at idle may mean the engine mount material has hardened or cracked. • Erratic shifting may signal that the valve body harness is defective. • If the gear selector lever is hard to operate, it's likely that the lower manual shaft in the transfer case has excessive rust. • An inoperative AC may have a corroded pressure switch terminal assembly (see illustration below).

A/C Inop., P/S Pressure Sw. Terminal Assembly Corroded
Bulletin No. 001/00
Issued 02/07/00
Revised
Section
07
Applicable Model/s
1995-98 Protege
1996-97 Miata
Subject
A/C INOPERATIVE – P/S PRESSURE SWITCH TERMINAL ASSEMBLY CORRODED
DESCRIPTION

Some vehicles may exhibit the air conditioning (NC) system inoperative with the Malfunction Indicator lamp (MIL) ON. This may be due to the Power Steering Pressure (PSP) switch terminal assembly becoming corroded causing the Powertrain Control Module (PCM) to open the A/C relay circuit and set Diagnostic Trouble Code (DTC) P0550. A modified PSP switch terminal assembly is available to resolve this concern. Customers having this concern should have their vehicle repaired using the following procedure.

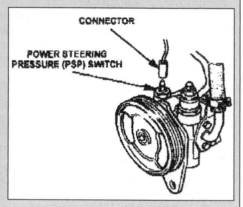

CONNECTOR

POWER STEERING
PRESSURE (PSP) SWITCH

1996–98—A noisy driveshaft can be silenced by installing a countermeasure dynamic damper. • If the door mirror cracks in freezing temperatures, install an upgraded mirror. **1997–98**—A 1–2 upshift shock at light throttle may require the replacement of the large and small accumulator spring with a single spring. • If the brake warning light is constantly lit even though the brakes check out OK, it's likely the speedometer assembly transistor has been damaged. • A thumping noise from the rear suspension can be corrected by installing a modified adjusting sheet.

323, Protegé Profile

	1992	1993	1994	1995	1996	1997	1998	1999
Cost Price ($)								
323	9,250	9,435	9,965	—	—	—	—	—
Protegé	12,425	12,675	13,265	13,370	13,895	14,685	14,675	14,970
Used Values ($)								
323 ↑	2,500	3,000	3,500	—	—	—	—	—
323 ↓	2,000	2,500	3,000	—	—	—	—	—
Protegé ↑	3,500	4,000	5,000	6,500	7,500	8,500	10,000	11,500
Protegé ↓	3,000	3,500	4,000	5,500	6,500	7,500	9,000	10,500
Extended Warranty	N	N	N	N	N	N	N	N
Secret Warranty	N	N	N	N	N	N	N	N

Reliability	②	③	④	④	④	④	④	④
Air conditioning	②	②	③	③	③	③	④	④
Auto. transmission	②	②	②	②	③	③	③	④
Body integrity	①	②	②	②	③	③	③	③
Braking system	①	②	②	②	③	③	③	③
Electrical system	①	②	③	③	③	④	④	④
Engines	③	③	③	③	③	③	③	④
Exhaust/Converter	②	②	②	②	③	⑤	⑤	⑤
Fuel system	②	③	③	④	④	⑤	⑤	⑤
Ignition system	③	④	④	④	④	④	⑤	⑤
Rust/Paint	②	②	②	③	③	③	③	④
Steering	③	③	③	④	④	④	④	④
Suspension	③	③	③	③	③	③	③	④
Crash Safety								
323	②	②	②	—	—	—	—	—
Protegé	—	—	—	③	③	③	③	④
Side Impact	—	—	—	—	—	—	—	③

NISSAN

Sentra

Rating: Recommended (1995–99); Above Average (1991–94); Average (1988–90); Not Recommended (1983–87). The redesigned 1995 version offers fresh styling, a longer wheelbase, a peppier powerplant, standard dual airbags, and side-door beams. **Maintenance/Repair costs:** Higher than average on early models, but anybody can repair these cars. **Parts:** Reasonably priced and easily obtainable.

Strengths and weaknesses: Late-model Sentras aren't expensive to buy, they're generally reliable, relatively easy and inexpensive to repair, and they give good fuel economy. On the other hand, ride and handling are mediocre and build quality is spotty at best. Until 1991, mechanical and body components suffered from poor quality control, making these cars quite unreliable and sometimes expensive to repair. Clutches and exhaust systems were particularly problematic. The 1.6L engine is much more reliable, but the oil pressure switch may still develop a leak that can lead to sudden oil loss and serious engine damage. Quality improved considerably with the 1991 version, yet the vehicle's base price rose only marginally, making these later model years bargain buys for consumers looking for a reliable "beater."

1991–94 Sentras are a bit peppier and handle better. Some owner-reported problems: faulty fuel tanks, leaking manual and automatic transmissions, a persistent rotten-egg smell, and noisy engine timing chains and front brakes. With the exception of electronic component failures, repairs are relatively simple to perform.

Redesigned for the 1995 model year, 1995–99 Sentra sedans are much improved, larger, and better-performing vehicles. The seatbelts are more comfortable, and dual airbags are a standard feature. Most owner complaints concern some stalling and hard starting, electrical glitches, premature brake wear and excessive brake noise, AC solenoid failures, and accessories that malfunction. Body assembly is also targeted with some complaints of poor body fits, paint defects, and air and water leaks into the interior.

Safety summary/Recalls: All models: 1998–99—Airbags failed to deploy or deployed inadvertently. • ABS failures. • Defective brake master cylinder. • Premature tire wear. • Excessive stopping distance. • Sudden acceleration. • Sticking throttle. • Brake and gas pedal set too close together. • Ignition key breaks off in the ignition. • Faulty power door locks. • Vehicle leaks when it rains. • Windshield wiper washer leaks and washer produces acrid fumes that enter the cabin. • Front seats jam when moved back. **Recalls: All models: 1995**—ABS may be defective. **1995–98**—Dealer will install a water diversion seal to prevent water from entering the windshield wiper linkage.

Secret Warranties/Service Tips

All models: 1991–92—Noisy front brakes can be silenced by installing upgraded, non-asbestos front disc brake pads (#41060-63Y90). • Timing chain rattle may be caused by insufficient oil in the chain tensioner. You can correct this by replacing the tensioner with a countermeasure part (#13070-53J03). **1991–93**—The manual transmission has no Reverse gear—install a Nissan upgrade kit. **1991–94**—Stiffer trunk torsion bars will help keep the trunk lid from falling. **1993–94**—Brake and steering wheel vibrations are most likely caused by excessive rotor thickness. **1994**—Door hinges may have received inadequate rust protection; Nissan will apply a sealer at no charge. **1995–96**—An engine that cranks but won't start may need TSB #96-032 for the correct repair. • An engine malfunction light that is constantly lit may be fixed by installing a new rear heated oxygen sensor under the emissions warranty. • An automatic transmission that won't shift out of Park may need a countermeasure interlock cable. • TSB #NTB96-001 gives lots of troubleshooting tips on finding and correcting various squeaks and rattles. • Nissan has a special kit to improve brake pedal feel, according to TSB #NTB96-041. **1995–99**—Harsh shifts and low power with the automatic transmission may be due to reduced movement of the A/T throttle wire cable inside the cable housing. • A self-activating horn can be fixed by replacing the horn springs and spring insulators. **1996**—An AC refrigerant leak may require an upgraded valve core.

Sentra Profile

	1992	1993	1994	1995	1996	1997	1998	1999
Cost Price ($)								
Sentra	8,990	9,590	10,990	12,290	13,448	13,698	14,498	15,398
Used Values ($)								
Sentra ↑	3,000	3,500	4,500	5,500	6,500	7,500	9,000	10,500

Sentra ↓	2,500	3,000	3,500	4,500	5,500	6,500	7,500	9,000
Extended Warranty	N	N	N	N	N	N	N	N
Secret Warranty	N	N	N	N	N	N	N	N
Reliability	②	③	④	④	④	⑤	⑤	⑤
Air conditioning	③	③	③	③	③	④	⑤	⑤
Auto. transmission	②	②	③	③	③	④	⑤	⑤
Body integrity	②	②	②	③	③	③	④	④
Braking system	①	②	②	②	②	②	③	③
Electrical system	②	③	③	②	②	②	③	③
Engines	③	③	③	③	③	④	⑤	⑤
Exhaust/Converter	②	②	③	③	④	⑤	⑤	⑤
Fuel system	②	②	③	③	③	③	③	④
Ignition system	②	③	③	③	③	④	④	④
Rust/Paint	②	③	③	③	③	③	④	④
Steering	③	③	③	③	④	④	⑤	⑤
Suspension	③	④	④	④	④	④	⑤	⑤
Crash Safety	④	⑤	④	④	—	④	④	③
Side Impact	—	—	—	—	—	—	—	③

SUBARU

Impreza, Loyale

Rating: Recommended (1996–99); Average (1993–95); Below Average (1984–92). The earlier models aren't recommended because of poor-quality emissions components and the premature wearout of major mechanical systems (CV joints, steering, etc.). **Maintenance/Repair costs:** Higher than average, and 4X4 repairs must be carried out by a dealer. Only buy a Subaru if you must have AWD and you're confident you can get dependable service from your local Subaru dealer. **Parts:** Expensive and hard to find. Emissions components are often back-ordered for months, but cheap aftermarket components can be found outside the dealer network.

Strengths and weaknesses: 1984–92 are the years to avoid. Performance, handling, and ride are mediocre. Engine breakdowns and premature clutch and exhaust system wearout are commonplace. Early hatchbacks came with a weak and growly 1.6L flat 4-cylinder motor; later models have a 1.8L version of the same anemic engine. Expensive catalytic converters are often replaced at the owner's cost before the five-year emissions warranty has expired. Subaru will reimburse the cost if you raise a fuss.

On 1988 and later models, steering assemblies, CV joints, and front brakes are the main problem areas. These parts generally need replacing after three to five years, and Subaru dealers charge the full rate for replacement.

In the early spring of 1994, the Impreza replaced the unpopular and aging Loyale. The Impreza, too, offered sluggish engine performance, jerky full-throttle downshifts, and mediocre fuel economy. Overall reliability was improved, however.

By 1995, when these small cars went AWD, overall quality control improved as well. Powertrain components function more smoothly, though there have been scattered reports of transmission failures under 80,000 km and electronic components have fewer glitches. Rusting is less of a problem than with the earlier models, which are particularly susceptible to rapid rusting of the bumpers, door bottoms, rear hatch, and hood. These models also came with the 2.2L engine borrowed from the Legacy.

For 1996, the Brighton AWD joined the lineup as a bare-bones entry-level model equipped with the smaller 1.8L engine mated to a manual transmission. The '97 lineup dropped the front-drives, gave the Imprezas a slight restyling and additional horsepower, and the more aggressive Outback "sport-utility wagon" made its debut. 1998 models were slightly reworked with a more user-friendly cabin, and the debut of the 2.5L RS model. The 1.8L engine was dropped, though. The '99 models got torquier engines, some transmission refinements, and a new spin-off, the Legacy Sport sedan.

Safety summary/Recalls: Impreza: 1994–99—Airbags are a serious problem with all Subarus: either they fail to deploy in an accident, or they deploy inadvertently while parked, when turning, if the underside of the car scrapes the road, if the car drives over a dip in the road, hits a pothole, is stuck in a ditch, is being washed, or the key is simply put into the ignition. • Two other common problems are the premature replacement of brake sensors, pads, and rotors; and wheel hubcaps that constantly fall off due to their poor design. **1996**—All four tires split their tread. • Intermittent brake loss. • Seatbelt failed to retract in an accident. • Windshield wiper motor nut falls off. • Short seatback and absence of head restraint could cause severe neck injuries in a collision. • Rear wheel bearing failure. **1997**—Airbags deployed in an accident and a brown liquid burned driver's arms. • Airbags failed to deploy and seatbelts failed to tighten in accident. • ABS brakes aren't effective and take a long distance to stop vehicle. • Sudden engine shutdown on the highway and won't re-start. • Sudden acceleration. • Hubcaps fall off. • Brake lights often fail. • Headlights are mistakenly turned off when turn signal lever is engaged. • Six-inch gash in steering wheel where airbag is deployed. **1998**—Front strut assembly failure. • Rear exterior light wiring covers continually fall off. • Tire blowouts. • Shorted interior dome light. **1999**—Wheel bearing failures. • Transmission plug fell out.

Secret Warranties/Service Tips

All models: 1991–92—Ignition relay failure is the likely cause of no-starts. **1992–94**—The heater mode door actuator may be the culprit of an annoying clicking in the heater area. **1995–97**—Tips on fixing transfer clutch binding and ABS relay sticking.

Impreza, Loyale Profile

	1992	1993	1994	1995	1996	1997	1998	1999
Cost Price ($)								
Impreza	—	—	12,995	17,995	—	—	—	—
Impreza 4X4	—	—	—	19,695	17,995	21,395	21,395	21,995
Loyale	11,899	12,265	—	—	—	—	—	—
Loyale 4X4	—	—	14,995	—	—	—	—	—
Used Values ($)								
Impreza ↑	—	—	5,000	6,000	—	—	—	—
Impreza ↓	—	—	4,000	5,000	—	—	—	—
Impreza 4X4 ↑	—	—	—	7,000	8,000	10,500	12,500	15,000
Impreza 4X4 ↓	—	—	—	5,500	7,000	9,500	11,000	13,000
Loyale ↑	2,500	3,000	—	—	—	—	—	—
Loyale ↓	2,000	2,500	—	—	—	—	—	—
Loyale 4X4 ↑	—	—	5,500	—	—	—	—	—
Loyale 4X4 ↓	—	—	4,500	—	—	—	—	—
Extended Warranty	Y	Y	Y	Y	Y	N	N	N
Secret Warranty	N	N	N	N	N	N	N	N
Reliability	❷	③	③	③	④	④	⑤	⑤
Air conditioning	❷	③	④	④	⑤	⑤	⑤	⑤
Auto. transmission	③	③	③	③	③	③	③	③
Body integrity	❷	❷	③	③	③	③	④	④
Braking system	❷	❷	❷	③	③	③	④	④
Electrical system	❷	❷	❷	❷	③	④	④	④
Engines	❷	③	③	③	④	⑤	⑤	⑤
Exhaust/Converter	❷	③	④	④	④	④	⑤	⑤
Fuel system	④	④	❷	❷	❷	④	④	⑤
Ignition system	❷	❷	❷	❷	④	④	④	⑤
Rust/Paint	❷	③	③	③	③	④	④	⑤
Steering	③	③	③	③	③	④	④	④
Suspension	③	③	④	④	④	④	④	④
Crash Safety								
Impreza, Impreza 4X4	—	—	—	—	④	④	—	—

SUZUKI

Esteem

Rating: Recommended (1996–99). An incredibly slow rate of depreciation means that bargains will be rare. Nevertheless, both the base GL and upscale GLX come loaded with standard features that cost extra on other models. The GL, for example, comes with power steering, rear window defroster, remote trunk and fuel-filler door releases, tinted glass, and a fold-down rear seat (great for getting extra cargo space). GLX shoppers can look forward to standard ABS, power windows and power door locks, and a host of other interior refinements. Shop around for a better-made, second-series 1996 Esteem (made after March 1996) rather than a 1997 version, inasmuch as they're practically identical and a late-model 1996 should be much cheaper. **Maintenance/Repair costs:** Higher than average. Repairs must be carried out by a Chevrolet or Suzuki dealer. **Parts:** Average cost, and parts are easily found.

Strengths and weaknesses: The Esteem, Suzuki's largest car, is a small four-door sedan that is a step up from the Swift (see under General Motors/Suzuki). Smaller than the Honda Civic and Chrysler Neon, it has a fairly spacious interior, offering rear accommodation (for two full-sized adults) that is comparable to or better than most cars in its class. Suzuki's top-of-the-line econobox stands out with its European-styled body and large array of such standard features as air conditioning, a fold-down back seat, and remote trunk and fuel-door releases.

The Esteem has been on the market for only a short time, but early reports indicate a high level of quality and dependability. In this respect, it competes well with rivals like the Chevrolet Cavalier, Ford Escort, and Honda Civic. However, some owners complain of premature front-brake wear, noisy front brakes, and occasional electrical short circuits.

Safety summary/Recalls: All models: 1996—Airbag failed to deploy. • ABS failure. • Engine crankshaft pulley broke while driving. • Transmission failure. **1997**—Sudden brake failure. • Seatbelts failed to secure occupants in a collision. • Sudden, total electrical shutdown. **1998**—Airbag failed to deploy. • Seatbelt failed to lock up in a collision. • Vehicle is unstable at high speed. • Door handle failures. **1999**—Stuck accelerator pedal. • Chronic stalling. • Transmission and brake failures.

Secret Warranties/Service Tips

All models: 1996–97—Uneven wear of the front disc brake pads can be corrected by modifying the upper bushing tolerance, says TSB #TS 5-03-04126. **1998–99**—Remote entry battery failure due to defective fob diode.

Esteem Profile

	1996	1997	1998	1999
Cost Price ($)				
GL	13,495	13,495	13,895	13,995
GLX	14,495	15,495	16,895	17,195
Used Values ($)				
GL ↑	6,500	7,500	8,500	9,500
GL ↓	5,000	6,000	7,500	9,000
GLX ↑	7,000	8,500	9,500	11,000
GLX ↓	6,000	7,000	8,000	10,000
Extended Warranty	N	N	N	N
Secret Warranty	N	N	N	N
Reliability	④	④	⑤	⑤

Note: The Esteem hasn't been crash-tested yet.

TOYOTA

Corolla

Rating: Above Average (1996–99); Average (1985–95). Be wary of serious safety deficiencies that include airbag malfunctions, airbag-induced injuries, and seatbelt failures. Since the 1997 model was "decontented" (less soundproofing, fewer standard features, etc.), there has been a noticeable reduction in quality control. The 1995–96 models combine the best array of standard features, quality control, and "reasonable" (for a Toyota) used prices. **Maintenance/Repair costs:** Lower than average, and repairs can be done anywhere. ECP extended warranty performance is unimpressive. **Parts:** Reasonably priced and easily found.

Strengths and weaknesses: Corollas are economical, high-quality, dependable little cars, but age can take its toll, especially in eastern Canada, where rust snacks on their little bodies. 1985–87 versions may carry the Toyota name and appear to be bargains at first glance, but they're likely to have serious rusting problems and need costly brake, steering, and suspension work. Stay away from the 1.8L diesel version; it lacks performance and parts aren't easy to find. 4X4 versions are also risky. Wiper pivot assemblies may seize due to corrosion. Front shocks on rear-drive models wear out more quickly than average. Exhaust parts aren't very durable.

Post-1987 models are much improved. The two-door models provide sporty performance and good fuel economy, especially when equipped with the 16-valve engine. The engines and drivetrains are exceptionally reliable. Front-drive sedans and five-door hatchbacks offer more room than their rear-drive counterparts. The base engine, however, lacks power and is especially deficient in low-end torque, making for agonizingly slow merging and passing on the highway. Owners report problems with premature front suspension strut and brake wear; brake vibration; faulty defrosting that allows the windows to fog up in winter; and rusting of body seams, especially door bottoms, side mirror mounts, trunk and hatchback lids, and wheel openings.

The 1990–94 Corolla's problems are limited to harsh automatic shifting, early front brake pad and strut/shock wearout, AC high-pressure tube leaks ($650), electrical glitches, ignition problems, windshield wiper linkage failures ($300), motor, and some interior squeaks and rattles. They do, however, still require regular valve adjustments to prevent serious engine problems. Less of a problem with later models, rusting is usually confined to the undercarriage and other areas where the mouldings attach to sheet metal.

1995–98 models have chronic seatbelt retractor glitches and airbag malfunctions. Additionally, owners report powertrain, brake, and electrical problems; poor rear windshield defrosting; and occasional squeaks and rattles, suspension vibrations, and body trim imperfections.

Safety summary/Recalls: All models: 1995—Fires originating in the defrost relay switch, starter, and battery storage area (not part of recall). • Steering wheel came off in driver's hands when making a left turn. • Dozens of reports that the airbag failed to deploy or deployed for no reason. • Many reports of injuries (one death) caused by airbag deployment. • Several reports of faulty seatbelt retractors. • Gearshift lever is easily knocked out of gear when under way. • Faulty door locks. **1996**—Fires originating in the fuel tank, dash, and engine compartment areas. • Airbag failed to deploy or deployed for no reason. • Brake failures and high maintenance costs. • Driver headrest too wide for adequate rear visibility. • Seatbelt failures and malfunctioning retractors. • Hood flew up while vehicle was under way. • Inoperative door locks. **1997**—Fires reportedly caused by faulty seatbelt wiring. • Brake failures. • Sudden acceleration. • Inadvertent airbag deployment (when the ignition is turned on) and no deployment during collisions. • Steering column grinding. • Interior water leaks. • Malfunctioning door locks. • Windshield wipers suddenly quit. • Poor visibility due to film on windshield interior and lack of an adequate rear defroster. • Frequent reports that the seatbelt retractors won't release or retract. • Researchers are looking into 20 incidents where the turn signal failed after the hazard warning light activated. **1998**—Airbag failures still lead the list of owner-reported problems recorded in NHTSA's database; however, '98 models also have a high incidence of airbag warning lights that stay lit when no fault can be found. • Other recurring problems are engine compartment fires, gas fumes in the interior, high-speed instability, brake and power-steering failures, and excessive steering column noise. **1999**—Airbags failed to deploy. • Inadvertent airbag deployment. • Engine compartment fire. • Loss of braking ability. • Defective tires (Firestone). • Sudden acceleration. • Cruise control self-activates. • Automatic transmission locked up while driving. • Vehicle went out of control after rear control-arm failure. • At cruising speed, vehicle tends to wander all over the road. • Windshield shattered when door was closed. • Poor headlight design causes blind spot and poor visibility. • Defective engine camshaft gets inadequate oil lubrication and loses compression. • Rear seatbelts aren't compatible with many child safety seats. • Three rear seat occupants causes muffler to scrape the ground. **Recalls: All models: 1993–95**—Liquid spilled onto the console could make the airbags deploy. **1995**—Defective terminal could drain the battery or make it explode. Dealer will replace the battery. • Cruise control may cause sudden acceleration. **1997**—To prevent inadvertent airbag deployment, Toyota will replace the airbag computer under a recall campaign. **1998**—For the same problem, the automaker will replace the airbag computer under a service campaign.

Secret Warranties/Service Tips

All models/years—Improved disc brake pad kits are described in TSB #BR94-004. • Brake pulsation/vibration, another generic Toyota problem, is fully addressed in TSB #BR94-002, "Cause and Repair of Vibration and Pulsation." • Complaints of steering column noise may require the replacement of the steering column assembly, a repair covered under Toyota's base warranty. • AM static noise on all vehicles with power antennas usually means the antenna is poorly grounded. • Toyota has developed special procedures for eliminating AC odours and excessive wind noise. These problems are covered in TSB #AC00297 and BO00397, respectively. **All models: 1993–96**—Toyota has upgraded the hazard switch to improve turn signal performance in cold climates. **1993–97**—Inoperative front passenger-side power window switch may be caused by lubricant from the wire harness contaminating the window switch contacts. **1994**—A loose rear-seat bolster cover is a common problem, according to TSB #B094-005. • Windshield A-pillar wind noise can be stopped by modifying the moulding lip. **1995–96**—To enhance the performance of the rear door glass, Toyota has upgraded the mounting channel rubber insert and offers it as a service part. **1996**—An axle hub squeaking noise can be fixed by installing an oil seal kit. • A fuel door that's hard to operate in cold weather should be replaced with one containing an upgraded inlet gasket. **1998**—Tips on reducing excessive engine V-belt noise. • Delayed upshift to Overdrive with cruise control engaged can be fixed by changing the cruise control ECU logic. • Water leakage into the rear cab can be plugged by installing an improved C-pillar moulding clip. • If the rear door glass malfunctions when temperatures dive, install an upgraded mounting channel insert bar. **1998–99**—A front suspension squeaking noise can be silenced by replacing the steering rack end shaft under the base warranty, only if customer requests the repair. **1998–2000**—In an attempt to reduce brake vibration complaints, Toyota will install a new front disk brake pad kit says TSB #BR002-00, which was issued March 10, 2000. This fix is covered by Toyota's base warranty, but customer must request the service.

Corolla Profile

	1992	1993	1994	1995	1996	1997	1998	1999
Cost Price ($)								
Base	12,788	14,598	14,798	15,628	13,508	13,968	14,928	15,200
Used Values ($)								
Base ↑	6,500	7,500	8,500	9,000	10,000	11,000	12,000	13,000
Base ↓	5,500	6,000	7,000	8,000	8,500	9,500	10,500	12,000
Extended Warranty	N	N	N	N	N	N	N	N
Secret Warranty	N	N	N	N	N	Y	Y	N
Reliability	③	③	③	④	④	④	⑤	⑤
Air conditioning	❷	⑤	⑤	⑤	⑤	⑤	⑤	⑤
Auto. transmission	③	④	④	④	④	④	⑤	⑤
Body integrity	❷	❷	❷	❷	③	③	④	④
Braking system	❷	❷	❷	❷	③	③	③	③
Electrical system	❷	③	③	③	③	④	⑤	⑤
Engines	④	④	④	④	④	④	⑤	⑤
Exhaust/Converter	❷	❷	③	④	④	⑤	⑤	⑤
Fuel system	❷	③	③	③	③	③	④	⑤
Ignition system	❷	❷	③	③	④	④	⑤	⑤
Rust/Paint	❷	❷	❷	❷	③	④	⑤	⑤
Steering	③	④	④	④	④	⑤	⑤	⑤
Suspension	③	③	③	④	④	④	④	④
Crash Safety	❷	③	④	④	④	④	④	④
Side Impact	—	—	—	—	—	③	③	④

Paseo

Rating: Recommended (1994–99); Above Average (1992–93). 1999 was the Paseo's last model year. **Maintenance/Repair costs:** Lower than average. Repairs can be done anywhere. **Parts:** Reasonably priced and easily found.

Strengths and weaknesses: This baby Tercel's main advantages are a peppy 1.5L 4-cylinder engine, a smooth 5-speed manual transmission, good handling, a supple ride, great fuel economy, and above-average reliability. On the other hand, this light little sportster is quite vulnerable to side winds; there's lots of body lean in turns; there's plenty of engine, exhaust, and road noise; front head room and leg room are limited; and there is very little rear seat space.

Technical service bulletins show that the 1993s may have defective Panasonic tape and CD players, as well as a radio hum at low volume caused by fuel pump interference. Later models have fewer reliability problems, except for some brake and drivetrain vibrations.

Safety summary/Recalls: All models: 1996–97—No airbag deployment and one report of an engine compartment fire of unknown origin. **Recalls:** N/A.

Secret Warranties/Service Tips

All models/years—TSB #B0003-97 recommends the use of a new wind noise repair kit. • TSB #AC002-97 gives lots of troubleshooting tips on eliminating AC odours. • AM radio static is likely caused by a damaged power antenna or by poor grounding due to corrosion. **All models: 1992**—Low-volume radio hum can be corrected by installing spacers (insulators) between the radio chassis and the printed circuit board. **1992–93**—Toyota will improve the shift "feel" on its automatic gearboxes by increasing the C1 accumulator control pressure. **1996**—Toyota has developed an upgraded thermostat to improve heater performance. **1997**—Fujitsu radios may not eject/accept CDs.

Paseo Profile

	1992	1993	1994	1995	1996	1997	1998	1999
Cost Price ($)								
Base	13,338	14,398	14,698	16,878	17,215	17,608	15,998	16,150
Used Values ($)								
Base ↑	3,500	4,000	5,000	6,500	8,500	9,500	11,000	12,500
Base ↓	3,000	3,500	4,500	5,000	7,000	8,000	9,000	11,000
Extended Warranty	N	N	N	N	N	N	N	N
Secret Warranty	N	N	N	N	N	N	N	N
Reliability	④	④	④	⑤	⑤	⑤	⑤	⑤
Crash Safety	③	③	—	—	—	—	④	—

Tercel

Rating: Recommended (1993–99); Above Average (1991–92); Average (1987–90). **Maintenance/Repair costs:** Inexpensive. Repairs can be done anywhere. **Parts:** Reasonably priced and easily obtainable.

Strengths and weaknesses: Don't buy a Toyota on reputation alone, because many early models (1985–90) can have serious braking, electrical, and rusting problems, and may be overpriced to boot. Also, stay away from the troublesome 4X4 versions made from 1984 to 1987.

All Tercels should be checked for door panel and underbody rust damage. 1987–90 Tercels are rust-prone around the rear wheels and side mirror mounts, and along the bottoms of doors, hatches, and rear quarter panels. Early models suffer from extensive corrosion of rear suspension components.

1987–88 Tercels give you more for your money with a restyled aero look; a better performing multi-valve, overhead-cam engine; the impressive performance of a 5-speed manual gearbox; and additional sound insulation. Their main shortcomings are insufficient power when merging into traffic or climbing hills (particularly when shifting from second to third gear with the automatic transmission), cruise control glitches, fuel system malfunctions, excessive carbon buildup on the engine intake valve, occasional air conditioner breakdowns, cracked front exhaust pipes, and exhaust system/catalytic converter rust-out. Tercels are also plagued by pulsating brakes that wear out much too quickly. Owners of the four-wheel-drive wagon complain of manual transmission failures and the occasional bug in the transfer case (these repairs are *very* expensive).

The redesigned 1989–90 versions are roomier, better performing, and acceptable in quality and reliability (except for some paint peeling and surface rusting). The sunroof is a frill that cuts head room drastically and causes irritating water leaks and wind noise. Tercels have a great reputation for exemplary durability, but overall performance is not outstanding and the interior is cramped.

1991–94 Tercels are pretty reliable, but they're not perfect. They were the first to be fuel-injected, which makes for livelier and smoother acceleration, and the interior space feels much larger than it is. Owners report faulty clutch-sleeve cylinders, hard shifting with the automatic transmission, premature brake and suspension-component wearout, brake pulsation, defective CD players, leaking radiators, windshield whistling, and myriad squeaks and rattles.

Redesigned 1995–99 Tercels offer a bit more horsepower, standard dual airbags, side-door beams, aero styling, and a redesigned interior. They continue, however, to have brake, electrical-system, suspension, and body/accessories problems.

Safety summary/Recalls: All models/years—Interestingly, there are far fewer safety-related Tercel and Paseo complaints recorded over the years than those listed for the Corolla or Camry. **1995**—NHTSA database top problems are: airbag failing to deploy, seatbelt lockup, and windshield seal leaks. • Other problems include brake failure, inadequate defrosting, stalling, vehicle jumping out of gear, and engine failure due to defective oil indicator. **1996**—No airbag deployment. • Fuel line explosion. • Fire caused by an overheated heater fan motor. • Brake failure. • Inadequate defrosting. • Light rear end makes car unstable at higher speeds. **1997**—No airbag deployment. • Seatbelt and brake failures. • Front ball joints snapped while car was underway. **1998**—No airbag deployment and seatbelt malfunctions. • Inoperative AC. • Excessive engine noise. **Recalls:** Nothing recent.

Secret Warranties/Service Tips

All models/years—TSB #B0003-97 recommends the use of a new wind noise repair kit. • Interior squeaks and rattles can be fixed with Toyota's kit (#08231-00801). • TSB #AC002-97 gives lots of troubleshooting tips on eliminating AC odours. • Older Toyotas with stalling problems should have the engine checked for excessive carbon buildup on the valves before any other repairs are done. • Improved disc brake pad kits are described in TSB #BR94-004. • Brake pulsation/vibration, another generic Toyota problem, is fully addressed in TSB #BR94-002, "Cause and Repair of Vibration and Pulsation." • A damaged power antenna or poor grounding due to corrosion are the most likely causes of AM radio static. **All models: 1989–90**—Fix harsh shifting from second to third on automatics by installing a new rubber check ball (#35495-22020). **1994**—A whistling noise coming from the windshield requires a urethane sealant applied at key points. • A steering column that's noisy or has excessive free play may need an upgraded steering main-shaft bushing. **1995**—Troubleshooting windshield moulding wind noise is covered in TSB #BO95-005. **1995–96**—Toyota has developed an upgraded thermostat to improve heater performance. • The company will also make available a longer passenger-side seatbelt. **1997**—Fujitsu radios may not eject/accept CDs.

Tercel Profile

	1992	1993	1994	1995	1996	1997	1998	1999
Cost Price ($)								
Base	8,798	9,098	9,618	10,998	11,948	12,498	12,498	12,625
Used Values ($)								
Base ↑	3,500	4,000	5,000	6,000	7,000	8,000	9,000	10,000
Base ↓	3,000	3,500	4,000	5,000	6,000	7,000	8,000	8,500
Extended Warranty	N	N	N	N	N	N	N	N
Secret Warranty	N	N	N	N	N	N	N	N
Reliability	③	③	③	④	⑤	⑤	⑤	⑤
Air conditioning	③	③	③	③	④	⑤	⑤	⑤
Auto. transmission	③	④	④	④	⑤	⑤	⑤	⑤
Body integrity	③	③	③	④	③	④	④	④
Braking system	❶	❷	❷	❷	❷	❷	❷	❷
Electrical system	③	③	③	④	④	④	④	④
Engines	❷	❷	❷	③	④	⑤	⑤	⑤
Exhaust/Converter	❷	③	③	③	④	④	⑤	⑤
Fuel system	③	③	③	④	⑤	⑤	⑤	⑤
Ignition system	④	④	④	④	⑤	⑤	⑤	⑤
Rust/Paint	❷	❷	❷	③	④	⑤	⑤	⑤
Steering	④	④	④	③	④	④	⑤	⑤
Suspension	③	③	③	③	③	③	③	③
Crash Safety	❷	❷	④	④	③	③	④	—
Side Impact	—	—	—	—	—	③	③	—

VOLKSWAGEN

Cabrio, Golf, Jetta

Rating: Above Average (1997–99); Average (1994–96); Below Average (1993); Not Recommended (1985–92). These small imports age particularly badly, and VW is not very generous with "goodwill" repairs. A Jetta is a Golf with a trunk; a Cabrio is a Golf without a roof. There was no 1994 model Cabrio. Interestingly, the early convertibles (Cabriolets) are real bargains inasmuch as they depreciate steeply after their first five years on the market. **Maintenance/Repair costs:** Higher than average. Repairs are dealer dependent. **Parts:** Expensive, but generally available from independent suppliers.

Strengths and weaknesses: On the positive side, these small Europeans are fun to drive and provide great fuel economy. The 1.8L gasoline engine is very peppy and the diesel engines are very reliable and good all-around performers. Both engines are easily started in cold weather. But here's the rub: Golfs and Jettas, like the failure-prone Rabbit they replaced, age badly. What you save in fuel, you lose in the car's high retail price carried over into the used-car market; and the ever-mounting maintenance costs as the vehicle gains years and mileage will easily wear you down.

Reliability is impressive—for the first three years. Then the brake components and fuel and electrical systems start to self-destruct as your wallet gets lighter. Exhaust system components aren't very durable, body hardware and dashboard controls are fragile, and the paint often discolours and is easily chipped.

Although the 1990–93 models are a tad improved, Volkswagen still has terrible quality problems. Owners report electrical short circuits; heater/defroster resistor and motor failures; leaking transmission and stub axles seals; and defective valve-pan gaskets, head gaskets, timing belts, steering assemblies, suspension components, alternator pulleys, and brake and electrical systems. Body problems are legion, with air and water leaks, faulty catalytic converters, inoperative locks and latches, poor-quality body construction and paint, plus cheap, easily broken accessories and trim items.

The redesigned 1994–96 models are a bit safer and more reliable. Nevertheless, problems disclosed in service bulletins for these model years include poor driveability, water leaks, trim defects, and premature rear tire wear. Owners report the following: electric door locks that take a long time to lock; paint that is easily nicked, chipped, and marked; a variety of trim defects; premature rear tire wear; and poor-quality seat cushions.

Factory defects on 1990–96 Golfs and Jettas are so numerous they make these models very risky buys. Problems include automatic-transmission, engine, suspension-component, and catalytic-converter failures; electrical short circuits; AC malfunctions; and fragile trim items. Body assembly and paint are second-class, leading to rattles and air leaks as the vehicles age.

For 1997, Golfs and Jettas equipped with the 116-hp 4-cylinder engine got a redesigned cylinder head that cuts engine noise. The Golf GTI VR6 rides lower, thanks to new shocks, springs, and anti-roll bars. The Cabrio Highline received standard AC, 14-inch alloy wheels, halogen driving lights, and leather upholstery. The base convertible lost its standard ABS and a few other goodies in an unsuccessful attempt to keep a lid on price. 1998 and 1999 models were returned relatively unchanged, except for side airbags and rear disc brakes; however, the 1999 Jetta debuted with junior-Passat features (adopted the following year by the Golf and GTI).

Jettas provide slightly more comfort and better road performance than their Golf hatchback counterparts. The 1.6L 4-cylinder found on early Jettas was surprisingly peppy, and the diesel engine is very economical, although quite slow to accelerate. Diesels have a better overall reliability record than gasoline models and are popular as taxis. Jettas are far more reliable than Rabbits, but they, too, suffer from rapid body deterioration and some mechanical problems after their fourth year in service. For example, on post-1988 Jettas, starters often burn out because they are vulnerable to engine heat; as well, sunroofs leak, door locks jam, window cranks break, and windows bind. Owners also report engine head gasket leaks and water-pump and heater-core breakdowns. It's axiomatic that all diesels are slow to accelerate, but VW's fourth gear can't handle highway speeds above 90 km/h. Engine noise is deafening when shifting down from fourth gear.

All 1996–99 models are much more reliable, but, nevertheless, owners still report chronic automatic-transmission, brake, and electrical-system malfunction problems, in addition to sub-par body construction and paint, leaky sunroofs, malfunctioning gauges and accessories, fragile locks and latches, bumpers that become brittle and crack as the temperature falls, and defective security systems.

Safety summary/Recalls: All models: 1995—NHTSA probes include: fuel tank punctures on '93–2000 Cabrios and Jettas, and light and wiper malfunctions on the '96 Jetta. **1995–98**—The NHTSA database shows the following problems are reported repeatedly: fires; airbags that fail to deploy or cause severe injuries when they go off; airbag light stays on for no apparent reason; transmission and wheel-bearing failures; transmission pops out of gear; electrical malfunctions leading to chronic stalling; self-activating alarms; lights going out; erratic cruise control operation; brake, tire, and AC failures; inadequate defrosting; AC mould and mildew smell; and poor quality body components. • Also, doors may open suddenly; locks jam shut, fall out, or freeze; power window motors and regulators self-destruct; hood suddenly flies up; cigarette lighter pops out of holder while lit; the seat heater may burn a hole in the driver's seat; and battery acid can leak onto the power steering reservoir and cause sudden steering loss. **1996**—Rear wheel and axle may separate. • Door mouldings fall off. **1997**—Fire caused by faulty driver seat wiring. • Battery exploded. **1998**—Engine damaged after water was ingested through the air intake system. • Transmission locked into third gear. • BS brake failures. • Head restraints suddenly drop down. • Michelin tire failure. • Noisy brakes. • Inaccurate fuel gauge. • Faulty factory alarm. **1999**—Plastic fuel line fails in cold weather. • Engine burns oil. • Vehicle may suddenly spin out of control. • Chronic stalling in traffic with engine warning light lit. • Headlight failures. **Recalls: All models: 1993–95**—The jack could collapse during use. • Rear brake lines may leak from rubbing against the fuel tank; dealers will re-route and replace damaged lines. • Radiator fan motor could seize. **1993–96**—Hood may fly up. **1999**—Sound-absorbing mat in B-pillar could ignite in an accident.

Secret Warranties/Service Tips

All models: 1988–94—Poor driveability may be caused by a deteriorated oxygen sensor wire shield or poor ground connection. **1990**—Hard winter starting may require the installation of a new high-energy ignition coil, high-tension wires, and spark plugs. **1992–94**—Poor engine performance or a rough idle may be due to a misrouted EVAP vacuum hose. **1993–94**—TSB #95-04 gives simple service tips for frozen door locks. **1994**—Water leaks into the engine bulkhead. **1996–97**—Tape player may have distorted sound or may snack on tapes. • A shifter that's hard to move side-to-side or won't go into Reverse may signal that the selector shaft is binding in the selector-shaft housing bearing. **1997**—Erratic electrical functions may be caused by a loose ground at one of two grounding studs located under the battery tray. • If the transmission pops out of gear, check for a hairline crack on the selector shaft shift detent sleeve. • Buzzing noise from right-side air outlet may be caused by loose outlet mounting screws. **1999**—Humming noise from front of vehicle when turning may be caused by the differential spider gear.

Cabrio, Golf, Jetta Profile

	1992	1993	1994	1995	1996	1997	1998	1999
Cost Price ($)								
Cabrio	21,395	19,990	—	26,495	26,495	25,230	25,300	25,300
Golf	10,710	10,710	12,600	12,995	14,325	14,690	16,765	15,610
Jetta	13,140	13,140	15,370	18,995	17,650	18,050	18,620	18,620
Used Values ($)								
Cabrio ↑	8,500	9,500	—	12,000	13,500	16,000	18,000	20,000
Cabrio ↓	7,000	8,000	—	11,000	12,000	14,000	16,000	18,500
Golf ↑	3,500	4,000	5,500	6,500	8,500	9,000	11,500	12,500
Golf ↓	3,000	3,500	4,500	5,500	7,500	8,000	10,500	11,500
Jetta ↑	5,000	6,000	7,500	9,000	11,500	13,000	14,000	15,000
Jetta ↓	4,500	5,500	6,500	8,000	10,000	11,500	13,000	14,000

Extended Warranty / Secret Warranty	Y N	Y N	Y N	Y N	Y N	Y N	Y N	Y N
Reliability	❶	❶	❷	❷	❷	③	③	③
Air conditioning	❷	❷	❷	❷	❷	③	④	⑤
Auto. transmission	❶	❶	❶	❶	❶	❷	❷	③
Body integrity	❶	❶	❶	❶	❶	❷	❷	❷
Braking system	❶	❶	❶	❷	❷	❷	❷	③
Electrical system	❶	❶	❶	❶	❶	❷	❷	❷
Engines	❷	❷	❷	❷	③	④	⑤	⑤
Exhaust/Converter	❷	❷	❷	③	③	④	④	⑤
Fuel system	❷	❷	❷	❷	③	③	③	④
Ignition system	❷	❷	❷	❷	❷	③	④	④
Rust/Paint	❷	❷	❷	❷	❷	③	④	⑤
Steering	③	③	③	③	④	⑤	⑤	⑤
Suspension	③	③	③	③	④	④	④	⑤
Crash Safety								
Golf	—	—	—	③	③	③	—	—
Jetta	—	—	—	③	③	③	—	—
Side Impact								
Jetta	—	—	—	—	—	—	③	③

MEDIUM CARS

Medium-sized cars, often referred to as "family" cars are a trade-off between size and fuel economy, offering more room and comfort but a bit less fuel economy (12.5–9.5 L/km) than a small car. These cars are popular because they combine the advantages of smaller cars with those of larger vehicles. As a result of their versatility and upsizing as well as downsizing throughout the years, these vehicles shade into both the small and the large car niches. The trunk is usually large enough to meet average baggage requirements, and the interior is spacious enough to meet the needs of the average family (seating four persons in comfort and five in a pinch). These cars are best for combined city and highway driving, with the top three choices traditionally dominated by Japanese automakers: the Honda Accord, the Mazda 626, and the Toyota Camry. VW's Passat has just recently taken top honours. Ford's Taurus and Sable are in a sales-death spiral following persistent owner complaints of drivetrain deficiencies.

Recommended

Acura 1.6 EL (1997–99)   Toyota Camry (1994–96)

Above Average

Acura CL-Series (1998–99)
Acura Integra (1990–99)
GM Bonneville, Cutlass Supreme,
 Delta 88, Grand Prix, LeSabre,
 Regal (1984–87 rear-drives)
Honda Accord (1990–99)
Hyundai Sonata (1999)

Mazda 626, MX-6 (1996–99)
Nissan Altima (1998–99)
Subaru Forester, Legacy
 (1997–99)
Toyota Camry, Solara (1997–99);
 Camry (1988–93)
Volkswagen Passat (1998–99)

Average

Acura CL-Series (1997)
Acura Integra (1986–89)
Chrysler Breeze, Cirrus,
 Stratus (1999)
GM Bonneville, Cutlass, Cutlass
 Supreme, Delta 88, Grand Prix,
 Intrigue, LeSabre, Lumina,
 Malibu, Monte Carlo,
 Regal (1997–99)
GM Beretta, Corsica (1993–96)

GM Century, Ciera (1998–99)
Honda Accord (1985–89)
 Hyundai Sonata (1995–98)
 Mazda 626, MX-6 (1994–95)
Nissan Altima (1993–97)
Toyota Camry, Solara (1985–87)
Subaru Forester, Legacy
 (1991–96 AWD; 1989–96
 front-drives)
Volkswagen New Beetle (1998–99)
Volkswagen Passat (1995–97)

Below Average

Chrysler Breeze, Cirrus,
  Stratus (1995–98)
Ford Contour, Mystique (1995–99)

GM Century, Ciera (1997)
GM Achieva, Grand Am,
  Skylark (1995–99)

Not Recommended

Ford Sable, Taurus
  (1986–99)
Ford Tempo, Topaz (1985–94)
GM Century, Ciera (1982–96)
GM Achieva (Calais), Grand Am,
  Skylark (1985–94)
GM Beretta, Corsica, Tempest
  (1987–92)

GM Bonneville, Cutlass, Cutlass
  Supreme, Delta 88, Grand Prix,
  Intrigue, LeSabre, Lumina,
  Malibu, Monte Carlo,
  Regal (1988–96 front-drives)
Hyundai Sonata (1986–93)
Mazda 626, MX-6 (1985–93)
Volkswagen Passat (1989–94)

ACURA

1.6 EL

Rating: Recommended (1997–99). Reasonably priced. **Maintenance/Repair costs:** Average. Repairs aren't dealer dependent. **Parts:** Average parts cost, thanks to the use of generic Honda Si parts sold through independent suppliers.

Strengths and weaknesses: The first Japanese automobile built exclusively in and for the Canadian market, the EL is essentially an all-dressed Civic sedan, sold under the Acura moniker. It came about as an answer to Canadian Acura–dealer pleadings for a more affordable Acura.

Based on the topline Civic Si, the EL comes with a peppy 127-horsepower VTEC 1.6L 4-banger that's both reliable and economical to run. Add to this the Civic's chassis and upgraded suspension components and you have outstanding performance as good as or better than the Civic Si—without all the noise.

The quieter-running EL's engine emits less clatter; the door, trim, and body panels are better assembled than what you find in the Si; and Acura has invested in a substantial amount of noise insulation throughout the EL's body to reduce NVH (noise, vibration, harshness). Additionally, the EL's modified-Civic suspension uses different dampers and a new ball joint link to better isolate EL passengers from the road. It improves the ride, but handling remains Civic-like.

Style-wise, the $17,800-base '97 EL still looks like a Civic—large, square headlights; upgraded cloth and plastic; and standard features that include a standard AM/FM cassette four-speaker audio system, dual vanity mirrors, tilt steering wheel, and cruise control. In 1997,

$20,000 got you the upscale sport version with a CD player, Acura's Acoustic Feedback Audio system, and air conditioning. For 2,000 additional loonies, there was the Premium version, which offered both the cassette and CD players, power sunroof, and leather covered seats.

In just over four years on the market, the EL has done quite well, and done so without cannibalizing Civic Si sales. First-year models go for about $5,000 less than their initial cost price (MSRP) and owner complaints have been practically non-existent.

Luc Lamirande, a '97 1.6L EL owner writes:

> This is a clone or sister of the Honda Civic sedan but with the drivetrain of the Civic's Si Coupe and is assembled in Alliston Ontario. It was marketed and released in Canada a year or so before the US. It was touted to have "special" windshield fluid nozzles, heated exterior mirrors and extra insulation for Canadian winters. It definitely has much more spunk than a Civic sedan.

Safety summary/Recalls: Recalls: All models: 1997—Passenger airbag modules may have been improperly assembled.

Secret Warranties/Service Tips

All models/years—Acura says it will replace any seatbelt's tongue stopper button for the life of the vehicle. **All models: 1997–99**—Most Honda TSBs allow for special warranty consideration on a "goodwill" basis even after the warranty has expired or the car has changed hands. Referring to this euphemism will increase your chances of getting some kind of refund for repairs that are obviously related to a factory defect.

1.6 EL Profile

	1997	1998	1999
Cost Price ($)			
1.6 EL	17,800	18,800	19,800
Used Values ($)			
1.6 EL ↑	12,500	14,500	16,500
1.6 EL ↓	11,000	13,500	15,000
Extended Warranty	N	N	N
Secret Warranty	Y	Y	Y
Reliability	⑤	⑤	⑤

Note: These vehicles have not been crash-tested.

CL-Series

Rating: Above Average (1998–99); Average (1997). Overpriced and hard to find; be wary of the first-year models. You may have to be astute in negotiating a fair price, particularly in rural areas; there's an unusually high $2,000 margin between the high (dealer) and low (private) values. Most vehicles show a $1,000–1,500 difference. **Maintenance/Repair costs:** Lower than average. Repairs can be done practically anywhere. **Parts:** A bit higher than average cost, but not hard to find.

Strengths and weaknesses: The only difference between the 2.2L CL and the 3.0L CL is the 3.0L CL's larger engine, different wheels, and larger exhaust tip. The 2.2L CL's engine was upgraded to a 2.3L on the 1998 models. Other vehicles worth considering, but with fewer standard features: BMW 318, Honda Accord, Lexus SC300, Nissan Maxima, and Toyota Camry.

The most distinctive features of the 2.2L CL and its 3.0L CL twin are the larger engine and upgraded wheels found on the 3.0L version. These cars are stylish, front-drive, five-passenger, American-designed-and-built luxury coupes. They have a flowing, slanted back end and no apparent trunk lock (a standard remote keyless entry system opens the trunk from the outside and a lever opens it from the inside). And while other Japanese automakers are taking content out of their vehicles, Acura has put content into the CL, making it one of the most feature-laden cars in its class.

Sure, we all know that the coupe's mechanicals and platform aren't that different from the Accord's, but when you add up all of its standard bells and whistles, you get a fully loaded medium-sized car that costs thousands of dollars less than such competing luxury coupes as the BMW 318 and the Lexus SC300. Consider this array of standard features: power windows, power mirrors, power moon roof, six-way power driver's seat, remote keyless entry system, ABS, leather-wrapped steering wheel, simulated wood trim, automatic climate control, dual airbags, tilt steering wheel, cruise control, and CD player and AM/FM stereo with six speakers.

Although no one would consider the CL a high-performance car, it gets plenty of power from its quiet and smooth-running 3.0L 24-valve SOHC Variable Valve Timing and Lift Electronic Control (VTEC) V6, as well as from the Accord's 2.2L, single overhead cam 4-cylinder VTEC engine (upgraded to a 2.3L on the '98 models). The latter engine's 145 horses take the CL from 0 to 100 km in a respectable nine seconds, but the engine works hard and is noisy. Handling is better than average, thanks to the Accord's upgraded suspension, variable assisted steering, and 16-inch wheels, which are one inch larger than the Accord's (I told you there was a lot of Accord in the CL). Confirming that fact, the 2000 coupe is set on the Accord's platform.

Now that I've whetted your appetite with all that's right about these little Acuras, let's look at some of the problems reported with the

1997–99 models. This is not a car for seating passengers in the rear. Backseat room is insufficient, unless the front seats are pushed all the way forward. And the rear windows don't roll down all the way. Furthermore, owners have become so incensed at what they perceive as Acura's arrogant stonewalling of customer complaints that one owner, Michael Hos, set up his own Acura Lemon website to air Acura gripes and put pressure on the company. He got his money back after a few months and took down his website as part of the bargain. Nevertheless, he shows how others can do the same in Part Two of this guide (see page 95).

Some of the common defects reported on the Hos website: faulty transmission-control unit; transmission downshift problems; chronic brake rotor pulsation and other brake problems leading to resurfacing of brake rotors and replacement of brake pads, rotors, calipers, and springs; repeated front-end realignments; door and wind noise leading to replacement of door; and a sunroof that won't stop at closed position, requiring replacement of sunroof switch and controller.

Consider the following two free repair programs: Honda's 14-year EPA-mandated tune-ups and engine emission component repairs applicable to all 1996–97 Acuras, except for the type R models and the free replacement of defective oil seals on four-cylinder-equipped 1994–97 models.

Safety summary/Recalls: All models: 1997—Complete brake failure; vehicle hit a wall. • Frequent brake rotor replacement. • Chronic hesitation and stalling. • When accelerating, vehicle will appear to stall, and then suddenly accelerate. • Inadvertent airbag deployment. • Passenger front seatbelt locks up and won't retract. • Leaky oil pan seals. • Premature catalytic converter failure. • Subframe out of alignment, causing vehicle to pull to one side. • Complete automatic transmission failure or transmission locks in fourth gear. • Main computer failure. **1998**—When driving on a flat surface at 45 km/h, or 1500 rpms, vehicle will jerk and pull for about 30 seconds. • Transmission seals failed. • Chronic electrical shorts. • Premature shock failure. • Sudden power steering loss. • Excessive steering play due to faulty steering column coupling. • Vehicle will sometimes accelerate when slowing for a stop. **Recalls: All models: 1997–98**—Ball joints could wear out prematurely and cause loss of steering control. **1998**—Defective shifter/parking pawl may allow vehicle to roll down an incline with shift lever ostensibly in Park. Dealer will put a collar on the pawl.

Secret Warranties/Service Tips

All models/years—Acura says it will replace any seatbelt's tongue stopper button for the life of the vehicle. **All models: 1997**—Remedy for front seat that won't slide forward or backward. • Freeing up seatback adjustment lever • Silencing a dash pop or creak. • Fix for incorrect fuel gauge and speedometer readings. • Correction for brake fluid leaking from the ABS modulator. • Fix for wind noise from front side windows. **1997–99**—Most Honda TSBs allow for special warranty consideration on a "goodwill" basis even after the warranty has expired or the car has changed hands. Referring to this euphemism will increase your chances of getting some kind of refund for repairs that are obviously related to a factory defect.

CL-Series Profile			
	1997	**1998**	**1999**
Cost Price ($)			
2.2L/2.3L CL	27,800	30,000	30,900
3.0L CL	30,650	34,000	35,000
Used Values ($)			
2.2L/2.3L CL ↑	17,500	19,700	22,500
2.2L/2.3L CL ↓	15,500	17,000	20,500
3.0L CL ↑	18,000	20,500	24,000
3.0L CL ↓	16,000	19,000	21,500
Extended Warranty	N	N	N
Secret Warranty	Y	Y	Y
Reliability	④	⑤	⑤

Note: These vehicles have not been crash-tested.

Integra

Rating: Above Average, compromised by a stiff price for the Acura cachet and limited passenger room (1990–99); Average (1986–89). **Maintenance/Repair costs:** Lower than average. Repairs can be done practically anywhere. **Parts:** A bit higher than average cost, but can be bought from cheaper independent Honda suppliers.

Strengths and weaknesses: A Honda spin-off, early Integras (1986–89) came with lots of standard equipment and are a pleasure to drive, especially when equipped with a manual transmission. The 4-speed automatic saps the base engine's power considerably. Engine and tire noise are intrusive at highway speeds. The car corners well and is more agile than later 1990–93 models. Its hard ride can be reduced a bit by changing the shocks and adding wide tires. The front seats are very comfortable, but they're set a bit low, and the side wheelwells leave little room for your feet. Rear seat room is very limited, especially on the three-door version.

Overall, assembly and component quality are good but not exceptional, as you can see from the "Secret Warranties/Service Tips" list. To avoid costly engine repairs, check the engine timing belt every 2 years/40,000 km.

For model years 1990–93, the high-revving 1.7L powerplant growls when pushed and lacks guts (read, torque) in the lower gears. The 1.8L engine runs more smoothly but delivers the same maximum horsepower as the 1.7L it replaced, until the '94 model year, when it gained 10 extra horses. Surprisingly, overall performance has been toned down and is seriously compromised by the 4-speed automatic gearbox. Interior design is more user-friendly, with the front seating roomier than in previous years, but reduced rear seating is still best left to small children.

Mechanical reliability is impressive, but that's the case with most Hondas that sell for far less, and many mechanical components are so complex that self-service can pretty well be ruled out. The Integra's front brakes may require more attention than those of other Hondas. Surprisingly, what Integras give you in mechanical reliability they take away in poor quality control of body components and accessories. Water leaks, excessive wind noise, low quality trim items, and plastic panels that deform easily are all commonplace. Owners also report severe steering shimmy, excessive brake noise, premature front brake pad wearout, and radio malfunctions.

In the 1994 model year, the Integra was dramatically restyled with a more aerodynamic profile, and a few more horses were wrung out of the venerable 1.8L 4-banger through variable valve timing. The 1994–99 models also offer a smoother ride than previous versions. On the other hand, the powerful VTEC engine requires lots of shifting and interior room is still problematic. Overall, there are too few improvements to justify the high prices that late-model Integras command.

Owners report that steering wheel shimmy, fit and finish deficiencies, and malfunctioning accessories continue to be problematic on later models. Premature front brake wear is also an ongoing concern. Squeaks and rattles frequently crop up in the door panels and hatches, and the sedan's frameless windows often have sealing problems.

Safety summary/Recalls: All models: 1998—Sudden steering lockup. • Battery leak could have caused fire by burning hole in charcoal canister. • Driver's seatbelt won't loosen. • Horn failure. • Sunroof malfunctions. • Window motor inoperative. • Windshield wipers suddenly stopped working; resumed operation when car was restarted. **Recalls: All models: 1994**—Automatic transmission retaining clip may show wrong gear.

Secret Warranties/Service Tips

All models/years—Severe and persistent steering wheel shimmy is likely due to an imbalanced wheel/tire/hub/rotor assembly. **All models: 1990–91**— TSB #91-015 is an excellent troubleshooting guide to the myriad squeaks and rattles in the dash, front doors, hatch, steering shaft, and sunroof. **1990–97**—Rear trailing arm bushing noise can be corrected by installing plastic shims. **1991–99**— Most Honda TSBs allow for special warranty consideration on a "goodwill" basis even after the warranty has expired or the car has changed hands. Referring to this euphemism will increase your chances of getting some kind of refund for repairs that are obviously related to a factory defect. **1992–99**—A defective seatbelt tongue stopper will be replaced free of charge with no ownership, time, or mileage limitations. **1994**—Rear-hatch rattles are usually caused by a poorly adjusted striker. • Power door locks that cycle from locked to unlocked require a new power-door lock control unit. **1994–95**—Rattling from a partially open window may be caused by excess clearance between the window guide pin and the centre sash guide or by the glass run channel having come out of the centre channel. These are also likely causes of moon roof chattering or shuddering. **1994–97**—Rear seatback rattles need the latch to be readjusted. Exhaust system buzzing can have two sources: the flexible joint connections may have insufficient spring tension or the inner exhaust pipe is vibrating against the outer pipe. **1994–99**—The window guide channel cover may be loose. **1996–97**—A squeaking steering wheel heard when turning, signals the need to grease the pinion shaft and grommet. In a settlement with the U.S. Environmental Protection Agency, Honda paid fines totalling $17.1 million (U.S.) and extended its emissions warranty on 1.6 million 1995–97 models to 14 years or 150,000 miles. This means that costly engine components and exhaust system parts, like catalytic converters, will be replaced free of charge, as long as the 14-year/150,000 mile limit hasn't been exceeded. Canadian owners may wish to use this settlement as leverage for free repairs in Canada, or use the full-terms of the settlement when visiting the States. One thing is certain, neither Transport Canada nor Environment Canada are sufficiently enthused to render any assistance.

Integra Profile

	1992	1993	1994	1995	1996	1997	1998	1999
Cost Price ($)								
LS/SE	18,495	20,155	22,095	23,095	23,245	23,800	23,800	21,800
RS	15,495	16,250	17,655	18,595	18,795	19,500	21,000	—
Used Values ($)								
LS/SE ↑	6,000	7,000	8,500	11,000	12,500	14,500	16,500	18,000
LS/SE ↓	5,500	6,500	7,000	9,500	11,500	13,500	15,500	17,000
RS ↑	4,500	6,000	6,500	9,500	11,000	12,500	14,500	—
RS ↓	4,000	5,000	6,000	7,500	9,000	10,500	12,500	—
Extended Warranty	N	N	N	N	N	N	N	N
Secret Warranty	N	N	N	N	Y	Y	N	N
Reliability	④	④	④	④	④	④	⑤	⑤
Air conditioning	❷	③	④	④	⑤	⑤	⑤	⑤
Auto. transmission	③	③	③	④	④	④	④	④
Body integrity	❷	❷	❷	❷	❷	③	③	④
Braking system	❷	❷	❷	❷	❷	③	④	④
Electrical system	③	③	③	③	③	④	④	④
Engines	④	④	④	④	④	④	④	④
Exhaust/Converter	❷	❷	❷	③	④	④	⑤	⑤
Fuel system	③	③	③	④	④	⑤	⑤	⑤
Ignition system	❷	③	④	④	④	④	④	④

Rust/Paint	❷	③	③	③	③	③	④	④
Steering	③	③	④	④	④	④	④	⑤
Suspension	③	③	④	④	④	④	④	⑤
Crash Safety	—	—	—	④	④	—	—	—

CHRYSLER

Breeze, Cirrus, Stratus

Rating: Average (1999); Below Average (1995–98). Stay away from any model carrying the anemic and failure-prone 4-cylinder engine. Fewer mechanical and safety problems than found on the Ford and GM competition, nevertheless, be prepared to experience a number of nasty safety-related failures such as blown engine head gaskets, airbags that don't deploy, sudden acceleration, and loss of braking. **Maintenance/ Repair costs:** Higher than average, but repairs aren't dealer dependent. **Parts:** Higher-than-average cost (independent suppliers sell for much less), but they are not hard to find. Recall parts, though, tend to dribble in; a month's wait isn't unusual. Don't even think about buying any one of these cars without a 3- to 5-year supplementary warranty.

Strengths and weaknesses: Roomy and stylish, well appointed, comfortable, and smooth, the Chrysler Cirrus and Dodge Stratus are midsized sedan replacements for the LeBaron. The Breeze, launched as a 1996 model, is essentially a "decontented" version of the more expensive Cirrus.

Most components have been used for some time on other Chrysler models, particularly the Neon subcompact and Avenger and Sebring sports coupes. Power is supplied by one of three engines: a 2.0L 4-cylinder engine (shared with the Neon), a 2.4L 4-banger, or the recommended optional 2.5L V6. Carrying Chrysler's "cab-forward" design a step further up the evolutionary ladder, these cars have short rear decks, low noses, and massive sloping grilles. A wheelbase that's two inches longer than the Ford Taurus makes these cars comfortable for five occupants, with wide door openings and plenty of trunk space.

These cars aren't all that impressive, either from a performance or a quality control standpoint. Furthermore, owners have serious misgivings as to whether these vehicles can withstand a harsh climate. One Saskatchewan CBC radio producer relates the following "adventure" with his 1995 Cirrus:

> As I left a shopping mall parking lot, I heard a slight "pop." I instantly lost power steering. I had it towed to Triple Seven. They diagnosed the same problem that the university professor had: it appears Chrysler engineers made the sender hose from the power

steering pump too long. In our severe climate, the line freezes, contracts, starves the power steering pump, and sends it into coronary arrest. And the professor and I weren't alone. Two other Cirruses with the same problem were seen Saturday at this dealer alone. Probably, this model was collapsing in large numbers across the West this last week in our record-breaking low temperatures....

Other problems reported by owners include the following: excessive road noise and vibrations, chronic automatic transmission failures, early and frequent engine head gasket failures through early '99 models (no doubt part of the Neon engine legacy) and erratic engine operation, ABS malfunctions (faulty solenoid—$1,000 repairs) and sudden brake loss, paint delamination, electrical short circuits, weak headlights, AC underperforms, water leaks into the trunk area and interior, easy-to-break trim items, lots of squeaks and rattles, and head restraints that are set too far back. Incidentally, in 1999 the manual seat height adjuster was dropped, making it difficult for short drivers to distance themselves safely from the airbag deployment. Additionally, this complicates both forward and rearward visibility, which is already seriously compromised by the cars' styling.

Safety summary/Recalls: 1997–98—NHTSA is looking into complaints of steering shaft binding. **All models: 1995–96**—Frequent reports of engine fires. • Chronic engine oil leaks and oil galley plug failures. • Repeated engine head gasket failures, some resulting in engine compartment fires. • Timing belt failure after recall correction. • Chronic stalling or loss of engine power blamed on timing belt tensioner and pulley failure. • Engine sometimes loses power, then quickly accelerates. At other times, while at highway speeds, vehicle won't slow down when foot is taken off the gas pedal; instead, it speeds up. • Check Engine light, often lit for no reason. • Reports of sudden acceleration in Drive and Reverse. • Owner claims that sudden acceleration is caused by a design flaw in cable to throttle body. • Airbags often fail to deploy. • Frequent ABS brake failures and prematurely worn rotors, calipers, and pads. • Rear brake failures also reported. • Faulty master cylinders are the cause of some early brake failures. • Floormat can catch the steering shaft clamp and jam the steering column assembly, causing the steering to lock up. • While driving off the highway at 100 km/h, steering tie-rod came apart, resulting in complete steering loss. • Steering components worn out prematurely. • Main computer failed seven times. • Oxygen sensor prone to early failure and fluid leakage. • Alternator burned out. • Child was able to take parked vehicle out of gear without applying brake. • Vehicle jumped out of third gear. • Defective electrical switch causes transmission to stick in second gear. • Sudden transmission lockup. • Transmission won't engage or upshift to third or fourth gear. • Leaking transmission front pump seal. • Prematurely worn strut links and wheel bearings. • Heat is unevenly

distributed, causing front and rear passengers to be cold. • Heater failures. • Defogger doesn't adequately defrost windshield. • AC fails to
cool interior unless vehicle is travelling at high speed. • AC failures. •
Dash reflection into windshield hampers view. • Inadequate headlight
illumination. • Windshield wipers don't run fast enough to clear windshield in a heavy downpour. • Rear brake lights and brake switch failure. • Sloping hood design creates poor visibility for parking. • Fuel
tank gauge indicates empty when tank is half full. • Trunk lid closes on
its own; this gave one owner a mild concussion. • Plastic on seatbelt
clinch bar is self-destructing. • Seatbacks collapsed when vehicle was
rear-ended. • Seat frame and anchor broke as driver sat down. • Power
window motor failures. • Door locks work intermittently. • Binding
door hinges make for difficult closing. • Door handle design pinches
fingers. • Key sticks in the ignition when vehicle is shut off. • Weak
front speakers prevent radio balance. **1997**—Engine compartment fire
ignited while car was parked in garage. • Reports of sudden acceleration in Drive and Reverse. • Chronic stalling at highway speeds. •
Vehicle rolled away while parked with shifter in Park position and keys
pulled from ignition. • Shifter came off in hand when shifting. •
Airbags fail to deploy. • Floormat can catch the steering shaft clamp
and jam the steering column assembly, causing the steering to lock up.
• Frequent engine head gasket failures. • When the head gasket blew,
one driver believes it overheated the transmission causing it to lock up.
• It's common for the engine timing belt idler pulley to fail and damage the timing belt. • Sudden brake and power-steering loss. • Brake
pads and rotors fail prematurely. • Noisy brakes. • AC emits odour and
white flakes through ventilation system, causing headaches, burning
sensation, and congestion. • Noise coming from the high-pressure
power-steering line. • Missing part causes seatbelt to twist. • Seat buckle
design is too short, causing difficulty in latching. • Driver-side shoulder
belt failed to restrain driver in a collision. • Starter short caused fuse to
blow. • Fuel sender for dash gauge often defective. • Inoperative power
door lock motor. **1998**—Airbag exploded rather than inflated. •
Airbags fail to deploy. • Frequent complaints of ABS brake failures; ABS
brakes failed five times on one owner despite dealer attempts to correct
the problem. • There is excessive brake noise whenever brakes are
applied. • Floormat jammed the steering column assembly causing the
steering to lock up. • Automatic transmission (floor console design)
throw from Drive to Reverse to Park is too long, resulting in consumer
thinking vehicle is in Park when it's really in Reverse. • Floor shift indicator on the dash doesn't give a true reading of which gear is engaged.
• Gear shift lever can be moved into Drive without putting foot on
brakes to engage the transmission/brake interlock system. • High trunk
lid makes it impossible to see directly behind the vehicle. **1999**—Several
trunk fires reported from a too intense trunk-mounted light bulb. •
Airbags failed to deploy in a collision. • Airbag deployed inadvertently,
knocking driver out and causing an accident. • Sudden acceleration;

stuck throttle. • Stalling upon acceleration and when foot is taken off of the gas pedal. • Steering locks up when making left-hand turns. • Automatic transmission has a short life span; sensors are the first to go. • Transmission lever can be shifted into Drive without first depressing brake pedal. • Cracked axle. • Dash reflects onto front windshield. • Many incidents reported of sudden brake failure without any prior warning. • While driving, brake vacuum hose separated, causing complete brake failure. • Chronic brake rotor warpage around 8,000 kilometres resulting in severe brake vibrations, noise, and extended stopping distance. • Engine fumes invade the cabin causing driver drowsiness. • Frequent electrical shorts cause gauges, wipers, and windows to function erratically. • Engine, ABS, and airbag warning light often come on for no reason. • Seatbelts fail to tighten. **Recalls: All models: 1995**—Install plugs to prevent engine cylinder head from leaking oil. • Master cylinder could leak brake fluid. **1995–96**—Rusting in the ABS unit could cause the car to jerk to one side when stopping. **1995–97**—Dealers may replace, free of charge, prematurely corroded ball-joint components. Ball joint may wear prematurely and cause sudden steering loss. **1995–98**—Transmission/brake interlock may be faulty. **1996–97**—The hood could fly up. **1998**—The right rear brake tube may leak, increasing stopping distance. **Breeze: 1996–97**—An engine oil leak correction will, hopefully, eliminate fire hazard in the 2.4L engine. • Faulty ignition switches, console shifter, and cables may cause the vehicle to roll away or render the ignition-park interlock system inoperative. **Cirrus, Stratus: 1995**—Following an NHTSA lawsuit, Chrysler has been ordered to replace the rear seatbelt anchor belts. **1995–98**—Faulty ignition switches, console shifter, and cables may cause the vehicle to roll away or render the ignition-park interlock system inoperative.

Secret Warranties/Service Tips

All models/years—Anecdotal reports confirm Chrysler has a 7-year/ 160,000 km secret warranty covering engine head gasket failures. **All models: 1995–96**—Water leaks into the passenger compartment from behind the door trim panel. Correct the leakage by installing new door panel clips, door watershields, and additional tape to seal the watershield.

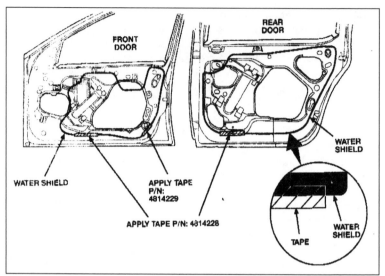

Water leakage from both doors is a common problem.

• Front brake lining wears prematurely (see TSB #05-01-96). **1995–97**—Troubleshooting tips are available to correct poor AC performance. • A powertrain "bump" when the AC engages is normal, according to Chrysler. • Transmission shudder could be caused by using the wrong transmission fluid. **1995–98**—Repair procedure for the evaporator failure (see following).

NO: 24-04-98
GROUP: Air Conditioning
DATE: Apr. 17, 1998
SUBJECT:
A/C Systems Performance
MODELS:
1995-1998 (JA) Breeze/Cirrus/Stratus
1996-1998 (JX) Sebring Convertible
SYMPTOM/CONDITION:
A/C performance complaints and/or A/C compressor failure (seized) in high ambient
temperatures (90°+F). This condition is aggravated by start and stop city driving and/or
extended periods of idling with the A/C running.
DIAGNOSIS:
If the is vehicle operated in high ambient temperatures or A/C compressor has failed
(seized) or system passes the Performance Test Procedure as described on page 24-5 of
the Breeze/Cirrus/Stratus Service Manual (Publication No. 81-270-8121) perform the
Repair Procedure.
PARTS REQUIRED:

1	05011395AA	Kit, A/C Condenser
		Contains: A/C Condenser
		Foam Seals, Radiator to Condenser Label,
		Refrigerant Charge Level
1	04796282AB	Kit, Retaining Strap Transmission Cooler
5	06502625	Retainer, Fascia
AR(1)	04886129AA	SP-15 PAG Oil
AR(1)	04883308	Air Seal, Radiator Right Side
AR(1)	04883308	Air Seal, Radiator Left Side

POLICY: Reimbursable within the provisions of the warranty.

1995–99—Chrysler will replace faulty 4-cylinder engine head gaskets free
of charge. • Paint delamination, peeling, and fading (see Part Two).
1995–2000—A steering wheel rattle or clunk can be silenced by replacing
the steering gear. **1997**—Send a rattling CD changer back to the factory. •
A low-frequency rumble heard while at highway cruising speed can be
silenced by replacing the front hub bearing assemblies. **1997–98**—
Excessive cold crank time, start die-out, or weak run-up may be corrected
by replacing the powertrain control module (PCM) under warranty,
according to TSB #18-18-98. **1999**—A metallic noise heard from the rear
doors can be silenced by modifying the window regulator channel.
1999–2000—No-starts and stalling may be caused by a malfunctioning sen-
try key immobilizer system.

Breeze, Cirrus, Stratus Profile

	1995	1996	1997	1998	1999
Cost Price ($)					
Breeze	—	18,200	18,865	19,505	21,090
Cirrus	22,115	23,235	24,125	—	22,180
LXi	24,555	25,695	26,465	26,465	24,840
Stratus	17,895	18,200	18,865	19,505	21,090
V6	19,750	20,100	24,060	24,475	25,025

Used Values ($)

Breeze ↑	—	8,500	10,000	12,000	14,500
Breeze ↓	—	7,000	8,500	10,500	13,000
Cirrus ↑	7,500	9,500	11,500	—	15,500
Cirrus ↓	6,000	8,000	10,000	—	14,000
LXi ↑	8,500	9,500	12,500	14,000	16,500
LXi ↓	7,000	8,000	11,000	12,500	15,000
Stratus ↑	7,500	9,000	10,000	12,000	15,000
Stratus ↓	6,000	7,500	8,500	10,500	13,500
V6 ↑	8,500	9,500	12,000	14,000	15,500
V6 ↓	7,000	8,500	10,500	12,500	14,000
Extended Warranty	Y	Y	Y	Y	Y
Secret Warranty	Y	Y	Y	Y	Y
Reliability	❷	❷	❷	❷	③
Crash Safety	③	③	③	③	③
Side Impact	—	—	③	③	③

Crash ratings are applicable to all models.

FORD

Contour, Mystique

Rating: Below Average (1995–99). Mazda's 626 is a worthwhile alternative to the Contour and Mystique—it's a more stylish, reasonably priced, highway-proven sedan with a better reliability record. For the latest reports on problems, look at the Contour website listed in Appendix II. **Maintenance/Repair costs:** Higher than average. Most repairs are dealer dependent. **Parts:** Higher-than-average cost, and body parts are sometimes hard to find.

Strengths and weaknesses: These front-drive, mid-sized twin sedans (Contour has a more angular nose and different dashboard) are based on the European-designed Mondeo, which has met with respectable sales after many years on the market. The four-door, five-passenger Contour sells for a bit less than its practically identical Mercury counterpart.

These vehicles are set on a wheelbase slightly larger than that of the Taurus and come with a choice of two engines and transmissions: a base 16-valve 125-hp 2.0L 4-cylinder or an optional 24-valve 170-hp 2.5L V6. Either engine may be hooked to a standard 5-speed transaxle or an optional 4-speed automatic. A smooth but firm ride and crisp handling are guaranteed by the standard MacPherson-strut front suspension, an anti-roll bar, and fully independent rear suspension.

The main advantages of the Contour and Mystique are exceptional handling and a powerful, limited-maintenance V6 engine. Their drawbacks are a plethora of safety-related defects; cramped rear seating; a wimpy, noisy 4-banger; and atrocious quality control that is highlighted by powertrain failures, electrical system shorts, poor body assembly, and ineffective, noisy brakes that are costly to maintain.

Owners report frequent computer module failures and a long wait for parts—even those parts needed to carry out safety-related recall campaigns. One CompuServe member had the following to say:

> My '95 Mystique ran fine for six months, but has been in the dealer repair shop—still not fixed—for three weeks now. First the "over-lock" froze, so you couldn't shift out of Park—even with a foot on the brake. The dealer said an "electrical short circuit kept mak-ing a module fail." They told me the part was part of a recall that had not yet been announced. No sooner had they fixed that when the Overdrive on-off button on the automatic gearshift stopped working. That's still not fixed after 11 working days. First the dealer claimed they couldn't "locate the cause." They sent the car out to a transmission expert who found another "failed mod-ule." The current problem is that the replacement part is "much in demand," and they're "trying to locate one."

Safety summary/Recalls: All models: NHTSA has opened an official probe into front-suspension coil spring failures and engine cooling fan fires on the 1995 Contour, headlight switch failures on 1996s, and blower switch/resistor or wiring harnesses on 1995–99 models. **1995–98**—Many reports of fuel tank leaks, fuel and oil odours perme-ating the interior, difficulty in filling the fuel tank, and inaccurate fuel readings. • Malfunctioning airbags that go off when they shouldn't or don't go off when they should. • Reports of serious injuries caused by airbag deployment. • Airbag light stays on for no reason. • Chronic stalling at idle or after attaining cruising speed. • Complete electrical shutdown. • Lights shut off unexpectedly. • Seatback often collapses for no reason or after a rear fender-bender. • Brakes often fail, make a grinding noise when applied, and often need replacing (warped rotors and prematurely worn pads). • Frequent engine and transmission fail-ures. • Transmission will not hold vehicle in Park. • Check Engine light stays lit for no reason. **Recalls: All models: 1995**—The rear door win-dow will be replaced. • The addition of a ground strap prevents an elec-trostatic charge from building up and igniting fuel vapours when refueling. • The hardware that attaches the outboard ends of the front seatbelts to the front seat frames may be cracked or fractured. • The passenger airbag may not inflate properly. • The fuel-filler-pipe open-ing reinforcement may leak fuel. Tank replacement includes a new fuel filter and a *free fill-up!* The last item in the recall procedure involves fill-ing up the tank (at Ford's expense) in order to confirm that there are no leaks at the tank-to-filler-neck seal. **1995–96**—Faulty traction control throttle cables may prevent the engine from returning to idle.

1996–97—Natural gas–equipped vehicles may explode in a collision.
1996–98—The floor shift indicator may give an incorrect reading.

Secret Warranties/Service Tips

All models: 1995–97—Air that blows out the defroster ducts only may signal that the defrost actuator door linkage has become disconnected from
the crank. • Transaxle fluid seepage can be corrected by servicing with a
remote vent kit or by replacing the main control cover. • Parking brakes
that stick or bind need a parking brake cable service kit. • Front end accessory drivebelt slippage can be corrected by installing an upgraded FEAD
belt, steel idler pulley, and splash shield kit. **1995–98**—Stall and/or exhaust
sulfur smell requires a revised power control module. • Stall, or hooting or
moosing noise from engine compartment can be fixed by replacing the air
intake-duct idle air resonator, and idle air hose, with a revised duct and resonator assembly (#F6RZ-9B659-CA). **1995–99**—Upgraded front brake pads
have been put into service to silence front brake groaning. • Tips for fixing
windshield water leaks. • Paint delamination, peeling, and fading (see Part
Two). **1998**—Harsh automatic shifting is likely caused by a mis-calibrated
PCM. • Frequent shut-off when fueling can be fixed by installing a new flap-
per baffle in the fuel filler pipe. • Inaccurate fuel gauge readings may be
corrected by installing either a new fuel tank or a fuel pump.

Contour, Mystique Profile

	1995	1996	1997	1998	1999
Cost Price ($)					
GL/LX	15,470	15,980	16,020	17,305	17,595
SE V6	18,355	18,865	19,350	19,475	19,695
Used Values ($)					
GL/LX ↑	6,000	8,000	9,000	11,000	12,000
GL/LX ↓	5,000	6,000	7,500	9,000	9,500
SE V6 ↑	7,500	8,000	11,000	12,500	14,000
SE V6 ↓	6,000	6,500	9,500	11,000	12,500
Extended Warranty	Y	Y	Y	Y	Y
Secret Warranty	Y	Y	Y	Y	Y
Reliability	❷	❷	❷	❷	❷
Crash Safety	⑤	⑤	⑤	⑤	—
Side Impact	—	—	③	③	③

Note: The GL was replaced by the '99 LX.

Sable, Taurus

Rating: Not Recommended (1986–99). These cars aren't bargains at any price, despite their rapid depreciation. Besides an appointment with a psychiatrist, an extended powertrain warranty is a prerequisite for anyone seriously thinking of buying a Sable or Taurus. True, the high-performance Taurus SHO (Super High Output) has fewer engine breakdowns (it's Yamaha-sourced); however, it shares most of the other generic safety- and performance-related defects that have long plagued these family sedans and wagons.

These cars are aging badly. Chronic 3.8L engine head gasket and automatic transmission failures; a plethora of hazardous airbag, fuel system, brake, suspension, and steering defects; and chronic paint/rust problems are the main reasons their rating is so low this year. Plus, owners are reporting that engine and transmission repairs don't last: some owners are routinely putting in new engines or transmissions every year, as the following American reader's email relates,

> I own a '95 Taurus. I bought it as a program car with 14,792 miles on it, on 4/23/96. It still had time on the original warranty. I bought it with extended 6 year/100,000 mile coverage. Thank goodness!
>
> I'm on my second transmission and am awaiting my FOURTH 3.8L engine!!! Even with the Ford 6 year/100,000 mile extended warranty I am certain that this engine will fail outside the warranty period.
>
> My dealer at first told me I had to pay for labor charges to install the FOURTH engine. They say the warranty (I believe 12 months) applies only from the time the first engine is installed!
>
> That means they can keep installing bad engines until the warranty runs out. Which is just what they did!!!
>
> I change engines on an average of every 20,000 miles. This is a terrible inconvenience! I am now driving my car in 20 degree [Fahrenheit] weather without heat!!! My dealer told me to keep it until the FOURTH engine arrives....

I've recommended these cars in the past because Ford's "goodwill" programs usually compensated owners for most of the above-noted failures once the warranty had expired. Unfortunately, these refund programs are drying up and owners are now frequently faced with $3,000 automatic transmission repair bills in addition to thousand of dollars in repairs for defective fuel systems, brakes, suspension and steering assemblies.

And the situation isn't likely to improve, judging by Ford's rejection of more and more consumer complaints on the grounds that repairs were done by independent agencies, the vehicle was bought used, or it is no longer under the original warranty. Furthermore, some key consumer allies at Ford, like Ford Canada President Bobbie Gaunt, have retired, leaving consumers to fend for themselves before a corporation that values stonewalling over integrity.

After exchanging dozens of letters and meeting with Ford officials over the past three years, I've come to the conclusion that Taurus, Sable, and Windstar engine and transmission defects are so widespread that Ford's customer relations department has been overwhelmed by the enormity of the problem and is routinely stonewalling and then rejecting most claims for after-warranty assistance (AWA in Ford lingo). I recognize that Ford Canada has been far more generous and not mean-spirited like its American counterpart. However, customer assistance, particularly for transmission failures, is still unfairly allocated, if given at all. Consequently, I cannot recommend the purchase of any new or used Taurus, Sable, or Windstar. Furthermore, you can count on me keeping these ratings low until I see all Ford owners are being treated fairly through a refund program identical to its 3.8L engine Owner Notification Program (ONP). **Maintenance/Repair costs:** Higher than average, but repairs aren't dealer dependent. **Parts:** Average cost (independent suppliers sell for much less) and very easy to find, except for the SHO's Yamaha engine, which is practically indestructible anyhow.

Strengths and weaknesses: Although they lack pickup with the standard 4-cylinder engine, these mid-sized sedans are competent family cars, offering lots of interior room, nice handling, a good crash rating, and many convenience features. The best powertrain combination for all driving conditions (it's also the worst combination from a reliability standpoint): the 3.8L V6 hooked to a 4-speed for the family sedan, and the Yamaha powerplant harnessed to a manual gearbox on the high-performance SHO.

SHO

The Taurus SHO sedan, debuting in 1989, carries a Yamaha 24-valve 3.0L V6 with 220 horsepower; a stiff, performance-oriented suspension; and 5-speed manual transmission. As of 1993, a 4-speed automatic transmission became available. In mid-1996, a redesigned SHO debuted with a standard Yamaha 32-valve V8. Unfortunately, the manual transmission was dropped at that time, a move that has turned off most die-hard performance enthusiasts.

The SHO is an impressive high-performance car that is apparently better built than regular-production Sable and Taurus versions. In fact, early SHOs escaped Ford's powertrain problems because of their reliance upon Yamaha for their engines and the wide use of a manual gearbox.

Is the SHO a good buy? The answer is yes, but only if you're willing to spend big bucks for your performance thrills. SHOs hold their value well and give impressive performance. On the other hand, they're hard to find (only 10,000 units a year are sold, and only three percent of

Taurus buyers opt for an SHO), they're expensive, and engine repairs may become a problem if Ford abandons the model. The SHO's price is likely to remain stable, or even drop somewhat, inasmuch as most buyers feel the vehicle is already overpriced and they are becoming increasingly wary of Ford's reputation for poor quality control.

Reliability: Not job 1!

Since their 1986 debut, Sables and Tauruses (joined by the Lincoln Continental in 1991) have been subject to a multitude of safety-related recalls, secret warranties, and service adjustments. They've distinguished themselves for being unsafe, unreliable, and costly to maintain and repair (see "Dead Ford" "Ford Suckz," and "Ford Taurus, Sable Automatic Transmission Victims" website links in Appendix II). Their deficiencies fall into the following major categories: powertrain (engines and transmissions) and brake failures; costly brake maintenance; faulty fuel, steering, suspension, and air conditioning systems; poor body fits; clunks and rattles; and paint peeling and delamination.

Automatic transmission failures

Since 1991, Ford's automatic transmissions have been failure-prone, function erratically, and are slow to shift—an annoying drawback if you need to rock the car out of a snowbank, and fairly dangerous if you need to pull out onto a busy roadway. These problems are caused principally by a cracked aluminum forward clutch piston, although dozens of other causes, including major hardware and software components, have been linked to the above failures. Breakdowns usually occur after three years of use, around the 80,000–120,000 km mark, and can cost $3,000–$3,500 to repair at the dealer, or half that much at an independent garage.

When Ford modified the automatic transmission in 1991 for easier shifting, it also made it less reliable. (Chrysler had a similar experience with its A604 automatic transmission.) In fact, *Consumer Reports'* annual member survey shows that almost 20 percent of owners of 1991 Tauruses, Sables, and Continentals experienced a serious transmission failure—four times the average for 1991 vehicles. Ford subsequently extended the warranty on these transmissions for up to six years under a special Owner Notification Program (ONP).

So why aren't we applauding Ford's earlier generosity? Because the company has been systematically dishonest with its customers.

First, although the automaker's 1991 model ONP established the benchmark for automatic transmission durability as 6 years/160,000 km, Ford never extended its application to 1992–98 models—vehicles afflicted by the same defect. Secondly, when the company recently announced *another* ONP, this time covering 1999 Taurus, Sables, and Windstars transmissions, 1992 through 1998 models were once again excluded, even though customer complaints indicate that these are the model years with the most problems. Furthermore, the company's own internal bulletins shout out the fact that Ford has known about the transmission's premature failures and erratic shifting since 1986! Yet Ford continued using the cheaper, though failure-prone, aluminum forward clutch piston—which has been principally responsible for the above failures—for over a decade.

Let's take a look at what Ford's bulletins disclose, as background and as arguing points with Ford, before or after your small claims filing:

Detroit, We Have a Problem! (1986–95)

Article No
94-24-7
11/28/94
TRANSAXLE - AXOD, AXOD-E, AX4S - FORWARD/REVERSE ENGAGEMENT CONCERN - REVISED FORWARD CLUTCH PISTON
FORD:
1986-95 TAURUS
1993-95 TAURUS SHO
LINCOLN-MERCURY:
1986-95 SABLE
1988-94 CONTINENTAL
LIGHT TRUCK:
1995 WINDSTAR
ISSUE:
The forward clutch piston may crack on its outside diameter, seal groove or apply wall (bottom of piston). This condition could allow internal clutch leakage resulting in engagement concerns.
STEEL CLUTCH PISTON PART APPLICATIONS
F4DZ-7A262-A   F4DZ-7A262-B
3.0L TAURUS
3.0L SABLE
3.8L TAURUS
3.8L SABLE
3.8L CONTINENTAL
3.8L WINDSTAR   3.2L TAURUS SHO
NOTE:
Use a magnet to verify the forward clutch piston being installed is the new steel piston. The magnet will adhere to the steel piston and not to the aluminum piston.
Do not use any service stock of aluminum forward clutch pistons. Return stock to parts depot for credit.

PART NUMBER	PART NAME	CLASS
F4DZ-7A262-A	Forward Clutch Piston	A
F4DZ-7A262-B	Forward Clutch Piston (SHO)	C

This first bulletin updates others going back several years and lists 1986–95 as the model years affected. Note how Ford clearly blames the aluminum piston as the culprit causing what the automaker understates as "engagement concerns."

Surprise! Upgraded Steel Piston Fails, Too (1994–98)

Article No.
98-3-7
02/16/98
TRANSAXLE - AX4N - INTERMITTENT NEUTRAL CONDITION - NO FORWARD OR REVERSE MOVEMENT - VEHICLES BUILT
THROUGH 2/1/98
FORD:
1994-98 TAURUS
LINCOLN-MERCURY:
1994-98 SABLE
1995-98 CONTINENTAL

ISSUE:
Some vehicles may experience an intermittent Neutral condition after driving and coming to a stop. This may be caused by
the bonded seal on the forward clutch piston intermittently not sealing during the 3-2 downshift.
ACTION:
Replace the forward clutch piston with a revised Forward Clutch Piston (F8DZ-7A262-AB). Refer to the following Service
Procedure for details.

PART NUMBER	PART NAME
F5DZJ153-AA	Seal And Gasket kit
F8DZ-7A262-AB	Forward Clutch Piston
F8DZ-7B164-AC	Forward Clutch Plates - Friction (4)
F2DZ-7B442-A	Forward Clutch Plates - Steel (4)

Apparently, the move to a steel piston didn't make Ford's transmissions
more reliable or durable, as the above bulletin clearly demonstrates. Hence,
my ratings downgrade Ford's latest models.

3.8L engine failures

Ford's other major powertrain problem is the 3.8L engine's chronic
head gasket failures. Symptoms include engine overheating; poor
engine performance; and a thin film deposited on the inside of the
windshield, thus cutting down night driving visibility. Repairs range
$700–$1,000 depending upon what other damage has occurred from
overheating. Left untreated, the failure can "cook" your engine, requiring $3,000–$4,000 in repairs. And, even if treated in time, this defect
can cause emissions component failures (oxygen sensors and various
computer modules) and other hardware malfunctions that can lead to
other expensive repairs.

There have been hundreds of cases reported to me of head gasket
failures after three to five years or 60,000–100,000 km of use. Although
these engine repairs are covered by Ford's 00M09 "goodwill" engine
warranty up to seven years or 160,000 km (see page 57 for Ford's ONP
letter), many Sable, Taurus, and Windstar owners have had their claims
rejected because their vehicles fell outside of the 1994–95 limit set out
in the above warranty extension. This makes no sense whatsoever, especially since Ford's own bulletin (see following) traces the problem back
to the 1988 models and through to 1996.

3.8L V6 Engines Blow Their Tops (1988–96)

98-4-9
03/02/98
COOLING SYSTEM - OVERHEATING AND/OR LOSS OF COOLANT - 3.8L VEHICLES
FORD:
1988-96 TAURUS
LINCOLN-MERCURY:
1988-94 CONTINENTAL
1988-95 SABLE
LIGHT TRUCK:
1996 WINDSTAR
ISSUE:
Coolant may leak from the head gaskets and/or the vehicle may overheat. There may also be concerns of reduced heater
output due to low coolant levels. This may be caused by insufficient sealing of the head gaskets.
ACTION:
Replace the head gaskets and head bolts. The revised head gaskets and bolts provide improved sealing capability and higher
clamping force between the cylinder head and block. Refer to the following Service Procedure for details.
PART NUMBER   PART NAME
F5PZ-6051-AA   Head Gasket And Bolt Kit (One Side)
WARRANTY STATUS: Eligible Under The Provisions Of Bumper To Bumper Warranty Coverage

*Interestingly, the above head gasket failures have also been reported with
3.8L V6 engines equipping Ford's Mustang through 1998.*

Paint delamination

Over the past decade, there have been frequent complaints of paint
delamination, peeling, and premature rusting affecting 1986–97
Taurus and Sables.

*A paint-delaminated Ford Taurus. Chrysler, Ford, and GM will repaint
their vehicles for free, if threatened with a small claims lawsuit.*

One owner of a 1990 Sable found pinpoint rust spots during the first year of ownership and had the entire car repainted at Ford's expense. Unfortunately, the problem didn't go away. The owner reports the following:

> I have recently noticed continued paint defects causing the car to rust prematurely, specifically under the front edge of the hood...I maintain that the sealer and paint were improperly applied when the car was manufactured and that this is a defect that the Ford Motor Company should correct.

That *Lemon-Aid* reader is right, and that's why Ford is the target of multiple class action paint lawsuits and is settling most small claims court cases, although more class actions may still be imminent.

Ford's warranty performance
In the States, Ford CEO Jac Nasser has not only led Ford's coverup of Explorer safety hazards and Firestone tire–related deaths and injuries (check the tire settlement gag orders throughout the States over the past decade), he is also responsible for turning his back on Ford Canada's request for a transmission refund program (ONP) for owners of 1992–98 models. Bolstered by Nasser's mean-spirited edict, Ford's U.S. assistance centres don't acknowledge the transmission problem and rarely offer "goodwill" refunds. However, once a small claims court case is filed, Ford reps usually make a fair settlement offer, if they show up at all, as this owner relates in his November, 2000 email:

> Dear Phil,
> I emailed you earlier in the year seeking help on my small claims case against Ford. I'm happy to report that I won my case and received a $1900 settlement check from Ford in the mail yesterday!
> As you may recall I have a 1991 Explorer that has a significant paint peel problem. I followed all the steps recommended by your web site. I ended up in small claims court. Ford had indicated in court documents that they were going to send a representative to the hearing, but nobody showed. The judge made a quick ruling in my favor and I was out the door, I didn't even get a chance to show the load of material I had brought to make my case.
> I'm spreading the word about your web site (and my victory) to all the paint peel victims I see!
> Thanks for all your help.
> Mark Granger

As stated earlier, Ford's after-warranty assistance is easier to obtain in Canada than in the United States because Ford agents don't habitually force you to file suit before offering a fair settlement. Plus, Canada's customer assistance centre is staffed by usually competent, empowered

Ford employees, not subcontracted, third-party flunkies. This having been said, don't get the idea that Ford's Canadian customer assistance agents are pushovers. Quite the opposite, actually.

Canadian owners tell me that they still have to threaten small claims court action to get Ford employees to accept repairs done by independent garages, repeat failures, or failures that occur in the 100,000 to 160,000 km ("no man's land") range, where warranty decisions are particularly inconsistent. That's why an ONP is so important; it'll take out the "hit or miss" element from the refund process and treat everyone equally.

As always, I'll continue monitoring Ford's customer assistance activities throughout the year, and invite readers to use *www.lemonaidcars.com* for the latest updates and Appendix II, "Best Internet Gripe Sites," to link up with websites specifically oriented toward Ford transmission, head gasket, and warranty servicing deficiencies.

In the meantime, anyone seeking assistance should call Ford's toll-free number, 1-800-565-3673 (FORD). I have been assured that each owner will have his or her claim reviewed fairly. I hope this will be the case; however, keep in mind what one Ford customer assistance whistle-blower told me recently:

> Ford has just received a J.D. Power report that shows giving out goodwill refunds for repairs doesn't improve car sales. Since then, the company has taken a harder line in reviewing customer claims. THE ONLY THING THAT GETS OUR ATTENTION IS IF A SMALL CLAIMS LAWSUIT IS THREATENED OR HAS BEEN FILED. These are kicked upstairs to Legal Affairs and are settled right away....

Other problems

The 4-cylinder engine is a dog that no amount of servicing can change. It's slow, noisy, prone to stalling and surging, and actually consumes more gas than the V6.

The 3.0L 6-cylinder is noted for engine head bolt failures and piston scuffing, and is characterized by hard starting, stalling, excessive engine noise, and poor fuel economy. Transmission cooler lines leak and often lead to the unnecessary repair or replacement of the transmission— note the advice given to this vacationing owner of a 1993 Taurus:

> ...
>
> While in Florida a month ago the local Ford dealer plugged a tester in our car and announced that our problem with the transmission could only be fixed by a new one—at an estimated $2,800 US. Another garage checked the colour of the transmission fluid and came to the same conclusion...a new transmission, but the estimate was lower, about $1,800 US. They added oil which temporarily fixed the problem. On our long drive home, towing a boat, we kept the fluid level topped up.
>
> On arrival, we visited our local CTC station in Port Hope, and discovered that a transmission cooling line had been leaking. The two mechanics who listened while I described the problem, immediately guessed what it would likely be. It turns out they have seen a lot these rusted lines on Fords. The fix cost $150, because the radiator had to be removed to get at the line. In fairness to the mechanics in Florida, perhaps this rusting problem is limited to climates where salt is used on roads.
>
> ...

Other things to look out for: blown heater hoses, malfunctioning fuel gauge sending units, and brakes that need constant attention—in front, they're noisy, pulsate excessively, tend to wear out prematurely, require a great deal of pedal effort, and are hard to modulate. Master cylinders need replacing around 100,000 km.

1988–95 models continue to have defective ignition modules, oxygen sensors, and fuel pumps, which cause rough running, chronic stalling, hard starting, and electrical-system short circuits. Other problem areas include the following: biodegradable tie-rods, ball joints, coil springs, and motor mounts; an automatic transmission that is slow to downshift, hunts for Overdrive, and gives jerky performance; air conditioners that are failure-prone and can cost up to $1,000 to fix; malfunctioning heaters that are slow to warm up and don't direct enough heat to the floor (particularly on the passenger side); a defective heater core that costs big bills to replace (buy from an independent supplier); and noisy, prematurely worn rack-and-pinion steering assemblies. Front suspension components also wear out quickly.

Electrical components, like windshield wipers, fuel pumps, and the rear defroster, interfere with radio reception. The automatic antenna often sticks, electric windows short-circuit, power door locks fail, and the electronic dash gives inaccurate readings. Owners report that electrical short circuits—which illuminate the Check Engine light and cause flickering lights and engine surging—are frequently misdiagnosed. Customers end up paying for the unnecessary replacement of the alternator, voltage regulator, or battery, in addition to unnecessary tune-ups. The speedometer is noisy and often inaccurate in cold weather.

Body/trim items are fragile on all cars (did somebody mention door handles?). Paint adherence is particularly poor on plastic components, weld joints, and the underside—even with mudguards. Owners also report that water leaks into the trunk through the taillight assembly and that 1986–95 versions produce an annoying sound of fuel sloshing when accelerating or stopping.

1996–99 models were radically redesigned with a totally new, more rounded styling that turned off as many buyers as it turned on. Other changes included upgraded engines, new electronic controls for the LX, and a revamped, oval dash panel. Other improvements: better handling and ride quality, more effective soundproofing, and some transmission refinements (beginning with the 1997 models, but ineffective from a reliability standpoint). Despite these changes, owners still report serious safety-related deficiencies (see "Safety summary/Recalls") and other performance-related problems, like the non-upgraded engines being noisy, slow and hard to start; the automatic transmission shifting erratically, or not at all; engine gaskets still failing; front end failures including the outer tie-rods, ball joints, and stabilizer bar links; and an assortment of rattles, buzzes, whines, and moans. The most annoying? Power windows that fail constantly and cost big bucks to repair. Finally, there's the incessant snapping and creaking of the plastic in the centre console and dash from the plastic sections binding against each other when the body flexes, especially if the sun has been shining on it.

Technical service bulletins: All models: 1992–95—Hesitation, no-start, reduced power, stalling, no-crank due to solenoid corrosion. **1993**—Poorly performing air conditioning systems caused by a slipping clutch at high ambient temperatures. • Growling AC FX-15 compressor. • Fuel odours in the passenger compartment. • Noisy power-steering units. • Inoperative power door locks. • Under-hood squeaks, chirps, and knocks; wind noise coming from front door windows. • Intermittent long cranks or no-starts. • A service engine light that has a mind of its own and may go on for no apparent reason. **1994**—A faulty 3.8L engine rocker arm assembly may be the cause of squeaking, chirping, and knocking noises. • A rough idle, hesitation, and excessive fuel consumption. • Faulty electric rear window defrosters. • Inadequate AC operation caused by a faulty cold engine lockout switch and hose assembly. **1994–95**—Defective fuel pumps often produce extraneous noise in radio speakers. **1995**—Delayed transmission engagement and shift errors, harsh shifts, no 3–4 shift, erratic shifts, Forward/Reverse gear malfunctions, and transaxle click when in Reverse. • Insufficient AC cooling or excessive clutch end gap; AC compressor has moans, chirps, or squeaks coming from the blower motor at low speeds. • Faulty temperature gauge. • No-crank caused by a corroded starter solenoid (carried over several model years). • Brake roughness upon application and a clacking/thumping noise when braking. • Premature inner-edge wear on the rear tires. • A fuel tank sloshing noise. **1996**—No-start or stall. • Stall or hard start after one- to four-hour soak • Cold engine hesitation/stumble. • Click from transmission when going into Reverse. • Transaxle driveline noises. • Case breakage at rear planet support. • Grunt or groan noise during steering wheel return. • Reduction in power-steering assist. • Door hinge correction. • Fog/film on windshield/interior glass. • Musty and mildewy odours. • Dead battery diagnosis. • Acceleration or deceleration clunk noise. • Wind noise at A-pillar at highway speeds. • A-pillar creaking noise. • Front suspension creak/groan. • Hard starting, long crank, stalling. • Rear headliner sag. • Door handle malfunctions. • High idle, surge, stall, harsh transmission engagement. • Loose catalyst or muffler heat shields. • Click noise when going into Reverse. • Warm-weather stalling. • Thump, clunk, or chuckle noise from front end. • Troubleshooting driveline noises. • Excessive wind noise. **1996–97**—Harsh automatic transmission shifting. • Excessive blower motor noise. • AM band radio static. • Water leaks onto passenger floor area. **1997**—Chronic dead battery. • Acceleration or deceleration clunk. • Front suspension clunk. • A-pillar creaking noise. • Front end accessory drivebelt (FEAD) may slip during wet conditions, causing a reduction in steering power assist. • Steering wheel grunt or honk noise. • Loose catalyst or heat shields. • Stall or surging with automatic transmission engagement. **1998**—Numerous automatic transmission failures, including no fourth gear, torque converter clutch not engaging, intermittent shifting into Neutral, no Forward or Reverse. • Other problems include hard starts, excessive spark knock, power steering moan, rattling upon acceleration, AC lack of temperature control, faulty trunk-mounted CD player, and inoperative power windows. **1999**—Harsh 3–2 downshift/shudder when accelerating or turning; no Reverse engagement. • Lack of engine braking. • Whining or buzzing in speakers. • Troubleshooting tips to correct reduce NVH (noise, vibration, or harshness) when driving. • Windshield sealing for water leaks. • Defining what is abnormal ABS noise. • Windnoise around side doors. • Fuel gauge concerns. • Self-activating front wipers.

Safety summary/Recalls: All models: 1995—Sudden windshield shattering. • AC failures. • Headlight failures. **1995–96**—Fuel pump failures. • Airbag fails to deploy or is accidentally deployed. • Transmission slips out of Park. • Engine compartment fires. • Defective door locks. **1995–97**—Sudden acceleration. • Stalling. • ABS failures. **1996**—Chronic stalling. • Cruise control won't slow vehicle on slopes. • Left front wheel may separate from car. • Loss of steering when it rains. • Loss of power steering. • Frequent engine head gasket failures. • Transmission fails or shifts erratically. • Dash reflects into the windshield. • Faulty door lock switch. • Defective heating/defrosting system causes excessive windshield fogging. **1997**—Transmission jumps from Park to Reverse. • Sudden steering loss. • Wheels fly off. • Several engine head gasket failures. • Chronic transmission failures. **1998**—Accelerator and brake pedals are too close to each other. • Vehicle won't slow when accelerator pedal is released. • Faulty cruise control won't slow vehicle down. • Automatic transmission malfunctions. • Chronic brake failures. • Defective rotor and wiring assembly caused ABS failure. • Loss of steering when steering belt pulley and pump failed. • Defective rack-and-pinion steering spring yoke. • Sudden steering lockup. • Trunk lid fell on owner's head due to defective torsion bar. • Trunk light burned garment in the trunk. • Faulty headlights. • Headlights don't give enough light to the sides. • Daylight running lights flicker due to defective module. • Dashboard reflects in the windshield, causing reduced visibility. • Heater system failed. • Driver's seatbelt won't retract or lock into position. • Hatchback window suddenly exploded while vehicle was parked. **1999**—Engine fires. • No airbag deployment and inadvertent air deployment. • Frequent complaints of sudden acceleration or high idle when taking the foot off the gas pedal, at a standstill, when shifting into Reverse, slowly accelerating, or applying the brakes. • Reports of accelerator sticking. • Many reports of no-starts or sudden stalling caused by fuel pump failure. • Defective power-steering pump causes sudden steering lockup. • ABS brakes locked up when applied and vehicle suddenly accelerated. • Many reports of brake pedal having been pushed to the floor with no braking effect. One Taurus owner recounts the following tragic experience in his NHTSA complaint:

> Sudden brake loss, cruise control wouldn't disengage, brakes to floor, emergency brake pulled to no effect, death of four....

Every element of this owner's story is repeated throughout the NHTSA database from reports of other Taurus and Sable owners. • Cruise control fails to disengage when vehicle is going downhill. • Frequent automatic transmission failures that include: slipping, hesitation, lurching into gear, failure to engage first gear, and a defective fluid pump destroying the catalytic converter. • Transmission in Park position allowed vehicle to roll downhill. • Transmission may leak fluid onto the exhaust manifold. • Steering wheel and brakes vibrate excessively when braking. • These vehicles eat brake rotors, calipers, and pads every 8,000 kilometres. • Brakes produce a grinding, growling noise in addition to an acrid smell. • Front passenger's seatbelt won't retract or lock into position. • Seatbelt broke. • Seatbelts fail to retract in a collision. • In the morning and evening, the light tan dashboard reflects upon the windshield, causing reduced visibility. • Rear defroster/defogger works poorly. • Rear windshield exploded when defroster/defogger activated. • In another incident, rear windshield exploded while vehicle was underway. • Headlights dim when brakes are applied. • Trunk light bulb burned part of luggage. • Electrical system shorts lead to the erratic operation of power door locks (they unlock while vehicle is underway) and windows. • AC discharges a foul odour that causes eyes to water and burn. • Fuel tank leaks. • Vehicle will stall out when fuel gauge shows the tank is one-quarter full. In fact, the gauge is so inaccurate that it will vary its reading by a half a tank depending upon whether you are going uphill or downhill. **Recalls: 1991–95**—Cruise control units and throttle control cable are faulty. **1992**—The inner tie-rod may collapse suddenly. The son of a West Coast owner of a 1992 Taurus relates this incident:

The right inner tie-rod, a piece of the suspension critical to the steering and thus safety of my 1992 Taurus, broke while my father was attempting to make a right turn from a stop sign. The car lost all steering control and the front wheels were seized. Fortunately, the car was barely moving, and no collision occurred...I can tolerate a radio or AC failure on a "medium aged" car but critical safety components should have a longer service life designed into them. I hope you can inform all Taurus/Sable owners of the inherent dangers lurking in their steering system. And for those cars still under warranty, specify that the part be thoroughly inspected by first removing the rubber protecting boot...

• Children could lock themselves in the footwell area or storage area of wagons. • The wagon liftgate could open while the vehicle is in motion. **1992–95**—The engine cooling fan may freeze and cause the cooling fan motor to overheat, in turn causing wiring damage and sparking a fire (3.0L and 3.8L engines only). • The throttle can stick and not return to idle if water enters the throttle cable area and freezes (3.8L engines only). **1993**—The following is not a safety problem in accordance with U.S. Federal Regulation 573; however, it is deemed a safety improvement campaign by NHTSA. Ford is providing an extended warranty through the year 2001 for replacement of front springs due to fracture. The front coil springs can fracture as a result of corrosion in combination with small cracks in the springs. The front tire could deflate due to a broken front coil spring contacting the tire, increasing the risk of a vehicle crash. Dealers will install a spring catcher bracket that will prevent a fractured spring from contacting a tire. Owners can contact Ford at 1-800-392-3673. • Rear-drive controllers in models with ABS were installed in error. **1995**—Brake master cylinder may be defective. **1996**—Although apparently in Park, the vehicle can roll away. • The brake fluid indicator may malfunction. • Fuel may leak from a faulty fuel pressure regulator. • The brake system fluid level indicator lamp switch may be faulty. **1996–98**—Dealers will replace the dash insulator retainer clip so it doesn't interfere with the accelerator cable or pedal. **1998**—On vehicles equipped with manual seat tracks, the front seatbelt buckle attaching stud may be defective. **SHO: 1996**—Faulty fuel pressure regulator could cause a fire. **Sable, Taurus: 1996–97**—The transmission may not engage. • PRNDL may give a false reading, allowing vehicle to move although it appears to be in Park. • Defective fuel rail may deliver fuel to the injectors at more than 43 psi; it may cause chronic stalling under low-speed deceleration or acceleration. • Transmission fluid leakage could cause a fire. **1998–99**—Dealers will replace the seatbelt buckle mounting bracket and stud assembly on models with manual seats.

Secret Warranties/Service Tips

All models: 1986–89—If the accessories frequently cut out, install a new ignition switch wire harness. **1986–90**—Extended or no 3–4 shift may require a reassembled direct clutch piston and spring retainer. • No-shifts, harsh shifts, or extended shifts may be due to faulty oil pump body and valve body check balls. • AC evaporator water leaks onto the carpet require a new core and seal assembly (#E9DZ-19860-A). • Poor AM radio reception may be caused by interference from the heated windshield system. **1986–91**—Poor forward shifting may require a new clutch piston. • Engine knocking at idle may require the installation of a new, thicker thrust plate to reduce camshaft end play. **1986–94**—A squeak or chirp coming from the blower motor can be stopped by installing an upgraded blower motor with improved brush-to-commutator friction. • A rear suspension clunk or rattle when a wagon goes over a bump may be caused by a loose rear tension strut. • A speaker whine or buzz caused by the fuel pump can be stopped by installing an electronic noise RFI filter. **1986–95**—A cracked forward clutch piston may cause Forward/Reverse problems. Install the improved clutch piston and ask Ford to cover part of the cost inasmuch as their bulletins confirm it's a design defect. **1986–98**—A buzz or rattle from the exhaust system may be caused by a loose heat shield catalyst. **1988–92**—Cold hesitation when accelerating, rough idle, long crank times, and stalling may all signal the need to clean out excessive intake valve deposits. **1989–93**—A persistent fuel odour in the interior when the AC is running signals the need to install a new auxiliary vapour-tube service kit and relocate the vapour tube near the rear bumper. **1990–93**—Noise coming from the power-steering pump may be caused by air in the system; purge the system. **1991–93**—Growling from the FX-15 AC compressor can be eliminated by installing a new compressor rubber damped disc and hub assembly. **1991–95**—A sloshing noise from the fuel tank when accelerating or stopping requires the installation of an upgraded tank. Cost may be covered under the emissions warranty for 1995 models. **1992**—A 3.0L engine that stalls or idles roughly after a cold start may require a new EEC IV processor. **1992–95**—A corroded solenoid may be the cause of starter failures (see following).

Article No. 94-25-3
12/26/94
NO CRANK — POSSIBLE CORROSION AT STARTER SOLENOID — VEHICLES WITH 3.0L AND 3.8L
ENGINES
FORD:
1992—95 TAURUS, THUNDERBIRD
LINCOLN-MERCURY:
1992–94 CONTINENTAL
1992—95 COUGAR, SABLE
LIGHT TRUCK:
1996 WINDSTAR
ISSUE: Some vehicles may exhibit a "No-Crank" condition due to corrosion at the starter solenoid
connector.
ACTION: Replace the corroded connector with a service wiring and connector assembly. Applying
di-electric grease, along with replacing the wiring and service connector, to the terminal connector
will aid in corrosion protection.

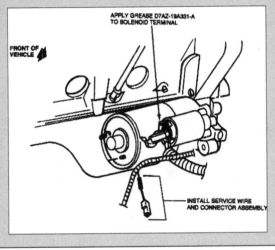

This is one inexpensive-to-repair cause of no-starts on 1992–96 cars and minivans equipped with 3.0L and 3.8L engines. Check it out before authorizing other costly repairs.

1993—Free replacement through the year 2001 of front coil springs that fracture or may fracture due to excessive corrosion (see "Safety summary/ Recalls"). **1993–94**—An inoperative AC blower probably needs an improved cold engine lockout switch and hose assembly. • Stalling or hard starts in high ambient temperatures or high altitudes may be due to fuel tank contamination, which causes damage to the fuel pump. Ford paid for a fuel tank flush and a new fuel pump/sender and in-line fuel filter until May 31, 1997, under Service Program 94B48. **1993–97**—If the front end accessory drive belt (FEAD) slips during wet conditions, it can cause a reduction in steering power assist; Ford suggests the belt be replaced. **1993–99**—Paint delamination, fading, and peeling (see Part Two). A rotten-egg odour coming from the exhaust probably means that you have a faulty catalytic converter; replacement may be covered under the emissions warranty. • Ford has been repairing premature engine head gasket, ring, and valve wear for free when the emissions warranty applies. • Two other

components that frequently benefit from Ford "goodwill" warranty extensions are fuel pumps and computer modules. If Ford balks at refunding
your money, apply the emissions warranty for a full or partial refund.
1994–95—A thumping or clanking noise heard from the front brakes signals the need to service the front disc brake rotors. **1994–98**—No fourth
gear may signal the need to install an upgraded forward clutch control
valve retaining clip. • Forward clutch piston returns as the most likely suspect in malfunctioning automatic transmissions (see page 201). **1994–99**—
Service tips to silence wind noise around doors. **1995–98**—No-starts may be
cause by a defective fuel pump. **1995–99**—Tips for sealing windshield water
leaks and reducing noise, vibration, and harshness while driving.
1995–2000—A harsh 3–2 downshift/shudder when accelerating or turning
may have a simple cause: air entering the fluid filter pickup area due to a
slightly low ATF fluid level. **1996–97**—An acceleration or deceleration
clunk is likely caused by the rear lower subframe isolators allowing movement between the mounts and the subframe. • A front suspension clunk
may signal premature sway bar wear. • Harsh automatic 1–2 shifting may be
caused by a malfunctioning electronic pressure control or the main control
valves sticking in the valve body (see following).

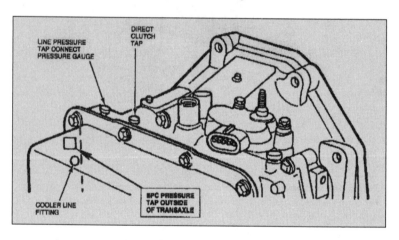

1996–98—Troubleshooting tips for a torque converter clutch that won't
engage. Hard starts or long cranks may be caused by a mis-calibrated PCM,
a faulty IAC, or a malfunctioning fuel pump. • Install a power-steering service kit to silence steering moan. • A rattle heard when accelerating may be
corrected by replacing the exhaust pipe flex coupling. • Inoperative power
windows may need a new motor and lubrication of the glass run weather
stripping. • Water leaking onto the passenger floor area is likely caused by
insufficient sealing of the cabin air filter to the cowl inlet. **1996–99**—
Frequent no-starts, long cranks, or a dead battery may be caused by excessive current drain or water entry in the ABS module connector.
1997—Stalling or surging of 3.0L engines when shifting may signal the need
to reprogram the power control module (PCM). **1997–98**—Lack of AC temperature control may be corrected by replacing the blend air door actuator.
1999—Self-activating front wipers need an upgraded multifunction switch

(covered under warranty or "goodwill"). • No Reverse engagement is likely caused by the Reverse clutch lip seals shearing or tearing during Reverse engagement in cold weather.

Sable, Taurus Profile

	1992	1993	1994	1995	1996	1997	1998	1999
Cost Price ($)								
Sable GS	18,995	19,470	20,995	21,195	22,595	23,595	24,395	24,595
LS Wagon	23,550	23,570	24,196	24,195	25,496	26,596	25,096	25,795
Taurus GL	17,495	18,195	19,295	20,695	22,195	23,195	—	—
Taurus LX	21,195	22,595	23,495	23,895	25,095	26,195	23,295	23,495
L Wagon	18,895	—	—	—	—	—	—	—
GL Wagon	20,250	18,196	19,296	20,636	22,196	23,196	—	—
SHO	28,595	30,095	30,095	31,095	32,430	32,695	37,795	37,995
Used Values ($)								
Sable GS ↑	3,300	3,800	5,500	7,500	9,000	11,000	13,000	15,500
Sable GS ↓	2,800	3,000	3,800	5,000	7,000	9,000	11,000	13,500
LS Wagon ↑	4,500	5,500	6,500	9,000	11,000	13,500	15,500	16,500
LS Wagon ↓	4,000	4,500	5,000	7,000	9,000	11,500	13,500	15,000
Taurus GL ↑	3,000	3,500	5,000	7,000	9,000	11,000	—	—
Taurus GL ↓	2,500	3,000	4,000	5,000	7,000	9,000	—	—
Taurus LX ↑	3,300	3,800	5,500	7,500	9,000	11,000	13,500	15,500
Taurus LX ↓	2,800	3,000	3,800	5,000	7,000	9,000	11,500	13,500
L Wagon ↑	5,000	—	—	—	—	—	—	—
L Wagon ↓	4,000	—	—	—	—	—	—	—
GL Wagon ↑	4,000	4,500	5,500	6,500	9,000	11,000	—	—
GL Wagon ↓	3,500	4,000	4,500	5,000	7,000	9,000	—	—
SHO ↑	5,000	6,500	7,500	9,000	13,000	16,500	20,500	24,000
SHO ↓	4,500	5,500	6,000	8,000	11,000	14,500	18,000	22,000
Extended Warranty	Y	Y	Y	Y	Y	Y	Y	Y
Secret Warranty	N	Y	Y	Y	Y	Y	Y	Y
Reliability	①	①	②	②	②	②	②	③
Air conditioning	①	①	①	②	②	③	③	③
Auto. transmission	①	①	②	②	②	②	②	②
Body integrity	②	②	②	②	②	②	③	③
Braking system	②	②	②	②	②	②	②	②
Electrical system	③	③	③	③	③	③	③	③
Engines	②	②	②	②	②	③	③	③
Exhaust/Converter	②	②	②	②	③	③	③	④
Fuel system	②	②	②	②	②	②	③	③
Ignition system	③	③	③	③	③	③	④	④
Rust/Paint	②	②	②	②	②	②	②	③
Steering	②	②	②	②	②	②	②	③
Suspension	②	②	②	③	③	③	③	③
Crash Safety	④	④	④	④	④	④	④	⑤
Side Impact	—	—	—	—	—	③	③	③

Tempo, Topaz

Rating: Not Recommended (1985–94). The V6 is the powerplant of choice, but it's found only on 1992 and later versions. Stay away from the 4X4 versions. In 1994, these cars were replaced by the 1995 Contour and Mystique. **Maintenance/Repair costs:** Higher than average. Repairs aren't dealer dependent, but troubleshooting usually costs an arm and a leg. **Parts:** Higher-than-average cost, but can be bought for much less from independent suppliers.

Strengths and weaknesses: This front-drive compact's strong points are its attractive, rounded styling; smooth, quiet V6, which works well with the automatic gearbox; a reliable, fuel-efficient manual gearbox; and a roomy interior. On the downside, these cars are underpowered with the base 2.3L 4-cylinder engine, fuel-thirsty when coupled with an automatic transmission, and failure-prone. They are riddled with design and manufacturing bugs. The engine, transmission, electrical systems, electronic modules, fuel pump, power steering, suspension components, and cruise control all tend to fail prematurely. The 2.0L Mazda diesel engine is unreliable and doesn't deliver traditional diesel durability. Plus the four-wheel drive is failure-prone and difficult to repair (parts are also expensive, if they can be found).

The 2.3L gas engine isn't much better. Cylinder head gaskets tend to leak and the engine's cooling, fuel, and ignition systems are plagued by a multitude of breakdowns.

For all models, stalling and hard starting are often caused by a malfunctioning catalytic converter. If the car still won't start, mechanics advise owners to tap the solenoid switch behind the battery. The starter motor is weak and the oil pan gasket tends to leak. There are many complaints of prematurely worn front axles and leaking seals. The air conditioning fails frequently and is expensive to repair. Heater noise often signals the need to change the heater motor. Power-steering rack seals deteriorate quickly. Suspension components, such as tie-rod ends and strut bearings, need replacement almost annually. Shocks, for example, last barely 30,000 km. Front brakes wear out almost as quickly, and rotors are easily damaged. Even though these cars have been dropped, parts are plentiful; but they cost more than the North American average.

Body components are substandard and poorly assembled on all models and all years, with peeling paint and premature rusting being the main offenders. The front door seal tears every time the seatbelt doesn't retract properly, the car's air dam often works loose, and the hood cable-release mechanism tends to jam. Radio reception is mediocre.

Safety summary/Recalls: All models: 1991–94—Engine cooling fan motor may overheat and catch fire. • Door locks are a major problem; they frequently fail and cost over $200 to replace. Replacement locks last barely two years. • Owners report that their cars' chronic stalling places them constantly at risk. Other owners report the opposite problem with their 1993 Topaz—the car may suddenly accelerate. **1990**— Fan motor could overheat and cause engine damage. **1992–94**—Engine cooling-fan motor may overheat and cause a fire.

Secret Warranties/Service Tips

All models: 1992–94—If the idle speed fluctuates excessively in cold weather, you may need to change the powertrain control module (PCM). **1993–94**— Paint delamination, peeling, or fading (see Part Two). • If the transmission seems erratic in shifting from second to third gear, or downshifting from third to second, a newly designed governor spring will have to be installed. • A rotten-egg odour coming from the exhaust is the result of a malfunctioning catalytic converter.

Tempo, Topaz Profile

	1987	1988	1989	1990	1991	1992	1993	1994
Cost Price ($)								
L	9,520	9,794	10,695	11,695	10,695	—	—	—
GL	10,087	10,697	11,536	12,547	11,395	11,295	9,995	10,995
LX	11,814	12,208	12,751	13,497	12,295	12,995	10,775	16,195
4X4	—	—	14,864	15,607	14,195	—	—	—
Used Values ($)								
L ↑	500	900	1,400	1,700	2,000	—	—	—
L ↓	500	500	1,100	1,500	2,300	—	—	—
GL ↑	800	1,000	1,500	2,000	2,500	3,000	3,500	4,000
GL ↓	800	800	1,200	1,500	2,000	2,500	3,000	3,500
LX ↑	900	1,200	1,800	2,000	2,500	3,500	4,000	5,000
LX ↓	900	1,000	1,500	1,800	2,000	3,000	3,500	4,000
4X4 ↑	—	—	2,000	2,500	3,000	—	—	—
4X4 ↓	—	—	1,500	2,000	2,500	—	—	—
Extended Warranty	Y	Y	Y	Y	Y	Y	Y	Y
Secret Warranty	N	N	N	N	N	N	Y	Y
Reliability	❶	❶	❶	❶	❷	❷	❷	❷
Crash Safety	—	—	—	--	—	—	④	④

GENERAL MOTORS

Achieva (Calais), Grand Am, Skylark

Rating: Below Average (1995–99); Not Recommended (1985–94). Only the Grand Am survived through the 1999 model year. The 1992 Achieva replaced the Calais; except for styling, this Achieva is practically identical to the others. **Maintenance/Repair costs:** Higher than average. Repairs aren't dealer dependent. **Parts:** Higher-than-average cost, but can be bought for much less from independent suppliers.

Strengths and weaknesses: These cars come with a standard 150-hp Quad SOHC engine, a 5-speed transaxle, and ABS. The basic front-wheel-drive platform continues to be a refined version of the Sunfire (Sunbird) and Cavalier J-body. They are too cramped to be family sedans (rear entry/exit can be difficult), too sedate for sporty coupe status, and too ordinary for inclusion in the luxury car ranks.

In their basic form, these cars are unreliable, unspectacular, and provide barely adequate performance. An upgraded and more reliable 3.1L V6 powerplant gives you only five more horses than the base 4-banger. There's been a lot of hype about the Quad 4 16-valve engine, available with all models, but little of this translates into benefits for the average driver. A multi-valve motor produces more power than a standard engine, but always at higher rpms and with a fuel penalty and excess engine noise. The Quad 4 is rougher than most multi-valve engines when revved to cruising speed, and so does little to encourage drivers to get the maximum power from it.

These cars ride and handle fairly well but share chassis components with the failure-prone J-bodies. This explains why engine, transmission, brake, and electronic problems are similar. Fortunately, manual transmissions are much more reliable and are also the better choice for fuel economy. Water leaks and body squeaks and rattles are so abundant that GM has published a six-page troubleshooting TSB that pinpoints the noises and lists fixes (see "Secret Warranties/Service Tips").

The 2.5L 4-cylinder engine doesn't provide much power and has a poor reliability record. Avoid the Quad 4 and 3.0L V6 engines with SFI (sequential fuel injection) because of their frequent breakdowns and difficult servicing. If you have a blown head gasket or other problems with the Quad 4 engine, keep in mind that GM has a 7-year/100,000 km secret warranty covering its free repair or replacement; ask for a pro rata refund for the repair, even though the warranty coverage may have expired (see "Secret Warranties/Service Tips"). Poor engine cooling and fuel system malfunctions are common; diagnosis and repair are more complicated than average, however. The engine computer on V6 models has a high failure rate, and the oil pressure switch often malfunctions. The electrical system is plagued by gremlins that cause gauges and controls to go haywire and result in the car shutting down on the highway. Seals and pumps in the power-steering rack deteriorate rapidly. Front brake discs, rotors, and pads need replacing every 8,000 kilometres. Locks and headlights self-activate.

Among body deficiencies, owners note: chronic hubcap rattling, windshield mouldings fall off, water leaks into the trunk and through the doors, door panels often need replacing, the sun visor fails to stay in place, seat cushions aren't durable, and paint defects are quite common.

Technical service bulletins: All Models: 1992–95—TSB #43-1007A gives an exhaustive review of all the possible causes and remedies for body squeaks and rattles afflicting these models. **1995**—Oil leaks at the rocker cover. • Engine tick/rattle on cold start-up. • Cold-start stall or tip-in hesitation. • Grinding/growling when in Park on an incline. • AC cut-off after an extended idle. • A cold-start rattle with the 4T60E automatic transmission. • Introduction of longer-life front brake linings. • Brake vibration and/or pedal pulsation. • Rear wheel brake drag. • Inoperative washer pump. • A low voltage reading or dim lights at idle. • Check Oil and Check Gauges lights flicker. • Water entering into spoiler (Grand Am). • Poor paint application and rust spots. • Right rear-quarter window wind noise and water leaks. • **1996**—Second-gear starts, poor 1–3 shifting. • Driveability problems, whistling noise, or reduced fuel economy. • Engine overheating/faulty cooling fan. • Excessive engine roll. • Air conditioning odours. • Front seatbelt webbing twists and won't retract. • Fuel-filler door won't open. • Radio frequency interference diagnosis. • Wind noise at front-door outer-belt sealing strip. • Water entering rear compartment at taillight area. • Water leaking into taillight harness. **1997**—Cold-start rattle noise is normal, according to GM, and no fix is planned. • Inoperative power door locks. • Noisy instrument panel. • Intermittent loss of Drive at highway speeds. • No-starts. • Engine popping noises. • Power window malfunctions. • Front suspension squawk noise. **1998**—Reducing AC odours. • Correcting hard starts. • Excessive steering and front suspension noise. • Plugging water leaks. **1999–2000**—No third or fourth gear (Grand Am). • Hesitation or lack of power when accelerating. • Curing brake vibrations. • A remedy for hot-running engines. • Preventing paint chipping from the Grand Am SE's rocker panel and lower-quarter panel. • And stopping water leaking onto the front or rear carpet.

Safety summary/Recalls: All models: 1995—Fire ignited in the engine compartment while vehicle was on the road. • Sudden acceleration due to weak pedal return spring. • Chronic stalling. • Airbag failed to deploy. • Malfunctioning airbag causes horn to suddenly go off. • Driver's seatbelt failed to restrain driver. • Frequent brake failures and extended stopping distance. • Power-steering fluid leak due to high pressure hose chafing by the two fuel-injector tabs. • Brake caliper seizure damages pads and rotors. • Transmission jumps out of gear. • Shoulder belt rides across driver's neck. • Driver-side door handle popped out. • Erratic fuel gauge operation. • Headlights suddenly shut off. • Passenger seat not anchored securely. **1996**—Inadvertent airbag deployment. • Airbag failed to deploy. • Sudden acceleration and stalling. • When putting car in Reverse, it suddenly accelerated forward. • Left wheel came off after the stud that holds the wheel unbolted from the wheel. • Oxygen sensor failures cause Check Engine light to come on. • Frequent brake failures. • Excessive brake noise. • Defective master cylinder, drums, pads, and rotors. • Engine, transmission, and AC failures. • Seatbelt sticks into driver's side or will not fasten properly. • Insufficient insulation under steering column allows draft to come in under left lower dash area. • Headlight failure. • Water leaks into the trunk. • Cracking around the outside edge of all tires. • Passenger power door lock and window lock do not work properly. **1997**—Many reports of vehicle first losing power and then suddenly accelerating. • Accelerator cable snapped, causing pedal to go to the floor. • While vehicle was being driven, the hood suddenly flipped backwards, hitting the windshield. • Windshield reflection obstructs vision. • Premature brake replacements. • Seatbelt improperly fitted. • Design flaw allows wheels to rub against front fender. • Mirrors aren't adjustable enough to see other vehicles, and seatbacks are too high for some drivers to see over. • Driver-side bucket seat isn't anchored properly; rocks from side to side. • Intermittent windshield wiper failures. • Headlights sometimes cut out. **1998–99**—Vehicle caught fire while parked. • Airbag failed to deploy, or deployed inadvertently. • Premature brake pad wearout and warped rotors every 5,000–8,000 kilometres. • Sudden acceleration. • Cruise control is either inoperative or fails to disengage. • Chronic hesitation and stallout, accompanied by dash lights and other electrics going haywire. • Enhanced traction system engages when not needed. • Complete electrical system shutdown while underway. • Rainwater leaks through the dash panel into the fuse box. • Wheel lug nuts sheared off, causing wheel to fall away. • Severe brake, steering, and body vibrations; vehicle intermittently violently jerks to one side. • Sudden steering loss; steering pump failure. • Fuel pressure regulator leaks fumes into the interior. • Sunroof exploded when side window was opened while vehicle was underway. • Windows run off their channels and shatter; power window motors often need replacing. • Windshield washer fluid freezes due to poor tubing design. • Headrests obstruct rear visibility. • Locks and headlights self-activate. • Headlights give inadequate illuminate on turns. • Faulty fuel level sensor gives a false Empty reading. • Seatbelts tend to twist when retracting. **Recalls: All models: 1996**—Front or rear hazard warning lights could be faulty. • The airbag could deploy behind the instrument panel. • A loose steering column bolt could cause loss of steering. **1997**—Fire may ignite due to a fuse short in the wiring harness.

Secret Warranties/Service Tips

All models: 1990–93—2.3L Quad 4 engine is notoriously bad. Head gasket leaks are covered under GM's 7-year/160,000 km secret warranty—oops, I mean Special Policy. **1991–95**—Front brake linings can be made to last longer by replacing the front brake pads with a new 8100 lining compound (#18022600) **1992–93**—A front-end engine knock troubleshooting chart is found in TSB #306001. **1992–94**—Corrosion of the ECM connectors can lead to a host of driveability problems (TSB #338109A). • TSB #431007 is an excellent troubleshooting guide to finding and correcting squeaks and rattles. **1992–97**—Inoperative power door locks may need an upgraded external bumper on the actuator arm. **1993–98**—A front suspension/engine squawk may be reduced by applying ultra high molecular tape to the area producing the noise. **1993–99**—A rotten-egg odour coming from the exhaust may be the result of a malfunctioning catalytic converter—possibly covered by the emissions warranty. Stand your ground if GM or the dealer claims you must pay. • Tips on removing AC odours. • Paint delamination, peeling, or fading (see Part Two). **1994**—Gear whine with the 4T60E automatic transaxle can be stopped by replacing the final drive and updating the PCM calibration. • Insufficient AC cooling may be due to a leak at the low-charge primary-port seal. • Loss of Drive or erratic shifts may be caused by an intermittent short to ground on the A or B shift solenoid or an electrical short circuit in the transaxle. • A front-end clunking noise when driving over rough roads may require the repositioning of the diagonal radiator support braces. **1995–97**—Intermittent loss of Drive at highway speeds may require the replacement of the control valve body assembly. • Engine popping noises can be silenced by tightening the torque strut mount bolts. **1995–98**—A steering squeak or squawk may be reduced by installing a rack-and-pinion service kit. **1996–98**—Install a seatbelt webbing stop button if the seatbelt latch slides to the anchor sleeve. • Passenger compartment water leaks can be plugged by applying silicone sealer to the top vent grill assembly. **1997**—No-starts may be due to an improperly routed and pinched wire from the generator to the wiring harness. • Excessive oil consumption in the 2.5L engine may be caused by one or more damaged intake valve guides. • Hard starting and engine pinging can be fixed by the installation of a new PROM module (#16121217), TSB #88-6E-11. **1997–98**—Hard starting or a weak or dead battery may signal the need to repair the B+ stud and/or starter wiring. **1999–2000**—No third or fourth gear may signal a defective direct clutch piston. • Upgraded pads and rotors will fix brake pulsation/vibration (see Malibu entry). • A front or rear wet carpet may mean the front door water deflectors need to be replaced. • Simply changing the radiator cap may cure your hot-running engine. **Grand Am: 1999**—Hesitation or lack of power when accelerating on vehicles equipped with the 3.4L engine may simply need a reprogramming of the power control module. • Paint chipping from the Grand Am SE's rocker panel and lower quarter panel can be prevented by installing upgraded driver and passenger side rocker moldings. **Skylark: 1995–97**—Intermittent Neutral/loss of Drive at highway speeds can be fixed by replacing the control valve body assembly.

Achieva (Calais), Grand Am, Skylark Profile

	1992	1993	1994	1995	1996	1997	1998	1999
Cost Price ($)								
Achieva S	15,098	15,298	16,698	18,485	19,925	20,735	21,200	—
Grand Am	13,698	14,898	15,798	17,365	18,000	19,035	19,610	21,795
Skylark	16,350	15,298	16,398	19,035	20,035	21,220	22,965	—
Used Values ($)								
Achieva S ↑	3,500	4,500	5,000	7,500	9,500	11,000	13,500	—
Achieva S ↓	3,000	3,500	4,000	5,500	7,500	9,000	11,000	—
Grand Am ↑	3,500	4,500	5,500	7,000	8,500	10,500	12,000	14,500
Grand Am ↓	3,000	3,500	4,500	5,500	6,500	8,000	10,000	12,500
Skylark ↑	3,500	4,500	5,500	7,500	9,500	11,000	13,500	—
Skylark ↓	3,000	4,000	4,000	6,000	7,500	9,000	11,500	—
Extended Warranty	Y	Y	Y	Y	Y	Y	Y	Y
Secret Warranty	Y	Y	Y	Y	Y	Y	Y	Y
Reliability	②	②	②	②	②	③	④	④
Air conditioning	②	②	③	③	④	④	④	④
Auto. transmission	②	②	②	②	②	②	②	④
Body integrity	②	②	②	②	②	②	②	②
Braking system	①	①	②	②	②	③	③	③
Electrical system	①	②	②	②	②	②	②	②
Engines	②	②	②	②	③	③	③	③
Exhaust/Converter	①	②	③	③	③	④	⑤	⑤
Fuel system	②	②	②	②	②	③	③	③
Ignition system	②	②	③	③	③	③	③	④
Rust/Paint	①	①	②	②	②	③	③	③
Steering	②	②	②	③	④	⑤	⑤	⑤
Suspension	③	③	③	⑤	⑤	⑤	⑤	⑤
Crash Safety								
Achieva 2d	①	①	④	④	—	④	—	—
Achieva 4d	—	①	—	④	④	⑤	—	—
Grand Am 2d	①	—	④	④	—	④	—	—
Grand Am 4d	—	①	—	—	④	⑤	—	④
Skylark 2d	—	—	④	④	—	④	—	—
Skylark 4d	①	①	—	—	④	⑤	—	—
Side Impact								
Achieva 4d	—	—	—	—	—	①	①	—
Grand Am 4d	—	—	—	—	—	①	①	③
Skylark 4d	—	—	—	—	—	①	①	—

Bonneville, Cutlass, Cutlass Supreme, Delta 88, Grand Prix, Intrigue, LeSabre, Lumina, Malibu, Monte Carlo, Regal

Rating: Rear-drives, if you can find them, are Above Average (1984–87); early front-drives are Not Recommended (1988–96); recent models are Average buys (1997–99). Although these GM models are generally classed as medium-sized cars, some of them move in and out of the large car class as well. **Maintenance/Repair costs:** Higher than average, but repairs aren't dealer dependent. **Parts:** Higher-than-average cost (independent suppliers sell for much less), but not hard to find. Nevertheless, don't even think about buying one of the front-drives without a three- to five-year supplementary warranty.

Strengths and weaknesses: Body assembly on all models is notoriously poor and is no doubt one of the main reasons why GM has lost so much market share over the past decade. Premature paint peeling and rusting, water and dust leaks into the trunk, squeaks and rattles, and wind and road noise are all too common. Accessories are also plagued by problems, with defective radios, power antennas, door locks, cruise control, and alarm systems leading the pack.

No Tears Shed Over Olds Demise
Say goodbye to your father's Oldsmobile, and it's none too soon. Despite an investment of $3 billion over the past few years, Oldsmobile sales have skidded 18 percent over the past year while most of the auto industry has posted record sales. This has prompted GM to announce it will phase out the Oldsmobile division over the next two years.

Ever since the Olds division went front-drive in the mid-'80s, we've seen a classic case of "the bland leading the bland" with little innovation and even less dependability. Gone are the days when teens gushed over the high-performance '67 442 sedan, or the airbag-equipped front-drive '74 Toronado. Today, I defy the average buyer to name one Oldsmobile model (try Alero, Aurora, Bravada, Intrigue, and Silhouette) still in production. Yet everyone remembers the Toronado, 88, 98, and all the other Cutlass derivatives. They remember them for their powerful 350 engines and automatic transmissions that worked smoothly with a minimum of maintenance, unlike today's biodegradable front-drive powertrains.

Two suggestions for Olds owners in light of the GM announcement: don't worry about servicing—the phase-out will be gradual and there are plenty of generic parts in the GM bin—and don't expect your vehicle to become a "collectors" item—the only place where post-'86 models are collected are junkyards.

Incidentally, when the first Oldsmobile was sold in Michigan in 1901, it came equipped with a five-horsepower, one-cylinder engine; purchase price: $650.

Rear-drives

The rear-drives are competent and comfortable cars, but they definitely point to a time when handling wasn't a priority and fuel economy was unimportant. Their overall reliability isn't impressive, but at least repairs are easy, defects are obvious, and any independent garage can service them. Models equipped with diesel engines or with the turbo-charged gas V6 should be approached with extreme caution. These cars have a higher-than-average incidence of repairs, but parts are inexpensive and all mechanical work is very easy to perform.

Original-equipment shock absorbers and springs aren't durable, and electrical malfunctions increase proportionally with extra equipment. The AC module and condenser and wheel bearings (incredibly expensive) also have short life spans. The 4-speed automatic transmission available in later models isn't reliable. Surface rust caused by poor paint quality and application is common. The rear edge of trunk lids, roof areas above doors, and the windshield and windshield posts rust through easily.

Front-drives

The front-drives are a different breed of car: less reliable and more expensive to repair, with a considerable number of mechanical and electrical deficiencies directly related to their front-wheel drive configuration. Nevertheless, acceleration is adequate, fuel economy is good, and they're better at handling than their rear-drive cousins—except in emergencies, when their non-ABS brakes lock up and directional stability is the first to go. The front-drive's many design and manufacturing weaknesses make for unimpressive high-speed performance, mediocre interior comfort, a poor reliability record, and expensive maintenance costs. That's why most fleets and police agencies use rear-drives when they can get them. They've seen the rear-drive's safety and operating cost advantages.

These aren't driver-friendly cars. Many models have a dash that's replete with confusing push-buttons and gauges that are washed out in sunlight. At other times, there are retro touches, like the Intrigue's dash-mounted ignition, that just simply seem out of place. The keyless entry system often fails, the radio's memory is frequently forgetful, and the fuel light comes on when the tank is below the "?" fuel-level mark. The electronic climate control frequently malfunctions and owners report that warm air doesn't reach the driver-side heating vents. Servicing, especially for the electronic engine controls, is complicated and expensive.

Other major problem areas: the engine, automatic transmission, leaking and malfunctioning AC systems (due mainly to defective AC modules), faulty electronic modules, rack-and-pinion steering failure, bursting steering hoses on 1991 models, weak shocks, excessive front brake pad wear, warping rotors, seizure of the rear brake calipers, rear brake/wheel lockup, myriad electrical failures requiring replacement of the computer module (a $500–$750 repair if the emissions warranty has expired), leaking oil pan, and suspension struts.

The base 2.3L and 2.5L engines found on pre-'95 models provide insufficient power. The more powerful 3.1L V6 is peppier, but it's seriously hampered by the 4-speed automatic transaxle. The high-performance 3.4L V6, available since 1991 gives out plenty of power, but only at high engine speeds. Other deficiencies: the instruments and steering column shake when the car is travelling over uneven road surfaces; and lots of road and wind noise come through the side windows thanks to the inadequately soundproofed chassis. Seating isn't very comfortable due to the lack of support caused by low-density foam, knees-in-your-face low seating, and the ramrod-straight rear backrest. The ride is acceptable with a light load, but when fully loaded, the car's back end sags and the ride deteriorates. Owners report that 3.8L engines won't continue running after a cold start, the exhaust system booms, 3T40 automatic transmissions may have faulty Reverse gears, and the instrument panel may pop or creak.

Intrigue
Strikingly similar to the Alero, the Oldsmobile Intrigue is GM's replacement for the Cutlass Supreme and represents the most refined iteration of the W-body shared by the Century, Grand Prix, Lumina, and Regal. It's more luxurious than the Lumina and performs as well as the Accord, Camry, and Maxima. Its rigid chassis has fewer shakes and rattles than are found on GM's other models, and its 3.8L engine provides lots of low-end grunt but lacks the top-end power that makes the Japanese competition so much fun to toss around. The '99 versions got a torquier 3.5L V6 coupled to standard traction control. This engine's a bit more refined, but it's still not smooth and the automatic transmission still struggles to get past its first two gears.

1995–99 Lumina and Monte Carlo
The redesigned Lumina and Monte Carlo are popular two- and four-door versions of Chevy's "large" mid-sized cars, featuring standard dual airbags, ABS, and 160-hp V6 power. The Monte Carlo was formerly sold as the Lumina Z34. Powertrain enhancements have increased horsepower and fuel efficiency. Each car has been given a slightly different appearance and a distinct "personality." A 3.1L V6 is the standard engine, a standard 3.4L 210-hp V6 powers the coupe and is optional with the LS Lumina, and a 3.8L V6 equips the more upscale versions. In 1996, the 3.4L got a slight horsepower boost, and all-disc braking was adopted on the Monte Carlo Z34 and upscale versions of the LS. For 1997, a better performing transmission, mated to the 3.4L engine, gives smoother shifts. The '98 and '99 models got few changes, except for the addition of the 3.8L V6 to the Monte Carlo Z34 and Lumina LTZ.

Except for the automatic transmission upgrade, owners report that newer versions still have some of the same shortcomings seen on earlier front-drive models. For example, in spite of some noise reduction progress, body construction is still below par, with loose door panel mouldings, poorly fitted door fabric, and misaligned panels. Other common problems: fuel pump whistling, frequent stalling, vague steering, premature paint peeling on the hood and trunk, heavy accumulation of hard-to-remove brake dust inside the honeycomb-design wheels, and front tires that scrape the fenders when the wheel is turned. Despite its own recent redesign, the 3.1L engine isn't entirely problem-free. Electronic fuel-injection systems and engine controls have created many problems for GM owners. The 4-speed automatic transmission still has some bugs. The front brakes wear quickly, as do the MacPherson struts and shock absorbers. Steering assemblies tend to fail prematurely. The electrical system is temperamental. The sunroof motor is failure-prone. Owners report water leaks from the front windshield. Front-end squeaks may require the replacement of the exhaust manifold pipe springs with dampers.

Cutlass and Malibu

These two front-drive, medium-sized sedans are slotted in between the Cavalier and Lumina in both size and price. This niche was once filled by the Corsica, Beretta, Tempest, Celebrity, and Ciera. Malibu and Cutlass are boringly styled cars that use a more rigid body structure to cut down on noise and improve handling. Standard mechanicals include a 2.4L twin-cam 4-cylinder engine or an optional 3.1L V6. There's plenty of passenger and luggage space. Although head room is tight, the Malibu can carry three rear passengers and gives much more leg room than either the Cavalier or Lumina.

Other points to consider: the base 4-cylinder is loud, handling isn't on par with the Japanese competition, there's lots of body lean in turns, outside mirrors are too small, there's no traction control, and the ignition switch is mounted on the dash (a throwback to your dad's Oldsmobile).

In addition to the generic front-drive problems listed above, owners also report: fuel-injector deposits cause chronic stalling, poor idling, or hard starts; excessive vibration occurs at any speed; transmission doesn't lock when the key is in the accessory position; steering is very loose; backfires caused by defective computer modules; premature suspension strut failures (vehicle bottoms out with four or more passengers aboard); excessive AC noise; and the high-beam light switch fails intermittently.

Technical service bulletins: All models: 1991–97—Bulletin #83-20-06 outlines procedures for fixing prematurely rusted door bottoms. **1995**—A knocking noise from the accessory drive belt tensioner. • Continuous spark knock. • Excessive oil consumption and oil leaks at the rocker cover. • Coolant leak near the throttle body. • Grinding/growling when in Park on an incline and a cold-start rattle with the 4T60E automatic transmission. • Harsh 1–2 upshifts. • Brake vibration and/or pedal pulsation. • Low voltage reading or dim lights at idle. • Headlights/parking lights remain on. • An upgraded wire protector shield is needed to correct a noisy steering column. • Squeak/creak from rear of vehicle, whistle noise from the heater/AC unit, and excessive radio static. • Door window rattle, popping noise during moderate braking or acceleration, front suspension pop noise, and rear strut–related squeaking/thumping noise. • Left rear door binds. • Poor paint application and rust spots. • Frequent reports of wind noise affecting the 1990–95 Cutlass, Grand Prix, and Regal and the 1988–94 Lumina have led to the publication of TSB #53-15-16, which outlines the causes of and remedies for persistent wind noise. **1996**—Second-gear starts, poor 1–3 shifting. • Steering column noise. • Air conditioning odours and diagnosis of AC noises. • Whistle noise from HVAC. • Diagnosis and correction of fluttering, popping, ticking, and clunking noises. • Popping noise from the front of the vehicle when turning. • Radio frequency interference diagnosis. • Rear door rattle when closing. • Excessive wrinkles in seat cushion trim. • Condensation on exterior light. **1997**—AC flutter or moan. • Cold-start rattle. Engine cranks but will not run. • Engine oil leak at oil pan sealing flange and rear of engine near flywheel cover. • Engine oil level indicates over-full. • Excessive vibration of electrochromic mirror. • High beams are intermittent. • Inoperative power door locks. • Intermittent Neutral/loss of Drive at highway speeds. • Instrument panel buzzes and rattles when the brakes are applied. • Popping or thump noise from the left rear of vehicle is normal, according to GM. • Transmission gear whine at 40–70 km/h. **1997–2000**—Front disc brake pulsation will be corrected by installing upgraded pads and rotors, says TSB #00-05-23-002 (see Malibu). **1998**—Engine runs rough. • Power steering shudder and vibration. • Front suspension scrunch/pop. • Reducing AC odours. • Inaccurate speedometer. **1999–2000**—No third and fourth gear may mean the direct clutch piston assembly needs to be replaced. An engine that runs hot, overheats, or loses coolant may only need an upgraded radiator cap (check this before authorizing any expensive repairs). **Cutlass and Malibu: 1997–99**—Front disc brake pulsation will be corrected by installing upgraded pads and rotors, says TSB #00-05-23-002. Another bulletin (see following) outlines under what conditions repair will be done for free.

Bulletin No:
00-05-22-002
February, 2000
Brake Rotor Warranty Service Procedure
Models:
1995-2000 Passenger Cars and Light Duty Trucks
The following are examples of pulsation conditions and reimbursement recommendations:
1. If a customer noticed the condition after 4800-11300 kilometers (300-7000 miles)
    and it gradually got worse, normally the repair would be covered. The customer
    may tolerate the condition until it becomes very apparent.
2. If a customer indicated that they had wheel service, ask who performed the service.
    Then:
    If a dealer performed the service, consider paying for the repair and then strongly
    reinforce the use of torque sticks at that dealer. Two common size torque sticks cover
    90% of all GM products. Each technician needs to use torque sticks properly every
    time the wheel nuts are tightened.
    If the customer had the wheel service done outside of our dealer network, normally
    GM would not offer any assistance.
Customer assistance concerning brake pulsation and brake wear should always take into
account the individual circumstances on a case by case basis. The recommendations pre-
viously should only be used as a general guide. REMEMBER THAT CUSTOMER SATIS-
FACTION IS CRITICAL TO GM AND THAT OFTEN IT IS IN GM'S BEST INTEREST TO
SATISFY AND EDUCATE THE CUSTOMER CONDERNING FUTURE BRAKE SERVICE.

*GM's guidelines for free brake vibration/pulsation repairs can be extra-
polated to other models, as well.*

• Front seatbelt is slow to retract. • Premature wear of leather seatcover
material requires replacing the material. **1998–99**—Road or water
noise in the rear seat area may require the installation of foam insulat-
ing pads. **Cutlass Supreme: 1996**—Stalls at low rpm and high loads,
extended crank time. • Front suspension popping. • HVAC blower
motor noise/vibration. • Loose left side instrument panel access cover.
• Inoperative antenna, power mirrors and door locks.

Safety summary/Recalls: All models: 1988–93—Corroded brake
calipers may cause brake failures. **1990**—ABS is tough to modulate; it
doesn't always engage quickly enough or it's sometimes too sensitive.
1997—Airbag failed to deploy. • Seating design forces driver to sit too
close to airbag mechanism in the steering column. • Chronic stalling.
• Throttle sticks. • Frequent cruise control failures. • Inadequate braking; ABS brake failures are common. • Emergency brake doesn't work
properly; it won't remain locked. • Ventilation system emitted fumes
that made occupants ill. • Frequent AC compressor failures. • Seatbelt
didn't restrain passenger sufficiently in an accident. • Inoperative rear
seat buckles. • Rear seatbelts are too short to secure a child's seat or
large person. • Plastic part of buckle came off when trying to buckle
up. • Rear seatbelt design forces user to sit on buckles; they are too
close to the seat and difficult to fasten. • Turn signal lever won't return
to neutral position. • Excessive wind noise comes in around the door
openings. • Many reports that door locks continually engage and

disengage while driving. • Power window motor failure. • Outside rear-view mirrors positioned too far back for a clear view. • Dash reflection in windshield cuts visibility. • Windshield wipers operate erratically. • Water collects in the headlight lenses, causing them to fog or malfunction. • Headlights often dim for no apparent reason. • Stop lights and taillights aren't very durable. **1998**—Airbags failed to deploy. • Sudden acceleration; faulty fuel pressure regulator suspected. • Power seat puts occupant too close to airbag. • Headrest can't be raised high enough for someone over six feet tall. • Engine hesitates when accelerating. • Many reports of vehicle suddenly stalling in traffic. • Ignition coil failure also causes engine to stall and backfire. • Flexible hose line from fuel pump rests against sharp metal edge of the heat shield. • Trunk popped open while driving. • Excessive wind noise enters the interior. **1998–99**—Windshield wiper failures are under study. **Cutlass: 1998**—Inadvertent airbag deployment is being investigated. **Grand Prix: 1999**—Similar airbag probe. **Intrigue: 1997–98**—Rear shoulder belt malfunctions are also under investigation. **Monte Carlo: 1995–98**—NHTSA is looking into complaints of poor braking. **Recalls: All models: 1996–97**—Backfire can break upper intake manifold, making car hard to start and possibly starting a fire. **1997**—Seatbelt may not latch properly. **Lumina, Regal: 1996**—Brake line could rub against the transaxle mounting bracket. **Bonneville, Delta 88, LeSabre with 4T60-E automatic transmission: 1992–93**—Oil cooler line can leak transmission fluid, posing a fire hazard. **Cutlass Supreme: 1994–95**—Washer wiper may malfunction. **1995**—Seatbelt anchor could fracture in a crash. • If cracks appear in the centre rear seatbelt anchor, the dealer must replace the entire centre rear seatbelt system. **Delta 88: 1994–95**—Headlight switch may not work. **Lumina: 1996**—Improperly located brake booster tab may cause extended stopping distance. **Regal: 1994–95**—Improperly installed brake hoses could leak fluid. **1995**—Steering could fail. **Bonneville, LeSabre: 1992**—Parking brake may not hold well enough, allowing the car to roll when the brake is on. **Monte Carlo: 1996**—Improperly installed brake booster.

Secret Warranties/Service Tips

All models: 1980–89—First gear malfunctions with the THM 125C transmission may require new forward clutch piston seals (#8631986). **1984–89**—No third gear with the automatic 440-T4 transmission means that a new thrust bearing assembly should be installed. **1986–88**—3.8L V6 engines have a history of low oil pressure caused by a failure-prone oil pump. A temporary remedy is to avoid low viscosity oils and use 10W-40 in the winter and 20W-50 in the summer. **1988–93**—A vehicle equipped with a 3300 or 3800 engine that stalls when decelerating or is hard to start may need a new air control motor (IAC). **1989–92**—Hard coldstarts may require a new MEMCAL. **1991–94**—Loss of Drive or erratic shifts may be caused by an intermittent short to ground on the A or B shift solenoid or an electrical short circuit in the transaxle. • Harsh automatic transmission upshifts can be corrected by installing an upgraded accumulator valve in the control valve body. **1992–94**—A front-end engine knock troubleshooting chart is found in TSB #306001. • Water leaking from the doors into the passenger compartment has a number of causes and remedies, according to TSB #431003. **1993–94**—Knocking from the accessory drive belt tensioner requires an upgraded replacement. • Owners who complain of automatic transmission low-speed miss, hesitation, chuggle, or skip may find relief with an improved MEMCAL module. **1993–99**—Odours can be eliminated by using a coil coating kit. • A rotten-egg odour coming from the exhaust is probably caused by a malfunctioning catalytic converter (covered by the emissions warranty). • Paint delamination, peeling, or fading (see Part Two). **1994–98**—A cold engine tick or rattle heard shortly after start-up may be fixed by replacing the piston/pin assembly. • A front suspension scrunch or pop may be silenced by merely installing a jounce washer (see following illustration).

Front Susp Scrunch/Pop Noise
File In Section: 3 – Steering/Suspension
Bulletin No.: 53-33-07B
Date: July, 1998
Subject:
Front Suspension Scrunch/Pop Noise
(Install Front Suspension Jounce Washer)
Models:
1994-96 Buick Regal
1994-98 Chevrolet Lumina
1995-98 Chevrolet Monte Carlo
1994-97 Oldsmobile Cutlass Supreme
1994-96 Pontiac Grand Prix
Condition
Some vehicles may exhibit a scrunch/popping type noise coming from the front of vehicle that is apparent during low speed turning maneuvers.
Cause
Slip-stick condition that occurs between front suspension strut bumper and front strut closure nut.

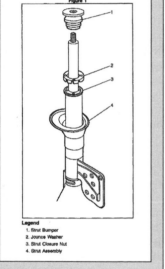

Figure 1

Legend
1. Strut Bumper
2. Jounce Washer
3. Strut Closure Nut
4. Strut Assembly

1995–96—Wind noise around front and rear doors; diagnosis and repair. **1995–97**—Intermittent Neutral/loss of Drive at highway speeds can be fixed by replacing the control valve body assembly. **1997–98**—A rough-running engine may be fixed by merely changing the plug wires. **1997–99**—A low-speed steering shudder or vibration may be corrected by replacing the steering pressure and return lines with revised "tuned" hoses. • Front disc pads have been upgraded to reduce brake squeal. • A shaking sensation at cruising speed may be fixed by replacing the transmission mount. **1998**—A wet right rear floor signals the need to reseal the stationary glass area. **1998–99**—Power steering shudder/vibration may be fixed by replacing the pressure pipe/hose assembly (see following bulletin).

Bulletin No.: 99-02-32-001
Date: March, 1999
TECHNICAL
Subject:
Power Steering Shudder/Vibration at Low Speed
(Replace Power Steering Pressure Pipe/Hose Assembly)
Models:
1998-99 Chevrolet Lumina, Monte Carlo
Built Prior to VIN Breakpoint 132824 with 3.8L V-6 Engine (VIN K – RPO L26)
Condition
Some customers may comment on a shudder/vibration condition at low speeds during parking lot type steering maneuvers. This low frequency condition can be felt in the steering wheel/body structure and is audible inside the vehicle's passenger compartment.
Cause
This condition may be caused by a mechanical vibration of the power steering gear rack, tie rods and tires that is reinforced by the hydraulic pressure generated in the power steering system.
Correction
Replace the existing power steering pressure pipe/hose assembly with the new "tuned" pie/hose assembly, P/N 26075972, using the following procedure.

• Poor AM reception on vehicles with a windshield-mounted antenna may be improved by installing an in-line antenna jumper. **All models with a 2.3L Quad 4 engine: 1990–91**—Head gasket leaks are a problem that was once covered by a secret warranty extension. **LeSabre: 1991–94**—A scraping noise or increased effort required to open the front doors can be fixed by bending the door's lower check ear. • Water leaking from the doors into the passenger compartment has a number of causes and remedies (TSB #431003). **1995–97**—Transmission gear whine at 30–80 km/h means the final drive assembly may have to be replaced. **Lumina: 1990–91**—Late transaxle upshifts may be fixed by resetting the TV cable. **1994**—Excessive brake-pedal effort when cold can be fixed by installing upgraded brake pads. **1994–95**—A steering wheel clicking or scrubbing noise when turning can be fixed by installing an upgraded wire protector shield. **Regal: 1991–94**—Loss of Drive or erratic shifts may be caused by an intermittent short to ground on the A or B shift solenoid or an electrical short circuit in the transaxle. **1992**—Front-door wind noise and water leaks can be fixed by replacing the run channel retainer and adding sealer between the retainer and the door frame. **Grand Prix, Regal: 1997**—Insufficient heater performance on passenger-side floor area can be fixed by installing a new I/P insulator panel and bracket. **Lumina, Regal: 1990–92**—Vehicles equipped with the 3T40 automatic transmission may experience slippage in manual Low or Reverse. Install service package #8628222. **1991–92**—A delayed shift between Drive and Reverse is likely caused by a rolled or cut input-clutch-piston outer seal. **1991–94**—Loss of Drive or erratic shifts may be caused by an intermittent short to ground on the A or B shift solenoid or an electrical short circuit in the transaxle. **1992–93**—No Reverse or slipping in Reverse can be corrected by installing an upgraded Low/Reverse clutch return spring and spiral retaining ring.

Bonneville, Cutlass, Cutlass Supreme, Delta 88, Grand Prix, Intrigue, LeSabre, Lumina, Malibu, Monte Carlo, Regal Profile

	1992	1993	1994	1995	1996	1997	1998	1999
Cost Price ($)								
Bonneville	22,898	23,498	25,298	28,175	29,440	31,175	33,255	29,000
Cutlass GL	—	—	—	—	—	—	23,140	—
Cutlass Supreme	18,398	18,858	21,398	24,310	25,285	26,355	—	—
Delta 88	22,250	23,098	25,598	28,320	30,190	32,185	32,950	32,515
Grand Prix	17,598	18,498	22,098	24,555	23,940	26,305	26,035	27,489
Intrigue	—	—	—	—	—	—	27,998	27,994
LeSabre	23,198	23,997	25,498	28,235	29,560	32,370	33,100	28,845
Lumina	15,998	17,798	19,898	20,730	21,455	22,340	22,980	23,074
Malibu	—	—	—	—	—	19,995	20,595	20,895
Monte Carlo	—	—	—	22,578	23,625	24,275	24,895	24,715
Regal	19,398	20,006	21,898	20,060	25,035	27,795	28,410	27,695
Used Values ($)								
Bonneville ↑	5,500	7,500	9,000	11000	12,500	14,000	17,500	21,000
Bonneville ↓	4,500	6,500	7,500	9,000	10,000	12,000	15,000	18,000
Cutlass GL ↑	—	—	—	—	—	—	15,500	—
Cutlass GL ↓	—	—	—	—	—	—	13,000	—
Cutlass Supreme ↑	4,000	5,000	7,000	9,000	11,000	13,500	—	—
Cutlass Supreme ↓	3,500	4,000	5,500	7,500	9,000	11,000	—	—
Delta 88 ↑	5,000	7,000	9,000	10,500	12,000	14,500	19,500	21,000
Delta 88 ↓	4,500	5,500	7,000	8,500	10,000	12,500	17,000	19,000
Grand Prix ↑	4,500	5,500	7,000	8,500	11,000	14,000	16,000	20,500
Grand Prix ↓	4,000	4,500	5,000	7,000	9,000	12,000	14,000	19,000
Intrigue ↑	—	—	—	—	—	—	17,000	19,500
Intrigue ↓	—	—	—	—	—	—	14,500	17,000
LeSabre ↑	5,000	7,000	9,000	11,000	12,500	15,000	18,000	20,500
LeSabre ↓	4,500	5,500	7,000	9,000	10,000	12,500	15,500	18,000
Lumina ↑	4,000	5,000	6,000	7,500	9,000	10,500	13,000	14,500
Lumina ↓	3,500	4,500	5,000	6,000	7,500	9,000	11,000	13,000
Malibu ↑	—	—	—	—	—	10,000	12,000	14,000
Malibu ↓	—	—	—	—	—	8,000	10,000	12,000
Monte Carlo ↑	—	—	—	8,500	10,500	12,500	15,000	17,500
Monte Carlo ↓	—	—	—	7,500	9,000	11,000	13,000	16,000
Regal ↑	4,500	5,500	7,000	9,000	11,000	14,000	16,500	19,500
Regal ↓	4,000	5,000	5,000	7,500	9,000	12,500	14,000	17,000
Extended Warranty	Y	Y	Y	Y	Y	Y	Y	Y
Secret Warranty	Y	Y	Y	Y	Y	Y	Y	Y
Reliability	❶	❶	❶	❷	❷	③	③	③
Air conditioning	❷	❷	❷	❷	③	③	③	③
Auto. transmission	❶	❶	❶	❶	❶	❷	③	③
Body integrity	❶	❶	❶	❶	❶	❷	❷	③

Braking system	❶	❶	❶	❷	❷	❷	❷	③
Electrical system	❶	❶	❶	❷	❷	③	③	③
Engines	❷	❷	❷	❷	③	③	③	④
Exhaust/Converter	❷	❷	❷	③	③	④	④	④
Fuel system	❷	❷	❷	❷	③	③	③	④
Ignition system	❷	❷	③	③	③	③	③	④
Rust/Paint	❶	❶	❶	❶	❶	❶	❷	③
Steering	❷	❷	❷	❷	③	③	③	③
Suspension	❷	❷	❷	❷	③	③	③	③
Crash Safety								
Bonneville 4d	⑤	④	⑤	⑤	⑤	⑤	⑤	—
Cutlass 4d	—	—	—	—	—	④	④	④
Cutlass Supreme 2d	—	—	—	—	④	—	—	—
Cutlass Supreme 4d	④	❷	④	—	—	—	—	—
Delta 88 4d	④	④	—	—	④	—	—	—
Grand Prix 2d	—	—	④	④	—	—	—	—
Grand Prix 4d	❷	❷	—	—	—	④	—	—
Intrigue	—	—	—	—	—	—	④	④
LeSabre 4d	④	④	—	—	—	④	④	④
Lumina 4d	❷	❷	④	—	⑤	⑤	④	④
Malibu	—	—	—	—	—	④	④	④
Monte Carlo	—	—	—	④	④	④	—	—
Regal 2d	⑤	—	—	—	④	—	—	—
Regal 4d	❷	❷	④	—	—	—	—	④
Side Impact								
Cutlass 4d	—	—	—	—	—	❶	❶	❶
Intrigue	—	—	—	—	—	—	③	③
LeSabre 4d	—	—	—	—	—	—	—	③
Lumina	—	—	—	—	—	④	④	④
Malibu	—	—	—	—	—	❶	❶	❶
Regal 4d	—	—	—	—	—	—	③	③

Century, Ciera

Rating: Average (1998–99); Below Average (1997); Not Recommended (1982–96). In the early years, the same failure-prone components were used year after year. The 1996 Century isn't in the same league as the revised 1997 version, which adopted the W platform used by the Chevrolet Lumina, Pontiac Grand Prix, and 1998 Oldsmobile Intrigue. A 1996 Ciera is cheaper, but you won't have the important mechanical and body upgrades offered by its 1998 replacement, the '98 Oldsmobile Cutlass. The new Cutlass is an upgraded mid-sized sedan similar to the new Malibu (be careful not to confuse the new Cutlass with the Cutlass Supreme, a 10-year-old model that was replaced by the Intrigue, which is equipped like the Century). **Maintenance/Repair costs:** Higher than average, but repairs aren't dealer dependent. **Parts:** Higher-than-average cost (independent suppliers sell for much less), but not hard to find. Nevertheless, don't even think about buying one of these front-drives without a three- to five-year comprehensive warranty.

Strengths and weaknesses: The A-body line, long a mainstay in GM's family sedan market, has disappeared. This is good news, because these cars are outclassed by the competition and are in desperate need of high-quality components and fresher styling. Overall quality has improved somewhat since the introduction of these cars in 1982, but with the arrival of better quality Japanese imports, these derivatives of the X-bodies aren't really in the running.

Nevertheless, these cars were consistently popular with fleet buyers and car rental agencies because they were useful as comfortable family sedans and wagons. Handling and other aspects of road performance varied considerably depending on the suspension and powertrain chosen.

1988–96 models are particularly unreliable. The 2.5L 4-cylinder engine suffers from engine-block cracking and a host of other serious defects. The 2.8L V6 engine hasn't been durable either; it suffers from premature camshaft wear and leaky gaskets and seals, especially the intake manifold gasket. The 3-speed automatic transmission is weak and the 4-speed automatic frequently malfunctions. Temperamental and expensive-to-replace fuel systems (including the in-tank fuel pump) afflict all models/years, causing chronic stalling, hard starting, and poor fuel economy (use the emissions warranty as leverage to get compensation). Fuel system diagnosis and repair for the 3.0L V6 are difficult, and the electronic controls are often defective. Air conditioners frequently malfunction and the cooling system is prone to leaks.

Prematurely worn power-steering assemblies are particularly commonplace. Brakes are weak and need frequent attention due to premature wear and dangerously rapid corrosion, front brake rotors warp easily, excessive pulsation is common, and rear brake drums often lock up, particularly when damp. Shock absorbers and springs wear out quickly. Rear wheel alignment should be checked often. Electric door locks frequently malfunction. Water leaks onto carpeting. Premature and extensive surface rust—due to poor paint application, delamination, and defective materials—is common for all years. Far more disturbing are scattered reports of severe undercarriage/suspension rusting, possibly making the vehicles unsafe to drive. This problem also costs lots of money to correct, as the owner of a 1990 Century relates:

> Recently I was doing an oil change on my car and I noticed a small divot in the engine cradle (or sub frame). I poked at it and put my finger right through it! I discovered that the cradle was rotted on both sides near the idler arm. The car is only 8 years old and has only 112,000 km on it. I have had it into two collision repair places and they both said they have never seen a rotted engine cradle. One man has been in the business 25 years!

The 1997 Century received a complete make-over that includes the following: gobs of room and trunk space (rivaling that of the Taurus, Concorde, Accord, and Camry); sleeker styling; a much quieter interior; and an upgraded, standard ABS system that produces minimal pedal pulsation. Engine noise was also reduced, although insufficient firewall insulation means a considerable amount of noise still gets into the interior. Other new features include upgraded door seals, steering-wheel-mounted radio controls, and additional heating ducts for rear passengers. '98 models come with reduced-force airbags; '99 versions offer a revised ABS system and better traction control. On the downside, you can get only the 160-hp 3.1L V6 engine; the new Century's speed-dependent power steering is too light and vague; and its suspension and handling are more tuned to comfort than performance. The Century's front air deflector shield has also been the object of many complaints. Its low placement causes the shield to hit the roadway whenever passing over a small dip or bump. Furthermore, the bumper pulls off when passing over parking blocks, forcing drivers to park away from the blocks, with the rear end hanging out in the laneway.

Safety summary/Recalls: All models: 1996—Vehicle suddenly accelerated on its own. • Cruise control speed increases upon descending a hill. • Sudden brake loss. • Chronic stalling. • Oxygen sensor failures believed to be cause of stalling problems. • Steering radius is too large, and steering response is sluggish. • Dash reflection in windshield causes poor visibility. • Cannot read clock in daylight. • Airbag assembly on steering wheel blocks view of instrument panel. • Back windows often shatter. • Frequent battery failures. • Fuel pump failures. • Transmission failures; gear shift lever fell off in driver's hand. • Front door power motors failed. **1997**—Sudden brake loss. • Car moved forward when put into Reverse. • Battery exploded twice. • Poor design of magnetic variable steering results in difficult handling with vehicle swaying at 60 km/h and struts contributing to instability. • Sway bar links failure. • Horn buttons difficult to access and depress due to their small size; must take eyes off the road. • Fuel tank warning system activates prematurely. • Dash reflection in windshield causes poor visibility. • Poor headlight design makes for poor visibility. • Defroster system button breaks easily. • Windshield wipers fail frequently. • Defective airbag cover. • Power door lock failures. • Driver's seatbelt won't fully retract. **1998**—Airbags failed to deploy. • Idle surge after releasing brake due to faulty oxygen sensor. • Leaking lower intake manifold. • Engine oil pan leakage. • Chronic stalling. • Transmission shifts erratically. • Transmission hard to put into Reverse; faulty gear shift lever. • Sudden loss of electrical power. • Climate control switch failures. • Dash reflection on windshield causes poor visibility. • Excessive brake vibrations. • Headlights provide poor visibility. • Headlight switch failure. • Windshield wiper arm failures. • Water leaks into trunk. • Drivers report that the head restraints don't stay up. • Horn buttons hard to access in an emergency because of the airbag located directly under the horn and the radio control on the steering wheel. • Horn blows on its own when car is not running. **1999**—Airbags failed to deploy in a collision. • Engine fire upon startup. • Chronic engine hesitation when accelerating or changing gears. • Vehicle suddenly accelerated when brakes were applied. • Sudden, unintended acceleration once car was underway. • Cruise control failed to disengage. • Premature transmission failure; won't go into Reverse, shift lever hangs up; Drive gear won't hold vehicle when stopped on an incline. • Seatbelt trapped child around waist, had to be cut free. • Dash and seatcover reflect upon the windshield. • Front right window suddenly exploded. • Horn isn't loud enough and "sweet" spot to sound horn is hard to locate. • Headlights are too dim and have a narrow beam. • Front seat headrests won't stay in the raised position. • Tire jack won't hold vehicle's weight. **Recalls: All models: 1988–95**—Rear outboard safety belt anchorages will be reinforced. **Century: 1997**—Faulty windshield wiper linkage will be replaced. **Ciera: 1989–96**—Rear seat anchor bolts don't meet federal load standards.

Secret Warranties/Service Tips

All models/years—Low oil pressure in 3.8L V6 engines is likely caused by a failure-prone oil pump. A temporary remedy is to avoid low-viscosity oils and use 10W-40 in the winter and 20W-50 for summer driving. • THM 44C-T4 automatic transaxles with V6 engines are particularly failure-prone, due to pinched or kinked vacuum lines that cause oil starvation. **All models: 1984–90**—Frequent loss of Drive with 440-T4 transmissions is likely caused by a maladjusted 1–2 band stop unit. **1986–90**—Vehicles equipped with the 3T40 automatic transmission may experience slippage in manual Low or Reverse gears. Install service package #8628222, which includes a Low/Reverse clutch release spring (#8664961) and a clutch retainer and snap ring (#656/657). **1990**—Door lock rods that fall off need an upgraded inside handle to lock the rod. **1993–99**—A rotten-egg odour coming from the exhaust is probably the result of a malfunctioning catalytic converter; replacement cost may be covered by the emissions warranty. • Eliminate AC odours by installing an evaporator cooling-coil coating kit. • Paint delamination, peeling, or fading (see Part Two). **1994**—Loss of Drive or erratic shifts may be caused by an intermittent short to ground on the A or B shift solenoid or an electrical short circuit in the transaxle. • A front-end clunking noise when driving over rough roads may require the repositioning of the diagonal radiator support braces. **1994–95**—TSB #43-81-29 troubleshoots cruise controls that fail to engage. **1995–97**—Intermittent Neutral/loss of Drive at highway speeds can be fixed by replacing the control valve body assembly. **1997**—Rear brake clicking or squealing may be caused by a misadjusted park brake cable. • Insufficient heater performance on the passenger-side floor area can be fixed by installing a new I/P insulator panel and bracket. **Century: 1994–98**—A cold engine tick or rattle heard shortly after start-up may be fixed by replacing the piston/pin assembly. **1997–99**—A low-speed steering shudder or vibration may be corrected by replacing the steering pressure and return lines with revised "tuned" hoses. • Front disc pads have been upgraded to reduce brake squeal. • A shaking sensation at cruising speed may be fixed by replacing the transmission mount. • TSB #00-03-06-001 gives a comprehensive list of common front end noises and what's needed to silence them. • Install a new steering wheel inflatable restraint module to make it easier to sound the horn. • Install an upgraded low level fuel sensor to fix a fluctuating fuel gauge. **1998**—A wet right rear floor signals the need to reseal the stationary glass area. **1998–99**—Poor AM reception on vehicles with a windshield-mounted antenna may be improved by installing an in-line antenna jumper. **1999–2000**—Simply changing the radiator cap may cure your hot-running engine and prevent coolant loss.

Century, Ciera Profile

	1992	1993	1994	1995	1996	1997	1998	1999
Cost Price ($)								
Century	17,798	17,298	20,398	23,080	23,820	24,545	25,215	25,199
Ciera S/SL	16,398	17,298	20,598	22,960	23,625	—	—	—
Used Values ($)								
Century ↑	3,500	5,500	7,000	8,500	10,500	14,000	16,000	18,000
Century ↓	3,000	3,500	5,500	6,500	8,500	11,500	14,000	16,000
Ciera S/SL ↑	3,000	5,000	6,500	7,500	9,500	—	—	—
Ciera S/SL ↓	2,500	3,500	5,500	6,000	8,000	—	—	—
Extended Warranty	Y	Y	Y	Y	Y	Y	Y	Y
Secret Warranty	N	Y	Y	Y	Y	Y	Y	Y
Reliability	❷	❷	❷	❷	❷	❷	③	③
Air conditioning	❷	❷	❷	❷	③	③	③	③
Auto. transmission	❷	❷	❷	❷	❷	❷	❷	③
Body integrity	❶	❶	❶	❶	❶	❷	❷	❷
Braking system	❷	❷	❷	❷	❷	❷	❷	❷
Electrical system	❷	❷	❷	❷	❷	❷	❷	③
Engines	❷	❷	❷	❷	③	③	③	③
Exhaust/Converter	❷	❷	③	③	④	⑤	⑤	⑤

Fuel system	❷	❷	❷	❷	❷	③	③	③
Ignition system	❷	❷	❷	❷	❷	③	④	④
Rust/Paint	❶	❶	❶	❶	❶	❷	❷	❷
Steering	❷	❷	❷	❷	③	③	③	④
Suspension	❷	❷	❷	❷	❷	❷	③	④
Crash Safety								
Century 4d	④	④	④	④	④	—	—	④
Ciera	—	④	—	—	—	—	—	—
Side Impact								
Century 4d	—	—	—	—	—	—	③	③

HONDA

Accord

Rating: Above Average (1990–99); Average (1985–89). Accord has lost its Recommended status this year because models built during the last few years have racked up an unusually large number of safety- and performance-related complaints. They include reports of sudden acceleration and stalling, brake failures, and airbag malfunctions that cause the devices to go off when they shouldn't and fail to deploy when they should. Also be wary of Honda servicing and sales practices; they're not of the same caliber as Honda's products. Consumer complaints aside, the Accord is fast and nimble without a V6, making it the car of choice in the compact sedan class for drivers who want maximum fuel economy and comfort along with lots of space for grocery hauling and occasional highway cruising. **Maintenance/Repair costs:** Lower than average. Repairs aren't dealer dependent. **Parts:** Higher-than-average cost, but can be easily found for much less from independent suppliers.

Strengths and weaknesses: The Accord doesn't really excel in any particular area; it's just very, very good at everything. It's smooth, quiet, mannerly, and competent, with outstanding fit and finish, inside and out. Every time Honda redesigned the line it not only caught up with the latest advances, it went slightly ahead. Strong points are comfort, fit and finish, ergonomics, impressive assembly quality, reliability, and driveability. With the optional 16-valve 4-cylinder engine or V6, the Accord is one of the most versatile compacts you can find. It offers something for everyone, and its high resale value means there's no way you can lose money buying one.

Despite all the foregoing praise, this hasn't always been a great car. During the '80s, Accords were beset with severe premature rusting, frequent engine camshaft and crankshaft failures, and severe front brake problems. Engines leaked or burned oil and blew their cylinder head gaskets easily, and carbureted models suffered from driveability problems through 1986.

Between 1986 and 1989, the brakes, automatic transmission (particularly the 2–4 clutch assembly), rack-and-pinion steering, suspension (coils are practically biodegradable), and electrical system became the major problem areas. Also, water pumps and alternators need replacing about every three years. Rapid front brake wear and frequent brake rotor replacements are common. The automatic transmission shifts a bit harshly upon hard acceleration. Shock absorbers go soft quickly, and replacement prices are often less at independent suppliers. To avoid costly engine repairs, check the engine timing belt every 2 years/ 40,000 km.

Early Accords were surprisingly vulnerable to paint chipping, flaking, and premature surface rust. If left untreated, sheet metal perforations develop unusually quickly. Especially vulnerable spots are front fender seams, door bottoms, areas surrounding side view mirrors, door handles, rocker panels, wheel openings, windshield posts, front cowls, and trunk and hatchback lids.

1990–93 models got more room (stepping up to the mid-size car niche) and additional power through a new and quieter 2.2L 4-cylinder engine. Nevertheless, rear seating is still inadequate, the added weight saps the car's performance, and the automatic transmission shifts harshly at times. Owners report prematurely worn automatic transmissions, constant velocity joints, and power-steering assemblies. Poor quality control in the choice of body trim and assembly leads to numerous air and water leaks.

Redesigned again for the 1994 model year, the Accord continues to add interior room and other refinements. However, the addition of the V6 powerplant in the 1995 model year gives the Accord plenty of power in reserve without the high rpms. The automatic transmission still works poorly with the 4-banger, producing acceleration times that are far from impressive, and owners still complain of excessive road noise and tire whine. Nevertheless, no significant reliability problems have been reported with that redesign. 1996 models were slightly restyled, the trunk opening was enlarged, and a rear-seat pass-through feature increased cargo space. Although the '97s were carried over unchanged, the '98 Accord was substantially reworked. Notable changes: no more wagon version, more powerful 6- and 8-cylinder engines, a more refined suspension and automatic transaxle, upgraded ABS, additional interior space, and more glass. The '99s were mostly carried over unchanged, except for standard ABS on the LX.

Confidential technical service bulletins show that the 1994–97 models are susceptible to AC malfunctions, engine oil leaks, Check Engine light coming on for no reason, transmission glitches, power-steering pump leaks, windows falling off their channels, and numerous air and water leaks. Usually, these problems are simple to repair and Honda customer relations staff are helpful; however, Honda staffers and dealers are reluctant to admit their mistakes and may be getting a bit too arrogant in their dealings with the public. Witness the company's failure to publicly disclose its 1994–97 engine oil leak problems over the past seven years and its delay in setting up a free repair program until the end of year 2000. Honda has also asked that ALLDATA no longer share Honda service bulletin information with owners. Yet, these service bulletins help owners and independent garages to quickly zero in on a problem without wasting time and money. One *Lemon-Aid* reader wrote the following:

> We returned the car to the dealer several times (at least six) to have the doors adjusted to reduce wind noise affecting my 1994 Accord LX sedan. They were finally able to reduce the noise a small amount. A letter written to Honda explaining our dissatisfaction with the car resulted in a response letter with very definite "screw you" overtones.

This owner's problem is covered in the Honda bulletin shown below, which is on file with the U.S. government agency National Highway Traffic Safety Administration (NHTSA) in Washington D.C. The bulletin not only clearly identifies the problem as affecting the Accord, it actually allows for the repair to be done for free under a "goodwill" warranty.

Why would Honda want to keep this info out of owners' hands?

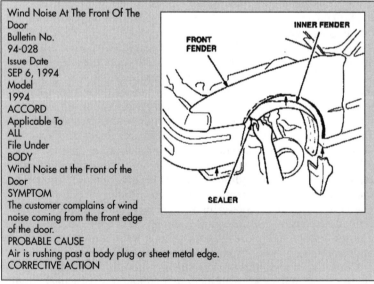

Wind Noise At The Front Of The Door
Bulletin No.
94-028
Issue Date
SEP 6, 1994
Model
1994
ACCORD
Applicable To
ALL
File Under
BODY
Wind Noise at the Front of the Door
SYMPTOM
The customer complains of wind noise coming from the front edge of the door.
PROBABLE CAUSE
Air is rushing past a body plug or sheet metal edge.
CORRECTIVE ACTION

Honda makes some fine vehicles; but mistakes do happen.

In another email posting that reinforces owner comments I've received over the past few years, a 2000 Accord owner had praise for his car but felt that Honda's sales practices and servicing were sub-par:

I have been buying new Honda Accords since 1987 and the car just keeps getting better but the service and dealer ethics just keep getting worse.

When I bought my latest 2000 Accord the dealer wouldn't budge from the MRSP but threw in a "free" cruise to make the deal...I have been trying to collect on this free cruise for a year, but the only way to retrieve your money is to buy a cruise at an inflated price.

As part of the deal, I also ordered the Keyless Accessory feature that the salesman showed me in the Honda brochure. Several months after numerous complaints the dealer finally admitted they had farmed this work out to a one-man shop who installed a $100.00 system even though I was charged the Honda accessory price. In reviewing my service bills, I actually discovered that they had doctored the documentation to pretend it was a Honda system. All they have done for me is to have this piece of junk replaced 3 times; who knows what my wiring harness looks like by now.

The regular warranty service has also been a rip-off being charged at least 3 times what the work was actually worth. I have since discovered that I can apparently get the work done at an independent garage at a fraction of the price. (What would we do without the internet?)

I have written 3 letters to Honda Canada complaining about the dealer with only one response that basically said that they don't care how their dealers carry on their business as long as they sell cars, have a nice day but quit bothering us.

The lesson to be learned in all of this for both Honda and potential Honda customers is that just because Honda is a great car don't expect the service to match the product. In fact, the service can be quite lousy because the cars sell themselves regardless of what the dealer does or doesn't do....

Bulletins and owner complaints relative to the reworked '98 and '99 models show a surprisingly large number of factory-related powertrain and body defects, undoubtedly due to the Accord's redesign. Some of those deficiencies affecting both safety and performance are: chronic lurching, hesitation, and stalling while on the highway, accompanied by the Check Engine light coming on; hard starting; frequent transmission failures; poor tracking allows vehicle to wander; defective rear-computerized motor mounts; electrical shorts; coolant and brake master cylinder leakage; ABS and AC failures; poor radio reception.

Body and accessory problems for these same model years include: a plethora of squeaks, creaks, groans, and rattles; wind noise; water leaks; and fuel gauge defects; paint chipping, bubbling and peeling on hood, trunk, and roof (Honda blames it on bird droppings); leaky sunroof; windshield has vertical lines of distortion; driver's side mirror shakes excessively; faulty fuel-sending unit makes for inaccurate fuel readings (when full, indicates three-fourths full); speedometer off by 10 percent.

Technical service bulletins: All models: 1995—Noise from the front passenger's footwell, exhaust system, and shoulder belt anchors; rear shelf will buzz. • The dash panel and clutch pedal may creak. • A screeching noise occurs when the driver's window is lowered. • A wind whistle emanates from the top of the windshield. • Heater control indicators may not light. • TSB #95-017 shows which rear brake pads produce less noise and which ones last the longest. **1996**—Instrument panel creaking. • Poor fit of wheel centre cap. • Screeching noise when lowering the driver's window. • Seatbelt is slow to retract. **1997**—AC won't blow cold air (we're talking secret warranty here). • Oil seepage from the engine block. • Torque converter won't lock up. • Fifth gear grinds during upshift. • Leak from the power steering pump. • Rear wheel bearing noise. • Static when adjusting the radio volume. • Front door glass comes out of run channel. • Cracking paint on passenger-side airbag cover. • Missing alloy wheel centre cap. **1998**—Trunk spoiler damages paint. • Brake system indicator stays on. • Creak from the rear shelf area, headliner, windshield, and rear window. • Front ABS wheel sensor harness rubs against wheel. • Rattle from rear stabilizer bar. • Water leaks from the rear doors. • Wind noise from the top of the windshield. **1999**—Automatic transmission vibration at low speeds. • Wrinkled rear door sash trim. • Glove box door rattling, wheels clicking, and clutch pedal and rear wheel bearing noise. • Loose AC, heater, temperature, and fan control knobs. • Inaccurate fuel gauge.

Safety summary/Recalls: All models: 1995—Rear seatbelt buckle has insufficient slack, preventing buckle from latching. • Airbag warning light stays on. • Excessive windshield glare. • AC failure. • Headlight failure. • Cruise control malfunctions. • Premature front/rear brake wear. **1995–96**—Faulty power windows. • Brake failures/lockup. • Airbag failed to deploy or accidentally deployed. • Injury from airbag. • Sudden acceleration, stalling. • Passenger-side seatbacks won't stay upright. **1996**—Front passenger seatbelt locks up. • The door lock design gives a boost to thieves. • The Check Engine light is always on. • The defroster could be faulty. • Faulty power door locks. • The steering column separates from the shaft. **1997**—Airbags failed to deploy. • Inadvertent airbag deployment. • Fire caused by faulty wiring harness. • Sudden acceleration while braking. • Cruise control doesn't accelerate properly and won't downshift the transmission. • Transmission shifted into Reverse and vehicle moved forward. • ABS brakes lock up. • Sudden brake failure. • Location of the oil filter allows oil to leak onto the exhaust system and catalytic converter. • Faulty brake master cylinder. • All four front brake pads cracked right down the centre. • Power-steering fluid leakage. • Oil plug fell off into the oil pan and sprayed oil everywhere. • Left side seatbelt fails to retract. • Seatbelt tightened and locked up; occupant had to cut belt. • Seatbelt continually ratchets tighter. • When sun visor is opened, it blocks driver's vision due to its large size. • Check Engine light stays on continually. • Defroster fails to defrost side windows, and actually causes them to fog up. • Power windows fail to operate properly in cold weather. • Door continually out of adjustment. **1998**—Sudden acceleration while vehicle stopped in traffic. • Sudden acceleration occurred when vehicle hit from the rear. • Chronic stalling. • ABS brake light comes on continually. • Gas and brake pedals are too close together and often get pressed at the same time. • Airbag failed to deploy. • Frequent brake failures. • Sudden brake lockup. • Brake master cylinder failures. • Floormat bunches under the brake pedal. • Engine oil leakage. • Power-steering fluid leakage, causing sudden loss of steering control. • Vehicle rolled back when parked. • Automatic transmission gears disengage and make a loud noise when engaging. • Transmission fails to engage at slow speeds. • Transmission fails to fully lock up in Overdrive. • Transmission hunts for the right gear. • Clutch pedal failure. • Automatic transmission parking mechanism failure. • Due to design of dashboard lights, it's hard to read odometer, digital clock, and radio indicator. • Can't see high-beam indicator light in the daytime. • Light tan dash reflects too much sunlight into the eyes. • Instrument panel lights are too bright at night and can't be dimmed enough. • To activate horn, driver must remove hand from steering wheel. • Fuel gauge shows two-thirds when the gas tank is full, or indicates an empty tank with warning light on while 19 litres remain in the tank. • Poor seatbelt design allows for belt to wrap around the release lever and get stuck, or causes seatback to suddenly recline. • Seatbelts get trapped underneath the seatback electric switch. • Seatbelts ratchet too tight, trapping occupants. • Rear passenger-side door won't unlock. • Sunroofs and headliners often need replacing. **1999**—Airbags failed to deploy. • Over-sensitive airbag sensors caused airbags to deploy when bumper touched curb while parking. • Airbag deployment caused extensive neck and head injuries. • Sudden acceleration. • Gas and brake pedals placed too close together; foot easily slips off brake pedal. • Sudden brake loss. • Emergency brakes failed to hold on hill, allowing car to roll into lake. • Brake master cylinder leakage. • Driver's seatback suddenly fell back. • Steering knuckle broke while driving. • Bolt that holds the lower control arm assembly broke away from the frame, causing wheel to come out of fender. • Many complaints of chronic lurching, hesitation, and stalling while on the highway accompanied by Check Engine light coming on (dealers can't duplicate the problem). • Sudden tire tread failures (Michelin MXV4). • Engine sputters at half throttle. • Hard starting. Frequent transmission failures. • Vehicle doesn't track well; wanders all over the road. • Engine mount makes a clunking sound. • Defective rear computerized motor mounts on '98 and '99 models. • Loose oil pan plug may drip oil onto exhaust pipe. • Seatbelts fail to retract or continually tighten up, choking occupant. • Right front passenger window exploded while driving. • Windshield has vertical lines of distortion. • Driver's side mirror shakes excessively.

Recalls: All models: 1995—Airbags may deploy for no reason. **1995–97**—Models with 4-cylinder engines (excluding DX version) have improperly routed air conditioning wires that may short and cause fires or other electrical malfunctions; dealers must install protective plastic tubing on the harnesses, re-route the wires, and replace damaged harnesses. **1997–98**—Ball joints may wear out prematurely. **1998**—Vehicle may roll away with transmission lever in Park.

Secret Warranties/Service Tips

All models/years—Steering wheel shimmy is a frequent problem, and is taken care of in TSB #94-025. **All models: 1988–93**—A creaking sound coming from the window regulator can be corrected by installing an upgraded regulator spiral spring. **1990**—Delay after shifting into Drive is corrected by adjusting the cable (#87-040). • An interior roaring noise can be silenced by installing blind body plugs (#95550-15000) in the door rocker panels. • If the front inside door handle doesn't work, check for a loose or broken actuator rod clip. • A moaning sound heard when the steering wheel is turned may mean that the steering-pump outlet-hose orifice has slipped out of position or that the outlet hose is faulty. • Water leaks behind the dashboard require sealing near the windshield-locating blocks and frame-panel seams in the cowl. • Whistling from the front of the car is likely caused by poor hood sealing. • Defective front door handle may prevent entry or exit. Honda will replace the mechanism free of charge. **1994–97**—Poor radio reception may be caused by a corroded coaxial connector. • If the AC doesn't blow cold air, Honda will consider replacing both the evaporator and the receiver/dryer free of charge under a "goodwill" program. • Oil seepage from the engine block requires sealing and the installation of a new exhaust manifold bracket. (The following two bulletins give more details on the above 1994–97 problems.)

97-031
Applies To:
1994-97 Accord - ALL
1994-97 Civic - ALL
1994-95 del Sol - ALL
August 4, 1997
A/C Does Not Blow Cold Air
SYMPTOM
The air conditioning system does not blow cold air.
PROBABLE CAUSE
The evaporator tubes corrode from ocean salt spray, causing pinholes that allow refrigerant to leak. This problem is limited to areas where a hot, humid climate is combined with ocean air (Florida, Hawaii, Puerto Rico, or Gulf Coast areas).
CORRECTIVE ACTION
Replace only the evaporator if the vehicle comes in with some refrigerant in the high side line. Replace both the evaporator and the receiver/dryer if the vehicle comes in without any refrigerant in the high side line.

This secret warranty pays for major AC components plus two hours of labour needed to get the job done. It also establishes that AC failures are routinely covered by Honda up to four years. Smart owners of other models should argue that any failure of the AC during that time, whether caused by salty air, road salt, or any other defect, falls within these "goodwill" parameters. Repairs required after four years of use should get partial refunds.

```
97-060
September 22, 1997
Applies To: 1994-97 Accord 4-door - All
Front Door Glass Comes Out of Run Channel
SYMPTOM
When operating a front window (power or manual), the rear edge of the glass comes out of the B-pillar run channel.
PROBABLE CAUSE
The window regulator is out of adjustment.
CORRECTIVE ACTION
Adjust the window regulator, the front channel, and the glass.
WARRANTY CLAIM INFORMATION
In warranty:
The normal warranty applies.
Failed part:        P/N 72250-SV4-A11, H/C 4272282
Defect code:        030
Contention code:    B01
Skill level:        Repair Technician
Out of warranty:
Any repair performed after warranty expiration may be eligible for goodwill consideration by the District Service Manager
or your Zone Office. You must request consideration, and get a decision, before starting work.
```

This job also falls under Honda's "goodwill" policy.

• Acura CL, Honda Accord, Prelude, and Odyssey models equipped with 4-cylinder engines may have defective engine oil seals that can slip, causing the engine to drain of oil and eventually seize. Although Honda maintains this isn't a safety recall (hmm, sudden engine seizure on the highway sounds scary to me), the company will, at no charge, inspect and replace the seal and install a clip to ensure the seal cannot move. There are about 1.4 million vehicles involved in this worldwide program. Repairs had been delayed due to poor parts availability (Source: December 1, 2000, edition of *The National Post* and Associated Press wire copy). • Power-steering pump fluid leakage requires a new O-ring, which is also eligible for "goodwill" consideration, says Honda. **1995**—A whistling or howling noise coming from the top of the windshield can be silenced by applying sealant under the upper windshield moulding. • Honda will supply an exhaust buzz silencing kit for free on a case-by-case basis. • The Accord's noise problems will be fixed for free only if the dealer makes the request to Honda. **1995–96**—A creaking noise coming from the instrument panel can be silenced through a variety of measures outlined in a series of Honda bulletins. **1996–97**—In a settlement with the U.S. Environmental Protection Agency (EPA), Honda paid fines totaling $17.1 million and extended its emissions warranty on 1.6 million 1995–97 models to 14 years/150,000 miles (see Honda Civic rating for full details, page 155). **1998**—If the brake system indicator stays on, install an improved master cylinder reservoir cap float. • A flickering ceiling light may be caused by a poor ground contact in the switch. • An inaccurate fuel gauge must be replaced with an upgraded unit. • Tips on eliminating wind noise from the top of the front windshield, and a creaking noise from the rear shelf, headliner, and windshield area. • Coolant leakage from the radiator drain plug may require the replacement of the drain plug/O-ring assembly. • Rear door water leaks may be plugged simply by removing excess weather stripping. **1998–99**—A clutch pedal squeak or groan is likely due to insufficient lubrication of the piston cup seal. **1999–2000**—Automatic transmission vibration at low speeds requires an upgraded torque converter covered by the base warranty or by a "good-will" program.

A/T – Vibration While Driving at Low Speeds
00-038
April 25, 2000
Applies To:
1999 Accord V6- 4-door from VIN 1HGCG1...XA050000 thru 1HGCG1...XA068508
2-door from VIN 1HGCG2...XA026000 thru 1HGCG2...XA033528
2000 Accord V6- 4-door from VIN 1HGCG1...YA000001 thru 1HGCG1...YA028000
2-door from VIN 1HGCG2...YA000001 thru 1HGCG2...YA006000
Vibration While Driving At Low Speeds
SYMPTOM
A shudder or judder when driving at speeds between 20 and 40 mph. This vibration is most noticeable when the torque converter lock-up clutch is in the partial lock-up mode.
PROBABLE CAUSE
Irregularities in the torque converter face prevent the lock-up clutch from smoothly engaging.
CORRECTIVE ACTION
Replace the torque converter.
Out of warranty: Any repair performed after warranty expiration may be eligible for goodwill consideration by the District Service Manager or our Zone Office. You must request consideration, and get a decision, before starting work.

Take note that Honda covers this five-hour repair under its "goodwill" policy even if your warranty has expired.

Accord Profile

	1992	1993	1994	1995	1996	1997	1998	1999
Cost Price ($)								
LX	15,690	17,195	18,695	19,795	20,295	20,995	23,800	23,800
EXi/EX	18,695	20,545	21,495	22,595	22,995	23,495	26,800	26,801
Used Values ($)								
LX ↑	4,500	5,500	7,500	9,000	11,000	13,000	15,500	18,000
LX ↓	4,000	5,000	6,000	7,500	9,500	11,000	14,000	16,000
EXi/EX ↑	6,000	7,500	9,000	11,000	13,000	15,000	18,500	20,500
EXi/EX ↓	5,500	6,000	7,500	9,500	11,500	13,000	16,500	19,000
Extended Warranty	N	N	N	N	N	N	N	N
Secret Warranty	Y	Y	Y	Y	Y	Y	Y	Y
Reliability	③	④	⑤	⑤	⑤	⑤	⑤	⑤
Air conditioning	③	③	③	③	③	④	④	④
Auto. transmission	③	③	③	④	④	④	④	④
Body integrity	❷	❷	❷	❷	③	③	③	④
Braking system	❷	❷	❷	❷	❷	③	③	④
Electrical system	❷	③	③	③	④	⑤	⑤	⑤
Engines	④	④	④	⑤	⑤	⑤	⑤	⑤
Exhaust/Converter	❷	❷	❷	④	④	⑤	⑤	⑤

Fuel system	④	④	④	⑤	⑤	⑤	⑤	⑤
Ignition system	③	③	④	⑤	⑤	⑤	⑤	⑤
Rust/Paint	③	③	④	④	④	④	④	③
Steering	❷	❷	③	③	③	④	⑤	⑤
Suspension	③	③	③	④	⑤	⑤	⑤	⑤
Crash Safety								
2d	—	—	—	—	—	④	④	④
4d	④	④	④	④	④	④	④	④
SE	—	④	—	—	—	—	—	—
Side Impact								
2d	—	—	—	—	—	—	—	③
4d	—	—	—	—	—	❷	④	④

HYUNDAI

Sonata

Rating: Above Average (1999); Average (1995–98); Not Recommended (1986–93). The 1994 model year was skipped. These cars haven't registered one-tenth the number of safety complaints as has the higher-rated Honda Accord. For maximum savings, I suggest you buy a 1996–99 version, with some of the original warranty left, plan to keep it at least five years to shake off the depreciation, and put some of the savings on the purchase price into a comprehensive supplementary warranty to protect yourself when the warranty ends. (I exclude the '95 version because it was the first year of its redesign.) **Maintenance/Repair costs:** Higher than average. Repairs aren't dealer dependent. **Parts:** Higher-than-average cost, and often back-ordered.

Strengths and weaknesses: This mid-sized front-drive sedan was built under Mitsubishi licensing, but its overall reliability isn't anywhere near as good as what you'll find with Mitsubishi's cars and trucks sold in Canada under the Chrysler and Eagle monikers. Acceleration is impressive with the manual gearbox, but only passable with the automatic. Handling and performance are also fairly good, although emergency handling isn't confidence inspiring, particularly due to the imprecise steering and excessive lean when cornering. As with other Hyundai models, the automatic transmission performs erratically, the engine is noisy, and reliability is a problem—it's way below average for the 1989–93 models; the 1995–98 models are moderately improved (remember, Hyundai skipped the 1994s).

Redesigned for the 1995 model year, the car got additional interior room, more horsepower, and an upgraded automatic transmission. Nevertheless, acceleration with the automatic is still below average with the 4-banger, and the automatic gearbox still downshifts slowly. (The manual transmission is still more reliable and fuel efficient.) The 1996 model Sonatas came with more standard features, like air conditioning, power steering, a split-folding rear seatback, liquid-filled engine mounts, and additional sound deadening to make for a more comfortable ride. The 1997–98 versions returned virtually unchanged, but the '99 version arrived with a redesigned body and suspension, side airbags, two new engines, and a huge price increase that's not reflected in its resale value.

Consumer Reports magazine reports that owners of 1990–92 Sonatas had 120 percent more complaints than the average car owner. Sonatas have body-assembly and preparation deficiencies that show that Hyundai doesn't yet have a firm grip on quality control. For example, the sloppily applied paint pits like an orange peel, and the sun visors and headliner look cheap and fragile. If the experience of Stellar and Pony owners is any guide, Sonata owners will notice serious deficiencies by the third and fourth year.

Hyundai technical service bulletins indicate that the Sonata's automatic transmission could exhibit what Hyundai describes as "shift shock," as well as delayed shifting. Problems reported by owners in the past: poor engine performance (hard starting, poor idling, stalling); the engine runs hot, and when you're stopped at a traffic light it shakes like a boiling kettle; #3 spark plug often needs replacing or cleaning; rough engine rattle; high oil consumption (one litre every two to three months); excessive front brake pulsation and premature wear; steering defects (when the steering wheel is turned to either extreme, it makes a sound like metal cracking); cruise control malfunctions and electrical short circuits; battery life of only 18 months; malfunctioning lights; radio failures; falling interior roof liner; faulty hood locks; rotten-egg smell coming from the catalytic converter; broken muffler; faulty resonator; defective exhaust pipe; poor door and window sealing (water leaking into the interior when the car is washed); premature paint peeling; and rusting.

The 1995–99 Sonatas haven't elicited as many quality-control and safety complaints as previous versions. However, automatic transmissions, brakes, airbags, and electrical-system components still top the list of parts most vulnerable to premature failure or malfunctioning.

Safety summary/Recalls: All models: Emergency handling leaves a lot to be desired. **1996**—Tire fell off car. • Battery blew up while car was idling. • Airbag light is continuously lit. • Brake malfunctions. • Chronic stalling, particularly when AC is engaged. • Frequent engine valve cover gasket failures. • Poor-quality spark plugs cause sluggish acceleration. • Check Engine light is lit continuously. • Frequent automatic transmission failures. • Water leaks from the front of the car. **1997**—Airbags fail to deploy. • Frequent engine failures. • Transmission gearshift will not stay in place. • Power window switch failed. **1998**—Frequent inadvertent airbag deployment. • Sudden transmission failure while driving. **1999**—Complete brake failure. • Airbag failed to deploy; airbag warning light comes on for no reason. • Sudden alternator failure causes entire vehicle to shut down. • Hyundai does not offer a seatbelt extension for large occupants. **Recalls: All models: 1989–94**—Motorized shoulder belt may be defective or need lubrication. **1995**—There is the potential of loss of rear spring support. **1996–97**—The wiper motor may be faulty.

Secret Warranties/Service Tips

All models/years—Troubleshooting tips for delayed engagement of the automatic transmission. Harsh shifting when coming to a stop or upon initial acceleration is likely caused by an improperly adjusted accelerator pedal switch TCU. • A faulty air exhaust plug could cause harsh shifting into second and fourth gears on vehicles with automatic transmission. • Brake pedal pulsation can be corrected by installing upgraded front discs and pads. • Troubleshooting tips for reducing brake noise. **All models: 1989–98**—Revised measures to reduce AC odours. **1990**—Difficult shifts into fourth gear require a new transmission restrict ball assembly. **1992–93**—Hyundai has a field fix for manual transaxle gear clash/grind (TSB #9440-004). **1992–95**—Difficult-to-engage Reverse gear needs an upgraded part. **1995–99**—Tips are offered on getting the automatic transmission to shift properly. **1995–98**—Harsh shifting might be fixed by installing an upgraded Transaxle Control Module (TCM) under a "goodwill" warranty. • If wind noise makes a "kazoo" sound, try installing an additional drip rail moulding. **1999**—Shudder or vibration during acceleration can be eliminated by correcting a sticking inboard CV—tripod joint assembly. • A humping/knocking noise heard from the left front side of the vehicle on hard right turns may be caused by the left rear corner of the transaxle mounting bracket base touching the body. • Tips on silencing front wheel-bearing noise. **1999–2000**—No-starts, hard starting, or erratic idling may all be caused by a canister purge valve that's stuck open.

Sonata Profile

	1991	1992	1993	1995	1996	1997	1998	1999
Cost Price ($)								
Base	12,595	13,095	13,495	15,595	16,595	16,995	17,495	19,495
Used Values ($)								
Base ↑	1,500	2,000	3,000	5,000	6,500	8,500	10,000	13,500
Base ↓	1,000	1,500	2,000	4,000	5,500	7,000	8,500	12,000
Extended Warranty	Y	Y	Y	Y	Y	Y	Y	Y
Secret Warranty	N	N	N	N	Y	Y	Y	N
Reliability	②	②	②	②	③	③	③	③
Air conditioning	②	②	③	③	③	③	④	④
Auto. transmission	②	②	②	②	②	③	③	③
Body integrity	②	②	②	②	②	②	②	③
Braking system	②	②	②	②	②	③	③	③
Electrical system	②	②	②	②	②	④	④	④
Engines	③	③	③	③	②	②	③	③

Exhaust/Converter	②	②	③	④	④	⑤	⑤	⑤
Fuel system	③	③	③	⑤	⑤	④	⑤	⑤
Ignition system	③	④	④	④	⑤	⑤	⑤	⑤
Rust/Paint	②	②	②	②	③	③	③	④
Steering	③	②	②	③	③	③	③	④
Suspension	②	②	③	④	④	⑤	⑤	⑤
Crash Safety	—	—	—	③	③	③	③	—
Side Impact	—	—	—	—	—	❶	❶	—

MAZDA

626, MX-6

Rating: Above Average (1996–99); Average (1994–95); Not Recommended (1985–93). 1997 was the last model year for the MX-6 and the Probe, its Ford twin. Make sure the car fits your size: tall drivers should be wary of the low headrests that can be hazardous in a collision, and short drivers will want to ensure they can see adequately without getting dangerously close to the airbag housing. All drivers are warned that the airbags often go off for no reason. **Maintenance/ Repair costs:** Higher than average. Repairs aren't dealer dependent. Mazda suggests changing the engine timing chain after 100,000 km. **Parts:** Easily found, but sometimes costly. Although Mazda has promised to cut prices, still compare prices with independent suppliers.

Strengths and weaknesses: Although far from being high-performance vehicles, these cars ride and handle fairly well and still manage to accommodate four people in comfort. The 1988–92 versions incorporated a third-generation redesign that added a bit more horsepower to the 4-banger. Apart from that improvement, these cars are still easy riding, fairly responsive, and not hard on gas. On the downside, the automatic transmission downshifts roughly, the power steering is imprecise, and the car leans a lot in turns.

Four-wheel steering was part of the sedan's equipment in 1988, and it was added exclusively to the MX-6 a year later. Wise buyers should pass over this option and look instead for anti-lock brakes and airbags on 1992 LG and GT versions. The manual transmission is a better choice because the automatic robs the engine of much-needed horsepower, as is the case with most cars this size. A passenger-side airbag was added to all '94 models.

A mid-sport and mid-compact hybrid, the MX-6 is a coupe version of the 626. It has a more sophisticated suspension, more horsepower, and better steering response than its sedan alter ego. The 1993 model gained a base 2.5L 165-hp V6 powerplant. Overall reliability and durability are on par with the 626.

1995–99 models offer improved performance, handling, and overall reliability, plus reasonable fuel economy. Owners still complain, though, of sub-par body construction, electrical system and cruise control glitches, dim headlights, brakes and AC compressors that wear out prematurely, and automatic transmissions that shift poorly and are prone to premature failure. The Check Engine comes on and goes off repeatedly due to oil spilling into the air flow sensor or the intake manifold gasket leaking. Expect jerky downshifts when the 4-cylinder is at full throttle. Shocks and struts (MacPherson) aren't very durable and are expensive to replace (especially when the model is equipped with the electronic adjustment feature).

Body problems include door and hatch locks that often freeze up, the right side of the dash is often loose, the interior door panel pulls away, interior colours fade, headliner rattles, and the metal surrounding the rear wheelwells is prone to rust perforation, as are hood, trunk, and door seams. The paint seems particularly prone to chipping. The underbody and suspension components on cars older than five years should be examined carefully for corrosion damage. The exhaust system rarely lasts more than two years, and wheel bearings fail repeatedly within the same period.

1998 models underwent a major redesign, making them the better buy on the used-car market today. Some of the '98's best new features were attractive Millenia-type styling, a longer wheelbase and larger cabin, a reinforced body to keep creaks and rattles to a minimum, and more powerful engines. The '99 models were carried over unchanged, except for a larger selection of standard accessories.

Safety summary/Recalls: All models/years—Head restraints are too low. One Canadian neurologist wrote *Lemon-Aid* that the 626's head restraints are set too low and cannot extend to a safe level; he says there is an additional two inches required for a six-foot-tall occupant. When informed of his assessment, the dealer replied that Mazda "cannot help you with your problem." The doctor maintains his Mazda 626 cannot be safely operated by a driver over five feet and ten inches in height. He concludes: "As a result of my occupation, I see many motor vehicle accident neck injuries and have a keen interest in making my new vehicle, and those of others, safe." **All models: 1995–96**—Inadvertent airbag deployments. **1997**—Airbags continue to deploy for no reason, injuring occupants (recall announced). • Several incidents where the steering failed without warning. • Frequent transmission failures. • Premature tire wear. • Brake failures and extended stopping distance. • Chronic electrical shorts. • Exhaust fumes enter into the interior. • Horn button hard to locate in an emergency. • Poor braking on wet roadways. • Headrest too low for tall drivers. Vehicle started on its own, then fire erupted. • Hesitation or stalling while driving. **1998**—Sudden, unintended acceleration. • Many incidents continue to be reported where airbags deployed for no reason. • Airbags failed to deploy in a collision. • Front axle pulled out of the transmission. • Steering rack gear broke in two without prior warning. • Sudden automatic transmission downshifts. • Frequent transmission failures. • Many reports of tire tread separation. • Poor braking leads to extended stopping distance. • Driver's seat is so low it must be brought dangerously close to the airbag housing for maximum visibility. **1999**—Left lower strut bolts loose, bent, and broken, causing the driver-side wheel to fall. • Premature tire wear. • When AC engages, engine hesitates, causes car to jerk. • Automatic transmission shift shock. • Transmission fails upon deceleration, it downshifts harshly, O/D light flashes, and then engine compartment starts to fill with transmission fluid. • Headlights dim intermittently. • Excessive vibration at low speeds. • Seatbelts won't properly secure a child safety seat. **Recalls: All models: 1995**—Airbags malfunction. **1995–96**—Inadvertent airbag deployment when passing over bumps in the road. Sensors will be reprogrammed. **1997**—Tensioner spring may break and get caught in the engine timing belt, stalling the engine; dealers will replace the tensioner. **1998**—Faulty computer module causes stalling.

Secret Warranties/Service Tips

All models/years—Non-turbo models that idle roughly after a warm restart could have fuel vapourizing in the distribution pipe (TSB #023/87R). • Excessive rear brake squealing can be reduced with improved brake pads (TSB #015/89-11). • Excessive vibrations felt in the brake pedal, steering wheel, floor, or seat when applying the brakes can be fixed by installing a redesigned brake assembly. • TSB #50901898 gives tips for eliminating wind noise around doors. **All models: 1993–94**—Freezing door and hatch lock cylinders are addressed in TSB #021/94. • Headliner rattles can be fixed by using Mazda's fastener kit. • The driver-side power seat might not work if the wiring harness touches the seat frame. • A clunking noise coming from the steering gear is caused by excessive backlash in the steering gear assembly. **1993–97**—Engine camshaft noise may be corrected with a new friction gear spring and lock nut. **1995–96**—A 3–4 shift hunt is probably caused by failure in the 3–4 shift solenoid hydraulic circuit. • Front strut squeaks on turns could be caused by interference between the upper seat spring and the strut dust cover, or between the dust cover and the rubber bump stopper. **1996–97**—Unwanted 4–3 downshifts or intermittent shifting into Overdrive is covered in bulletin #015/98. **1997–98**—Tips on fixing faulty sunroofs, a seatbelt warning buzzer that sounds for no reason, rough automatic transmission shifts, excessive idle vibration, rear brake squeal, coolant leaks, and hard-to-close trunk lid. **1998–2000**—Tips on silencing a rear end tapping noise, and preventing AC odours.

626, MX-6 Profile

	1992	1993	1994	1995	1996	1997	1998	1999
Cost Price ($)								
626	15,595	17,395	18,725	19,365	19,995	19,995	20,140	21,000
MX-6	15,825	19,375	20,695	21,835	22,780	23,325	—	—

Used Values ($)

626 ↑	5,000	6,500	8,500	10,000	11,000	13,000	15,000	16,000
626 ↓	4,000	5,500	7,000	8,500	9,500	11,500	13,500	14,500
MX-6 ↑	7,000	8,000	10,500	12,000	13,500	15,000	—	—
MX-6 ↓	6,000	7,000	9,000	10,500	12,000	13,500	—	—

Extended Warranty	Y	Y	Y	Y	N	N	N	N
Secret Warranty	N	N	N	N	N	N	N	N
Reliability	②	②	②	②	③	④	④	④
Air conditioning	②	③	③	③	③	③	④	④
Auto. transmission	②	②	②	②	②	②	③	③
Body integrity	②	②	②	②	③	③	④	④
Braking system	②	②	②	②	②	③	③	③
Electrical system	②	②	②	③	③	③	③	③
Engines	④	④	⑤	⑤	③	③	④	④
Exhaust/Converter	①	①	①	②	②	③	③	④
Fuel system	④	③	④	④	④	⑤	⑤	⑤
Ignition system	②	②	②	③	④	⑤	⑤	⑤
Rust/Paint	②	②	②	②	③	③	④	④
Steering	③	③	④	④	⑤	⑤	⑤	⑤
Suspension	②	②	③	③	④	④	④	④
Crash Safety								
626 4d	④	④	④	④	④	—	④	④
Side Impact								
626 4d	—	—	—	—	②	③	③	③

NISSAN

Altima

Rating: Above Average (1998–99); Average (1993–97). The 4-cylinder engine barely provides the necessary versatility needed to match the competition: the Toyota Camry, Mazda 626, updated Ford Probe, or larger Ford Sable and Taurus. Although the SE gives the sportiest performance, the less expensive GXE is the better deal from a price/quality standpoint. **Maintenance/Repair costs:** Higher than average. Repairs are dealer dependent. **Parts:** Owners complain of parts shortages, and parts may be more expensive than those for most other cars in this class.

Strengths and weaknesses: The Altima's wheelbase is a couple of inches longer than the Stanza's, and the car is touted by Nissan as a mid-size, even though its interior dimensions put it in the compact league. The small cabin seats only four, and rear seat access is difficult to master due to the slanted roof pillars, inward-curving door frames, and narrow clearance.

The base engine gives average acceleration and fuel economy. Manoeuvrability is good around town. There are no reliability problems reported with the 16-valve powerplant, although the automatic transmission's performance has been problematic through the '96 model year. The manual transaxle is a better choice for all years from a reliability and fuel-economy standpoint. The uncluttered under-hood layout makes servicing easy. Body assembly is only so-so with more than the average number of squeaks and rattles.

With its noisy and rough engine performance, this car cries out for a V6 like the one used in the Maxima. The 4-banger has insufficient top-end torque and gets buzzier the more it's pushed. In order to get the automatic to downshift for passing, for example, you have to practically stomp on the accelerator. The 5-speed manual transmission is sloppy. The Altima's sporty handling is way overrated; there's excessive body roll and front-end plow in hard cornering, tires squeal at moderate speeds, and steering isn't as precise or responsive as befits a car with performance pretensions. In spite of the car's independent suspension, it gives a busy, uncomfortable ride that's punishing over bumps. Lots of engine, road, and tire noise.

Redesigned '98 and '99 models came with depowered airbags and a more powerful powertrain setup. Prior to the '98 redesign, Altimas had a fairly good reliability reputation; only problem areas then were prematurely worn, noisy front brakes; transmission and electrical malfunctions; and body glitches. Since then, most complaints concern front brakes, transmission problems, and poor body fit and finish.

Safety summary/Recalls: All models: 1997—Fire ignited in the engine compartment while vehicle was parked. • Fire started by fuse box in passenger compartment. • Sudden acceleration. • Frequent reports that the airbag failed to deploy. • Poor braking performance. • Poor design causes electronic control unit failure. • Defective automatic transmission solenoid. • Windshield wiper fails periodically. • Water leaks into trunk area, causing premature rusting. • Automatic door lock failure. • Seat and shoulder belts lock up and don't retract. **1998**— Stalling when accelerating. • Rear seats won't lock upright. • Windows rattle excessively. • Wheel cover failure. **1999**—Several incidents where engine or electrical fires ignited while vehicle was parked. • Sudden acceleration. • Vehicle unstable on wet roadway. • Airbags failed to deploy. • Airbag light comes on for no reason. • Gearshift lever sticks in Park. • Transaxle snapped in half taking suspension and steering knuckle with it. • Sudden tire separation; tires gradually lose air (Continental-General). • Premature tire wear (Firestone). • Chronic brake problems. • Exhaust fumes (rotten-egg smell) enters into the interior. • Driver's seat moves forward when braking. **Recalls: All models: 1995**—Automatic shift lever plate can break causing unintended vehicle movement. • Brake hose may leak. **1996**—AC refrigerant leaks. • Leaking AC evaporator drain hose causes ECM damage. **1997**— Defective seatbelt buckles.

Secret Warranties/Service Tips

All models and years: Diagnostic and correction tips for brake vibration and steering wheel shimmy. • TSB #NTB99-028 outlines the procedures necessary to fix slow-to-retract seatbelts. **1993–96**—No-starts or hard starts may be caused by an automatic transmission control cable that's too short; TSB #96-032 gives additional diagnostic tips. • If the transmission won't shift into Reverse, it may mean the Reverse clutch drum, snap ring, and two dish rings need replacing. • A worn differential pinion shaft may require an upgraded transmission differential case. • Rear brake squeal can be reduced by installing improved rear brake shoes. • TSB #NTB96-046 gives lots of useful tips for troubleshooting squeaks and rattles. **1995**—An AC refrigerant leak at the charge port may be corrected by replacing the Schrader valve. **1995–96**—If the MIL light stays lit, it may mean the rear heated oxygen sensor needs replacing. **1999–2000**—Remote keyless entry controllers that don't work need to be re-programmed. • A sunroof that jams when opening rearward requires a re-adjustment of the sunroof links. This half-hour repair is covered by Nissan's base warranty. • Guidelines as to what constitues suspension strut leakage that qualifies for warranty coverage are found in TSB # NTB99-001.

Altima Profile							
	1993	1994	1995	1996	1997	1998	1999
Cost Price ($)							
XE	16,491	17,690	18,990	20,598	20,798	19,398	19,898
GXE	18,690	19,990	21,690	23,298	23,498	21,398	21,998
Used Values ($)							
XE ↑	5,500	6,500	8,000	9,500	11,000	13,000	15,000

XE ↓	4,500	5,500	6,500	8,000	9,000	11,500	13,000
GXE ↑	5,800	7,000	9,000	11,000	12,500	14,500	16,000
GXE ↓	4,800	6,000	7,000	9,500	11,000	12,500	14,500
Extended Warranty	N	N	N	N	N	N	N
Secret Warranty	N	N	N	N	N	N	N
Reliability	③	③	④	④	④	⑤	⑤
Air conditioning	❷	③	④	④	④	⑤	⑤
Auto. transmission	❷	❷	❷	❷	③	③	④
Body integrity	❷	❷	❷	❷	③	③	④
Braking system	❷	❷	❷	③	③	③	④
Electrical system	❷	❷	❷	③	③	③	⑤
Engines	④	⑤	④	⑤	⑤	⑤	⑤
Exhaust/Converter	③	③	③	④	⑤	⑤	⑤
Fuel system	③	③	③	③	④	⑤	⑤
Ignition system	④	⑤	⑤	⑤	⑤	⑤	⑤
Rust/Paint	❷	❷	③	③	③	③	③
Steering	③	③	③	④	④	③	④
Suspension	③	③	③	③	③	③	③
Crash Safety	④	④	—	④	④	③	③
Side Impact	—	—	—	—	—	③	③

SUBARU

Forester, Legacy

Rating: Above Average (1997–99); Average for AWD (1991–96); Average for front-drives (1989–96). The 1995–99 AWD models are way overpriced. Furthermore, you may wish to budget an extra $500 or more for an extended powertrain warranty to protect you from premature and repeated clutch failures. The only reason to buy a Subaru is for its 4X4 capability, and on most used models you'll have to pay a $1,000–$2,000 premium to get it. If it's not what you need for your basic driving requirements, pick a Honda, Mazda, or Toyota instead—you'll appreciate the additional leg room and more user-friendly drivetrain. **Maintenance/ Repair costs:** Higher than average. Repairs are dealer dependent. **Parts:** Higher-than-average cost can't be attenuated through purchasing from independent suppliers.

Strengths and weaknesses: First launched in 1989 as front-drives, these compacts are a bit slow off the mark. The 5-speed is a bit notchy, and the automatic gearbox is slow to downshift, has difficulty staying in Overdrive, and is failure-prone. Early Legacys are noisy, fuel-thirsty cars with bland styling that masks their solid, dependable AWD performance.

Actually, the availability of a proven four-wheel-drive powertrain in a compact family sedan and wagon makes these cars appealing for special use. In spite of their reputation for dependability, though, Subarus are not trouble-free—engine, clutch, turbo, and driveline defects are common on the early models through to the 1998 versions.

The redesigned 1995–98 models have sleeker styling, additional interior room (though leg room is still at a premium), a bit more horsepower with the base engine, and a new 2.5L 4-cylinder driving the 1996 AWD GT and Lsi. The Outback, a Legacy–Madison Avenue spin-off, was transformed into a sport-utility wagon with a taller roof. Even with the improvements noted above, acceleration is still only passable (if you don't mind the loud engine), but highway handling and ride are remarkably good. Overall, it's a competent car with only one outstanding advantage—AWD. If you don't need that feature, there are better-performing, less-expensive vehicles available. Another word of warning: the Outback's off-road handling isn't as competent as that of the regular Legacy (something to do with the higher centre of gravity, no doubt).

Subaru's overall product lineup for 1997 marked a return to the company's four-wheel-drive roots, with the repackaging of its Legacy and Impreza 4X4 lineup as Outbacks (half of all Legacys sold are Outbacks). A Legacy 2.5L GT all-wheel-drive sporting sedan, or wagon variant, also joined the group that year. In addition to these redesignated models—and the squeezing out of a bit more horsepower from its limited range of engines—Subaru continued to tap the sport-utility craze by offering a greater variety of AWD vehicles.

1998 models were carried over practically unchanged, while the '99s were given an upgraded 2.2L engine.

Are Subarus good buys? Devotees will insist that there's no other car as versatile, and the manufacturer is justifiably proud of the high J.D. Power owner-satisfaction rating earned in the U.S. On the other hand, I have found that a Subaru can be a good used-car choice only if its AWD feature is essential for your driving needs and you can accustom yourself to its jerky, abrupt downshifts; the car's been maintained carefully; there's an extended warranty covering the transmission; the body isn't rust-perforated; and dealer servicing is easily available. This last point is crucial because these cars are very dependent on the dealer network for parts and servicing. And if you have an early transmission failure, you'd better have the dealer on your side buttressing your request for a "goodwill" repair refund.

Through 1999, automatic transmission (front seals, especially) and clutch breakdowns are the more common complaints. Transmission downshifts abruptly and without warning while descending a long grade or on snow-packed highways, causing swerving and loss of control. Front brakes require frequent attention, and the Check Engine and ABS warning lights come on constantly for no reason. Shock absorbers, constant velocity joints, and catalytic converters often wear out prematurely. Other problems that appear over most model years include starter and ignition relay failures, steering and alignment problems, and front-end suspension noises. Subarus are also rust-prone: fenders, door bottoms, rocker panels, wheel openings, bumpers and supports, rear quarter-panels, tailgates, trunk lids, and hoods are particularly vulnerable. Additionally, the underbody and chassis components should be examined very carefully for corrosion damage.

Forester
The 1998–99 Forester is a cross between a wagon and a sport-utility. Built on the Impreza's platform, it uses the Legacy Outback's peppy 2.5L, 165-hp Boxer engine that can outlug Toyota's RAV4 and Honda's CR-V by about 1,000 lb. Although not crash-tested by NHTSA, the Subaru Forester was given a "Good" crashworthiness rating by IIHS. The Outback is not for serious off-roaders, but it's nice to have for the occasional use during inclement weather. The question you must answer is, Does your expected bad-weather use justify the high cost of ownership? Are Foresters and Outbacks good buys? Yes, until Honda adds the Accord's VTEC engine and a 5-speed manual transmission to the CR-V.

Safety summary/Recalls: All models: 1996—Sudden acceleration. • When the vehicle is being driven, transmission may suddenly jump out of Drive into Neutral. • Inadvertent airbag deployment. • Airbags failed to deploy. • ABS brakes locked up. • Brake failures. • ABS performs poorly on snow and ice. • Floor carpet prevented brake pedal application. • Complete engine failure at 18,000 km. • Chronic stalling. • Computer sensor control unit failure. • Excessive shaking at highway speeds. • Windshield wiper bolt failure. • Alternator failures while driving. • Left turn signal fails intermittently. • Climate control button sticks. • AC seizure. • O-ring failure causes AC to leak freon. • Bridgestone tires frequently blow out. • Keyless entry failed due to pinched wire in driver's door. • New-design headlights give poor illumination. **1997**—Airbags deployed but failed to inflate. • Airbags failed to deploy. • Sudden acceleration. • Cruise control failed to disengage when brakes were applied. • Igniter failed, allowing unburned fuel to flow into catalytic converter. • AC blew fumes into interior, causing driver to black out. • Stalling caused by igniter failure. • Complete engine failure due to defective valves and pistons. • Sudden loss of steering. • Poor braking performance; anti-lock brakes frequently fail or lock up. • Front brake pad failure. • Premature wearout of all brake components. • Transmission surges when cold, or shifts into Neutral at low speed or when descending a small hill. • Transmission failures. • Frequent electronic control unit failures. • Rear seatbelts are too long to properly secure child safety seat, and the locking mechanism doesn't lock properly. • Brake and engine lights continually on. • Three alternators replaced by one owner. • Shorted hazard switch drained battery. • Alternator belt snapped, causing battery and brake warning lights to come on and making car hard to steer. • Alternators frequently quit while vehicle is under power. **1998**—Many instances where the airbags failed to deploy. • Oil leak from oil filter seam caused fire. • Sudden brake loss after linings, calipers, and master cylinder had been replaced. • Cruise control failed to disengage when brakes were applied. • Excessive shaking at highway speeds. • Seatback collapsed when vehicle was rear-ended. • Subaru told car owner that tendency to pull to the right was a design feature. **1999**—Airbags failed to deploy. • Sudden acceleration. • Chronic cold engine hesitation, stalling. • Engine failure due to cracked #2 piston. • When accelerating or decelerating, vehicle will begin to jerk due to excessive play in the front axle. • Total brake system failure; pedal went to the floor with no braking effect. • Tire blowout; air slowly escapes. • Front bumper skirt catches on parking blocks, resulting in bumper twisting and being ripped off. • The centre rear seatbelt's poor design prohibits the installation of many child safety seats. **Legacy: 1996**—False deployment of airbag injured passenger. • Serious burns caused by airbag gases. • Car suddenly fishtails out of control when making a lane change. • Electrical system fire. • Cruise control won't disengage. • Premature tire failures (Bridgestone) • Hood flew up while driving; engine replaced at 18,000 km. • AC condenser and alternator failures. • Sudden electrical shutdown. • Chronic hesitation, high-speed miss, and stalling. • Five times fuse blew out causing stall. • Faulty gas gauge. • Low rear bench seat and no head restraints. **Recalls: All models: 1985–87**—Corrosion of the rear suspension inner arms could affect the control of the vehicle. **1997–99**—ABS may fail (vehicles equipped with 2.2L engines are excluded); dealers are to replace the brake master cylinder. **1998**—Due to poor welds, ignition keys can stick, shift levers and linkages can break, and shift levers can move; dealers will replace the automatic transmission shift lever assembly. • The Purolator oil filter may fracture and pose a fire hazard as oil spews out.

Secret Warranties/Service Tips

All models/years—Troubleshooting tips on a sticking anti-lock brake relay are offered. This problem is characterized by a lit ABS warning light or the ABS motor continuing to run/buzz when the ignition is turned off. • Diagnostic and repair tips are offered on transfer clutch binding and/or bucking on turns. • A rotten-egg smell could be caused by a defective catalytic converter. It will be replaced, after a bit of arguing, free of charge, up to five years under the emissions warranty. **All models: 1990–93**—The manual gearbox in the AWD could leak, causing the transmission to seize. **1993**—Legacys could have a headliner droop, which is addressed in a March 1994 TSB. **1994**—Torque converter squeaking is addressed in a June 1993 TSB. **1995**—Tips are provided on silencing excessive front strut noise and engine oil pump leaks. **1995–96**—If the antenna won't fully retract, Subaru suggests cleaning the antenna mast and replacing the dress nut. **1997–99**—Excessive driveline vibration is covered in TSB #05-33-98R. Subaru's fix requires modifying the differential. **Legacy 1997–99**—Troubleshooting body driveline vibration.

Forester, Legacy Profile

	1992	1993	1994	1995	1996	1997	1998	1999
Cost Price ($)								
Forester	—	—	—	—	—	—	26,695	26,695
Legacy	16,888	16,888	19,995	17,995	23,195	—	—	—
Legacy 4X4	18,969	19,126	22,695	24,695	25,195	26,495	25,695	25,995
Used Values ($)								
Legacy ↑	3,500	4,500	7,000	8,000	11,000	—	—	—
Legacy ↓	2,500	4,000	5,000	6,000	9,500	—	—	—
Legacy 4X4 ↑	4,500	5,500	7,500	9,500	12,500	15,000	17,500	19,000
Legacy 4X4 ↓	4,000	4,500	6,000	8,000	11,000	13,000	15,500	17,500
Forester	—	—	—	—	—	—	26,695	26,695
Used Values ($)								
Forester ↑	—	—	—	—	—	—	17,500	20,500
Forester ↓	—	—	—	—	—	—	16,000	19,000
Extended Warranty	Y	Y	Y	Y	Y	Y	Y	Y
Secret Warranty	N	N	N	N	Y	Y	Y	Y
Reliability	②	③	②	②	③	④	④	④
Air conditioning	②	②	③	③	④	⑤	⑤	⑤
Auto. transmission	②	②	②	②	②	②	③	③
Body integrity	②	②	②	②	②	③	③	③
Braking system	②	②	②	②	②	②	②	②
Electrical system	②	②	②	②	③	③	③	④
Engines	③	④	④	③	③	③	④	④
Exhaust/Converter	①	①	②	②	③	④	⑤	⑤
Fuel system	③	③	④	④	④	④	⑤	⑤
Ignition system	②	②	③	③	④	⑤	⑤	⑤
Rust/Paint	②	②	②	③	③	③	④	⑤
Steering	③	③	④	④	⑤	⑤	⑤	⑤
Suspension	③	③	③	③	⑤	⑤	⑤	⑤
Crash Safety								
Legacy 4d	③	④	④	④	④	④	④	④
Side Impact	—	—	—	—	—	—	③	③

TOYOTA

Camry, Solara

Rating: Above Average (1997–99); Recommended (1994–96); Above Average (1988–93); Average (1985–87). 1996 was the wagon's last model year. The Solara, a two-door Camry clone, is outrageously over-priced. For the past four years, Camrys have elicited an unusually high number of safety complaints that are carried over from one model year to the next. The complaints include severe wandering at highway speeds; sudden acceleration; engine-compartment fires; brake failures; poor headlight illumination; and transmission interlock failures, which allow a parked vehicle to roll away. **Maintenance/Repair costs:** Higher than average, but repairs aren't dealer dependent. **Parts:** Parts are more expensive than for most other cars in this class (alternator and ignition module, for example). Parts availability is excellent.

Strengths and weaknesses: Safety complaints aside, the Camry is an excellent family-car buy because of its spacious, comfortable interior; good fuel economy; and impressive reliability and durability.

1988–93 models have few problems, although they're far from perfect. Main areas of concern are failure-prone cylinder head gaskets; suspension and electrical system failures; defective starter drive and ring gear; leaking low-pressure and high-pressure power-steering lines; outer CV boots that split, causing grease to leak; premature brake wear; and some paint peeling and rusting. Mufflers last only two years on earlier models, and sunroofs are rattle-prone.

Persistent problems with all Toyota vehicles are premature brake wear, and excessive noise and vibrations. Stung by consumer criticism that these problems haven't been fixed for over a decade and that owners are charged for useless repairs, Toyota published a "Brake Repair" service bulletin (POL94-18) in October 1994, which defines those repairs that will be done under warranty. Toyota states that premature brake wear and noise will be fixed under warranty for the first 12 months/ 15,000 miles, and that vibrations will be attended to, under warranty, up to 3 years/50,000 miles. Canadians should use these parameters as their guide in requesting "goodwill" repairs.

Front suspension bushings wear out quickly, leading to clunking and squeaking noises when going over bumps or when stopping quickly. There's also the so-called Camry chop (exceptionally rough rides when passing over uneven roadways) reported by owners of 1992–94 models. Cruise control fails frequently on all years. Owners of the 1992 Camry have reported that a chronic drone noise, along with a vibration felt from the floor and the gas pedal, occurs mostly when the automatic transmission changes from second to third gear at 1800–2000 rpm. Incidentally, manual transmissions are exceptionally reliable and fuel-efficient.

1994–99 Camrys are quite reliable, but they too have their shortcomings. Owners report premature brake failures; faulty window regulators;

smelly ACs; and myriad rattles, clunks, and groans that seem to come from everywhere. There is also an annoying surging and shuddering when decelerating, which appears to be more common with the 1995–96 models. It seems as though it's a sticking throttle position sensor, but mechanics say that the problem is intrinsic to the way the engine/transmission computer module is calibrated. Other deficiencies reported by owners: brake vibrations, premature brake pad wear, AC malfunctions, and defective automatic transmissions that slip out of gear when parked. Reliability problems include engine failure due to sludge buildup, premature torque converter failures, persistent drifting, uneven and premature tire wear, premature front and rear brake wear, early replacement of the inner tie rod and steering rack, and excessive vibration at 90 km/h. 1994–99 model body problems include excessive wind noise coming from the front windshield, back doors, and sunroof. Trim items rust and fall off, door handles pull away, and mufflers have a short life span. No reports of rust perforation problems, but weak spots are door bottoms, rear wheel openings, and trunk and hatchback edges. There are complaints concerning premature rusting on cars painted white. Toyota generally corrects these rust/paint deficiencies for free.

The totally redesigned 1997 Camry is taller, longer, wider, more powerful, and cheaper, in both a literal and a figurative sense. Gone are the coupe and station wagon variants. The wheelbase was extended by two inches, giving backseat passengers more room. Other changes: it's powered by a base 2.2L 133-hp 16-valve 4-cylinder engine and an optional 3.0L 24-valve V6 that unleashes 194 horses. Either engine will be mated to a 5-speed manual or an electronically controlled 4-speed automatic. ABS and traction control are standard on all V6-equipped Camrys, rear seats have shoulder belts for the middle passenger, low beam lights are brighter, and optional heated mirrors are available, as well as more cup holders, a sunglasses holder, and an additional power port in the centre console.

"De-contenting" hit Toyota's 1997 lineup hard, resulting in many changes that cheapened the Camry. Although Toyota admits to engine head gasket leaks for the first time (see "Secret Warranties/Service Tips"), overall reliability doesn't appear to have been affected, notwithstanding a sharp increase in noise complaints and airbag malfunctions. The changes include less expensive S-rated tires on models with 4-cylinder engines, cheaper heating/ventilation system components, no more assist handles for front occupants, no more chrome trim around the windshield, one door seal instead of three (greater chance for wind and water leaks), fewer airbag sensors, an LCD odometer, a distributorless ignition with the 4-cylinder, and a windshield-embedded antenna. Owners report the 1997 models have limited rear visibility (due to the side pillars and high trunk lid), less steering "feel," and more squeaks and rattles than previous versions.

Similar problems continue to plague the 1998–99 models. Specifically, owners report that the vehicle often hesitates or stalls when accelerating; front power windows often run off their channel; the steering wheel vibrates excessively; brake components (calipers, rotors, pads, master cylinder and the ABS valve) often fail within the first year or 20,000 km; warning lights constantly come on, charcoal canister failure; suspension "bottoms out" when carrying four adults; struts leak and are noisy; and moonroof leaks are commonplace.

The '98 models returned unchanged, except for optional side airbags and an improved anti-theft system. The '99 models changed little, apart from adjustable front headrests, new upholstery, a revised accessory list, and the addition of a new coupe, called the Solara.

Solara

The Solara's small, but it's not cheap. Built in Cambridge, Ontario, a base model Solara is reasonably priced, but put in the Sienna and Lexus ES 300's V6 powerplant and you drive up its cost considerably. Introduced in the summer of 1998, as a '99 model, the Solara is essentially a longer, lower, bare-bones, two-door coupe or convertible Camry with a sportier powertrain and suspension and a more stylish exterior. But don't let this put you off. Most new Toyota model offerings, like the Sienna, Avalon, and RAV4s, are Camry derivatives.

You have a choice of either a 4- or 6-cylinder powerplant. Unfortunately, if you choose the V6, you also get a gimmicky rear spoiler and a head room-robbing moon roof. The stiff body structure and suspension, as well as tight steering, make for easy sports car–like handling, with lots of road feel and few surprises.

Technical service bulletins: All models: 1995—Front brake noise. • AC evaporator odour. • Moon-roof panel wind noise. • Improved power window regulator. • Rear brake squeak. • Rear suspension noise. **1996**—Front brake noise. • AC evaporator odour. • Charcoal canister humming noise. • Rear window rattle. • Rear brake squeak. • Rear suspension noise. • Moon-roof panel wind noise. **1997**—Engine head gasket coolant leak. • AC evaporator odour. • Charcoal canister humming noise. • Difficulties with moon roof operation. • Exterior rear-view mirror improvement. • Steering rack housing bushing noise. • Front shoulder belt anchor buzzes. • Front suspension groans. • Suspension rattle and popping. • Tailpipe contact with heat shield. • Headliner buzzes or rattles. • Moon roof rattles. • Manual front seat movement/noise. • Power front seat chattering. • Radio volume control too sensitive. • Rubbing noise from door trim. • Seatcover loose at lower rear corners. • Seat movement field-fix procedure. • Armrest improvement • CD player won't accept/eject CDs. • Fuel door operation improvement. • Wind noise repair kit. **1998**—Revised countermeasures for front brake noise. • Rear console box improvements. • Preventing carpet stains. • Steering noise. • Front suspension groans. **1999**—Door glass displacement (see "Secret Warranties/Service Tips"). • Front brake noise countermeasures. • Loose seat covers. • Wind noise from the door mirror. • Power steering rack squeaks.

Safety summary/Recalls: All models: Owners report that the Dunlop D60 A2 tire is a poor wet-weather performer. **1987–91**—Leaking fuel tanks. **1995**—Injury from airbag. • Premature front/rear brake wear. • Defective, poor-performance (when wet) Goodyear Invicta tires. • Windshield reflects dashboard image. **1995–96**—Brake failure. • Noisy, vibrating brakes. • Premature front and rear brake wear. • Excessive engine noise. • Transmission lever can slip from Drive to Neutral. • Airbag fails to deploy or is accidentally deployed. • Sudden acceleration, stalling. • Passenger-side seatbacks won't stay upright. • Passenger seatbelts over-retract. • Defective radio antenna. • Taillight and turn signal bulbs frequently burn out. • **1996**—Vehicle wanders over road. • Door bottom/undercarriage rusting. • Airbag warning light and Check Engine light always on. • Windshield film buildup. • Window water leaks. • "Rocking" driver and passenger seats. • Steering system leaks. **1997**—Engine compartment fire following ABS brake failure. • Airbags failed to deploy. • Violent deployment of airbag during an accident caused death. • Sudden acceleration when brakes were applied. • Tendency for car to wander all over the roadway. • Steering wheel suddenly locked up, causing an accident. • Many reports of transmission interlock system failures. • Many other reports, probably related to the interlock system, that vehicle was put in Park and keys taken out of ignition and car then proceeded to roll away. • Century infant seat won't fit in the centre of rear seat. • Seatbelts continually ratchet tighter; rear seatbelt was strangling child, who had to be cut free. • Plastic part fell behind the dash and lodged behind the brake pedal arm, causing an accident. • Frequent brake failures. • Premature brake pad and caliper wear or failure. • Loud grinding brake noise when braking. • Excessive noise coming from underneath the car at highway speeds. • Vehicle sits too low, has minimal ground clearance. • Driver's knee can hit the steering wheel adjuster lever, making steering wheel go up and down. On several occasions, steering wheel suddenly tilted all the way up while on the highway. • Very poor headlight illumination; headlight safety cap cover design cuts visibility severely; there's a blind spot on the driver-side headlights. • Low beam lights aren't bright enough. • Dash indicator lights are too small and low in intensity. • Inoperative rear window defroster. • Driver's seatback rocks back and forth. • Power door lock relay failure. • Car locks and unlocks on its own. • Fuel door doesn't open fully when lever is pulled. • Rear windshield exploded while car was parked overnight. **1998**—Several reports of engine fires. • Vehicle stalled, oil light came on, and fire ignited in engine compartment. • Sudden acceleration. • Many reports that airbags failed to deploy. • Frequent complaints that vehicle wanders at highway speeds and is difficult to control in a crosswind. • Overly soft suspension allows the chassis to scrape the roadway when passing over a small bump. • Frequent ABS brake failures. • Excessive brake noise and extended stopping distances. • Transmission gearshift lever went from Neutral to Drive without pressing button. • Airbag service indicator light stays on.

• Engine malfunction light stays on. • Inadequate night illumination from headlights; low beam halogen headlights don't carry very far; dark spot cast from left headlight results in poor visibility; metal deflector inside the concealed headlights blocks out all light beyond 10 metres. • Electrical system failure; running lights won't shut off. • Lock design allows for occupants to be temporarily locked in vehicle if someone gets out before them and locks the doors. • Power door locks fail intermittently. • Front restraints lock up when vehicle is parked on an incline. • Sun visors are too small to block the sun, and cut visibility. • Back windshield shattered. • Fumes from inside the vehicle fog up the windshield. • Gas tank makes sloshing noise when brakes are applied. • Tire (General) wears excessively on the inside tread. • Frequent complaints of moon roof leaks, which may cause electrical short. • Doors have to be slammed shut. **1999**—Incredible as it may seem, the Camry continues to have serious safety-related defects that aren't much different than what's been recorded for previous model years. They include, in order of frequency: sudden unintended acceleration; airbags not deploying during a collision; inadvertent airbag deployment injuring occupants; complete brake failure, or extended stopping distances caused by poor braking; sudden acceleration; chronic engine hesitation when accelerating or stalling; engine, airbag and ABS warning lights come on constantly; premature tire wear or blowout (Cooper and General tires); optically distorted windshield; and the transmission won't hold when stopped on a hill. **Recalls: All models: 1994–98**—The steering wheel nut may not have been sufficiently tightened. **1995–98**—Steering wheels may come off. **1996**—Taillight assembly lacks sufficient heat resistance. **1997**—Ignition key can be removed when vehicle not in Park. • Brake failure may occur due to moisture freezing in the brake vacuum hose.

Secret Warranties/Service Tips

All models/years—A wind noise repair kit is now available. • A decade-old brake pulsation/vibration problem is fully described and corrective measures are detailed in TSB #BR94-002, issued February 7, 1994. Sometimes only the parts are covered; the owner has to pay for labour. • To reduce front brake squeaks on ABS-equipped vehicles, ask the dealer to install new, upgraded rotors (#43517-32020). • Owner feedback over the last decade plus dealer service managers who wish to remain anonymous tell me that Toyota has a secret warranty that will pay for replacing front disc brake components that wear out before 2 years/40,000 km. If you're denied this coverage, threaten small claims court action. **All models: 1987–91**—A front inner shoulder belt guide is available to keep the belt away from the neck and face. This free accessory is covered under the seatbelt warranty. **1993**—AC units may fail to cool due to a faulty expansion valve. **1993–96**—Suspension squeaks and groans are addressed in TSB #SU95-003. **1994**—A steering column clicking noise calls for the replacement of the steering main shaft assembly and steering column tube assembly. • Rear window wind noise can be stopped by replacing the front centring-type bolt with a non-centring-type bolt and a washer. **1995–96**—Use upgraded brake pad material to eliminate brake groaning, according to TSB #BR002-96. **1996–97**—A charcoal canister humming noise can be silenced by installing an upgraded vacuum hose. **1997**—Head gasket leaks are covered by a special Toyota program that is applied only if the customer complains. • If the driver's seat "rocks," Toyota has an upgraded assembly that will secure the seat. **1997–98**—A front suspension groan can be fixed by replacing the front spring bumper under Toyota's 3-year warranty. • Toyota will replace the carpeting, free of charge, to prevent asphalt insulation stains. • Steering rack bushing noise (see following illustration).

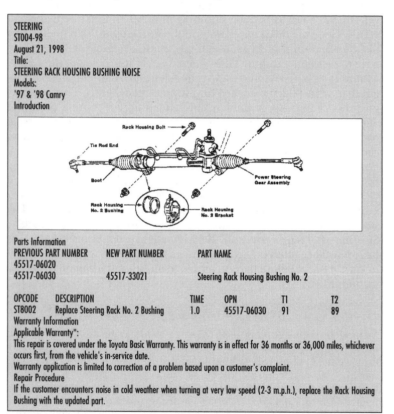

STEERING
ST004-98
August 21, 1998
Title:
STEERING RACK HOUSING BUSHING NOISE
Models:
'97 & '98 Camry
Introduction

Parts Information

PREVIOUS PART NUMBER	NEW PART NUMBER	PART NAME
45517-06020		
45517-06030	45517-33021	Steering Rack Housing Bushing No. 2

OPCODE	DESCRIPTION	TIME	OPN	T1	T2
ST8002	Replace Steering Rack No. 2 Bushing	1.0	45517-06030	91	89

Warranty Information
Applicable Warranty*:
This repair is covered under the Toyota Basic Warranty. This warranty is in effect for 36 months or 36,000 miles, whichever occurs first, from the vehicle's in-service date.
Warranty application is limited to correction of a problem based upon a customer's complaint.
Repair Procedure
If the customer encounters noise in cold weather when turning at very low speed (2-3 m.p.h.), replace the Rack Housing Bushing with the updated part.

Toyota won't give you the upgraded steering component unless you ask for it.

1997–99—Fuel door operation improvement, tips on reducing steering noise. • New front brake pad kits will reduce brake grinding or groaning, says bulletin #BR001-99. • To enhance headlight performance, the alignment process has been modified. **1998–99**—Door glass that runs off its channel is a common factory-related problem that Toyota admits is covered under its base warranty. Here's the catch: the dealer isn't authorized to upgrade the channel (a half-hour procedure), unless the customer asks for the service (see following bulletin).

Door Glass Displacement
November 26, 1999
BO017-99
Introduction
On some 1998 and 1999 Camry vehicles the door glass may be displaced from the front door glass run if the door is closed forcefully with the window partially down. A field fix has been developed to remedy this condition.
Warranty Information
Applicable Warranty *:
This repair is covered under the Toyota Basic Warranty. This warranty is in effect for 36 months or 36,000 miles, whichever occurs first, from the vehicles in-service date.
* Warranty application is limited to correction of a problem based upon a customer's specific complaint.

Camry, Solara Profile

	1992	1993	1994	1995	1996	1997	1998	1999
Cost Price ($)								
Camry Coupe	—	—	19,238	19,998	20,488	—	—	—
Sedan	17,948	18,778	20,138	20,638	21,138	21,178	21,348	21,680
LE	20,998	23,058	24,918	24,718	25,458	25,268	26,508	27,070
Wagon V6	26,008	27,668	29,708	31,278	32,178	—	—	—
Base Solara	—	—	—	—	—	—	—	26,245
V6	—	—	—	—	—	—	—	29,815
Used Values ($)								
Camry Coupe ↑	—	—	8,000	9,500	11,000	—	—	—
Camry Coupe ↓	—	—	6,500	8,500	9,000	—	—	—
Sedan ↑	5,500	7,000	8,500	10,000	11,500	13,000	14,500	17,000
Sedan ↓	4,500	6,000	7,000	9,000	9,500	11,000	13,000	15,500
LE ↑	6,500	8,000	9,500	12,000	13,500	15,500	18,500	21,000
LE ↓	5,500	7,000	8,000	10,000	12,000	14,000	17,000	19,500
Wagon V6 ↑	7,500	9,000	10,500	13,500	16,500	—	—	—
Wagon V6 ↓	6,500	7,500	8,500	12,000	15,000	—	—	—
Solara ↑	—	—	—	—	—	—	—	20,000
Solara ↓	—	—	—	—	—	—	—	18,500
V6 ↑	—	—	—	—	—	—	—	22,000
V6 ↓	—	—	—	—	—	—	—	20,000
Extended Warranty	N	N	N	N	N	N	N	N
Secret Warranty	N	Y	N	N	Y	Y	Y	N
Reliability	⑤	⑤	⑤	⑤	⑤	⑤	⑤	⑤
Air conditioning	③	③	③	③	❷	❷	③	③
Auto. transmission	③	③	③	③	③	③	③	③
Body integrity	❷	❷	❷	❷	③	③	③	③
Braking system	❷	❷	❷	❷	❷	❷	❷	❷
Electrical system	③	③	③	③	③	③	③	④
Engines	③	④	④	④	⑤	⑤	③	⑤
Exhaust/Converter	❷	❷	④	④	④	⑤	⑤	⑤

Fuel system	③	③	③	④	④	③	④	⑤
Ignition system	③	③	③	④	④	④	⑤	⑤
Rust/Paint	③	③	③	④	④	④	⑤	⑤
Steering	③	③	③	③	③	⑤	⑤	⑤
Suspension	③	③	④	④	④	⑤	⑤	⑤
Crash Safety	④	④	④	④	④	④	④	④
Side Impact	—	—	—	—	—	③	③	④
Solara	—	—	—	—	—	—	—	③

VOLKSWAGEN

New Beetle

Rating: Average (1998–99). The New Beetle is an expensive trip down memory lane. Personally, I don't think it's worth it—with or without its speed-activated spoiler and dash-mounted bud vase. Another negative is the large number of safety-related complaints registered by NHTSA involving electrical fires, chronic stalling, and transmission failures. Other cars worth considering are the Honda Civic, Mazda Protegé, Nissan Sentra, Toyota Corolla, and VW Cabrio. **Maintenance/Repair costs:** Estimated to be higher than average, and only a VW dealer can repair these cars. **Parts:** Easily found since they're taken mostly from the Golf parts bin. Body parts may be harder to find.

Strengths and weaknesses: The New Beetle was a hands-down marketing and public relations winner when the model was re-introduced AS A '98 model year after being absent since 1979. By the end of March 1998, over 56,000 were sold and sales for '99 versions are tracking first year sales.

Why so much emotion for an ugly German import that never had a functioning heater, was declared "Small on Safety" by Ralph Nader and his Center for Auto Safety, and carried a puny 48-hp engine? The simple answer is that it was cheap and represented the first car most of us could afford as we went through school, got our first job, and dreamed of...getting a better car. Time has taken the edge off the memories of the hardships the Beetle made us endure—like having to scrape the inside windshield with our nails as our breath froze—and left us with the cozy feeling that the car wasn't that bad after all.

But it was.

Now VW has resurrected the Beetle and produced a competent front-engine, front-drive, compact car—set on the chassis and running gear of the Golf hatchback—that's much safer than its predecessor, but oddly enough is still afflicted by many of the same deficiencies we learned to hate with the original.

Again, without the turbocharger, the 115-hp base engine is underwhelming (the 90-hp turbodiesel isn't much better). And even when you get it up to cruising speed, there's still not much room for rear passengers, engine noise is disconcerting, radio buttons and power accessory switches located on the door panels aren't user-friendly, front visibility is hindered by the car's quirky design, and storage capacity is at a premium.

On the other hand, the powerful, optional 1.8L turbocharged engine makes this Beetle an impressive performer; the heater works fine; steering, handling, and braking are quite good; and the interior is not as spartan or tacky as it once was.

In a nutshell, here are the New Beetle's strong and weak points: standard side airbags; easy handling; sure-footed, comfortable, though firm, ride; impressive braking; comfortable and supportive front seats with plenty of head room and leg room; cargo area that can be expanded by folding down the rear seats; and top-quality mechanical components and workmanship. The Insurance Institute for Highway Safety (IIHS) has given the Beetle a "good" rating for offset crashworthiness and front seat head restraint protection and an "acceptable" rating for the rear.

On the minus side: serious safety defects have been reported by owners (see "Safety Summary/Recalls" below), powertrain performance is unimpressive, and body construction is second-rate. Specific owner gripes: the base engine runs out of steam around 100 km/h; diesel engines lack pep and produce lots of noise and vibration; faulty O2 sensor causes the Check Engine light to come on; frequent ECM (electronic control module) failures; faulty fuses and relays; delayed shifts from Park to Drive, or failure to shift into fourth gear; car is easily buffeted by crosswinds; optional high-mounted side mirrors, large head restraints, and large front roof pillars obstruct front and rear visibility; limited rear leg and head room; difficult rear entry/exit; excessive engine and brake noise; awkward-to-access radio buttons and door panel–mounted power switches; and skimpy interior storage and trunk space; interior vent louvre loosens and breaks; starter horn, window switch and radiator failures, hatchback rattles and sometimes fails to open; AC disengages when decelerating; low-slung chassis causes extensive undercarriage damage when going over a curb; and engine cover often gets pulled back and scrapes on the ground.

Technical service bulletins: All models: 1998–99—Erratic, harsh, or delayed automatic transmission shifting. • Troubleshooting tips on silencing instrument panel, front door lock/latch, and door speaker squeaks or rattles. • Possible causes and fix for wind noise or whistle coming from the instrument panel. • Diagnosing humming noise from front of vehicle when cornering. • No adjustment of air flow from centre air outlets. • Throttle pedal and shifter lever vibration or knocking vibration. • AM radio static. • Eliminating musty AC odours.

Safety summary/Recalls: All models: 1998—Driver's head restraint sits too high and can't be lowered, seriously restricting rear visibility. • Oil pan hole leaked oil and caused vehicle to stall. • Sudden loss of power while driving 100 km/h, forcing driver to reset computer by restarting the vehicle. • While driving at any speed, vehicle goes into emergency mode and suddenly slows down to about 20 km/h. • Instrument cluster failure. • Vehicle was smoking under the hood because a faulty hose leaked oil onto the engine. • While stopped at a traffic light, vehicle just exploded into flames and was a total loss (see photo below).

1999—Vehicle caught fire on inside of ignition switch box. • Another fire reportedly ignited in the wiring harness behind the dashboard. • Brake and accelerator pedals are too close together. • Sudden, unintended acceleration, and steering locked up. • Cruise control wouldn't disengage when brakes were applied. • Airbags failed to deploy; airbag warning light often comes on for no reason. • Sudden tread separation on the low-profile sporty tires. • When brakes are applied in a panic stop, one of the rear wheels will lock up along with one of the front wheels, causing vehicle to go into a spin. • Chronic hesitation and stalling on the highway (one fatality reported). • Vehicle won't start when facing down on a slope. • Frequent automatic transmission breakdowns. • Clutch failure causes vehicle to stall. • Left side driveshaft cracked twice. • Driver's seat broke in a collision, causing severe injuries. • Driver's side seat came off its track and fell into back seat. • Tire jack fails to hold vehicle. • Cracked battery leaked acid onto power steering fluid reservoir. • Vehicle shakes and shudders when driven with the sunroof fully open. • Headrest cannot be adjusted down to permit driver to see through rear and side windows; it's also quite uncomfortable for short drivers. **Recalls: All models: 1998**—A malfunctioning fuel pump could cause the vehicle to stall or catch fire.

Secret Warranties/Service Tips

All models: 1998–99—An erratic-shifting automatic transaxle is likely caused by an improper throttle angle setting. VW will correct the problem under its base warranty.

New Beetle Profile

	1998	1999
Cost Price ($)		
Base	19,940	21,500
Used Values ($)		
Base ↑	16,000	18,500
Base ↓	15,000	17,000
Extended Warranty	Y	Y
Secret Warranty	N	N
Reliability	③	③
Crash Safety	—	④
Side Impact	—	⑤

Passat

Rating: Above Average (1998–99); Average (1995–97); Not Recommended (1989–94). Don't buy any Passat without a comprehensive extended warranty. If you must have a Passat, wait until the Audi spin-off 1998 Passats come off their two-year leases. Recent models stick you with a high cost price due to their slow depreciation. **Maintenance/Repair costs:** Much higher than average. Most major repairs are dealer dependent. **Parts:** Parts and service are more expensive than average; long waits for parts are commonplace.

Strengths and weaknesses: This front-drive compact sedan and wagon uses a standard 2.0L engine and other mechanical parts borrowed from the Golf, Jetta, and Corrado. However, a 2.8L V6 became the standard powerplant, beginning with the '99 wagon. Its long wheelbase and squat appearance give the Passat a massive, solid feeling, while its styling makes it look sleek and clean. As with most European imports, it comes fairly well appointed.

As far as overall performance goes, the Passat is no slouch. The multivalve 4-cylinder engine is adequate, and its handling is superior to that of most of the competition. The 2.8L V6 provides lots of power when revved and is the engine that works best with an automatic transmission.

The redesigned 1995 version came with standard dual airbags, a restyled interior, rear headrests, a softened suspension, and a much-improved crashworthiness rating. The 1998 Passat, however, is practically an entirely different car, based upon the Audi A4 and A6, and offers much better performance.

Passats are infamous for transmission malfunctions and fuel-system glitches that are hard to diagnose and costly to repair. Even when they're operating as they should, Passat's manual and automatic gearboxes leave a lot to be desired. For example, the 5-speed manual transmission gear ranges are too far apart: there's an enormous gap between third and fourth gear, and the 4-speed automatic shifts poorly with the 4-banger. Also, owners report problems with clutch slave cylinder leaks and transmission not shifting from lower gears. Other problem areas as the car ages include: front brakes (master cylinder replacements, brake booster failure, rotor warpage, premature wear, and excessive noise), MacPherson struts, and fuel and electrical systems. Owners mention that defective tie-rod and constant velocity joint seals allow debris to enter into system, effectively causing premature wearout of internal components; engines often leak oil; power steering assembly requires early replacement; fuel and computer module problems lead to hard starts and chronic stalling.

On the body side, there's a helicopter-type wind noise when cruising with the windows or sunroof open; a persistent water leak from the pollen filter; fragile interior trim and controls; door speakers require frequent replacement; fuel gauge malfunctions, indicating fuel in tank when it's empty; windshields may be optically distorted; rear-view passenger side mirrors are too small and cause several blind spots.

Owners report that VW dealer servicing is the pits. Cars have to be brought in constantly to fix the same problem, recall campaign repairs are often slow because parts aren't available, and warranty coverage is spotty because VW headquarters doesn't empower/pay dealers sufficiently to take the initiative. Competent servicing and parts are particularly hard to find away from the larger cities, and many of the above-mentioned deficiencies can cost you an arm and a leg to repair.

Technical service bulletins: All models: 1995—Poor fuel-system performance. • Engine won't start. Drifting, pulling to one side. • Instrument cluster loss of memory. **1996–97**—Transmission fluid seepage. • Shifter is hard to move or won't go into Reverse. • Knocking/vibrating shift lever. • Transmission pops out of gear. • Vehicle will not move into any forward gear. • Eliminating musty odour from AC. • Malfunctioning CD player. **1998**—Reducing musty odours from the AC. • Door speaker noise. • Delayed and erratic shifting. **1999**—Engine cranks, but won't start. • Delayed shift on cold-start warm-up. • Poor AM radio reception. Malfunctioning windshield wipers. • Engine misfire. • Door speaker rattling or vibrating.

Safety summary/Recalls: All models: 1993–2000—NHTSA probe of fuel tank punctures. **1996**—Many complaints that transmission slips out of third gear into Neutral. • Vehicle suddenly accelerated forward as lever was put into Reverse. • Intermittent stalling due to electronic control module failure. • Check Engine light constantly goes on and off. •

Engine-valve cover gasket failures. • Plastic shroud on top of engine rubs against the fuel line. • Leaking windshield and door seals. • Premature wheel-bearing failure on the driver's side. • Door lock failure allows door to open while under power, or makes doors difficult to open. • Instrument cluster wiring harness failures. • Repeated trunk-switch failures. • Chronic trunk water leaks. • Premature brake pad wearout. • All dash gauges suddenly stop working. **1997**—When manual transmission lever is put into Reverse, it often goes into first gear instead. • Sudden steering-wheel lockup. • Cooling fan control module failure. • Rear window defroster power button works only when held in the ON position. • Door handle failures. • Frequent window regulator failures. **1998**—Engine head gasket leaks. • Erratic transmission performance. • Gas tank can't be filled without the pump shutting off repeatedly. • AC recirculation switch failure. • Serious blind spots caused by the small size and narrow view of the three mirrors. • Front seats move back and forth when braking or accelerating. • Total electrical-system failure. **1999**—Electrical fire. • Airbags failed to deploy; airbag light comes on for no reason. • Sudden unintended acceleration; cruise control doesn't disengage, or engages on its own. • Accelerator pedal fails to return after full throttle. • Chronic stalling on the highway. • Early transmission clutch failure. • Clutch depressed to the floor and gear stayed engaged. • Front suspension's lower right arm failure due to a faulty bushing. • Front left wheel came off when making a turn. • Premature failures of the Michelin MXV4 tire; when rear tires blow out, they wreak havoc on vehicle's undercarriage (wheelwell and well lining), in some cases, causing the fuel tank to leak. • Other complaints of ruptured fuel tanks. • Oil line ruptured while driving. • Missing power-steering cap caused fluid to leak out. • Driver seat has excessive fore and aft movement. • Windshield cracked while vehicle was parked in direct sunlight. **Recalls: All models: 1993–95**—Faulty radiator fan motor could cause engine to overheat and stall in models equipped with a VR6 engine. **1997–98**—Possibility of sudden acceleration, unless a special retaining ring is used to secure the air screen in place. **1998**—Poor tie-rod sealing may cause loss of vehicle control.

Secret Warranties/Service Tips

All models/years—Vehicles that won't move into any forward gear could have broken retaining lugs for selector plugs of B2/K1, which causes the selector valve to partially protrude or fall out of the valve body. **All models: 1990–91**—If the radiator fan stays on high speed with the ignition off and thus runs down the battery, replace the fan's high-speed relay with part #321-919-505A. **1990–95**—On Passats equipped with an automatic transmission, an engine that won't start could have a loose contact in the ECM power supply relay. **1991–93**—AC expansion valve noises require the installation of an upgraded expansion valve. • Poor driveability could be caused by magnetic interference due to a deteriorated oxygen sensor wire shield or improper oxygen sensor wire shield ground connection. **1992–94**—Poor 2.8L engine performance or a rough idle could be due to a misrouted EVAP vacuum hose or an improperly routed positive crankcase ventilation hose, which will cause a vacuum leak. **1993**—If the ABS warning light won't go out, a faulty start switch/lock is the likely culprit. **1995–96**—Troubleshooting tips are offered on automatic transmission fluid seepage. **1995–99**—An erratic-shifting automatic transmission may be due to an improper throttle angle setting. **1996–97**—If the transmission pops out of gear, check for a hairline crack on the selector shaft shift detent sleeve. **1998–99**—Tips on fixing a door speaker rattle or vibration. • VW says a delayed upshift after a cold start is normal and a wait of 40 seconds isn't too long (typical of German logic, "Our cars are perfect, our customers aren't.").

Passat Profile

	1991	1992	1993	1995	1996	1997	1998	1999
Cost Price ($)								
Base	18,995	19,790	21,525	25,870	27,230	28,620	28,450	29,100
Used Values ($)								
Base ↑	5,000	6,000	7,500	9,500	12,500	16,000	19,000	23,000
Base ↓	4,000	5,000	6,500	8,500	11,000	14,500	17,000	22,000
Extended Warranty	Y	Y	Y	Y	Y	Y	Y	Y
Secret Warranty	N	N	N	N	N	N	N	N
Reliability	❷	❷	❷	③	③	④	⑤	⑤
Air conditioning	❷	❷	❷	④	④	④	④	⑤
Auto. transmission	❶	❶	❶	❷	❷	③	④	④
Body integrity	❷	❷	❷	③	④	④	④	④
Braking system	❷	❷	❷	❷	③	③	④	④
Electrical system	❷	❷	❷	③	③	③	③	③
Engines	⑤	⑤	⑤	⑤	⑤	⑤	⑤	⑤
Exhaust/Converter	⑤	⑤	⑤	⑤	⑤	⑤	⑤	⑤
Fuel system	❷	❷	❷	④	⑤	⑤	⑤	⑤
Ignition system	❷	❷	❷	④	⑤	⑤	⑤	⑤
Rust/Paint	③	③	⑤	⑤	⑤	⑤	⑤	⑤
Steering	③	③	③	④	④	⑤	⑤	⑤
Suspension	③	③	③	④	④	⑤	⑤	⑤
Crash Safety	❷	❷	❷	④	④	④	—	—

LARGE CARS/WAGONS

For motorists who can write off relatively high gasoline consumption, maintenance, and insurance premiums, these are excellent cars for extensive highway driving.

The term "large car" is relative. It once designated vehicles that had a wheelbase of more than 114 inches and that weighed about 3,200 lb. (1,450 kg). But now that the automakers have shortened most of the wheelbases of their large cars, reduced their weight, and switched to front-wheel drive, traditional definitions of "large" may no longer be accurate indicators of a car's size. Some large cars, like GM's Caprice and Roadmaster, bucked this trend, however, and remained long and heavy.

Owners have to pay a premium for these vehicles, which usually come fully loaded with performance and convenience features, but they are happy to do so because these vehicles offer considerable comfort and stability at high speeds. Large cars also depreciate slowly, can seat six adults comfortably, and are ideal for motoring vacations.

These vehicles generally incur less damage from front, rear, and side collisions, although recent U.S. government crash tests show that many smaller cars absorb frontal crash just as well.

Recommended

Ford Crown Victoria,
  Grand Marquis (1997–99)

Above Average

Ford Cougar, Thunderbird
  (1995–97)
Ford Crown Victoria,
  Grand Marquis (1994–96)

GM Caprice, Impala SS,
  Roadmaster (1995–96)

Average

Ford Crown Victoria, Grand
  Marquis (1984–93)

GM Caprice, Impala SS,
  Roadmaster (1994)

Below Average

Chrysler revised LHS, 300M (1999)

Ford Cougar, Thunderbird
  (1985–94; 1999)

Not Recommended

Chrysler Concorde, Intrepid,
  LHS, New Yorker, Vision
  (1993–99)

GM Caprice, Impala SS,
  Roadmaster (1982–93)

273

Station wagons (full-sized)

If passenger and cargo space and carlike handling are what you want, a large station wagon may not be the answer—a used minivan, van, light truck, or compact wagon can fill the same need for less cost and will probably still be around a decade from now. Popular (though troublesome) wagons—like the Caprice and Roadmaster (both axed in 1996)—in which you could cram a Little League team are an endangered species, losing out to the van and minivan craze.

Some disadvantages of large station wagons: difficulty in keeping the interior heated in winter, atrocious gas consumption, sloppy handling, and poor rear visibility. Exterior road noise is also a frequent problem, since the vehicle's interior has a tendency to amplify normal road noise. Rear hatches tend to be rust prone. Crash safety is variable.

No full-sized station wagons are recommended.

CHRYSLER

300M, Concorde, Intrepid, LHS, New Yorker, Vision

Rating: Concorde, Intrepid, LHS, New Yorker, and Vision are Not Recommended buys (1993–99); revised LHS and 300M are Below Average in their first year of production (1999), Average buys thereafter. If you want maximum passenger room and engine performance, choose a 1995 or 1996 LHS or New Yorker. They're about five inches longer, use a larger engine, and are a bit more refined. Whichever vehicle you're considering buying, before paying a cent, make sure you get an extended warranty and take a test drive at night to assess the efficacy of the headlights. Only vehicles that carry an extended powertrain and body warranty are worthy of any consideration. Be wary of original equipment Goodyear tires; they're prone to early wearout. These cars have elicited fewer safety-related complaints than the competition (think GM and Ford, here). Nevertheless, they have chronic problems with unintended acceleration that has carried over year after year. **Maintenance/Repair costs:** Higher than average, but most repairs aren't dealer dependent. **Parts:** Higher-than-average cost (independent suppliers sell for much less), but not hard to find.

Strengths and weaknesses: These full-sized cars share the same chassis and offer most of the same standard and optional features. They provide loads of passenger space and many standard features that usually sell as options, such as four-wheel disc brakes and an independent rear suspension. The Concorde is marketed to the more conservative buyer, while the Intrepid, the more popular model, is the entry-level version. Base models are equipped with a 2.7L V6 aluminum engine that delivers 200 hp. Higher line variants get a more powerful 3.2L V6 225-hp powerplant, or a 242-hp 3.5L V6. Earlier models, carried a 3.3L 153-hp

6-banger, but 70 percent of buyers chose the 3.5L for its extra horses. Both engines provide plenty of low-end torque and acceleration, but this advantage is lost somewhat when traversing hilly terrain: the smaller V6 powerplant strains to keep up. These are more reliable vehicles, with better handling and steering response than in the Sable and Taurus, and the independent suspension maximizes control, reduces body roll, and provides lots of suspension travel so that you don't get bumped around too much on rough roads.

With all these positives, why aren't these cars recommended? Simple: they're unsafe and unreliable. One 1994 Intrepid owner's comments posted on the Internet sum it up: "The lack of overall quality and dangerous headlights made me dump the car after only 15 months' use."

A perusal of technical service bulletins and comments from car rental agencies and owners tells me that these cars continue to have many serious safety- and performance-related shortcomings that can no longer be explained away as the "first series" teething problems that all new cars experience.

The automatic climate control system operates erratically, blowing cold air when it's set for warm, and warm air when it's set for cool. The instrument panel must be removed before servicing the ventilation system because the AC ducts are molded into the plastic panel. The shift console needs lighting, the radio and climate controls are too small, the trunk release is hidden in the glove compartment, the hood release is on the floor, the rear-view mirror is too narrow, and the fuel-filler door needs a lock. The trunk has a high deck lid, making for difficult loading and unloading, and there's no inside access by folding down the rear seat, as in the Camry.

Owner reports confirm that there are chronic problems with leaking 3.3L engine head gaskets and noisy lifters that wear out prematurely around 60,000 km. Water pumps often self-destruct and take the engine timing chain along with them (a $1,200 repair). Other common complaints: a poor fit between the exhaust manifold and the engine block often results in oil leaks and noisy engine operation; if you wash your car during extremely cold weather, the resulting ice buildup and leaking deck lid seals can easily damage the heater fan motor.

The 4-speed LE42 automatic transmission is a spin-off of Chrysler's failure-prone A604 version—and owner reports show it to be troublesome as well. Owners tell of chronic glitches in the computerized transmission's shift timing and other computer malfunctions, which result in driveability problems (stalling, hard starts, and surging).

Body problems abound, with lots of interior noise, uneven fit and finish, poor quality trim items that break or fall off easily, exposed screw heads, faulty door hinges that make the doors rattle and hard to open, distorted windshields, windows that come off their tracks or are misaligned and poorly sealed, power window motor failures, and steering wheel noise when the car is turning. Other body defects specifically addressed in Technical service bulletins include the following: noisy front suspension, glue oozing out at the back centre brake light and windshield moulding, water collecting in the park/turn lights, noisy rear upper strut mounts, water draining into the trunk when the deck lid is raised, and water entering into the AC/heater housing.

AC failures are commonplace and costly to repair. The problem has become so prevalent that Chrysler has a little-known warranty extension that will pay for the replacement of the evaporator up to seven years. Chrysler has tried to limit compensation to a limited number of models, but the company can't escape its 7-year benchmark or arbitrarily exclude owners of other vehicles made by the company (see page 55).

Upscale LHS and New Yorker versions haven't escaped Chrysler's notorious poor-quality body components and sloppy assembly. In addition to the above-mentioned owner and bulletin-related problems, additional service bulletins for these cars indicate that they're likely to have their own persistent problems—such as faulty fuel pumps causing stalling, reduced power, or erratic transmission shifting; radio lockups; water leaks coming from the heater/AC housing; and moisture in the headlights. Bulletins also address how to silence a noisy AC compressor, a squeaking or creaking noise coming from the rear window when travelling at slow speeds over rough roads, and a high-pitched whistling noise caused by a defective idle air control motor.

300M and LHS

These two models represent the near-luxury and sport clones of the Chrysler Concorde. Although they use the same front-drive platform as the Concorde, their bodies are shorter and they're styled differently. In fact, the 300M is the shortest of Chrysler's mid-sized sedans. Both cars are powered by a 253-hp 3.5L V6 and mated to Chrysler's AutoStick semi-automatic transmission. Only a few months after their launch in the summer of '98, Chrysler made engineering changes to reduce noise and vibration and smooth out what was thought to be an overly harsh ride.

Although mechanical and body deficiencies generally mirror those of the Concorde and Intrepid, 1999 model 300M and LHS owners report the following problems: a rough-running engine and transmission, excessive road and wind noise, and only five-passenger capacity. The 300M has limited rear leg room, no side airbags, mediocre fit and finish, and questionable reliability. A narrow rear windshield reduces rear visibility, and the trunk and trunk opening are smaller than the LHS.

Technical service bulletins: All models: 1995—Glitches in the computerized transmission's shift timing cause driveability problems (stalling, hard starts, and surging). Amazingly, the 4-speed LE42 automatic transmission—a spin-off of Chrysler's failure-prone A604—appears to be just as problem-plagued as its predecessor. • AC refrigerant leaks. •

Heater/AC housing leaks water and there's moisture in headlights. • Excessive engine noise is likely caused by carbon buildup on the top of the pistons. • Engine mount rattles. • Transmission clicks and clunks. • Fuel line rattles caused by faulty fuel rail assembly. • Squeaking front or rear brakes require upgraded brake linings. • A-pillar wind noise. • Rattling C-post appliqué or poor fit of the appliqué to the back glass. • Front hub clicks and clunks. • B-pillar and rear spring rattles. • Upper strut mount squeaks. • Excessive road noise from the front wheels and rear seat requires reduced tire pressure and the addition of foam/sealer insulation to the front upper load beam or the C-pillar. **1996**—3.3L, 3.5L lower engine oil leaks. • Reduced transmission limp-in default sensitivity. • Shuddering on upshift or whenever the torque converter is engaged. • Upgraded Overdrive clutch hub. • Front suspension clunking or rattling. • Metallic knocking from front of vehicle when passing over bumps. • High-speed windshield washer spray knockdown. • Water leaks into trunk (see "Secret Warranties/Service Tips"). • Polycast wheel centre falls off. • Cupholder improvements. **1997**—Tips on troubleshooting noisy brakes. • AC evaporator leaks. • AC suction line failure. • Warped or poor-fitting passenger-side airbag door. • A metallic popping noise might be heard coming from the front of the vehicle. • Sticking sunroof or sunshade. • Rear drum brake ticking. • Water ingestion into heater/AC housing. **1998**—Delayed automatic transmission shifts; defective door locks, interior lights, radio, climate control, heater, and AC; squeaks, squawks, and rattles; and water leaks are the most frequent problems covered. **1999**—Water leaks in the trunk area and on the carpeting, wind noise, squeaks, clunks, and rattles are still paramount concerns. • Bulletins also target: a rough idle and poor driveability; loose, clunky steering; loose rear door trim; cold engine growling; poor AC and heater performance; vehicle leading or pulling at highway speeds; and inoperative or erratically performing power windows.

Safety summary/Recalls: All models/years: Headlights may be too dim for safe motoring, and some owners report that the headlights sometimes cut out completely. • Defrosting is inadequate, allowing ice and moisture to collect at the base of the windshield. Chrysler has a fix for these two problems that requires the installation of a new headlight lens and small foam pads into the defroster outlet ducts. • Both ABS and non-ABS brakes perform poorly, resulting in excessively long stopping distances—more so than for other cars in this class. • The overhead digital panel is distracting and forces you to take your eyes from the road. • The emergency brake pedal catches pant cuffs and shoelaces as you enter or exit the vehicle. • A high rear windowsill obstructs rear visibility. **1994–96**—Steering failures are under study by NHTSA. **1994–97**—NHTSA is looking into reports that the front suspension may collapse, causing the driver to lose control of the vehicle. This government agency knows of 26 complaints and 105 warranty claims for 1994 models, and another 49 complaints covering 1995–97 years that used an upgraded suspension. Broken welds or cracks where the lower control arm attaches to the front cradle may be the cause of the failures. **1996**—Sudden acceleration when starting out in Drive. • Airbags fail to deploy. • Driver's pant leg gets caught on the parking brake assembly upon entering the vehicle. • Many reports that while the vehicle is being driven at 100 km/h, there's a sudden loss of power, the engine shuts down, power steering and brakes become inoperative, and the Check Engine light comes on. • High-pressure fuel lines between the two cylinder heads leak gas onto the engine. • When shifting into Reverse from Park, automatic transmission acts as if it's in Neutral, and the engine races when the accelerator is pressed. • ABS brake failures. • Brake rotors rust prematurely and warp easily, and pads have to be changed every 15,000 km. • Vehicle shakes violently when ABS brakes are applied. • Inadequate headlight illumination. • Dashboard reflection in the windshield hampers visibility. • Horn buttons difficult to access in emergency situations. • Stuck right rear door lock won't allow door to open. • Door hinges don't hold door open securely, causing injury to occupants when door closes unexpectedly. • Frequent water pump, AC, and battery failures. **1997**—Fire ignited in trunk. • Fuel line hoses disconnected from the engine, spilling fuel into the engine area. • ABS brake failures. • Airbags failed to deploy. • Engine hesitates and surges. • Vehicle decelerates while driving. • Premature wearout of front brake pads and rotors (rotors warp or become rust-pitted). • Excessive brake noise. • Several reports that Goodyear Eagle tires tend to hydroplane. • Steering linkage failure causes vehicle to wander all over the roadway. • Power steering failure— extremely hard to turn. • Many reports of sudden transmission failures, many due to cracked transmission casings. • Transmission fluid leakage caused by defective transmission casing bolt. • Seat backrest failure. • Frequent windshield replacements due to distortion—particularly annoying at night when combined with poor headlight illumination. • Intermittent turn signal operation. • Flawed interior door panels. • Frequent instrument panel malfunctions: lights, gauges, AC all go out at once. • Cigarette lighter shoots out so hard it shoots under driver's seat—while red hot. **1998**—Several reports of sudden acceleration when shifting into Reverse. • When transmission relay fails, it causes a harsh downshift to second gear while at highway speeds. • Airbags failed to deploy. • Rear brakes improperly adjusted by Chrysler result in overloaded front brakes and warped front brake rotors. • Windshield distortions. **1999**—Many complaints of sudden acceleration, accompanied by brake failure. • Vehicle suddenly accelerated when shifted into Reverse at a car wash. • The bolt that holds the fan and engine pulley came loose, resulting in complete loss of steering ability. • Brakes continually lock up, grind when applied, and result in extended stopping distance. • With cruise control engaged, brakes will suddenly lock up. • Chronic automatic transmission failures (the speed

sensor often fails, causing the engine warning light to come on). •
Vehicle will suddenly shudder or lurch violently while underway at
cruising speed. • The #4 engine cylinder failed, causing vehicle to lose
power. • Check Engine light comes on constantly. • Fuel smell invades
the interior. • Shifter pin to interlock cable broke off, causing the ignition key to be removable while vehicle is in gear. • Glove box can't be
locked. • Frequent failure of the power window motors. **300M: 1999—**
Airbags suddenly deployed for no reason when changing lanes. •
Airbags failed to deploy in a collision. • Many complaints of sudden,
unintended acceleration. • Transmission jumped from Park to Reverse
with engine running. • Driver's son took shifter out of Park without key
in ignition, and vehicle rolled down hill. • Premature wearout of brake
rotors. • Vehicle constantly shakes and shimmies; wobbles and bobbles
on the highway. • Early wearout of original equipment Goodyear tires.
Recalls: All models: 1993—Dealers will reroute the wiring harness to
prevent shorting. **1994**—Faulty transmission wiring might cause the car
to allow starting when not in the Park position. **Intrepid, Vision: 1993—**
Defective lower control arm washers could cause loss of steering.
Concorde, Intrepid, LHS, Vision: 1993–97—Models with 3.5L V6
engines may have a faulty O-ring in the engines' fuel-injection system
that may harden and let fuel escape.

Secret Warranties/Service Tips

All models/years—A rotten-egg odour coming from the exhaust is probably caused by a malfunctioning catalytic converter; this is covered by
Chrysler's original warranty *and* the emissions warranty. Don't take "no" for
an answer. The same advice goes for all the squeaks and rattles and the
water and wind leaks that afflict these vehicles. Don't let Chrysler or the
dealer pawn these problems off as maintenance items. They're all factory
related and should be covered for at least five years. **All models: 1993**—
Failure of the fuel pump check valve could cause start-up die-out, reduced
power, or erratic shifting. • Doors that are hard to open or close or that
make a snapping sound likely need four-check door straps, which Chrysler
will provide free of charge. • More importantly, AC evaporator failures will
be covered under a special 7-year program, according to Chrysler service
honchos. Although limited to 1993s, it's logical (to me, at least) that this
warranty extension sets up a benchmark that owners of other, more recent
models can rely upon to get their ACs repaired under warranty (even if the
evaporator isn't the cause of the failure). **1993–97**—The blower motor
could seize or freeze from water seeping into the heater/AC housing. • AC
evaporator leaks caused by premature corrosion can be prevented by
installing a cowl plenum screen; Chrysler confirms this is a warranty repair.
1993–98—Delayed transaxle engagement can be corrected through
upgraded hardware and software components. **1993–99**—Troubleshooting
tips for correcting a severe lead or pull when driving. • Trunk water and
dust leaks. • Paint delamination, peeling, or fading (see Part Two).
1993–2000—If the vehicle leads or pulls at highway speeds, TSB #02-16-99
suggests a whole series of countermeasures, including replacing the engine
mounts, if necessary. Chrysler will apply the base warranty to this repair. •

Loose or noisy steering may be corrected by servicing the inner tie rod bushings or simply replacing the tie rod. • Harsh, erratic, or delayed transmission shifts can be corrected by replacing the throttle position sensor (TPS) with a revised part. **1994–95**—The intermittent or total loss of air conditioning can be corrected by installing a revised AC pressure transducer. **1995–99**—More troubleshooting tips are offered on diagnosing and fixing trunk water leaks.

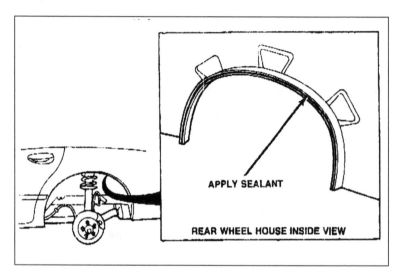

APPLY SEALANT

REAR WHEEL HOUSE INSIDE VIEW

1995–97—If the AC suction line fails, replace it and install a revised right-side engine ground strap; the original ground strap probably caused the failure. **1996–97**—If you hear a metallic popping noise coming from the front of the vehicle when you accelerate from a stop, install two new upper and two new lower cradle mounting isolators. • Rear drum brake ticking can be silenced by burnishing the rear brakes. **1998**—Tips on correcting inadvertent door lock operation. **1998–99**—A rough idle or poor driveability may require the testing and replacing of the EGR valve and power control module (PCM). • An engine hiss noise can be silenced by replacing the throttle body assembly. • Delayed shifts and other transmission malfunctions affecting a broad range of models are addressed in TSB #21-03-98. This is proof positive that Chrysler's transmission woes are far from over. • Troubleshooting tips for no hot air or lack of cold air. • Poor heater performance may mean the PCM should be simply reprogrammed. • Window sticks in the up position. • Countermeasures for correcting excessive road noise and a variety of squeaks, rattles, and squawks. • Troubleshooting tips for correcting water leaks on top of and/or under floor carpets. • Poor AM radio reception can be fixed by installing a new electronic back light module. **1998–2000**—Poor AC performance can be fixed by first carrying out Customer Satisfaction Recall #857 and then re-programming the power control module. • Repair procedures are outlined for re-attaching the rear door trim panel. • Guidelines for silencing wind noise emanating from the sunroof and forward of the B-pillars. •

Front suspension strut squeaking can be stopped by installing a revised front strut striker cap.

300M, Concorde, Intrepid, LHS, New Yorker, Vision Profile

	1993	1994	1995	1996	1997	1998	1999
Cost Price ($)							
300M	—	—	—	—	—	—	39,150
Concorde	20,425	22,590	24,420	26,005	26,815	26,915	27,635
Intrepid	17,555	19,170	21,010	22,980	24,055	24,395	25,060
LHS	—	35,020	37,625	38,420	40,500	40,500	41,150
New Yorker	—	29,990	32,080	34,490	—	—	—
Vision	18,450	21,485	22,910	23,770	24,775	—	—
Used Values ($)							
300M ↑	—	—	—	—	—	—	26,000
300M ↓	—	—	—	—	—	—	24,000
Concorde ↑	6,000	7,500	9,500	11,000	13,500	16,500	18,500
Concorde ↓	5,000	6,000	7,500	9,500	11,500	14,500	16,500
Intrepid ↑	4,500	5,500	7,500	9,000	11,000	14,000	17,000
Intrepid ↓	4,000	4,500	5,500	7,500	9,500	13,000	15,000
LHS ↑	—	8,500	11,500	14,000	18,000	21,000	26,000
LHS ↓	—	7,000	9,500	12,000	16,000	19,000	24,500
New Yorker ↑	—	8,000	10,000	12,000	—	—	—
New Yorker ↓	—	6,000	8,500	10,500	—	—	—
Vision ↑	4,000	5,500	7,500	9,000	11,000	—	—
Vision ↓	3,000	4,500	6,000	7,500	9,500	—	—
Extended Warranty	Y	Y	Y	Y	Y	Y	Y
Secret Warranty	Y	Y	Y	Y	Y	Y	Y
Reliability	❶	❶	❶	❷	❷	❷	❷
Air conditioning	❶	❶	❶	❷	❷	③	③
Auto. Transmission	❶	❶	❶	❷	③	③	③
Body integrity	❶	❶	❶	❷	❷	❷	❷
Braking system	❶	❶	❶	❶	❶	❷	③
Electrical system	❶	❶	❷	❷	❷	❷	❷
Engines	③	③	③	④	④	④	④
Exhaust/Converter	③	③	③	③	④	④	④
Fuel system	③	③	③	③	④	④	④
Ignition system	❷	❷	③	④	④	④	④
Rust/Paint	③	④	④	④	④	④	④
Steering	③	③	③	③	③	③	③
Suspension	❷	❷	❷	❷	❷	③	③
Crash Safety							
Concorde	④	④	④	④	④	—	—
Intrepid	④	④	④	④	④	—	④
LHS	—	④	④	④	④	—	—
New Yorker	—	④	④	④	—	—	—

Vision	④	④	④	④	④	—	—
Side Impact							
Concorde	—	—	—	—	④	—	—
Intrepid	—	—	—	—	④	—	④
Vision	—	—	—	—	④	—	—

Note: All these vehicles are practically identical and should have similar crashworthiness scores, even though not every model was tested each year.

FORD

Cougar, Thunderbird

Rating: Below Average (1999); Above Average (1995–97); Below Average (1985–94). Just about when Ford was getting its act together with the T-Bird and Cougar, it took both off the market and returned a year later with a poor-quality, unreliable Contour-*cum*-Cougar. Considering the millions invested and advertising hype we've endured, that's frankly an embarrassment. For readers wondering how the Cougar could go from a below average rating to above average, and then fall again to below average, remember we are reviewing distinctly different vehicles. The early rear-drives improved over the years; however, its front-drive 1999 iteration carries all of the deficiencies of Ford's front-drives, coupled to the Contour and Mystique's own sub-set of problems. Plus, as a first-year vehicle, the Cougar's quality control suffered even more (see "Safety Summary" and "Service Tips"). Get rid of the original equipment Firestone Firehawk tires: they're too risky. **Maintenance/Repair costs:** About average, and most repairs aren't dealer dependent. **Parts:** Moderately priced (independent suppliers sell for much less), and not hard to find for rear-drives. Front-drive parts, however, are more expensive and not as easily found. And, they will likely become rarer when the Contour is taken off the market in 2001. Despite the fact that 1997 was the last model year for both rear-drive models, parts should remain plentiful.

Strengths and weaknesses: These are no-surprise, average-performing, two-door, rear-drive, luxury cars that have changed little over the years. Nevertheless, they offer more comfort and performance, and greater reliability than GM rear-drives and most of the Big Three–produced front-drives. Handling and ride are far from perfect, though, with considerable body lean and rear-end instability when taking curves at moderate speeds.

Overall reliability of these models has been average, as long as you stay away from the turbocharged 4-cylinder engine and watch out for 3.8L V6 engine head gasket failures and automatic transmission glitches.

Dear Phil,

Thank you for your help with my '94 T-Bird.
I pressed Ford armed with the information from your site and received a new engine, carte blanche. It was a $4500 Christmas present from Ford (and you).

Thank you, once again.

Sincerely, Paul Vallas

True, these cars offer lots of power, but excessive noise and expensive repairs are the price you pay when they're pushed too hard. Front suspension components wear out quickly, as do power-steering rack seals. Owners of recent models have complained of ignition module defects, electrical system bugs, premature front brake repairs, steering pump hoses that burst repeatedly (one owner of a 1994 Cougar wrote that he replaced the hose twice in the same year), erratic transmission performance, early AC failures, defective engine intake manifolds, excessive vibrations when driving, numerous squeaks and rattles, faulty heater fans, and failure-prone power window regulators.

1999 Cougar

Essentially a Contour spin-off, this Cougar's main attributes are its attractive styling and pleasant handling. On the other hand, owners have to accept so-so acceleration with the base models, problematic transmission performance, a four-seater with a narrow, claustrophobic interior, limited rear-seat room, obstructed rear visibility, an ugly and superfluous trunklid spoiler, and excessive interior noise.

The front-drive Cougar, restyled as a hatchback, is equipped with a 16-valve, 125-hp 2.0L inline-four and a 24-valve, 170-hp 2.5L V6, later replaced with an upgraded 200-hp powerplant, and optional ABS and side airbags. It shares the Contour's chassis (with an inch added), base 4-banger, and V6, but its suspension and steering are much tighter.

Emergency handling is acceptable, but not in the same league as Japanese sedans. The firm suspension and quick, responsive steering make the Cougar both nimble and stable when cornering under speed, especially with the optional Sport Group's rear disc brakes and larger wheels (you'll have to put up with a harder, noisier ride, though). The car is also quite peppy around town, with good amount of low-end torque. Braking is also quite good with little fading after successive stops.

Acceleration is only so-so with the base four or V6 engine and they both run roughly; the base four-cylinder engine is not as refined or fun to push as the Japanese competition. 170-hp V6 lacks passing or merging power: 0–100 km/h takes about 10 seconds. The automatic transmission tends to "hunt" the proper gear when going over hilly terrain and there's no way to lock out Overdrive in fourth gear. The 5-speed hooked to the V6 also shifts roughly. The base suspension doesn't absorb bumps very well and the optional Sports Group tires produce a busy, jostling ride on any surface that's less than perfect. Steering is also a bit heavy in city traffic.

Owner-reported problems include automatic transmission failures accompanied by slipping, humming, and clanking noises; electrical glitches; chronic stalling, rough running, and hard starts; premature front and rear brake wear and a low grinding noise or squeak heard when the brakes are applied; trunk, sunroof, door, and side window jamming; a sun visor that keeps falling down; door latch failures; doors that lock and unlock themselves; faulty driver-side door weather stripping that produces excessive wind noise; and water leakage into the interior.

Safety summary/Recalls: All models: 1995–99—NHTSA probe of blower switch/resistor or wiring harness. **1996**—Vehicle caught fire after being parked for 13 hours. • Airbags failed to deploy. • Airbag indicator light comes on for no reason. • Right rear wheel came off. • During inclement weather, design of engine allows water to saturate the air filter, causing engine to die out. • PCM chip defect causes engine to cut out and the Check Engine light to come on. • Malfunctioning crankshaft and oxygen sensors may cause chronic stalling and no-starts. • Cracked intake manifold allows coolant leakage. • Frequent motor mount failures. • Transmissions are noisy, won't shift properly, and frequently won't shift at all. • Excessive driveshaft vibrations. • Power steering works poorly at low speeds and sometimes cuts out completely when cruising on the highway. • Heater and AC compressor failures. • Defective AC fan switch. • Frequent reports of sudden brake failures, front brake rotor warpage, and noisy brakes. • Brake pedal sinks below the accelerator pedal level, causing driver to depress the accelerator. • Hood struts are too weak to keep hood in open position. • Crooked steering wheel replaced. • Power window regulator failures. • Electric door locks are failure-prone. • Doors fit poorly. • Headlights require constant adjustment and don't provide as much illumination as with other model years. • Seatbelt doesn't release properly. • Defective sunroof guides, and the gasket barely lasts two years. • Sun visor hits driver in the head when it's adjusted. • Speedometer and gauges work erratically. **1997**—Sudden acceleration while stopped at a traffic light. • Left vehicle in Park with engine running and it suddenly lurched into Reverse. • Car suddenly pulled to the left when braking, and steering locked up. • Excessive vibrations while cruising that increase in intensity when braking. • Premature front brake wear. • Headrests can't be raised high enough to protect the head. • Seat won't latch. • Brake caliper moves in its bracket. • Transmission fluid leakage. • Water leaks onto passenger-side floor due to missing wiring harness plug. • Dash reflection on the windshield obstructs visibility. • Dealer can't correct windshield washer spray to prevent it from spraying the rear window. • Multiple Firestone tire failures. **1998**—Airbag failed to deploy. • Tire side-wall failure. • Engine increases rpms when shifting. • Sudden stalling with locked-up steering. • Engine and airbag service lights stay on for no apparent reason. • Key won't work in the ignition. • Hard to find a child safety seat that fits in the rear. • The silly, non-functional rear spoiler is both distracting and cuts rearward vision. **1999**— Inadvertent airbag deployment. • Driver's airbag deployed after collision and seatbelt failed to lock up. • Sticking throttle causes sudden, unintended acceleration. • Cruise control wouldn't disengage. • Chronic hesitation or stalling (electrical shorts, or a faulty fuel pump, fuel regulator, intake gaskets, or IAC solenoid are the prime suspects). • No-start due to faulty ignition or starter. • Transmission failures. • While driving at 110 km/h, transmission downshifted on its own. • Sudden brake failure (locked up). • Total brake failure when ABS brake master cylinder "exploded." • Brake pads, calipers, and rotors need replacing after only 32,000 kilometres.• Power steering fails and dash lights go out when car is driven through a rain puddle. This may be caused by the serpentine belt getting wet. • Plastic fuel tank is prone to early disintegration, contributing to stalling; vehicle bought back by Ford. • Gas tank seal swells and breaks, spilling fuel. • Fuel tank wiring harness melted. • Brake lights don't come on when brakes are applied. • Electrical failures tend to blow out the fuel pump. • On another occasion, dash lights suddenly came on, engine died, and brakes and steering ability were gone. • Steering failures due to a broken suspension strut, or the tie rod bolt shearing off. • Wheel may crack, causing a tire blowout. • Frequent reports of tire tread separation at the side walls or prematurely wearing out (Firestone Firehawk). • Lug nut wrench doesn't work. • Trunk won't open or close and remote release is useless. • Horn is hard to activate. • Inadequate rear windshield defogger. **Recalls: All models: 1996**—The automatic transmission may disengage or fail to engage when shift lever is moved to Park. • Driver's door may not sustain the specified load when it's in the secondary latch position. • The semi-automatic temperature control blower may malfunction.

Secret Warranties/Service Tips

All models/years—Ford's "goodwill" warranty extensions cover engine and transmission breakdowns up to about seven years. There's nothing like a small claims court action to focus Ford's attention. The same advice applies if you notice a rotten-egg odour coming from the exhaust. **All models: 1985–97**—A buzz or rattle from the exhaust system may be caused by a loose heat shield catalyst. **1989–97**—Water dripping from the floor ducts when the AC is working requires a relocated evaporator core. **1992–95**—A corroded solenoid may be the cause of starter failures. **1993–97**— Roughness when braking from 105 km/h is likely caused by a distorted rear brake drum. • Paint delamination, peeling, or fading (see Part Two). **1993–2000**—Brake vibration diagnosis and correction. **1994**—Automatic transmissions with delayed, no forward engagement, or a higher engine rpm than expected when coming to a stop are covered in TSB #94-26-9. • A no-crank condition in cold weather may be due to water freezing in the starter solenoid. • Hesitation or stumble in vehicles equipped with a 3.8L engine may be fixed by installing an upgraded PCM that allows for low-grade fuel. **1994–95**—A thumping or clacking noise heard from the front brakes signals the need to machine the front disc brake rotors. **1994–97**—

An erratic or prolonged 1–2 shift can be cured by replacing the cast aluminum piston with a one-piece stamped steel piston that has bonded lip seals, and by replacing the top accumulator spring. • A simple solution for correcting a transmission shudder or vibration in third or fourth gear may be to simply change the transmission fluid or recalibrate the PCM. **1995–97**—Tips on sealing windshield water leaks and reducing noise, vibration, and harshness while driving. **1996–97**—A stuck door latch or handle should be replaced with upgraded parts. **1999**—Three bulletins target automatic transmission failures, suggesting that either that the Overdrive/Reverse ring gear be replaced, or an ugpgraded transaxle assembly be installed. • Front brake groaning during city driving can be silenced by installing revised brake pads under warranty, says TSB #99-8-9. **1999–2000**—Engine hesitation and a rough idle may be corrected by reprogramming the power control module. • Automatic transmission fluid leaks. • An exhaust sulphur odour evident just after highway cruising may signal the need to replace the catalytic converter under the emissions warranty. • Water leaks and wind noise troubleshooting tips.

Cougar, Thunderbird Profile

	1991	1992	1993	1994	1995	1996	1997	1999
Cost Price ($)								
Cougar	18,295	19,395	19,650	21,395	22,095	23,495	24,995	19,995
T-bird	17,495	18,795	19,695	21,895	22,995	23,595	25,095	—
Used Values ($)								
Cougar ↑	3,500	4,000	5,000	6,000	8,500	10,500	12,500	15,500
Cougar ↓	3,000	3,500	4,000	4,500	7,000	9,000	10,500	14,000
T-bird ↑	3,500	4,000	4,500	6,000	8,500	10,500	12,500	—
T-bird ↓	3,000	3,500	4,000	4,500	7,500	8,500	11,000	—
Extended Warranty	Y	Y	Y	Y	Y	Y	N	N
Secret Warranty	Y	Y	Y	Y	Y	Y	Y	Y
Reliability	②	②	②	②	②	③	④	④
Air conditioning	②	②	②	②	②	③	③	④
Auto. transmission	②	②	②	②	②	②	③	③
Body integrity	②	②	②	②	②	③	③	③
Braking system	②	②	②	②	②	②	②	②
Electrical system	②	②	②	②	②	②	③	③
Engines	③	③	④	④	④	⑤	⑤	⑤
Exhaust/Converter	②	②	②	③	③	③	④	⑤
Fuel system	②	②	③	③	③	③	③	③
Ignition system	③	③	③	③	③	④	④	⑤
Rust/Paint	①	①	②	②	②	②	②	③
Steering	②	②	②	③	③	③	③	⑤
Suspension	②	②	③	③	④	④	④	⑤
Crash Safety	④	④	—	⑤	⑤	⑤	⑤	—
Side Impact	—	—	—	—	—	—	③	—

Crown Victoria, Grand Marquis

Rating: Recommended (1997–99); Above Average (1994–96); Average (1984–93). Overall, these cars aren't as reliable as Japanese luxury vehicles, but they're the best of the domestic crop when it comes to price, power, performance, and overall comfort. Don't waste your money buying a 1998 or 1999 version if you can find a low-mileage 1996. It'll cost much less and give you most of the same features. The Marquis is a slightly more luxurious version that costs more but gives little of consequence for the extra expense. Make sure you check out the headlight illumination. **Maintenance/Repair costs:** Average, but some electronic repairs can be carried out only by Ford dealers. **Parts:** Higher-than-average cost (independent suppliers sell for much less), but not hard to find.

Strengths and weaknesses: These cars are especially suited to people who need lots of room or who prefer the safety blanket provided by road-hugging, gas-guzzling weight. Handling is mediocre, but it's about average for cars this size. Both the 4.6L and 5.0L V8s provide adequate though sometimes sluggish power, with most of their torque found in the lower gear ranges. The fuel pump, sender, fuel filter, and fuel hose assemblies are failure prone. There are many complaints of EEC IV ignition module and fuel cut-off switch malfunctions that cause hard starting and frequent stalling. Brakes (rotors, calipers, and pads), shock absorbers, and springs wear out more quickly than they should. Chronic front suspension noise when passing over small bumps. Inadequate inner fender protection allows road salt to completely cover engine wiring, brake master cylinder, and suspension components; frequent inspection and cleaning is required. Hubcaps frequently fall off. An undercarriage inspection is a prerequisite to buying models year three years or older, since there is such a high number of safety-related complaints concerning brake and fuel lines, suspension, and steering components.

Technical service bulletins: All models: 1995—Delayed transmission engagement and shift errors, loose transmission connector, intermittent loss of torque at 3–4 upshift, irregular or no-torque converter operation, and shifts to Neutral at heavy throttle. • Insufficient AC cooling or excessive clutch end gap. • Water intrusion of the MLP/TR sensor. • A clacking/thumping noise when braking, and brake roughness upon application. • A fuel pump buzz/whine heard through the radio speaker. **1996**—Stalling or hard starts. • Delayed 1–2 shift. • Transmission valve body cross leaks. • Chatter during turns. • Fog/film on windshield/interior glass. • Musty and mildew-type odours. • Right front door window requires much effort to roll up. **1997**—ABS brakes may activate on their own or produce a grinding, pulsing, fluttering effect on the brake pedal. • AC emits musty odour. • Air rush and/or flutter noise from centre register. • Erratic or prolonged 1–2 shift. •

Spark knock during acceleration. • Door latch sticks open. • Driver-side seat cushion is uncomfortable, sags. • Fog/film on windshield/interior glass. • Front door panel crack on rear edge. • Loose catalyst or muffler heat shields. • Wind noise around doors. • Shudder or vibration while in third or fourth gear. • Steering wheel noise or vibration. • Suspension leans to right side. • Axle whine at 100 km/h. **1998**—Hesitation when accelerating and traction control self-activates. • Automatic transmission delayed shift or no 2–3 upshift. • Pull or drift when braking with wet brakes. • Steering wheel vibration or buzzing. Vibration or buzzing caused by a loose catalytic converter or heat shield. • Front windshield buzzing or whistling. • AC musty odours and lack of temperature control. **1998–99**—Rough idle and exhaust system resonance. • Spark knock. • Inadvertent disabling of the brake/shift interlock. • Procedures for correcting brake vibrations and ABS noise. • Dome lamp malfunction. • Headliner sags. • Side door wind noise. • Speaker whining or buzzing. • Noise, vibration, and harshness countermeasures.

Safety summary/Recalls: All models: 1995—A number of fires have been reportedly caused by faulty ignition switches:

> Hi Phil.
> I am e-mailing you from Humboldt Saskatchewan, Canada. My parents were proud own-
> ers of a '95 Grand Marquis. Last Friday (Dec 8/00) at approximately 11:30 pm, it self-
> combusted in their garage. From talking to some mechanic friends, I have learned that
> Ford has a faulty ignition switch, which could have been the cause.

1996—Fire caused by a short in the electrical system. • Airbag failed to deploy. • ABS brake failures. • Engine surges without warning or shuts down when brakes are applied. • Cruise control won't disengage when brakes are applied. • Oil pan/gasket leaks. • Many reports that the left frame bracket broke at weld, causing vehicle to pull sharply to the right when brakes were applied. • Reports of ball joint and lower control arm failures say that the vehicle's front wheel assembly is also affected. • Police department inspectors report their vehicles have shown excessive play in the Pitman arms. • Brake lines are routed too close to the body and chafe excessively. • Brake pedal went to the floor due to failure of the stop switch and clip on pedal. • Frequent replacement of front brake components. • Steering locks up, will not return, or is so loose it won't steer vehicle. • Cracked intake manifolds cause loss of coolant. • Frequent catalytic converter failures. • Inoperative rear window defroster. • Seatbelt buckle doesn't stay latched. • Seatbelts failed to restrain occupants during a collision. **1997**—Fire caused by a faulty fuel line. • Other engine compartment fires reported, cause unknown. • Sudden acceleration due to a design flaw of the throttle linkage and bracket. • Floormats can shift under the gas or brake pedals, causing them to jam. • Vehicle left in Park position with engine on slipped into

Reverse. • Many reports of brake failures caused by brake line rubbing against body components. • Collapsed body mounts allow undercarriage to rub flat spots on steel brake lines, causing brake failure. • Steering wheel lockup while driving. • Front suspension ball joint failure after having recall campaign correction done. • Lower passenger-side control arm fell off when vehicle was in first gear. • Sharp door edges have injured three people. • Engine intake manifold failures that cause anti-freeze to leak into the engine compartment. • Front doors are too large and difficult to manoeuvre around. **1998**—NHTSA investigators are looking into reports that the inertia fuel shutoff switch operates when it shouldn't, stalling the vehicle. • Vehicle caught fire in the engine compartment while parked in garage overnight. • Sudden acceleration after vehicle stalled and was restarted. • Airbags failed to deploy. • Sudden loss of power, stalling. • Traction control engages for no reason, causing loss of power and control. • Steering too sensitive when changing lanes, easy to lose control. • Dome light switch is poorly designed; it can only be activated by the driver due to its location. • Loss of lighting caused by sudden electrical system failure. • Rubber hose leading from the fuel tank is easily hit when going over a bump or pothole. **1998–99**—NHTSA probe of rear axle trailering arm frame mounting. **1999**—Engine compartment fire. • Vehicle suddenly surges forward or backward. • Sudden stalling while underway (fuel inertia cut-off switch self-activates when vehicle hits a pothole or goes over a small bump). • Steering shaft failure when turning. • Cracked rear trailing arm assembly frames. • Transmission jumps from Park into gear. • Premature brake rotor warpage and pad wearout causes excessive brake noise (grinding), vibration, and extended stopping distance. • Sticking front calipers cause vehicle to veer to the right or left. • Premature wear of the lower control arm. • Headlights aren't bright enough. • Loose rear outer door handles. • Driver's seat misalignment places steering wheel and gas/brake pedals too far to the right. **Recalls: All models: 1995**—Fuel could leak from the tank and pose a fire hazard; dealer will replace the fuel-filler pipe seat. • Faulty headlight and power window circuit breakers may unexpectedly turn the headlights off. • Rear seatbelt attachments may be faulty. • Airbag may not inflate properly and the end cap could separate. **1995–96**—Pitman arm corrosion on fleet cars can cause abnormal wear. **1996**—Driver's door may not sustain the specified load when in the secondary latch position. **1996–99**—Prematurely worn ball joint could break, causing loss of steering. **Grand Marquis: 1994**—The metal cylinder that holds the airbag can be projected into the passenger area as the airbag deploys.

Secret Warranties/Service Tips

All models/years—Three components that frequently benefit from Ford "goodwill" warranty extensions are engine head gaskets, automatic transmissions, brakes, and computer modules. **All models: 1993–99**—An exhaust buzz or rattle may mean you have a loose catalyst or muffler heat shield. • Paint delamination, peeling, or fading (see Part Two). **1994–99**—

Tips on preventing wind noise around the doors. **1995–97**—ABS brakes that activate on their own or produce a grinding, pulsing, fluttering effect on the brake pedal probably need upgraded wiring connectors at the ABS sensors. **1995–99**—Tips on reducing noise, vibration, and harshness and plugging windshield water leaks. **1996–97**—Spark knock during acceleration can be silenced by replacing the MAF sensor and reprogramming the power control module. **1996–98**—A steering vibration or buzzing when making right turns can be silenced by replacing the power steering pressure hose. **1997–98**—Lack of AC temperature control may require a new air door actuator. **1997–99**—Delayed upshifts, may require a new 2–3 accumulator along with a revised piston. • A rough idle or exhaust system resonance can be fixed by installing an exhaust system mass damper. **1998–99**—A pull or drift when braking in rainy weather can be corrected by installing upgraded front brake linings that are less sensitive to water, says TSB #98-13-4. • A poorly performing AC that also makes a thumping noise may need a new suction accumulator and suction hose assembly.

Crown Victoria, Grand Marquis Profile

	1992	1993	1994	1995	1996	1997	1998	1999
Cost Price ($)								
Crown S/LTD	22,095	23,195	22,495	24,695	27,195	29,895	30,995	31,895
Grand Marquis GS	23,995	24,595	23,795	26,695	30,295	32,195	32,895	33,695
Used Values ($)								
Crown S/LTD ↑	5,000	5,500	6,500	10,000	11,500	14,500	17,000	19,000
Crown S/LTD ↓	4,000	5,000	6,000	8,000	9,500	13,000	15,000	17,500
Grand Marquis GS ↑	5,500	6,000	8,500	11,000	12,500	16,000	18,000	21,000
Grand Marquis GS ↓	5,000	5,500	7,000	9,500	11,000	14,500	16,500	19,000
Extended Warranty	Y	Y	Y	Y	N	N	N	N
Secret Warranty	Y	Y	Y	Y	Y	Y	Y	Y
Reliability	③	③	③	④	④	④	⑤	⑤
Air conditioning	❷	❷	❷	❷	③	③	③	④
Auto. transmission	❶	❶	❷	❷	❷	❷	④	④
Body integrity	❶	❶	❶	❶	❷	❷	❷	③
Braking system	❶	❶	❶	❶	❷	❷	❷	③
Electrical system	❷	❷	❷	❷	③	③	③	④
Engines	④	④	④	④	④	④	⑤	⑤
Exhaust/Converter	❶	❶	③	③	③	④	⑤	⑤
Fuel system	❷	❷	③	③	③	③	③	④
Ignition system	❷	❷	❷	③	③	③	③	④
Rust/Paint	❷	❷	❷	❷	③	③	③	④
Steering	❷	❷	③	③	③	③	③	④
Suspension	❷	❷	❷	❷	❷	❷	③	③
Crash Safety	⑤	③	③	③	④	⑤	⑤	⑤
Side Impact	④	—	—	—	—	—	④	④

GENERAL MOTORS

Caprice, Impala SS, Roadmaster

Rating: Above Average (1995–96); Average (1994); Not Recommended (1982–93). This group of cars ceased production in 1996. A good alternative would be any rear-drive Buick LeSabre or a Ford Crown Victoria or Grand Marquis. **Maintenance/Repair costs:** Maintenance is inexpensive and easy to perform, plus repairs can be done by any corner garage. **Parts:** Average parts costs can be cut further by shopping at independent suppliers, who are generally well stocked.

Strengths and weaknesses: These cars are large, comfortable, and easy to maintain. The trunk is spacious. Overall handling is acceptable, but expect a queasy ride from the too-soft suspension. Gas mileage is particularly poor. Despite the many generic deficiencies inherent in these rear-drives, they still score higher than GM's front-drives for overall reliability and durability. The Impala SS is basically a Caprice with a 260-hp Corvette engine and high-performance suspension.

On 1988–91 models, engine problems include crankshaft and head gasket failures, cracked cylinder heads, injection pump malfunctions, and oil leaks. Engine knocking is another common problem on early models that's hard to correct inexpensively, due to the various possible causes that have to be eliminated. Early V8s, in particular, suffer from premature camshaft wear, and the 350-cubic-inch V8s often fall prey to premature valve guide wear caused by a faulty EGR valve. Cars equipped with the 5.7L diesel V8 should be approached with caution; they aren't very durable and cost an arm and a leg to troubleshoot and repair. The 4-speed automatic transmission was troublesome until 1991, with burnt-out clutches and malfunctioning torque converters being the most common failures.

The 1991–96 models have elicited few engine and transmission complaints, although they have shown the following deficiencies: chronic AC and ignition glitches; prematurely worn brakes (lots of corrosion damage), steering, and suspension components, especially shock absorbers and rear springs; serious electrical problems; and poor-quality body and trim items.

Body assembly is not impressive, but paint quality and durability is fairly good, considering the delamination one usually finds with GM's other models. Wagons often have excessive rust around cargo-area side windows and wheelwells, and hubcaps on later models tend to fly off.

Safety summary/Recalls: All models: 1994–96—NHTSA probes are looking into reports that coolant in vehicles with heavy-duty cooling systems may leak into the rear of the engine compartment, where it may ignite. **1996**—Child was able to shift gear into Neutral. Jumped out, and was run over. • Airbags failed to deploy. • Airbag light stays lit for no apparent reason. • Gas pedal sticks on initial application. ABS brakes lock up. • Transmission torque converter/engine flywheel breakage. • Broken torque converter bolts. • Steering box loosens despite new bolts. • Steering lockup. • Sometimes vehicle fishtails uncontrollably while at moderate speed. • Front coil spring failure. • Premature tire wear caused by faulty suspension components that can't be fixed by repeated alignments. • Fuel pump failure caused by wiring harness short. Faulty Uniroyal Agua Grip tires (steel wires sticking out). **Recalls: All models: 1985**—Leaking fuel feed and return pipe may cause a fire. • Cars equipped with a 4.3L engine could have a battery-cable short, which creates a fire hazard. **1985–88**—Faulty cruise control could lead to sudden acceleration. **1987**—Cars equipped with 200-4R automatic transmissions could start in gear or engage the wrong gear. **1989**—GM will inspect and replace the AC condenser inlet pipe. **1991**—Seatbelts malfunction because of defective shoulder belt guide loop. **1991–92**—Rear seatbelts that are uncomfortable will be changed for free by GM. • Corrosion could prevent the hood from latching properly, making it hard to open or causing it to fly open. **1992**—A rattling front door lock rod can be silenced by installing a corrective kit (#10222731). **1994**—A leaking oil cooler inlet hose is a fire hazard. • Fractured wheel studs may allow the wheel to separate from the car. • Faulty fuel tank strap fasteners. **1994–95**—Accelerator pedal may stick. **Roadmaster, Caprice: 1995–96**—Loose wheel lug nuts could cause the wheel to fall off.

Secret Warranties/Service Tips

All models/years—A rotten-egg odour coming from the exhaust is usually the result of a malfunctioning catalytic converter possibly covered by the emissions warranty. **All models: 1982–91**—Hydramatic 4L60/700R4 automatic transmission may have no upshift or appear to be stuck in first gear. The probable cause is a worn governor gear. It would be wise to replace the retaining ring as well. **1982–93**—Vehicles equipped with a Hydramatic 4L60 transmission that buzzes when the car is in Reverse or at idle may need a new oil pressure regulator valve. **1987–91**—A bulletin lists the different types of tailpipe smoke signals that alert you to the need for different repairs: cars with V8 engines that emit blue or bluish-white smoke may require a valve seal kit (#12511890); models with port fuel-injection that emit black smoke after long starter cranks may have fuel leaking into the engine from the injectors; models with throttle body injection and port fuel-injection that emit white or bluish smoke and have normal oil consumption likely have poor sealing between the intake manifold joint and the cylinder head. **1989–91**—If the transmission won't go into Reverse or is slow to shift into Reverse, GM suggests that the Reverse input clutch housing be changed. **1991**—A poor-running 5.0L engine may require an EGR valve kit and PCV valve in addition to a new PROM. **1993–96**—Paint delamination, peeling, or fading (see Part Two). **1994**—Excessive oil consumption is likely due to delaminated intake manifold gaskets. Install an upgraded intake manifold gasket kit. • GM campaign 94C15 will adjust at no charge a misadjusted automatic transmission shift linkage that could, if left alone, burn out the Low/Reverse clutch. **1994–96**—Excessive engine noise can be silenced by installing an upgraded valve stem oil seal. • A chuggle or surge condition in vehicles with a with 5.7L engine will require a reflash calibration. **Roadmaster: 1991**—If the starter makes a grinding noise or won't engage the engine, the fault could be a weak starter spring. • Front doors that won't stay open on an incline or are hard to open need an improved hold-open door spring. **1992**—Water leaks into the trunk from the fixed mast antenna; install an upgraded antenna base (#25610633) and bezel (#25609129). • If the front seat doesn't have enough upward travel, GM has a special kit (#12520796) to raise it. • A chuggle or shudder at 44 mph (70 km/h) on vehicles equipped with a 5.7L engine may be corrected by installing a new torque converter assembly. **1994**—Excessive oil consumption is likely due to delaminated intake manifold gaskets. Install an upgraded intake manifold gasket kit. • Poor AC performance can be improved by replacing the temperature control cable. • Delayed automatic transmission shift engagement is a common problem addressed in TSB #47-71-20A. **1995–96**—Delayed automatic transmission shift engagement may require the replacement of the pump cover assembly.

Caprice, Impala SS, Roadmaster Profile

	1990	1991	1992	1993	1994	1995	1996
Cost Price ($)							
Caprice	20,128	19,698	20,298	20,806	22,500	25,455	28,345
Caprice wagon	21,347	20,398	21,598	22,138	24,985	29,120	30,980
Impala SS	—	—	—	—	—	29,005	30,675
Roadmaster	—	—	25,398	26,298	29,798	32,930	34,230
Used Values ($)							
Caprice ↑	3,500	5,000	6,000	7,000	8,500	10,500	12,500
Caprice ↓	3,000	4,000	5,000	6,000	7,500	8,500	11,000
Caprice wagon ↑	4,500	5,500	6,500	7,500	9,000	11,000	13,000
Caprice wagon ↓	4,000	4,500	5,000	6,500	8,000	9,000	11,000
Impala SS ↑	—	—	—	—	—	14,500	17,500
Impala SS ↓	—	—	—	—	—	12,000	16,000
Roadmaster ↑	—	—	5,000	6,500	9,000	12,000	15,000
Roadmaster ↓	—	—	4,000	4,500	6,500	9,500	12,500
Extended Warranty	Y	Y	Y	Y	N	N	N
Secret Warranty	Y	Y	Y	Y	Y	Y	Y
Reliability	②	②	②	②	③	③	③
Air conditioning	②	②	②	②	②	③	④
Auto. transmission	②	③	③	③	③	④	④
Body integrity	②	②	②	②	②	③	③
Braking system	②	②	②	②	②	②	③
Electrical system	②	②	②	②	②	②	③
Engines	③	③	③	③	③	④	④
Exhaust/Converter	②	②	②	②	③	④	④

Fuel system	③	③	③	③	③	③	③
Ignition system	❷	❷	❷	❷	❷	❷	③
Rust/Paint	❷	❷	❷	❷	❷	③	③
Steering	❷	❷	❷	❷	③	④	④
Suspension	❷	❷	❷	③	③	④	④
Crash Safety							
Caprice	—	④	④	④	④	④	④

LUXURY CARS

Used luxury cars can be great buys—if you know how to separate the wheat from the chaff. These high-end cars project a flashy image and come loaded with high-tech safety, performance, and comfort features. They can be bought, after three years or so, for half of what they sold for new. Furthermore, if you can get servicing and parts from independent garages, you'll save even more. On the downside, there *are* overpriced luxury lemons out there with unreliable, hard-to-service electronics and servicing costs that rival Neiman-Marcus.

And do remember this: spending more on a luxury car doesn't always mean you'll get a safer vehicle, as thousands of Cadillac owners, with airbags exploding whenever the carpet gets wet, will confirm. See "Safety summary/Recalls" for more sorry facts about General Motors and Ford safety-related failures.

Traditionally, the luxury-car niche has been dominated by American and German automakers. During the past decade, however, buyers have gravitated towards Japanese models. This shift in buyer preference has forced Chrysler out of the market and made Ford and GM adopt down-sized front-drives. Despite these moves to better respond to buyers' preferences, American luxury cars are still seen by most consumers as overweight and unreliable land yachts.

Okay, so you're well-advised to choose a Japanese model, but doesn't that mean you'll have to dig deep in your wallet, wiping out most of your expected savings? Not necessarily. You don't always have to spend big bucks to get true luxury and ironclad reliability. Smart buyers can target the fully equipped Toyota Camry or Avalon, Honda Accord, Nissan Maxima, and Mazda 929, all of which offer the same equipment, reliability, and performance as Lexus, Infiniti, and Acura models, but for much, much less.

It's sad but true. There aren't any American luxury cars that can match an equivalent Japanese or German model for overall reliability, durability, and value. And this isn't because German or Japanese products are that well made; far from it, as anyone who's purchased a quirky Saab 9000 or a transmission-challenged Lexus will attest. No, it's simply because GM, Ford, and Chrysler's vehicles are so poorly made that they make everyone else look better. This fact is reflected in the head-spinningly high depreciation rates and plummeting market share seen with most large-*cum*-luxury cars put out by the Big Three. Ford's rear-drive Crown Victoria, Grand Marquis, and Lincoln Town Car come closest to meeting the imports in overall reliability and durability, yet, they still come nowhere near the quality level of many *entry-level* imports. Examples of lousy American luxury cars abound: the Chrysler front-drive New Yorker and LHS are unremarkable and are plagued by serious powertrain reliability problems; GM's Cadillacs have been

295

characterized by innovative, albeit unreliable, technology like variable-cylinder engines (the 4-6-8 engine), cobbled-together diesel power-plants, and poorly-engineered, high-maintenance, low-quality, front-drive components. Only Ford, with its aforementioned luxury rear-drives has presented any credible competition. And now with the dropping of the Lincoln Town Car, and the Crown Victoria reserved solely for fleet sales, it's just a matter of time before it is taken out of the running.

What does this foretell for the future of used luxury cars? Firstly, fewer cars will be available due to the mergers between American, Japanese, and European automakers. Also, entire automotive divisions will be axed (Oldsmobile, Mercury, and Plymouth) and we'll pay higher prices because of less competition. Finally, we'll likely see the renaissance of rear-drives, with Cadillac and Ford leading the parade.

Recommended

BMW 5 Series (1992–99)
BMW M3 (1997–99)
BMW Z3 (1996–99)
Lexus ES 300, GS 300,
  LS 400, SC 400 (1996–99)

Mercedes-Benz 300 Series, 400
  Series, 500 Series, E-Class
  (1993–99)
Nissan Maxima (1996–99)
Volvo 850 Series (1995–97)

Above Average

Acura RL (1996–99)
Acura TL (1996–99)
Audi 90, A4, A6 (100), A8, S6
  (1995–99)
BMW 3 Series (1995–99)
Ford/Lincoln Mark VII, Mark
  VIII (1995–98)
Ford/Lincoln Town Car
  (1995–99)
GM/Cadillac Brougham,
  Fleetwood RWD (1993–96)
  (1993–99)
Infiniti G20, I30, J30, Q45
  (1995–99)

Lexus ES 300, GS 300, LS 400,
  SC 400 (1990–95)
Mazda Millenia (1995–99)
Mercedes-Benz 300 Series,
  400 Series, 500 Series,
  E-Class (1992)
Mercedes-Benz C-Class
  (1995–99)
Nissan Maxima (1989–95)
Toyota Avalon (1995–99)
Volvo 850 series, 70 series
Volvo 900 series, 90 series, S80
  (1989–96)

Average

BMW 3 Series (1994)
BMW 5 Series (1985–91)
Ford/Lincoln Mark VII, Mark
  VIII (1994)
Ford/Lincoln Town Car
  (1988–94)
GM 98 Regency, Park

GM/Cadillac Brougham,
  Fleetwood RWD (1984–92)
  (1997–99)
GM Concours, DeVille,
  Fleetwood front-drives (1995–99)
Infiniti G20, I30, J30, Q45
  (1991–94)

Avenue (1997–99)
GM Aurora, Riviera, Toronado,
  Trofeo (1995–99)

Mercedes-Benz C-Class (1994)
Nissan Maxima (1986–88)
Saab 900, 9000 (1998–99)
Volvo 900 series, 90 series, S80

Below Average

BMW 3 Series (1984–93)
Ford/Lincoln Continental
  (1988–98)
Ford/Lincoln Mark VII, Mark
  VIII (1986–93)
GM 98 Regency, Park
  Avenue (1991–96)

GM/Cadillac Allanté, Catera,
  Eldorado, Seville (1992–99)
GM Concours, DeVille,
  Fleetwood front-drives (1985–94)
Mercedes-Benz 300 Series,
  400 Series, 500 Series
  E-Class (1985–91)
Saab 900, 9000 (1995–97)

Not Recommended

Acura Legend (1986–88)
Audi 90, A4, A6 (100), A8, S6
  (1984–94)
GM 98 Regency, Park
  Avenue (1985–90)
GM/Cadillac Allanté, Catera,
  Eldorado, Seville (1986–91)

GM Riviera, Toronado,
  Trofeo (1986–93)
Mercedes-Benz 190 Series
  (1984–93)
Saab 900, 9000 (1985–94)

ACURA

RL

Rating: Above Average (1996–99). The RL is basically a fully-loaded, longer, wider, and heavier TL, equipped with a larger engine that produces less horsepower than its smaller brother. Resale value is high on all Acura models. Also consider BMW's 5 Series, Infiniti's redesigned I30, and the Lexus GS 300/400. You may want to take a look at the TL sedan: it's not as expensive, and is a better performer, though passenger room is more limited. **Maintenance/Repair costs:** Average, and most repairs are dealer dependent. **Parts:** Most mechanical and electronic components are easily found and moderately priced. Some reports indicate that recall repairs are often delayed because corrected parts aren't available (transmission/transfer case, for example). Body parts may be hard to come by and can be expensive.

Strengths and weaknesses: Strong points: Good acceleration that's smooth and quiet in all gear ranges, exceptional steering and handling, comfortable ride, top-quality body and mechanical components, and it's loaded with goodies. Weak points: Numb steering and problematic navigation system controls.

The 3.5 RL is Honda's—Oh, I mean, Acura's!—flagship sedan. It's loaded with all the innovative high-tech safety and convenience features one would expect to find in a luxury car. These include heated front seats, front and rear climate controls, rear-seat trunk pass-through, Xenon headlights (get used to oncoming drivers flashing you their headlights), "smart" side airbags, ABS, traction control, and an anti-skid system. No engine other than the 3.5L is available. The only option offered is Acura's ubiquitous GPS navigation system, which is tough to read, hard to calibrate, and subject to malfunction. Invest in maps instead.

The 3.5L 210-hp V6 mated to a 4-speed automatic transmission provides good acceleration that's a bit slower and more fuel-thirsty than the TL, due partly to the RL's extra pounds. Power is nevertheless delivered in a smooth and quiet manner. The car handles nicely, with a less firm ride than the TL, although steering response doesn't feel as crisp. Interior accommodation for four occupants is excellent up front and in the rear, due to the RL's use of a larger platform than the TL. All seats are well-cushioned and give plenty of thigh support. Cockpit controls and instruments are easily accessed and the climate control system is both efficient and easy to adjust, both fore and aft. Good all-around visibility; however, the optional navigation system is annoyingly distracting and not easily mastered.

Crash tests give four stars for driver and passenger crash protection in a frontal collision. On the other hand, head restraints are given a "marginal" rating by IIHS; overall insurance claim rate is average for models in this category.

Owner-reported problems: The only areas that have proved troublesome in the past have been malfunctioning accessories and premature brake wear. Service bulletin problems: moon roof rattle, driver's seat squeaks, steering wheel may be off-centre, and damaged paint.

Safety summary/Recalls: All models: It's interesting to note that the RL has had remarkable few complaints registered by NHTSA. Short-statured drivers should be wary of the Acura airbag's tendency to deploy in fender-benders; severe injury or death may ensue. **1996—**Airbags failed to deploy in a collision. **1998—**Premature wearout of the front and rear brake pads around 15,000 miles (24,000 km). **1999—**ABS failed to respond, resulting in rear-end collision. **Recalls: All models: 1997–98—**Ball joint may wear out prematurely, causing front suspension to collapse. **1999—**Driver's seatbelt buckle may be faulty.

Secret Warranties/Service Tips

All models/years—Like Honda's, most of Acura's TSBs allow for special warranty consideration on a "goodwill" basis even after the warranty has expired or the car has changed hands. Referring to this euphemism will increase your chances of getting some kind of refund for repairs that are obviously factory defects. • Seatbelts that fail to function properly during normal use will be replaced for free under the company's lifetime seatbelt warranty. • Diagnostic procedures and correction for off-centre steering wheels. **All models: 1996**—Rapid rear brake pad wear can be corrected by installing upgraded pads (eligible for "goodwill"). • Moon roof wind noise can be corrected by replacing the visor clips and mounting hardware. • If the driver's seatback piping wears out prematurely, Acura suggests it be replaced. **1996–97**—Details of Acura's 14-year free engine repairs/tuneups agreement with the the U.S. Environmental Protection Agency (EPA). • Front window wind noise can be reduced by aligning the glass and sash. • Window noise during operation can be silenced by replacing the glass stabilizers and sashes and the glass, if it's scratched (eligible for "goodwill"). • Drivers who find the footrest is positioned too far away may obtain a replacement footrest from Acura. **1996–98**—A growling or whining coming from the rear wheels can be fixed by replacing the hub bearing unit. Brake squeal during light application can be fixed by replacing the front pads (eligible for "goodwill"). **1996–2000**—Moon roof rattles can be silenced by replacing the moon roof glass. **1999**—A navigation system that locks up or resets can be corrected by rewriting the units software; a remanufactured unit may also be considered. **1999–2000**—A squeaking, creaking driver's seat is addressed in TSB #00-010.

RL Profile				
	1996	**1997**	**1998**	**1999**
Cost Price ($)				
Base	52,300	54,600	55,000	52,000
Used Values ($)				
Base ↑	21,500	26,500	32,000	37,000
Base ↓	18,500	23,500	30,000	34,000
Extended Warranty	N	N	N	N
Secret Warranty	Y	Y	Y	Y
Reliability	④	④	⑤	⑤
Crash Safety	—	—	—	④

TL

Rating: Above Average (1996–99). Resale value is high on all Acura models. **Maintenance/Repair costs:** Higher than average, and most repairs are dealer dependent. Consider the Audi A4, BMW's redesigned 3-Series, Infiniti's redesigned I30, and the Lexus ES 300. You may want to take a look at the CL coupe: it's not as expensive, and is as close as you can get to the Accord, with lots of standard bells and whistles thrown in. Don't pay extra for the satellite navigation system; it's confusing to calibrate and hard to see. **Parts:** Higher-than-average cost (some independent suppliers sell for much less under the Honda name), but not hard to find.

Strengths and weaknesses: Strong points: Accelerates impressively, handles well, rides comfortably, and is well put together with quality mechanical and body components. Weak points: Suspension that may be too firm for some, uncomfortable rear seating, excessive road noise, and problematic navigation system controls.

Filling the void left by the discontinued Vigor, the 3.2 TL combines luxury and performance in a nicely styled front-drive five-passenger sedan that uses the same chassis as the Accord and CL coupe. The only engine available, a 3.2L 225-hp V6 mated to a 4-speed automatic transmission, provides impressive acceleration (0–100 km/h in just over 8 seconds) in a smooth and quiet manner. Handling is exceptional with the firm suspension, and responsive, precise steering makes it easy to toss the TL around turns without losing control. Bumps can be a bit jarring, though, but this is a small price to pay for the car's high-speed stability.

Interior accommodations are better than average up front, but rear occupants may discover that leg room is a bit tight and the seat cushions lack sufficient thigh support. The cockpit layout is very user-friendly due in part to the easy-to-read gauges and accessible controls (far-away climate controls, the only exception). Visibility fore and aft is unobstructed; however, the optional navigation system is best avoided (see comments in RL).

Standard safety features include ABS, traction control, childproof door locks, three-point seatbelts, and a transmission/brake interlock. Crash tests give four stars for driver and passenger crash protection in a frontal collision. On the other hand, head restraints are given a "poor" rating by IIHS. The overall insurance claim rate is average for other models in this category, but higher than average for the TL.

The only areas that have proved troublesome in the past have been poor body fits, malfunctioning accessories, and premature brake wear. Owners point out that the window regulator may need replacing, ignition switch buzzes, trunk lock jams, and the rear bumper is often loose.

Safety summary/Recalls: Short-statured drivers should be wary of Acura airbag fender-bender deployments; severe injury or death may ensue. **All models: 1996**—Both airbags suddenly deployed for no reason while vehicle was underway. • Driveline whines upon acceleration. • Rear brake failure; brakes are frequently in need of repair. • Prematurely worn rear brake pads. • Passenger side window suddenly shattered. **1997**—Several incidents where car suddenly accelerated. • Chronic stalling as vehicle decelerates. • Steering column fire. • Complete brake loss. • Bridgestone tire side wall bulge. • Horn is difficult to locate in emergency situations. • Check Engine light comes on often. **1998**—Too-small horn buttons are poorly designed. **1999**— Airbags deployed in a collision and severely burned driver's hands. • Seatbelt failed to retract in a collision, allowing driver to hit windshield. • Transmission fails to downshift or upshift. • Front rotors warp within 10,000 miles (16,000 km). • Door locks operate erratically. • Wiper blades leak graphite, smearing windshield. • Instrument panel is washed out in sunlight; odometer is practically invisible. **Recalls: All models: 1996–98**—Automatic transmission sealing bolt may fall out, causing the extension shaft to disconnect from the differential. **1997–98**—Ball joint may wear out prematurely, causing the front suspension to collapse.

Secret Warranties/Service Tips

All models/years—Like Honda's, most of Acura's TSBs allow for special warranty consideration on a "goodwill" basis even after the warranty has expired or the car has changed hands. Referring to this euphemism will increase your chances of getting some kind of refund for repairs that are obviously factory defects. • Seatbelts that fail to function properly during normal use will be replaced for free under the company's lifetime seatbelt warranty. • Diagnostic procedures and correction for off-centre steering wheels. **All models: 1996**—Rapid rear brake pad wear can be corrected by installing upgraded pads (eligible for "goodwill"). • Moon roof wind noise can be corrected by replacing the visor clips and mounting hardware. • If the driver's seatback piping wears out prematurely, Acura suggests it be replaced. **1996–97**—Details of Acura's 14-year free engine repairs/tuneups agreement with the U.S. Environmental Protection Agency (EPA). • Front window wind noise can be reduced by aligning the glass and sash. • Window noise during operation can be silenced by replacing the glass stabilizers and sashes and the glass, if it's scratched (eligible for "goodwill"). • Drivers who find the footrest is positioned too far away may obtain a replacement footrest from Acura. **1996–98**—A growling or whining coming from the rear wheels can be fixed by replacing the hub bearing unit. **1996–98**—Brake squeal during light application can be fixed by replacing the front pads (eligible for "goodwill"). **1999**—A navigation system that locks up or resets can be corrected by rewriting the units software; a remanufactured unit may also be considered. **1999–2000**—A squeaking, creaking driver's seat is addressed in TSB #00-014. A wrinkled rear door sash trim will be covered under a "goodwill" policy, even if correction was done by an independent bodyshop.

TL Profile

	1996	1997	1998	1999
Cost Price ($)				
Base	34,900	36,600	37,000	35,001
Used Values ($)				
Base ↑	14,500	18,000	20,000	26,000
Base ↓	12,500	15,500	18,000	24,000
Extended Warranty	N	N	N	N
Secret Warranty	Y	Y	Y	Y
Reliability	④	④	④	⑤

AUDI

90, A4, A6 (100), A8, S6

Rating: Above Average (1995–99); Not Recommended (1984–94).
Maintenance/Repair costs: Higher than average, and almost all repairs
have to be done by an Audi dealer. **Parts:** Way-higher-than-average cost,
and independent suppliers have a hard time finding parts. Don't even
think about buying one of these front-drives without a three- to five-
year supplementary warranty backed by Audi.

Strengths and weaknesses: These cars are attractively styled, handle well,
are comfortable to drive, and provide a spacious interior. Yet the pre-
1993 models, including the old 90 and 100, have a worse-than-average
reliability record and are plagued by mechanical and electrical components that don't stand up to the rigors of driving in cold climates.
Furthermore, it seems that Audi has written off these failure-prone cars
in favour of the better built and more recent A4 and A6 models. The
dealer body isn't strong enough to adequately service all of these vehicles when things go wrong, so owners of older models are generally left
to independent garages to serve their needs. Premium fuel is required
for vehicles equipped with the 6-cylinder engine. Airbags became a
standard feature during the 1994 model year.

The 1995 and later models are the pick of the Audi litter (when all-
wheel-drive became an optional feature on all entry-level models).
These cars substantially improved upon the cars they replaced. The A6,
the reincarnation of the 100 Series, is packed with standard features,
and is a comfortable, spacious, front-drive or all-wheel-drive luxury
sedan that comes with dual airbags and ABS. It uses the same V6 powerplant as the A4, its smaller sibling, but has 47 additional horses.
Unfortunately, the engine is no match for the car's size (0–100 km/h
in 13 seconds) and steering and handling is decidedly truck-like. The

A8, the first luxury car with an all-aluminum body, competes with the BMW 7 Series and the Mercedes S-Class. Equipped with a WHO 174-hp 2.8L V6 or a 300-hp V8, the A8 is an above-average buy. Its only drawbacks: high price, steering is a bit imprecise for an Audi, and its aluminum body can only be repaired by an Audi dealer.

The S6 is a solid performer with its turbocharged 227-hp 2.2L 5-cylinder engine. Its reliability is better than average and its sports performance leaves the A6 in the dust. The S6 is equipped with sports suspension, a turbocharger, and four-wheel-drive. It was joined by the S4, a limited-production, high-performance spin-off that carries a 227-hp turbocharged rendition of the old 5-cylinder powerplant.

These alphabetically named cars are conservatively styled, slow off the mark (in spite of the V6 addition when hooked to an automatic), and plagued by electrical glitches. The 4-speed automatic shifts erratically (delayed and abrupt engagement) and the 2.8L V6 engine needs full throttle for adequate performance. Handling is acceptable, but the ride is a bit firm and the car still exhibits considerable body roll, brake dive, and acceleration squat when pushed. Handling is on a par with the BMW 300 Series and acceleration times beat out those of the Mercedes. The AWD is extended to entry-level models at a time when most automakers are dropping the option on passenger cars.

Overall quality control has really improved during the past several years, with fewer body, brake, and electrical glitches than exhibited by previous models. A perusal of 1996–99 internal service bulletins shows a dramatic improvement in quality control over earlier versions.

90

The 90 has appeared in various incarnations over the years. Launched in 1988, these entry-level Audis share the same wheelbase and front-drive and 4X4 components. Equipped with an efficient but wimpy 4-cylinder (dropped in 1991) or the more powerful 2.3L 5-cylinder engine, four-wheel disc brakes, and galvanized body panels, these small sedans are leagues ahead of Audi's mid-1980s vehicles. The 1991 models are clearly a better choice; they use an improved 4-speed automatic transmission hooked up to a more powerful engine. 1992 was basically a carry-over year in which unsold 1991 models were recycled. Audi's first convertible, the Cabriolet, first appeared in 1994. It's essentially a 90 model set on a shorter wheelbase with a standard automatic transmission. The 90 was redesigned in 1995 (replacing both the 80 and the old 90) as the Sport 90, a stylish, sporty version that was more show than go—it was dropped shortly thereafter. Common problems include AC, electrical system, and brake malfunctions.

Technical service bulletins: All models: 1995—Oil leakage from the rear and upper engine. • Coolant circulation pump leakage. • Delayed first- and second-gear shift. • A malfunctioning climate control. • Inaccurate fuel gauge and temperature gauges. • Door lock key bind-

ing. • Skipping wiper blades. **1996**—ABS light comes on inadvertently.
• Front speaker buzzing. • Cruise control won't maintain set speed. •
Delayed 1–2 shift on cold-start warm-up. • Inaccurate Delta Bose radio
display. • Friction noise from front and rear door seals. • Fuel gauge
doesn't register full. • Carbon buildup in the intake valve and combustion chamber. • Exhaust popping and rasping noise. • Radio volume
goes to maximum when adjusted. • Binding rear ashtray lid. • Rear differential noise and vibration while driving. • Loose rear reading light.
• Tachometer sticking and erratic AC display. **1997**—False ABS light
warning. • Delayed 1–2 shift on cold-start warm-up. • Friction noise from
front and rear door seals. • Rasping noise from exhaust. **100: 1992–94**—
Quirky AC systems that often malfunction and have to be constantly
readjusted. The fresh air fan will also misbehave, suddenly going into
high-speed operation for no reason. **1993**—Misaligned deck lids that are
hard to close. • Noisy steering column and squeaking and rattling coming from the front seats and inside the B-pillar. • Excessive wind noise
because of poor window sealing. • Smearing, chattering wiper blades.

Safety summary/Recalls: A4: 1997–2000—NHTSA probe of degraded
breaking in wet weather. **A6 sedan: 1998–99**—During refueling, gasoline spits back violently from the filler pipe. **100, S4, A6, S6: 1992–95**—
NHTSA is looking into complaints of foul gasoline line leaks. **Recalls:
100: 1992**—Audi will modify the brake vacuum booster system to
improve brake pedal assist. **A4: 1996**—A fuel gauge that won't register
full signals a short circuit. • Inoperative horn is due to insufficient electrical ground contact. **1997–98**—Dealer will install a retaining ring to
hold the air screen in place. **90 (V6-equipped Cabriolets), 100:
1993–95**—Leaky fuel-injectors will be replaced, free of charge. **90, A6
(100): 1994–96**—Defective ignition switches will cause malfunctioning
turn signals, windshield wipers, lights, power windows, and air conditioners. **90, A4, A6: 1995–96**—If the cruise control won't maintain
speed, add additional vacuum or change the vacuum servo unit.
1995–97—Static electricity can set off driver airbag.

Secret Warranties/Service Tips

All models/years—Defective catalytic converters that cause a rotten-egg
smell may be replaced free of charge under the emissions warranty. **A4:
1996–99**—Audi will install upgraded front brakes on a case-by-case basis to
"fix" problems related to premature corrosion (*Automotive News,* February
8, 1999). **A4, A6, S6: 1995–97**—Delayed 1–2 shift on cold-start warm-ups is
a normal condition resulting from the emissions control settings, according to Audi. **A4, A6: 1998–2000**—Diagnostic and repair procedures for disc
brake squeal, an engine that will crank but not start, and engine misfires.
1999—AC doesn't provide enough cooling. • Tips to silence rear window
creaking or popping.

90, A4, A6 (100), A8, S6 Profile

	1992	1993	1994	1995	1996	1997	1998	1999
Cost Price ($)								
90	—	28,450	—	—	—	—	—	
4X4, Sport	—	38,750	35,250	38,750	—	—	—	—
A4	—	—	—	—	36,250	31,600	32,700	
A6 (100)	—	37,600	48,250	47,480	48,904	49,270	48,800	
A8	—	—	—	—	—	89,850	90,540	
S6	—	—	—	59,900	61,400	63,550	—	—
Used Values ($)								
90 ↑	—	5,500	—	—	—	—	—	—
90 ↓	—	4,000	—	—	—	—	—	—
4X4, Sport ↑	—	7,000	8,500	12,500	—	—	—	—
4X4, Sport ↓	—	5,500	7,000	11,000	—	—	—	—
A4 ↑	—	—	—	—	14,000	17,500	21,000	24,000
A4 ↓	—	—	—	—	12,000	15,000	18,500	21,500
A6 (100)↑	—	7,500	10,500	16,500	20,000	26,000	31,000	36,000
A6 (100)↓	—	5,500	8,500	14,000	17,000	23,000	28,000	34,000
A8 ↑	—	—	—	—	—	42,000	53,000	60,000
A8 ↓	—	—	—	—	—	39,000	49,000	56,000
S6 ↑	—	—	—	21,000	22,500	32,000	—	—
S6 ↓	—	—	—	17,500	21,000	29,000	—	—
Extended Warranty	Y	Y	Y	Y	Y	Y	Y	Y
Secret Warranty	N	N	N	N	Y	Y	Y	Y
Reliability	❶	❶	❷	❷	③	④	④	④
Air conditioning	❶	❶	❶	❶	❷	❷	❷	③
Auto. transmission	❷	❷	④	④	④	⑤	⑤	⑤
Body integrity	④	④	④	④	④	④	④	④
Braking system	❷	❷	❷	❶	❷	❷	❷	③
Electrical system	❶	❶	❶	❶	❶	❷	❷	③
Engines	❶	❶	❶	❷	③	③	③	④
Exhaust/Converter	❷	❷	❷	❶	④	⑤	⑤	⑤
Fuel system	❶	❷	❷	③	④	④	④	④
Ignition system	❷	❷	❷	❶	③	③	③	③
Rust/Paint	❷	❶	④	④	④	④	④	④
Steering	❷	❷	③	③	③	③	③	④
Suspension	❷	③	③	③	③	③	③	③
Crash Safety								
A4	—	—	—	—	④	④	—	—
A6 (100)	—	—	—	—	⑤	⑤	⑤	—
A8	—	—	—	—	—	—	⑤	⑤

BMW

3 Series, 5 Series, M3, Z3

Rating: 3 Series: Above Average (1995–99); Average (1994); Below Average (1984–93). **5 Series:** Recommended (1992–99; there was no 1996 version); Average (1985–91). **M3:** Recommended (1997–99). **Z3:** Recommended (1996–99). These cars come with a reputation that far exceeds what they actually deliver. Don't take my word for it; look at the BMW Lemon website at *www.bmwlemon.com.* Pre-'94 prices drop dramatically, making these years the bargain buys of the 3 Series group. **Maintenance/Repair costs:** Higher than average, but many repairs can be done by independents who specialize in BMW repairs. Unfortunately, the specialists are concentrated around large urban areas. **Parts:** Higher-than-average cost, and often back-ordered.

Strengths and weaknesses: These vehicles exhibit great 6-cylinder performance with the manual gearbox, and ride and handling are commendable. The 318's small engine is seriously compromised, however, by an automatic transmission. The 325e is more pleasant to drive and delivers lots of low-end torque. The 4-cylinder engines that first appeared on the 1991 models aren't well suited to the demands of the automatic gearbox. Through 1998, rear passenger and cargo room is limited.

BMW's Z3 roadster arrived on the scene for the 1996 model year (an optional 2.8L engine was added in 1997) and was followed a year later by the M3, a high-performance coupe equipped with a potent 240-hp, 3.0L engine, a manual shifter, firmer suspension, and 17-inch tires. Although the M3 debuted in the States in the spring of 1994, it arrived in Canada for the 1997 model year, when a four-door version was offered for the first time.

Overall reliability has been very poor with early Bimmers, but has improved of late. Nevertheless, whenever a problem does arise, repair costs are particularly high due to the small number of dealers, the relative scarcity of parts, and the acquiescence of affluent owners.

The electrical system is the source of most complaints. The automatic transmission isn't durable and front brakes require frequent attention. Owners also report chronic surging at idle and a rotten-egg smell from the exhaust (all models/years). Door seams, rocker panels, rear-wheel openings, and fender seams are particularly prone to rust. Early BMWs were poorly rustproofed and deteriorated very quickly, especially along the door bottoms and within the front and rear wheelwells. Check the muffler bracket for premature wear, and weather seals and door adjustments for leaks.

Models after 1991 provide peppy 4-cylinder acceleration only with high revs and a manual transmission. Keep in mind that city driving requires lots of manual gear shifting characterized by an abrupt clutch. If you must have an automatic, look for a used model with the 6-cylinder engine. The larger 1.9L 4-cylinder that went into the mid-'96 models doesn't boost performance appreciably.

Although the 1997 models came with traction control, it is not very effective in giving these vehicles acceptable wet pavement traction. A problem since the early '90s, the rear end tends to slip sideways when the roadway is wet (much like Ford's rear-drive Mustang).

In 1998 the 3 Series models, called the 323, were given a 2.5L inline-six, which had been standard on 1992–95 models, and standard side airbags. The '99 models were revamped with a better-performing 2.5L base engine and 2.8L six, and a more refined transmission and chassis. Nevertheless, handling is still tricky on wet roads, despite the ASC+T traction control. Rear seat access is problematic, rear passenger space is limited, and styling is the essence of bland.

There is no problem with rear seat or cargo room with the 5 Series Bimmer. Handling and ride are superb, although these weighty upscale models do strain when going over hilly terrain if they have the automatic gearbox.

5 Series owners report numerous electrical and fuel glitches, faulty turn signal indicators, starter failures, self-activating emergency flashers, rotten-egg odours from the exhaust, and excessive steering-wheel/brake vibration.

Technical service bulletins: 3 Series: 1995—Excessive brake squealing. • Insufficient interior air distribution. • Leaking door contact switches; binding air-distribution knobs; and noisy, ineffective wipers. **1996–97**— AC evaporator ices up. • ABS warning light glows for no reason. • CD skips when road surface is rough. • Delayed gear engagement or adapter case leak. • Electrical troubleshooting tips. • Electronic mobilizer malfunctions. • False alarms caused by glass breakage sensor. • General module malfunctions. • Noise from AC expansion valve on 318ti. • Noise from AC compressor area. • Sun visor pops out of clip. • Sunroof fails to close. • Transmission shudders. • Whistle noise when cooling fan runs on high speed. • Wind noise troubleshooting tips. **1998**—No start caused by faulty oil level sensor. **1999**—Hard or no shift. • Transmission clunk noise. • Inoperative cruise control. • Poor AM reception. **5 Series: 1995**—AC belt tensioner noise. • Leaking door contact switches. • Faulty trunk lock actuator. • Noisy, ineffective wipers. **528, 540: 1997**—Brakes momentarily won't release. • CD skips when road surface is rough. • Electronic mobilizer malfunctions. • Glove-box lock broken. • Radio with DSP switches off intermittently. • Right front door won't lock. • Wind noise troubleshooting tips. **1998**— No-start caused by faulty oil level sensor.

Safety summary/Recalls: 318: 1995—During an accident, the driver-side seatbelt and airbags failed to operate as they should. • Other reports of airbags not deploying. • Sudden steering lockup. • AC expansion valve failures. • Noisy exhaust manifold. • Erratic automatic-transmission

---

---

shifting: hesitation and jerky shifts. • Transmission slips when accelerating, causing vehicle to stall. • Clutch pressure plate failures. • Electrical-system malfunctions. **1996**—Airbags failed to deploy. • AC failures. **1997**—Gas and brake pedals are too close together. • Airbag safety light keeps coming on. **1998**—Sudden acceleration. **M3: 1998**—Sudden acceleration. • Brake failure. • Airbags failed to deploy. • Chronic horn failures. • Rear-view mirror blocks a substantial portion of the field of vision. • Inadvertent deployment of side airbags. **Recalls: All models: 1988–95**—Radiator caps replaced free of charge. Original caps failed to relieve excess pressure, causing heater cores or hoses to rupture. **325i, 325iS: 1992–94**—Brake light switch may fail. **1993–94**—Defective front transmission cross-member support. **318i, 318iS, 325i, 325iS: 1992**—Airbag may not deploy. **1992–93**—Fuel lines can harden and become brittle over time. **M3: 1995**—Brake lights may fail. **1995–97**—Plastic bushing for cruise control and throttle cable could break, causing the vehicle not to decelerate as it should. **1997–99**—Inadvertent deployment of side airbags.

Secret Warranties/Service Tips

All models: 1996–99—Frequent crankshaft position sensor failures result in chronic Check Engine light illumination. Can be corrected by changing the sensor and installing an adapter harness under warranty or under a BMW "goodwill" policy. **3 Series: 1992–95**—Automatic transmission may be slow to shift after sitting overnight because fluid has drained out of the torque converter. **1996**—Transmission shuddering requires the installation of a modified transmission control module. **1996–97**—Delayed gear engagement or adapter case leak requires the installation of a new transmission seal kit (#21-41-422-762). **1998**—A no-start condition may signal that the oil level sensor is faulty. • A "clunk" heard during downshifts, release of the accelerator pedal, or when shifting into Reverse is likely caused by excessive axial clearance between the transmission output shaft and the output shaft. **1998–2000**—Hard, or no shifts can be corrected by exchanging the valve body. **1999**—Tips for improving AM radio reception. • An inoperative cruise control may need a new brake light switch (strange but true). **1999–2000**—Guidelines for plugging manual transmission oil drain plug leaks. **5 Series: 1998**—A no-start condition may signal that the oil level sensor is faulty. **525i: 1990–94**—Brake light switch may fail. **525iT: 1992–94**—Brake light switch may fail. **525i, 535i: 1991–92**—Airbag may not deploy. **1993–94**—Emergency flashers may self-activate. • Tips on fixing starter motor failures.

3 Series, M3, Z3 Profile

	1992	1993	1994	1995	1996	1997	1998	1999
Cost Price ($)								
318ti	—	—	—	24,900	25,900	26,900	27,800	27,800
318i 4d	25,700	28,430	26,900	28,900	30,900	32,300	33,300	34,301
Convertible	33,270	34,760	—	40,900	42,900	43,900	44,900	45,900
325i, 328i	38,800	39,750	38,200	41,900	43,900	46,900	47,900	50,902

Convertible	42,365	45,780	52,900	53,900	55,300	57,900	58,900	58,900
323 Coupe	—	—	—	—	—	—	39,900	39,900
M3 2d	—	—	—	—	—	61,900	62,900	62,900
Z3 1.9/2.3	—	—	—	—	38,900	40,500	41,500	43,900
Z3 2.8	—	—	—	—	—	49,900	51,900	52,900
Used Values ($)								
318ti ↑	—	—	—	11,500	13,500	15,000	17,500	21,500
318ti ↓	—	—	—	9,500	11,000	13,000	15,500	19,000
318i 4d ↑	7,500	9,000	10,500	13,500	17,000	19,000	22,000	25,500
318i 4d ↓	6,000	7,500	9,500	11,000	14,000	17,000	19,000	23,500
Convertible ↑	10,500	12,000	14,000	—	23,000	28,000	33,000	38,000
Convertible ↓	9,500	10,000	12,000	—	20,000	25,000	31,000	36,000
323 Coupe ↑	—	—	—	—	—	—	25,000	30,900
323 Coupe ↓	—	—	—	—	—	—	23,000	27,000
325i, 328i ↑	9,500	12,000	14,000	19,000	24,000	28,000	32,000	35,000
325i, 328i ↓	8,500	10,000	12,000	16,000	21,000	25,500	29,000	32,000
Convertible ↑	12,500	14,000	17,000	25,000	31,000	37,000	40,000	43,000
Convertible ↓	11,500	13,000	14,000	22,000	28,000	34,000	37,000	40,000
M3 2d ↑	—	—	—	—	—	37,000	42,000	47,000
M3 2d ↓	—	—	—	—	—	34,000	39,000	45,000
Z3 1.9/2.3 ↑	—	—	—	—	22,000	26,000	29,000	33,000
Z3 1.9/2.3 ↓	—	—	—	—	19,000	23,000	26,000	30,000
Z3 2.8 ↑	—	—	—	—	—	32,000	36,000	41,000
Z3 2.8 ↓	—	—	—	—	—	29,000	33,000	39,000

Extended Warranty	Y	N	N	N	N	N	N	N
Secret Warranty	N	N	N	N	Y	Y	Y	Y
Reliability	②	②	③	③	③	③	③	④
Air conditioning	②	②	②	②	③	④	④	④
Auto. transmission	③	③	③	③	③	③	④	④
Body integrity	②	②	②	③	③	③	③	④
Braking system	②	②	②	③	③	③	③	③
Electrical system	②	②	②	②	②	②	②	③
Engines	②	②	②	③	④	④	④	⑤
Exhaust/Converter	②	②	②	③	③	③	③	④
Fuel system	②	②	③	③	③	③	④	④
Ignition system	③	③	③	③	④	④	④	④
Rust/Paint	②	②	③	④	④	⑤	⑤	⑤
Steering	③	③	③	④	④	⑤	⑤	⑤
Suspension	④	④	④	④	④	⑤	⑤	⑤
Crash Safety								
325i 4d	④	④	—	④	—	—	—	—
328i	—	—	—	—	④	④	—	—

5 Series Profile

	1991	1992	1993	1994	1995	1997	1998	1999
Cost Price ($)								
525i, 528i	45,200	47,830	51,210	49,750	52,900	54,900	56,200	58,500
535i	52,150	54,760	58,520	—	—	—	—	—
Used Values ($)								
525i, 528i ↑	8,500	10,000	12,500	16,000	22,000	30,000	35,000	40,000
525i, 528i ↓	7,500	9,000	10,000	13,500	18,500	27,500	31,000	35,000
535i ↑	10,000	11,500	13,000	—	—	—	—	—
535i ↓	9,000	12,500	11,000	—	—	—	—	—
Extended Warranty	Y	N	N	N	N	N	N	N
Secret Warranty	N	N	N	N	N	Y	N	N
Reliability	❷	③	③	③	④	⑤	⑤	⑤

Note: The above models haven't been crash-tested.

FORD/LINCOLN

Continental, Mark VII, Mark VIII, Town Car

Rating: Lincoln Continental: Below Average (1988–99); **Lincoln Mark VII, Mark VIII:** Above Average (1995–98); Average (1994); Below Average (1986–93). 1998 was the Mark series' last model year. **Lincoln Town Car:** Above Average (1995–99); Average (1988–94). Redesigned for 1998. Although the 1992–94 Continentals are dirt-cheap, their low quality makes them risky buys. **Maintenance/Repair costs:** Higher than average, and they must be done by a Ford or Lincoln dealer. **Parts:** Higher-than-average cost, but not hard to find (except for electronic components and body panels).

Strengths and weaknesses: These large luxury cruisers are proof that quality isn't proportional to the money you spend. Several designer series offer all the luxury options anyone could wish for, but the two ingredients most owners would expect to find—high quality and consistent reliability—are sadly lacking, especially with the front-drive versions. All models, however, have poor-quality automatic transmissions, electrical systems, brakes, body hardware, and fit and finish. NHTSA-recorded safety complaints also target more front-drive than rear-drive Lincolns with engine, transmission, airbag, and brake failures cropping up repeatedly over the years—with increasing severity and frequency.

Continental (front-drive)

When the Continental went front-drive in 1988, what was a mediocre luxury car became a luxury lemon with serious safety-related deficiencies.

The frequency and cost of repairs increased considerably, and parts became more complex, complicating easy diagnosis and repair. The automatic transmission tends to self-destruct, particularly on 1988–99 models; engine head gaskets blow (see Part Two); electrical components are unreliable; stopping performance is compromised by premature brake wear and wheel lockup; and body hardware continues to be an embarrassment. The redesigned 1995 Continental featured a new V8 powerplant, more aerodynamic styling, and fiberglass panels. However, engine, transmission, electrical-system, and brake problems actually worsened.

These cars don't offer the kind of trouble-free driving one would normally expect in a luxury vehicle selling for over $40,000. The automatic levelling air-spring suspension system makes for a stiff ride (especially on early models), while still allowing the Continental to "porpoise" due to its heavy front end. The Continental's anemic V6 powertrain is poorly suited to a car of this heft. The engine hesitates in cold weather and the automatic transmission shifts roughly due to malfunctioning computer modules.

Other major mechanical defects include frequent engine flywheel and transmission forward clutch piston replacements; failure-prone ABS, electrical, suspension, and steering systems; as well as glitch-ridden electronic modules causing hard starts and sudden stalling. The mass of electrical gadgets increases the likelihood of problems as the cars age. For example, automatic headlight doors fail frequently, and the electronic antenna seldom rises to the occasion. The computerized dashboard is particularly failure-prone.

Other reliability complaints concern transmission fluid leakage due to misplaced bolts, rough upshifting caused by a defective valve body, and air conditioning and heating that sometimes work in reverse order (you often get heat when opening the AC, and air conditioning frequently comes on when the heater is engaged).

Town Car
The rear-drive Town Car is the pick of the Lincoln litter. Thanks to its rear-drive configuration, it's relatively inexpensive to repair and parts aren't hard to find. Nevertheless, it's still afflicted by the Lincoln's generic problems: transmission, AC, and electrical glitches, and body hardware deficiencies. Try to find a 1992 or later version with the 4.6L engine to optimize performance and economy.

Technical service bulletins: Continental: 1995—Engine misfires, no-start, hard start, and spark plug fouling. • Faulty in-tank fuel delivery modules causing the engine to stall and not restart will be replaced for free under Ford Program #95B71. • The Virtual Image Cluster will also be replaced at no charge under Program #95B71. • Harsh shifts, no 3–4 shift, erratic shifts, delayed transmission engagement and shift errors, low transaxle-fluid level improperly setting the DTC and causing serious transmission malfunctions, and clicking noise when shifting into Reverse. • Insufficient AC cooling or excessive clutch end gap. • Brake roughness upon application or a thumping, clacking noise when braking. • Power-steering grunt or groan. • Rocker arm noise. • A ticking noise from the cooling fan or AX4N transaxle. **1996**—Stall or hard start after 1–4 hour soak. • Vehicle drifts or pulls while driving. • Transaxle click noise during Reverse engagement. • Transaxle driveline noises. • Transfer case breaks at rear planet support. • Air suspension leaks down overnight. • Fog/film on windshield/interior windows. • Musty and mildew-type odours. **1997**—Harsh automatic shifting. • Chronic dead battery. • Excessive blower motor noise. • Acceleration or deceleration clunk. • Front suspension clunk. • A-pillar creaking noise. • Front end accessory drive belt (FEAD) may slip during wet conditions, causing a reduction in steering power-assist. • Steering-wheel grunt or honk noise. • Loose catalyst or heat shields. • Stall or surging with automatic transmission engagement. **1998**—Bulletins cover poor engine and transmission performance; troubleshooting tips on eliminating various body, suspension, brake and radio noises, and overcoming lack of AC temperature control. **1999**—Hesitation when accelerating. • No Reverse engagement with the automatic transmission. • Steering wheel vibration/moaning. • Noisy ABS. • Creaking or popping when turning or braking. • Guidelines for correcting brake vibration under warranty. **Mark VIII: 1994–97**—An erratic or prolonged 1–2 shift can be cured by replacing the cast aluminum piston with a one-piece stamped steel piston with bonded lip seals, and replacing the top accumulator spring. These upgraded parts will increase the transmission's durability, says Ford. **1995**—Intermittent loss of torque at 3–4 upshift, shifts to Neutral at heavy throttle, delayed transmission engagement and shift errors, and irregular or no torque converter operation. • Brake roughness upon application. • Insufficient AC cooling or excessive clutch end gap. • Faulty fuel gauge. • Hard start in low temperatures. **1996**—Stall or hard start after 1–4 hour soak. • Transmission valve body cross-leaks and shudder/downshift bump. • Growling noise from steering column when vehicle turns. • Squealing noise from the engine compartment. • Fog/film on windshield/interior windows. • Musty and mildew-type odours. **1997**—Erratic transmission shifting, especially the 1–2 shift. • Chirping and squeaking from blower motor. • No-start or crank; anti-theft system not responding. • Radio AM band static while driving. • Troubleshooting wind noise around doors. **Town Car: 1995**—Problems with the 1995 Town Car are identical to those listed for the Crown Victoria (see page 287). **1996**—Stall or hard start after 1–4 hour soak. • Squealing noise from the engine compartment. • Transmission valve body cross-leaks. • Chatter during turns. • Creaking from A-pillar area. • Rough idle or stalling at high altitudes. • Inoperative power-assisted deck lid. • Fog/film on windshield/interior windows. • Musty and mildew-type odours. **1997**—Erratic transmission shifting, especially the 1–2 shift. • Spark knock upon acceleration. • Door latch stuck open. •

Fog/film on windshield/interior windows. • Loose catalysts or muffler heat shields. • Diagnosing and correcting wind noise around doors. • Shudder or vibration while in third or fourth gear. • Steering wheel noise and vibration. • Suspension leans to right side. • Whining noise from rear axle at highway speeds.

Safety summary/Recalls: Continental: 1995—While parked, vehicle rolled backward and suddenly accelerated forward. • Steering locks when driving through deep puddles. • Frequent reports of seatbelts failing to retract during an accident. • Defective inner tie-rod and strut causes severe steering shake. • Brake failures due to premature wear of rear drums and rotor warpage. • Inadequate defogging leaves two small circles to see through. • Console lights reflect into driver's portion of windshield and rear-view mirror. • Rear deck stereo hump obstructs rear visibility. **1996**—Sudden acceleration while driving on the highway. • While parked, vehicle suddenly jumped out of Park, rolled forward, and hit another car. • Several reports that the front suspension collapsed. • Front strut failures. • Clock spring broke, causing loss of steering. • Steering wheel jams intermittently. • Power steering is inoperative when it rains. • Transmission jumped out of gear while driving. • Power seats malfunction. • Vehicle cannot be properly aligned, causing premature tire wear. **1997**—Sudden, unintended acceleration. • Gas pedal sticks. Inadvertent airbag deployment, breaking passenger's arm. • Airbag failed to deploy in a collision. • Blown engine head gasket. • Engine suddenly stalls in traffic. • Vehicle often won't start; starter whirrs, but won't crank. • Premature failure of the tie rod ends. • Several incidents of steering failure; cracked steering gear. • Front brake failure; ABS operates erratically. • Excessive shaking when brakes are applied. • Gasoline smell permeates interior. • Broken rear side door handle disables the door. • Poor visibility with rear-view mirror. • Rear-view mirror distortions; leaks oil onto the dash. • Speedometer is difficult to read in daylight and gas gauge is often in error. • Frequent complaints that Michelin XW4 and Green X tires split open. • Horn suddenly blows on its own. **1998**—Cracked high pressure plastic line on top of engine caused fuel to spew out and catch fire. • Several complaints that engine coolant leaks and bubbles up onto the engine compartment, risking a fire. • Premature engine timing chain failure. • Sudden acceleration in Forward and in Reverse gear occurs when brakes are applied. • Gas pedal set higher than brake pedal, causing unintended acceleration. • Cruise control speeds up when vehicle goes downhill. • Airbags failed to deploy in a collision. • Frequent stalling and no-starts likely caused by a sensor failure. • Sudden steering failure. • Right front wheel assembly came off as vehicle came to a stop. • Power-steering pump fails periodically. • Front suspension failed as vehicle came to a stop. • ABS brake failures. • Interior lights fail, smoke. • Many complaints that the interior ventilation system leaks exhaust fumes. • Rain leaks through right rear door. • Excessive front windshield glare. **1999**—Driver's front airbag deployed for no reason. Two other incidents where the driver's side airbag deployed inadvertently. • Headlights fail to adequately light side of the road. • Visual image speedometer can't be seen by colour-blind drivers. **1999–2000**—NHTSA probe of inadvertent side airbag deployment. **Town Car: 1996**—Vehicle fires reportedly ignited in the engine compartment wiring. • Frequent reports of sudden acceleration. • Many reports of sudden acceleration while in Reverse, leading to the replacement of the speed control servo and servo cable. • Frequent complaints of chronic stalling. • ABS brakes often malfunction. • Airbag failed to deploy during collision. • Airbag packing gets hard in cold weather, leaving horn inoperative. • Trunk lid flew open on highway. • Many incidents where seatbelts either are too short for adults, won't retract, or ratchet tighter while being worn. • Two front seatbacks collapsed rearward when vehicle was rear-ended. • Excessive noise when braking. • Wind noise comes in through windshield. **1998**—Fuel may spit out of filler pipe when refueling. **Recalls: Continental: 1995–96**—"Autolamp" control module may fail. **1996–97**—Transmission may not engage; PRNDL may give a false reading. **Town Car: 1995**—Fuel could leak from tank. • Passenger airbag may not deploy properly. **1996**—Driver's door may not sustain specified load. • Seatbelts with switchable retractors for child restraints may not have the right components. **1997**—Driver's airbag may malfunction.

Secret Warranties/Service Tips

All models/years—Lincoln components that frequently benefit from Ford "goodwill" warranty extensions are catalytic converters, 3.8L engines, transmissions, and computer modules. If Ford balks at refunding your money, ask that the emissions warranty be applied for a full or partial refund. **All models: 1993–99**—Paint delamination, peeling, or fading (see Part Two). **Continental: 1984–94**—A hum from the air suspension system can be corrected by replacing the compressor isolators with upgraded parts. **1994–95**—A thumping or clacking heard from the front brakes signals the need to machine the front disc brake rotors. Ford will pay for this repair under its base warranty. **1994–99**—Tips on plugging door, window, and moon roof wind noise. **1995–97**—An acceleration or deceleration clunk is likely caused by the rear lower subframe isolators allowing movement between the mounts and the subframe. • A front suspension clunk may signal excessive sway bar wear. **1995–98**—No fourth gear may mean you have a defective forward clutch control valve retaining clip. • Condensation buildup on the inside of windows may be stopped by installing an upgraded pressure cycling switch. • An intermittent shifting into Neutral or loss of Forward or Reverse gear is likely caused by a defective forward clutch piston (a problem that has haunted Ford and Lincoln for over 12 years). • Front brake groaning, moaning, or squealing can be silenced by installing upgraded brake pads under the bumper-to-bumper warranty. **1995–99**—Troubleshooting tips for silencing a creak or pop while turning or braking, and wind noise coming from the side doors. **1996–98**—No-starts may be due to fuel pump wire chafing. **1997–98**—Lack of AC temperature control may signal the need for a new air blend door actuator. **1998**—Inaccurate fuel gauge readings may be corrected by installing a new fuel limit vent valve. **1998–99**—Steering wheel vibration/moaning can be fixed by installing a longer power steering hose. **1999**—No Reverse engagement with the automatic transmission, may be caused by torn Reverse clutch lip seals. Ford will cover the repair under a special "goodwill" policy (see Part Two). **1999–2000**—Hesitation when accelerating can be fixed by reprogramming the PCM. • Guidelines for diagnosing and preventing front brake vibration. **Mark VII, Mark VIII: 1985–99**—An exhaust buzz or rattle may be caused by a loose heat shield catalyst. **1986–94**—The in-tank fuel pump is the likely cause of radio static. Install an electronic noise RFI filter (#F1PZ-18B925-A). **1993–94**—A squeak or chirp coming from the blower motor can be stopped by installing an upgraded blower motor. • Automatic transmissions with delayed or no forward engagement, or a higher engine rpm than expected when coming to a stop, are covered in TSB #94-26-9.

Continental Profile

	1992	1993	1994	1995	1996	1997	1998	1999
Cost Price ($)								
Continental Ex.	37,895	38,842	40,295	50,995	51,896	49,995	51,995	52,795
Used Values ($)								
Continental Ex. ↑	6,500	8,500	10,000	12,000	16,000	21,000	25,000	31,000
Continental Ex. ↓	4,500	7,000	7,500	9,000	12,000	18,000	22,000	29,000
Extended Warranty	Y	Y	Y	Y	Y	Y	Y	Y
Secret Warranty	Y	Y	Y	Y	Y	Y	Y	Y
Reliability	❶	❷	❷	❷	❷	③	③	④
Air conditioning	❶	❶	❶	❶	❷	③	③	③
Auto. transmission	❶	❷	❷	❷	❷	❷	❷	❷
Body integrity	❷	❷	❷	❷	❷	③	③	③
Braking system	❶	❶	❶	❶	❷	❷	❷	③
Electrical system	❶	❶	❶	❷	❷	❷	❷	③
Engines	❶	❶	❷	❷	③	③	④	④
Exhaust/Converter	③	③	③	③	③	③	③	④
Fuel system	❷	③	③	③	③	③	③	④
Ignition system	❶	❷	③	③	③	③	④	④
Rust/Paint	③	③	③	④	④	④	④	④
Steering	❷	③	③	③	③	③	③	④
Suspension	❶	❶	❶	❷	❷	❷	③	④
Crash Safety	③	③	③	—	—	—	—	—

Mark VII, Mark VIII Profile

	1991	1992	1993	1994	1995	1996	1997	1998
Cost Price ($)								
Mark VII, VIII	38,895	41,010	43,968	47,995	50,996	51,895	53,695	56,595
Used Values ($)								
Mark VII, VIII ↑	8,000	9,000	10,000	12,000	16,000	18,500	22,500	29,000

Mark VII, VIII ↓	7,000	8,000	9,000	10,000	12,500	15,000	20,000	26,000
Extended Warranty	Y	Y	Y	Y	Y	Y	Y	Y
Secret Warranty	N	N	Y	Y	Y	Y	Y	Y
Reliability	②	②	②	②	②	③	③	③
Air conditioning	②	②	②	③	③	③	③	③
Auto. transmission	②	②	②	②	②	③	③	③
Body integrity	②	②	②	②	②	②	②	③
Braking system	②	②	②	②	②	③	④	④
Electrical system	②	②	②	②	②	②	②	②
Engines	④	④	③	③	④	④	④	④
Exhaust/Converter	②	②	③	③	③	③	③	④
Fuel system	③	③	③	③	③	③	④	④
Ignition system	③	③	③	③	③	③	④	③
Rust/Paint	②	②	②	②	③	③	③	④
Steering	②	②	③	③	③	④	⑤	⑤
Suspension	②	②	②	③	③	③	③	④

Note: The Mark series hasn't been crash-tested.

Town Car Profile

	1992	1993	1994	1995	1996	1997	1998	1999
Cost Price ($)								
Town Car	37,695	38,637	40,495	44,495	44,895	45,895	52,795	55,000
Used Values ($)								
Town Car ↑	9,000	11,000	15,000	17,000	22,000	25,000	32,000	37,000
Town Car ↓	8,000	9,000	12,000	14,000	19,000	22,000	29,000	33,000
Extended Warranty	N	N	N	N	N	N	N	N
Secret Warranty	Y	Y	Y	Y	Y	Y	Y	
Reliability	②	②	③	④	④	④	④	④
Air conditioning	②	②	③	③	③	③	④	④
Auto. transmission	①	①	①	①	①	①	①	②
Body integrity	②	②	②	②	②	②	③	③
Braking system	①	①	①	①	②	③	③	②
Electrical system	①	①	②	②	③	③	③	③
Engines	④	④	②	②	③	④	④	④
Exhaust/Converter	③	④	④	④	⑤	⑤	⑤	⑤
Fuel system	②	③	③	③	③	③	④	④
Ignition system	②	②	③	③	③	③	③	③
Rust/Paint	②	③	③	③	③	④	⑤	⑤
Steering	②	③	④	④	③	③	④	④
Suspension	③	③	③	③	④	④	④	④
Crash Safety	⑤	⑤	⑤	⑤	④	④	—	—
Side Impact	—	—	—	—	—	—	④	④

GENERAL MOTORS

98 Regency, Park Avenue

Rating: Average (1998–99); Below Average (1991–97); Not Recommended (1985–90). Although a new Park Avenue commands a higher price than a new 98 Regency, the value of a used Park Avenue trails slightly. **Maintenance/Repair costs:** Higher than average, but repairs aren't dealer dependent. **Parts:** Higher-than-average cost (independent suppliers sell for much less), but not hard to find. Nevertheless, don't even think about buying one of these front-drives without a three- to five-year extended warranty backed by the automaker.

Strengths and weaknesses: These attractive, luxurious cars are billed as six-seaters, but only four passengers can ride in comfort. Although the 1991–96 Park Avenue and 98 Regency were improved over the years, they've compiled the worst repair history among large cars. Main problem areas are the engine, automatic transmission, fuel system, steering, brakes, electrical system (including defective PROM and MEMCAL modules), starter and alternator, and badly assembled, poor-quality body hardware. The 3.0L V6 engine is inadequate for cars this heavy, and the 3.8L has been a big quality disappointment. Stay away from the failure-prone diesel engine. Under-hood servicing is complicated. Automatic transmission and engine computer malfunctions are common. The fuel-injection system is temperamental. Window mechanisms are poorly designed. The power-steering assembly is failure-prone. There are frequent electrical failures. Front brake pads and rotors require frequent replacement. Shock absorbers leak or go soft very quickly. Extensive surface corrosion has been a problem because of poor and often incomplete paint application at the factory.

Like the LeSabre, the 1997 Park Avenue and Ultra (its fully dressed version) were redesigned to include a reworked powertrain, a stiffer body, improved interior amenities, upgraded four-wheel disc brakes, and an upgraded ventilation system. The following model year adopted depowered airbags. The '99 models were carried over without any significant changes.

Aficionados of full-sized luxury sedans love the flush glass, wraparound windshield and bumpers, and clean body lines that lend the latest makeover an aerodynamic and pleasing appearance. But these cars are more than just pretty packages; they provide lots of room, luxury, style, and (dare I say) performance. Plenty of power is available with the 205-hp 3.8L V6 engine and the 240-hp supercharged powerplant. It does 0–100 km/h in under 9 seconds (impressive, considering the heft of these vehicles), and improves low- and mid-range throttle response. Power is transmitted to the front wheels through an electronically controlled transmission that features "free-wheeling" clutches designed to eliminate abrupt gear changes. Both the Park Avenue and Ultra use a stretched version of the more rigid Riviera and Aurora platform.

The revised 1997 Park Avenue models have had fewer complaints, perhaps because of the short time they've been out and the fact that GM's warranty is still in effect. Nevertheless, the main problem areas continue to be the following: powertrain malfunctions; engine and transmission leaks; a concerto of squeaks, rattles, moans, and whines; AC not performing properly; and numerous body and trim defects. Since the '98s and '99s returned relatively unchanged, don't expect any major improvements quality-wise.

Technical service bulletins: All models: 1995—Noise while driving up medium grades or accelerating. • Stall upon deceleration. • Cold-start rattle with the 4T60E automatic transmission. • Grinding/growling when in Park on an incline. • A coolant leak from the belt tensioner assembly. • Throttle body noise upon acceleration from stop. • Brake vibration and/or pedal pulsation. • Whistle coming from the heater/AC unit. • Low-voltage reading or dim lights at idle. • Headlights/parking lights remain on. • Squeak/creak from rear of vehicle. • Poor paint application and rust spots. **1996**—Second-gear starts, poor 1–3 shifting. • AC defrost valve creaks when changing modes. • AC odour at start-up in humid climates. • AC flutter or moan. • Noisy steering column. • Cold-start rattle. • Engine cranks but won't start. • Engine oil leaks. • Excess vibration of electrochromatic rear-view mirror. • Exterior light condensation. • Fluttering, popping, ticking, and clunking noises. • Inoperative door locks. • AC thump noise upon start-up. • Intermittent Neutral/loss of Drive at highway speeds. • Instrument-panel buzz or rattle when the brakes are applied. • Popping noise from front of vehicle when turning. • Troubleshooting radio frequency interference. • Rattle in rear door when closing. • Transaxle gear whine. • Whistle noise from HVAC (climate control system). • Wind noise around front and rear doors. **1997**—AC thump noise. • Driver's seat rocks. • Noisy front brakes. • Engine oil leaks. • Engine oil level indicates over-full. • Harsh shift from Reverse to Drive. • Excess vibration of electrochromatic rear-view mirror. • Erratic wiper operation in automatic mode. • Spontaneous horn activation or inoperative horn. • Instrument-panel buzz or rattle when the brakes are applied. • Popping noise from front of vehicle when turning. • Growl or vibration when turning or accelerating. • Paint chips on rear compartment lid. • Roof panel running front to back has a wavy/dimpled appearance and transmits excessive rain noise. • Steering vibration/moan when parking. • Transaxle gear whine. **1998**—Bulletins address excessive brake noise, whistling, rattling, clunking, and groaning from the front and rear; a rough-running engine that lacks power; engine knocking; intermittent stalling; vehicle shudder when accelerating; inaccurate fuel gauge reading; and AC odours. **1999**—Engine runs hot, overheats, or loses coolant. • Low power, or stumbling when accelerating. • Gear shift lever hard to shift. • Transmission whine in Park or

Neutral. • Slips, harsh upshift or garage shifts, and launch shudders. • Front strut noise. • Front end clunk or rattle. • Passenger compartment popping noise. • Front door locks won't re-open. • Front brake pad design change to improve wear. • Measures to reduce excessive steering wheel and floor shake or vibration.

Safety summary/Recalls: All models: 1998—Chronic stalling, loss of electrical power, particularly when braking. • Vehicle also suddenly accelerates when braking. • With cruise control engaged, vehicle picks up speed when going downhill. • Faulty fuel sending unit; fuel gauge failure. • Cracked engine head gasket. • Transmission failures. • Brakes or steering fail in rainy weather. • ABS failure may be caused by defective computer module. • Steering failure caused by broken serpentine belt. • Premature failure of brake rotors, pads, and calipers. • Goodyear tire tread separation. • Faulty air level ride filled up rear shocks so rear end sticks up high in the air. • Seatbelts jam in the retractor; fail to extend or retract. • Door locks don't work properly. • Windshield dash glare. **1999**—Sudden acceleration after vehicle jumped from Park into Drive. • Frequent stalling; Check Engine light comes on. • Loss of steering due to premature steering pump failure. • Brake rotor overheating and warpage creates excessive vibration and pulling to one side when brakes are applied. • Transmission jerks when going from Reverse to Drive. • Airbag light comes on for no reason. • Shoulder belt twists in retractor. • Premature failure of Goodyear tires. • Keys won't lock or unlock the doors. • Battery often goes dead. **98 Regency: 1994–95**— Headlight switch may not work. **1995**—Current leakage in models with Twilight Sentinel can cause loss of headlights and parking lights, or the lights may suddenly come on while the car is parked. **1996**—Damaged capacitor could cause confusing electronic warnings to be displayed. • Backfire upon start-up can damage the intake manifold and cause hard starting or a fire. **Park Avenue: 1997**—Centre seatbelt anchor bolts were improperly installed. • Brake/Traction Control Module could cause ABS to lose its effectiveness and make for longer stopping distances.

Secret Warranties/Service Tips

All models/years—The THM 44C-T4 automatic transaxles on front-drive models equipped with V6 engines are particularly failure-prone: their pinched or kinked vacuum lines result in low oil pressure. **1993–99**—AC odours can be reduced by applying a cooling coil coating. • A rotten-egg odour coming from the exhaust is probably caused by a malfunctioning catalytic converter and may be covered under GM's emissions warranty. • Paint delamination, peeling, or fading (see Part Two). **1995–96**—Wind noise around front and rear doors; diagnosis and repair. **1995–97**— Transmission gear whine means the final drive assembly may have to be replaced. **1995–98**—A noise, growl, or vibration from the front when making a right turn or when accelerating may signal the need to replace or reposition the rear transaxle mount. **1997–99**—Excessive brake noise can be reduced by installing upgraded pads and rotors. **1998**—Spark plug electrode erosion is the likely cause of engine knock, a rough-running engine, or lack of power. • A fuel gauge that gives inaccurate readings probably needs a new fuel level sensor. • Rattling from the rear may mean the fuel tank strap is loose or defective. **1998–99**—Low power, stalling, or stumbling when accelerating can be cured by re-calibrating the PCM. **1998–2000**—A hard to shift gear shift lever may need a new cable assembly. **1999–2000**—An engine that runs hot, overheats, or loses coolant may simply need a new radiator cap. • Transmission whine in Park or Neutral may be silenced with a new drive sprocket support bearing. • Slips, harsh upshift or garage shifts, and launch shudders have a variety of causes and corrections, says TSB #00-07-30-002. • Diagnostic procedures for an engine that runs hot, overheats, or loses coolant are outlined in TSB #00-06-02-001.

98 Regency, Park Avenue Profile

	1992	1993	1994	1995	1996	1997	1998	1999
Cost Price ($)								
Park Avenue	30,898	31,798	33,798	37,115	38,150	40,865	41,850	41,060
98 Regency	28,798	31,798	34,498	35,525	36,610	—	—	—
Used Values ($)								
Park Avenue ↑	6,500	7,500	9,000	12,500	13,500	18,000	21,000	26,000
Park Avenue ↓	5,500	6,500	7,500	10,000	11,000	15,000	18,500	23,500
98 Regency ↑	6,000	7,000	9,000	12,000	13,500	—	—	—
98 Regency ↓	5,000	6,000	7,000	9,500	11,500	—	—	—
Extended Warranty	Y	Y	Y	Y	Y	Y	Y	Y
Secret Warranty	Y	Y	Y	Y	Y	Y	Y	Y
Reliability	❷	❷	❷	❷	❷	❷	③	③
Air conditioning	❷	❷	❷	❷	❷	③	③	③
Auto. transmission	❷	❷	❷	❷	❷	③	③	③
Body integrity	❶	❶	❶	❶	❶	❶	❶	③
Braking system	❷	❷	❷	❷	❷	③	③	③
Electrical system	❷	❷	❷	❷	❷	❷	❷	❷
Engines	❷	❷	❷	③	③	③	③	③
Fuel system	❷	❷	❷	❷	❷	❷	③	③
Ignition system	❷	❷	❷	❷	③	③	③	③
Rust/Paint	❶	❶	❶	❶	❶	❶	❷	③
Steering	❶	❶	❶	❶	❷	❷	❷	③
Suspension	❷	❷	❷	❷	❷	③	③	③
Crash Safety								
98 Regency	⑤	⑤	⑤	—	—	—	—	—

Aurora, Riviera, Toronado, Trofeo

Rating: Riviera, Toronado, Trofeo: Average (1995–99); Not Recommended (1986–93). GM skipped the 1994 model year and introduced an all-new 1995 version. **Aurora:** Average (1995–99). Now that GM is phasing out its Oldsmobile division, resale values are likely to suffer. **Maintenance/Repair costs:** Higher than average, but repairs aren't dealer dependent. **Parts:** Higher-than-average cost (independent suppliers sell for much less), but not hard to find. GM's phaseout won't affect availability or costs, since these vehicles use the same generic parts found on many other GM products. Nevertheless, don't even think about buying one of the earlier front-drives without a three- to five-year supplementary warranty.

Strengths and weaknesses: Although the redesigned 1988–93 cars got performance, handling, and ride upgrades, they kept the same low level of quality control with multiple design and manufacturing defects, including serious fuel-injection, engine-computer, and electrical-system problems. One particularly poor design was the complex Graphic Control Centre, which used an oversensitive video screen and small push buttons. It's both distracting and expensive to repair. The automatic transmission is notoriously failure-prone, and brakes wear out prematurely and perform poorly. Surface rust and poor paint quality are the most common body complaints on all years. Shock absorbers wear out quickly and the diesel engine seldom runs properly. Mechanical parts are easy to find, but body panels have to be ordered from GM at a premium.

The 1995 Riviera was totally redesigned with standard dual airbags, ABS, a 3.8L V6, and a supercharged variant. These upgrades were carried over for the '96 model. However, the '97s got additional standard features and a smoother-shifting automatic transmission. The supercharged engine became a standard feature on the '98s and traction control became standard a year later.

Overall, 1995–99 models offer many more luxury features but continue their checkered repair history. GM improved the quality over the years, but generic deficiencies affecting the automatic transmission, engine, computer modules, brakes, steering, suspension, and fit and finish make these cars less than luxury from a quality-control standpoint.

Aurora

This front-drive Olds luxury sedan is aimed at the Acura, Infiniti, and Lexus crowd. It uses the same basic design as the Riviera but doesn't share the same major mechanical features or popular styling.

The Aurora's main advantages are its sporty handling and unusual aero styling. In contrast to the Riviera and Toronado, the Aurora seats five only and uses a 4.0L V8 derived from the Cadillac 4.6L V8 Northstar engine. Acceleration is underwhelming (this is a heavy car) but adequate for highway touring. Road and wind noise is omnipresent and the rear trunk's small opening compromises the large trunk's ability to handle odd-sized objects. Owner complaints mostly concern electrical shorts, poor AC performance, frequent brake repairs, and sub-par fit and finish.

Technical service bulletins: All models: 1995—Engine misfires, rough idle, white exhaust smoke, and a continuous spark knock. • Excessive oil consumption. • A cold-start rattle with the 4T60E automatic transmission. • A starter motor that runs continuously. • Reduced heater performance on the driver's side. • Brake vibration and/or pedal pulsation. • Instrument panel trim may separate from the upper trim pad. • Low-voltage reading or dim lights at idle. • A scraping noise and increased effort needed to open the doors. • Inoperative fuel-filler door. • ABS/traction light stays on. • Poor paint application and rust spots. **1996**—Second-gear starts and erratic 1–3 shifts. • AC odour in humid climates. • Steering column noise. • Cold-start rattle noise. • Engine cranks but won't start. • Engine oil leaks. • Excessive vibration of electrochromatic mirror. • Exterior light condensation. • Troubleshooting tips for fluttering, popping, ticking, and clunking noises. • Gap between door-opening weather strip and roofline. • Inoperative power door locks. • Intermittent Neutral/loss of Drive at highway speeds. • Instrument-panel buzz or rattle when the brakes are applied. • Popping noise, growl, or vibration when making a right turn. • Reduced heater performance on the driver's side. • Reduced retention of door trim lace. • Roof panel running front to back has a wavy/dimpled appearance and transmits excessive rain noise. • Underbody noise from rear of vehicle. • Wet or smelly carpet from water leaks. **1997**—Front brake noise. • Engine cranks but won't start. • Engine oil leaks. • Engine oil level indicates over-full. • Excessive vibration of electrochromatic mirror. • Harsh shift from Reverse to Drive. • Inoperative power door locks. • Instrument-panel buzz or rattle when the brakes are applied. • Popping noise, growl, or vibration when making a right turn. • Steering vibration, shudder, or moan when parking. • Roof panel running front to back has a wavy/dimpled appearance and transmits excessive rain noise. **Aurora: 1995**—White exhaust smoke, engine oil leak at the rear main seal or T-joint, and loss of oil pressure or lack of power. • A popping noise is heard during cranking, or the starter motor continues to run or crank after shut off. • Reduced heater performance on the driver's side. • Brake vibration and/or pedal pulsation. • A clicking noise emanating from the dash or hood, creak noise at the right side of vehicle, and a thumping from the rear of the vehicle. • Loose, rattling headliner and clicking emanating from the sunroof. • Excessive radio static. • Instrument panel trim that may separate from the upper trim pad. • Wet, smelly carpet from water leaks. • Wind noise at the front door A-pillar. **1996**—Engine oil leaks from upper to lower crankcase joint. • Oil leakage from the oil pan to lower crankcase attaching bolts. • Loss of oil pressure and/or lack of power. • Steering column noise. • Popping noise from front of vehicle when turning. • Underbody noise from rear of vehicle. • Reduced heater performance. • Rear compartment lid assist rod separating from lid. • Gap between door-opening weather strip and roofline. • Reduced retention of door trim lace. • Condensation on exterior light. • Wet or smelly carpet from water leaks. **1997–98**—Tips on reducing AC odours and squeaks, rattles, groans, and clunks from the front and rear of the vehicle. • Several bulletins address excessive front brake noise.

Safety summary/Recalls: Recalls: All models: 1991–93—Front shoulder seatbelt may stick in retractor. • Poorly aligned rear shoulder seatbelt retractor assemblies. **1992**—Possible steering loss due to the disengagement of the steering shaft. **1996**—Driver-warning alarms and displays may malfunction. • Backfire can break the intake manifold and cause a fire.

Secret Warranties/Service Tips

All models: 1993–99—AC odours can be reduced by applying a cooling coil coating. A rotten-egg odour coming from the exhaust is likely the result of a malfunctioning catalytic converter, covered by GM's emissions warranty up to five years. • Paint delamination, peeling, or fading (see Part Two). **1995–96**—Intermittent Neutral/loss of Drive at highway speeds can be fixed by replacing the control valve body assembly. **1995–98**—A noise, growl, or vibration from the front when making a right turn or when accelerating may signal the need to replace or reposition the rear transaxle mount. **1997–99**—Excessive front brake noise can be reduced by installing upgraded pads and rotors. **1998**—A fuel gauge that gives inaccurate readings probably needs a new fuel level sensor. • Rattling from the rear may mean the fuel tank strap is loose or defective. **Aurora: 1995–99**—A cold engine knock or ticking may be caused by excessive carbon deposits in the engine. **1997–98**—Excessive front brake noise can be reduced by installing upgraded pads and rotors. **1998**—Harsh or delayed gear shifts may require the installation of an enhanced garage shift package. • Accessory drive noise may be caused by a misaligned accessory drive pulley. • Delayed or no engine braking in D3 may require the replacement of the forward and coast latch piston assemblies. **1998–99**—Diagnostic and repair tips for a faulty cruise control and speedometer. • Front end clunks and rattles can be silenced by a judicious use of anti-friction materials. **Riviera: 1990–93**—An engine ticking at idle can be traced to rattling piston pins that must be replaced with upgraded parts. **Toronado, Trofeo: 1990–92**—A body-mount creak that occurs whenever the vehicle passes over a bump may be due to one or more of the body mounts being poorly positioned in the frame; correct by installing a new, lower insulator. • Chronic wind noise coming from the front door window can be corrected by reinstalling the run-channel retainer. • A shake or vibration in the front end when going over smooth roads may be caused by an internal leak in the engine mount.

Aurora Profile

	1995	1996	1997	1998	1999
Cost Price ($)					
Aurora	43,020	43,695	46,045	47,250	46,190
Used Values ($)					
Aurora ↑	12,000	15,500	20,500	25,000	30,000
Aurora ↓	9,500	12,500	17,500	21,500	27,000
Extended Warranty	Y	Y	Y	Y	Y
Secret Warranty	Y	Y	Y	Y	Y
Reliability	③	③	③	③	④
Crash Safety	③	③	③	③	③

Riviera, Toronado, Trofeo Profile

	1991	1992	1993	1995	1996	1997	1998	1999
Cost Price ($)								
Riviera	29,698	29,898	30,790	39,525	40,700	42,415	44,950	44,125
Toronado	29,698	28,799	—	—	—	—	—	—
Trofeo	32,698	31,998	—	—	—	—	—	—
Used Values ($)								
Riviera ↑	5,000	6,000	8,000	11,000	14,000	17,000	22,000	28,000
Riviera ↓	4,500	5,000	7,000	8,500	11,500	14,500	19,000	25,000
Toronado ↑	5,500	6,500	—	—	—	—	—	—
Toronado ↓	4,500	5,500	—	—	—	—	—	—
Trofeo ↑	5,500	7,000	—	—	—	—	—	—
Trofeo ↓	5,000	5,500	—	—	—	—	—	—
Extended Warranty	Y	Y	Y	Y	Y	Y	Y	Y
Secret Warranty	Y	Y	Y	Y	Y	Y	Y	Y
Reliability	❷	③	③	③	③	③	③	③
Air conditioning	③	③	③	③	③	③	③	③
Auto. transmission	❷	❷	③	③	③	③	③	③
Body integrity	❷	❷	❷	❷	❷	❷	❷	③
Braking system	❷	❷	❷	❷	❷	❷	③	③
Electrical system	❷	❷	❷	❷	❷	❷	❷	❷
Engines	③	③	③	④	④	④	④	④
Exhaust/Converter	③	③	③	④	⑤	⑤	⑤	⑤
Fuel system	❷	③	③	③	③	③	④	⑤
Ignition system	③	③	③	③	③	③	④	⑤
Rust/Paint	❷	❷	❷	❷	❷	❷	③	⑤
Steering	③	③	③	④	④	④	④	④
Suspension	❷	③	③	③	③	④	④	④

Note: These vehicles haven't been crash-tested.

Cadillac Allanté, Catera, Eldorado, Seville

Rating: Below Average (1992–99); Not Recommended (1986–91). **Maintenance/Repair costs:** Higher than average, but repairs aren't dealer dependent. **Parts:** Higher-than-average cost (independent suppliers sell for much less), but not hard to find (Allanté excluded). Don't buy one of the front-drives without a three- to five-year supplementary warranty.

Strengths and weaknesses: The early Cadillacs are luxury embarrassments and later models barely pass muster. Even though most use the same mechanical components with the same deficiencies as the Riviera and Toronado models, they're far more failure-prone due to the complexity of their different luxury features and hard-to-find Allanté parts.

Allanté

Introduced in 1987, the Allanté was essentially a "kit car" Cadillac two-seat roadster with body components flown in from Italy and mechanicals assembled in Detroit. This car got the more powerful Northstar V8 in 1993—the same year the car was discontinued. Originally selling for $77,475, a 1987 model would fetch no more than $8,000 today. Does it have any value as a collector's item? Not a chance.

Owners report many reliability problems—especially with brake, electronic-control, and powertrain glitches—and woefully poor quality body assembly. Also, the convertible top is a chore to put up or down. Allanté owners have expressed a few other concerns: chronic and costly ABS brake repairs; emergency brake rattles, particularly if the emergency brake is not used often (the cause is prematurely worn rear brake pads, or defective brake "springs" or clips); turn signals sticking (simply squirt TV Tuner Cleaner from Radio Shack into the assembly); defective intake manifolds; and faulty alarms. For more detailed information from Allanté owners who both love and hate their car, access *www.allante.org* on the Internet.

Catera

Assembled in Germany and based on the Opel Omega, the rear-drive, mid-sized Catera comes with a 200-hp V6 engine, 4-speed automatic transmission, 16-inch alloy wheels, 4-wheel disc brakes, a limited-slip differential, traction control, and standard dual front airbags. The conservatively styled 200-hp, V6-equipped 1997 Catera (the uninspired styling has Lumina written all over it) was designed to compete with the BMW 328i, Lexus ES 300, and Mercedes-Benz C280. GM hoped not to drive away its more traditional "empty-nesters" (I guess that's a polite term for "old folks"), while luring more baby boomers to its higher-performance variations. The '98 versions got depowered airbags, while the '99s adopted even more complex electronics and emissions systems to meet federal fuel economy and emissions standards.

The last time Cadillac introduced an entry-level model was 1981, when the automaker launched the Cimarron, a fully loaded, Chevrolet Cavalier–derived Cadillac that carried a $4,000 premium over the comparably equipped Cavalier. Back then, most auto critics and consumer advocates considered the Cimarron to be at the rear of the pack as far as performance and quality control were concerned. The Catera, on the other hand, has received good reviews from the European press for its quiet, spacious, and comfortable interior; responsive handling; precise steering; fine-tuned suspension; and almost nonexistent lean or body roll when cornering. Without a doubt, this is one Cadillac that's meant to be driven. On the downside, though, the controls aren't easy to figure out, some gauges are hard to read, and the driver's rear view is hindered by the large rear head restraints and narrow back windshield. Furthermore, owners report chronic stalling and hard starts, possibly due to a malfunctioning idle-control valve, constant warning-light illuminations, poor AM radio reception (requiring an additional amplifier), and loose interior panels. Two other performance problems reported by owners: when you pass over a large expansion joint, the floorpan vibrates annoyingly; if you drive over a bump when turning, the steering wheel kicks back in your hands.

A few other points you may wish to consider: GM dealers are notoriously bad when it comes to understanding and repairing European-transplanted cars (just ask any Saab owner). As well, low-volume cars generally don't have an adequate supply of replacement parts in the pipeline until they've been on the market for a while. Add in the Catera's European connection and you'd best be ready to endure long service waits and high parts costs for those repairs not covered under warranty.

Finally, the fact that Cateras are European built doesn't necessarily mean that these Cadillacs will be reliable or durable. Based on the past performance of Big Three European imports, it's a safe bet that these cars will be less reliable and more troublesome than the competition. GM first learned that lesson with the British-built, failure-prone Vauxhall Firenza it unleashed on an unsuspecting Canadian public in the '70s. A few years later, it settled out of court on several class actions that I piloted, and paid a $20,000 fine to the federal government for misleading advertising. (On a nationally advertised road trip across Canada, GM said the cars excelled. Truth is, they were a mess. They required a team of engineers just to get started.)

Eldorado and Seville

From 1992 on, the Eldorado's styling became more distinctive, even though the vehicle shares most powertrain and chassis components with the Seville. Although the base 4.9L V8 provides brisk acceleration, the 32-valve Northstar V8, first found on the 1993 Touring Coupe, gives you almost 100 more horses with great handling and a comfortable ride. Overall, the Touring Coupe or Sport Coupe will give you the best powertrain, handling, and braking features. Of course, you'll have to contend with poor fuel economy, rear visibility that's obstructed by the huge side pillars (a Seville problem, as well), confusing and inconvenient climate controls, and a particularly complex engine compartment.

Sitting on the same platform as the Eldorado, the Seville has European-style allure with a more rounded body than the Eldorado. Apart from that, since its redesign in 1992 its engine, handling, and braking upgrades have followed in lockstep fashion the Eldorado's improvements.

Whether you buy a used Eldorado or Seville, keep in mind that the improved versions came out with the 1995 models, which carried on unchanged until their redesign for 1998. So, if you must buy one of these models, remember that the only distinguishing feature between them is styling, not performance.

The 4.1L V8 is best avoided. It may be simpler to work on, but it too is fuel thirsty and easily overpowered by the Eldorado's weight.

These cars have generic deficiencies that fall into common categories: poorly calibrated and failure-prone engines, transmissions, and fuel and ignition systems; a multiplicity of electrical short circuits; and sloppy body assembly using poor-quality components. Specifically, engines and fuel systems often produce intermittent stalling, rough idling, hesitation, and no-starts; the Overdrive automatic is prone to premature failure; oil pumps fail frequently; front brakes and shock absorbers wear out quickly; often, paint is poorly applied, fades, or peels away prematurely; fragile body hardware breaks easily; and there are large gaps between sheet-metal panels and doors that are poorly hung and not entirely square. Other body problems include cracking of front outside door handles, door rattles (Eldorado), poor bumper fit, loose sun visor mounting, rear taillight condensation, fading and discolouring appliqué mouldings (Seville), interior window fogging, "creaking" body mounts, water leaking into trunk from licence-plate holder (Eldorado), noisy roof panels and seatback lumbar motors, and a creaking noise at the front-door upper hinge area.

Technical service bulletins: Catera: 1997—Brake squealing. • Clunk noise from engine compartment on vehicles with cruise control. • Ignition key binds, drags, or sticks in ignition. • Loose fuel cap. • Low-voltage reading or dim lights at idle. • Noise in radio AM band when rear defogger on. • Oil leak from engine timing cover. • Inoperative power door locks. **1998**—Inoperative rear defogger. • Windshield wiper slap/flop noise. **1999**—Engine overheats or loses coolant. **Eldorado: All years**—Squeaks and squealing after a cold start. • Warped windshield and rear-window moulding. **1995**—Engine cranks but won't start; no fuel pressure; loss of oil pressure or lack of power. • Engine oil leak at the rear main seal or T-joint. • Starter motor runs continuously. • Metallic knocking sound from the engine. • A grinding or scraping noise in Park or Neutral. • Front brake vibration and/or pedal pulsation. • Annoying AC odour. • A low-voltage reading or dim lights at idle. • Remote keyless entry malfunctions. • Rattle noise from front of vehicle, front-seat clicking noise, clicking noise from under the hood or dash, and rubbing noise when the front wheels are turned all the way. • Door window slaps or rattles when closing door. • Excessive radio static. • Wet or smelly carpet from water leaks. • Poor paint application and rust spots. **1996**—Engine oil leaks from upper to lower crankcase joint. • Loss of oil pressure and/or lack of power. • Oil leakage from the oil pan to lower crankcase attaching bolts. • Second-gear starts, poor 1–3 shifting. • Steering column noise. • Poor AC cooling in traffic and high ambient temperatures. • Insufficient heat distribution or lack of airflow. • Coolant temperature gauge always reads hot. • Erratic or inaccurate instrument-panel displays and gauges. • Insufficient remote keyless entry operating range. • Positive battery cable won't tighten properly. • Radio clock stuck on 12:00. • Radio frequency interference diagnosis. • Whistle noise from HVAC. • Exhaust rattles. • Rattling heard when vehicle goes over bumps. • Clicking noise from front seats. • Squawk noise from rear of vehicle in cold temperature. • Slow parking brake release or slow HVAC mode changes. • Water leak from rear-door side-window area. • Wet or smelly carpet from water leaks. • Abnormal condensation in taillights and other lights. • Faulty cup holders. **1997**—Front brake noise. • Remote won't open doors or trunk. • Excessive vibration of electrochromatic mirror. • Fuel tank won't fill to capacity/always reads full. • Horn hard to operate when cold. • Inoperative power door locks. • Metallic buzz or rattle at the instrument panel when the brakes are applied. • No warning light or driver information centre message. • Power window inoperative after express down feature is used. • Torque converter clutch buzz or moan. **1998**—Bulletins give troubleshooting tips relating to body, brake, and engine noises; reducing AC odours; and curing automatic transmission harsh or delayed shifts. **1999**—Engine overheats or loses coolant. • Diagnostic and repair tips for a faulty cruise control and speedometer. • Front end clunks and rattles.

Safety summary/Recalls: Allanté: 1987–92—Owners report frequent brake problems on the Allanté Appreciation Group website (*www.allante.org*). **Recalls: All models: 1993–94**—Leaking engine oil cooler hose may cause a fire. **1994**—Faulty throttle cable. **Eldorado, Seville: 1995–96**—Excessive moisture (due to a window left open when it rains, for example) may cause the airbag to deploy when the ignition is switched on.

Secret Warranties/Service Tips

All models: 1993–99—A cold engine knock or ticking may be caused by excessive carbon deposits in the engine. • AC odours can be reduced by applying a cooling coil coating. • Defective catalytic converters that cause a rotten-egg smell in the interior may be replaced free of charge under the emissions warranty. • Paint delamination, peeling, or fading (see Part

Two). **1994**—Condensation dripping from the heater duct requires the installation of a watertight dam in the HVAC case. • An inoperative cruise control or brake/transmission interlock may signal a misadjusted stop-light switch assembly. • A binding parking brake may need a new parking-brake vacuum-release switch. **1996–97**—A torque converter clutch buzz or moan requires the installation of an upgraded case-cover-assembly spacer plate and the upper-control-valve body. **1997**—Excessive front brake noise can be cured by installing upgraded front brake pads. **1997–98**—Excessive brake noise can be reduced by installing upgraded pads and rotors. **1998**—Harsh or delayed gear shifts may require the installation of an enhanced garage shift package. • Accessory drive noise may be caused by a misaligned accessory drive pulley. • Delayed or no engine braking in D3 may require the replacement of the forward and coast latch piston assemblies. **1998–99**—Diagnostic and repair tips for a faulty cruise control and speedometer. • Front end clunks and rattles can be silenced by a judicious use of anti-friction materials. **1999–2000**—An engine that runs hot, overheats, or loses coolant, may simply need a new radiator cap. **All models with 4.9L engines: 1991–95**—GM will install a new computer chip that reduces stalling. **Catera: 1997**—Brake squealing can be silenced by installing redesigned calipers. • Oil leakage from the engine timing cover can be corrected by installing a new oil-pump gasket. **1999–2000**—An engine that runs hot, overheats, or loses coolant may simply need a new radiator cap.

Cadillac Allanté, Catera, Eldorado, Seville Profile

	1992	1993	1994	1995	1996	1997	1998	1999
Cost Price ($)								
Allanté	74,198	71,998	—	—	—	—	—	—
Catera	—	—	—	—	—	42,690	43,250	42,310
Eldorado	39,840	40,998	46,498	50,430	50,745	52,015	53,000	52,660
Seville	42,640	44,488	49,998	55,315	55,635	57,000	59,900	59,195
Used Values ($)								
Allanté ↑	21,000	25,000	—	—	—	—	—	—
Allanté ↓	19,000	23,000	—	—	—	—	—	—
Catera ↑	—	—	—	—	—	18,000	23,000	27,000
Catera ↓	—	—	—	—	—	15,000	20,000	23,000
Eldorado ↑	6,500	8,500	10,500	13,500	18,000	23,500	29,000	35,000
Eldorado ↓	5,500	6,000	8,000	11,000	15,000	20,000	26,000	31,000
Seville ↑	7,500	9,000	11,500	15,000	20,000	26,000	32,000	38,000
Seville ↓	6,500	7,000	9,000	12,000	17,000	23,000	28,000	34,000
Extended Warranty	Y	Y	Y	Y	Y	Y	Y	Y
Secret Warranty	Y	Y	Y	Y	Y	Y	Y	Y
Reliability	❷	❷	❷	❷	❷	❷	③	③
Air conditioning	❷	❷	❷	❷	❷	③	③	④
Auto. transmission	❷	❷	❷	❷	③	③	③	④
Body integrity	❷	❷	❷	❷	❷	❷	❷	❷
Braking system	❷	❷	❷	❷	❷	❷	③	③

Electrical system	②	②	②	②	②	②	②	③
Engines	②	②	②	②	③	③	③	③
Exhaust/Converter	②	②	②	③	③	④	④	⑤
Fuel system	②	②	②	③	③	③	④	④
Ignition system	②	②	②	②	③	③	③	③
Rust/Paint	②	②	②	②	②	②	③	③
Steering	②	②	②	②	④	④	④	④
Suspension	②	②	②	②	②	②	③	④
Crash Safety								
Seville	④	—	—	—	—	—	—	—

Note: Reliability figures apply to the Eldorado and Seville only; Allanté and Catera reliability information is given in the text.

Cadillac Brougham, Fleetwood (RWD)

Rating: Above Average (1993–96); Average (1984–92). A smart car for retirees, it's on par with the Ford Crown Victoria and Grand Marquis when it comes to comfort and reliability. **Maintenance/Repair costs:** Average, and repairs aren't dealer dependent. **Parts:** Reasonably priced (independent suppliers sell for much less) and not hard to find, despite the fact that these rear-drives were dropped in '96.

Strengths and weaknesses: The quintessential land yacht, these cars emphasize comfort over handling with their powerful engines and large chassis. Nevertheless, with their spacious interior and many convenience features, these large cars are ideal for vacationing and light trailer pulling.

The most serious problem areas are the fuel-injection system, which frequently malfunctions and costs an arm and a leg to repair; automatic transmissions that shift erratically; a weak suspension; computer-module glitches; poor body assembly; and paint defects. From a reliability/durability standpoint, the rear-drives are much better made than their front-drive counterparts.

GM technical service bulletins show that these vehicles also have noisy power-steering units and cooling fans, the AC bi-level mode produces extreme temperature differences, the instrument panel squeaks and rattles, there are rear quarter-panel gaps and rusting at the rear side-door window moulding, and water leaks into the passenger side of the front compartment.

Safety summary/Recalls: All models: 1995—Dashboard reflects into windshield. • Vehicle accelerated while braking. • Frequent stalling. • Trunk lid opened while driving. • Brakes require extended stopping distances. **1996**—Airbags failed to deploy. • Seatbelts didn't restrain driver and passenger during a collision. • Chronic stalling due to fuel-sending unit failure. • Engine head gaskets failures. • Transmission pounds when shifting gears. • Water-pump leakage on the serpentine belt may cause steering to lock up. • Power-steering hose and pump failure. • Brakes often lock up when applied. • Excessive brake noise caused by the premature wearout of brake rotor and drum. • AC cooling switch and high-pressure hose failures. • Instrument cluster hard to read in daylight. • Power door locks and trunk lock frequently fail to operate properly. • Loose windshield moulding. • Defective keyless entry module. **Recalls: All models: 1993**—Passenger-side airbag may have a defective igniter. **1994**—Oil-cooler inlet hose leaks. • Lug nuts may loosen. • Fuel-tank strap fasteners can detach. **1994–95**—Throttle control spring may stick in low temperatures.

Secret Warranties/Service Tips

All models: 1993–96—Defective catalytic converters that cause a rotten-egg smell in the interior may be replaced free of charge under the emissions warranty. • Paint delamination, peeling, or fading (see Part Two). **1995**—A popping noise during cranking, the engine cranks but won't start, no fuel pressure, or extended crank time after cold soak. • Lack of power. • Engine oil leak at the rear main seal or T-joint. • Low oil pressure, loss of oil pressure, or lack of power. • AC odour. • Grinding or scraping noise in Park or Neutral • A cold-start rattle with the 4T60E automatic transmission. • Front-brake vibration and/or pedal pulsation. • A rubbing noise when the front wheels are turned all the way. • Door window scraping noise or sticking, rattle noise from front of vehicle, and excessive radio static. • A clicking noise from under the dash or hood. • A front-seat clicking noise. • Erroneous fuel-gauge readings, a low-voltage reading or dim lights at idle, and frequent blown fuse or battery drain. • Malfunctioning remote keyless entry. • Wet or smelly carpet from water leaks. • Poor paint application and rust spots. **1996**—3–2 part throttle downshift flare. • Engine noise (install new valve stem oil seal). • Transmission chuggle/surge. • Transmission fluid leak from pump body (replace bushing). • Crunch/pop noise in steering system. • AC odours. • Radio frequency interference diagnosis. **All models with 5.7L engines: 1994–96**—A chuggle or surge condition will require a reflash calibration. • Excessive engine noise can be silenced by installing an upgraded valve-stem oil seal. **1995**—Intermittent Neutral/loss of Drive at highway speeds can be fixed by replacing the control valve body assembly. **1996–97**—A torque converter clutch buzz or moan requires the installation of an upgraded case-cover assembly spacer plate and the upper control valve body. **1997–98**—Excessive front brake noise can be reduced by installing upgraded pads and rotors. **1998–99**—Diagnostic and repair tips for a faulty cruise control and speedometer. • Front end clunks and rattles can be silenced by a judicious use of anti-friction materials. **1999–2000**—An engine that runs hot, overheats, or loses coolant may simply need a new radiator cap. **Fleetwood (RWD): 1993**—Noisy transmissions, power-steering units, and cooling fans. • Instrument panel squeaks and rattles. • Rusting at the rear side door window moulding. • Water leaks into the passenger side of the front compartment.

Cadillac Brougham, Fleetwood (RWD) Profile

	1990	1991	1992	1993	1994	1995	1996
Cost Price ($)							
Brougham, Fleetwood (RWD)	39,816	37,298	37,488	39,988	41,798	46,830	46,965
Used Values ($)							
Brougham, Fleetwood (RWD) ↑	5,000	6,000	7,000	8,500	10,500	13,500	17,500
Brougham, Fleetwood (RWD) ↓	4,000	5,000	6,000	7,500	8,000	10,500	14,500
Extended Warranty	Y	Y	Y	Y	Y	Y	Y
Secret Warranty	Y	Y	Y	Y	Y	Y	Y
Reliability	③	③	③	③	③	④	④

Note: The Brougham and Fleetwood (RWD) haven't been crash-tested.

Cadillac Concours, DeVille, Fleetwood (FWD)

Rating: Average (1995–99); Below Average (1985–94). There are two major safety problems affecting 1995–99 models: inadvertent side and front airbag deployment and chronic stalling in traffic. Ask dealer to shut off the airbags until GM fixes your vehicle. **Maintenance/Repair costs:** Higher than average, and most repairs must be done by a dealer. **Parts:** Higher-than-average cost (independent suppliers sell for much less), but not hard to find. All of these front-drives require a three- to five-year supplementary warranty.

Strengths and weaknesses: Although they have better handling and are almost as comfortable as the old series, the early models of these luxury coupes and sedans aren't worth considering because of their dismal reliability and overly complex servicing. Redesigned 1995–99 versions have posted fewer complaints; however, they are still far below the industry norm for quality and reliability. As with the Eldorado and Seville, you get the best array of handling, braking, and performance features with the 1996 and later versions. They do ride more quietly and comfortably, but fuel economy is still poor, the dash controls and gauges are confusing and not easily accessible, and the rear view is obstructed by the high trunk lid and large side pillars.

The 4.3L V6, 4.1L V8, and 4.5L V8 engines and 4-speed automatic transmission suffer from a variety of terminal maladies including oil leaks, premature wear, poor fuel economy, and excessive noise. The electrical system and related components are temperamental. The suspension goes soft quickly, and the front brakes often wear out after only 18 months/20,000 km. Problems with the digital fuel-injection and engine control systems are very difficult to diagnose and repair. Poor body assembly is characterized by premature paint peeling and rusting, excessive wind noise in the interior, and fragile trim items.

Technical service bulletins: Concours, DeVille: 1995–96—Engine oil leaks from upper to lower crankcase joint. • Loss of oil pressure and/or lack of power. • Oil leakage from the oil pan to lower crankcase attaching bolts. • Poor AC cooling in traffic and high ambient temperatures. • AC defrost creaking noise. • AC odours. • Steering column noise. • Insufficient heat distribution or lack of airflow. • Erratic or inaccurate instrument-panel displays and gauges. • Insufficient remote keyless entry operating range. • Inaccurate fuel gauge. • Exhaust rattles. • Rattling heard when vehicle goes over bumps. • Clicking noise from front seats. • Squawk noise from rear of vehicle in cold temperatures. • Slow parking-brake release or slow HVAC mode changes. • Vertical seat height adjustment tips. • Abnormal condensation in taillights and other lights. • Wet or smelly carpet from water leaks. **1997**—Fuel tank won't fill to capacity/always reads full. • Front brake noise. • Remote won't open doors or trunk. • Excessive vibration of electrochromatic mirror. • Front-door front auxiliary weather strip loose. • Uncomfortable front seatback. • Horn hard to operate when cold. • Inoperative power door locks. • Metallic buzz or rattle at the instrument panel when the brakes are applied. • No warning light or driver information centre message. • Power window inoperative after express down feature is used. • Torque converter clutch buzz or moan. **1997–98**—Tips on reducing AC odours, squeaks, rattles, groans, and clunks from the front and rear of the vehicle. • Other bulletins address excessive front brake noise, harsh or delayed shifting, and delayed or no braking through engine compression. **1999**—Diagnostic and repair tips for a faulty cruise control and speedometer. • Engine runs hot, overheats, or loses coolant. • Front end clunks and rattles.

Safety summary/Recalls: DeVille: 1998—Inadvertent side airbag deployment (see below). • Wheel flew off car after wheel studs failed. • Vehicle suddenly accelerated killing one person and injuring others. • Accelerator sticking. • Cruise control self-activates. • Chronic stalling while underway. • Can't read speedometer in daylight. • Many complaints of front and rear brake rotor warpage and premature pad and caliper failure. • Sudden loss of power steering. • Vehicle tends to wander all over the road. • Leaking engine oil cooler. • Windshield washer fluid doesn't pump high enough. • Gas tank sensor failure causes inaccurate fuel readings. • Tire failure (Vogue). • Exterior mirrors are too small and when vehicle is in Reverse, rear-view mirror automatically tilts down. • Interior light frequently malfunction. • Chronic battery failure. **1999**—Airbags explode when vehicle is started, idles, accelerates, or is parked. Several occupants have been injured. NHTSA looked into a flood of complaints of inadvertent side airbag deployment on 1998 and 1999 models and forced GM to recall these cars. Problem is, GM says it won't have the parts to correct the defect before April 2001. Drivers are demanding that dealers disconnect the system until it is corrected. • Incidents where front and side airbags failed to deploy in a collision. • Engine overheating, loose head bolts, and excessive oil consumption. • Stalling when coasting or coming to a stop. • Vehicle rolls backward when in gear. • Fuel tank leaks fuel. • Premature warpage of the front and rear brake rotors. • Failure-prone ignition and electronic control module. • Tire flew off while vehicle was underway. • Factory-equipped jack inadequate to support vehicle. • Instrument panel lighting hard to read in daylight. • Power door locks operate erratically. • Windshield wipers won't come on unless turned on high setting. • Driver's seatbelt constantly tightens up. **DeVille, Concours: 1995–96**—A short circuit caused by wet carpets could cause the airbags to suddenly deploy. **Recalls: All models: 1994–95**—Accelerator pedal may stick. **1996**—Hood may fly up. **1997**—Faulty Brake Traction Control module could increase stopping distance. **All models with 4.9L engines: 1991–95**—GM will install a new computer chip that reduces chronic stalling. **DeVille with 4.9L engines: 1991–93**—Upper transaxle oil cooler hose could come loose and create a fire hazard.

Secret Warranties/Service Tips

All models/years: Defective catalytic converters that cause a rotten-egg smell in the interior may be replaced free of charge under the emissions warranty. • Paint delamination, peeling, or fading (see Part Two). **1994**—Condensation dripping from the heater duct requires the installation of a watertight dam in the HVAC case. • An inoperative cruise control or brake/transmission interlock may signal a misadjusted stop-light switch assembly. • TSB #476003 goes into great detail about how to troubleshoot the various engine oil leaks afflicting 1994 models. • Doors that won't stay open on slight grades require upgraded door springs. • Noisy fuel pumps can be silenced only by installing an upgraded fuel pump under warranty. • TSB #476506 gives lots of tips on fixing 4.6L engines that run roughly, miss, surge, or hesitate. • Poor heat distribution (driver's feet get cold) can be fixed by replacing the floor outlet assembly. • Rear compartment water leaks are addressed in TSB #311510. **1998**—Harsh or delayed gear shifts may require the installation of an enhanced garage shift package. • Delayed or no engine braking in D3 may require the replacement of the forward and coast latch piston assemblies.

Cadillac Concours, DeVille, Fleetwood (FWD) Profile

	1992	1993	1994	1995	1996	1997	1998	1999
Cost Price ($)								
Concours	—	—	49,498	53,690	54,340	56,985	58,600	57,490
DeVille	37,388	39,685	41,998	46,635	48,125	49,400	50,495	49,710
Fleetwood (FWD)	37,389	39,988	41,798	46,830	46,965	—	—	—
Used Values ($)								
Concours ↑	—	—	10,000	13,500	18,000	24,000	31,000	37,000
Concours ↓	—	—	7,500	11,500	15,500	21,000	28,000	34,000

DeVille ↑	6,000	7,500	9,000	12,000	16,500	22,000	27,000	33,000
DeVille ↓	5,000	6,500	7,000	10,000	14,000	19,000	24,000	30,000
Fleetwood (FWD)↑	6,500	8,500	10,500	13,000	17,000	—	—	—
Fleetwood (FWD)↓	5,500	6,500	8,000	10,000	14,500	—	—	—
Extended Warranty	Y	Y	Y	Y	Y	Y	Y	Y
Secret Warranty	N	N	Y	Y	Y	Y	Y	Y
Reliability	②	②	②	②	②	③	③	③
Air conditioning	②	②	②	③	③	③	④	④
Auto. transmission	④	④	④	④	④	⑤	⑤	⑤
Body integrity	②	③	③	②	②	②	③	③
Braking system	②	②	②	②	②	②	②	③
Electrical system	②	②	②	②	②	②	③	③
Engines	②	②	②	③	③	③	④	④
Exhaust/Converter	③	③	④	④	④	④	⑤	⑤
Fuel system	②	②	②	②	③	③	③	③
Ignition system	②	②	②	②	③	③	③	③
Rust/Paint	②	③	③	③	④	④	④	⑤
Steering	②	②	②	②	③	④	④	④
Suspension	②	②	③	③	③	③	④	④
Crash Safety								
DeVille	④	—	③	④	④	—	—	④
Side Impact								
DeVille	—	—	—	—	—	④	④	④

INFINITI

G20, I30, J30, Q45

Rating: Above Average (1995–99); Average (1991–94). The fully equipped Maxima, Accord, Camry, Avalon, Millenia, and 929 are better buys from a price/quality standpoint, but they don't have the same luxury cachet. The 1997–99 Q45s were "de-contented" by Infiniti, meaning they sold for less because they were made more cheaply, came with fewer standard features, and were equipped with a smaller, less powerful engine. Despite obvious cost-cutting in the manufacturing process, though, these vehicles have had surprisingly few safety-related defects reported to the federal government. **Maintenance/Repair costs:** Higher than average, and repairs must be done by either an Infiniti or a Nissan dealer. This is worrisome inasmuch as Nissan dealers have had a string of poor-sales years and may be tempted to make up the profit loss through their service bays. **Parts:** Higher-than-average cost, but not hard to find (except for body panels).

Strengths and weaknesses: With its emphasis on sporty handling, the Infiniti series takes the opposite tack from the Lexus, which puts the accent on comfort and luxury. Still, the Infiniti comes fully equipped and offers owners the prestige of driving a comfortable, reliable, and nicely styled luxury car. One serious weakness, however, is the 1994 airbag-equipped J30's poor crash rating—all the more surprising when one considers that the 1992 Nissan Maxima passed the NHTSA 57 km/h crash tests with flying colours.

G20

The least expensive Infiniti, the G20 is a front-drive luxury sports sedan that uses a base 2.0L 140-hp 16-valve, twin-cam, 4-cylinder powerplant to accelerate smoothly, albeit noisily, through all gear ranges. Dual airbags came on line midway through the 1993 model year and ABS is standard. Cruise control is a bit erratic, particularly when traversing hilly terrain. Unlike the engine, the automatic transmission is silent and power is reduced automatically when shifting. Steering is precise and responsive on the highway. However, the rear end tends to swing out sharply following abrupt steering changes. Early Infiniti G20s rode a bit too firmly, which led to the suspension being softened on the 1994 model. Now drivers say that the suspension tends to bounce and jiggle occupants whenever the car goes over uneven pavement or the load is increased.

Overall, however, the Infiniti G20s aren't as refined as their entry-level Lexus counterparts in interior space, drivetrain, or convenience features. Owners have complained that the engine's lack of low-speed torque means that it has to work hard above 4000 rpm—while protesting noisily—to produce brisk engine response in the higher gear ranges. The automatic transmission shifts roughly, particularly when passing (a problem corrected in the 1994 models); the power steering needs more assist during parking maneuvers; and the dealer-installed fog lights cost an exorbitant $500 to replace. Poorly thought-out control layout is best exemplified by the hard-to-reach heat/vent controls, an armrest-mounted trunk and filler release that's inconvenient to operate, and centre console–mounted power window switches that are difficult to find while driving. Tall drivers will find the leg room insufficient. The trunk is spacious, but its small opening is limited by the angle of the rear window.

There are three helpful bulletins containing troubleshooting tips for AC compressor leaks and noise, Code 45 driveability alerts, and brake shudder and steering-wheel shimmy.

I30, J30

Resembling the 929 Serenia, the rear-drive, four-door J30 and its high-performance variant, the I30, are sized and priced midway between the G20 and the top-of-the-line Q45. The J30 uses a modified version of the Nissan 300ZX's 3.0L 210-hp V6 engine. Although the vehicle is replete with important safety features and accelerates and handles well, its engine is noisy, passenger and cargo room have been sacrificed to styling, and fuel economy is underwhelming. The more spacious, better-performing I30 replaced the J30 in 1997.

The J30 comes with a standard airbag (or dual airbags, depending on the model year), ABS, and traction control. It's changed very little over the years, meaning that there's no reason to choose a more recent model over a much cheaper older version. Alternatively, consider buying an Acura Legend, Lexus ES 300, or a fully equipped Accord, Maxima, 929, Cressida, or Camry.

Technical service bulletins list the following two defects affecting the '95s: a front seat rattling noise and a loose B-pillar lower finisher. For all J30 model years, there are a number of other helpful bulletins containing troubleshooting tips for AC compressor leaks and noise, brake clunking noises and pedal pulsation, hard starts, rough idle, water leaks, Code 45 driveability alerts, and brake shudder and steering-wheel shimmy.

Q45

This luxury sedan provides performance while its chief rival, the Lexus ES 400, provides luxury and quiet. Faster and glitzier than other cars in its category, the Q45 uses a 32-valve 278-hp 4.5L V8 tire burner not frequently found on a Japanese luxury compact. It accelerates faster than the Lexus, going 0–100 km/h in 7.1 seconds without a hint of noise or abrupt shifting. Unlike the base engine of the G20, though, the Q45's engine supplies plenty of upper-range torque as well. The suspension was softened in 1994, but the car still rides much more firmly than its Lexus counterpart. The four-wheel steering is precise, but the standard limited-slip differential is no help in preventing the car's rear end from sliding out on slippery roads, due mainly to the original equipment "sport" tires designed mainly for 190 km/h autobahn cruising. There's not much foot room for passengers, and cargo room is disappointing. Fuel economy is nonexistent. ABS is standard, but a passenger-side airbag wasn't available before 1994. A redesigned 1994 version got a restyled front end, a chrome grille, and an updated instrument panel.

Three years later, the car was again made over with the addition of a downsized 4.1L V8 set on a smaller platform, effectively changing the character of the car from a sporty performer to a highway cruiser. Other changes in the ensuing model years were minor: front seatbelt pretensioners for the '98s; and minor interior and exterior restyling of the 1999 models.

Owners report excessive wind noise around the A-pillars, sunroof wind leaks, tire thumping noise, cellular telephone echoing, faulty CD players, and a popping sound from the radio. Owners of 1999 Q45s report that the paint scratches and flakes off so easily that it has to be constantly touched up.

Technical service bulletins list the following defects affecting the 1994–96 models: AC not blowing cold, front brake pad noise, low or rough idle, doors locking/unlocking themselves, and windshield cracking. You may also be interested in reviewing other helpful bulletins that contain troubleshooting tips for AC compressor leaks and noise, brake clunking noises and pedal pulsation, booming/drone noise and vibration, cold-weather hard starts, rough idle, suspension noise, Code 45 driveability alerts, and brake shudder and steering-wheel shimmy.

Bulletins for the 1997 model don't cover much that's new, concerning themselves principally with clunking noises and pedal pulsation, cold-weather starting tips, hard starting, and rough idle and suspension noise diagnostic tips. 1998 bulletins contain no useful tips and the 1999 TSBs are integrated into the "Secret Warranties/Service Tips" section.

Safety summary/Recalls: G20: 1995—Driver seriously injured by airbag deployment when vehicle was pushed into a wall at low speed. • Faulty cruise control wouldn't disengage, brakes failed, and collision ensued. • Defective fuel-filler tube/fuel-vent tube. • Frequent stalling. • Large sun visor blocks driver's view of stoplights. • Passenger-side power windows operate erratically. • Defective speaker amplifier. • Centre console handle broke. **1996**—Violent deployment of airbag during collision resulted in permanent eye damage. • Brakes were applied to disengage cruise control and vehicle suddenly accelerated. • Noisy brakes; dealer cannot fix the problem. • Oil pressure switch failure. **1999**—Carbon monoxide poisoning. • When car is put into Reverse, driver's seat reclines, without warning. **J30: 1995**—Airbag failed to deploy. • Airbags deployed during low speed (11 km/h) fender-bender, causing extensive injuries to occupants. • Rear end swings out when accelerating. • Excessive vibrations when accelerating make vehicle difficult to steer. • Driver's seatbelt won't retract. **Q45: 1995**—Sudden acceleration when coming to a stop. • Gas and brake pedals are set too close together. • Failure of driver's power seat adjuster motor. • Hood flew up while driving along the highway at about 100 km/h. **1996**—Airbag indicator flashes due to ECM failure. • Premature failure of the shock absorber and power window. **1997**—Owner alleges that vehicle design causes the vehicle to hydroplane where other cars wouldn't. • Airbag warning light comes on for no reason. • When car is put into Reverse, driver's seat reclines, without warning. • Severe front end vibration continued after tires were replaced. **1998**—Airbag failed to deploy. • Accelerator pedal stuck while vehicle was stopped. **Recalls: G20: 1991–92**—Rear seatbelt buckle may only partially engage. **1991–96**—Possible fuel leakage from a corroded fuel-filler tube. **1993–95**—Harness connector protector near seatbelt pretensioner can ignite. • Cabin may catch fire in a collision. **J30: 1993–94**—Cabin may catch fire in a collision. **Q45: 1991–92**—On models with Bose speakers, circuit board may short out, overheat, and burn. **1997–98**—Key can be removed when shift lever is not in Park and engine is shut off; dealers will replace the shift lock control unit.

Secret Warranties/Service Tips

All models/years—Troubleshooting tips to correct hard starts. • Vehicles with sunroofs may have wind noise coming from the sunroof area because of a small pinhole in the body sealer at the rear C-pillar. • Windshield cracking. • Erratic operation of the power antenna requires that the antenna rod be replaced. • Slow retraction of the front seatbelt can be fixed by wiping off any residue found on the seatbelt D-ring. **G20: 1999**—Excessive blower noise can be reduced by installing a new cover. • Coolant leakage may be caused by a defective intake manifold expansion plug. • Replace the window glass run rubber if window makes a popping sound when opened. **I30: 1996–1998**—If either one of the front power seats won't move, check for a broken power seat drive cable. **1996–2000**—Excessive blower noise can be reduced by installing a new cover. **Q45: 1990**—The following noises require the following repairs, according to TSB #ITB90-039: valve ticking—replace valves/guides; front engine block knocking—replace tensioners; tapping from valves during warm-up—replace pivot/rocker; tapping from valves at all times—check cam bearings. **1990–91**—A driveline vibration or drone at moderate speeds can be eliminated by installing a new balance propshaft assembly. **1991**—Transmission overheating and failures forced Infiniti to extend the warranty to seven years in order to compensate owners whose transmissions had insufficient cooling and filtration. Furthermore, the company installed an external cooler and filter at no charge. **1994–96**—Doors that intermittently lock by themselves require the installation of countermeasure front door lock actuators (TSB #NTB96-027). **1997–99**—A lumbar support mechanism that's inoperative should be replaced with an upgraded support mechanism. • If either one of the front power seats won't move, check for a broken power seat drive cable. • Excessive blower noise can be reduced by installing a new cover. • TSB #ITB98-062 gives an exhaustive listing for a variety of squeak and rattle repairs. **1997–2000**—TSB #ITB00-010 gives a detailed list of brake shudder countermeasures. **1998–99**—An automatic transmission that produces a "double thump" noise when coming to a stop likely needs a new transmission control module.

G20, I30, J30, Q45 Profile

	1992	1993	1994	1995	1996	1997	1998	1999
Cost Price ($)								
G20	25,275	23,440	26,440	29,540	31,440	—	—	29,950
I30	—	—	—	—	40,600	41,000	41,350	41,950
J30	—	41,500	45,000	48,100	51,600	52,600	—	—
Q45	54,000	59,500	72,000	75,450	72,000	65,000	66,500	71,000
Used Values ($)								
G20 ↑	5,500	8,000	9,500	11,000	13,500	—	—	20,000
G20 ↓	4,500	6,000	7,000	9,000	11,000	—	—	19,000
I30 ↑	—	—	—	—	16,000	20,000	24,500	28,000
I30 ↓	—	—	—	—	14,000	18,000	22,000	26,000
J30 ↑	—	9,000	11,000	15,500	19,000	25,000	—	—
J30 ↓	—	7,500	9,000	13,000	17,000	23,000	—	—
Q45 ↑	8,500	10,500	14,000	20,000	27,000	34,000	40,000	45,000
Q45 ↓	7,500	8,000	11,000	16,000	23,000	31,000	36,000	42,000
Extended Warranty	N	N	N	N	N	N	N	N
Secret Warranty	N	N	N	N	N	N	N	N
Reliability	❷	❷	❷	④	④	⑤	④	④
Air conditioning	❷	③	③	③	③	③	④	⑤
Auto. transmission	❷	❷	❷	③	④	④	④	⑤
Body integrity	❷	❷	❷	③	③	③	❷	③
Braking system	❷	❷	❷	❷	❷	❷	❷	③
Electrical system	❷	❷	❷	③	③	③	❷	③
Engines	❷	③	④	④	⑤	⑤	④	④
Exhaust/Converter	④	④	④	④	⑤	⑤	⑤	⑤
Fuel system	❷	❷	③	④	④	③	④	④
Ignition system	④	⑤	⑤	⑤	⑤	⑤	⑤	⑤
Rust/Paint	③	③	④	⑤	⑤	⑤	⑤	⑤
Steering	❷	③	④	④	④	⑤	③	⑤
Suspension	③	③	③	④	⑤	⑤	③	⑤
Crash Safety								
I30	—	—	—	—	④	④	④	—
J30	—	—	④	④	④	—	—	—
Side Impact								
I30	—	—	—	—	—	④	—	—

LEXUS

ES 300, GS 300, LS 400, SC 400

Rating: Recommended (1996–99); Above Average (1990–95). More reliable and better built than the Infiniti, but more costly too. The 1996 and 1998 models were the first to incorporate important safety, performance, and styling improvements. A fully equipped Legend, Accord, Maxima, or Camry will provide airbags, comparable highway performance, and reliability at far less initial cost. But, if you do pay top dollar for a used Lexus, its slow rate of depreciation virtually guarantees that you'll get much of your money back. Keep in mind that Lexus airbags pack a mighty wallop and may cause severe injuries; install an off-switch or look for depowered airbags. Keep in mind that the LS 400 depreciates much more slowly than the SC 400, resulting in the SC 400 costing far less used, despite the fact it sold originally for almost as much as the LS 400. **Maintenance/Repair costs:** Higher than average, and repairs must be done by either a Lexus or a Toyota dealer. **Parts:** Higher-than-average cost, but not hard to find (except for body panels).

Strengths and weaknesses: These are benchmark cars known for their bulletproof reliability and impressive performance. Sports cars, they're not. But if you're looking for your father's Oldsmobile (if your dad was Japanese), these luxury cars fill the bill. Like the Acuras and Infinitis, Lexus models all suffer from some automatic transmission, front-brake, electrical, body, trim, and accessory deficiencies that are confirmed by confidential technical service bulletins.

ES 300
Resembling an LS 400 dressed in sporty attire, the entry-level ES 300 was launched in 1992 to fill the gap between the discontinued ES 250 and the LS 400. In fact, the ES 300 has many of the attributes of the LS 400 sedan for much less money. A five-passenger sedan based on the Camry, it comes equipped with a standard 3.0L 24-valve engine that produces 181–210 horsepower coupled to either a 5-speed manual or a 4-speed electronically controlled automatic transmission. Unlike the Infinitis, the ES 300 accelerates smoothly and quietly, while averaging about 14L/100 km in mixed driving. The suspension is soft and steady. Passenger and cargo room are plentiful, with lots of leg and head room (except on sunroof-equipped versions).

ABS is standard, but a second airbag became available only on the 1994 model, which also introduced a new 3.0L 6-cylinder that boosted horsepower a bit. The '95 and '96 models were carried over unchanged, but the '97 ES 300 was completely revamped, offering a restyled interior and exterior, increased interior dimensions, and additional horsepower. The '98s got depowered airbags along with side airbags and an upgraded anti-theft system. The 3.0L V6 got another small horsepower boost for the 1999 model year.

Surprisingly for a vehicle this well made, government-reported safety-related defects are legion. Airbag-induced injuries, sudden acceleration, ABS and Goodyear tire failures, interior window fogging, and AC toxic emanations are only a few of the ES 300 complaints that carried over many years and have been reported with other Lexus models.

GS 300

The rear-drive GS 300 is a step up from the front-drive ES 300 and just a rung below Lexus's top-of-the-line LS 400. It carries the same V6 engine as the ES 300, except it has 20 more horses. This produces sparkling performance at higher speeds, though the car is disappointingly sluggish from a start. Fuel economy is sacrificed for performance, however, and the base suspension and tires pass noisily over small bumps and ruts. Visibility is also less than impressive, with large rear pillars and a narrow rear window restricting the view. There's not much usable trunk space either, and the liftover is unreasonably high.

This sports sedan, first launched as a 1993 model, carrying standard dual airbags and ABS, didn't change much until the 1996 model year when it got a light rear end restyling and a 5-speed automatic transmission. The car was totally reworked, however, for the '98 model year when it was once again restyled and given an overhead cam V8.

LS 400

The Lexus flagship, the LS 400 rear-drive outclasses all other luxury sedans in reliability, styling, and function. The base engine is a 242- to 290-hp 4.0L V8 that provides smooth, impressive acceleration and superior highway passing ability at all speeds. Its transmission is smooth and efficient. The suspension gives an easy ride without body roll or front-end plow during emergency stops, thereby delivering a major comfort advantage over other luxury compacts. There's an absence of engine and wind noise.

ABS and dual airbags are standard. A passenger airbag, alloy wheels, larger tires and brakes, interior upgrades, and revised exterior styling characterized the '93 models. Two years later, the '95 version got increased interior and exterior dimensions, a more powerful engine, and a better-performing drivetrain for quicker acceleration. Side airbags were added to the '97s. The '98 models got a whole slew of improvements that included a 4-cam V8 with continuously-variable valve timing, a new 5-speed automatic transmission, Vehicle Skid Control (VSC), and a host of interior upgrades. There were no significant changes to the 1999 LS 400.

Owners have complained that the brakes don't inspire confidence, owing to their mushy feel and average performance. Furthermore, there's limited rear foot room under the front seats, and the rear middle passenger has to sit on the transmission hump. This gas-guzzler is thirsty for premium fuel.

SC 300, SC 400

These two coupes are practically identical, except for their engines and luxury features. The cheaper SC 300 gives you the same high-performance 6-cylinder engine used by the GS 300 and Toyota Supra, while the SC 400 uses the same 4.0L V8 engine found in the LS 400. You're likely to find fewer luxury features with the SC 300 because they were sold as options. Nevertheless, look for an SC with traction control for additional safety during poor driving conditions. On the downside, V8 fuel consumption is horrendous, rear seating is cramped, and trunk space is unimpressive. Also, invest in a good anti-theft device, or your Lexus relationship will be over almost before it begins.

The 1993 models gained a passenger airbag; '95s were slightly restyled; and the '96 400 series was given the LS 400's V8. The '98 model year SC 400 got a 4.0L, 4-cam aluminum V8 engine, while the SC 300 continued to use the previous year's inline-six, but ditched its 5-speed manual transmission. Other upgrades: variable-valve timing, a more-refined 5-speed automatic transmission, a new anti-theft system, and depowered airbags.

Technical service bulletins: All models: 1996—Front brake groan. • Static noise on weak AM stations. **1998**—Inoperative Nakamichi radio. **ES 300: 1992–96**—Upgraded components to reduce front brake noise. **1995–96**—CD changer won't eject magazine. • Direct clutch improvements. • Front brake groan. • Static noise on weak AM stations. **1995–98**—Moon roof panel wind noise. **1997**—Steering rack noise. **LS 400: 1995**—Engine knocking, front seat cushion noise, front stabilizer bushing noise, strut bar cushion noise, and sun visor rattling. **SC 300, SC 400: 1995**—Rear suspension rattling or clacking, probably caused by a faulty rear spring bumper (replace with an upgraded spring bumper).

Safety summary/Recalls: All models: 1995—Airbags failed to deploy. • Both front seatbelts failed to lock during a collision. • Seatbelt failed to restrain passenger during collision. • Goodyear Eagle tire blowout. • Premature failure of the electronic control unit. • Transmission leaks. • Brake pedal design makes it difficult for someone with a shoe size larger than men's 9 to use the brakes. • Excessive noise when braking. • Faulty windshield mouldings cause excessive wind noise. **1996**—Fire in the engine compartment. • Frequent reports that the airbag failed to deploy. • Weak seatback collapsed rearward in a collision. • Entire vehicle shimmies. • Sudden steering failure when turning. **1997**—Vehicle left in Park rolled backward and hit another car. Same thing occurred with a vehicle parked in a garage, but this time cause was isolated to a failure of the shift lock actuator fuse. • Owner says airbags are a hazard for short people. Also, floor pedals are located too high and are too far apart for short people. • Middle rear shoulder belt locks up, making it very difficult to get occupant out; owner had to cut the belt. • Instrument cluster lights aren't bright enough for night driving. • AC assembly panel failure. **1998**—Vehicle accelerated as brakes were applied. • Premature front brake pad wearout. • Seat adjustment motor failure. **ES 300: 1993**—Engine compartment fire. • Airbags fail to deploy. • Airbag deployed and caught on fire. • Airbag deployment burned driver severely. • Airbags deployed when vehicle at a standstill, causing severe burns to driver's nose and hands. • In another incident, car was bumped slightly, airbags deployed 10 seconds later, and driver received severe facial injuries. • ABS system failures. • Goodyear tires experience blowouts and are worn out prematurely at 15,000 km. • Steering tie-rod broke while driving, causing loss of steering and an accident. • Transmission doesn't engage right away, but when it does engage, it jumps forward. • When vehicle goes over a bump, the steering wheel jumps out of hand. • Foul odour from AC caused occupants to fall ill with bronchial infection. • Several reports that dashboard emits fumes that fog inside window glass. • Headlights provide poor illumination. • Driver can't read speedometer when sun shines onto dash. • Seatback collapsed backward when vehicle was rear-ended. **Recalls: ES 300: 1994–98**—Steering wheel may come off while driving. **GS 300: 1993–94**—Premature ball joint wear could affect steering and handling. An upgraded ball joint socket will be installed. **LS 400: 1990**—Cruise control may not return to its former position. • Prolonged illumination of the centre-mounted brake light. **1995–97**— A faulty starter-motor magnetic switch may cause a fire or render the starter inoperative. **SC 400: 1996–97**—A faulty starter-motor magnetic switch may cause a fire or render the starter inoperative.

Secret Warranties/Service Tips

ES 300: 1992—Inaccurate fuel gauges require an improved indicator needle. **1992–93**—Rear stabilizer bar bushing noise can be eliminated by installing upgraded bushings. **1992–96**—Upgraded front brake pads and a shim kit will eliminate excessive brake noise. **1993**—Problems with hot start or poor engine performance when going downhill require the installation of an upgraded ECM. • Front seat headrest rattles can be corrected by installing an improved headrest support. **1996–99**—A knocking noise from under the floor in the rear of the car can be fixed by following the field fix outlined in TSB #SU005-96. **1997–99**—New front brake pads have been developed to reduce brake grind and groan. Toyota will install them for free under its "goodwill" policy. **1997–2000**—Front suspension noise may be silenced by installing an upgraded suspension support, says TSB #SU002-99. **1999**—If the vehicle shudders during a 2–3 shift, try changing the transaxle valve body under warranty, before moving on to other repairs. **LS 400: 1990**—Front brake popping can be corrected by installing a modified pad support plate and applying new adhesive. • Moon roof wind noise may be corrected by realigning the roof panel. • Faulty cruise control assemblies will be replaced with an improved assembly (SSC 901). • **1990–91**—To prevent transmission clicking when shifting from Neutral to Drive or Reverse, reduce the depth of the flange yoke assembly. • AC groaning can be eliminated by reducing the expansion valve flow rate and adding an O-ring to the EPR piston. **1998–99**—An upgraded blower motor that is better at maintaining blower speed will be installed under warranty.

ES 300, GS 300, LS 400, SC 400 Profile

	1992	1993	1994	1995	1996	1997	1998	1999
Cost Price ($)								
ES 300	34,400	37,300	41,300	44,700	45,600	42,960	43,820	44,235
GS 300	—	54,700	57,800	66,100	71,400	71,400	58,900	59,220
LS 400	63,000	67,200	71,100	75,900	78,700	78,700	78,300	78,690
SC 400	57,000	61,000	64,600	74,600	80,800	82,100	84,000	—
Used Values ($)								
ES 300 ↑	8,000	10,000	13,500	16,000	19,500	23,000	26,000	30,000
ES 300 ↓	7,000	8,500	12,000	14,000	17,500	20,000	24,000	28,000
GS 300 ↑	—	12,000	15,000	19,000	23,000	28,000	33,000	39,000
GS 300 ↓	—	10,000	13,000	16,000	20,000	25,000	31,000	37,000
LS 400 ↑	12,000	15,000	20,000	26,000	32,500	40,000	48,000	54,000
LS 400 ↓	10,500	11,500	16,000	22,000	28,500	36,000	44,000	51,000
SC 400 ↑	13,000	16,000	21,000	28,000	34,000	42,000	50,000	—
SC 400 ↓	11,500	13,000	18,000	24,000	31,000	38,000	46,000	—
Extended Warranty	N	N	N	N	N	N	N	N
Secret Warranty	N	N	N	N	N	N	N	N
Reliability	③	④	④	⑤	⑤	⑤	⑤	⑤
Air conditioning	②	②	③	④	⑤	⑤	⑤	⑤
Auto. transmission	③	④	⑤	⑤	⑤	⑤	⑤	⑤
Body integrity	②	②	③	④	⑤	⑤	⑤	⑤
Braking system	②	②	②	②	②	③	④	④
Electrical system	②	②	③	③	④	④	④	④
Engines	②	③	③	③	⑤	⑤	⑤	⑤
Exhaust/Converter	④	④	⑤	⑤	⑤	⑤	⑤	⑤
Fuel system	④	④	⑤	⑤	⑤	⑤	⑤	⑤
Ignition system	③	④	⑤	⑤	⑤	⑤	⑤	⑤
Rust/Paint	⑤	⑤	⑤	⑤	⑤	⑤	⑤	⑤
Steering	④	④	⑤	⑤	⑤	⑤	⑤	⑤
Suspension	②	②	③	④	⑤	⑤	⑤	⑤
Crash Safety								
ES 300	—	—	—	—	⑤	—	④	④
GS 300	—	—	③	③	③	③	—	—
Side Impact								
ES 300	—	—	—	—	—	—	⑤	⑤

MAZDA

Millenia

Rating: Above Average (1995–99). Lots of power and sophisticated mechanicals make this luxury tourer a winner. From a performance standpoint, the Camry V6 (with its less complicated powertrain) out-runs the Millenia. Unusually rapid depreciation for a Japanese luxury car means there are plenty of bargains out there—just make sure the engine and transmission are functioning properly. **Maintenance/ Repair costs:** Higher than average, and repairs must be done by a Mazda dealer. **Parts:** Higher-than-average cost, despite Mazda's recent pledge to lower prices. Parts are easily found, except for the Miller-Cycle 6-cylinder engine.

Strengths and weaknesses: Smaller than the Mazda 929, the front-drive Millenia carries the same 2.5L 170-hp V6 used by the 626. An optional 2.3L Miller-Cycle "S" 6-cylinder engine, although smaller than the base powerplant, still manages to pump out 210 horsepower. Both engines use a standard 4-speed automatic transmission that shifts a bit harshly when pushed. As with all luxury cars, the Millenia comes with a wide array of standard features that would normally cost thousands of dollars more. Although billed as a five-passenger car, the middle occupant in the rear seat is cramped and has to sit on a hump—a problem that 929 owners are familiar with. Incidentally, all model years have been carried over relatively unchanged, although the '99 models did get a slight restyling of the front and rear ends.

Assembly and component quality are fairly high (in fact, these cars have never been recalled); however, there have been some reports of Miller-Cycle engine failures and front-brake and electrical glitches. Among the powertrain problems, owners cite transmission failures and defective engine head gaskets with the base 2.5L powerplant. Paint delamination has also been a common complaint on 1995–96 models.

Technical service bulletins: All models: 1995—Cruise control surging. • Transmission position indicator light failure. • AC evaporator freeze-up. • Battery discharge due to the trunk light staying on. • Snap noise around the A-pillar. • Steering wheel may be off centre. • Roof insulator peeling off. **1996**—Brake pulsation repair. • Cracked centre sun visor holder. • Creaking or knocking noise from rear of vehicle. • Rattle noise from rear package tray. **1997**—Brake pulsation repair. **1998**—Bulletins address brake pulsation (a chronic problem over the years), harsh automatic transmission shifting or erratic performance, wind noise around doors, and inaccurate fuel-gauge readings.

Safety summary/Recalls: All models: 1995—Many complaints that vehicle surges when shifted into Reverse. • Inadvertent airbag deployment;

failure to deploy. • Steering-wheel back is open, allowing objects to jam the steering mechanism. • Driver's automatic seatbelt came loose when vehicle was rear-ended. • While vehicle was being driven on the highway, engine locked up due to leakage from the oil pan. • ABS brake failures. • Many reports of cracked engine valve cover gaskets, which allowed oil to leak onto the wiring and spark plugs. • Because the engine intake valve is set so low, whenever it comes in contact with water, the car stalls. • Premature AC and CV joint failures. • Sudden electrical system failure. • Defroster doesn't do an adequate job in cold weather; collects water or quits altogether. • When AC is on, the headlights go dim. • Low-beam lights are inadequate for night driving. • Battery connections become loose, making it impossible to unlock or start vehicle. • When driver turned the ignition switch, the battery cable popped off; this caused the automatic door locks to become inoperative, trapping occupants. • Trunk won't open with inside latch release. • The location of the cup holder allows drinks to be spilled into the shifter mechanism, causing the shifter to lock up. • Cup holder doesn't always release. • Seatbelt buckle on passenger's side fell completely apart in driver's hand. • Aluminum alloy wheel cracked. **1996—** Airbag failed to deploy. • Transmission failures. • Intermittent starting problems. • Loose dashboard and interior trim. • It's easy to hit your head on the low trunk lid and latch. **1997**—Traction-control system failure. **1998**—Fuel smell permeates the interior. • Car wouldn't accelerate. • Vehicle stalls in traffic, particularly when it rains. • Automatic transmission shifts erratically and jerks upon acceleration. • Brake pedal goes to floor and brakes don't react. **1999**—Front airbag failed to deploy in a collision. • Emergency brake doesn't hold. • Front bumper cracked; dealer says it's a common defect with the 626, as well. • Engine surges forward and hesitates. • Excessive AC fan noise. **Recalls:** N/A.

Secret Warranties/Service Tips

All models/years—Troubleshooting tips for plugging wind noise around doors, and excessive brake pulsation. **All models: 1995–96**—A creaking or knocking noise from the rear of the vehicle is likely caused by loose diagonal braces behind the rear seat. **1995–98**—Rough shifting or erratic automatic transmission performance may indicate a fluid leak at the oil pan and transfer case. • A stuck tach needle must be reset manually. **1997–98**— Inaccurate fuel gauge readings can be fixed by changing the sender and instrument cluster. **1998–99**—If the Low Fuel light constantly comes on, or only 38–49 litres can be pumped into the fuel tank, Mazda will install modified components to allow a 53–litre fill-up. • An exhaust system rattling can be cured by replacing the pre-silencer. • Guidelines for correcting wind noise around doors and removing musty AC odours. • If the steering wheel is slightly off centre, Mazda suggests re-positioning the tie-rod ends.

Millenia Profile					
	1995	1996	1997	1998	1999
Cost Price ($)					
Base	38,055	42,035	42,900	38,660	36,535
Used Values ($)					
Base ↑	13,000	15,000	18,000	21,000	24,000
Base ↓	12,500	14,000	16,500	20,000	22,000
Extended Warranty	N	N	N	N	N
Secret Warranty	N	N	N	Y	Y
Reliability	③	④	⑤	⑤	⑤
Crash Safety	④	④	④	—	—

MERCEDES-BENZ

190 Series, C-Class

Rating: 190: Not Recommended (1984–93). C-Class: Above Average (1995–99); Average (1994). Although these cars are above average in reliability and comfort, every model—other than the 300 series—is overpriced and overrated. The 190 version is not recommended. Consider buying a 1997 C-Class only if you feel you need the 2.3L engine's 12 additional horses and improved automatic gearbox. Keep in mind, though, that you'll have to keep the car much longer to amortize its higher cost. **Maintenance/Repair costs:** Higher than average, and most repairs must be done by a Mercedes dealer if you don't live in an area where independent shops have sprung up. **Parts:** Higher-than-average cost. Parts supply and servicing have become problematic now that the 190 series has been off the market since 1993.

Strengths and weaknesses: Mercedes introduced the 190 "baby" Benz in 1984 in an effort to downsize its entry-level compact and make it more affordable. It never caught on due to its serious drivetrain deficiencies, cramped interior, and rounded styling (a real departure from Mercedes's traditional squared-off look). The best choice from a quality/price standpoint is any post-1989 version equipped with the inline 6-cylinder powerplant.

The 1994 models were renamed the C-Class, and gained interior room and more powerful engines. The standard 2.6L 6-cylinder motor is a real powerhouse in this small car, and its power is used effectively when coupled to the manual 5-speed transmission. The 4-speed automatic is a big disappointment—it requires a lot of throttle effort to downshift and prefers to start out in second gear. The 1994 versions add much-needed horsepower, but lack the manual 5-speed transmission that would set those extra horses free. Rear seat room is limited and a lot of road noise intrudes into the passenger compartment.

The base 2.3L engine is acceptable around town, but highway cruising requires more grunt to handle the car's heft and accessories. And speaking of grunt, the 2.8L engine is ideally suited to these small cars. Although its power is used most effectively when coupled to the new 5-speed manual transmission, its performance with the 5-speed automatic is quite good. On 1996 models, some owners have complained that the 4-speed automatic requires a lot of throttle effort to downshift.

The 1997 C-Class replaced the standard 2.2L engine with the more robust 2.3L (C230) and revised headlamps. Bigger changes were in store for the following year's models: a new 2.8L engine (C280), BabySmart car seats, brake assist, and side airbags. The 1999 models got the SLK's 2.3L supercharged engine replacing the C230's normally aspirated powerplant, a better-performing drivetrain, and standard leather upholstery.

Keep in mind that owner surveys give the entry-level C-Class cars a *just* better-than-average rating, while the 300 and higher series have always scored way above average in owner satisfaction. The 190's reliability is a notch below that of other Mercedes vehicles; the 1994 model C-Class is the better buy from a quality and reliability standpoint, although 1995 and later models have had fewer bugs. Nevertheless, owners report frequent problems with drivetrain noise and vibration, and slipping or soft shifts. Brakes, AC, and the electrical system are also failure-prone.

Technical service bulletins: C-Class: 1995—Drivetrain noise and vibration. • High coolant temperature. • Slipping or soft shifts. **190: 1993, 220C: 1994**—Drivetrain noise and vibration. • Harsh shifts or erratic shift quality. • High coolant temperature. • Rough reverse release. • Handling of fuel system complaints.

Safety summary/Recalls: All models: 1993—Vehicle stalled while on the highway. • After vehicle was towed home, fire ignited in the engine compartment. • ABS brake failures cause the brakes to lock up. • Premature replacement of the front wheel bearings. • Climate control module failures. • Hard starting. • Driver's master door lock failed to unlock other doors. • Power door lock vacuum control pump failure. • Bent upper control arm/camber MIKE link caused right rear wheel to turn out. **1995**—Check Engine light remains on for no apparent reason. • Frequent stalling due to defective idle-speed control unit. • Missing left rear wheelwell inside panel allows tire to spray debris into area. **1996**—Airbags failed to deploy. • Airbag light stays on for no apparent reason. • After parking the vehicle and turning off the ignition, the vehicle lurches forward or rocks backward. • In another incident, vehicle was put in Park on an incline and keys were removed; vehicle rolled backward down the hill. • Brakes are noisy when applied and don't brake well. • While car is being driven, engine light comes on for no apparent reason. • Complete electrical system failure. • Windshield washer fluid sensor failure. **1997**—While in Reverse, vehicle suddenly accelerated in backward. **1998**—Airbag warning light came on and then airbag suddenly exploded. • Transmission fluid leakage. • Faulty gas gauge sensor. • Rear suspension bouncing makes it difficult to maintain directional control. • Noisy heat shield. • Inoperative windshield wipers. • Car is very vulnerable to sidewind buffeting. • Window failures. **1999**—Vehicle suddenly accelerated and brakes couldn't stop it. • Brakes failed on incline. **280: 1994**—Vehicle suddenly accelerated forward in garage. • Another report that, while coming to a stop at an intersection, vehicle will accelerate when foot is on the brake. • Airbag failed to deploy. • Upon braking, ABS pedal went to the floor, resulting in extended stopping distance. • Extreme pressure is needed to push horn button. • Cruise control failure. • Premature rear wheel-bearing failure. • Windshield wiper is inadequate; poor visibility. **1998**—Vehicle suddenly accelerated while stopped at a traffic light. Premature tire failure. • Excessive vibration or shimmy escalates with speed. Faulty gas gauge sensor. • Horn doesn't work. **Recalls: All models: 1994–95**— Secondary hood latch may not work properly.

Secret Warranties/Service Tips

All models/years—Excessive engine valve train noise may be caused by a stretched timing chain. After 48,000 km, the camshaft and timing chain drive should be checked carefully, especially if excessive noise is heard. **All models: 1989–92**—Excessive oil consumption may be corrected by replacing the valve stem seals with upgraded Viton seals. **1990–91**—A jerking that occurs when driving downhill with the cruise control engaged can be corrected by installing a relay to disable the deceleration fuel shut-off switch. **230: 1999–2000**—If the brake pedal is hard to apply, replace the brake booster and crankcase vent hoses.

190 Series, C-Class Profile

	1992	1993	1994	1995	1996	1997	1998	1999
Cost Price ($)								
190E 2.3	38,150	38,050	—	—	—	—	—	—
190E 2.6	45,250	45,050	—	—	—	—	—	—
220C	—	—	34,350	34,995	35,995	—	—	—
230C	—	—	—	—	—	36,950	37,550	37,950
280C	—	—	47,650	48,750	49,995	50,995	49,950	49,950
Used Values ($)								
190E 2.3 ↑	8,500	10,500	—	—	—	—	—	—
190E 2.3 ↓	7,500	8,000	—	—	—	—	—	—
190E 2.6 ↑	10,000	13,000	—	—	—	—	—	—
190E 2.6 ↓	9,000	11,000	—	—	—	—	—	—
220C ↑	—	—	11,000	14,000	18,000	—	—	—
220C ↓	—	—	8,500	12,500	15,000	—	—	—

230C ↑	—	—	—	—	—	22,000	25,000	29,000
230C ↓	—	—	—	—	—	19,000	23,000	26,000
280C ↑	—	—	21,000	25,000	30,000	35,000	40,000
280C ↓	—	—	18,000	23,000	27,000	31,000	37,000

Extended Warranty	Y	Y	Y	Y	Y	Y	Y	Y
Secret Warranty	N	N	N	N	N	N	N	N
Reliability	❷	❷	❷	③	③	④	④	⑤
Air conditioning	❷	❷	❷	③	③	④	④	⑤
Auto. transmission	④	④	⑤	⑤	⑤	⑤	⑤	⑤
Body integrity	❷	❷	❷	❷	③	③	③	③
Braking system	❷	❷	❷	❷	③	④	⑤	⑤
Electrical system	❷	❷	❷	❷	❷	③	③	③
Engines	❷	③	③	④	④	⑤	⑤	⑤
Exhaust/Converter	④	④	④	⑤	⑤	⑤	⑤	⑤
Fuel system	❷	③	③	③	④	⑤	⑤	⑤
Ignition system	④	④	④	④	④	⑤	⑤	⑤
Rust/Paint	④	④	④	④	④	④	⑤	⑤
Steering	③	③	④	④	⑤	⑤	⑤	⑤
Suspension	③	③	④	④	⑤	⑤	⑤	⑤
Crash Safety								
C220, C230	—	—	④	④	④	④	④	—
Side Impact								
C230	—	—	—	—	—	—	③	③

300 Series, 400 Series, 500 Series, E-Class

Rating: Recommended (1993–99); Above Average (1992); Below Average (1985–91). The 1994 and later models are referred to as E-Class, with the entry-level model a 300 diesel. Interestingly, with the increase in diesel fuel prices, early diesel versions are now depreciating more rapidly than gasoline-powered models. **Maintenance/Repair costs:** Higher than average, and repairs must be done by a Mercedes dealer. **Parts:** Higher-than-average cost and limited availability.

Strengths and weaknesses: These cars are ideal mid-sized family sedans. They're reliable, depreciate slowly, and provide all the interior space that the pre-1994 190 series and C-Class leave out. Their only short-comings are a high resale value that discourages bargain hunters and a weak dealer network that limits parts distribution and drives up parts costs. The 300 Series offers a traction control system that prevents wheel spin upon acceleration—somewhat like ABS in reverse.

Another interesting feature is a 24-valve 220-hp high-performance version of the inline 6-cylinder engine that powers the 300 Series. All this has its price, though. If, ironically, you'd like to drive one of these cars but are of an economical frame of mind, choose the 260E—it offers everything the 300 does, but for much less. The 300CE is a coupe version, appealing to a sportier crowd, while the 300TE is the station wagon variant.

Technical service bulletins: Bulletins show that the 1995 300 Series may have transmission gasket leaks in addition to drivetrain noise and vibration, and slipping or soft shifts. The 1996–99 models have no bulletins listing factory-related problems or troubleshooting tips.

Safety summary/Recalls: 300 series: 1994—Sudden acceleration caused accident and injuries. • Defective ABS brakes; brakes locked up and caused driver to lose control of vehicle. • Emergency brake cable failed twice. • Vehicle rolls backward when stopped on a hill. • Driver's seatbelt failed. • Accelerator pedal is too hard to press, causes fatigue in driver's leg. • Frequent power door lock and automatic antenna failures. • Front panels were cracked and loose. • Rear axle and fuel pump failures. **1995**—Sudden acceleration caused an accident. • Brake rotor and caliper failure. • Headlights cast dark shadows. • Windshield wipers fail to keep glass clean. • Automatic transmission slips or shifts erratically, as if hunting for the right gear. **1996**—Check Engine light flashes on and off at will. • AC fan starts and stops intermittently. • Door rattles. • Failure-prone headlight bulbs. **1997**—Airbag deployed for no reason. • Airbags failed to deploy in a collision. • Brakes locked up, causing extended stopping distance. • Premature failure of the automatic transmission, AC compressor, and hatch door release. • Single windshield wiper doesn't clear windshield adequately. • Instrument gauge cluster doesn't light gauges sufficiently. • Double-pane windows, rear windshield, and rear-view mirrors blur images. **1998**—Sudden, unintended acceleration while on the highway. • Airbag failed to deploy in a collision. • While parking, steering went out and car caught fire. • Total loss of braking; pedal went to floor. • Premature failure of the automatic transmission, tie-rod, belt tensioner, fuel pump, fuel-level sensor, oxygen sensor, windows, power-assisted sunroof, electric seats turn-signal switch, and brake lights. • Excessive wind noise emanating from the windows and sunroof. • Blue-tinted headlights cause glare and are too bright. • Power seat suddenly moved back and reclined while vehicle was in traffic. • Bumper cracks from minor impacts. **1999**—Sudden acceleration when turning. • Engine fuel line leakage. • Fuel pump failures. • Inaccurate fuel gauge: says tank is full, but it can take almost five more gallons. • Sudden stalling while underway, especially when going over a bump in the road. • Excessive vibration when decelerating. • Transmission leaks oil, disengages, and then suddenly locks up. • ABS suddenly activated; threw vehicle to side of the road. • Self-activating door locks. • Severe window hazing in rainy weather. **Recalls: 300 Series, E-Class: 1992–95**—Front passenger's footrest could abrade the wiring harness underneath. The ensuing short circuit could stall the engine or deploy the airbag.

Secret Warranties/Service Tips

All models: 1987–92—Excessive brake vibrations can be reduced by installing upgraded Jurid 226 front brake pads. **1988–90**—A gurgling heater core noise can be silenced by Mercedes's "gurgling kit." **1990–91**—Excessive exhaust noise between the exhaust manifold flange and rear muffler may be caused by a leak at the clamped joints. If this isn't the cause, change the catalytic converter.

300 Series, 400 Series, 500 Series, E-Class Profile

	1992	1993	1994	1995	1996	1997	1998	1999
Cost Price ($)								
300E	67,275	68,050	55,995	—	—	—	—	—
300CE	79,800	80,800	—	—	—	—	—	—
300D	58,551	—	—	—	—	—	—	—
300ED	—	—	55,995	55,995	58,500	59,950	59,950	59,950
320E 4d	—	—	58,895	60,950	64,750	65,900	66,450	66,750
420E, 430	—	—	71,000	72,950	101,900	73,300	73,950	70,500
500E, 500S	103,900	108,600	108,00	124,900	132,500	132,950	117,900	122,900
Used Values ($)								
300E ↑	15,000	17,000	18,500	—	—	—	—	—
300E ↓	14,000	15,000	16,000	—	—	—	—	—
300CE ↑	18,000	21,000	—	—	—	—	—	—
300CE ↓	17,000	18,500	—	—	—	—	—	—
300D ↑	15,000	—	—	—	—	—	—	—
300D ↓	13,500	—	—	—	—	—	—	—
300ED ↑	—	—	21,000	23,000	28,000	34,000	39,000	45,000
300ED ↓	—	—	19,000	21,000	25,000	30,000	36,000	42,000
320E 4d ↑	—	—	20,500	26,000	32,000	38,000	45,000	51,000
320E 4d ↓	—	—	18,000	24,000	29,000	35,000	42,000	48,000
420E, 430 ↑	—	—	21,000	28,000	46,000	43,000	49,000	57,000
420E, 430 ↓	—	—	18,000	24,000	43,000	39,000	46,000	53,000
500E, 500S ↑	17,000	22,000	28,000	47,000	55,000	63,000	74,000	83,000
500E, 500S ↓	15,000	17,500	24,000	41,000	48,000	58,000	69,000	80,000
Extended Warranty	N	N	N	N	N	N	N	N
Secret Warranty	N	N	N	N	N	N	N	N
Reliability	③	③	③	③	④	④	⑤	⑤
Air conditioning	❷	③	③	③	③	④	⑤	⑤
Auto. transmission	③	③	③	④	④	⑤	⑤	⑤
Body integrity	③	④	⑤	⑤	⑤	⑤	⑤	⑤
Braking system	❷	③	③	③	③	③	③	③
Electrical system	❷	❷	❷	❷	❷	❷	③	③
Engines	❷	❷	❷	❷	③	④	⑤	⑤
Exhaust/Converter	③	④	④	④	⑤	⑤	⑤	⑤
Fuel system	③	③	④	④	⑤	⑤	⑤	⑤

Ignition system	③	③	④	⑤	⑤	⑤	⑤	⑤
Rust/Paint	④	④	④	④	④	④	⑤	⑤
Steering	③	③	③	③	④	④	④	⑤
Suspension	③	③	③	③	⑤	⑤	⑤	⑤

Note: The above model years haven't been crash-tested by NHTSA.

NISSAN

Maxima

Rating: Recommended (1996–99); Above Average (1989–95); Average (1986–88). The redesigned 1995–99 version offers a peppier engine, more rounded styling, and a bit longer wheelbase. **Maintenance/ Repair costs:** Higher than average, but repairs can be done practically anywhere. **Parts:** Higher-than-average cost, but easy to find.

Strengths and weaknesses: These front-wheel drive sedans are very well equipped and nicely finished, but cramped for their size. Although the trunk is spacious, only five passengers can travel in a pinch (literally!). The 6-cylinder, 190-hp engine, borrowed from the 300ZX in 1992, offers sparkling performance; the fuel injectors, however, are problematic. The '93 models got standard driver-side airbags and the Maxima remained unchanged until the 1995 model's redesign.

Early Maximas are less expensive to buy, but more costly to maintain— for example, the exhaust manifold, a component that commonly fails, will set you back $300–$500 to replace. Owners report that the '95 Maxima's suspension was cheapened, to the detriment of both the ride and the handling.

Minor electrical and front suspension problems afflict early Maximas. Brakes and engine timing belts need frequent attention in all years. Newer models have a weak automatic transmission and the ignition system can malfunction. There have also been reports of "cooked" transmissions. This is due to a poorly designed transmission cooler. Mechanics say that this breakdown can be avoided by installing an externally mounted transmission cooler with a filter and replacing the transmission filter cooler at every oil change.

Owners report that the V6-equipped Maxima is sometimes hard to start in cold weather because the engine tends to flood easily. The cruise control unit is another problematic component. When it's engaged at moderate speeds, it hesitates or "drifts" to a lower speed, acting as if the fuel line were clogged. It operates correctly only at much higher speeds than needed. Incidentally, owners say that a new fuel filter will *not* correct the problem. Additionally, though warped manifolds were once routinely replaced under a "goodwill" warranty, Nissan now makes the customer pay. The warpage causes a manifold bolt to break off, thereby causing a huge exhaust leak. Most fuel-injector malfunctions are caused by carbon clogging up the injectors; there are additives you can try that might reduce this buildup. There have also been internal problems with the coil windings on the fuel-injectors. Your best bet is to replace the entire set.

Nissan has had problems with weak window regulators for some time. If the window is frozen, don't open it. The rubber weather stripping around the window is also a problem. It cuts easily and causes the window to go off track, which in turn puts stress on the weak regulators. Driver-side window breakage is common and can cost up to $300 to repair. Costly aluminum wheels corrode quickly and are easily damaged by road hazards. There have been a few reports of surface rust and paint problems. Pre-1990 Maximas suffer from rust perforation on the sunroof, door bottoms, rear wheelwells, front edge of the hood, and bumper supports. The underbody should also be checked carefully for corrosion damage. Premature wearout of the muffler is a frequent problem; it's often covered by Nissan's "goodwill" warranty, wherein the company and dealer will contribute 50 percent of the replacement cost.

1995–99

These redesigned Maximas have a longer wheelbase (adding to interior room), a new 3.0L engine, and more rounded styling. They compete well with fully equipped Camrys, entry-level Infinitis, and Lexus models. Nevertheless, tall passengers will find the interior a bit cramped, and the automatic transmission is often slow to downshift and isn't always smooth. The '97 models got a new front-end restyling, and optional side airbags were offered with the '98s; however, the '99s were the first Maximas to get optional traction control.

Quality control and overall reliability are apparently much better with these more recent iterations. Nevertheless, owners still report a variety of safety-related deficiencies, in addition to brake, electrical-system, fuel-system, and body glitches.

Safety summary/Recalls: All models: 1996—Fire ignited from shorted wires under the passenger-side seat. • Airbag failed to deploy. • ABS failures. • Vehicle constantly pulls to the right. • Engine warning light flashes for no apparent reason. • Sudden loss of power resulting in inoperative brakes and steering. • Chronic stalling. • Power steering failure. • Erratic transmission performance. • Hard to shift transmission out of Park. • Key can be taken out of ignition while vehicle isn't in Park. • Power door locks failed. • Defective AC expansion valve. • Several reports of headlight explosions. **1997**—Door latch won't engage in cold weather. • Front wheel suddenly locked up while driving. • Power steering leaks fluid. • Trunk lid opened while driving. • Pedal went to the floor when brakes were applied, resulting in extended stopping distance. **1998**—Vehicle intermittently accelerates while braking. • Hazy, milky pattern on glass exterior causes poor visibility. • Frequent windshield wiper failures. **Recalls: All models: 1986**—Windshield may detach in a collision. **1992–93**—Dealers will install a new airbag sensor so that the airbags won't inadvertently deploy whenever the car passes over a speed bump. **1993–94**—Loose wheel nuts on aluminum wheels could allow wheels to fall away.

Secret Warranties/Service Tips

All models/years—Defective catalytic converters that cause a rotten-egg smell may be replaced free of charge under Nissan's emissions warranty. • Bulletin P195-006 looks at the many causes and remedies for excessive brake noise. **All models: 1995–96**—Timing chain rattling noise can be silenced by replacing the timing chain tensioner and slack guide. • Brake squeak or squeal can be corrected by installing front and rear brake kits. **1995–98**—An inoperative power seat may require a new drive cable. **1995–99**—Blower motor noise can be cured by installing a new blower motor cover. • A front brake groan when stopping is addressed in TSB #99-032. • A rear brake groan or hum can be fixed by readjusting the parking brake cable. • If the rear brakes squeak or squeal when cold, replace the rear brake pads with upgraded ones. • Guidelines for correcting steering pull or drift. • Tips on eliminating a foul odour emanating from the sunroof sunshade. **1996–99**—Diagnostic tips for fixing a front seatbelt that's slow to retract. **1998–99**—An on-off transmission throttle shock can be atenuated by installing an upgraded ECM. **1999**—Guidelines for correcting rocker panel creaking or popping.

Maxima Profile

	1992	1993	1994	1995	1996	1997	1998	1999
Cost Price ($)								
Base	23,190	24,690	25,690	25,990	27,998	27,998	27,998	28,598
Used Values ($)								
Base ↑	5,500	6,500	8,500	11,000	13,500	15,500	18,000	20,000
Base ↓	4,500	5,000	6,500	9,000	11,500	13,500	16,000	18,000
Extended Warranty	N	N	N	N	N	N	N	N
Secret Warranty	N	N	N	N	N	Y	Y	Y
Reliability	③	④	④	④	④	④	⑤	⑤
Air conditioning	③	④	④	⑤	⑤	⑤	⑤	⑤
Auto. transmission	③	③	③	④	④	⑤	⑤	⑤
Body integrity	❷	❷	❷	③	③	③	④	④
Braking system	❷	❷	❷	❷	❷	③	③	③
Electrical system	❷	❷	❷	❷	③	③	④	④
Engines	③	④	④	④	⑤	⑤	⑤	⑤
Exhaust/Converter	❷	③	③	③	③	⑤	⑤	⑤
Fuel system	③	③	③	③	③	③	③	④
Ignition system	③	③	③	③	③	④	⑤	⑤
Rust/Paint	③	③	③	④	④	⑤	⑤	⑤
Steering	③	③	④	④	④	⑤	⑤	⑤
Suspension	③	③	④	④	④	⑤	⑤	⑤
Crash Safety	③	③	③	③	④	④	④	—
Side Impact	—	—	—	—	—	④	④	④

SAAB

900, 9000

Rating: Average (1998–99); Below Average (1995–97); Not Recommended (1985–94). Interestingly, the upscale 9000 series isn't as crashworthy as the cheaper 900 versions, nor is it more reliable, exhibiting similar generic deficiencies to its entry-level brother. Be wary of the aluminum wheels; they're easily damaged and costly to replace. **Maintenance/Repair costs:** Higher than average, and repairs must be done by a GM or Saab dealer. **Parts:** Higher-than-average cost and limited availability outside major urban areas.

Strengths and weaknesses: These Swedish-built luxury cars combine excellent handling and great interior ergonomics (one of the few imports with the EPA's "large car" label), but without all the bells and whistles found in domestic luxury breeds. Convenience items like a fuse box in the glove compartment, a toolbox in the hatchback, and easy-to-replace bulbs, etc., add to your comfort.

Unfortunately, Saabs aren't Volvos, and they don't live up to the Swedish reputation for exceptional reliability. Quirky in design, servicing is inadequate—and will probably get much worse in the future now that GM has acquired the company and GM dealers are responsible for servicing.

Generally, the 900 and 9000 series have similar deficiencies affecting the engine, cooling (biodegradable water pumps) and electrical systems, brakes, automatic transmission (clutch O-rings), and body hardware (alloy wheels are easily bent). The 9000 is assembled with greater care, but owner reports show only a marginal improvement in overall reliability and durability.

Short circuits are legion and run the gamut from minor annoyances to fire hazards (see "Safety summary/Recalls"). Electrical glitches in the traction control system's relay module give a false reading that the tires are spinning, which shuts the engine down.

Turbos produce much stronger acceleration and better handling than other 9000s without compromising their overall reliability. Nevertheless, they should be approached with caution because owner abuse or poor maintenance can quickly lead to turbocharger deterioration. Air conditioners and exhaust-system parts have a short life span, and leaky seals and gaskets are common. Rust perforations tend to develop along door bottoms and the rocker panels. The underbody, especially the floor, should be inspected for corrosion damage on older models.

Over the years, Saab's 900 and 9000 have changed little. The '93 9000s got a 225-hp version of the inline 4-cylinder, while the 900 received more standard features. A year later, the 900 was revamped, getting a new V6 and an upgraded optional automatic transmission, while the 9000 offered, for the first time, standard dual airbags. The following year, the '95 9000s got a new turbocharger and a V6 powerplant coupled with an automatic transmission. The 9000 sedans were dropped in the '96 model year, but 900 models got engine upgrades and standard seat lumbar support.

Major changes were incorporated into the 1999 model year. The entry-level 900 was re-named the 9-3 and given suspension, steering, and interior upgrades, plus a high-performance 200-hp 2.0L engine and a more responsive drivetrain. The 1999 9000 models were re-designated the 9-5, limited to sedans, and equipped with either a turbocharged 4-cylinder or V6.

Safety summary/Recalls: 900: 1996—Under-hood fire ignited as vehicle was idling with transmission lever in the Park position. • Several reports that when shifting from Reverse to Drive, vehicle suddenly accelerated forward without braking or steering control. • Airbags failed to deploy, and the warning light comes on for no apparent reason • Fuel-filter failures caused fuel leak. • Car drifts to the right while driving. • Defective exhaust check valve lifters. • Transmission failures and excessive vibrations. • Repeated gear shifting problems cause the shifter bushings and motor-mount housing to be prematurely worn. • Sundry electrical system shorts and failures affecting the stereo and CD player, anti-theft system, and battery. • Frequent trunk latch release, door handle, and passenger seat adjuster failures. • Glass headlight cover is often broken. • Left side-view mirror can't be adjusted properly to see blind spots to left rear of vehicle. **1997**—Faulty power seat. • Aluminum wheels are easily bent. **1998**—Airbag deployed inadvertently. • Car can start in gear. • Alloy wheels are easily bent. • Power seat fails to respond to commands. **1999**—Airbag failed to deploy. • Cruise control fails to disengage when brakes are applied. • Early automatic transmission failure. • Vehicle tends to wander on the highway. • Shock absorber failure. • Wheel rims are easily bent. • Door lock won't unlock from the inside. **Recalls: All models with 2.3L engines: 1995**—Faulty electronic system. **900: 1994**—Hatchbacks show fatigue cracks, which could allow seat to suddenly fold backward. **1995**—Convertibles may experience a possible loss of steering control due to a misaligned steering shaft. **900 Turbo: 1988–95**— Transmission may be in Neutral when shifter is in Reverse. • Car could roll away if it's parked with the parking brake disengaged. **1996**—Seatbelt anchorage may not hold. **5d, Coupe (manual transmissions): 1994–95**—A shift linkage defect may cause an unexpected movement if transmission is in gear. **9000: 1992–93**—Dealers will install a new fuel filler and fuel-filler vent hose to prevent fuel leakage. • Vehicles equipped with an engine oil cooler may catch fire in a collision. **1992–94**—ABS corrosion can lead to loss of full braking power. **1993–94**—Brake lights may operate erratically.

Secret Warranties/Service Tips

All models/years: Tips for finding and fixing windshield noise are outlined in TSB #841-15772. **900: 1993–94**—Binding ignition switch contacts can lead to electrical failures. **1994**—A-pillar wind noise is addressed in TSB #08194-0486. • TSB #88/94-0480 lists the causes and remedies of AC malfunctions. **1994–98**—Diagnostic procedures and correction for brake vibration are addressed in TSB #510-1919. • If you find your battery has died, it may have drained though the trunk light switch. • A Low Oil light may come on for no apparent reason; fix the problem by re-programming the SID module. **1997–98**—Customer Satisfaction Campaign #443 calls for the free replacement of the fuel pump. Its durability is compromised by its lack of a carbide coating on the pump spindle. **9000: All years**—Saab offers a pedal-raising kit free of charge to short drivers wishing to sit farther away from the airbag housing. **1992–94**—A noisy climate control unit may have excess pressure building up at the fresh air intake. **1993–94**—A stuck shift lever may be caused by a blown #3 fuse. • A faulty sun visor/vanity mirror causes the short circuit. **1994–98**—Noise or vibrations from the gear shift lever when accelerating are addressed in TSB #471-1937. **1995–98**—Sunroof rattling can be silenced following TSB #812-1983. **1997–98**—If the hood is difficult to open, install an upgraded lock. **1998**—Poor AM/FM reception is a common problem addressed in TSB #367-2015.

900, 9000 Profile

	1992	1993	1994	1995	1996	1997	1998	1999
Cost Price ($)								
900/9-3	24,965	26,715	27,000	26,995	28,500	29,901	30,700	33,800
9000/9-5	31,795	33,875	35,000	35,995	36,400	37,100	50,300	39,800
Used Values ($)								
900/9-3 ↑	4,000	5,000	7,500	9,000	11,000	13,000	16,000	19,000
900/9-3 ↓	3,000	4,000	5,000	6,500	8,500	11,000	14,000	17,000
9000/9-5 ↑	6,000	7,000	9,000	10,000	14,000	16,000	27,000	23,000
9000/9-5 ↓	5,000	6,000	7,000	8,000	11,000	13,500	24,000	21,000
Extended Warranty	Y	Y	Y	Y	Y	Y	Y	Y
Secret Warranty	N	N	N	N	N	N	N	N
Reliability	②	②	②	②	②	②	③	③
Air conditioning	②	②	②	②	③	③	③	③
Auto. transmission	②	②	②	②	②	③	③	④
Body integrity	②	②	②	②	③	③	④	④
Braking system	②	②	②	②	②	②	②	③
Electrical system	❶	❶	❶	②	②	②	②	③
Engines	②	②	②	③	③	③	④	④
Exhaust/Converter	②	②	②	②	③	③	④	④
Fuel system	③	③	③	③	③	③	③	③
Ignition system	②	②	③	③	③	③	③	③
Rust/Paint	③	③	③	③	③	③	④	⑤

Steering	③	③	④	⑤	⑤	⑤	⑤	⑤
Suspension	❷	❷	③	③	③	③	④	④
Crash Safety								
900	—	—	—	④	④	④	④	—
9000	—	④	—	—	—	—	—	—

TOYOTA

Avalon

Rating: Above Average (1995–99). A Camry knock-off; if you want a more driver-involved experience in a Toyota, consider a Lexus ES 300 or GS 300. The Avalon's rating has been lowered this year in view of the car's many safety-related failures recorded in NHTSA's database. **Maintenance/Repair costs:** Higher than average. Repairs must be done by a Toyota dealer. **Parts:** Higher-than-average cost and limited availability.

Strengths and weaknesses: This near-luxury four-door offers more value, interior space, and performance than do other cars in its class that cost thousands of dollars more. A front-engine, front-drive, mid-sized sedan based on a stretched Camry platform, the six-passenger Avalon is bigger than the rear-drive Cressida it replaced and similar in size to the Ford Taurus. Sure, there's a fair amount of Camry in the Avalon, but it's quicker on its feet than the Camry, better attuned to abrupt manoeuvres, and two inches longer. In fact, there's more rear-seat leg room than you'll find in either the Taurus or the new Chevrolet Lumina. It's close to the Dodge Intrepid in this respect.

Dual airbags are standard, along with power locks, windows, and mirrors. The '97 models were given more power, torque, and standard features, while the '98s got seatbelt pretensioners, side airbags, new headlights and taillights, and a new trunk lid and grill. The 1999 Avalon was carried over without any significant changes.

Quality control is better than average, though steering, suspension, and fuel system components are failure prone. Owners have some performance gripes, however. They include numerous electrical system glitches, engine failure due to sludge buildup, premature torque converter failures, persistent drifting, uneven and premature tire wear, premature front and rear brake wear, early replacement of the inner tie rod and steering rack, and excessive vibration at 90 km/h, premature front brake repairs and suspension strut failures, power steering that's a bit too light, hydroplaning, excessive body lean, and under-steer when cornering. Body construction and assembly are fairly good, although rattles are commonplace for all model years and trunk leaks have been reported on the '99 models.

Safety summary/Recalls: All models: 1995—Researchers are looking into 20 incidents of turn-signal failures after the hazard warning lights have been activated. **1997**—Airbags deployed while stopped at a light. • Airbags failed to deploy in an accident. • Sudden engine failure; engine leaks oil. • Engine cylinder failure. • Fuel damper and fuel pump failed twice, leaking fuel. • Brakes failed due to freezing vacuum hose. • ABS controller failure. • Frequent complaints of steering fluid leaks. • Many reports of premature failure of the steering assembly (upper steering knuckle) and front strut support. • Front suspension bar suddenly broke. • Transmission failure caused by loss of internal pressure. • Vehicle hydroplanes on the slightest wet pavement; Bridgestone tires don't help. • Early replacement of Bridgestone/ Firestone tires due to hydroplaning, excessive wear, and substandard performance. • Several incidents of Bridgestone Potenza tire tread separation. • Driver seat moves when vehicle turns. • Wind blew trunk lid shut on driver's neck. • Taillight bulbs have a short life span. **1998**— Many incidents where vehicle suddenly accelerated in Drive and in Reverse. • Vehicle caught fire at fuel filler neck when getting gas. • Gas tank fuel hose leaks fuel. • Front and side airbags fail to deploy in collisions. • Airbag deployment caused severe chest and chin injuries. • Front seat reclined suddenly when vehicle was hit from the rear. • Engine surges and drops rpms rapidly and unexpectedly when engaging cruise control or when taking foot off of the gas pedal. • Power steering pump failure and fluid reservoir leakage. • Early replacement of brake pads, calipers, and rotors. • Dunlop Sport 4000 tread separation. • Premature tire wear. • Front suspension bangs and clanks when going over any size bump and rear suspension bottoms out. • Constant vibration in steering wheel and accelerator while driving caused by fuel pressure regulator. • Loose driver seat. • Kick panel falls off repeatedly. **1999**—Vehicle suddenly accelerated; surges at intersections. • Airbag failed to deploy. • Airbag warning light comes on for no reason. • Cruise control operates erratically. • Brake pedal went to floor with little effect. • Car shifts poorly (hesitates and jerks) when you let off the gas and then accelerate, or do a rolling stop.

Secret Warranties/Service Tips

All models: 1995–96—Use an upgraded rear brake pad material to eliminate rear brake moan. • To reduce wind noise from the front door A-pillar area, consult TSB #B0010-97. **1995–97**—Countermeasures are listed to reduce front suspension groan under the base warranty. **1995–2000**—A power steering squeak can be silenced by installing a new rack end shaft. **1996**—Tips on reducing engine noise, front door wind noise, and front suspension and rear popping noise. • Upgraded hazard switch. **1997**—AC odour troubleshooting. • Fixing front suspension crunch. **1997–99**—A front brake grind or groan can be silenced by installing a new front brake pad kit under warranty. • Front suspension noise can be eliminated by changing the suspension support. **1998–99**—Door weather-strip improvements are detailed in TSB #B0-009-99.

Avalon Profile

	1995	1996	1997	1998	1999
Cost Price ($)					
XL	31,058	33,368	33,718	34,688	35,605
XLS	34,458	35,778	36,188	37,868	42,515
Used Values ($)					
XL ↑	13,000	15,500	18,000	21,000	25,000
XL ↓	12,500	13,000	15,000	19,000	23,000
XLS ↑	14,500	17,000	20,000	24,000	28,000
XLS ↓	13,000	14,500	17,000	21,000	26,000
Extended Warranty	N	N	N	N	N
Secret Warranty	N	N	Y	Y	Y
Reliability	⑤	⑤	⑤	⑤	⑤
Crash Safety	—	④	④	④	—
Side Impact	—	—	—	③	—

VOLVO

850 series, 70 series

Rating: Above Average (1993–99). Surprisingly, for a car company that emphasizes its commitment to safe cars, the 850 and 70 series have quite a few safety-related defects reported by owners, including engine and seat fires, loss of steering, sudden acceleration, transmission failures, electrical shorts, light failures, and tire blowouts. Don't waste your money on a 1997 850; the 1996 models are virtually identical to the more expensive 1997 versions and are a real bargain if the selling price has been reduced sufficiently. The 1998 model 850s were renamed the C70, S70, and V70; they also have a disappointingly high number of safety-related deficiencies reported to the federal government. **Maintenance/Repair costs:** Higher than average, and repairs must be done by a Volvo dealer. **Parts:** Higher-than-average cost and limited availability.

Strengths and weaknesses: Bland, but practical to the extreme, with plenty of power, good handling, and lots of capacity. For 1997, the 850 GLT got a bit more lower-end torque, while the turbo version was upgraded with electrically adjusted front passenger seats and an in-dash CD player. The base 850 sedan uses a 2.4L 24-valve 168-hp 5-cylinder engine hooked to a front-drive powertrain. (An all-wheel-drive version is available only in Canada and Europe.) Wagons use the same base powerplant, hooked to a 5-speed manual or optional 4-speed electronic automatic. GLTs have a torquier, turbo variant of the same powerplant that boosts horsepower to 190.

The "sports" sedan T5 is a rounder, sportier-looking Volvo that delivers honest, predictable performance but comes up a bit short on the "sport" side. Volvo's base turbo boosts horsepower to 222, but its new T-5R variant uses an upgraded turbocharger that boosts power to 240 horses—for up to seven seconds.

Passenger space, seating comfort, and trunk and cargo space are unmatched by the competition. Braking on dry and wet pavement is also exemplary. The ride of both the sedan and the wagon deteriorates progressively as the road gets rougher and passengers are added. Turbo versions are particularly stiff, and passengers are constantly bumped and thumped.

The 850 hasn't escaped the traditional AC, electrical-system, and brake problems that afflict its predecessors. Additionally, owners have complained that the early models have uncomfortable seatbelts, insufficient rear travel for the front seats, and some body hardware deficiencies, resulting in excess noise invading the interior.

70 series
Making its debut for the 1998 model year, the 70 series is basically the discontinued 850 using a *nom de plume*. The letters S, V, and C preceding the

numerical designation stand for sedans, wagons, and coupes. The 90 series is a redesignated rear-drive 960, and, as with the 70 series, "S" indicates sedan and "V" indicates wagon. Both the 70 and 90 series are carried over relatively unchanged, except for their names.

With the front-drive 70 series, all-wheel drive is offered with the wagons and the base 2.4L, 5-cylinder engine comes with three horsepower ratings: 168, 190, and 236. Only two transmissions are available: a manual 5-speed (relatively rare) and an automatic 4-speed.

Handling is superb with the suspension dampened somewhat for a more comfortable ride than what many European imports offer. AWD performs flawlessly, road and body noise are muted, and the cars are well-appointed with a full array of standard safety features, with the exception of traction control, which is optional.

On the downside, rear seating is cramped for three adults, and the instrument panel appears to be overly busy with a confusing array of gauges, instruments, and controls on the centre console. Plus, the three rear head restraints induce claustrophobia while severely restricting rear visibility.

The 90 series has plenty of room for three rear seat passengers and its 181-hp V6 performs very smoothly and fairly quietly, providing plenty of power for passing and merging. The car's tight turning circle makes parking a snap and the suspension has been tuned for comfort rather than performance. Still handling is quite good. Once again, the large rear head restraints obstruct rear visibility.

As far as quality control and dealer servicing are concerned, Volvo technical service bulletins and owner complaints indicate that factory defects on all models have been on the rise for the past several years. For example, the electrical system shuts down in rainy weather or when passing over puddles; headlights, turn signal lights, and other bulbs burn out monthly; dash lights suddenly go berserk when passing through puddles; power window switches fail; wheels are easily bent; turn signal lever doesn't return; airbags deploy for no reason; and springs are noisy.

The above defects clearly show there's less stringent quality control at the factory level since Ford acquired the company and that Volvo is counting on Ford and Volvo dealers to repair their engineering mistakes. On the other hand, Volvo *has* improved service and warranty relations by accelerating service training programs and allowing its dealers to carry out most warranty and extra-warranty repairs without obtaining prior authorization from the company. Ford's impact upon the dealer network has been minimal and is likely to stay that way as long as Volvo products continue to be hot sellers.

C70

Good acceleration with lots of torque, exceptional steering and handling, first-class body construction and finish, predicted better than average reliability. Weak points: Difficult rear-seat entry/exit, some engine turbo lag, excessive engine noise, a jarring suspension, and an uncertain future due to its high price and a shaky market.

Seating four comfortably, this $54,695 luxury coupe and convertible is based on the 850 (pardon, S70) platform, and marketed as a high-performance Volvo. It comes with two turbocharged engines: a base 2.4L 190-hp inline 5-cylinder, and a 2.3L 236-hp variant. Either engine can be hooked to a 5-speed manual or a 4-speed automatic transmission. Of the two engines, the 190-hp appears to offer the best response and smoothest performance.

Acceleration is impressive, despite the fact that the car feels underpowered until the turbo kicks in at around 1,500 rpm—a feature that drivers will find more frustrating with a manual shifter than with an automatic. Steering and handling are first class, fit and finish above reproach, and mechanical and body components are top quality.

The only things not to like are a high resale price, turbo lag, tire thumping caused by the high-performance tires, excessive engine and wind noise, and power-sliding rear seats that require lots of skill and patience.

Safety features include dual driver/passenger airbags, side airbags, ABS, traction control, and a platform designed to give maximum passenger protection in a collision. The IIHS has awarded the C70 its highest rating for front and rear seat head restraint protection.

Safety summary/Recalls: All models: 1996—A handful of reports that while vehicle was being driven, it suddenly lost all power and the engine compartment caught fire. • Inadvertent airbag deployment injured driver. • ABS brake failures. • Vehicle suddenly downshifts while cruising on the highway. • Transmission slipped out of Park, rolled down incline, and hit a house. • During rainy periods, the steering wheel locks up or the dashboard suddenly lights up. • Repeated tire blowouts. • Premature failure of the engine cooling fan and the evaporator pump fan relay for the exhaust manifold. Owners also cite cruise control, power-steering pump, and front seatbelt failures. • Electrical glitches affect the speedometer, radio cassette player, and battery. • Broken driver-side door hinge. **1997**—Heated seat caught fire. • Driver seatback frame broke when vehicle accelerated. • Sudden acceleration, spinning wildly, when backing up. • Pirelli (205/45-17) tires blew out; the design and size for this vehicle is inappropriate. • Original equipment tires bubble. • Total brake loss in rainy weather. • Rain also causes vehicle to shut down, without steering control. • Vehicle drifts left when being driven, even after the steering mechanism replaced. • Gas odour in the interior after driving a short distance. • Driver's seatbelt retractor locks up. • Steering also locks up in rainy weather. • Air pump and AC compressor failures. **1998**—Passenger-side airbag suddenly deployed while vehicle was parked. • Front and side airbags failed to deploy in a collision. • Right front wheel assembly disengaged from car while vehicle was underway, causing loss of control and an accident. • Vehicle suddenly accelerated; brakes locked up. • Stalling while underway caused by defective air mass sensor. • A piece of the vacuum brake system came loose causing engine rpms to surge and spontaneously locking up the brakes. • Transmission randomly fails to engage in Reverse gear, or kicks strongly when going into Reverse. • Frequent battery failures due to battery not holding its charge. • Headlights and other lights burn out frequently. • Two incidents where the front turn-signal socket smoldered and charred. • Driver seatbelt doesn't retract when disconnected. • Continental tires tread separation. • Frequent tire blowouts. • Wheels are easily bent, causing excessive vibration. • Defective door lock pin makes it difficult to open or close door. • Weak trunk lid struts allow lid to fall. • Dashboard causes excessive glare on windshield. • Tall front seats and head restraints obstruct visibility. **1998–99—** NHTSA probe of overheating front seat heaters and faulty turn signals. **1999**—Sudden acceleration when applying brakes. • Vehicle shuts down when making a left turn. • Airbags failed to deploy. • While underway, driver seat suddenly moved backward. • Fuel fumes leak into interior. • Brake pedal locks up. • Chronic light failures. • Automatic door locks and trunk lock fail to open. • Automatic gas tank door jams shut. • Hot tailpipe extends beyond bumper. • Inside door handles pinch fingers. **Recalls: All models: 1993–96**—Block heater could loosen and overheat, seriously damaging the engine. **1994**—Frozen throttle linkage could result in erratic engine operation. **1995**—The threaded insert that attaches the seatbelt catch to the front seat was incorrectly manufactured. • Some jacks may fail. **1996–97**—Throttle may not return to idle when foot is taken off the accelerator pedal.

Secret Warranties/Service Tips

All models/years—Campaign #92 provides improvements to the clutch control cylinder to make for smoother, more-efficient shifting. • Check the valve cover nuts at every servicing interval to prevent oil leakage. • Availability of free front seatbelt extenders. **All models: 1992–97—** Upgraded parts have been produced to correct a steering-column knocking noise. • Tips on silencing an automatic transmission whining noise. **1993**—A jerking sensation while accelerating may be caused by electrical interference between the rpm sensor wiring and the secondary ignition system. • Accessory drive-belt noise due to water infiltrating the system can be corrected by installing a special right-front-fender liner extension manufactured by Volvo to fix the problem. • Headlight wiper and washer motors may cause radio interference on the FM band; eliminate this noise by installing suppressed wiper motors and a suppressor between the washer pump and the existing wiring. • Under Service Campaign No. 62, Volvo dealers may install, at no charge, an improved engine accessory mounting bracket. **1993–94**—Steering column spring noise can be silenced by using upgraded bolts to secure the upper bracket to the airbag retaining plate. **1993–96**—Tips on repairing roof panel unevenness. **1993–97**—A number of bulletins have been issued to reduce cargo compartment and interior noise and trim rattles. **1995**—If the cruise control won't engage, check the vacuum supply and vacuum-supply pipe first. **1996**—An upgraded engine control module (ECM) has been released to improve engine function; it will be installed under the five-year emissions warranty. **1996–99**— Automatic transmission final drive whining sound can be eliminated by putting a damper on the driveshaft. This is covered under warranty "claim Type 01." **1997**—Correct high oil consumption. • New shims will minimize low-speed braking vibrations. • Tips on correcting hard starting. • AC odour troubleshooting tips. • Measures for improved ventilation and defrosting. • Engine may run too lean. **1997–99**—Rear axle whining countermeasures. • Automatic transmission whining correction tips. **1998–2000**—Installation of protective door lock covers. **1999**—Measures to reduce upper windshield moulding noise. **C70: 1997–99**—There are at least a half-dozen bulletins addressing water leaks affecting the C70. • Rear axle whining countermeasures. • Automatic transmission whining correction tips. **1998–2000**—Automatic transmission correction tips. • Power window noise can be silenced by following the procedures outlined in TSB #8330033. Poor FM reception (static) can be improved by modifying the ground strap. This gives additional benefit of bringing in more stations in scan mode. **1998–2001**—Upgraded rear brake pads will be installed under warrantry for more-efficient and quieter brakng.

850 series, 70 series Profile

	1993	1994	1995	1996	1997	1998	1999
Cost Price ($)							
850	29,950	29,095	29,995	31,995	32,995	—	—
Turbo	—	37,495	40,640	41,695	43,995	—	—
TLA/AWD	—	—	—	48,695	48,495	—	—
C70	—	—	—	—	—	54,675	49,995
S70	—	—	—	—	—	33,995	34,995
V70	—	—	—	—	—	33,295	36,295
Used Values ($)							
850 ↑	11,000	13,000	15,000	18,000	21,000	—	—
850 ↓	9,000	10,500	12,500	15,500	19,000	—	—
Turbo ↑	—	16,000	20,000	24,000	22,000	—	—
Turbo ↓	—	14,000	18,000	21,000	19,000	—	—
TLA/AWD ↑	—	—	—	26,000	29,000	—	—
TLA/AWD ↓	—	—	—	23,000	27,000	—	—
C70 ↑	—	—	—	—	—	34,000	36,500
C70 ↓	—	—	—	—	—	31,000	34,000
S70 ↑	—	—	—	—	—	21,000	25,000
S70 ↓	—	—	—	—	—	18,500	22,000
V70 ↑	—	—	—	—	—	22,000	26,000
V70 ↓	—	—	—	—	—	19,000	23,000
Extended Warranty	Y	Y	Y	Y	Y	Y	Y
Secret Warranty	Y	N	N	N	N	N	N
Reliability	③	④	⑤	⑤	⑤	⑤	⑤
Air conditioning	❷	❷	③	③	④	⑤	⑤

Auto. transmission	②	②	②	②	②	②	③
Body integrity	②	②	③	③	③	④	⑤
Braking system	③	③	③	③	③	③	③
Electrical system	②	②	②	②	③	③	③
Engines	⑤	⑤	⑤	⑤	⑤	⑤	⑤
Exhaust/Converter	③	③	③	④	⑤	⑤	⑤
Fuel system	③	④	④	⑤	⑤	⑤	⑤
Ignition system	③	③	④	⑤	⑤	⑤	⑤
Rust/Paint	③	④	⑤	⑤	⑤	⑤	⑤
Steering	⑤	⑤	⑤	⑤	⑤	⑤	⑤
Suspension	③	③	④	⑤	⑤	⑤	⑤
Crash Safety	—	⑤	⑤	⑤	⑤	—	⑤
Side Impact	—	—	—	—	④	—	④

900 series, 90 series, S80

Rating: Average (1997–99); Above Average (1989–96). The 1998 model 900s were renamed the S90 and V90 and have apparently inherited similar brake and electrical deficiencies. The base model was once again renamed—now the S80—for the 1999 model year. It's interesting to note that as the years progress the 960 series becomes cheaper to acquire than the 940 series. Unfortunately, as the revamped Volvos have gotten more popular during the past few years, their reliability and safety have become more problematic. For this reason, their rating has been downgraded this year. **Maintenance/Repair costs:** Higher than average, and repairs must be done by a Volvo dealer. **Parts:** Higher-than-average cost and limited availability.

Strengths and weaknesses: Practical to the extreme, with plenty of power, good handling, lots of carrying capacity, many standard safety features, and impressive crashworthiness ratings and accident injury claim data. Weak points: a jarring ride with vehicles equipped with 16- and 17-inch wheels; limited rear visibility; excessive engine, wind, and road noise; fuel-thirstiness (turbo models); declining quality control and increased frequency of safety-related deficiencies; and limited availability causing soaring resale prices for recent reworked models, with little room for negotiating.

Having debuted as essentially repackaged 760s, these flagship rear-drive sedans and wagons have a much better reliability record than do the 240 and 700 series, and have been on par with the 850 and S70/V70 over the last few model years. Both the 940 and 960 offer exceptional roominess and comfort, and are capable of carrying six people with ease. The wagon provides lots of cargo space and manages to do it in great style. Some owner gripes: the base 114-hp 2.3L engine is overpowered by the car's weight, excessive fuel consumption with the turbo option, and excessive road and wind noise at highway speeds.

Most of the 900 and 90 series' deficiencies are identical to the S70s, with some exceptions, like miscalibrated engine computer modules that cause random misfiring; rotten-egg and other exhaust odours that permeate the interior even after the catalytic converter is replaced; ignition switch, rear spring, and climate control unit failures; excessive on-road shudder/vibration, drifting, and hard steering; frequent fuel leaks; children suffering burns from the extended tailpipe; battery boil-over causing acid to spray into engine compartment; and seatbelt catching in the door after failing to retract properly. Drivers also report that the front bumper is too low; it hits the wheel stop in parking lots, causing extensive bumper and wheelwell damage. Also, brakes continue to require frequent and expensive maintenance due to the poor durability of front and rear pads and the premature warpage of the brake rotors (15,000 to 30,000 kilometres).

The S80 is the long overdue redesign of the S90 and offers several interestingly new features like a powerful, 268-hp, transverse inline 6-cylinder engine and a sophisticated automatic transmission called the Geartronic—a 4-speed automatic with a feature for manually changing gears, if one so desires. Additionally, the car is chock-full of safety features, has the largest interior of any Volvo, gives impressive performance and handling, and is attractively styled.

Unfortunately, the S80s defects closely resemble the problems reported on prior year's models (see "Safety summary/Recalls") and seriously undermine Volvo's much-touted safety claims. Some of the problems reported: pumps, lights, automatic door lock and window closing mechanism failures. Additionally, speaker grills warp and crack, and rear seatbelts malfunction.

Safety summary/Recalls: All models: 1986–91—Front seat/centre console fires. **1991–95**—Airbags deploy for no reason. **1998**—Engine fire. • Airbags didn't deploy in a collision. • Fuel system leak (T junctions and clamps replaced). • Other fuel leaks reported where owners claim problem may relate to the fuel expansion tank or its hoses. • Vehicle suddenly accelerated. • Tire tread separation. • Premature failure of the headlight, taillight, and turning signal, driveshaft, front and rear brake pad and rotor, tailgate struts, window switches, and door locks. • Turn signal bulbs are scorched and plastic melted. • Total loss of braking ability. • Inappropriate placement of the tailgate handle causes one to pull the tailgate close to one's face causing nose injury. • Brakes didn't work on an incline after vehicle stalled out. **1999**—Electrical short caused under-hood fire. Another fire occurred as vehicle was backing into a parking space. • Airbags deployed inadvertently while car was in Park. • Vehicle suddenly accelerated while parking. • Accelerator pedal became stuck when passing another vehicle on the highway. • Several incidents where electrical switches continually malfunction, console and console knobs are hot to the touch, and tapes have melted in the tape deck. • Chronic headlight and turn-signal light short circuits leading to lights constantly burning out; wires melted in turn signal socket. • Engine wire harness cracked and fell apart; shorted out near engine and radiator. • Fuel pump leaks and other unspecified leaks from the gas tank area. • Fuel tank wouldn't accept fuel. • Fuel line sprayed small amounts of fuel from impact with a rock. It should have some kind of protective shield. • Tire tread separation. • Transmission grinding and vibration when underway. • Suddenly stalled while turning. • Steering wheel locks up when making a left turn. • Total brake failure and excessive brake fade after successive braking. • Defective steering rack replaced by dealer. • Front wheel fell off the axle. • Sudden ball joint failure (see "Recalls") also causes premature tire wear. • Chronic front end shimmy. • Subframe bushing problem. • Clunking sound when automatic transmission is put into Reverse. • Power windows operate erratically. **Recalls: All models: 1989–90**—Fuel may seep from fuel tank. **1992–93**—Front seatbelts may detach from anchorage. • The seatbelt webbing guide may break. **1995**—Driver-side airbag may not deploy properly. **1996–97**—Throttle may not return to idle when foot is taken off the accelerator pedal. **1997–99**—Faulty ball joint may cause suspension to collapse. **Turbo 944, 945: 1991**—Throttle may jam. • Child car seat may not conform to federal safety standards. **1993**—Erratic throttle operation.

Secret Warranties/Service Tips

All models/years—Campaign #92 provides for improvements to the clutch control cylinder to make for smoother, more efficient shifting. Check the valve cover nuts at every servicing interval to prevent oil leakage. • New steering components will reduce power steering knocking. • AC evaporator odours can be controlled by installing a new fan control module. • Tips on silencing noise from the manual front seats. **All models: 1989–93**—To improve cold starting, ask Volvo to install an improved fuel-injection control module. Volvo may also have to replace the MFI E PROM. **1992**—Volvo Special Service Campaign #59 provides for the free replacement of AC pressure switches and harness, the Regina fuel control units, and Rex ignition control units. These repairs are to be carried out regardless of the vehicle mileage or the number of previous owners. **1992–94**—A decrease in idling speed when the AC engages can be corrected by installing a capacitor kit. **1992–98**—Oil pump leaks are usually due to loose pump retaining screws. **1997–99**—Rear axle whining countermeasures. • Automatic transmission final drive whining correction tips. • Upgraded rear brake pads to reduce grinding. • Upgraded weather stripping to reduce upper windshield moulding noise. • Installation of protective covers for door locks. • Improvements for door handle operation in cold weather. **1998**—Service Campaign #83 provides for the free replacement of faulty AC compressors. • Service Campaign #83A and 83B provide for the free replacement of the front panel to prevent it from interfering with the AC. **1999–2001**—New rear brake pads have been developed to reduce vibration.

900 series, 90 series, S80 Profile

	1992	1993	1994	1995	1996	1997	1998	1999
Cost Price ($)								
940 GLE	33,275	29,995	26,995	28,460	—	—	—	—
Wagon	33,900	30,995	27,995	29,490	—	—	—	—
960	40,986	43,045	35,495	41,300	46,400	47,400	—	—
S90	—	—	—	—	—	—	47,400	—
V90	—	—	—	—	—	—	49,075	—
S80	—	—	—	—	—	—	—	49,995
Used Values ($)								
940 GLE ↑	7,000	8,000	9,000	10,000	—	—	—	—
940 GLE ↓	6,000	7,000	8,000	8,000	—	—	—	—
Wagon ↑	7,000	8,000	9,000	10,500	—	—	—	—
Wagon ↓	6,000	7,000	8,000	8,000	—	—	—	—
960 ↑	8,500	10,000	12,000	14,000	17,500	23,000	—	—
960 ↓	7,500	8,500	9,500	12,000	16,000	20,000	—	—
S90 ↑	—	—	—	—	—	—	23,500	—
S90 ↓	—	—	—	—	—	—	22,000	—
V90 ↑	—	—	—	—	—	—	25,500	—
V90 ↓	—	—	—	—	—	—	23,000	—
S80 ↑	—	—	—	—	—	—	—	33,000
S80 ↓	—	—	—	—	—	—	—	31,000
Extended Warranty	Y	Y	Y	Y	Y	Y	Y	Y
Secret Warranty	N	Y	N	N	N	N	N	N
Reliability	③	③	④	⑤	⑤	③	③	③
Air conditioning	❷	❷	❷	③	④	⑤	⑤	⑤
Auto. transmission	❷	③	③	④	⑤	⑤	⑤	③
Body integrity	❷	❷	❷	❷	③	③	③	③
Braking system	❷	❷	❷	❷	❷	③	③	❷
Electrical system	❷	❷	❷	❷	❷	③	③	③
Engines	④	④	④	④	⑤	⑤	⑤	⑤
Exhaust/Converter	⑤	⑤	⑤	⑤	⑤	⑤	⑤	⑤
Fuel system	④	④	⑤	⑤	⑤	⑤	⑤	⑤
Ignition system	③	④	④	⑤	⑤	⑤	⑤	⑤
Rust/Paint	⑤	⑤	⑤	⑤	⑤	⑤	⑤	⑤
Steering	⑤	⑤	⑤	⑤	⑤	⑤	⑤	⑤
Suspension	③	③	④	⑤	⑤	⑤	⑤	⑤

Note: The 900 series was not crash-tested.

SPORTS CARS

The average sports car model, like the Mazda Miata, should be able to go from 0 to 100 km/h in under 10 seconds and top 130 km/h at the end of a quarter mile. Meanwhile, luxury sports sedans, like the Infiniti Q45 and Lexus LS 400, have produced exceptional acceleration times of 100 km/h in less than 8 seconds and have exceeded 145 km/h after a quarter mile. But most sports cars, or "high-performance vehicles" as they're euphemistically named, don't offer the comfort or reliability of an Infiniti or Lexus. Instead, they sacrifice reliability, interior space, and comfortable suspension for speed, superior road handling, and attractive styling. They also need a whole slew of expensive high-performance packages, because many entry-level sports cars aren't very sporty in their basic form. Keep in mind as well that sports cars often have serious accident damage that may not have been repaired properly, resulting in serious tracking problems because of a bent chassis. This risk can be attenuated only by a thorough check-up by a body shop before you purchase.

Browse carefully through classified ads and dealer car lots and you'll find many fully loaded offerings at a fraction of their original cost. Remember that most models that have been taken off the market, like the Toyota Supra, Nissan 300ZX, and Chevrolet Corvette ZR1, aren't likely to become collectors' cars with soaring resale values. In fact, discontinued Japanese sports cars like the Nissan 1600 haven't done nearly as well as some of the British roadsters taken off the market at about the same time.

Recommended

Ford Probe (1995–97)
GM Camaro, Firebird,
  Trans Am (1997–99)

Honda Prelude (1993–99)
Mazda Miata (1996–99)
Toyota Celica (1995–99)

Above Average

Chrysler Talon (1997–99)
Ford Mustang (1998–99)
Honda Prelude (1985–92)

Hyundai Tiburon (1997–99)
Mazda Miata (1990–95)
Toyota Celica (1986–94)

Average

Ford Probe (1993–94)
GM Camaro, Firebird,
  Trans Am (1994–96)

GM Corvette (1997–99)

Below Average

Chrysler Avenger, Sebring
  (1995–99)
Ford Cobra, Mustang (1980–97)

Ford Probe (1989–92)
GM Camaro, Firebird
  Trans Am (1992–93)

Not Recommended

Chrysler Laser, Talon
  (1990–96)

GM Camaro, Firebird,
  Trans Am (1982–91)
GM Corvette (1977–96)

CHRYSLER

Avenger, Sebring

Rating: Below Average (1995–99). The Avenger and its more luxuriously appointed Sebring twin have had fewer factory-related defects than other new Chrysler designs, though this is faint praise, indeed. New V6-equipped versions cost about $3,000–$5,000 more than the base models, but a used V6 is a real bargain, only costing a bit more. Drive a hard bargain, because the money you save will be eaten up in transmission, engine head gasket, and AC evaporator repair bills if you don't threaten small claims court action. Of course, an extended powertrain warranty is a must. **Maintenance/Repair costs:** Higher than average. Repairs must be done by a Chrysler dealer. **Parts:** Higher-than-average cost and limited availability.

Strengths and weaknesses: The Avenger and Sebring, designed by Chrysler and built by Mitsubishi in Illinois, are both surprisingly agile—they share the same components, except for grille and taillights. Since Avengers come with fewer standard features, they're usually priced a bit lower than Sebrings. The convertible, made in Mexico, is six inches longer than the Sebring coupe and is powered by a standard 2.0L twin cam, while the upscale JXi gets a performance injection with the 2.5L 6-cylinder powerplant. ABS was standard on ES versions and optional on base Avengers; dual airbags were standard on all models. From 1995 through the 1999 model, neither the Avenger nor the Sebring have changed much, except for minor restyling touches and the dropping of the 4-cylinder engine in mid-1999.

Acceleration is fairly good, though noisy, with the base 140-hp engine and a manual transmission; however, the optional V6 powerplant is the engine of choice to overcome the power-hungry automatic transmission and to avoid a persistent 4-cylinder engine head gasket defect affecting all model years. Handling is better than average, and the ride is generally comfortable, except for a bit of choppiness due to the firm suspension. Engine, tire, and road noise at higher speeds can be annoying. Rear-seat

Sports Cars

access can be a pain (literally), and rear seating may be uncomfortable for long trips. Small gauges and sound system controls that are set way too low are disconcerting. Plus, the car's narrow back window, tall shelf, and wide roof pillars impede rear visibility and create a claustrophobic interior environment. Incidentally, small horn buttons on the steering-wheel spokes can be hard to reach in an emergency.

Mitsubishi quality control has slipped considerably as of late and is compounded by the increased use of Chrysler poor-quality generic parts. Owners single out the automatic transmission (shuddering from a stop and defaulting to second gear); 4-cylinder engine head gasket failures; premature brake wear and brake failures; ignition, electrical-system, and power control module glitches; sunroof malfunctions; and sloppy body construction as the areas most needing attention. Would you believe the driver's seat motor burns out because it doesn't have a fuse? Replacement cost: $2,000! Furthermore, the convertible top is prone to fly off on early models, leaks water and air, and operates erratically.

Safety summary/Recalls: All models: 1995–99—Avengers had only one safety-related incident reported to NHTSA: no airbag deployment in an accident. Sebring safety failures over the same period were frequent and serious. **Sebring: 1995**—Fuel line connection fire. • Rear window explosion from defroster short circuit. • No airbag deployment. • Premature transmission failure; sticks in second gear or won't go into Park or Reverse. • ABS brake failures. • Premature brake wear, due to a defective sensor relay, forces rotor and pad replacement every 10,000–20,000 km and makes the car jerk and vibrate when braking. • Faulty seatbelts. • Anti-theft alarm self-activates. • Front windshield moulding peels away. • Trunk supports gave out, causing lid to slam down. • The low front end causes the front bumper to hit the pavement whenever passing over a speed bump. • Annoying engine ticking noise and head gasket failure. **1996**—Same problems generally as '95 models except for more frequent reports of the following problems. • Convertible top flies off. • Fire ignites inside the driver and passenger doors and shift console. • Key trapped in ignition. • Transmission jumps out of gear while in Park with key removed. • Engine head gasket failures. • Transmission defects. • ABS failures. • Brake rotor warpage. • Sudden failure of suspension and steering components. • New problems also abound. • Water leaks into the interior and collects under the back seat cushion and on the floor. • Carpeting may cause the steering to lock up. • Horn doesn't blow. • Digital mileage and gear shift screen goes blank. • Rotten-egg smell. • Electrical shorts cause the car to suddenly shut down. **1997**—As unbelievable as it seems, Chrysler still carries on with almost identical safety problems as those reported earlier. • Reports of transmission failures have increased. • Sudden acceleration due to the throttle jamming is still a danger. • Brake failures are common. • Rotors and pads must be replaced. • Seatbelts frequently lock up. • Owners report the transmission still permits the vehicle to roll away even though the lever was put into Park. • Trunk leaks. • Noisy steering. • Inadequate and hard-to-find spare tire also make this year's list. • Interestingly, head gasket failure reports have tapered off (too early to tell?). **1998**—After only two years on the market, you'd expect few complaints, right? Wrong! More of the same old same old. However, virtually no engine failures have been reported, but most of the same complaints as enumerated above have continued. • There has also been a greater number of safety-related reports. • Electrical shorts. • Brake problems. • Airbag malfunctions. • Sudden acceleration. • Loss of steering control due to the floor mat blocking the steering column. • Bent wheel rims cause tire blowouts. • Seatbelts lock up. • Alternator/battery failures. • One new item: an unusually large number of complaints that the side door panel cladding falls off while cruising. **1999**—Vehicle caught fire after hitting bumper of other car at 5 mph (8 km/h). • Other fire reported from a leaking fuel hose. Front airbags failed to deploy upon impact. • Many incidents where the throttle stuck while engaging Reverse. • Premature replacement of the lower lateral sway bar. • Automatic transmission rebuild after 38,000 miles (60,000 kilometres). • Split transmission line. • Delayed, noisy transmission shifting. • Slipped into Reverse and rolled downhill, despite being in Park with ignition off. • Constant-velocity joint flew off in heavy traffic on highway. • Brakes don't grab sufficiently; complete loss of braking due to loss of vacuum. • Defective rear defroster clip. • Windshield wipers suddenly stop working. • Toxic tar substance leaks out of the doors and body cladding (door panels) falls off on the highway (see "Technical service bulletins"). • Convertible boot flew off while vehicle underway. • Replaced ignition switch because key couldn't be inserted. • Front end too low. **Recalls: All models: 1995–96**—Front ball joints fail, suspension collapses. **1996**—Faulty power mirror switch. • Power brake booster hose mislocated. **1997**—Front passenger head restraint support bracket may break. Dealers must replace the entire seatback assembly. **Sebring: 1996–98**—Faulty ignition switches, console shifter, and cables in convertible models may cause the vehicle to roll away or render the ignition-park interlock system inoperative.

Secret Warranties/Service Tips

All models: 1995—One of the causes of premature brake wear, shudder, and noise is a misadjusted brake light switch. **1995–96**—Engine compartment ticking can be silenced by replacing the duty cycle purge solenoid with a quieter solenoid assembly. **1995–97**—Engine compartment popping or knocking may require an upgraded EGR valve. **1995–98**—Delayed transaxle engagement can be corrected by installing an upgraded trailing arm bushing. **1995–99**—Front coil spring creak, pop, or squeak can be silenced by putting in coil spring insulators. • Intermittent loss of speed control can be prevented by installing new speed sensors. • Wind noise coming from the front windshield area is caused by wind lifting the windshield moulding at the glass. • Tips on reducing excessive front brake pulsation or shudder. • Paint delamination, peeling, or fading (see Part Two).

1997–99—A light knocking noise from the rear shock area may mean you need to install various upgraded rear shock components. • New software will prevent the transmission from shifting erratically or falling into a second gear "limp" mode. **1997–2000**—To prevent the door cladding from falling off, Chrysler recommends replacing the lower mounting clips under warranty (TSB #23-40-99). **1999–2000**—A black, tar-like residue can be cleaned under warranty by following guidelines found in TSB #23-56-99.

Avenger, Sebring Profile

	1995	1996	1997	1998	1999
Cost Price ($)					
Avenger	17,175	18,954	18,780	19,280	20,360
Avenger V6	21,275	22,544	23,820	24,320	23,545
Sebring	18,155	19,514	21,420	21,500	23,380
Sebring V6	24,025	25,538	24,135	24,360	28,675
Convertible	—	25,210	27,030	27,530	—
Used Values ($)					
Avenger ↑	8,000	9,500	10,000	12,000	14,500
Avenger ↓	6,500	8,000	9,000	10,500	13,000
Avenger V6 ↑	8,500	10,500	12,000	14,000	16,000
Avenger V6 ↓	7,000	9,000	10,500	13,000	14,500
Sebring ↑	8,000	10,000	11,500	14,000	16,500
Sebring ↓	6,500	9,000	10,000	12,500	15,000
Sebring V6 ↑	9,000	12,000	13,500	16,000	18,500
Sebring V6 ↓	7,500	10,500	12,500	14,500	17,000
Convertible ↑	—	13,500	15,000	19,000	—
Convertible ↓	—	11,500	13,500	17,000	—
Extended Warranty	Y	Y	Y	Y	Y
Secret Warranty	Y	Y	Y	Y	Y
Reliability	❷	❷	❷	❷	❷
Crash Safety					
Avenger	—	⑤	⑤	—	—
Sebring	—	—	⑤	—	—

Laser, Talon

Rating: Above Average (1997–98); Not Recommended (1990–96). The '95 models offered fresh styling, dual airbags, and a more powerful engine. The 1997 versions are identical to the more expensive, restyled '98 models (Talon's last year), and are the better buy since they're substantially cheaper and don't have the first-year glitches found on earlier offerings. **Maintenance/Repair costs:** Higher than average, but routine repairs can be done practically anywhere. Make sure the engine timing chain is inspected regularly and check for head gasket failures—I've received about a dozen reports of owners having to pay huge repair bills for new engines. **Parts:** Good parts availability. Dealers have had some trouble adequately servicing high-tech components, and parts are a bit more expensive than other cars in this class.

Strengths and weaknesses: These sporty Mitsubishi-made cars combine high performance, low price, and reasonable durability. The base 1.8L engine is adequate and the suspension is comfortable, although a bit soft. The optional 16-valve, turbocharged 2.0L comes with a firmer suspension and gives more horsepower for the dollar than most other front-drive sports coupes, without much turbo lag. The 5-speed manual is the gearbox of choice. Torque steer makes the car appear to try to twist out of your hands when all 195 turbocharged horses are unleashed. The 4-speed automatic transmission cuts into the Laser's highway performance. Overall handling is impressive, with the 4X4 system giving sure-footed foul-weather stability. Keep in mind that the all-wheel-drive (AWD) model has a smaller trunk area than the front-drive.

All high-performance models cost thousands of dollars less than their Japanese competitors, without compromising quality or performance. The 16-valve Talon and its 4X4 variant are at the top of the trim list and provide five more horses than the turbocharged TSi.

Beginning with the 1990–94 models, owners report glitches with the 1.8L engine and electrical system, driveline vibrations, premature brake wear and excessive noise, and poor fit and finish that includes water leakage into the interior and paint delamination. Some problems reported with 1995–98 versions were unstable idling, poor idling, and reduced rpm when the AC is running; cold-weather hard starts and stalling; cold-weather transmission shift delays (2–3 and 3–4) that take up to two minutes; transmission defaults into second gear (limp-in mode); frequent wheel alignments; a tendency to drift or lead to the right; speed control undershoot or overshoot; chronic electrical system, brake, and transmission failures; false theft alarm; centre exhaust-pipe heat shield buzz; door buzz and rattle; misadjusted door glass and poor windshield sealing causing water leaks and wind noise; noisy clutch pedal; interior window film buildup; headliner sagging; power seat switch sticking; stress marks on the quarter-trim panel; buzz or rattle from the rear quarter-trim; inoperative, noisy, and jerky sunroof operation; faulty lever latch pin; and the sunroof may open by itself.

Safety summary/Recalls: All models: Standard brakes often lock up or require long stopping distances. Choose the optional ABS. • Head restraints block rear visibility. **1995–98**—Most of the following problems reappear each year in NHTSA records. • Engine and fuel tank fires. • Fuel leakage after recall repairs. • Sudden acceleration due to jammed throttle. • Airbags failed to deploy. • Chronic transmission failures that include transfer case leakage after recall repairs (automatic and manual transaxles), causing sudden wheel lockup. • Wheels fall off. • Engine timing belt breakage (100,000–120,000 km). • Loss of steering caused by going through a puddle of water. • Steering belt slipping off the pulley. • Collapse of suspension and steering components (front control arms and ball joints). • Frequent replacement of brake pads and warped rotors. • Electrical system failures. • Faulty door locks and windows. • Water leakage into interior. • Horn won't work or self-activates. • ABS and Check Engine lights come on for no reason. **Recalls: All models: 1990–98**—Transfer-case fluid leakage may cause sudden wheel lockup. **1995–96**—Incorrectly installed fuel gauge/pump gaskets may cause a fire; requires a new fuel tank. • Lower ball joint rubber boots may be defective. **1998**—Throttle control cable could jam. **Talon, Talon 4X4: 1997**—Front passenger head-restraint support bracket may break; dealers must replace the entire seat back assembly.

Secret Warranties/Service Tips

All models: 1993–98—Paint delamination, peeling, or fading (see Part Two). • A rotten-egg odour coming from the exhaust may be the result of a malfunctioning catalytic converter that may be covered by the emissions warranty. **1995–96**—Engine compartment ticking can be silenced by replacing the duty cycle purge solenoid with a quieter solenoid assembly. **1995–97**—Engine compartment popping or knocking may require an upgraded EGR valve. **1995–98**—Front coil spring creak, pop, or squeak can be silenced by putting in coil-spring insulators. • Delayed transaxle engagement can be corrected by installing an upgraded trailing arm bushing. **1995–98**—Intermittent loss of speed control can be prevented by installing new speed sensors. • Wind noise coming from the front windshield area is caused by wind lifting the windshield moulding at the glass. • Tips on reducing excessive front brake pulsation or shudder. **1997–98**—A light knocking noise from the rear shock area may mean you need to install various upgraded rear shock components. • New software will prevent the transmission from shifting erratically or falling into a second-gear "limp" mode. **1998**—Erratic automatic transmission performance can be corrected by installing new software.

Laser, Talon Profile

	1991	1992	1993	1994	1995	1996	1997	1998
Cost Price ($)								
Laser	13,000	13,735	14,145	14,145	—	—	—	—
Turbo RS	14,900	15,820	16,310	16,310	—	—	—	—
Talon	15,505	16,205	14,475	16,000	19,425	20,695	19,885	20,290

Talon TSi	18,100	19,365	19,365	19,975	28,360	29,985	30,225	30,675
Used Values ($)								
Laser ↑	2,500	3,000	4,000	5,000	—	—	—	—
Laser ↓	2,000	2,500	3,000	4,000	—	—	—	—
Turbo RS ↑	2,500	3,000	4,000	6,000	—	—	—	—
Turbo RS ↓	2,000	2,000	2,500	4,500	—	—	—	—
Talon ↑	3,000	3,500	4,000	5,000	8,000	10,000	10,500	12,000
Talon ↓	2,500	3,000	3,500	4,000	6,500	8,000	9,000	11,000
Talon TSi ↑	3,500	4,000	4,500	7,000	12,000	15,000	17,000	20,000
Talon TSi ↓	3,000	3,500	3,500	5,500	10,500	13,000	15,000	18,000
Extended Warranty	Y	Y	Y	Y	Y	Y	Y	Y
Secret Warranty	Y	Y	Y	Y	Y	Y	Y	Y
Reliability	②	②	②	②	②	②	④	⑤
Air conditioning	③	③	④	⑤	⑤	⑤	④	④
Auto. transmission	②	②	②	②	②	②	②	③
Body integrity	②	②	②	②	②	②	③	③
Braking system	②	②	②	②	②	②	③	④
Electrical system	②	②	②	②	②	②	②	③
Engines	①	①	①	①	②	②	③	④
Exhaust/Converter	③	③	③	④	⑤	⑤	⑤	⑤
Fuel system	①	①	①	①	①	②	③	④
Ignition system	③	②	②	③	③	④	⑤	⑤
Rust/Paint	②	③	③	③	③	③	③	④
Steering	③	③	③	③	③	④	④	⑤
Suspension	③	③	③	③	④	④	④	④
Crash Safety	—	—	—	—	—	④	—	—
Side Impact	—	—	—	—	—	—	①	①

FORD

Cobra, Mustang

Rating: Above Average (1998–99); Below Average (1980–97).
Unfortunately, Mustangs don't perform well in rough weather and they
have had a frighteningly high number of safety-related mechanical failures. GM's Camaro and Firebird are the Mustang's traditional competition as far as performance is concerned. Ford has the price advantage,
with a base Mustang costing a bit less than the cheapest Camaro, but it
lags from a performance standpoint—10 fewer horses with the V6 and
only 60 more horses with the V8. The GM models also offer more sure-
footed acceleration, crisper handling, standard ABS, a 6-speed transmission, and more comfortable rear seats. Don't waste your money on
a 1997 Mustang if a 1996 version, in good condition, is available. All
4-cylinder versions should be shunned. **Maintenance/Repair costs:**
Average, particularly because repairs can be done anywhere. Be wary of
cracked plastic intake manifolds on '96 and '97 models. They often fail
and cost almost $1,000 new, or $200 salvage. **Parts:** Average cost, and
parts are often sold for much less through independent suppliers. Some
parts are continually back-ordered, particularly if involved in recall
repairs (cruise control components, for example).

Strengths and weaknesses: This is definitely not a family car. For example, a light rear end makes the car dangerously unstable on wet roads
or when cornering at high speeds. But for those who want a sturdy and
stylish second car, or who don't need room in the back or standard
ABS, the 1996–98 Mustang is a pretty good sports-car buy. And if GM
carries out its threat to drop its rear-drive Camaro and Firebird after
the year 2001, the Mustang will be the main alternative for rear-drive
sports car enthusiasts. As stated earlier, Mustangs remain popular
because they offer sporty styling and high-performance thrills, usually
for less money than GM's Camaro and Firebird, the Mustang's main
domestic rivals.

Base models come equipped with a host of luxury and convenience
items, which can be a real bargain once the base price has sufficiently
depreciated, say, after the first three years. Off-lease models are particularly good buys these days.

1990–93

There are three body styles to choose from—a coupe, a coupe hatchback, and a ragtop—and two engines—a wimpy 2.3L 4-banger and a
5.0L V8. A driver-side airbag was a standard feature. The 1991 models
added 15 more horses to the base engine (105 hp), upgraded convertible tops, and a brake/shift interlock. The following year's models were
unchanged carryovers; however, the '93 model year saw the debut of
the high-performance Mustang Cobra sporting a 245-hp V8 marketed
in limited numbers in Canada.

Mustangs have never been very reliable cars, and the 1990–93 models were particularly troublesome. Yet when failures do occur, they aren't difficult or expensive to fix (engine head gaskets excepted). The first Mustang, launched in 1964, and now worth more than $25,000, had serious rusting, electrical, and suspension problems. And guess what? Thirty-six years later, Mustangs still have electrical systems and electronic modules that are constantly breaking down, transmissions that jump from Park to Reverse, and a base suspension and front brakes that wear out in the blink of an eye.

The less said about the infamous 2.3L 4-cylinder engine, the better. The V6 is also failure-prone (head gaskets, again), leaving the V8 engine with a definite performance and reliability edge. Turbocharged models aren't recommended because of their frequent and expensive mechanical breakdowns. If you want high-performance action, you'll have to pay a premium—and be prepared for some monstrous repair bills and white-knuckle acceleration on wet roadways. Sport trim models feature an upgraded suspension and wheel package that improves handling considerably.

Keep in mind that the electronic modules that govern engine and transmission performance are often on the fritz, producing chronic hard starts, stalling, and overall poor city and highway performance. Furthermore, the 3.8L 6-cylinder engine has begun to tally up a record number of head gasket failures around the 150,000 km mark. Other problem areas: the front brakes, fuel pumps, and front suspension remain consistent weak spots, and MacPherson struts and various steering components are likely to wear out before their time. The parking brake cable also seizes easily. The EEC IV engine computer can be temperamental, and electrical problems are common. Assembly quality is still not on par with Japanese vehicles.

The 4-cylinder engine, used through 1993, isn't just failure-prone— it also doesn't carry half the horses of the 5.0L V8 and has no redeeming qualities. Unfortunately, the 1993 Mustang fell behind the competition that year as GM radically restyled the Camaro and Firebird with additional safety features, a more rigid and dent-resistant body, better body fit and finish, and a more powerful base engine.

1994–99
Ford fought back with its own redesign of its 1994 model, replacing the 4-banger with a V6, adding four-wheel disc brakes and dual airbags, making the chassis more rigid (especially the convertible version), and dropping the hatchback. Mustangs now carry a base 3.8L V6 and an optional 4.6L V8. In addition, the high-performance limited edition Cobra variation delivers 90 more horses than the stock 4.6L V8 offers. The single and twin cam V8 options make the Mustang a powerful—if a bit unsophisticated—street machine. V6 models are an acceptable compromise, even though the engines fail to deliver the gobs of power most performance enthusiasts expect.

1995 models were simply carried over unchanged. The '96s got a 4.6L V8 with upgraded spark plugs and the Cobra received a 305-hp variant of the same powerplant; '97s returned mostly unchanged, except for new colours and option upgrades. For 1998, the GT version got a 10-horsepower performance boost and the '99s got fresh styling and another horsepower boost. That year, the V6 models also get suspension and steering gear upgrades.

Unfortunately, Ford's safety-related problems continue to be carried over as well (see "Safety summary/Recalls"). Additionally, both the V6 and V8 engines have a propensity for chronic stalling; blowing engine intake manifold and head gaskets; fuel system glitches highlighted by frequent fuel injector malfunctions; faulty differential carrier bearings; prematurely worn clutch pressure plates; electrical shorts causing instrument panel shutdown; early replacement of brake rotors, pads, and calipers; and paint defects and premature rusting reported on earlier models.

Safety summary/Recalls: Regularly equipped Mustangs, like most rear-drive Fords, don't handle sharp curves or wet pavement very well. The rear end swings out suddenly, and the car tends to spin uncontrollably. Furthermore, the car loses traction easily on wet roads and braking is barely adequate. **All models: 1994–95**—NHTSA is looking into parking brake failures. **1995**—Fuel-line failure caused several fires. • Front fan belt caught on fire with no warning. • Several reports of sudden acceleration due to a stuck throttle. • Airbag failed to deploy. • Airbag deployment caused severe injuries. • Inadvertent airbag deployment; several reports that when driver applied the brakes, the airbag deployed. • ABS brake failures, warped rotors, and frequent pad replacement. • Engine head gasket failures. • Power steering fails; steering wheel is off-centre or locks up. • Chronic stalling thought to be caused by defective fuel pump. • Transmission failure while driving caused accident. • Torque converter failure causes transmission to slip. • Many reports of vehicle jumping from Park to Reverse and rolling away. • Rear axle broke during normal driving conditions. • Front-end alignment doesn't hold, causing premature wear of steering and tie-rods. • On one occasion, tie-rods broke and caused vehicle to go out of control, resulting in several fatalities. • Front struts suddenly collapsed. • Weak rear struts allow vehicle to "bottom out." • Front stabilizer bar rusted and cracked. • Driver's door hinge broke. • Fuel gauge inoperative or gives an inaccurate reading. • Gas tank too small and requires frequent fillups. • Trunk leaks cause premature rusting. • Fog lights fill with water and blow their bulbs. • Frequent AC failures. • Seatbelt failed to restrain driver. **1996**—Many defects are carried over, including braking, automatic-transmission, and engine cooling problems (many allegations that the plastic intake manifold ruptures under pressure from the cooling system and may be a causative agent for an increase in head gasket failures). • Airbags fail to deploy, or deploy inadvertently causing injuries. • Stalling. • Sudden acceleration (now appears to be cruise control–related). • ABS failures. • Frequent brake rotor and pad replacement. • Fuel-tank leakage and fuel-line fire. • Sudden steering loss, and water leaking into lights. • Broken rear sway bar behind rear mounting bolt. • Excessive front-end vibrations. • Timing chain and fan belt failures. • Check Engine light comes on due to a defective evaporator canister solenoid. • Some airbag injuries traced to the use of sodium azide, the airbag propellent; apparently, it changes to the very toxic sodium hydroxide (caustic soda) when detonated. **1997**—Engine overheating caused by a defective intake manifold. • More reports of manual and automatic transmission failures (popping out of gear, grinding, clutch vibrations, no Reverse of second-to-third gear shift). • ABS and parking-brake failures. • Power-steering pump. • Seatbelt fails to retract. • Sway bar breakage. • Sudden acceleration. • Fuel leakage at fuel-tank connection. • Differential rear ring and pinion gear problems. • AC compressor fails. • Hood pops open. • Front brake line separation. • Front lower control arm/ball joint separation. **1998–99**—Fuel tank leaks. • Engine compartment fires. • Hood flew up unexpectedly while underway. • Sudden acceleration. • Throttle stuck under floor mat. • Frequent stalling, hesitation, and loses power. • No airbag deployment; airbag-induced injuries. • Parking brake doesn't hold (traced to a broken ratchet assembly). • Vehicle rolled down hill with emergency brake applied. • Brake handle pulls up all the way up, without engaging. • Brake pedal goes to floor without braking. • Steering system failure. • Right ball joint fractured causing wheel to turn inward. • Tire side-wall tread separation. • Seatbelt tightens up continually. • Repeats of '97 problems: transmission, braking, and engine failures. • Fire ignited in the centre console and dash areas. • Defective seatbelt retractor and poor design allows belt to slip out of guide. • Stalling caused by fuel pump or fuel relay cut-off switch failure. • Original equipment tire blowouts (side wall splits). **Recalls: All models: 1988–93**—Faulty ignition module may pose a fire hazard. **1991**—Vehicle could roll away with the shift lever in Park position. **1994–96**—Hood catch may be defective. **1994–2001**—Emergency brake doesn't hold. **1995**—Defective tie-rod ends could cause an excessive shake or shimmy, resulting in an accident. **1998**—Steering may fail. • Fuel leak may cause a fire. **1998–99**—Cruise control may stick. **1999**—Defective seatbelt retractor jams belt. **Mustang GT: 1995**—Front seat cushion supports could abrade wiring harness, posing a fire hazard.

Secret Warranties/Service Tips

All models: 1982–90—An unusual engine metal-to-metal noise may be caused by the flexing of the torque converter; install six new flywheel bolts with reduced head height to provide additional clearance. **1985–97**—A buzz or rattle from the exhaust system may be caused by a loose heat shield catalyst. **1986–94**—The in-tank fuel pump is the likely cause of all that radio static you hear; stop the noise by installing an electronic noise RFI filter

(#F1PZ-18B925-A). **1987–90**—Excessive oil consumption is likely caused by leaking gaskets, poor sealing of the lower intake manifold, defective intake, and exhaust valve stem seals, or worn piston rings; install new guide-mounted valve stem seals for a more positive fit and new piston rings with improved oil control. **1988–92**—Cold hesitation when accelerating, rough idle, long crank times, and stalling may all signal the need to clean out excessive intake valve deposits. These problems also may result from the use of fuels that have low volatility, such as high-octane premium blends. **1990**—Excessive transmission noise, delayed shifts, or no engagements may be due to thrust washer metal particles that have plugged the filter or burnt out the clutch plates. **1993–99**—Paint delamination, peeling, or fading (see Part Two). • Ford "goodwill" warranty extensions usually cover engine and transmission components, catalytic converters, and computer modules. If Ford balks at refunding your money, apply the emissions warranty for a full or partial refund. **1994**—Automatic transmissions with delayed or no forward engagement, or a higher engine rpm than expected when coming to a stop, are covered in TSB #94-26-9. • A cracked cowl top vent grille should be replaced with an upgraded version. • A driveline boom can be silenced by replacing the rear upper control arms. • A noisy fuel pump needs to be replaced by an improved "guided check valve" fuel pump. • Models with laser-red paint may have serious paint decay problems, requiring a repainting of the entire body. • A ticking or tapping sound coming from the engine at idle can be silenced by installing an improved fuel hose/damper assembly. **1994–95**—A thumping or clacking heard from the front brakes signals the need to machine the front disc brake rotors. • Loss of torque during or just after 3–4 shift may be caused by a hydraulic condition in the transmission or an intermittent signal from one of the powertrain system sensors. **1994–97**—An erratic or prolonged 1–2 shift is likely caused by a defective aluminum piston. **1994–98**—Loose rocker panel mouldings will be fixed under the bumper-to-bumper warranty. **1996**—Stalling or hard starts may be due to the idle air control valve sticking. **1996–97**—The engine's lower intake manifold side and front-cover gaskets might leak coolant, a problem that can cause overheating and severe engine damage (see refund program letter on next page).

A.R. O'Neill
Director
Vehicle Services and Programs
Ford Customer Service Division

Ford Motor Company
P.O. Box 1904
Dearborn, MI 48121-1904

January, 2000

Ford Motor Company is providing a no-charge Service Program, Number 99B29, to owners of certain 1996 and 1997 model year Mustang, Thunderbird, Cougar, and 1997 F-Series vehicles equipped with 3.8L or 4.2L engines.

What Is The Reason For This Program?	The affected vehicles may experience engine coolant leaks at the engine front cover gasket; this could cause severe engine damage if not corrected. To avoid engine damage, you should make an appointment to have this service performed on your vehicle at your Ford or Lincoln Mercury Dealer as soon as possible.
No Charge Service:	At no charge to you, your dealer will replace the engine from cover gasket with a redesigned gasket and change the engine oil and filter. This service will reduce the likelihood of coolant leaks at the engine front cover, and will help avoid the potential inconvenience of breakdowns and costly engine repairs.
	Your vehicle is eligible for this program until March 31, 2001, regardless of mileage.

Ford asks owners to call their dealers immediately to have the gasket replaced even if they have not experienced any problem. Consumers who have already had the repair will be reimbursed for their expenses.

1997–99—Delayed, or no 2–3 upshift may be caused by a leaking accumulator seal. • Road noise, or dust/water leaks in the luggage compartment can be fixed by sealing the wheelhouse flange. **1997–2000**—Automatic transmission fluid leaks at the radiator can be stopped by installing an O-ring onto the transmission oil cooler fitting. **1998–99**—Tips on spotting abnormal ABS braking noise. **1999–2000**—An erratically operating front windshield wiper probably has a faulty multifunction switch. Replace it under warranty, says TSB #00-9-6.

Cobra, Mustang Profile

	1992	1993	1994	1995	1996	1997	1998	1999
Cost Price ($)								
Cobra GT	17,995	18,995	—	—	—	—	—	—
Mustang LX/Coupe	12,095	10,995	15,595	17,595	18,595	19,795	22,595	20,995
Convertible	19,995	20,495	24,995	26,095	25,895	26,795	29,295	24,995
Used Values ($)								
Cobra GT ↑	4,500	6,000	—	—	—	—	—	—
Cobra GT ↓	3,500	4,500	—	—	—	—	—	—
Mustang LX/ Coupe ↑	3,000	3,500	6,000	8,500	10,000	12,500	14,500	16,000
Mustang LX/ Coupe ↓	2,500	3,000	4,500	7,000	8,500	11,000	13,000	14,500
Convertible ↑	4,500	6,500	9,000	12,000	14,000	16,000	18,500	21,000
Convertible ↓	4,000	4,500	7,000	10,000	12,500	14,500	17,000	19,000

Extended Warranty	Y	Y	Y	Y	Y	Y	N	N
Secret Warranty	Y	Y	Y	Y	Y	Y	Y	Y
Reliability	❷	❶	❷	❷	❷	③	③	④
Air conditioning	❶	❶	❶	❶	❶	❷	④	⑤
Auto. transmission	❶	❶	❶	❶	❷	❷	❷	❷
Body integrity	❶	❶	❷	❷	❷	❷	③	③
Braking system	❶	❶	❶	❶	❷	❷	❷	❷
Electrical system	❶	❶	❶	❶	❷	❷	③	④
Engines	❶	❶	❶	❶	❶	❷	③	④
Exhaust/Converter	❷	③	③	③	③	③	③	④
Fuel system	❷	❷	❷	③	③	③	③	④
Ignition system	③	③	③	③	④	④	④	④
Rust/Paint	❶	❶	❶	❶	❶	③	③	④
Steering	❷	③	③	③	③	④	⑤	⑤
Suspension	❷	③	③	③	③	④	⑤	⑤
Crash Safety								
Base	—	—	④	④	④	④	⑤	④
Convertible	④	④	—	—	⑤	⑤	—	—
Side Impact								
Base	—	—	—	—	—	—	③	③

Probe

Rating: Recommended (1995–97); Average (1993–94); Below Average (1989–92). **Maintenance/Repair costs:** Average, and repairs can be done by independent garages or Mazda dealers. Nevertheless, the under-hood layout is crowded, making for high routine maintenance costs. **Parts:** Despite the fact that 1997 was the Probe's last model year (Mazda's MX-6 bit the dust as well), parts should remain plentiful and reasonably priced.

Strengths and weaknesses: The four-seater Probe sporty coupe was launched in May 1988 as the front-drive replacement for the aging Mustang. Don't get the impression that the Mazda MX-6 and Probe are twins because they share most mechanical features. In fact, they differ markedly in handling and appearance. Ford engineers took more control of the chassis tuning and suspension geometry to give the car a smoother and firmer sporty demeanor, and its stylists chopped and pulled the body to give it a more aerodynamic, aggressive personality.

Available only as a two-door hatchback, there are two models, each with its own powerplant: a 2.0L 4-cylinder for the GL and a 2.5L V6 engine powering the GT. These engines give the car much-needed power and smoothness not found in the anemic and brutish power-trains used in the past.

Mazda's mechanicals are above reproach, but despite gobs of torque, the GT doesn't give the muscle-car performance found in the less refined 5.0L Mustang GT. Performance is sapped considerably by the automatic transmission. Early models are beset by severe "torque steer," a tendency for the chassis to twist when the vehicle accelerates. Nevertheless, overall handling is precise and predictable on all models without sacrificing ride quality, which is a bit on the hard side.

Refinements of the 1993 and later versions include two new Mazda-designed engines that give the car a small horsepower boost, more interior room, all-disc brakes on the GT, and less torque steer. The '94s were the first to get dual airbags.

The Probe's overall mechanical reliability is fairly good, but like its Mustang cousin, body assembly is the pits (no surprise here—Mazda did the mechanicals; Ford did the body work.) Paint quality and rust protection are mediocre at best. The turbocharged engine has been relatively trouble-free, but owners have complained of frequent stalling and stumbling with the base powerplant. Many experience excessive ABS noise and vibrations when braking, and the front brakes tend to wear out very quickly. AC components have a short life span of three to five years and are outrageously expensive to troubleshoot and repair.

The car is essentially a 2+2 with the rear reserved for children or cargo. The interior is short on head room for tall drivers (especially on vehicles equipped with a sunroof), but cargo room is increased with the folding rear seatbacks. Multiple squeaks and rattles, wind and water leaks, and cheap interior appointments are the most common body complaints. The digital read-outs are distracting and often incorrect.

Safety summary/Recalls: All models: The driver's motorized shoulder belt is literally a pain in the neck. It rides high on the neck, fails to retract properly, tangles easily, and often hangs too loose. It also requires that the driver attach the lapbelt separately, which isn't done very often, resulting in decapitation in high-speed collisions. • Beware of coil spring corrosion causing the spring to suddenly break. Ford will pay for the repair on a case-by-case basis. • There are far fewer and less dramatic safety-related complaints on the Probe than one finds with the Mustang. For example, the '95 Probe has about half as many incidents reported to NHTSA as does the '95 Mustang. **1995**—Engine fire. • Leaking fuel-tank connection. • Sudden acceleration. • Airbag fails to deploy. • Windshield cracks near the outside moulding. • Hatchback collapses. • Driver's door pops open. **1995–97**—Chronic stalling, possibly due to a defective catalytic converter, wiring harness, spark-plug wiring, or throttle valve. • Check Engine light comes on for no apparent reason. • Poor brake performance and lockup. **1996**—Engine failure. • Seatbelt fails to retract. • Wind noise around glass. • Cruise control won't disengage. • Ventilation system emits a strong odour. **1996–97**—Sudden loss of steering, lockup, and premature rack-and-pinion failure. • Transmission failures. • Stalling. • Loose outside door

handles (defective retention rings). **1997**—Engine fire. • Timing chain
failure. • Poor heater performance. **Recalls: All models: 1991**—Vehicle
could roll away when in Park. **1993**—A faulty rear hatch strut may cause
the hatch to drop without warning. **1994–95**—Passenger-side airbag
may not inflate properly. **1997**—Timing belt tensioner spring may
break and jam the belt. **GL: 1991**—There's a free fix for welds that
anchor the front shoulder belt retractors.

Secret Warranties/Service Tips

All models: 1989–94—A no-start condition or inoperative heater or lights
may be caused by water and corrosion in the wiring connector, or a short-
to-ground at splice 102 (circuit 9). **1990–94**—A speaker whine or buzz
caused by the fuel pump can be stopped by installing an electronic noise
RFI filter. **1993–94**—A clunk or knock from the steering assembly when
turning the steering wheel is likely due to an insufficient yoke plug (pinion) preload. • Wind/water leaks require the readjustment of the front
door glass, as outlined in TSB #994-5-4. • Inoperative power door locks may
have a corroded wiring harness connection. • Frozen door locks, a common problem, are addressed in TSB #94-8-6. • A ticking noise coming from
the 2.0L engine's hydraulic lash adjusters can be stopped by a longer oil-
pump control plunger that prevents air from passing through to the oil
pump. **1993–97**—Ford "goodwill" warranty extensions often cover powertrain components, catalytic converters, and computer modules. If Ford
balks at refunding your money, apply the emissions warranty for a full or
partial refund. • Paint delamination, peeling, or fading (see Part Two).
1994—A rough idle affecting 2.0L engines could be caused by spark leakage from a damaged number 1 or number 2 spark plug wire. **1994–97**—
Transaxle fluid seepage can be corrected by servicing with a remote vent
kit or by replacing the main control cover. **GT: 1990**—Service Program
No. 96 provides for the rerouting of the wiring harness and hose clamp to
prevent transmission failure.

Probe Profile

	1990	1991	1992	1993	1994	1995	1996	1997
Cost Price ($)								
GL	14,972	13,795	14,795	15,165	16,495	17,895	18,395	19,095
GT	21,760	19,895	17,795	18,240	20,195	21,595	22,195	22,995
Used Values ($)								
GL ↑	3,000	3,500	4,000	4,500	6,000	8,000	9,500	11,500
GL ↓	2,000	3,000	3,500	4,000	4,500	6,000	8,000	10,000
GT ↑	4,500	5,000	5,500	6,000	7,500	9,500	11,500	13,500
GT ↓	3,500	4,500	4,500	5,500	6,000	7,500	9,500	11,500
Extended Warranty	Y	Y	Y	Y	Y	N	N	N
Secret Warranty	N	N	N	Y	Y	Y	Y	Y
Reliability	③	③	③	③	④	④	⑤	⑤
Air conditioning	❷	❷	❷	❷	❷	❷	❷	③

Auto. transmission	③	③	③	④	④	⑤	④	⑤
Body integrity	❶	❶	❶	❶	❶	❶	❷	❷
Braking system	❶	❶	❶	❶	❶	❷	❷	❷
Electrical system	❶	❶	❷	❷	❷	❷	❷	③
Engines	③	③	③	④	⑤	⑤	⑤	⑤
Exhaust/Converter	❷	❷	❷	③	④	④	④	⑤
Fuel system	③	③	③	③	④	⑤	⑤	⑤
Ignition system	❷	③	③	⑤	⑤	⑤	⑤	⑤
Rust/Paint	❶	❶	❶	③	③	③	③	③
Steering	③	③	③	③	④	④	④	⑤
Suspension	③	③	③	③	④	④	④	⑤
Crash Safety	—	④	④	③	⑤	⑤	⑤	⑤

Note: Although the 1990 Probe wasn't crash-tested, the 1989 crash test results showed minimal injury would be sustained by the driver and front-seat passenger.

GENERAL MOTORS

Camaro, Firebird, Trans Am

Rating: Recommended (1997–99); Average (1994–96); Below Average (1992–93); Not Recommended (1982–91). As with the Mustang, the Camaro and Firebird have elicited many safety-related complaints, including airbag deployment injuries, sudden acceleration, brake failures, and steering loss. Be especially wary of brake rotor warpage requiring rotor replacement every two years (about a $300 job). The 1996 Camaro and Firebird are essentially the same as the more expensive 1997 versions. A V8-equipped Camaro or convertible is the best choice for retained value a few years down the road. But you can do quite well with a used base coupe equipped with the performance handling package and high-performance tires. GM has announced it may drop the Camaro and Firebird after the year 2002. If it does, this move is unlikely to affect the cars' resale values or parts supply. **Maintenance/Repair costs:** Average, and repairs can be done by any independent garage. **Parts:** Reasonably priced parts are easy to find.

Strengths and weaknesses: When compared with the Mustang, Camaros and Firebirds are better performing rear-drive muscle cars that produce excellent crash protection scores and high resale values. They also take the lead over the Mustang with their standard ABS and slightly better reliability record. However, brute power is combined with almost-as-brutal repair charges. Camaro and Firebird overall performance varies a great deal depending on the engine, transmission, and suspension combination in each particular car. Base models equipped with the V6 powerplant accelerate reasonably well, but high-performance enthusiasts will find them slow for sporty cars. Handling is compromised by poor wet-road traction, minimal comfort, and a suspension that's too soft for high-speed cornering and too bone-jarring for smooth cruising. The Z28, IROC-Z, and Trans Am provide smart acceleration and handling, but at the expense of fuel economy.

1982–92

Relatively unchanged since its last redesign in 1982, a convertible was added in 1987. In 1990 GM offered a standard driver-side airbag, tilt steering wheel, tinted glass, intermittent wipers, and halogen headlamps. That same year the IROC-Z debuted with a standard limited-slip differential and 16-inch alloy wheels.

For 1991, the V8-equipped Z-28 returned after a 3-year hiatus and the IROC-Z was axed; '92 models were carried over unchanged.

During this period, performance and reliability problems are commonplace. Much like Ford's embarrassing 4-banger, the puny and failure-prone 2.5L 4-cylinder powerplant was the standard engine up to 1986—part of the legacy of an earlier fuel crisis and the subsequent downsizing binge. The turbocharged V8 offered on some Trans Am models should be viewed with caution because of its many durability problems.

Body hardware is fragile, poor paint quality and application are common and lead to premature rusting, and squeaks and rattles are legion. Body integrity is especially poor on cars equipped with a T-roof. Areas particularly vulnerable to rusting are the windshield and rear wheel openings, door bottoms, and rear quarter panels. The assorted add-on plastic body parts found on sporty versions promote corrosion by trapping moisture along with road salt and grime. Also note that the Camaro's flat seats don't offer as much support as the better contoured Firebird seats.

These cars are also plagued by chronic fuel-system problems, especially on the Cross-Fire and multi-port fuel-injection controls. Automatic transmissions, especially the 4-speed, aren't durable. The standard 5-speed manual gearbox has a stiff shifter and a heavy clutch. Clutches fail frequently and don't stand up to hard use. The 2.8L V6, used through 1989, suffers from leaky gaskets and seals and premature camshaft wear. The larger 3.1L 6-cylinder has fewer problems. Malfunctioning dash gauges and electrical problems are common. Exhaust parts rust quickly. Dual outlet exhaust systems on V8 engines are expensive to replace. Front suspension components and shock absorbers wear out very quickly.

1993–99

The 1993s were totally redesigned and given a more aerodynamic body style. Dimensions were slightly enlarged, weight was added, power boosted, and the dashboard was reworked. Dual airbags and ABS also became standard safety features. There was no '93 convertible.

For the '94 model year, the convertible returned with an upgraded top and 6-speed gearbox. The '95s added a 3.8L V6 engine and optional traction control. '96 models carried the 3.8L engine as the base powerplant, the 5.7L V8 gained 10 extra horses, and a new high-performance SS option was offered for the first time on the Z28. On 1997 models, GM offered a 30th birthday styling package for the Camaro and some interior upgrades, V6 engine dampening for smoother running at high speeds, optional Ram Air induction, and racier-looking ground-effects body trim for the Firebird. The '98 model got a minor facelift and the Z28 and SS both received a slight horsepower boost. Optional traction control became available on the '99s, along with standard electronic throttle control on V6-equipped versions and a new Zexel Torsion differential used in the limited-slip rear axle.

Of this grouping, you should stick with the 1996–99 models for the best performance and price. All of these cars are much better overall performers than previous models, and additional standard safety features are a plus.

These sporty convertibles and coupes are almost identical in their pricing and in the features they offer (the Firebird has pop-up headlights, a more pointed front end, a narrower middle, and a rear spoiler). As noted above, both cars got a complete make-over in 1995, making them more powerful and aerodynamic with less spine-jarring performance.

As one moves up the scale, overall performance improves considerably. The V8 engine gives these cars lots of sparkle and tire-spinning torque, but there's a fuel penalty to pay. A 4-speed automatic transmission is standard on the 5.7L-equipped Z28; other versions come with a standard 5-speed manual gearbox or an optional 6-speed. Many of these cars are likely to have been ordered with lots of extra performance and luxury options, including a T-roof package guaranteed to include a full assortment of creaks and groans.

Both the Camaro and the Firebird may be equipped with an impressively effective pass-key theft-deterrent system similar to the one used successfully in the Corvette. A resistor pellet in the ignition disables the starter and fuel system when the key code doesn't match the ignition lock.

Not everything is perfect, however. Owners report that the base engine is noisy, though the 3.8L doesn't have the head gasket failures seen with Ford's 3.8L powerplant. Fuel economy is unimpressive, the air conditioner malfunctions (but not to the same extent as Ford-produced units), front brakes and MacPherson struts wear out quickly, servicing the fuel-injection system is an exercise in frustration, and body problems are worse than with the Mustang and just won't go away.

These cars are still afflicted by door rattles, misaligned doors and hatch, a sticking hatch power release, and poor fit and finish. Owners also complain that the steering wheel is positioned too close to the driver's chest, the low seats create a feeling of claustrophobia, visibility is limited by wide side pillars, and trunk space is sparse with a high liftover.

Safety summary/Recalls: All models: 1995—Severe injuries caused by airbag deployment. • Airbag deployed, projecting dash panel into the passenger's face. • Airbag deployed and caught fire. • Rear brakes rusted out. • Left rear caliper grabs when making turns. • Faulty cruise control. • The tie-rod broke while driving, forcing the car off the road. • Broken gas-tank weld. • Stabilizer bar failure. • Transmission bolts came off. • Trunk latch failure allows trunk to open while driving. • Two reports that double-locking T-top flew off from passenger side while driving with both locks engaged. • In another incident, the sun-roof flew off. • Convertible top latch failure. • Door windows leak. • Inadequate defroster; causes windows to fog. • Headlight dimmer switch failures. • Driver's seatbelt failed during accident. **1995–96—** Many reports that car caught fire near the fuel tank. • Fuel-line retaining clamp could fail, causing the plastic fuel lines to come into contact with the exhaust manifold cover. • Other fires ignited near the radio and in the engine compartment. • Many reports claiming sudden acceleration. • Airbag failed to deploy. • Frequent ABS brake failures; pedal goes to the floor. • ABS particularly ineffective in rainy weather. • Rear brake caliper failure. • Emergency brake fails frequently, allowing car to roll away even though shift lever is placed in Park. • In wet conditions, or when passing over a puddle, the power-steering pump fails, resulting in steering lockup. • Frequent transmission failures while driving. **1996—**Transmission jumps out of gear. • Traction control fails in cold weather. • Right rear axle broke. • Rear main oil seal leakage and failure. • ABS light remains lit due to defective jumper. • Seatbelts slip off their guides and their anchorages may break. • Faulty ignition control module. • Windshield wipers stay on one speed, don't clean enough of the right side, and their placement blocks right-side visibility. **1997—**Fire caused by a short in the defroster wiring. • Engine intake manifold gasket and valve cover failure. • Faulty power-steering pumps. • Stalling in the rain. **1997–98—**Four recurring problems are: prematurely worn brake pads and warped or cracked rotors, sudden acceleration, no airbag deployment, and failure of the emergency brake to hold. **1998—**Dash fire. • Axle seal, tie-rod, serpentine belt, fuel pump, brake caliper bolt, AC blower motor, fuel gauge, and wiper failures. **1999—**Interestingly, both the Camaro and Firebird have about one-third fewer safety-related complaints registered against them by NHTSA than does the Ford Mustang. • Airbags failed to deploy upon impact. • Cracked fuel tank leaks fuel. • Accelerator pedal sticks. • Prematurely warped front brake rotors jerking to one side when brakes are applied and cause pulsation, excessive noise, and extended stopping distance. • Many incidents of clutch slippage at low mileage. • Frequent complaints that the stock shifter causes mis-shifts. • Electrical system shorts cause instrument panel and assorted gauges and lights to operate erratically. • Turn signal lights don't flash, headlights often dim about 50 percent of their brightness, heater slows down, and power windows run slowly. **Recalls: All models: 1991–92—**Fuel-filler neck may leak. **1992—**The automatic transmission shift control cable may separate and hamper shifting. **1994—**Fuel line on V8-equipped cars may leak fuel into the engine compartment. **1995—**Faulty lower steering shaft coupling could lead to loss of steering. **1997**—Seatbelt retractor may fail.

Secret Warranties/Service Tips

All models: 1982–93—Vehicles equipped with a Hydramatic 4L60 transmission that buzzes when the car is in Reverse or idle may need a new oil pressure regulator valve. **1985–91**—Hydramatic 4L60/700R4 automatic transmission may have no upshift or appear to be stuck in first gear. The probable cause is a worn governor gear. It would be wise to also replace the retaining ring. **1989**—If the rear brakes moan when they're applied slightly while backing up or turning, a redesigned caliper mounting plate may be needed (TSB #89-162-5). • Knocking from a cold 5.0L engine means that the PROM module has to be replaced (TSB #89-284-6E). **1989–90**—Campaign 90-C-11 provides for free convertible top latch handles. **1993–96**—Uneven rear brake pad wear or premature wear can be corrected by replacing the caliper anchor bracket, guide pins, and the brake pads with upgraded parts. **1993–97**—Oil leaks between the intake manifold and engine block are most often caused by insufficient RTV bonding between the intake manifold and cylinder block. **1993–99**—Eliminate AC odours by applying an evaporator core cooling coil coating. • A rotten-egg odour coming from the exhaust is probably the result of a malfunctioning catalytic converter, which may be covered by the emissions warranty. • Paint delamination, peeling, or fading (see Part Two). • GM guidelines to dealers on troubleshooting exterior lamp condensation complaints. **1994**—Excessive oil consumption is likely due to delaminated intake manifold gaskets. Install an upgraded intake manifold gasket kit. • Delayed automatic transmission shift engagement is a common problem addressed in TSB #47-71-20A. • Install a new "flash" PROM to cure engine surging or hesitation and stalling upon acceleration for cars with automatic transmissions. **1994–98**—GM guidelines for repairing front brake problems. **1995–96**—Delayed automatic transmission shift engagement may require the replacement of the pump cover assembly. **1997**—New switches will fix inoperative door locks. • Fixing automatic transmission slippage. • Engine oil leak diagnosis. • Theft alarm sounds when vehicle gets wet. • Diagnosing engine miss and poor driveability. **1998**—Tips on eliminating roof panel ticking. **1998–2000**—An engine that loses coolant or runs hot may simply need a new radiator cap or the radiator filler neck polished. • Install upgraded disc pads to eliminate rear brake chirp or groan and front brake squeal when braking. • Silence accessory drive belt chirping or squeaking by installing a new double row idler pulley, generator bracket, and serpentine belt. **1999**—If the convertible top closes with difficulty, it may be because the headliner is too short. **Models with 2.5L engines: All years**—Spark knock can be fixed with the free installation of a new PROM module (#12269198) if the emissions warranty applies. • Frequent stalling may require a new MAP sensor (TSB #90-142-8A). **1990–91**—Stalling on deceleration or at stops requires a new MEMCAL that refines idle speed control and throttle follower operation. **3.8L V6: 1996–98**—These engines have a history of low oil pressure caused by a failure-prone oil pump. A temporary remedy is to avoid low-viscosity oils and use 10W-40 in the winter and 20W-50 for summer driving.

Camaro, Firebird, Trans Am Profile

	1992	1993	1994	1995	1996	1997	1998	1999
Cost Price ($)								
Camaro/RS	14,298	15,998	16,498	18,995	20,195	22,075	22,790	23,100
Z28	18,998	19,898	20,498	23,650	25,530	27,270	27,840	28,670
Convertible	25,098	—	24,370	26,045	28,365	29,080	29,795	30,105
Firebird	14,798	15,168	17,198	19,795	20,955	23,120	24,580	24,865
Trans Am	20,998	23,265	24,500	27,390	28,755	30,780	34,080	34,750
Used Values ($)								
Camaro/RS ↑	4,000	5,000	6,500	8,500	11,000	13,000	15,000	17,000
Camaro/RS ↓	3,500	4,500	5,500	7,000	9,500	11,000	13,500	16,000
Z28 ↑	6,500	7,500	8,500	11,500	14,000	16,000	18,500	21,000
Z28 ↓	5,500	6,500	7,000	9,500	12,500	14,000	17,000	19,000
Convertible ↑	7,500	—	9,000	12,000	15,000	17,000	20,000	22,000
Convertible ↓	7,000	—	7,500	10,500	13,500	15,500	18,000	21,000
Firebird ↑	5,000	5,500	6,500	8,500	11,500	13,000	15,000	18,000
Firebird ↓	4,500	5,000	6,000	7,000	10,000	11,500	13,500	16,500
Trans Am ↑	6,500	7,500	9,500	13,000	15,000	17,500	19,500	25,000
Trans Am ↓	6,000	7,000	7,500	10,500	12,500	15,500	18,000	23,500
Extended Warranty	Y	Y	Y	N	N	N	N	N
Secret Warranty	Y	Y	Y	Y	Y	Y	Y	Y
Reliability	❶	❷	❷	③	③	④	④	⑤
Air conditioning	❷	③	③	③	④	⑤	⑤	⑤
Auto. transmission	③	③	③	④	④	⑤	⑤	❷
Body integrity	❶	❶	❶	❶	❷	❷	❷	③
Braking system	❶	❶	❶	❶	❶	❷	❷	❷
Electrical system	❶	❶	❶	❶	❶	❶	❷	❷
Engines	❷	④	④	③	③	③	③	❷
Exhaust/Converter	❶	❶	③	③	③	④	④	⑤
Fuel system	❶	❷	❷	③	③	④	④	⑤
Ignition system	❷	❷	❷	❷	③	③	④	④
Rust/Paint	❶	❶	③	③	③	④	⑤	⑤
Steering	③	③	③	③	③	③	④	⑤
Suspension	④	③	④	④	④	④	④	⑤
Crash Safety								
Camaro	⑤	⑤	⑤	⑤	⑤	⑤	④	④
Side Impact								
Camaro	—	—	—	—	—	③	③	③

Corvette

Rating: Average (1997–99); Not Recommended (1977–96). The cheaper 1996 Corvette won't have the cachet or the mechanical and body refinements of the redesigned 1997 version. If you choose the 1997 model, try to get a second-series car that was made after June 1997. Keep in mind that premium fuel and astronomical insurance rates will further drive up your operating costs. Plus, don't discount the serious safety-related problems you're likely to experience on 1997–99 models. They run the gamut of sudden steering lockup when underway, electrical shorts causing vehicle shutdown, a non-functioning parking brake, brake failures due to premature rotor warpage (around 16,000 kilometres), and seatbelts that jam in the retractor. The locked-up steering is particularly scary because it apparently has carried over to year 2000 models and traffic accident investigators may simply conclude accident was due to driver inexperience or unsafe driving. **Maintenance/Repair costs:** Higher than average, although most repairs can be done by any independent garage. Long waits for recall repairs. **Parts:** Pricey, but easy to find. Surprisingly, it is often easier to find parts for older Corvettes, through collectors' clubs, than to find many of the high-tech components used today.

Strengths and weaknesses: Corvettes made in the late '60s and early '70s are acceptable buys, due mainly to their value as collector cars and their uncomplicated repairs. Unfortunately, the Corvette's overall reliability and safety have declined over the years as its price and complexity have increased. This is due in large part to GM's updating its antiquated design with high-tech, complicated add-ons rather than coming up with something original. Consequently, the car has been gutted and then re-tuned using failure-prone electronic circuitry. Complicated emissions plumbing, braking and suspension systems have also been added to make the Corvette a fuel-efficient, user-friendly, high-performance vehicle—goals that General Motors has missed by a large margin.

The electronically controlled suspension systems have always been glitch-plagued. Servicing the different sophisticated fuel-injection systems is a nightmare—even (especially) for GM mechanics. The noisy 5.7L engine frequently hesitates and stalls, there's lots of transmission buzz and whine, the rear tires produce excessive noise, and wind whistles through the A- and C-pillars. These, and the all-too-familiar fibreglass body squeaks and paint delamination, continue to be unwanted standard features throughout all model years. The electronic dash never works quite right (speedometer lag, for example).

On the other hand, Corvette ownership of more recent models does have its positive side. For example, the ABS vented disc brakes, available since 1986, are easy to modulate and fade-free. The standard European-made Bilstein FX-3 Selective Ride Control suspension can be preset for touring, sport, or performance. Under speed, an electronic module automatically varies the suspension setting, finally curing these cars of their earlier endemic over-steering, wheel spinning, breakaway rear ends, and other nasty surprises.

All used Corvettes are high-risk buys, but the 1977–93 models have been particularly troublesome. These models are notorious for failure-prone and complicated safety, emissions, and performance "innovations" that were routinely brought in one year and dropped shortly thereafter—making for difficult troubleshooting and hard-to-find parts. There's also a greater chance you'll get stuck with a turned-back odometer or an accident-damaged car, written off by the insurance company and then re-sold by scam artists.

To protect yourself from these scams all you need to do is give the Corvette's VIN number to any GM garage and you'll get a printout of the previous owners' names and all the repairs carried out and at what mileage. As far as body damage is concerned, this too should be checked out by a Chevrolet dealer's body shop.

There is one other precaution you should take when buying a Corvette; get a GM-backed supplementary warranty, or look for a recent model that has some of the original warranty left. The frequency of repairs and the high repair costs make maintenance outrageously expensive. Keep reading to get an idea of the problems that might put a large dent in your wallet if they haven't been fixed already.

1977–83
Major mechanical failings affect the fuel and emissions systems, air conditioning, transmission, clutch, shift linkage, camshaft lifters and rear half-shaft soft yokes, carburetor, steering, brakes, and starter and electrical systems, including the lights. As far as body assembly goes, the major deficiencies are poor panel fits, faulty and fragile interior/exterior parts and trim items, quirky instruments, cheap upholstery, and defective window lifts. Owners also complain of poor workmanship/shoddy assembly causing a cacophony of squeaks and rattles, poor dealer servicing, unavailable and expensive parts, and excessive labour charges.

1984–90
These model years are incredibly difficult to service. One *Lemon-Aid* reader had a faulty engine bearing at 16,000 km and spent $2,500 to remove the engine. It takes half a day to change the spark plugs on the passenger side. Likely mechanical problem areas are the emissions control system (injectors, computer-controlled sensors, fuel-injection, and engine gaskets), air conditioning, and ignition/distributor. Owners also experience engine and drivetrain failures, Bosch radio malfunctions, and the need to make frequent wheel alignments. Fragile body hardware, poor fit and finish, wind/road noise, and water intrusion into the interior are still major weaknesses. Owners complain of faulty controls and window lifts, as well as defective paint (base coat comes through the finish), interior/exterior parts and trim, glass and weather stripping, instruments, lights, door locks, upholstery, and carpeting.

1991–99

Though the restyled 1991 Corvette remained the same mechanically, all models got the convex tail and square taillights previously used only on the upscale ZR-1 coupe. Acceleration Slip Regulation on 1992–96 models effectively reduces the horrendous wheel spin that threw many Corvettes out of control when accelerating on slippery surfaces. A new LTI engine with 55 more horses came on the scene with the 1992 'Vette, and the following year the ZR-1 got a 405-hp variant of the same powerplant, shortly before the model was replaced in the spring of 1995 by the Grand Sport. Incidentally, the super-powered ZR-1's depreciated price makes the car a bargain when one totes up the cost of its standard performance features.

A more substantial redesign was carried out in mid-1997. Although styling remained practically unchanged, the transmission was moved back, creating a roomier cockpit; the interior was made much more user-friendly; structural improvements reduced body flexing (a problem with most convertibles) and made for a more rigid hatchback; and a new aluminum 340-hp LSI V8 engine arrived on the scene. The '98 and '99 versions are pretty much carryovers of the redesigned '97 and aren't worth the higher prices. A high-performance hardtop model was launched for the '99 model year.

Owners rave about the redesigned '97 models' improved performance, better handling, and additional safety features, but they still find fault with the stiff ride, poor fuel economy, and excessive interior noise. From a reliability standpoint, these later models are much improved, with problems limited to the emissions, electronic and electrical systems, body hardware, fit and finish, suspension, and air conditioning.

Technical service bulletins: All models: 1995—A high effort to shift into gear in cold, wet weather; high shift effort into Reverse. • A 3–2 downshift flare and erratic downshifting with the automatic transmission. • Starter clicks but won't start engine. • Front brake pulsation. • A low-voltage reading or dim lights at idle. • Right-hand wiper blade chatter • Excessive radio static. • Door glass scratches. • Poor paint application. **1996**—Oil leaks between the intake manifold and engine block. • 3–2 part throttle downshift flare and delayed transmission engagement. • Transmission fluid leak from pump body (replace bushing). • Steering column noise. • Radio frequency interference diagnosis. • Low-voltage reading or dim lights at idle. • Door trim armrest lid hard to open. • Water leak diagnostic guide. • Condensation on exterior light. **1997**—Air temperature from HVAC outlets doesn't change. • Erratic fuel gauge readings. • Low-voltage reading or dim lights at idle. • Hatch won't pop up when activated in cold weather. • Water drips into rear compartment. **1998**—Troubleshooting squeaks and rattles, AC odours, possible causes for the Low Engine Coolant light coming on, diagnosing water leaks, window rattles, and poorly fitted body panels. **1999**—Engine loses coolant or runs hot. • Low Engine Coolant light comes on at start-up. • Accessory drive squeak. • Inoperative or noisy window motor. • Rattling from the left fuel tank area. • Shift boot squeak when shifting. • Premature wear of seatback leather. • Tips for removing AC odours.

Safety summary/Recalls: All models: 1995—Fire ignited in the wiring harness. • Sudden acceleration. • Electrical system failure. • Defective convertible top, fuel gauge, and ABS brakes. • **1996**—Fire started in the engine computer system. • Faulty front wheel-bearing hub, fuel pump, intake manifold, and tire-pressure sensor (no parts available). • Transmission failures and fluid leakage. • Excessive vibration when top is taken off. **1997–98**—Sudden loss of power, engine shuts down, and warning lights come on everywhere. • Defective throttle control module, parking brake, brake rotors and pads, seatbelt retractors, fuel-line clips, and Check Engine light. **1998**—NHTSA is looking into complaints of steering column lock module failures, non-functional parking brake, and jammed seatbelts on 1997–99 models. • Fuel tank leakage. • No airbag deployment. • Transmission failure, leaks. • Emergency brake won't hold. • Excessive vibrations when driving. • Poor headlight illumination.

www.nhtsa.dot.gov
Office of Defects Investigation
Complaints Database
Call the Auto Safety Hotline toll free at (888) 327-4236 to report safety defects or to obtain information on cars, trucks, child seats, highway or traffic safety.

People Saving People
http://www.nhtsa.dot.gov

Report Date: January 22, 2001 08:42:57 AM
ODI ID: 737643
Make: CHEVROLET
Model: CORVETTE
Year: 1999
Date of Failure: Thursday, September 21, 2000
Incident: No
Fire: No
Number of Injuries: 0
Component: STEERING:WHEEL AND COLUMN
Summary: STEERING LOCKING UP, IS A REAL SCARY PROBLEM THAT APPEARS TO BE WIDE SPREAD. I AM GRATEFUL THAT IT ONLY WAS A QUICK LOCK UP.

ODI ID: 730883
Make: CHEVROLET
Model: CORVETTE
Year: 1999
Date of Failure: Friday, September 08, 2000
Incident: No
Fire: No
Number of Injuries: 0
Component: STEERING:WHEEL AND COLUMN
Summary: ON ATTEMPTING TO DRIVE CAR THE VEHICLE STARTED BUT THE STEERING WHEEL DID NOT UNLOCK LEAVING ME STRANDED.

ODI ID: 729995
Make: CHEVROLET
Model: CORVETTE
Year: 1999
Date of Failure: Thursday, August 31, 2000
Incident: No
Fire: No
Number of Injuries:
Component: STEERING:WHEEL AND COLUMN
Summary: YOU BETTER ISSUE A RECALL BECAUSE I'M PISSED ANY DAY YOU WAIT IS IMORAL THERE ARE MORE THAN ENOUGH COMPLAINTS ANY OTHER RESPONSE IS BULLSHIT.

Highway homicide: misdiagnosed as driver error, when it's really GM's error and public-be-damned attitude. Can you imagine, after all these years, GM still hasn't recalled these Corvettes. Wonder how many drivers have died or been injured by this safety defect?

1999—Epidemic of complaints relating to sudden steering column lockup. • Also, frequent complaints that the steering wheel won't unlock with ignition key. • Sudden, unintended acceleration. • Fuel tank leaks when gassing up; vehicle caught fire as raw fuel was ignited by the catalytic converter. • Fuel pump failures. • Parking brake won't hold car. • Chronic premature warpage of the brake rotors. • Front lap-belts jam in the retractor. • Electrical shorts cause headlights to stick open, melted rear-view mirror assembly, and a plethora of other electronic glitches leading to vehicle shutdown. • Engine serpentine belt and tensioner failures. • Poorly anchored driver's seat and warped trunk door. **Recalls: All models: 1988–89**—The rear wheel tie-rod end could fracture; GM will replace any defective tie-rod assembly free of charge. **1990**—Inoperative parking brakes will get a new brake lever assembly. • The fuel feed and return line connectors may leak fuel. **1992–93**—Power-steering hose leakage may cause an engine compartment fire. **1997**—Fuel tank leaks. • Seatbelts won't sufficiently absorb crash forces. • Rear suspension tie rod assembly may fracture. **1997–99**—Seatbelt webbing can twist and jam in the retractor.

Secret Warranties/Service Tips

All models: 1982–91—Hydramatic 4L60/700R4 automatic transmission may have no upshift or appear to be stuck in first gear; the probable cause is a worn governor gear. It would be wise to replace the retaining ring as well. **1987–89**—Revised cylinder head gaskets provide better sealing (TSB #89-283-6A). **1990–91**—Engine wiring short circuits may be caused by an abraded electrical harness at the mounting clamp just below the oil-pressure sensor. **1992**—5.7L engines may develop leaks at the oil filter area or backfire excessively when shifting from first to second gear with the throttle wide open; correct by changing the MEMCAL module. • Oil leaks from the rear of the same engine may be caused by insufficient sealing around the camshaft plug. Replace the plug and reseal. **1992–96**—Oil leaks between the intake manifold and engine block are most often caused by insufficient RTV bonding between the intake manifold and cylinder block. **1993–99**—A rotten-egg odour coming from the exhaust is probably caused by a defective catalytic converter that may be covered by the emissions warranty. • Clearcoat paint degradation, whitening, and chalking, long a problem with GM's other cars, is also a serious problem with the fibreglass-bodied Corvette, says TSB #331708. It too is covered by a secret warranty for up to six years (see Part Two). **1994**—Excessive oil consumption is likely due to delaminated intake manifold gaskets; install an upgraded intake manifold gasket kit. • Delayed automatic transmission shift engagement is a common problem, and is addressed in TSB #47-71-20A. **1995–96**—Delayed automatic transmission shift engagement may also require the replacement of the pump cover assembly. **1995–2000**—Guidelines for repairing brake rotor warpage under warranty. **1997**—Correcting water leaks into the rear compartment. • Inadequate heating, defrosting. • Correcting drivebelt noise. **1997–98**—What to do when the Low Engine Coolant light comes on. • A poor front fender–to-door fit can be fixed by installing an additional front fender clip. • Silence a muffler insulator rumble noise by installing upgraded insulators. • Countermeasures to eliminate water leaks above the door glass and door glass rattles. **1997–99**—A no start condition can be corrected by reprogramming the power control module. • TSB #99-06-02-016 has the remedy for a Low Coolant light that comes on at start-up. • Shift boot squeaking can be silenced by installing a new shift boot assembly. • Accessory drive squeaks can be corrected by installing a new idler pulley assembly. **1998**—Tips on correcting a faulty rear window defogger. **1998–2000**—An inoperative or noisy window motor can be corrected by replacing the window regulator and motor assembly. **1999**—Rattling from the left fuel tank area can be silenced by installing a fuel tank foam insulator pad. **1999–2000**—An engine that runs hot or loses coolant may simply need a new radiator cap of polishing of the radiator filler neck.

Corvette Profile

	1992	1993	1994	1995	1996	1997	1998	1999
Cost Price ($)								
Base	40,398	41,398	43,398	47,580	48,080	48,895	50,430	53,870
Convertible	48,098	48,298	50,498	55,020	56,335	—	58,430	60,850
ZR-1	76,998	78,898	80,798	86,765	—	—	—	—
Used Values ($)								
Base ↑	15,000	17,000	18,000	23,000	28,000	36,000	43,000	47,000
Base ↓	13,000	15,000	15,000	19,000	24,000	33,500	40,000	45,000
Convertible ↑	19,000	20,000	22,000	27,000	32,000	—	48,000	53,000
Convertible ↓	17,000	19,000	19,000	24,000	28,000	—	45,000	50,000
ZR-1 ↑	19,000	24,000	29,000	35,000	—	—	—	—
ZR-1 ↓	17,500	20,000	25,000	30,000	—	—	—	—
Extended Warranty	Y	Y	Y	Y	Y	Y	Y	Y
Secret Warranty	Y	Y	Y	Y	Y	Y	Y	Y
Reliability	❷	❷	❷	③	③	④	④	④
Air conditioning	❷	❷	❷	③	③	③	③	④
Auto. transmission	❷	❷	❷	❷	③	③	③	③
Body integrity	❷	❷	❷	❷	❷	❷	❷	③
Braking system	❷	❷	❷	❷	❷	❷	③	③
Electrical system	❷	❷	❷	❷	❷	❷	③	④
Engines	❷	❷	③	③	③	③	③	④
Exhaust/Converter	❷	❷	❷	③	③	④	④	⑤
Fuel system	❷	❷	❷	❷	❷	③	③	④
Ignition system	❷	❷	❷	❷	❷	③	④	⑤
Rust/Paint	❷	❷	❷	❷	③	③	③	④
Steering	❶	❶	❶	❶	❶	❶	❶	❶
Suspension	❷	❷	❷	❷	❷	③	④	④

Note: The Corvette hasn't been crash-tested.

HONDA

Prelude

Rating: Recommended (1993–99); Above Average (1985–92). **Maintenance/Repair costs:** Average. Repairs aren't dealer dependent. To avoid costly engine repairs, check the engine timing belt every 2 years/ 40,000 km and replace it every 96,000 km ($300). **Parts:** Higher-than-average cost, but independent suppliers sell parts for much less.

Strengths and weaknesses: Unimpressive as a high-performance sports car, the Prelude instead delivers a stylish exterior, legendary reliability, and excellent resale value.

The 1978–87 first-generation Preludes were described as luxury sporty cars, but didn't offer much of either. They should be inspected carefully for engine problems and severe underbody corrosion, particularly near the fuel tank. They're also prone to extensive rusting around wheel openings, door bottoms, the trunk lid, fenders, rear taillights, bumper supports, chassis members, and suspension components. Noisy front brakes, premature disc warpage, high oil consumption, and worn engine crankshaft/camshaft lobes are the main problem areas with these models.

The 1988–91 models offer more and smoother engine power, excellent handling, and improved reliability. There are some generic complaints that continue to crop up, including rapid front brake wear, scored and warped front brake rotors, automatic transmission failure, defective constant velocity joints, premature exhaust system rust-out, and a warping hood.

The 1992–96 models are shorter, wider, and heavier. They're not very fast. The four-wheel steering found on the 1992 4WS version is more gimmick than anything else. It was dropped after 1994. The automatic transmission is smoother, although it still saps some of the Prelude's power. Both the rear seating and tiny trunk are inadequate for most people. You can expect fewer but all-too-familiar glitches, including engine oil leaks (covered by a secret warranty), minor electrical problems, body and accessory defects, brake squealing, and prematurely warped front brake rotors. Most independent mechanics are ill equipped to service these cars because Preludes have become increasingly complicated to repair.

1997–99

The year for big Prelude changes was 1997, while 1998–99 models just coasted along with minor improvements. The '97 was restyled, repowered, and given handling upgrades that make it a better-performing, more comfortably riding sports coupe. It got an additional five horses for the base 2.2L VTEC engine, a new Automatic Torque Transfer System (ATTS), an upgraded suspension, and standard ABS, air conditioning,

16-inch wheels, and a CD player with six speakers. The Sequential SportShift automatic transmission (a variation of the one used in the NSX) equips the base Prelude. Overall, the car is roomier (the extended wheelbase gives added stability and provides more room in the rear seating area), has a more solid body structure, and includes a totally redesigned, user-friendly dash with analogue gauges.

On these more recent models, owners report that the engine tends to leak oil and air conditioner condensers frequently fail after a few years and often need cleaning to eliminate disagreeable odours. Other problems include minor electrical glitches, brake squealing, and prematurely warped front brake rotors. A host of new technical features adds to the Prelude's complexity and guarantees that you'll never stray far from the dealer's service bay. Again, most corner mechanics are poorly equipped to service these cars and the Automatic Torque Transfer System (ATTS) won't make their job any easier.

Technical service bulletins: All models: 1995—Creaking clutch pedal. • A jingling in the left side of the dashboard. • A slow-to-retract seatbelt. • A warped console. **1996**—Headliner rattles. • The seatbelt is slow to retract. **1997**—Details concerning Honda's EPA-imposed 14-year emissions warranty. • Loads of bulletins giving troubleshooting tips to silence squeaks, rattles, clunks, and whistles. • Fifth-gear grinding. • Opening a stuck door. **1997–98**—Power window clunking. **1999**— Power steering pump noise, rear suspension and trunk clunk, and moon roof rattles. • Deformed upper windshield moulding. • Doors are hard to open from the inside.

Safety summary/Recalls: 1999—Several incidents of sudden tire tread separation. • Several incidents of power steering loss; steering failure after steering pump replaced. • Airbags failed to deploy upon impact. • Engine loses power in cold weather or at cruising speeds. **Recalls: All models: 1978–85**—Severe chassis corrosion around fuel tank and body seams prompted Honda to provide free chassis repairs and replace suspension/steering components and fuel tanks under a "silent" recall campaign. **1983–87**—Road salt could cause the fuel filler and/or breather pipe to rust through, resulting in leaks. A recall campaign has been organized to fix this defect. **1986–91**—Takata seatbelt replacement. **1988**—Corroded coil spring breakage could cause loss of control. • Power-steering hose leaks could cause a fire.

Secret Warranties/Service Tips

All models/years—Steering wheel shimmy can be reduced by rebalancing the wheel/tire/hub/rotor assembly in the front end. • Seatbelts that fail to function properly during normal use will be replaced for free under Honda's lifetime seatbelt warranty. • Honda will also repair or replace defective steering assemblies, constant velocity joints, and catalytic converters free of charge up to 5 years/80,000 km on a case-by-case basis. •

Honda TSBs allow for special warranty consideration on a "goodwill" basis for most problems even after the warranty has expired or the car has changed hands. **All models: 1992–97**—Change the fifth gear shift fork if the transmission grinds when going into fifth gear. **1994–96**—Silence rear headliner rattling by applying EPT sealer 5T to the rear headliner where it contacts the wiring harness. **1994–97**—Engine oil leaks will be fixed for free under a Honda "goodwill" program (see Accord entry). **1997**—A squeaking seat may need a new seat pivot bushing. **1997–98**—Power window clunking can be stopped by changing the motor. **1997–99**—A rear suspension clunk can be fixed by replacing the coil springs under Honda's "goodwill" policies. • Doors that are hard to open from the inside may simply require a new inner door handle rod (a "goodwill" repair). • A rattling moon roof may need new guide rails and a re-adjustment of the glass brackets ("goodwill"). • A trunk clunking noise may be silenced by replacing the trunk spring clip. **1997–2000**—Deformed upper windshield mouldings are addressed in TSB #98-066. **1999–2000**—Try replacing the power steering pump bearing and seals to silence a noisy power steering pump.

Prelude Profile

	1992	1993	1994	1995	1996	1997	1998	1999
Cost Price ($)								
Base/SR	16,550	21,895	21,895	26,995	27,395	27,300	27,600	27,800
2.0L Si	19,650	—	—	—	—	—	—	—
VTEC	—	27,295	28,295	29,695	29,995	—	—	—
Used Values ($)								
Base/SR ↑	6,000	7,000	9,000	12,500	14,000	17,000	19,500	22,000
Base/SR ↓	5,000	6,000	7,500	11,000	13,000	15,500	17,500	20,000
2.0L Si ↑	7,000	—	—	—	—	—	—	—
2.0L Si ↓	6,000	—	—	—	—	—	—	—
VTEC ↑	—	8,500	11,000	14,000	15,500	—	—	—
VTEC ↓	—	7,500	9,500	12,500	14,000	—	—	—
Extended Warranty	N	N	N	N	N	N	N	N
Secret Warranty	Y	Y	Y	Y	Y	Y	Y	Y
Reliability	④	④	⑤	⑤	⑤	⑤	⑤	⑤
Air conditioning	③	③	③	④	⑤	⑤	⑤	⑤
Auto. transmission	③	③	④	⑤	⑤	⑤	⑤	⑤
Body integrity	③	③	③	③	③	③	③	④
Braking system	❷	③	③	③	③	③	④	⑤
Electrical system	❷	❷	③	③	③	③	④	⑤
Engines	③	③	③	③	③	③	⑤	⑤
Exhaust/Converter	❷	③	③	③	④	⑤	⑤	⑤
Fuel system	④	④	④	④	④	⑤	⑤	⑤
Ignition system	④	④	⑤	⑤	⑤	⑤	⑤	⑤
Rust/Paint	③	❷	③	③	④	⑤	⑤	⑤
Steering	❷	❷	③	③	③	③	④	④
Suspension	③	③	④	⑤	⑤	⑤	⑤	⑤
Crash Safety	④	④	—	—	—	—	—	—

HYUNDAI

Tiburon

Rating: Above Average (1997–99). A high-performance Elantra. Keep in mind that for about $1,000 more you can get the better-performing FX model. **Maintenance/Repair costs:** Higher than average, although most repairs can be done by any independent garage. **Parts:** Higher-than-average cost with limited availability.

Strengths and weaknesses: This is a fun-to-drive, budget sport coupe that's based on the Elantra sedan. Although it's too early to have a definitive opinion, overall reliability looks promising. The Tiburon is a credible alternative to the Ford Probe, Nissan 200SX, or Toyota Celica. On early models, the base 16-valve 1.8L 4-cylinder engine is smooth, efficient, and adequate when mated to the 5-speed manual transmission. Put in an automatic transmission and performance heads south and engine noise increases proportionally. Overall handling is crisp and predictable, due mainly to the Tiburon's long wheelbase and sophisticated suspension.

Since its debut as a '97 model, the Tiburon has changed little. The '97 FX got the more sprightly 2.0L engine along with optional ABS. Standard brakes are adequate though sometimes difficult to modulate. As with most sporty cars, interior room is cramped for average-sized occupants. Tall drivers, especially, might find rearward seat travel insufficient, making head room a bit tight. The 145-hp, 2.0L engine became a standard feature with the '98 versions. The '99 models were carried over unchanged.

Although no serious defects have been reported, be on the lookout for body deficiencies (fit, finish, and assembly), harsh shifting with the automatic transmission, oil leaks, and minor brake glitches.

Technical service bulletins: All models: 1997—Automatic transmission won't engage Overdrive. • Clutch pedal squeaking. • Tapping noise coming from the passenger-side dash panel/engine compartment area. • Exhaust system buzz. • Improved shifting into all gears. • Improved shifting into Reverse. • Clutch drag. **1998**—Countermeasures for faulty timing chains and harsh shifting. **1999**—Automatic transmission drain hole oil leak and fluid leak behind the torque converter. • Shift lever won't shift out of Park. Delayed engagement into Drive or Reverse. • Countermeasures for poor automatic transmission performance. • Timing belt noise. • Hard to fill fuel tank.

Safety summary/recalls: 1999—Brake failure on wet pavement. • Car jolts when accelerating. Transmission slippage. • Tires won't hold air. • Original equipment jack won't support vehicle. • Seatbelt webbing jams in retractor. **Recalls: All models: 1997**—A faulty wiper motor will be replaced. **1999**—Transmission slippage will be fixed for free.

Secret Warranties/Service Tips

All models/years—Hyundai has a new brake pad kit (#58101-28A00) that the company says will eliminate squeaks and squeals during light brake application. Hyundai also suggests that you replace the oil pump assembly if the engine rpm increases as the automatic transmission engages abruptly during a cold start. **1997**—A tip on eliminating clutch pedal squeaking is offered. • Tips on eliminating clutch drag are offered. **1997–98**—DOHC timing chain noise can be stopped by installing an upgraded timing chain. • Park–Reverse or Park–Drive harsh shifting may require an upgraded TCM. **1997–99**—Poor automatic transmission performance is addressed in TSB #97-40-031. • Automatic transmission drain hole oil leak and fluid leak behind the torque converter. • Delayed engagement into Drive or Reverse is addressed in TSB #99-40-006. **1999**—Tips on dealing with a hard-to-fill fuel tank. **1999–2000**—Timing belt noise may be caused by the belt rubbing against the front dust cover.

Tiburon Profile

	1997	1998	1999
Cost Price ($)			
Base	16,996	17,895	17,895
FX	18,895	19,895	19,895
Used Values ($)			
Base ↑	9000	10,000	11,000
Base ↓	7,500	8,500	9,500
FX ↑	10,000	11,000	12,500
FX ↓	9,000	10,000	11,000
Extended Warranty	N	N	N
Secret Warranty	Y	Y	Y
Reliability	④	⑤	⑤

Note: Tiburon has not been crash-tested by NHTSA.

MAZDA

Miata

Rating: Recommended (1996–99); Above Average (1990–95). There was no 1998 model. **Maintenance/Repair costs:** Higher than average, and dealer dependent. **Parts:** Higher-than-average cost and limited availability.

Strengths and weaknesses: The base 1.6L engine delivers adequate power and accelerates smoothly. Acceleration from 0 to 100 km/h is in the high 8-second range. The 5-speed manual transmission shifts easily and has well-spaced gears. The vehicle's lightness and 50/50 weight distribution make this an easy car to toss around corners, but it's quite jittery on uneven roads.

Owners' top gripes target the same characteristics that make other sports car enthusiasts swoon: inadequate cargo space, cramped interior for large adults, excessive interior noise, and limited low-end torque, which makes for frequent shifting.

Owners also say it's important to change the engine timing chain every 100,000 km. Other reported problems: 1990–91 model crankshaft failures, leaky rear end seals and valve cover gaskets, rear differential seal failure, a leaking or squeaky clutch, hard starts and stalling, torn drive boots, transmission whining in upper gear ranges, engine and exhaust system rattles, electrical system glitches, brake pulsation, valvetrain clatter on start-up (changing oil may help), prematurely worn-out shock absorbers and catalytic converter, soft-top cover coming off or breakimg, and minor body and trim deficiencies.

Technical service bulletins: 1995—Brake pulsation troubleshooting tips. • Clutch release bearing squeal. • Steering wheel may be off centre. • Clogged side sill drain holes. • Heater unit noise after long storage. **1996**—Brake pulsation repair. • Side sill paint damage from scuff plate. **1997**—Brake pulsation. **1998**—N/A. **1999**—Hard starting, exhaust rattles, AC odours, and problems with the soft-top cover.

Safety summary/Recalls: All models: Eighty percent of used Miatas are estimated to have some collision damage. Check your choice before signing the contract. **1995**—NHTSA is probing the unusually large number of reports that the airbag deployed for no reason, causing severe injuries. In one instance, a bolt in the convertible roof hinge assembly impaled the driver's skull when the airbag deployed. • Airbag failed to deploy. • Fire ignited in the engine compartment wiring. • Small triangular window exploded while driving. **1995–97**—Engine and horn failures. • Roof leaks. • Accelerator pedal cut a slit in the carpet, allowing the gas pedal to jam. **1997**—Airbag failed to deploy. • Convertible hard top flew off. • Cell phone usage caused battery failure.

• Gas tank expansion puts too much stress on the metal. **1999**—Airbags failed to deploy upon impact. • While passing another car on the highway, accelerator cable and the cable adjuster assembly disengaged from the horseshoe bracket that holds the cable. • Transmission suddenly failed, causing both rear wheels to seize. • Keizer aluminum wheel cracked, damaging brake caliper, rotor, and fender. • Car stalls whenever the clutch is released. • Miata performs poorly on wet roads. • At highway speeds, vehicle tends to wander all over the roadway. • Premature wearout of Yokohama tires. **Recalls: All models: 1990–93**— The optional hardtop's hoist accessory kit may have plastic buckles that break and allow the hardtop to suddenly fall. **1991**—Faulty ABS. **1999**— Vehicle may be hard to re-fuel; install a modified non-return valve.

Secret Warranties/Service Tips

All models/years—TSB #006/94 gives all of the possible causes and remedies for brake vibration. • TSB #N00198 addresses complaints that the steering wheel is off centre. • Other bulletins address the issue of AC musty odours. **All models: 1990**—A hard-to-close trunk lid requires an upgraded rubber cushion (#B48156786). • Poor AC performance is likely caused by the misalignment of the AC harness. • A rattling noise coming from the exhaust manifold may require the replacement of the insulator bracket. • Water may damage door speakers unless a speaker cover assembly (#B4Y5 7696X) is installed. • A musty odour coming from the AC system can be cured by installing an upgraded resin-coated evaporator core (#NA0J 61II0A). **1990–91**—Hard shifting into second gear before the vehicle has warmed up can be corrected by installing an upgraded second gear synchronizer ring and clutch hub sleeve (#JM1NA351-M-232720). **1990–95**—Dirt and debris can clog up side-sill drain holes, allowing water to collect and corrosion to occur; drill larger drain holes. **1990–99**—Paint damage caused by the trunk's rubber cushions will be repaired under the base warranty. **1992–94**—If the window won't open fully, install a new cable fastener. **1994**—Timing belt noise can be silenced by replacing the tensioner pulley with an upgraded part. **1996**—Soft-top water leakage may require a new soft-top link assembly. **1996–97**—An inoperative AC may need a new power-steering pressure switch; believe it or not, they are related. • Tips for troubleshooting power window glitches. **1999**—A hard-to-start engine may have debris accumulated at the fuel pressure regulator valve area causing the valve to stick open. • Engine rattling may be caused by premature wear of the engine thrust bearing or the engine harness clips rubbing against the car's frame. • Muffler rattling may be silenced by installing an upgraded unit under warranty. **1999–2000**—Additional tips on reducing AC odours.

Miata Profile

	1991	1992	1993	1994	1995	1996	1997	1999
Cost Price ($)								
Base	17,255	17,945	18,895	20,165	21,820	24,210	24,695	26,025
Used Values ($)								
Base ↑	5,500	7,000	8,000	10,000	12,000	13,000	15,000	17,500
Base ↓	5,000	6,000	7,000	8,000	10,000	11,000	13,000	16,000

Extended Warranty	N	N	N	N	N	N	N	N
Secret Warranty	N	N	N	N	N	N	N	N

Reliability	③	④	④	④	④	⑤	⑤	⑤
Air conditioning	④	④	④	⑤	⑤	⑤	⑤	⑤
Auto. transmission	⑤	⑤	⑤	⑤	⑤	⑤	⑤	⑤
Body integrity	❷	❷	③	③	③	④	④	⑤
Braking system	❷	❷	③	③	④	④	⑤	④
Electrical system	❷	❷	❷	③	③	④	④	⑤
Engines	❷	❷	③	④	④	⑤	⑤	⑤
Exhaust/Converter	③	④	④	④	④	④	⑤	⑤
Fuel system	③	③	④	④	④	⑤	⑤	⑤
Ignition system	❷	❷	③	③	③	④	④	⑤
Rust/Paint	❷	❷	③	③	③	④	④	④
Steering	④	⑤	⑤	⑤	⑤	⑤	⑤	⑤
Suspension	④	⑤	⑤	⑤	⑤	⑤	⑤	⑤
Crash Safety	—	③	③	—	—	④	④	—

TOYOTA

Celica

Rating: Recommended (1995–99); Above Average (1986–94). The 1996 and 1997 models are practically identical: choose the cheaper version. Keep in mind that the GT and GTS have a firmer suspension, a better-equipped interior, ABS, and a more sporting feel than do other versions. All handle competently and provide the kind of sporting performance expected from a car of this class. The extra performance in the higher-line versions does come at a price, but this isn't a problem given the high resale value and excellent reliability for which Celicas are known. Few safety-related complaints or recalls. **Maintenance/Repair costs:** Average, and most repairs can be done at any garage. **Parts:** Reasonably priced and easy to find.

Strengths and weaknesses: The pre-1986 Celicas weren't very sporty. Their excessive weight and soft suspension compromised handling and added a high fuel penalty. With the 1986 make-over, Celicas gained more power and much better handling—especially in the GT and GTS versions—but they're still more show than go, with limited rear passenger room.
Redesigned 1994 models are full of both show and go, with more aerodynamic styling, an enhanced 1.8L that gives more pickup than the ST's 1.6L, and better fuel economy. Among the upgraded models available, smart buyers should choose a used 1994 ST for its more reasonable price, smooth performance, quiet running, and high fuel economy.

Owner gripes target the excessive engine noise, limited rear seat room, and inadequate cargo space. Pre-1994 models get the most complaints regarding brakes, electrical problems, AC malfunctions, and premature exhaust wearout. The 1994 models may have a manual transmission that slips out of second gear, and hard starts caused by a faulty air flow meter (#22250-74200). Areas vulnerable to early rusting include rear wheel openings, suspension components, the area surrounding the fuel-filler cap, door bottoms, and trunk or hatchback lids.

1995–99

A GT convertible joined the lineup for the '95 model year; everything else was carried over practically unchanged; '96s got extra sound insulation and add-on skirts for a sportier appearance; '97s were mostly unchanged, except for the GT's five extra horses and the notchback GT getting axed. The 1998 Celica lineup dropped the ST and gave more standard features to the GT. In the following '99 model year, the GT Sport Coupe was dropped.

All late-model Celicas offer exceptional reliability and durability. Servicing and repair are straightforward, and parts are easily found. The front-drive series performs very well and hasn't presented any major problems to owners. Prices are high for Celicas in good condition, but some bargains are available with the base ST model.

Some common problems over the years include brake pulsation, rear defroster terminals breaking on convertibles, sunroof leaks, erratic CD changer performance, and smelly AC emissions.

Safety summary/Recalls: All models: Even if your vehicle has 4X4 capability, it's imperative that snow tires be fitted in order to avoid dangerous control problems on snow and ice. **1996**—Sudden brake failure. • Broken brake caliper bolt. • Clogged-up idle control valve makes for hard starts. **1997**—Convertible rear window glass shattered as top was lowered. • Headlights and instrument lights dim when brakes are applied. **1990**—Campaign L03 provides for the free replacement of the instrument panel light control switch. • Faulty airbag inflator. **1996**—Unintended acceleration caused by faulty cruise control. **Recalls: All-Trac Turbos: 1988–89**—The radiator and coolant will be replaced for free by Toyota.

Secret Warranties/Service Tips

All models/years—Older Toyotas with stalling problems should have the engine checked for excessive carbon buildup on the valves before any more extensive repairs are authorized. • Owner feedback and dealer service managers (who wish to remain anonymous) confirm the existence of Toyota's secret warranty that will pay for replacing front disc brake components that wear out before 2 years/40,000 km. • The decade-old problem of brake pulsation/vibration is fully outlined and corrective measures are detailed in TSB #BR94-002, issued February 7, 1994. • To reduce front brake squeaks on ABS-equipped vehicles, ask the dealer to install new, upgraded rotors (#43517-32020). **All models: 1986–91**—Rattling headrests are a common problem addressed in TSB #B091-010. **1994–96**—Rear brake squeaks can be silenced by installing countermeasure rear brake pads. **1995–97**—Convertible top chaffing may require a new convertible top covered by the base warranty. If that warranty has expired, ask for partial "goodwill" compensation.

Celica Profile

	1992	1993	1994	1995	1996	1997	1998	1999
Cost Price ($)								
Base	17,949	19,078	21,438	23,878	27,968	28,528	34,138	34,475
Used Values ($)								
Base ↑	5,000	6,000	9,000	11,500	16,000	18,500	22,000	25,000
Base ↓	4,000	5,000	7,500	9,500	14,500	17,000	20,000	23,000
Extended Warranty	N	N	N	N	N	N	N	N
Secret Warranty	N	N	N	N	Y	Y	Y	Y
Reliability	③	③	③	④	④	⑤	⑤	⑤
Air conditioning	❶	❶	❷	③	③	③	③	④
Auto. transmission	③	③	③	④	④	④	④	⑤
Body integrity	❷	❷	❷	❷	③	③	⑤	⑤
Braking system	❶	❶	❷	❷	❷	❷	③	③
Electrical system	❶	❶	❶	❷	③	③	④	④
Engines	③	③	③	③	③	③	④	⑤
Exhaust/Converter	❷	❷	❷	❷	③	③	④	⑤
Fuel system	④	④	④	④	④	④	④	④
Ignition system	④	④	④	④	④	④	⑤	⑤
Rust/Paint	❷	③	④	④	④	④	④	⑤
Steering	③	③	④	④	④	④	⑤	⑤
Suspension	④	④	④	④	④	④	⑤	⑤
Crash Safety	③	③	—	—	—	—	—	—

MINIVANS

Long on convenience, short on quality

Chrysler launched the modern minivan concept with its 1984 Caravan and Voyager and has dominated the area ever since. Although poorly assembled and riddled with deficiencies, the tall, boxy vehicle was an instant success because it combined fuel efficiency, carlike manoeuvrability, tons of convenience features, and increased cargo/passenger space in a smartly styled "garageable" van. As for the powertrain, AC, brake, body, and paint defects, Chrysler's comprehensive 7-year new-car warranty covered these factory defects so well that owner loyalty was retained—along with the same defects—year after year. But, don't take my word for it. Read what one of the truckers who hauls Chrysler products wrote me in December 2000:

> In your *Lemon-Aid* guides (I own at least 10 dating back to 1990), you frequently talk about the low quality and chronic problems with many Chrysler vehicles. I work for a trucking company that ships the Intrepids, Concordes, LHS's and 300M's out of the assembly plant in Bramalea, Ontario. I can tell you that in the six years I've worked there, I've seen Chrysler's product go "on hold" (that is, it can't be shipped) dozens of times, as much as once or twice a week.
>
> The reason that customers get defective cars is that the problem vehicles are rarely fixed by the factory!
>
> As an example, back in October, an engineer at the plant found a car where the rear suspension was not properly bolted to the frame. Everything went on hold while engineers searched the yard for more defective cars. Many were found, but someone at the plant must have decided that it wasn't a big deal, for less than 8 hours later, all of the cars were "okay" to ship. This sort of thing happens all the time. I guess the factory sends the cars to dealers for the dealers to fix, and I can see where a dealer might decide to sell the vehicle as is and process the inevitable customer complaint as a warranty claim.
>
> Let me repeat, this is not rare. This happens ALL THE TIME.
>
> The only time stuff gets fixed at the plant is when it is a safety issue, like (and I've seen these holds) brakes that can fail, wheels that might fall off, throttles that stick wide open, or fuel tanks that aren't attached to the cars properly. Anything else, like defective engine control computers that won't let the car start below freezing, doors that won't close properly, sunroofs that won't close, or transmissions that behave erratically, just gets shipped out. We even have a running joke about this—"I guess they waved their magic wands and POOF, the cars are fixed!"

I know that at Honda's Alliston, Ontario plant (home of the Civic), when some defect is discovered, they put everything on hold for days or even more than a week, so that they can fix everything before it gets shipped. I suppose Chrysler thinks that fobbing their problems off on their dealers is okay, but this is why I tell friends and family members in the market for a new car— "Don't buy a Chrysler!"

And still, some people I work with wonder why I bought a Toyota.

M. M.
Ontario

On the other hand, Volkswagen's minivan, which morphed into the EuroVan in the early '90s, had been on sale for almost four decades and never did very well. Used mostly as a camper, it suffered from decades-old styling, poor dealer support, insufficient heating, glacial acceleration, and a reputation for being reliably unreliable. Warranty protection was as elusive as a competent VW mechanic.

Fortunately, while Chrysler, Ford, and VW have apparently stood still or regressed from a quality-improvement standpoint, the competition has caught up and, in the case of Honda and Toyota, surpassed the American competition. In fact, imported vehicles produced during the past few years use more powerful engines; offer a greater variety of powertrains; and have better crash ratings, more safety features (airbags, etc.), more responsive road handling, better quality control, more competitive prices, and greater parts availability.

Rear-drive or front-drive?
If you must buy a minivan, remember that, much like sport-utilities, they usually fall into two categories: up-sized cars and down-sized trucks. The up-sized cars are "people movers." They're mostly FWD, handle like a car, and get great fuel economy. The 1999 Honda Odyssey and Toyota Sienna are the best examples of this kind of minivan. In fact, their road performance and reliability surpass the front- and rear-drive minivans built by Chrysler, Ford, and General Motors.

GM's Astro and Safari and the Ford Aerostar, on the other hand, are down-sized trucks. Using rear-wheel drive, 6-cylinder engines, and heavier mechanical components, these minivans handle cargo as well as passengers. On the negative side, fuel economy is no match for the front-drive minivans, and highway handling on rear-drives is also more trucklike. Nevertheless, rear-drive GM and Ford minivans are much more reliable performers than the front-drive Ford Windstar or Chrysler minivans.

Rear-drive vans are also better suited for towing trailers in the 3,500–6,500 lb. range. Although most automakers say their front-drive minivans can pull up to 3,500 lb. with an optional towing package (often costing almost $1,000 extra), don't you believe it. Owners report

Minivans

white-knuckle driving and premature powertrain failures caused by the extra load. It just stands to reason that Ford and Chrysler front-drive minivans equipped with engines and transmissions that blow out at 60,000–100,000 km under normal driving conditions are going to meet their demise much earlier under a full load. You will find lots of additional tips on minivan towing at *www.happycampers.net.*

Getting more for less

Most minivans are overpriced, and motorists needing a vehicle with large cargo- and passenger-carrying capacity should consider a cheaper GM Vandura or Chevy Van, even if it means sacrificing some fuel economy and convenience features (they can be added by most conversion shops at competitive prices). You just can't beat the excellent forward vision and easy-to-customize interiors that these large vans provide. Furthermore, parts are easily found and are competitively priced due to the large number of independent suppliers.

Recommended

No models are recommended.

Above Average

Ford Mercury Villager/Nissan
  Quest (1997–99)
GM Astro, Safari (1998–99)
GM Montana, Trans Sport,
  Venture (1997–99)

Honda Odyssey (1999)
Toyota Sienna (1998–99)

Average

Ford Aerostar (1995–97)
Ford Mercury Villager/Nissan
  Quest (1995–96)
GM Astro, Safari (1996–97)

GM Lumina, Lumina APV,
  Trans Sport (1995–96)
Mazda MPV (1996–98)
Toyota Previa (1991–97)

Below Average

Chrysler Caravan, Voyager,
  Grand Caravan, Grand Voyager,
  Town & Country (1997–99)

Honda Odyssey (1996–98)
Mazda MPV (1988–95)

Not Recommended

Chrysler Caravan, Voyager,
  Grand Caravan, Grand Voyager,
  Town & Country (1984–96)
Ford Aerostar (1986–94)
Ford Mercury Villager/Nissan
  Quest (1993–94)

Ford Windstar (1995–99)
GM Astro, Safari (1985–95)
GM Lumina, Lumina APV,
  Trans Sport (1990–94)

CHRYSLER

Caravan, Voyager, Grand Caravan, Grand Voyager, Town & Country

Rating: Below Average (1997–99); Not Recommended (1984–96). Don't consider any model year without being armed with the longest powertrain warranty you can afford. Also ditch the failure-prone Goodyear Conquest original equipment tires. Other minivans you may wish to consider: the GM front- and rear-drive minivans, Ford Mercury Villager, Nissan Quest, or Toyota Sienna. Major generic defects affecting the 1984–99 models make these minivans very risky buys. In spite of the poor reliability of the early versions, Chrysler minivans remained popular because Chrysler's comprehensive seven-year warranty paid for their shortcomings. But that warranty's gone and the defects remain. Another tip: as with many Chrysler vehicles, dim headlights are common; take a night test-drive before signing the contract. **Maintenance/Repair costs:** Higher than average, but any garage can repair these minivans. **Parts:** Expensive (especially for paint, AC, transmission, and ABS components, which are covered under a number of "goodwill" warranty programs and several recall campaigns).

There's presently an abundance of used Chrysler minivans on the market; however, very few have any of their original warranty coverage left. Count on spending at least another $1,000 for a supplementary bumper-to-bumper warranty to protect yourself from Chrysler's costly generic defects. ABS and transmission repairs alone could cost you $5,000. One radio listener recently asked me if my advice to get the extended warranty on the Caravan or Ford's Windstar should be seen as a "red flag" regarding the reliability of these vehicles. Yes, that's exactly what it is.

Strengths and weaknesses: Chrysler's minivans dominate the new- and used-minivan market because they offer pleasing styling and lots of convenience features. They can carry up to seven passengers in comfort and also ride and handle better than most truck-based minivans. The shorter-wheelbase minivans also offer better rear visibility and good ride quality, and are more nimble and easier to park than truck-based minivans and larger front-drive versions. Cargo hauling capability is more than adequate, with a 1,200–1,600 kg (2,700–3,500 lb.) maximum towing range, depending on engine size, passenger size, and luggage.

On the downside, these minivans pose maximum safety risks due to their chronic body and mechanical component failures. Owners report bizarre "happenings" with their minivans, suggesting that these vehicles require the services of an exorcist rather than a mechanic (seatbelts that may strangle children, airbags that deploy when the ignition is turned on, and sudden stalling on the highway when within radar range of airports or military installations).

Powertrain problems

These minivans are way underpowered with the base 4-cylinder engine. It has a history of head gasket failures, but it outshines the larger Mitsubishi 2.6L, which is guaranteed to self-destruct around the 100,000 km mark. The timing belt, piston rings, and valves are particular weak points on the 2.6L powerplant, and the two-piece camshaft oil seals are also prone to sudden leaks. The Mitsubishi 3.0L V6 is much more reliable than its smaller 2.6L version, but it lacks power on long climbs, has multiple fuel-injection and oil leak problems, and produces a loud piston "slapping" noise during cold starts. The Chrysler-built 2.5L engine is fairly dependable but sluggish; the 3.3L V6 is more reliable and better able to meet routine driving needs. The best engine choice of all, however, is the Chrysler 3.8L V6. It has the brawn to handle a full passenger load and pass and merge easily.

Since 1996, Chrysler's V6 engines have performed quite well, far better than similar 3.0L and 3.8L engines equipping Ford's Taurus, Sable, and Windstar minivan. Nevertheless, some owners have reported early engine head gasket failures, hard starts, stalling, and serpentine belt failures (causing loss of power steering), which are addressed in the following internal service bulletins.

Sags/Hesitation/Stumble/Start & Stall, A/C, Add LDP Test
NUMBER: 18-05-99
GROUP: Vehicle Performance
DATE: Feb. 26, 1999
SUBJECT:
Sags/Hesitation/Stumble/Start & Stall, A/C Bump Improvements, Addition of Leak Detection Pump (LDP) Monitor Test
OVERVIEW:
This bulletin involves selectively erasing and reprogramming the powertrain control module (PCM) with new software (calibration changes).
MODELS:
1997–1998 (NS) Town & Country/Caravan/Voyager
SYMPTOM/CONDITION:
1997/1998 3.0L ATX Powertrains
• Sags/Hesitation/Stumble/Start & Stall after a cold start in ambient temperatures of -7°–30° C (20°–86° F). This condition may persist for up to a minute into a drive cycle and is attributed to high driveability index (DI) fuel. See TSB 14-08-97 for more detail on Driveability Index fuel.
1997/1998 2.4/3.0/3.3/3.8L Powertrains
• Provides further enhancements to the software originally released in Technical Service Bulletins 18-19-97 Rev A dated Oct. 17, 1997 and 18-20-98 dated Apr. 17, 1998 for "Bump" Feel during A/C Compressor Engagement. See TSB 18-19-97A and/or 18-20-98 for further details regarding this subject.

Serpentine Belt Slips Off Idler Pulley
Number: 07-02-99
Group: Cooling
Date: June 4, 1999
SUBJECT:
Serpentine Belt Slips Off Idler Pulley
OVERVIEW:
This bulletin involves replacing the bracket that the idler pulley attaches to.
MODELS:
1996–1999 (NS) Town & Country/Caravan/Voyager
1996–1999 (GS) Chrysler Voyager (International Market)
NOTE:
THIS BULLETIN APPLIES TO VEHICLES EQUIPPED WITH A 3.3L OR 3.8L ENGINE.
SYMPTOM/CONDITION:
Loss of power steering assist occurs when driving through deep snow or standing water.
Snow or rain can enter the engine compartment from underneath the vehicle and force
the serpentine belt off of the idler pulley.

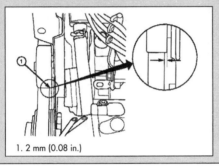

1. 2 mm (0.08 in.)

The manual transmission is fairly durable, but it's balky to use. The 3-speed automatic transmission is a throwback to another age. Its gearing puts unnecessary strain on the transmission and engine and it's constantly hunting for the right gear. Yet all of Chrysler's 41TE and 42LE automatic transmissions built over the past decade are a nightmare from a reliability and performance standpoint (see "Safety summary/Recalls"): imagine having to count to three in traffic before Drive or Reverse will engage, or "limping" home on the highway in second gear at 50 km/h. The disastrous A604 4-speed automatic was particularly troublesome on 1988–91 models. Then it was renamed the 41TE and 42LE—and continued to pile up complaints. Chrysler pledged that a free oil cooler by-pass valve would be installed on 1989–90 minivans to prevent transmission damage in cold temperatures (Customer Satisfaction Notification #281T), but automatic transmission failures continued unabated.

Automatic transmissions on the 1989–95 versions continue to leak, gear down to a limp-in mode, shift noisily, and hunt for the proper gear—the likely cause of some of the poor gas mileage claims. Software and hardware cures for these factory-related defects are listed in TSB #18-24-95.

The two following bulletins suggest that minivan automatic transmission "limping," shuddering, and delayed shifting continues well into the 1998 model year.

Delayed Transaxle Engagement
NO: 21-07-98
GROUP: Transmission
DATE: Apr. 24, 1998
SUBJECT:
Delayed Transaxle
Engagement
MODELS:

1989–1995	(AA)	Spirit/Acclaim/LeBaron Sedan
1989–1993	(AC)	Dynasty/New Yorker/New Yorker Salon
1990–1993	(AG)	Daytona
1990–1995	(AJ)	LeBaron Coupe/LeBaron Convertible
1992–1994	(AP)	Shadow/Shadow Convertible/Sundance
1990–1991	(AQ)	Chrysler Maserati TC
1989–1995	(AS)	Town & Country/Caravan/Voyager
1990–1993	(AY)	Imperial/New Yorker Fifth Avenue
1993–1995	(ES)	Chrysler Voyager (European Market)
1995–1998	(FJ)	Sebring/Avenger/Talon
1996–1998	(GS)	Chrysler Voyager (European Market)
1995–1998	(JA)	Cirrus/Stratus/Breeze
1996–1998	(JX)	Sebring Convertible
1993–1998	(LH)	Concorde/Intrepid/LHS/New Yorker/Vision
1996–1998	(NS)	Town & Country/Caravan/Voyager
1997	(PR)	Prowler

Symptom/Condition

Step	Symptoms	Yes	No
1	Was Fluid Level Checked, Test 1 and Test 2 completed?	Go to Step 2	Perform Fluid Level Check, Test 1 and Test 2 (described above)
2	Does the vehicle have a DTC 35? (Loss of Prime)	Perform test 35 in the latest applicable diagnostic publication. (See item #1 on DTC 35).	Go to step 3
3	Does the vehicle have a DTC 36 accompanied with DTC 50 or 51?	Go to step 4	Go to step 5
4	Is vehicle an **89-96** MY and is stop bump described by the customer along with DTC 36, 50 or 51? And/or is the delay experienced in both reverse and OD?	L – R inner and outer seals are not properly sealing. (See item #2 & #4 on L – R inner and outer seals).	Redefine symptom.
4a	Is vehicle an **89-94** MY and is delay experienced from N to OD during a cold start along with DTC 36 and 51 only?	UD inner seal is not properly sealing. (See item #3 & #4 on UD inner seal).	

| 5 | Is vehicle an **89-95** MY and is delay from <u>P to Reverse</u> during a <u>hot restart?</u> | Measure valve body #1 check ball clearance. (See item #5 measuring check ball clearance). | Go to step 6 |
| 6 | Is vehicle an **89-95** MY (pre TRS) with 41TE only and is the <u>delay</u> experienced <u>during</u> a cold start in <u>sub-freezing temperatures?</u> | PRNDL Switch condensation may be freezing in switch causing delay. Replace PRNDL switch. (See item #6 PRNDL switch). | Delay may be due to electrical noise in speed sensor circuit. (See item #7 output speed sensor). |

Intermittent delayed transaxle engagement greater than three seconds. The transaxle may be cold or hot based on the table as shown.

NOTE:
VEHICLES WITH DELAYED TRANSAXLE ENGAGEMENT ON START UP, AFTER BEING PARKED FOR SEVERAL DAYS, ARE CONSIDERED NORMAL AND WILL NOT BE AFFECTED BY THE INFORMATION IN THIS BULLETIN.

Transaxle Desensitization To Intermittent Faults
NO: 21-03-98
GROUP: Transmission
DATE: Feb. 13, 1998
SUBJECT:
Transaxle Desensitization To Intermittent Faults/Driveability Improvements
MODELS:
1998 (FJ) Avenger/Sebring/Talon
1998 (GS) Chrysler Voyager (European Market)
1998 (JA) Cirrus/Stratus/Breeze
1998 (JX) Sebring Convertible
1998 (LH) Concorde/Intrepid
1998 (NS) Town & Country/Caravan/Voyager
DISCUSSION:
New software has been released to address the following:
All models:
Be more tolerant of intermittent conditions that may cause MIL illumination, limp-in or DTC generation. Following is a list of symptom/conditions made more fault tolerant:
1. Corrects an error in extreme cold temperatures −27 C (−16 F) degrees or below. This allowed the transaxle to switch to the cold schedule too quickly. This may cause MIL illumination and limp-in conditions with associated DTC's due to slower than expected response from the fluid.
2. Reduce excessively long (more than 3 second) 3−2 shifts as the vehicle is coasting or braking to a stop with 4 C (40 F) degree or below fluid temperature. The driver may experience slight engine flare accelerating from a stop and/or sluggish acceleration due to the transaxle still being in 2nd gear instead of 1st.
On FJ/GS/JA/JX/NS models:
1. Improves the shift schedule while towing in hilly conditions. The driver may describe this condition as being in the wrong gear or delayed upshifts after cresting a hill.
On NS/GS models:
1. Reduces a shudder condition that may be experienced during a light to moderate throttle 1−2 upshift with −1 C (30 F) degree fluid temperature or higher. This condition can be experienced more frequently as the fluid becomes hotter.
2. Reduces a shudder condition that may be experienced during a 2−3 upshift just after a 3−2 or 4−2 kick-down.

Other mechanical weaknesses in early models include the premature wearout of front suspension components, wheel bearings, front brake discs, brake master cylinder, water pump, air conditioning unit, engine cooling system, and manual transmission clutch. Fuel-injectors on all engines have been troublesome, and engine supports may be missing or not connected.

Overall fit and finish has gotten worse, not better, over the years (see "Secret Warranties/Service Tips"). Body hardware and interior trim are fragile and tend to break, warp, or fall off (door handles are an example). After about a year's use, the Caravan and its various spin-offs become veritable rattle-boxes, with poorly anchored bench seats being a major player. Finish problems can be summed up in three words: paint, paint, paint. The paint tends to discolour or delaminate after the second year. Chrysler knows about this problem and often tries to get the owner to pay half the cost of a repainting job (about $1,500 on a $3,000 job), but will eventually agree to pay the total cost if the owner stands fast, threatens small claims court action, or belongs to a consumer protection group like Vancouver-based CLOG (Chrysler Lemon Owners Group). Moreover, minivan owners fed up with Chrysler's refusal to repaint their vehicles have filed a class action suit in Washington state, seeking damages for owners of 1986–97 cars, sport-utilities, minivans, and trucks. Several years ago, Chrysler Canada was sued by a Vancouver-based law firm acting on behalf of British Columbia Chrysler owners of paint-delaminated vehicles, in a class action similar to the Washington-state lawsuit. That case hasn't been decided, yet; call 1-800-689-2322 and get the latest info from Joe Fiorante or J.J. Camp, the lead litigators in this action.

Mechanical weaknesses on more recent models (1995–99) include the premature wearout of the engine tensioner pulley, automatic transmission speed sensors, the differential pin breaks through the automatic transmission casing, engine head gaskets, motor mounts, starter motor, front brake discs and pads (the brake pad material crumbles in your hands), front rotors and rear drums, brake master cylinder, suspension components, exhaust-system components, ball joints, wheel bearings, water pumps, fuel pumps and pump wiring harnesses, radiators, heater cores, and AC units. Fuel-injectors on all engines have been troublesome, the windshield washers freeze up in cold temperatures or bump into each other, sliding doors malfunction, engine supports may be missing or not connected, tie-rods may suddenly break, and the power-steering pump frequently leaks. Two further problems are batteries that last only 9–12 months, and factory-installed tires that fail prematurely at 40,000–65,000 kilometres and are hard to find—especially in the LT rating.

Cold-weather problems abound. One Hamilton, Ontario, owner says that her 1992 Voyager's rear heater coolant tubes were so badly corroded that they had to be replaced after two years at a cost of $160. Radiators and AC lines also quickly succumb to corrosion.

Chrysler owners organize and win

Chrysler's repeated attempts to blame drivers for its vehicles' ABS, automatic transmission, AC, and paint delamination problems continue to arouse consumer anger, despite the fact the company has settled many of its complaints through consumer pressure groups like CLOG. The CBC program *Marketplace* has made several references to these deficiencies; the Internet is replete with postings about failures all over the world (see Appendix II, "Best Internet Gripe Sites"); and Chrysler is currently the defendant in half a dozen class actions in the States, including the aforementioned suit in Washington state.

Surprisingly for a country not known for its consumer militancy, about 1000 dissatisfied Chrysler car owners have set up Chrysler Lemon Owners Groups (CLOGs) in Canada in the provinces of British Columbia, Alberta, Saskatchewan, and New Brunswick. These groups have submitted members' names to the automaker and have succeeded in getting sizeable refunds for brake, transmission, AC, and paint repairs from Chrysler Canada's Warranty Review Committee. If you have had any of these problems and want "goodwill" repairs or a refund for repairs already carried out, join a CLOG, or go through Chrysler's regular customer relations hot line, as outlined below. If this doesn't work within a reasonable period of time, phone, fax, or email the National Service Manager, Chrysler Parts, Service, and Engineering, tel: 519-973-2300; fax: 519-561-7005. Ask that your claim be reviewed by the Committee and that you be given a claim number.

Obviously with the Warranty Review Committee, Canadian consumers have a short-cut method of appealing Chrysler's decisions that American owners lack; however, with Daimler's cost-cutting edicts, I'm not sure how long the Warranty Review Committee will stay in existence (it's been five years, so far). I'm fearful it may be shut down or will simply rubber-stamp decisions taken earlier. If that occurs, your only inconvenience will be an estimated three-month wait for a settlement offer following your small claims court claim. A good way to judge whether a settlement offer is fair is to consult the links listed in Appendix II, "Best Internet Gripe Sites," or access *www.lemonaidcars.com* for an updated list of court victories and settlements.

If your claim is still rejected, file a small claims action that totals the costs for all the defects you believe are factory related and then wait for Chrysler's settlement offer. If no satisfactory offer is made, go to pretrial mediation or directly to court.

That's what *Lemon-Aid* reader John Cannell did in February 2000. He's a Toronto-based owner of a '90 Dodge Grand Caravan, bought used, who wasn't satisfied with Chrysler's low offer and insisted upon a trial to decide his claim relative to his transmission repair costs and paint estimates (Toronto Claim No. T16767/99, Judge Pamela Thomson). Here's what happened:

...The judge picked up on the fact that the vehicle's various transmissions had either failed or demonstrated major problems about every 2 to 2.5 years. I pointed out, as well, that none of the various Chrysler built/repaired transmissions had made it to 115,000 km.

The judge agreed that the paint problem was a defect (and stated she did not regard sunshine as "chemical fallout").

She allowed all my claim, except for the torque converter (she said that I had had my money's worth out of the 1993 component). As well, since I had offered to settle for less than the award, she doubled my costs and awarded me $340.

Total award was $3,030—although I only claimed $2,929!

The judge criticized Chrysler for not bringing any witnesses as well as for their refusal to supply me with the list of 47 service bulletins on the transmission, which I requested.

I made numerous references to *Lemon-Aid* to back up my paint and transmission claims and filed them with the court and Chrysler's lawyers (Gowling, Strathy, & Henderson), before the court date. I don't think that I would have had nearly as good an outcome without the inclusion of photocopies of sections of your book...

Model year changes: 1991—First major overhaul since the Caravan was launched in 1984. Restyled exterior and interior; problematic all-wheel drive (AWD) comes on the scene; optional ABS and driver-side airbag. **1992**—Standard driver-side airbag and optional integrated child safety seats. **1993**—Upgraded front shoulder belts; bucket seat tilts forward to ease access. **1994**—Standard passenger-side airbag; side door guard beams; redesigned dashboard; AWD limited to Grand versions; spruced-up exterior. **1995**—Carried over unchanged, except for trim and option packages. **1996**—Redesigned. More aerodynamic styling; driver-side sliding door; roll-out centre and rear seats; a longer wheelbase; standard dual airbags and ABS (ABS later became optional on base models); a more powerful 150-hp 2.4L 4-cylinder engine. **1997**—Grand models get optional AWD along with four-wheel disc brakes; LE models get optional traction control. **1998**—The 3.0L V6 engine gets a better-performing 4-speed automatic transmission and the 3.8L V6 gets 14 additional horses. **1999**—Cargo net between the front seats and middle and rear seat head restraints; Grand Caravan ES gets standard 17-inch wheels and some styling changes.

Technical service bulletins: All models: 1996—3.3L and 3.8L lower engine oil leaks. • Coolant seepage from rear heater hose connections. • Cold-start stumble. • Rough idle, hesitation, or sags after fuel tank is filled (see "Secret Warranties/Service Tips"). • Intermittent driveability problem near radar (again, explained more fully in "Secret Warranties/Service Tips"). • Intermittent powertrain shudder. • Transmission limp-in caused by a faulty speed sensor. • Reduced limp-in default sensitivity. • Excessive transmission downshifting/upshifting in cruise control. • Dealers will install an upgraded overdrive clutch hub. • Difficulty going into second gear or Reverse after a cold start. •

Upshift shuddering. • ABS activates below 16 km/h. • Front wipers activate while driving or will not turn off. • Vehicle drifts or leads at high speeds. • Underbody squeaks, buzzes, and rattles. • Exhaust drone at 2500–2800 rpm. • B-pillar area rattling. • Blower motor whine and AC-related moan/whine. • Power steering produces a clunk or popping noise at highway speeds. • Steering noise during parking lot manoeuvres. • Front door squeak/creak noise. • Ratcheting sound when coming to a stop. • Rear wheel rattle or click noise. • Rattling rear bench seat. • Rear brake noise (see "Secret Warranties/Service Tips"). • Integrated child safety seat seatbelt retractor may restrict seatbelt travel; dealer will replace assembly at no charge under Customer Satisfaction Note #650. • Child seat shoulder harness won't pull out. • Discoloured cowl grille or outside rear view mirrors. • Poor cowl cover fit. • Dust intrusion into rear of vehicle. • False info on fuel tank capacity and inaccurate fuel gauge. • Hard to unlatch rear bench seats. • HVAC control knobs or buttons may stick. • Interior window film buildup. • Intermittent operation of sliding door locks. • Liftgate-to-rear-fascia gap too small. • Paint chips at the upper front corner of the sliding doors. • Poor AM radio reception and RAS radio cassette malfunctions. • Faulty power vent windows. • Loose quad seats. • Roof panel is wavy or has depressions. • Inoperative sliding door and liftgate power lock motor; the sliding door may be difficult to open from the outside. • Suction-cup marks on door glass. • Unexplained theft alarm activation or dead battery. • Water leaks onto carpet from HVAC housing. • White stress marks on interior trim panel. • Flying hubcaps (see "Secret Warranties/Service Tips"). **1997**—1–2 shift shudder fix. • Delayed transaxle engagement. • 3.8L engine idle vibration. • Engine sags, hesitates, stumbles, stalls, or is hard to start. • Faulty speed control. • Engine misses or bucks. • Slipping serpentine belt. • Momentary loss of power steering. • Steering system honking or squealing during parking lot manoeuvres. • Rattling sliding door and B-pillar, quad seat latch, and roof rack. • Front end popping. • Underbody creak or knock. • Thumping noise coming from the rear. • Rear brake cyclic rubbing noise, moaning, or howling. • Power door lock motor noise. • Ticking noise from left B-pillar. • Low speed tire wobble. • Smooth-road shake, vibration, or wobble. • Loose or detached seatback assist handle. • High effort needed to unlatch rear bench seats. • Poor fit at rear of sliding door. • CV boot grease seepage. • Coolant seepage at rear heater line. • Inoperative radiator fans. • Self-activating front wipers. • Wipers won't park or wipe in intermittent mode. • Inoperative CD player. • AC evaporator odours. • Water leaks onto floor from HVAC housing. **1998**–Engine overheating. • Delayed transaxle engagement. • Transmission desensitization. • Intermittent loss of speed control, or power-assisted steering. • Sags, hesitation, stumble, hard starts, or stalling. • Serpentine belt slippage. • Snow/water ingestion into rear brake drums. • AC compressor lockup. • Ignition key stuck or won't turn. • Roof panel is wavy or has depressions. • Whistling when accelerating.

• Exhaust drone. • Steering wheel clicks and rattles. • Quad seat latch, roof rack, and sliding door rattling. • Front door glass wind noise. • Power door lock motor whirling noise. • Left B-pillar ticking. • Suspension strut bearing squeaks. • Poor radio reception (AM). • Taillight and HVAC housing water leaks. • Smooth road vibration, shake, or wobble. • Low-speed tire wobble. • CV boot grease seepage. **1999**—The defects affecting newer minivans are similar to those failures we've seen for over a decade, although automatic transmission breakdowns no longer figure prominently in Chrysler bulletins (see following 1999 Caravan TSB summary).

Number	Date	Name
23-23-00	Jun 00	Ignition Key Will Not Turn And/Or Cannot Be Removed
08-15-00	Apr 00	Intermittent instrument panel speaker operation/static
23-11-00	Mar 00	Roof Panel is Wavy or has Depression
22-01-00	Mar 00	Spare Tire Winches
02-03-00	Feb 00	Knock/Clunk Sound From Front Strut Area
19-09-99	Feb 00	Click/Rattle Sound In Area Of Steering Wheel
05-10-99	Jan 00	Snow/Water Ingestion Into Rear Brake Drum
08-45-99	Dec 99	AM Radio Reception
08-37-99	Nov 99	Airbag On/Off Switches
05-09-99	Nov 99	Rear Wheel Park Brake Actuator/Lever Service
21-15-99	Oct 99	Transaxle Seepage Mis-Diagnosis - Case Porosity
19-06-99	Sep 99	Ignition Switch Housing Service
08-27-99	Aug 99	Speed Control Does Not Maintain While Climbing A Grade
23-26-99	Aug 99	Rattle Noise At The Sliding Door Upper Track Or B-Post
24-10-99A	Aug 99	A/C System Blows Warm Air Intermittently.
23-33-99	Aug 99	Right Side Sliding Door Trim Panel Rubs Quarter Panel
23-27-99	Jul 99	Quad Seat Easy Entry Latch Rattle
24-14-99	Jul 99	A/C Suction And, Or Discharge Line Service
24-15-99	Jul 99	A/C Compressor Lock-up At Low Mileage
08-16-99A	Jun 99	Inoperative Or Intermittent RKE Transmitter
07-02-99	Jun 99	Serpentine Belt Slips Off Idler Pulley
23-01-99A	Jun 99	Tick Type Noise At Top Of Left B-Pillar.
829	May 99	Safety Recall # 829 - Daytime Running Lamp Labels
22-03-99	Apr 99	Smooth Road Vibration/Shake/Wobble.
23-11-99	Apr 99	Assist Handle On Back Of Front Seat Loose Or Pulled Out
22-02-99	Apr 99	Low Speed Tire Wobble.
21-06-99	Apr 99	Intermittent Loss of Speed Control
23-03-99	Feb 99	Power Door Lock Motor Whirling Noise
08-17-98C	Dec 98	Air bag On-Off Switches
23-59-98	Dec 98	Front Door Glass Adjustment/Windnoise
08-44-98	Dec 98	Memory Power Seat Travel Range
25-02-98	Oct 98	I/M Testing - OBDII CARB Readiness Monitor Information
03-06-98	Oct 98	CV Boot Grease Seepage
02-10-98	Sep 98	Squeaking Noise From Strut Bearings
18-32-98	Sep 98	Flash Programming Failure Recovery
08-40-98	Sep 98	Body Control Module/Signal Circuit DTC Code
19-05-98	Aug 98	Honk Or Squeal Noise During Parking Lot Maneuvers
18-25-98	Aug 98	Erroneous Body Control Module Diagnostic Trouble Code
23-34-98	Aug 98	Front Door Body Mounted Weatherstrip Retention
08-27-98	Jun 98	Perceived Loss or Change Of Radio Station Presets

Safety summary/Recalls: All models/years—Chrysler continues to downplay the seriousness of its minivan safety defects, whether in the case of ABS failures, inadvertent airbag deployments, or faulty rear latches. Nevertheless, the company continues to sustain heavy losses from lawsuits concerning airbag dangers (for example, a $69 million U.S. class action) and faulty minivan rear latches. • Owners report that cruise control units often malfunction, accelerating or decelerating the vehicle without any warning, and that sudden stalling and transmission failures also create life-threatening situations. The owner of a 1993 Caravan SE equipped with a 3.3L engine calls the transmission malfunction a safety hazard:

> I have experienced a transmission control module failure where the vehicle immediately dropped into second gear. This could have been tragic if it had occurred in heavy traffic.

• NHTSA is looking into complaints the fuel system may leak in an accident. Another probe targets 1996 model airbag clocksprings. **All models: 1991–93**—Seatbelts may become unhooked from the floor anchor. **1994**—Airbags deploy when the vehicle is started. **1994–95**—Airbags and wiper motor share the same fuse; if the wiper motor fails, the airbags are deactivated. **1995**—Engine fires. • Thieves love the door lock design. • Broken spare tire suspension cable allows tire to fall away while driving. • Right-side rear door suddenly flies open when vehicle passes over a small bump. • Seatbelt buckles jam or suddenly release. • Child shoulder-harness clip easily pulls out. • Roof drip rails allow water to leak inside. • Open glove-box back section allows for papers to be sucked into the AC blower. • Inoperative horn. **1995–96**—Brake failures, lockup, excessive noise, and premature wear. • Airbag fails to deploy or accidentally deploys. • Injury from airbag. • Sudden acceleration, stalling. • No steering. • Seatbacks fall backward. • Fuel tank is easily damaged. • Park won't hold vehicle. • Transmission fails, suddenly drops into low gear, won't go into Reverse, delays engagement, or jumps out of gear. • Rear windows fall out or shatter. • Power window and door lock failures. • Sliding door jams, trapping occupants. • Weak headlights. **1996**—Driver's side airbag deploys when the ignition is turned on. • Child safety seat harness over-retracts, trapping children or catching their hair. • Fuel tank leaks from tank top and fuel rail. • Incorrect fuel gauge. • Fuel sloshes around (no baffle), deforms tank, and makes noise. • Fuel leaks from vapour-recovery canister. • Broken steering belt tensioner causes the sudden loss of power steering and power brakes. • Wipers self-activate. • Sliding door falls off. • Faulty power door locks. • Cracked axle/drive shaft. • Cruise control drops speed and then surges to former setting. • With AC engaged, vehicle stalls, then surges forward. • Power-steering failure, excessive noise. • Parked vehicle, with gear in Park and with emergency brake applied, rolled into a lake. **1997**—Dashboard interior light switch started burning when ignition switch was turned on. • Inadvertent airbag deployment. • Airbags failed to deploy. • Facial injuries after airbag deployed when driving over a pothole. • Numerous complaints of 4-cylinder head gasket failures. • When driving through water, air breather intake ingests water and engine seizes. • Sluggish acceleration after cold starts. • Check Engine light comes on for no reason. • Slipping engine serpentine belt causes immediate steering loss. • Transmission hesitates and stumbles at turnpike speeds. • Constant stalling, often due to failure of the power control module (PCM) and oxygen sensor. • Chronic transmission failures. • Transmission allows vehicle to roll away when in Park. • One can move automatic transmission shift lever without applying brakes. • Several incidents where ignition was turned and vehicle went into Reverse at full throttle, although transmission was set in Park. • PRNDL indicator suddenly goes blank, comes back on only after vehicle restart. • ABS failure caused an accident. • Brakes activated by themselves while driving. • Prematurely warped rotors and worn-out pads cause excessive vibrations when stopping. • Rear drums often need replacing. • Often the rotors are rusted and pitted. • Steering may suddenly lock up. • Loss of steering control after running through a puddle. • Gas tank fuel leaks; replace fuel pump level unit. • Fuel moves violently in gas tank when accelerating, creating a thump-thump sound. • No standard head restraints on the second- and third-row seats. • Integrated child safety seat locked up and belts got tighter. • Seatback collapsed in collision. • Right front door latch failures and sliding door often opens while vehicle is underway. • Driver- and passenger-side locks failed on sliding doors. • Headlights are too dim. • Distorted windshields and exterior rear-view mirror. • Inadequate windshield defrosting caused by poor design. • Early burnout of the AC compressor clutch. • Inoperative blower motors caused by a defective resistor. • Chronic wiper failure or self-activation. • Frequent battery failures. • Vehicle must be lifted by a straight flat bed or the windows would pop out and the gas tank could blow out. **1998**—Right rear taillight caught fire. • Gas tank leaks caused by faulty fuel pumps or leaks from top of fuel tank responsible for a number of fires reported by owners. • Airbag deployment caused extensive facial and chest injuries. • Airbags failed to deploy. • Slipping engine serpentine belt causes immediate steering loss. • Sudden acceleration and chronic stalling. • Defective engine head gaskets, rocker arm gaskets, and engine mounts. • Chronic stalling caused by camshaft or oxygen sensor failures. • Surging and hesitation at highway speeds, especially with AC engaged. • Multiple transmission failures. • Vehicle rolled away while parked. • Many reports of vehicle suddenly jumping from Park into Reverse and speeding away. • Transmission fluid leaks due to defective front pump housing oil seal. • Sudden steering or brake loss. In one incident, the steering wheel separated from the steering column. • Power-steering loss often occurs when turning. • Frequent replacement of the steering column, rack, and pinion. • Front suspension strut failure. • Many reports of defective liftgate gas shocks. • Many incidents reported of electrical short circuits and total electrical system failure. • Water leaks from the passenger-side dash. • Difficult to see through windshield in direct sunlight. • Defroster vent reflects in the windshield, obscuring driver's vision. • Poor steering wheel design blocks the view of instruments and indicators. • Rear-view mirror often falls off. • Door cannot be unlocked with remote entry system. • Horn hard to find on steering hub. • Battery failures. **1999**—Airbag failed to deploy; airbag light comes on when braking. • Poor braking performance. • Van rolled away while in Park. • Transmission failures. • When put into Reverse, vehicle may accelerate or brakes may lock up. • Headlights aimed too low; not bright enough. • Sliding power door opens when vehicle passes over a bump. • Instrument panel fire. • Sudden, unintended acceleration. • When cruising on the highway, vehicle will suddenly shut down completely; problem also occurs at traffic lights. • When put into Reverse, vehicle may accelerate or brakes may lock up. • Van rolled away while in Park with ignition off. • Premature engine head gasket and automatic transmission failures. • Faulty speed sensors cause the automatic transmission to shift erratically and harshly. • With cruise control engaged, transmission won't downshift when going uphill. • 5-year-old was able to pull shift lever out of Park into Drive without engaging brakes. • Sudden tie-rod breakage, causing loss of vehicle control. • Chronic steering pump and rack failures. • Poor braking performance; brake pedal depressed to the floor with little or no effect; excessive vibrations or shuddering when braking. • Rusted-through front brake rotors and rear brake drums (see "Secret Warranties/Service Tips"). • Original equipment Goodyear Conquest tires leak air, or fail prematurely, with side-wall defects most evident; don't last half of their expected 80,000 kilometre (50,000 mile) rating. • Sudden Goodyear Conquest blowout and split wheel after passing over a small bump in the road. • Sliding power door opens when vehicle passes over a bump. • Power side windows fail to roll up. • Driver's lap and shoulder belt failed to lock up in a collision. • Horn often doesn't work. • Dash gauges all go dead intermittently. • Headlights aimed too low; not bright enough. • Windshield wiper bumps into other wiper. **Recalls: All models: 1984–95**—All minivans are subject to a voluntary service campaign that will fix a rear liftgate latch that may fail in a collision. **1985**—Dealers will install a protective cover over the brake proportioning valve. • The fuel supply tube leaks in vehicles equipped with a 2.2L engine. **1986–88**—On passenger models, first rear seats may detach in an accident. **1988**—Possible fuel tank leakage. **1988–90**—Notification #281T, applicable to vehicles with a trailer-towing package, provides for a free oil cooler by-pass valve to prevent transmission failure in cold weather. **1989–90**—Engine valve cover gasket may leak oil, creating a fire hazard. • Notification #466 provides for a free engine valve spring. • Safety recall #314T provides for the free installation of a reinforcing plate on the front seatbelt strap. **1990**—An incorrectly mounted proportioning valve may increase the chance of skidding.

1990–94—Liftgate bolts may fail causing liftgate to suddenly fall. **1991**—Faulty turn-signal flasher. • ABS hydraulic fluid leakage. **1991–92**—Steering wheel cracks may cause wheel to loosen. **1991–93**—Recall to fix two kinds of seatbelt problems: faulty buckle cover may prevent seatbelt from being fully latched, and seatbelt anchor hook could become detached from the anchor. • Chrysler ABS recall calls for the installation of a new pump and seal kit, if needed. The kit comes with a lifetime warranty, while all other ABS components will henceforth be covered for 10 years/160,000 km. **1992**—Replace liftgate supports, which may break from fatigue. • Safety recall #326T requires the replacement of all brake pedals that have been found to lack sufficient strength. • Faulty steering column shaft coupling bolts. • Improperly bent fuel tank flanges could cause a fire. **1993–94**—Rear liftgate struts and bolts will be replaced to prevent liftgate from falling down. **1993–95**—A wiring harness short may cause the driver-side airbag to deploy when the minivan is started. **1993–99**—Replace faulty wiper pivot drive arm. **1995–98**—Airbags may deploy for no reason. **1996**—Faulty bench seat attaching bolts. • Filler tube rollover valve. • Installation of a fuel-filler ground strap. • Improved retractors for child safety seats (service action) and upgraded seat module bolts (recall). • Defective engine cylinder head plug could cause a fire. • Defective fuel pump attaching nut could cause fuel leakage. **1997**—Goodyear Conquest tires will be replaced. • Dealers will clean the child safety seat latch and add a belt extender for anchoring the belts. • Brake master cylinder seals may be defective, allowing fluid to be drawn into the power-assist reservoir. • Wheels may have been damaged during mounting. **1998**—Install upgraded child safety seat belts.

Secret Warranties/Service Tips

All models/years—If pressed, Chrysler will replace the AC evaporator for free up to seven years (see Part Two). **All models: 1987–92**—The heater and air conditioning system may suddenly change to the defrost mode during a low vacuum condition, which can occur during trailer towing, hill climbing, and acceleration. Install a revised vacuum check valve to correct this problem. **1987–94**—3.0L engines that burn oil or produce a smoky exhaust at idle can be fixed by installing snap rings on the exhaust valve guides and replacing all of the valve guide stems or the cylinder head. **1988–90**—Intermittent rough running at idle signals a need for a new EGR. **1988–94**—A sticking AC heater blend door can be corrected by spraying an anti-rust penetrant into the assembly. **1989–90**—Oil leaks from the cylinder head cover with 2.5L engines are caused by poor sealing. The original cylinder head cover must be replaced with one that uses silicone sealant (RTV) instead of a gasket (TSB #09-17-89). • Defective valve stem seals are the likely cause of high oil consumption with 2.5L engines (TSB #HL-49-89C). • A604 automatic transmission clutch slippage is a common problem addressed in TSB #21-09-9. • A surge/buck at 60–90 km/h with an automatic transmission can be corrected by installing driveability kit #4419447. **1989–95**—An excellent summary of Chrysler's transmission glitches and corrections covering these seven model years can be found in

TSB #18-24-95. **1989–96**—Acceleration shudder that may be accompanied by a whine is likely the result of leakage in the transmission front pump, caused by a worn pump bushing. **1990–92**—Erratic idle speeds occurring after deceleration from a steady cruising speed can be corrected by replacing the idle air control motor with a revised motor. **1990–94**—Harsh automatic shifts may be tamed by installing the following revised parts: kickdown, accumulator, reverse servo cushion springs, and accumulator piston. • Cold-start piston knocking noise can be eliminated by replacing the piston and connecting rod assembly. • Erratic fuel gauge operation can be fixed by installing a revised sender assembly or fuel pump/sender assembly. **1991**—Loss of fuel pressure causing fuel-pump noise, erratic transmission shifting, engine power loss, or engine die-out may be due to a defective fuel pump. • An erratic idle with 2.5L engines can be cured by using an improved SMEC/SBEC engine controller. • Faulty power door locks may have a short circuit, need a new fuse, or require a new door latch with power door lock assembly. **1991–92**—If the engine knocks when at full operating temperature and during light to medium acceleration, it may mean that the single board engine controller (SBEC-Powertrain Control Module) needs replacing. • Engines with a rough idle and stalling following a cold start also may require a new SBEC. • The airbag warning light may light up constantly when the vehicle's ignition is in the ON position. This malfunction may be due to corrosion caused by water in the airbag's six-way connector. **1991–93**—Engines that stall following a cold start may need an upgraded Park/Neutral/start switch. **1991–94**—The serpentine belt may come off the pulley after driving through snow; install upgraded shield, screw, and retainers. • Noisy fuel pumps need to be replaced with upgraded pump, wiring harness, fuel tank isolators, and fuel tank straps. • Noise when shifting into Reverse or when turning is addressed in TSB #09-14-94. **1991–95**—Poor AC performance while the AC blower continues to operate is likely due to a frozen evaporator (ask for a "goodwill" refund). • TSB #24-05-94 looks at all the causes of, and remedies for, poor heater performance. • If the vehicle tends to drift left, cross-switch the tire and wheel assemblies, readjust the alignment, or reposition the front crossmember. **1992**—The brake pedal may not return to its fully released position, causing the brake lights to remain illuminated; install a pedal return kit (#4723625). • Front door forward hem separation (the door seems to sag) can be corrected by welding the inner door panel to the outer door panel along the front door forward hem. • Long crank times, a rough idle, and hesitation may be corrected by replacing the intake manifold assembly. • A vehicle that's hard to start may have a corroded ECT/sensor connector. • An oil leak in the oil filter area may be corrected by installing a special oil filter bracket gasket (#MD198554). • If the heater and ventilation system change to the defrost mode during acceleration, trailer towing, or hill climbing, install a revised vacuum check valve. • Intermittent failure of the power door locks, chimes, wipers, gauges, and other electrical devices can be corrected by replacing defective relays with revised relays (#4713737). **1992–93**—Some 41TE transaxles may produce a buzzing noise when shifted into Reverse. This problem can be corrected by replacing the valve body assembly or valve body separator plate. • A deceleration shudder can be eliminated by replacing the powertrain control module with an upgraded version. • Correct rough idling after a cold start with 2.5L engines by installing an upgraded powertrain control module (PCM). **1992–94**—AC duct odours are addressed in TSB #24-21-93. • Poor heater performance may be the result of a misadjusted clip on the blend air door cable. **1993**—A fuel pump check valve failure can cause start-up die-out, reduced power, or erratic shifting. **1993–94**—Improved automatic shifting can be had by installing an upgraded transmission control module. • AC evaporator whistling requires the installation of upgraded AC expansion valves and gaskets. • An AC moan may be silenced by installing an AC clutch plate with a damper ring. **1993–95**—Delayed automatic transmission engagement may be due to low fluid, a stuck or frozen PRNDL switch, or a transaxle front pump with excessive ground clearance. • Harsh low-speed automatic transmission shifting, accompanied by a fluctuating digital speedometer reading. This may be corrected by covering the wiring harness with aluminum wire, which prevents the spark plug wires from sending false signals to the outport speed sensor wiring that connects to the TCM. • Constant upshifting/downshifting on vehicles equipped with cruise control has a variety of causes, as set out in TSB #08-15-95. **1993–99**—Paint delamination, peeling, or fading (see Part Two). • A rotten-egg odour coming from the exhaust may be the result of a malfunctioning catalytic converter, probably covered under the emissions warranty. **1994**—Harsh, erratic, or delayed transmission shifts can be corrected by replacing the throttle position sensor (TPS) with a revised part. • A creaking left B-pillar can be silenced by repositioning the metal portion of the left B-pillar baffle. **1994–95**—Intake valve deposits are frequently the cause of poor driveability complaints. • Intermittent no-cranks can be corrected by modifying the battery-to-starter-cable terminal insulator at the starter connection. • A front suspension rapping noise heard when going over bumps can be corrected by providing additional clearance between the front coil springs and strut towers. **1996**—Poor engine performance near military installations or airports is caused by radar interference. Correct by installing a "hardened" crankshaft position sensor and/or reprogramming (flashing) the PCM with new software calibrations. • Rear brake noise that occurs at any time can be silenced by replacing the rear brake shoes and rear wheel cylinders. Another possibility is the addition of rear brake shoe springs. • Rough idle, hesitation, or sags after the fuel tank is filled can only be corrected by the installation of a new fuel tank, according to TSB #18-28-95. The repair is covered under warranty and should take about an hour. • Steering noise during parking lot manoeuvres may be fixed by installing a new power-steering gear and left-side attaching bolt. • Chrysler minivan wheel covers tend to take flight (and I thought that was only a Chevy Caprice problem). Chrysler will install upgraded covers under warranty. **1996–99**—A serpentine belt that slips off the idler pulley requires an upgraded bracket (see page 417). **1996–2000**—Snow or water ingestion into the rear brake drum calls for the installation of a revised rear drum brake support (backing) plate and the possible replacement of the rear brake shoes and drums under warranty (Failure Code: P8-New Part). **1997–98**—Engines that run poorly or stall may need the PCM reprogrammed under the emissions warranty. **1997–2000**—If the ignition key can't be turned or removed, TSB #23-23-00 proposes four possible corrections. **1998**—A faulty radiator fan relay may cause the engine to overheat; replace it with a new relay and reprogram the powertrain control module under Customer Satisfaction Notice #771. **1998–99**—Front brakes tend to wear out quickly on front-drive minivans. Owners say that Chrysler has paid half the cost of brake repairs for up to 2 years/40,000 km. • Silence a chronic squeaking noise coming from underneath the vehicle by installing a new strut pivot bearing (see following bulletin).

NO: 02-10-98
GROUP: Suspension
DATE: Sept. 25, 1998
SUBJECT:
Squeaking Noise From Strut Bearing(s)
MODELS:
1998–1999 (NS) Town & Country/Caravan/Voyager
1998–1999 (GS) Chrysler Voyager (International Market)
NOTE:
THIS BULLETIN APPLIES TO VEHICLES BUILT THROUGH OCT. 1, 1998.
SYMPTOM/CONDITION:
A squeaking/chirping noise is heard (inside or outside the vehicle) from the strut tower area(s) when turning the steering wheel or when the vehicle is driven over any irregularities in the road surface.
DIAGNOSIS:
With the vehicle on a level surface, hold a front suspension coil spring with your hands near 180° apart, and try to rotate the spring right and left. If a squeaking/chirping noise is heard from the top of the strut tower, perform the Repair Procedure. Repeat for the opposite side strut tower.
Parts Information:
AR (2) 04684418   Bearing, Strut Upper Pivot
POLICY: Reimbursable within the provisions of the warranty.

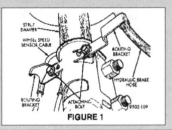

FIGURE 1

This repair should take about an hour for each side and is covered by Chrysler's base warranty.

Caravan, Voyager, Grand Caravan, Grand Voyager, Town & Country Profile

	1992	1993	1994	1995	1996	1997	1998	1999
Cost Price ($)								
Caravan	15,810	15,935	16,860	18,840	18,840	19,885	20,255	24,230
Caravan 4X4	20,750	20,900	—	—	—	—	—	—
Grand Caravan	19,105	19,685	20,425	22,120	20,320	21,465	23,160	25,890
Grand Caravan 4X4	21,300	21,860	23,680	27,450	—	—	—	—
Town & Country	31,470	32,490	34,874	35,980	38,280	40,350	41,040	41,260
Used Values ($)								
Caravan ↑		3,500	4,000	5,000	6,000	8,500	11,500	13,000	15,500
Caravan ↓		3,000	3,500	4,000	5,000	7,000	9,500	11,500	14,500
Caravan 4X4 ↑		4,000	5,000	—	—	—	—	—	—
Caravan 4X4 ↓		3,500	4,000	—	—	—	—	—	—
Grand Caravan ↑		4,500	5,500	6,500	7,500	9,500	12,000	15,000	17,500
Grand Caravan ↓		4,000	4,500	5,000	6,000	8,000	10,500	13,000	16,000
Grand Caravan 4X4 ↑	5,000	6,000	7,500	8,500	—	—	—	—

Grand Caravan 4X4 ↓	4,000	5,000	6,000	7,000	—	—	—	—
Town & Country ↑	9,000	10,500	12,500	14,500	17,000	21,000	25,000	28,000
Town & Country ↓	8,000	9,500	11,000	13,000	15,000	18,500	23,000	26,500
Extended Warranty	Y	Y	Y	Y	Y	Y	Y	Y
Secret Warranty	Y	Y	Y	Y	Y	Y	Y	Y
Reliability	①	①	②	②	②	②	②	②
Air conditioning	①	①	②	②	②	②	③	③
Auto. transmission	①	①	①	①	①	①	①	①
Body integrity	①	①	①	①	①	①	①	①
Braking system	①	①	①	①	①	①	①	①
Electrical system	①	①	①	①	①	①	②	③
Engines	①	①	②	②	②	③	③	③
Exhaust/Converter	②	②	②	②	②	③	③	③
Fuel system	①	①	①	②	③	③	③	④
Ignition system	②	②	②	②	②	②	③	④
Rust/Paint	①	①	①	①	①	①	①	①
Steering	③	③	③	③	③	④	④	④
Suspension	③	③	③	③	③	③	③	③
Crash Safety								
Caravan	④	④	④	④	—	④	③	—
Grand Caravan	—	—	—	—	③	③	③	④
Town & Country	④	④	④	④	—	④	③	—
Town & Country LX	—	—	—	—	③	③	③	④
Side Impact								
Grand Caravan	—	—	—	—	—	—	—	⑤
Town & Country LX	—	—	—	—	—	—	—	⑤

Note: Voyager and Grand Voyager prices and ratings are almost identical to the Caravan and Grand Caravan.

FORD

Aerostar

Rating: Average (1995–97); Not Recommended (1986–94). Brawnier and more reliable than Chrysler's or Ford's front-drive minivans; the Aerostar's last model year was 1997. **Maintenance/Repair costs:** Average, and any garage can repair an Aerostar. **Parts:** Plentiful, but not durable (especially AC; brake calipers, pads, and rotors; and electrical components).

Strengths and weaknesses: The 1986–94 models are at the bottom of the evolutionary scale as far as quality control is concerned. However, the last three model years showed lots of improvement. Repair costs are reasonable (except for high AC costs), and many of the Aerostar's myriad mechanical and body defects are covered by Ford warranty extensions (see "Secret Warranties/Service Tips"). The Aerostar's modern, swoopy shape belies its limited performance capabilities: the 3.0L and 4.0L engines are unreliable through the 1991 model year, and the 3.0L is a sluggish performer. Older 2.3L and 2.8L engines can barely pull their own weight. The 4-speed automatic transmission often has a hard time deciding which gear to choose, and the power steering transmits almost no road feel to the driver. The ride is bouncy, handling is sloppy, and braking performance is poor. Reliability problems on all models make early Aerostars risky buys, especially if the previous owner has been less than fastidious in maintenance and repairs.

Valve cover and rear main oil seal leaks are frequent, and leaks from the front axle vent tube often require the replacement of the front axle assembly. Even oil pans, which you wouldn't normally associate with leaks, tend to leak as a result of premature corrosion (a big-buck repair). Fuel-injectors are either faulty or plugged. Other problems include expensive automatic transmission failures; electronic and electrical system glitches; power steering, suspension, and brake defects; and premature and chronic air conditioner breakdowns involving AC condensers and compressors that tend to fail after the first three years of use. (Ford has consistently produced failure-prone AC systems in the Aerostar van since its birth in 1986; according to *Consumer Reports*, the failure rate was almost three times that of other vehicles in its class.) Auto air conditioning experts refer to the problem as the "Black Death"—in reference to the sludge these Ford ACs produce that leads to massive internal component failures in the FX–15 compressor. We have noted an above normal incidence in Aerostars ('91 and up), Explorers ('91 and up), Ford Taurus, Sable (up to 1994), T-Bird, Cougar ('89 and up), and F-Series ('92 and up).

A grinding/growling coming from the rear signals that the in-tank electric fuel pump is defective. Many mechanics find that the electronic engine controls are difficult to diagnose if problems arise. Routine repairs are very awkward because most components are buried under the windshield and dashboard. Windshield wipers are badly designed for winter driving. They freeze at the bottom of the windshield and wear out the wiper motor. Body hardware and integrity have earned low marks as well.

Model year changes: 1991—A new sport appearance package and minor body accents. **1992**—A standard driver-side airbag and front bucket seats, front-end restyling, redesigned dash and controls, automatic transmission moved from the floor to the steering column, and upgraded seatbelts for the rear outboard seats. **1993**—Optional rear integrated child safety seats. **1994**—A high-mounted third brake light. **1995**—Standard door-guard beams, no more manual transmissions offered, and AWD only available in extended-length Aerostars. **1996**—An upgraded 4-speed automatic transmission and upgraded sound and climate control systems. **1997**—A new 5-speed automatic transmission.

Safety summary/Recalls: All models: 1986–90—A draft of a January 20, 1993, Ford internal document lists "known incidents which are attributed to the ignition switch." It includes the 1986 Aerostar and Econoline full-sized vans. NHTSA documents show that the Aerostar has almost the highest rate of ignition switch fires of any Ford truck, second only to the 1988 Bronco. State Farm Insurance has filed an action against Ford to cover its payouts to policyholders whose Aerostars caught fire from an overheated ignition switch. • The hefty B-pillar (where the edge of the door meets the body behind the front seat) obstructs peripheral vision. • Some Aerostars don't have front-seat head restraints, unless the vehicles are equipped with the optional captain's chairs, and even then the restraints sit far too low for the average person. • Owners complain that the brake master cylinder and daytime running lights module may suddenly fail, and that 1990 Aerostars' rear brakes sometimes lock up in wet weather. **1990–97**—Transfer case and rear driveshaft failures. **1993–94**—Electrical malfunctions may cause overheating and/or fires at the fuel sender assembly on fuel tanks. **Recalls: All models: 1992–97**—Ford will fix wiring shorts that could cause a fire. • On models with AWD, the transmission or transfer case may crack or break. Dealers will install a new rear transfer case extension and a new aluminum rear driveshaft. **1995**—Spare tire may fracture the brake line. • Defective brake rotors. • Fuel pump and wiring electrical shorts. **1996**—Driver's door may not sustain specified load in the secondary latched position. • Defective brake rotors. • Defective electrical relay ignition switch. **1997**—Aftermarket brake rotors may crack. Call 1-800-264-3414 for Aimco manufacturer's free replacement.

Secret Warranties/Service Tips

All models/years—Two Aerostar components that often benefit from Ford's "goodwill" warranty extensions are automatic transmissions and computer modules that govern engine, fuel-injection, and transmission functions. **All models: 1986–94**—Rust perforations may occur in the front and/or rear lower rocker panel areas because the panels weren't coated with primer. Ford will replace the panel at no charge for up to 6 years/160,000 km; beyond those parameters, owners should seek partial refunds. **1989–96**—A chatter noise during sharp turns is likely due to an insufficient friction modifier, or over-shimming of the clutch packs within Traction-Lock differentials. **1990**—Delayed upshift or no upshift can be corrected by installing a new #4 thrust washer. • AC compressor shaft seal leaks can be best fixed by installing a new seal (#E9SZ-19D665-A). **1990–92**—A 4.0L engine oil leak may occur around the rocker gasket because of variations in the gasket quality; install two new rocker cover gaskets (Carrier type), along with conical spring screws. • Automatic transmission fluid leakage may be caused by a faulty or loose transfer case rear output seal. **1990–96**—Noisy power steering is likely caused by a pressure spike in the serpentine tube of the power-steering cooler. **1993–95**—A squeak or chirp coming from the blower motor can be stopped by installing an upgraded blower motor with improved brush-to-commutator friction. • An automatic transmission whine heard upon light acceleration can be silenced by replacing the front and rear planetary assembly and the front and rear sun gear. • Overheating or binding rear brakes can be corrected by backing off the self-adjusters. **1993–97**—Paint delamination, peeling, or fading (see Part Two). • Press Ford for "goodwill" warranty coverage if your AC is afflicted by the "Black Death" within 5 years/100,000 km. • Use the emissions warranty to cure rotten-egg odours caused by a defective catalytic converter. **1995–96**—Hard starts and stalling can be corrected by installing an upgraded idle air control valve under the emissions warranty. **1995–97**—Coolant leakage from the engine block heater requires the replacement of the block heater with an upgraded one that attaches better. **1997**—Delayed transmission engagement or constant shifting may be caused by a poorly calibrated torque converter (reprogram the powertrain control module).

Aerostar Profile

	1990	1991	1992	1993	1994	1995	1996	1997
Cost Price ($)								
Cargo	15,219	14,273	16,095	16,899	17,195	18,395	18,495	19,695
4X4	18,141	17,071	18,895	19,840	19,995	20,845	—	—
XL	—	—	16,395	17,215	18,095	20,195	19,995	20,195
Used Values ($)								
Cargo ↑	2,000	2,500	3,000	3,500	5,000	5,500	7,500	10,000
Cargo ↓	1,500	2,000	2,500	3,000	4,500	5,000	7,000	9,000
4X4 ↑	2,500	3,000	4,000	4,500	5,500	6,500	—	—
4X4 ↓	2,000	2,500	3,000	4,000	4,500	6,000	—	—
XL ↑	—	—	5,000	6,000	7,000	8,000	11,000	12,000
XL ↓	—	—	4,000	5,000	6,000	7,000	10,000	11,000
Extended Warranty	Y	Y	Y	Y	Y	Y	N	N
Secret Warranty	N	N	N	Y	Y	Y	Y	Y

Lemon-Aid

Reliability	❶	❷	❷	❷	③	③	④	④
Air conditioning	❶	❷	❷	❷	❷	③	④	④
Auto. transmission	❶	❷	❷	❷	❷	③	④	④
Body integrity	❷	❷	❷	❷	❷	❷	❷	❷
Braking system	❶	❶	❶	❶	❶	❷	❷	❷
Electrical system	❶	❶	❶	❷	❷	③	③	③
Engines	❷	❷	❷	④	④	⑤	⑤	⑤
Exhaust/Converter	❶	❶	❶	❷	③	④	④	⑤
Fuel system	❶	③	③	③	③	④	④	④
Ignition system	❷	❷	③	③	④	④	⑤	⑤
Rust/Paint	❶	❶	❶	❶	❷	❷	③	③
Steering	❷	❷	③	③	③	④	④	④
Suspension	❷	❷	❷	③	③	③	③	④
Crash Safety	—	—	④	④	④	④	④	④

Windstar

Rating: Not Recommended (1995–99). One of the worst minivan choices you can make; Jac Nasser, Ford's U.S. CEO should be ashamed of himself for putting this piece of crap on the market. Don't go anywhere near the Windstar, even if you have an extended warranty; it's not only unreliable, as is the Chrysler Caravan, but it's also very dangerous to drive. Sure, the Windstar combines an impressive five-star safety rating, plenty of raw power, an exceptional ride, and impressive cargo capacity. But the self-destructing automatic transmission is one black hole that will suck your wallet into its vortex (see website links in Appendix II). And, as a counterpoint to Ford's well-earned Windstar crashworthiness boasting, take a look at the summary of safety-related complaints recorded by the U.S. Department of Transportation (see "Safety summary/Recalls"): sudden acceleration, windows exploding, front springs puncturing tires, wheels falling off, horn failures, sliding doors that open and close on their own, and rolling away while parked. Kinda scary, for the AAA's "Minivan of the Year," eh? Other, more reliable minivans you may wish to consider: a late-model GM front-drive, a Ford Mercury Villager or Nissan Quest, or a Toyota Sienna. **Maintenance/Repair costs:** Average while under warranty; outrageously higher than average thereafter, due primarily to powertrain breakdowns not covered by warranty or insufficiently covered by parsimonious "goodwill" gestures. **Parts:** Reasonably priced parts are easy to find, mainly due to the entry of independent suppliers, lured by attractive profits sustained by parts that constantly need replacement. Speedometer electronics the exception; reports of $300–$500 bills run up on '95 and '96 models.

Strengths and weaknesses: Launched as a 1995 model in March 1994, the Windstar is a front-drive minivan that looks a bit like a stretched Mercury Villager. It's longer, larger, and lower than most other minivans.

It's also one of the few minivans not built on a truck platform (it uses the Taurus platform instead), and as a result, it has some of the carlike handling distinctions of Chrysler's minivans. It's offered in two body styles—a seven-passenger people-hauler and the less-expensive, basic cargo van.

There are a number of powertrain deficiencies that cut dramatically into the Windstar's performance and overall reliability. The automatic transmission, for example, is anything but smooth and has a scarlet history for running away when unattended, or simply packing it in early due to a failure-prone forward clutch piston, among other defective components ('99 Windstars, Tauruses, and Sables are covered by an extended warranty ONP, but 1993–98 model owners have been told to take a hike, unless they know Ford has a secret warranty covering the defect). At the best of times, the transmission pauses before downshifting or shifts roughly into a higher gear.

> Dear Phil
> I just want to thank you for saving us at least $1,500.00. The transmission in our '98 Windstar went BANG with only 47,300 miles [76,000 km]. After reading about Ford's goodwill adjustment on your site, we were told by our local Ford dealer that owner participation would be only $495. We received a new rebuilt Ford unit installed. Believe it or not, I am a fairly good mechanic myself and this came with no warning! We even serviced the transmission at 42,000 miles [68,000 km] and found no debris or evidence of a problem....

Over the past three years, I've been meeting with Ford executives to get the company to stop playing cat and mouse with its customers and set up a 7 year/100,000 mile (160,000 km) extended transmission warranty/Owner Notification Program (ONP) to fully compensate Windstar, Taurus, and Sable owners, without them having to file small claims court lawsuits.

As of December 2000, Ford of Canada was in favor of the program, but Ford USA (thanks to U.S. CEO Jac Nasser) squashed the whole idea.

In response to the many customer complaints of premature and outrageously expensive ($2,500–$3,000) automatic transmission failures, I have, again, dropped the ratings on these vehicles.

In a nutshell, it is the epitome of crass dishonesty for Ford to parade its CEO Jac Nasser in ads telling us of Ford's commitment to its customers in response to Explorer safety problems, while systematically forcing owners to pay thousands of dollars correcting what is essentially a factory-induced transmission defect, which also has serious safety implications (imagine losing all transmission power on a busy highway, or late at night, or when carrying your child's hockey or soccer teammates).

Windstar owners who do file small claims suits should realize that Ford reps are now filing standard form defense motions paraphrased below by one *Lemon-Aid* reader:

Phil: I was a victim of the faulty transmission on a '96 Sable within the parameters outlined in your book. Ford was difficult if not impossible to get through to prior to filing the claim, and now they have filed an interesting defense to the small claims notice they received.

These are the reasons they use to not honor their secret warranty:

If there was a failure of the transmission, the transmission failed due to improper use or maintenance of the Sable and its transmission, or the intervening act of the Plantiff or some other third party, and other unforeseeable factors beyond the control of Ford.

With regards to the warranty mentioned in the claim their response was that the Sable was subject to a specific warranty offered by Ford (the "Ford Warranty") which warranty was accepted by the Plaintiff in lieu of any other warranty with respect to the Sable.

The alleged defect is not covered under the warranty because it had expired at the time due to excess use and kilometers traveled; the Plantiff is not the original owner of the Sable; and the repairs done to the Sable were not completed by an approved representative.

In the event the warranty has not expired, Ford states that the Plaintiff breached the terms of the warranty.

Further, the "Program" referred to by the Plaintiff in the Civil Claim is a discretionary program, which is offered by Ford, but not mandatory.

I felt this information may be of use to you and future readers. I have taken some information from your book as part of my claim as well as some information on Ford's track record to date. I am confident the pretrial should go well. Again, many thanks for bringing this matter to my attention through your book...

Gosh, at least Ford admits it has a secret "goodwill" program—even if it is discretionary. I can see some of the straight-shooting Ford executives I've learned to respect, cringing at the above "weasel" defense, issued by the company's product liability section.

The 3.0L engine is overwhelmed by the Windstar's heft and struggles to keep up, but opting for the 3.8L V6 may get you into worse trouble. Owners report that the 3.8L engine head gaskets on '95 models need replacing shortly after the 60,000 km mark (see page 70). Even when it's running properly, the 3.8L knocks loudly when under load (1995–99 models). And if all these problems get you hot under the collar, too bad; you'll also have to contend with an air conditioning system that's generically dysfunctional, a false "door ajar" alert, a digital speedometer that won't glow, a horn that won't blow, and wipers that don't go.

But what's gotten many owners steaming in the past has been Ford's arrogant mishandling of their calls and letters, alerting the company to what is obviously a serious safety-related defect, as this owner of a '95 Windstar LX with 60,000 km relates:

We purchased a 1995 Ford Windstar LX which is inadequate and unsuitable for its intended purpose—namely, reliable family transportation....[T]ogether, the warranty work and retail work that directly relates to recalls, engine failures, transmission failures, and the like are in excess of $9,000....

As recently as last week, our van stalled out at an intersection when we were attempting a left hand turn, in front of traffic. Fortunately there was no accident and nobody was injured. The engine stalled out completely and would not start for a minute or two....

My concerns with Ford are twofold.

1) They have sold us a vehicle which is inadequate.

2) Ford's total failure to deal with the correspondence that I have sent.

With respect, the Corporate arrogance of the Customer Assistance Representative inflames a rather unsatisfactory relationship we have with Ford Canada. Further, to send us the identical form letter twice does little to assure us that Ford is at all responsive to our concerns, or for that matter, even reading our correspondence...

To be fair, let me add that Ford has always been aware of its customer relations deficiencies. Fortunately, recently retired Ford of Canada President, Bobbie Gaunt, had the courage to ditch the old system and upgrade Ford's customer assistance centre as of March 2000. With Gaunt gone, though, Ford runs the risk of drifting back into its former sadomasochistic mindset.

Windstar electrical and fuel system, suspension, brake, and body defects are legion. Paint peels off the roof; windows suddenly explode; water leaks through the headliner, doors, and hatch; mice get into interior through the firewall; heat shield and catalytic converter vibrate at highway speeds; and rattles, clunks, squeaks, clicks, and ticks can easily drown out your audio system.

Model year changes: 1996—The 3.8L V6 gets 45 more horses, upgraded seatbelts, and a tilt-slide driver's seat to improve rear seat access. **1997**—A bare-bones standard model makes its debut. **1998**—Wider driver's door improves rear seat access, a restyled front end, and the introduction of a fully equipped Limited version. **1999**—A standard fourth door, body stiffness was increased by 30 percent, optional seat-mounted side airbags, optional rear-bumper sonar sensors, improved steering and brakes, standard ABS, anti-theft system, new side panels, a new liftgate, larger headlights, and taillights, and a revised instrument panel. The second row bench seat can now be moved to the right or left to make it easier to access the third row seats. Exterior dimensions were decreased slightly; height was cut by an unusual 2.4 inches. The reworking of the hood makes it easier for drivers to see where the nose of the van is, particularly when parking.

Technical service bulletins: All models: 1995—Insufficient AC cooling or excessive clutch end gap. • Condensation leak at the auxiliary AC unit requires the installation of upgraded hose clamps. • Malfunctioning Drive/Reverse engagement, intermittent loss of torque at 3–4 upshift, and low transaxle fluid improperly setting the DTC causes major transmission malfunctions. • Solenoid corrosion causes a no-crank condition. • Chirp or squeak from the blower motor at low speeds. • Radio static, minor dash rattles, and false Door Ajar warnings. **1996**—Stall or hard start after 1–4 hour soak. • Case breakage at rear planet support. • Transaxle driveline noises. • Diagnostic tips on steering drift or pull. • Clunk in floor pan when accelerating/decelerating. • Clunk when moving gearshift out of Park. • Faulty power door locks. • Fuel gauge won't read over three-quarters. • Fog/film on windshield/interior glass. • Objectionable carpet odour. • AC musty odour. • Windshield wiper chatter/streaking. **1996–98**—Engine defects affecting newer Windstars mirror those failures we've seen on the first-year '95 model. All the more reason to be skeptical of Ford's claims that its quality control has improved. A prime example: the engine's lower intake manifold side and front cover gaskets might leak coolant, a problem that can cause overheating and severe engine damage (see page 445). **1997**—Harsh automatic transmission at 1–2 shift. • Intermittent Neutral condition when coming to a stop. • Parking brake may not release. • Tips on preventing brake vibration. • Water dripping onto floor from AC drain tube. • Inoperative rear auxiliary AC blower. • AC compressor moan. • Chirp or squeak from the blower motor at low speeds. • Clunking noise when moving gear shift lever out of Park. • Squeaking, creaking noise from upper A-pillar on turns. • Static noise heard at the low end of AM radio band. • Right rear quarter panel black soot deposits. • Fog/film on windshield/interior glass. **1998**—Harsh 3–2 downshift/shudder when turning or accelerating. • Harsh 1–2 upshift/intermittent Neutral after stop. • Inadvertent disabling of the brake/shift interlock. • Coolant loss/engine oil contamination with 3.8L engine. • Possible causes for chronic stalling. • Brake vibration diagnostic procedures. • Parking brake may not release. • Poor AC cooling. • Tips on eliminating AC odours and whistling. • Speaker noise. • Diagnostic procedures to rid vehicle of noise, vibration, and harshness. • Tips on preventing side door wind noise, rattling and clunking coming from the front of the vehicle, and measures to reduce ABS brake noise. • False low fuel indication. • Noisy liftgate and stress cracks. • Cargo area wet carpet and headliner. • Driver's seat squeaking or creaking. • Special program to rid right rear quarter panel of black soot deposits **1999**—See "Safety summary/Recalls" on next page.

Number	Date	Topic
00-11-4	May 00	Power Sliding Door Does Not Close
00-9-6	May 00	The Front Wipers Operate while Switch is in OFF position
00-4-4	Feb 00	Fuel Pump Handle Shuts Off Before Fuel Tank is Full
99-26-9	Dec 99	Fuel Economy-Customer Expectation vs. Vehicle Usage
99-25-1	Dec 99	Power Sliding Door Pops or Disengages When Fully Closed
99-24-2	Nov 99	Replace/Repair Any Lock Components and Individual Locks
99-23-4	Nov 99	Codes P0442, P0455/MIL On, No Driveability Concerns
99-21-6	Oct 99	A-Pillar Trim Warped
99-20-2	Oct 99	AX4S/AX4N-Redesigned Park System-Service Tip
99-19-4	Sep 99	Brake Vibration/Inspection/Friction Material Replacement
99-19-1	Sep 99	A/T-TCIL Illuminated/Trouble Codes P0715, P0717
99-18-4	Sep 99	Harsh 3-2 Downshift/Shudder When Accelerating-Turning
99-17-7	Aug 99	Reverse Park Aid-False Activation Of Warning Tone
99-17-6	Aug 99	Climate Control-Driver Side Door Glass Slow To Defog
99-17-3	Aug 99	Message Center-Falsely Displays Traction Control Error
99-13-9	Jun 99	Inadvertent Disabling Of Brake Shift Interlock
99-12-10	Jun 99	Industrial Fallout/Acid Rain Etching Neutralization
99-12-9	Jun 99	Whining/Buzzing Noise In Speakers Caused By Fuel Pump
99-11-1	Jun 99	Noise/Vibration/Harshness-TSB Special
99-8-4	May 99	Squeaking/Rattling Noise From Left/Right Rear Of Vehicle
99-8-15	May 99	Interior Door Trim Panel Replacement-Service Tip
99-7-6	Apr 99	A/T-No Reverse Engagement-AX4S/AX4N Built Thru 2/22/99
99-6-5	Apr 99	Windnoise Around Side Doors-Service Tips
99-6-6	Apr 99	Lack Of Cooling-Refrigerant Leak at Condenser Fittings
99-5-5	Mar 99	A/C-Lack Of Temperature Control In All Modes
99-4-10	Mar 99	Reverse Sensing System (RSS)-Service Tips
99-3-6	Feb 99	Power Sliding Door-Summary Of Concerns
99-3-1	Feb 99	Power Seat Switch Inoperative or Fuse 104 Opens
99-2-3	Feb 99	Windshield Sealing For Water Leaks-Service Tip
99-1-13	Jan 99	Trailer Tow Wiring Service Kit Available
98-26-2	Jan 99	Tips To Resolve Volatility Related Driveability Concerns
98-26-5	Jan 99	Anti-Lock Brake System (ABS) Noise
98-25-9	Dec 98	Interior Trim-Repairs To Vinyl Covered Surfaces
98-23-10	Nov 98	Mass Air Flow Sensor Contamination-Service Tip

Safety summary/Recalls: I'm both amazed and disgusted at the large number of safety complaints registered against recent-model Windstars; '98 Windstars, for example, have 616 complaints in the NHTSA database vs. a hundred or so for the imported competition. And, it gets worse the further you go back ('99 Windstars already have 230 complaints). Base models may not have head restraints for all seats, and the digital dash can be confusing. **All models: 1995–98**—NHTSA probe of sudden coil spring breakage puncturing tire. The following is a short summary of problems carried over, year after year; unfortunately, I don't have the space to list many other reported defects. Nevertheless, you can easily access NHTSA's website (see Appendix II) for the details of thousands of other Windstar complaints: Airbag failed to deploy. • Severe injuries caused by airbag deployment. • Sudden acceleration and chronic stalling. • Control arm and inner tie-rod failures cause the wheel to fall off. • Sudden steering lockup or loss of steering ability. • Engine head gasket failures. • Loose or missing front brake bolts could cause wheel lockup or loss of vehicle control. • Chronic ABS brake and transmission failures. • Almost a dozen reports that the vehicle jumps out of Park and rolls away when on an incline or slips into Reverse with the engine idling. • Transmission and axle separation. • Faulty fuel pump, sensor, and gauge. • Built-in child safety seat is easy to get out of, yet securing seatbelts are too tight; child almost strangled. • Faulty rear liftgate latches; trunk lid can fall on one's head. • Horn doesn't work properly. **1999**—This is a faithful summary of the 230 complaints in the NHTSA database. Keep in mind that many of these defects have been found in previous model year Windstars, but may not have been included due to space limitations: Airbag failed to deploy. • Vehicle suddenly accelerates—while parked, cruising, turning on the ignition, or braking. • Stuck accelerator causes unintended acceleration. • Chronic stalling caused by fuel vapour lock or faulty fuel pump. • Check Engine light constantly comes on due to a faulty gas cap or over-sensitive warning system. • Front passenger-side wheel fell off when turning at a traffic light; in another reported incident, dealer found the five lug nuts had broken in half. • Pops out of gear while parked and rolls away. • Frequent transmission failures, noisy engagement, won't engage forward or Reverse, slips or jerks into gear. • Transmission jumped from Park to Reverse and pinned driver against tree (this is a common problem affecting Ford vehicles for almost three decades). • Sudden loss of power steering; chronic leakage of fluid; and early replacement of steering components, like the pump and hoses. • Excessive brake fade after successive stops. • When brake pedal is depressed, it sinks below the accelerator pedal level, causing the accelerator to be pressed as well—particularly annoying for drivers with large feet. • ABS module wire burned out. • Complete electrical failure during rainstorm. • Horn button "sweet spot" is too small and takes too much pressure to activate; one owner says, "horn doesn't work, unless you hit it with a sledgehammer." • Windshield suddenly exploded when car was slowly accelerating. • Sliding door opens and closes on its own, sticks open or closed, or suddenly slams shut on a downgrade. • Sliding door closed on child's arm. • Door locks don't stay locked; passenger-side door opened when turning, causing passenger to fall out. • Many complaints that the side or rear windows suddenly exploded. • Rear defogger doesn't clear lower part of windshield in inclement weather when windshield wipers are activated. • Windshield wipers fail to clear windshield. • Water pours from dash onto front passenger floor. • Floor cupholder trips passengers. • Continental General tires lose air and crack between the treads. • Unspecified original equipment tires have sudden tread separation. • Large A-pillar (where windshield attached to door) seriously impairs forward visibility, hiding pedestrians. • Seatbelts aren't as described in owner's manual (supposed to be automatic retractable). • Two incidents where flames shot up out of fuel tank filler spout when gassing up. **Recalls: All models: 1995**—Hood may be defective. • A loose connection within the electrical power distribution box could ignite the electrical wiring under the hood. • A pinched instrument-panel wire harness could cause a short circuit and start an electrical fire. • The passenger airbag may not deploy properly. • An alternator wiring short circuit could cause a fire. • Fuel tank may leak. **1996**—Hood may be defective. • Transmission may not engage; PRNDL may give a false reading. **1997–98**—Servo cover can leak, creating a fire hazard. **1998**—Defective steering assembly. • Front brake rotors and pads will be replaced. **1998–99**—The overhead console may fall down.

Secret Warranties/Service Tips

All models: 1995—Blower motor squeaking or chirping can be silenced by installing an upgraded blower motor. **1995–96**—Intermittent no-starts may be caused by microscopic cracks on the fuel pump relay cover located inside the Constant Control Relay Module (CCRM); install a new CCRM. **1995–98**—Replace the seatbelt retractor if the integrated child safety seat's belt twists or binds. • A driver's seat that chucks or squeaks may need a seat track repair kit. • Ford says a clunking noise when shifting out of Park is normal. • A parking brake that won't release needs a new parking pawl actuating rod. • Power door locks that grind or won't work may need a new front door lock actuator. • Tips on finding and silencing instrument panel buzzing, rattling, squeaking, chirping, and ticking (see following).

Buzzing/Rattling/Squeaking/Ticking From Instrument Panel
Article No.
98-5-15
03/16/98
NOISE – "BUZZING" FROM INSTRUMENT PANEL
NOISE – "CHIRPING" FROM INSTRUMENT PANEL
NOISE – "RATTLING" FROM INSTRUMENT PANEL
NOISE – "SQUEAKING" FROM INSTRUMENT PANEL
NOISE – "TICKING" FROM INSTRUMENT PANEL
LIGHT TRUCK:
1995–98 WINDSTAR
ISSUE:
"Squeaking," "rattling," "chirping," "ticking," and/or "buzzing" noises may occur from the instrument panel area on some vehicles. These may be due to the tight fitting design of several components that make up the instrument panel.

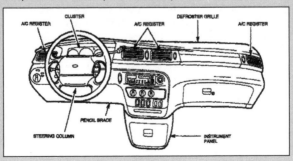

• The front end accessory drive belt (FEAD) slips during wet conditions, causing a reduction in steering power-assist; Ford suggests the belt be replaced. • A whistling noise from the front AC heater plenum requires a tighter seal. • Getting rid of AC odours requires a new moisture purge module and "disodorizer." • Water leakage onto carpet or headliner in rear cargo area is a factory-related defect covered in TSB #98-5-5 (see following bulletin).

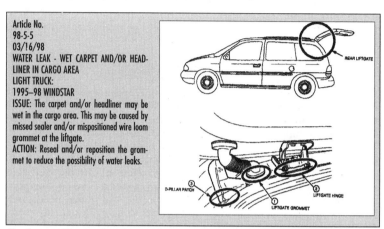

Article No.
98-5-5
03/16/98
WATER LEAK - WET CARPET AND/OR HEADLINER IN CARGO AREA
LIGHT TRUCK:
1995–98 WINDSTAR
ISSUE: The carpet and/or headliner may be wet in the cargo area. This may be caused by missed sealer and/or mispositioned wire loom grommet at the liftgate.
ACTION: Reseal and/or reposition the grommet to reduce the possibility of water leaks.

Ford says this repair takes an hour to carry out and is covered by the base warranty.

1995–99—Tips for correcting excessive noise, vibration, and harshness while driving; side door wind noise; and windshield water leaks. • An exhaust buzz or rattle may be caused by a loose catalyst or heat shield. • Paint delamination, peeling, or fading (see Part Two). **1995–2000**—A harsh 3–2 downshift/shudder when accelerating or turning may simply mean the transmission is low on fluid. • Diagnostic tips on brake vibration, inspection, and friction material replacement. **1996–98**—Harsh automatic shifting from first to second may be caused by a malfunctioning electronic pressure control or the main control valves sticking in the valve body. • Unwanted airflow from the AC vents can be stopped by replacing the evaporator case baffle. • A driver's seat that chucks or squeaks may need a seat track repair kit. • An intermittent Neutral condition when coming to a stop signals the need to replace the forward clutch piston and the forward clutch cylinder. • Black soot deposits on the right rear quarter panel can be avoided by installing an exhaust tailpipe extension under Ford's base warranty. • Engine oil mixed with coolant or coolant loss signals the need for revised 3.8L engine lower intake manifold side gaskets and/or front cover gaskets (see bulletin on next page).

Engine Oil Mixed With Coolant/Coolant Loss
Article No.
99-13-1
06/28/99
COOLING SYSTEM – 3.8L – UNDETERMINED LOSS OF COOLANT
COOLING SYSTEM – 4.2L – UNDETERMINED LOSS OF COOLANT
ENGINE – 3.8L – ENGINE OIL CONTAMINATED WITH COOLANT
ENGINE – 4.2L – ENGINE OIL CONTAMINATED WITH COOLANT
FORD:
1996–1997 THUNDERBIRD
1996–1998 MUSTANG, WINDSTAR
1997–1998 E-150, E-250, F-150
MERCURY:
1996–1997 COUGAR
ISSUE
Engine coolant may be leaking into the engine oil on some vehicles. The internal coolant leak may be difficult to identify. This may be caused by the lower intake manifold side gaskets and/or front cover gaskets allowing coolant to pass into the cylinders and/or the crankcase.
ACTION
Revised lower intake manifold side and front cover gaskets have been released for service.

The above engine defect is covered by Ford's emissions warranty for 5 years/160,000 km. Ford has another "goodwill" warranty that's far more generous; it's applicable to the 1996–97 Thunderbird, Cougar, Mustang, and 1997 F-150 pickup equipped with 3.8L or 4.2L engines (see page 385). Unfortunately, you are excluded from this "goodwill" program if you own a 1996–98 Windstar minivan, a 1997–98 E-150 or E-250 full-sized van, or a 1998 F-150 or Mustang—all vehicles afflicted by the same defect, as indicated by the service bulletin above. If you are refused compensation, fall back upon the emissions warranty for your refund.

1997–98—A rattling or clunking noise coming from the front of the vehicle may be caused by a loose front tension strut bushing retainer (see illustration on next page).

Rattling/Clunking Noise From Front Of Vehicle
Article No.
97-26-24
12/22/97
NOISE – "RATTLING" AND/OR "CLUNKING" NOISE FROM FRONT OF VEHICLE
LIGHT TRUCK:
1997-98 WINDSTAR
ISSUE:
A "rattling" and/or "clunking" noise may be heard from the front of the vehicle. This
may be caused by a loose front tension strut bushing retainer in the subframe front
crossmember.
ACTION:
Weld the front tension strut bushing retainer back into place. Refer to the following
Service Procedure for details.
SERVICE PROCEDURE

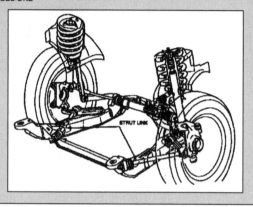

1998—Lack of AC cooling may be caused by refrigerant leak at the P-nut fitting. • AC may have a loose auxiliary climate control fan switch. • A Low
Fuel light lit for no reason signals the need for an upgraded fuel tank and
sender assembly. • A malfunction indicator light lit for no reason may simply show that the gas cap is loose. • An inaccurate metric speedometer
requires a new speedometer gear. • An overhead console that's loose or
hangs down needs a revised bracket. • Sliding door rattles and squeaks when
passing over bumps; requires adjusting and silicone. • Squeaks and creaks
from the left rear of the driver's seat can be silenced by lubricating the lateral stability bracket. • A driver's seat that chucks or squeaks may also need
a seat track repair kit. • Stalling when stopping, parking, coasting, or during
slow turns can be corrected by reprogramming the PCM. • An upper radiator hose leak requires an upgraded hose or protective sleeve. • Excessive
vibration at highway speeds may require new rear brake drums. **1998–99**—
Tips on spotting abnormal ABS braking noise, although Ford says some
noise is inevitable. **1999**—No Reverse engagement may be caused by torn
Reverse clutch lip seals. • To improve the defogging of the driver-side door
glass, install a revised window de-mister vent. • A squeaking, or rattling noise
coming from the left right rear of the vehicles is likely caused by a poorly
insulated parking brake cable. **1999–2000**—If the power sliding door won't
close, replace the door controller; if it pops or disengages when fully closed,
adjust the door and rear striker to reduce closing resistance. • Front wipers
that operate when switched OFF need a revised multifunction switch.

Windstar Profile

	1995	1996	1997	1998	1999
Cost Price ($)					
GL/Base	23,095	22,495	23,495	24,495	24,295
LX	27,195	27,495	28,995	28,995	28,195
Used Values ($)					
GL/Base ↑	9,000	11,500	14,000	15,500	18,000
GL/Base ↓	7,500	10,000	12,500	13,500	16,000
LX ↑	9,500	13,500	16,000	18,000	19,500
LX ↓	8,000	12,000	14,500	16,500	17,500
Extended Warranty	Y	Y	Y	Y	Y
Secret Warranty	Y	Y	Y	Y	Y
Reliability	❶	❶	❶	❷	❷
Air conditioning	❷	❷	❷	❷	❷
Auto. transmission	❶	❶	❶	❶	❶
Body integrity	❶	❶	❷	❷	❷
Braking system	❷	❷	❷	❷	❷
Electrical system	❶	❷	❷	❷	❷
Engines	❶	❶	❶	❶	③
Exhaust/Converter	❶	❷	❷	③	③
Fuel system	❷	❷	③	③	③
Ignition system	❶	❷	❷	③	③
Rust/Paint	③	③	④	④	⑤
Steering	③	③	③	③	④
Suspension	❶	❶	❶	❶	④
Crash Safety	⑤	⑤	⑤	⑤	⑤
Side Impact	—	—	—	—	⑤

FORD/NISSAN

Mercury Villager/Nissan Quest

Rating: Above Average (1997–99); Average (1995–96); Not Recommended (1993–94). More carlike than most of their competitors. The Quest, engineered by Nissan and built by Ford in Ohio, is practically identical to the Villager, except for some slight styling differences, more standard equipment, and a slightly lower rate of depreciation. By choosing a cargo van over a fully loaded wagon, you can save between $1,500 and $2,000. **Maintenance/Repair costs:** Higher than average. Any garage can repair these minivans. **Parts:** Both Mercury and Nissan dealers carry parts, and auto club surveys show that parts are less expensive than those of most other minivans in this class. The exception to this rule: broken engine exhaust manifold studs (a frequent problem), AC, and electrical components. There are plenty of 2- and 3-year-old models on the market that have just come off lease; the Nissan may cost a bit more, however, because it depreciates more slowly than the Villager. Other minivans you may wish to consider: the GM front-drives or Toyota Sienna.

Strengths and weaknesses: The Villager's and the Quest's strongest features are their impressive highway performance (as long as you're not carrying a full load) and easy, no-surprise, carlike handling. Additional assets are a 4-speed automatic transmission that's particularly smooth and quiet, and mechanical components that have been tested for years on the Maxima and various Ford vehicles. The ride on both smooth and uneven highways is comfortable, overall highway stability is above reproach, and braking performance is quite good, aided by standard ABS, which improves directional control by eliminating wheel lockup.

These fuel-thirsty minivans are heavier than the Aerostar by about 700 pounds, and the 3.0L engine has only 6–16 additional horses to carry the extra weight. GM's 2.8L engines produce more torque than what the Villager and Quest can deliver. Precise steering makes the Villager feel more responsive at highway speeds and in emergency manoeuvres than it really is. The control layout can be a bit confusing.

Interior space is impressive. The Villager is nearly a foot longer and two inches wider and higher than Chrysler's short-wheelbase minivans. There's better seating for three adults in the rear than with the Caravan, middle seatbacks fold flat, and the rear seats have tracks that allow them to slide forward all the way to the front or fold flat and convert to a serving area for tailgate parties.

There have been many reports of engine exhaust manifold stud and crankshaft failures (through 1995); electrical problems; brake failures; premature wear of the front disc brakes; and chronic stalling, possibly due to faulty fuel pumps or a shorted electrical system. One owner of a 1993 Villager GS tells of chronic vibrations at 100 km/h that can't be dampened even after frequent tire replacements and suspension re-tuning. Body integrity on model years up to 1996 is sub-par, with doors opening and closing on their own and poor fit and finish, allowing lots of wind noise to enter the interior. (Yes, Ford got the body work, while Nissan handled the mechanicals. You can tell, can't you?) There have also been some reports of panel and paint defects and premature rust-ing on the inside sliding door track.

Model year changes: 1994—A standard driver-side airbag and a Nautica Special Edition. **1995**—Carried over unchanged. **1996**—Motorized shoulder belts are dropped, a passenger-side airbag is added, and the dash and exterior are slightly restyled. **1997**—Buyers of the entry-level GS model may order captain's chairs. **1998**—Carried over unchanged in preparation for the redesigned '99 version. **Villager: 1999**—The Pathfinder's 3.3L V6 replaced the 3.0L V6, giving the Villager and Quest an additional 19 horses. Other changes: a fourth door; more interior room; a revised instrument panel that's easier to reach; restyled front and rear ends; improved shifting, acceleration, and brak-ing (ABS takes less effort and is supposedly more durable); the sus-pension was re-tuned to give a more carlike ride and handling; the old climate control system was ditched for a more sophisticated version with air filtration; and optional ABS was made available with all models. Mercury's top-of-the-line model, the Nautica, was dropped. **Quest: 1999**—An additional 4.6 inches in length and 1.2 inches in width, stan-dard ABS brakes, and a driver-side sliding rear door. The second row of seats can now be removed and the third row is set on tracks. Upgraded headlights and rear leaf springs. Owners gain an extra 10 cubic feet of storage space due to the addition of a cargo shelf behind the rear seats.

Safety summary/Recalls: All models: 1993–97—NHTSA is looking into fuel leaks into the engine compartment or from cracked fuel tank vent hoses that allow gas fumes to infiltrate the interior. **1994–96**—Vehicle suddenly accelerated forward. • Inadvertent airbag deployment. • Sudden stalling due to faulty fuel pump. • Both steering and brakes failed when turning into an intersection. • Steering wheel locked up while making a right turn. • Chronic ABS brake failures, brake pads and rotors need replacing every 5,000 km, and drums often need turn-ing. • Alarm system will lock and unlock the doors on its own. • Remote control door locks often won't respond, trapping occupants inside. • Faulty rear door latch and lock allow the door to come open while driv-ing. • The sliding door opens for no apparent reason. • Power windows often jam. • Seatbelts don't retract properly and ratchet too tightly. • Shoulder belt got caught around child's neck and had to be cut away. • Frequent rear windshield wiper failures. • Solar window at certain angles distorts vision by reflecting images. **1997–99**—Airbags fail to deploy. Power door locks self-activate. • Gas fumes leak into the inte-rior. • Gas pedal sticks. • Sudden acceleration and brake failures (extended stopping distance, noisy when applied). **Recalls: All models: 1992–98**—A faulty fuel pipe vent may cause a fire. **1993**—A faulty brake master cylinder or leaking fuel-filler hoses will be replaced for free. • Defective automatic seatbelt anchor bolts. • Leaves or other debris can accumulate in the fresh-air intake of the heating and AC system, creating a possible fire hazard. **1994–95**—A faulty electrical socket may cause the rear light to fail to operate. • Defective third-row sliding bench seat. **1996**—Power windows aren't in compliance with safety regulations. **1997**—Fuel-line hoses could crack or split. **Villager: 1997–98**—Faulty batteries may rupture or cause a fire.

Secret Warranties/Service Tips

All models/years—A rotten-egg odour coming from the exhaust is probably caused by a malfunctioning catalytic converter, which is covered by Ford's original warranty and the 5-year/80,000 km emissions warranty. • Two components that benefit from Ford's "goodwill" warranty extensions are fuel pumps and computer modules that govern engine, fuel-injection, and transmission functions. **All models: 1993**—Harsh automatic transmission upshifts may be caused by metal contamination in the solenoid assembly. • An inoperative air conditioning blower motor can be fixed by installing a new blower motor resistor. • Stalling whenever the vehicle is shifted from Park to Drive to Reverse may mean that the torque converter is stuck in the "lockup" mode; install an upgraded valve body assembly (#F3XY-7A100-D) and a transaxle oil pan gasket to fix the problem. • A ticking or clicking from the suspension strut area signals the need for an upgraded front strut spacer (#F3XY-3A120-A). • Fogging or frosting of the side windows may be caused by a misconnected C261 electrical connector. • If the Liftgate light/Door Ajar light flickers intermittently or the vehicle won't start, the rear liftgate latch may need to be changed. • A rear suspension clunk or thump when passing over bumps is likely caused by improperly calibrated rear shock absorbers. • Install an upgraded speed control module (#F3XY-9FS12-B) if the vehicle loses 5–8 km/h on hills or grades with the present module. • A clicking or ticking noise when accelerating can be corrected by installing a new EGR tube with a redesigned fitting. • A shudder or vibration that occurs during the 1–2 shift can be corrected by replacing the automatic transaxle valve body with an upgraded valve body and transaxle oil pan gasket. **1993–94**—A squeak or chirp coming from the blower motor can be stopped by installing an upgraded blower motor with improved brush-to-commutator friction. • Sliding door noise may need a new service spring in the upper hinge and a readjustment of the dovetail. • Body squeaks and rattles are thoroughly discussed in TSB #04-86-94. **1993–95**—Ford covered defective engine exhaust manifold studs on a case-by-case basis up to 5 years/100,000 km; owners exceeding these parameters ask for partial compensation. • The rear wiper motor may quit or stop intermittently because water has gotten into the motor printed circuit board. • Replace front brake pads that cause excessive brake squeaking or groaning with upgraded pads. **1993–96**—A crunch/grunt noise from the rear suspension may be caused by rear shackle bushings that need lubrication. **1993–97**—Front door windows that bind may have the glass rubber improperly installed into the door sheet metal channel. **1993–98**—Automatic transmission whining when accelerating may be caused by a faulty transaxle support bracket and insulators. **1993–99**—Inadvertent disabling of the brake shift interlock may occur when emergency vehicles have their brake lights and flashers modified. • Fuel pump may be cause of radio speaker noise. • Paint delamination, peeling, or fading (see Part Two). **1994–98**—If there's a strong fuel odour in the passenger compartment when refueling, it's likely there's a missing sealer between the fuel-filler opening upper flange and the fuel-filler base assembly. • Poor AC performance may be due to a faulty high-pressure cutoff switch. **1995–96**—Ford will replace, at no charge, 3.0L V6 engine blocks that produce excessive engine knock following a cold start, says its Owner Notification Program #96M89. **1995–99**—Tips for correcting windshield water leaks and excessive noise, vibration, and harshness. **1996–98**—Power door locks that intermittently self-activate (help, let me out!) are a common occurrence that's covered in TSB #98-22-5. **1997–98**—Tips on silencing rattles and creaks. • Hard starts, no-starts, stalling, or an exhaust rotten-egg smell can all be corrected by replacing the power control module (PCM) under the emissions warranty. **1997–99**—An exhaust buzz or rattle may be caused by a loose catalyst or muffler heat shield. **1999–2000**—Self-activating power door locks may be caused by a misadjustment of the front door lock linkage, excess solder in the front door power window switch, or water infiltration of a potential open wire harness connection inside the front doors.

Mercury Villager, Quest Profile

	1993	1994	1995	1996	1997	1998	1999
Cost Price ($)							
Villager GS	19,695	21,195	22,595	23,695	24,295	24,595	24,595
Villager LS	24,195	26,195	27,095	28,095	29,195	29,495	29,495
Quest XE/SE	20,231	23,490	24,598	25,598	25,598	25,598	32,498
Quest GXE	25,311	27,290	29,598	30,598	30,898	30,898	27,798
Used Values ($)							
Villager GS ↑	7,500	9,500	11,000	14,000	16,000	19,000	22,000
Villager GS ↓	7,000	9,000	9,500	12,000	14,500	17,500	20,000
Villager LS ↑	8,500	11,000	13,000	15,500	19,000	22,000	25,000
Villager LS ↓	7,500	9,500	11,500	13,500	17,000	20,000	23,000
Quest XE/SE ↑	7,000	9,500	11,500	14,500	17,000	20,000	26,000
Quest XE/SE ↓	6,500	8,500	10,500	12,500	15,000	18,000	25,000
Quest GXE ↑	8,500	11,500	14,000	17,000	19,500	22,000	25,000
Quest GXE ↓	7,000	8,500	12,500	15,000	17,500	20,000	23,000
Extended Warranty	Y	Y	Y	Y	N	N	N
Secret Warranty	Y	Y	Y	Y	Y	Y	Y
Reliability	②	②	③	④	④	④	⑤
Air conditioning	②	②	③	③	③	⑤	⑤
Auto. transmission	③	④	⑤	⑤	⑤	⑤	⑤
Body integrity	①	②	②	②	②	②	③
Braking system	②	②	②	②	②	③	③
Electrical system	①	②	②	②	②	②	③

Engines	➋	➋	③	③	④	⑤	⑤
Exhaust/Converter	➊	➋	③	③	④	⑤	⑤
Fuel system	③	③	③	④	⑤	⑤	⑤
Ignition system	③	④	④	⑤	⑤	⑤	⑤
Rust/Paint	➋	➋	③	④	④	④	⑤
Steering	③	④	⑤	⑤	⑤	⑤	⑤
Suspension	③	③	③	④	④	⑤	⑤
Crash Safety	④	④	④	④	④	—	—

GENERAL MOTORS

Astro, Safari

Rating: Above Average (1998–99); Average (1996–97); Not Recommended (1985–95). These vehicles are more mini-truck than minivan. Believe it or not, these run-of-the-mill minivans are beginning to look quite good when compared to the powertrain-challenged Chrysler and Ford minivans. They have fewer safety-related problems reported to the government, are easy to repair, and cost little to acquire. Stay away from the unreliable AWD models; they're expensive to repair and not very durable. **Maintenance/Repair costs:** Average. Any garage can repair these rear-drive minivans. **Parts:** Plentiful and reasonably priced. As with the Aerostar, the classified ads are jam-packed with sellers wanting to unload their Astros and Safaris simply because their vehicles have got high mileage or the owners are small businesses whose needs have moved up to a larger van. Whatever the reason, you can find some real bargains if you're patient. Other choices you may wish to consider: the later-model Ford Aerostar or a full-sized GM or Ford van.

Strengths and weaknesses: Introduced during the 1985 model year, these minivans are basically trucks dressed in minivan garb. Nevertheless, these spacious vans can be fitted to tow up to 2,700 kg (6,000 lb.) and carry eight people. The base 4.3L V6 gives acceptable acceleration, but the High Output variant of the same engine (first available in the 1991 model) is a far better choice, particularly when it's mated to a manual gearbox. The full-time AWD versions aren't very refined, have a high fail-ure rate, and are expensive to diagnose and repair.

Early versions suffer from failure-prone automatic transmissions, a poor braking system, and fragile steering components. The early base V6 provides ample power, but also produces lots of noise, consumes excessive amounts of fuel, and tends to have leaking head gaskets and failure-prone oxygen sensors. These computer-related problems often rob the engine of sufficient power to keep up in traffic. While the 5-speed manual transmis-sion shifts fairly easily, the automatic takes forever to downshift on the highway. Handling isn't particularly agile on these minivans, and the power steering doesn't provide the driver with enough road feel. Unloaded, the Astro provides very poor traction, the ride isn't comfortable on poor road surfaces, and interior noise is rampant. Many drivers find the driving position awkward (no left-leg room) and the heating/defrosting system inadequate. Many engine components are hidden under the dashboard, making repair or maintenance awkward.

Even on more recent models, highway performance and overall reliability remain mediocre. Through the 2000 model year, the 4-speed automatic transmissions are clunky, though much more reliable than the Ford or Chrysler gearboxes. Excessive rear-end clunking and clanging occurs whenever the transmission shifts or downshifts while under load. One worker at GM's Oshawa, Ontario, plant—a 1993 Safari owner—wrote GM's president the following angry letter:

> Do you as CEO really know what's going on or does middle management filter out the bad news? GM's policy on warranty service is atrocious, your service representative was rude and your parts are substandard....Your bulletin 93-4A-101, "Discouraging dealers from attempting to repair driveline clunk," is weaseling out on your responsibilities to the customer...

Other owners report that the front suspension, steering components, computer modules, and catalytic converter can wear out within as little as 60,000 km. There have also been lots of complaints about electrical, exhaust, cooling, and fuel system bugs; inadequate heating/defrosting; and axle seals wearing out every 12–18 months. Many owners write that they've had to endure a rotten-egg smell coming from the exhaust. Body hardware is fragile, and fit and finish is the pits. One 1994 Safari owner, frustrated by chronic water leaks, replaced the rear hatch moulding three times without any improvement. Squeaks and rattles are legion and hard to locate. Sliding-door handles often break off and the sliding door frequently jams in cold temperatures. The hatch release for the Dutch doors occasionally doesn't work and the driver-side vinyl seat lining tears apart. Premature paint peeling/delamination and surface rust are fairly common.

1995–99 models have similar problems as earlier years, with stalling, hard starts (see "Secret Warranties/Service Tips"), and expensive and frequent automatic transmission, power steering, wheel bearing, brake pad, caliper, and rotors repairs heading the list.

Model year changes: 1995—An extended body and a 190-hp V6. **1996**—A standard passenger-side airbag, a torquier V6, spark plugs touted to last 160,000 km, a new engine cover that gives more leg room, and an upgraded dash. **1997**—Speed-sensitive power steering. **1998**—Carried over unchanged, except for the introduction of a new automatic transmission. **1999**—Depowered airbags, a new standard anti-theft system, and an upgraded AWD active transfer case.

Safety summary/Recalls: All models: 1990–91—There were 31 complaints of dashboard fires recorded by NHTSA. **1995–98**—Fire ignited under the dashboard. • Headlight switch shorted out, resulting in a fire. • Driver-side airbag failed to deploy. • Vehicle continues to accelerate after foot is removed from accelerator. • Frequent stalling. • Erratic engine performance due to blocked catalytic converter. • Engine leaks oil. • Loose fan belts come off, causing loss of power steering and brakes. • Frequent brake failures. • Loss of braking when going over a bump. • ABS failed to engage. • ABS suddenly engaged for no reason and then wouldn't disengage. • ABS hesitates when applied. • Defective brake calipers. • Power brake hose fell off, causing loss of power brakes. • Front brake hoses collapsed, causing sudden brake failure. • Premature front brake wear. • Power-steering lockup. • Power-steering hose fell off, causing loss of power steering. • Power-steering fluid leaks. • Vehicle jerks to one side when braking. • Front wheels lock up when turning the steering wheel to the right from a stop while in gear. • Steering stuck when turning. • Seatbelts fail to work properly. • Shoulder belt failed to restrain driver in collision. • When the middle seat is removed, the seatbelt that is attached permanently to the headliner swings freely in the passenger compartment. • There is no room to latch the seatbelt. • Passenger-side seatbelt tightens up with every movement. • Seatbelt locks up unexpectedly. • Bench seatbelts are too short and cannot be adjusted. • Fresh-air ventilation system allows fumes from other vehicles to enter interior compartment. • With jack almost fully extended, wheel doesn't lift off ground. • Spare tire not safe for driving over 60 km/h. • Design of horn makes it difficult to use. • Horn buttons require excessive pressure to activate them. • Driver-side window failure. • Sliding door suddenly fell off. • Faulty door hinges allow the door to fall off. • Sliding door rattles. • Front passenger door won't close. • Passenger-side door glass fell out. • Rear hatch latch release failed. • Rear hatch hydraulic rods are too weak to support hatch. • Front passenger's seat reclining mechanism failed. • Poor traction. • Parked in gear and rolled downhill. • Transmission failures. • Left rear axle seal leaks, causing lubricant to burn on brake lining. • Excessive rear-end axle noise. • Sudden wheel bearing failure. • AC clutch fell apart. • Alternator bearing failure. • Windshield wipers fail intermittently. **1999**—Only 58 safety-related complaints compared with an average of a few hundred for most vehicles. Many of the 1999 model problems have been reported by owners of earlier model years, which isn't surprising since these vehicles have changed little over the years. • Airbag failed to deploy. • Chronic stalling can't be remedied by dealers. • Check Engine light is constantly lit and engines continues to misfire. • Difficult starting. • Hard shifting between first and second gear; transmission slippage. • Delayed shifting or stalling when passing from Drive to Reverse. • Leaking axle seals. • ABS brake failure; brakes grab suddenly or cause sudden lurching to the left or right when they're applied. • Premature front brake pad, calipers, and rotor wear causes extended stopping distance. • Early wheel bearing replacement. • Steering binds when turning and steering components aren't durable (pumps, gear boxes, and pressure lines). • Rear cargo door hinge and latch slipped off and door opened 180 degrees. • Floor mat moves under brake and accelerator pedals. • Brake pedal set too close to the accelerator. • Fuel gauge failure caused by faulty sending unit. **Recalls: All models: 1985–91**—The seatback may recline suddenly. **1995**—Possible separation of control arm from the frame. • Vehicles with the L35 engine may have fuel-line leakage. **1996–97**—Outboard seatbelt webbing on right rear bucket seat can separate during a crash. **1996–98**—Defective child safety seat attaching belts. **1997**—Defective right-hand rear bucket seatbelt webbing.

Secret Warranties/Service Tips

All models: 1985–93—Vehicles equipped with a Hydramatic 4L60 transmission that buzzes when the car is in Reverse or idle may need a new oil-pressure regulator valve. • A power-steering hiss can be silenced by replacing the power-steering valve assembly. **1988–92**—Hydramatic 4L60/700R4 automatic transmission may click or whine in third or fourth gear. There may also be a rattling noise coming from the rear of the transmission. Correct by installing five new fibre plates in the Low and Reverse clutch. The new plates have a different groove configuration that prevents third and fourth gear vibration. **1989–91**—THM 700-R4 automatic transmissions may exhibit a no-Reverse or delayed-Reverse condition in cold weather. This problem can be corrected by replacing the piston outer seal with a long lip design. If this design is already being used or there's no improvement, change the Reverse input clutch housing. • A binding sliding door requires the replacement of the centre track rolling bracket, the centre track assembly, and the lower track striker/bumper assembly. **1992–94**—The PCV hose may freeze, causing oil starvation to the engine and leading to engine failure. Alaska owners are eligible for free higher-flow calibrated PCVs under the emissions warranty. All other cold-weather operators are supposed to be told of the problem and given free servicing on a case-by-case basis. **1992–95**—A GM service campaign will install free ABS software to improve braking. **1993–94**—A faulty speedometer, inability to shift down into second gear, or a transmission stuck in second gear may all be corrected by replacing the C240 connector. • Poor cold starting can be traced to a defective fuel pump relay. **1993–95**—Malfunctioning gauges and driveability problems may be the result of a short circuit caused by the C110 connector wire rubbing against the AC accumulator pipe. **1993–2000**—GM says that a chronic driveline clunk can't be silenced and is a normal characteristic of its vehicles. **1993–99**—Tips on getting rid of AC odours. • Defective catalytic converters that cause a rotten-egg smell may be replaced free of charge under the vehicle's emissions warranty. • Paint delamination, peeling, or fading (see Part Two). **1995–2000**—Dealer guidelines for brake servicing under warranty. **1996–97**—Excessive engine noise can be curtailed by installing an upgraded valve stem oil seal. **1996–98**—Rough engine performance may be caused by a water-contaminated oxygen sensor, and a rough idle shortly after starting may be caused by sticking poppet valves. • Accessory drivebelt noise is likely caused by a misaligned power-steering pump pulley. **1996–2000**—A hard start, no-start, backfire, and kickback when starting may be corrected by replacing the crankshaft position sensor. • Silence a boom-type noise heard during engine warm-up by installing an exhaust dampener assembly. • A rough idle after start and/or a Service Engine light that stays lit may mean you have a stuck injector poppet valve ball that needs cleaning. **1997–98**—An engine ticking noise that appears when the temperature falls may require an EVAP purge solenoid valve. **1997–99**—A hard start, no-start, and rough idle can be fixed by replacing the fuel tank fill pipe assembly and cleaning the SCPI poppet valves. **1999**—Steering column squeaking can be silenced by replacing the steering wheel SIR module coil assembly. **1999–2000**—If the engine runs hot, overheats, or loses coolant, try polishing the radiator filler neck or replacing the radiator cap before letting any mechanic convince you that more expensive repairs are needed.

Astro, Safari Profile

	1992	1993	1994	1995	1996	1997	1998	1999
Cost Price ($)								
Cargo	16,798	17,638	18,198	22,640	23,475	25,110	25,110	23,290
CS/base	18,500	19,528	19,998	23,295	25,285	26,920	26,920	23,839
Used Values ($)								
Cargo ↑	3,500	4,000	5,500	7,500	10,000	11,500	15,500	18,500
Cargo ↓	3,000	3,500	5,000	6,500	8,500	10,000	13,500	16,500
CS/base ↑	5,000	6,000	7,500	10,500	13,000	15,500	17,500	20,500
CS/base ↓	4,000	5,000	6,500	9,000	11,000	14,500	16,500	18,500
Extended Warranty	Y	Y	Y	Y	Y	Y	N	N
Secret Warranty	Y	Y	Y	Y	Y	Y	Y	Y
Reliability	❶	❷	❷	❷	❷	③	③	④
Air conditioning	❷	❷	❷	❷	❷	③	④	④
Auto. transmission	③	③	③	③	③	③	③	③
Body integrity	❶	❶	❶	❶	❶	❶	❷	❷
Braking system	❶	❶	❶	❷	❷	❷	❷	③
Electrical system	❶	❶	❶	❶	❶	❶	③	③
Engines	③	③	③	④	④	④	⑤	⑤
Exhaust/Converter	❷	❷	❷	③	④	④	④	④
Fuel system	④	④	④	④	④	④	④	④
Ignition system	❶	❶	❷	❷	❷	③	④	④

Rust/Paint	①	①	①	①	①	①	②	②
Steering	②	③	③	③	③	④	④	④
Suspension	②	②	②	②	②	③	③	④
Crash Safety	①	①	①	—	③	③	③	③

Lumina, Lumina APV, Montana, Trans Sport, Venture

Rating: Above Average (1997–99); Average (1995–96); Not Recommended (1990–94). The Lumina's last model year was 1996; the Trans Sport was carried over to the 1998 model year. The Venture debuted as a 1997 model. The 1997–98 model ratings have been raised because owners have reported fewer powertrain problems. Pontiac dropped the Trans Sport for the '99 Montana moniker; before that, Montana was the name of a popular options package sold with the Trans Sport. **Maintenance/Repair costs:** Higher than average, but any garage can repair these minivans. **Parts:** Plentiful, but costly. Plastic body panels may soon be in short supply. There are plenty of reasonably priced 2- and 3-year-old models that have just come off lease on the market. Other minivans you may wish to consider: the Mercury Villager, Nissan Quest, or Toyota Sienna.

Strengths and weaknesses: Although the 1994 and later models have less of a Dustbuster look, GM's plastic-bodied, front-drive minivan resembles more a swoopy station wagon than the traditional minivan (like the popular, boxy Chrysler Caravan). These vehicles use the Chevrolet Lumina platform, and therefore have more carlike handling than GM's Astro and Safari. Seating is limited to five adults in the standard models (two up front and three on a removable bench seat), but this can be increased to seven if you order optional modular seats. Seats can be folded down flat, creating additional storage space. Incidentally, be careful not to drop your keys between the windshield and the dash because you'll need a fishing rod to get them back.

The chassis and mechanical components on early models come from GM's W-bodies (Lumina, Regal, Cutlass Supreme, and Grand Prix), which explains why these minivans had so many of the same factory-related defects as their smaller cousins—notably, electronic module (PROM) and starter failures; short circuits that burn out alternators, batteries, power door lock activators, and the blower motor; AC evaporator core failures; premature wearout of the inner and outer tie-rods; automatic transmission breakdowns; abysmal fit and finish; chronic sliding door malfunctions; and faulty rear seat latches. Other problems include a 4-speed automatic transmission that isn't as durable as the less fuel-efficient 3-speed automatic; a poorly mounted sliding door; side door glass that pops open; squeaks, rattles, and clunks in the instrument panel cluster area and suspension; and a wind buffeting noise around the front doors. By the way, don't trust the towing limit listed in GM's owner's manual. Automakers publish tow ratings that are on the optimistic side—and sometimes they even lie. Also, don't be surprised to find that the base 3.1L engine doesn't handle a full load of passenger and cargo, especially when mated to the 3-speed automatic transmission. The ideal powertrain combo would be the 4-speed automatic coupled to the optional "3800" V6 (first used on the 1996 versions).

The large dent- and rust-resistant plastic panels are robot-bonded to the frame with unique new adhesives, and they absorb engine and road noise very well, in addition to having an impressive record for durability. Some body shops complain, however, that the innovative panels are in short supply and that damaged panels can't be recycled. This drives up the cost of repairs and tempts insurance adjusters to simply write off repairable vehicles.

Model year changes: 1995—Carried over unchanged. **1996**—A new standard 3.4L V6, and the Lumina is replaced by the Venture at the end of the model year. **1997**—Optional driver-side sliding door on extended versions and standard dual airbags and ABS. **1998**—Sliding driver-side door available on more models, and side airbags are offered for the first time. **1999**—A five horsepower boost to the base V6 engine (185-hp), heated rear-view mirrors, and the debut of a Premiere model that offers a mobile entertainment centre that includes a videocassette player and colour monitor. **Venture:** Depowered airbags, upgraded electronically controlled automatic transmission, and a standard rear-window defogger.

Safety summary/Recalls: Some front door–mounted seatbelts cross uncomfortably at the neck. • A nasty blind spot on the driver's side should be corrected with a small stick-on convex mirror • NHTSA has closed an investigation of transaxle hose separation in exchange for GM's promise to conduct a regional recall. The agency has opened a probe of airbag ttearing upon deployment with 1998–99 models. **All models: 1995–99**—The following safety-related complaints have been reported year after year to NHTSA; recalls haven't fixed all the model years where the safety defects have been reported: sudden steering loss in rainy weather or when passing over a puddle (serpentine belt slippage); ABS brake failures; ABS light stays on for no reason; airbags fail to deploy; sliding doors suddenly open, close, come off their tracks, jam shut, stick open, injure children, and rattle; fire may ignite around the fuel filler nozzle or within the ignition switch; tie-rod failures may cause loss of control; during highway driving, transmission slips from Drive into Neutral, losing all forward motion. • Other recurrent 1995–99 safety complaints: transmission won't hold gear on a grade; headlight assembly collects moisture, burns bulb, or falls out; seatback suddenly collapses; windshield wipers fail intermittently; accelerator and brake pedals are too close together; fuel slosh/clunk when vehicle stops or accelerates (new tank useless); self-activating door locks lock occupants out or in; door handles break inside the door assembly; horn is hard to access; window latch failures. **Recalls: 1995**—The throttle cable support bracket needs to be replaced in order to enable the engine to decelerate. • Steering could fail. • Brake pedal arm could fracture. **1998**—Vehicle may roll away while in Park. • Install safety guards on seat latches.

Secret Warranties/Service Tips

All models: 1990–94—An engine ticking at idle can be traced to rattling piston pins, which must be replaced with upgraded parts. **1990–98**—An oil odour coming from the engine compartment may be eliminated by changing the crankshaft rear main oil seal. **1992–93**—No Reverse gear or slipping in Reverse can be corrected by installing an upgraded Low/Reverse clutch return spring and spiral retaining ring. **1992–94**—Loss of Drive or erratic shifts may be caused by an intermittent short to ground on the A or B shift solenoid, or an electrical short circuit in the transaxle. • A front-end clunking noise when driving over rough roads may require the repositioning of the diagonal radiator support braces. • A front-end engine knock troubleshooting chart is found in TSB #306001. **1993–94**—Owners who complain of automatic transmission low-speed miss, hesitation, chuggle, or skip may find relief with an improved MEMCAL module that GM developed to remedy the problem. **1993–95**—An engine coolant leak from the throttle body assembly may require an upgraded service seal kit. **1993–99**—Tips on eliminating AC odours. • Defective catalytic converters that cause a rotten-egg smell in the interior may be replaced free of charge under the emissions warranty. • Paint delamination, peeling, or fading (see Part Two). **1993–2000**—GM says that a chronic driveline clunk can't be silenced and is a normal characteristic of its vehicles. **1994**—Lazy front seatbelt retractors will be replaced free of charge. • A liftgate that fails to lock may have a loose or missing lock cylinder lock-out pin. • Manual sliding side doors that stick shut require a lock replacement. **1995**—A thud/clunk noise occurs when the fuel tank is more than three-quarters full; GM will replace the fuel tank and sender assembly. **1995–96**—Intermittent Neutral/loss of Drive at highway speeds can be fixed by replacing the control valve body assembly. **1995–2000**—Dealer guidelines for brake servicing under warranty. **1996–98**—A cold-engine tick or rattle after start-up can be silenced by installing all six pistons with pin assemblies. **1997**—Rear brake clicking or squealing may be caused by a misadjusted parking brake cable. • Brakes that don't work, drag, heat up, or wear out early may have a variety of causes, all outlined in TSB #73-50-27. • A rear suspension thud or clunk may be silenced by installing upgraded rear springs. **1997–98**—A fuel tank thud or clunk noise may require new fuel tank straps and insulators. • Loose lumber noise coming from the rear of the vehicle when it passes over bumps means upgraded rear shock absorbers are required. • Poor rear windshield wiper performance may require that the fluid line be purged. • Windshield wiper blade chatter can be reduced by changing the wiper arm. • Insufficient windshield clearing in defrost mode requires the installation of new seals. **1997–99**—Upgraded front disc pads will reduce brake squeal (see following illustration).

Front Disk Brake Pads Interim Design Change
Bulletin No.: 99-05-23-004
Date: April, 1999
INFORMATION
Subject:
Front Disk Brake Pads (Shoe/Lining Assemblies) Interim Design Change for Brake Squeal
Models:
1997–99 Buick Century, Park Avenue, Regal, Riviera
1997–99 Cadillac DeVille, Eldorado, Seville
1997–99 Chevrolet Venture
1997–99 Oldsmobile Aurora, Silhouette
1998–99 Oldsmobile Intrigue
1997–99 Pontiac Grand Prix, Montana, Trans Sport

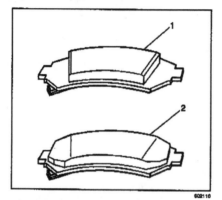

This pad lining configuration change (1) has shown to
provide a significant reduction in brake squeal during
light brake applications in comparison to the original
design (2).

1997–2000—Front door windows that are inoperative, slow, or noisy may need the window run channel adjusted or replaced, in addition to new weather stripping. **1998**—No-start, engine miss, and rough idle may indicate that melted slush has contaminated the fuel system. **1998–99**—An inoperative sliding door may have a defective control module. **1998–2000**—Poor AC performance in humid weather may be caused by an undercharged AC system. **1999–2000**—If the engine runs hot, overheats, or loses coolant, try polishing the radiator filler neck or replacing the radiator cap before considering more expensive repairs. An automatic transmission that whines in Park or Neutral, or a Service Engine light that stays on, may signal the need for a new drive sprocket support bearing. **1999**—Diagnostic tips for an automatic transmission that slips, produces a harsh upshift and garage shifts, or causes acceleration shudders.

Lumina, Lumina APV, Montana, Trans Sport, Venture Profile

	1992	1993	1994	1995	1996	1997	1998	1999
Cost Price ($)								
Lumina Cargo	16,698	17,398	17,998	20,110	20,110	—	—	—
Passenger	18,098	18,798	19,598	22,730	22,730	—	—	—
Montana	—	—	—	—	—	—	—	25,130
Trans Sport/SE	18,950	19,698	20,298	23,475	23,475	23,690	24,650	—
Venture	—	—	—	—	—	23,185	24,145	24,725
Used Values ($)								
Lumina Cargo ↑	4,000	6,000	5,000	6,500	8,500	—	—	—
Lumina Cargo ↓	3,000	5,500	4,500	5,500	7,500	—	—	—
Passenger ↑	5,000	6,500	7,500	10,000	12,000	—	—	—
Passenger ↓	4,500	5,500	6,500	8,500	10,000	—	—	—
Montana ↑	—	—	—	—	—	—	—	20,000
Montana ↓	—	—	—	—	—	—	—	18,000
Trans Sport/SE ↑	5,500	6,500	8,000	10,500	13,000	16,000	18,000	—
Trans Sport/SE ↓	4,500	5,500	6,500	9,500	11,000	14,000	16,000	—
Venture ↑	—	—	—	—	—	15,000	18,000	20,000
Venture ↓	—	—	—	—	—	13,500	16,000	18,000
Extended Warranty	Y	Y	Y	Y	Y	Y	Y	Y
Secret Warranty	Y	Y	Y	Y	Y	Y	Y	Y
Reliability	❶	❷	❷	❷	③	③	④	⑤
Air conditioning	❶	❷	③	③	④	④	④	⑤
Auto. transmission	③	③	③	❷	❷	❷	③	④
Body integrity	❶	❶	❶	❷	❷	❷	❷	❷
Braking system	❶	❷	❷	❷	❷	❷	③	④
Electrical system	❶	❶	❶	❷	❷	❷	③	③
Engines	③	④	④	④	④	④	④	⑤
Exhaust/Converter	③	④	④	④	④	④	④	⑤
Fuel system	④	④	④	④	⑤	⑤	⑤	⑤
Ignition system	❶	❷	❷	③	④	⑤	⑤	⑤
Rust/Paint	❶	❶	❶	❷	③	④	④	⑤
Steering	④	④	④	④	④	④	④	⑤
Suspension	❷	❷	③	③	③	④	⑤	⑤
Crash Safety	④	④	⑤	⑤	④	④	④	④
Side Impact	—	—	—	—	—	—	⑤	⑤

HONDA

Odyssey

Rating: Above Average (1999); Below Average (1996–98). Be wary of Honda's poor-quality sliding doors; they're both dangerous and unreliable. The only reason early Odysseys don't get a better rating is their small engine and interior—identical shortcomings embodied by Mazda's recently revised MPV minivan. Consider these smartly styled, fuel-efficient vehicles as full-sized, urban station wagons rather than highway-hauling minivans. The '99 model offered better performance and a larger interior, but it suffered from many first-year glitches. Ditch the original equipment Firestone tires: you don't need the extra risk. **Maintenance/Repair costs:** Higher than average, but any garage can repair these minivans. **Parts:** Limited supply and costly. There aren't many reasonably priced three-year-old Odysseys on the market. If you can't afford to wait, consider the Mercury Villager, Nissan Axxess (see Appendix I) and Quest, or the Toyota Sienna.

Strengths and weaknesses: One can sum up the strengths and weaknesses of the 1996–98 Odyssey (and its American twin through the 1998 model, the Isuzu Oasis) in three words: performance, performance, performance. You get carlike performance and handling, responsive steering, and a comfortable ride, offset by slow-as-molasses-in-January acceleration with a full load, a raucous engine, and limited passenger/cargo space due to the narrow body.

The 1996–98 Odysseys have proven to be more reliable and offer better handling than American rear-drive, truck-inspired minivans. But their high price on the used-car market, weak 2.2L 4-cylinder engine (given 10 extra horses in the '98 version), and small dimensions can't compete with GM's front-drive, or most rear-drive competitors. The upgraded 1999 models have powerful 6-cylinder engines and a larger interior, wiping out most of the previous model's deficiencies. The drivetrain, though, is a bit rougher than Toyota's Sienna and doesn't feel capable of handling as heavy a load. The timing chain may also have to be replaced frequently.

Like the Accord, component quality and assembly are fairly good, with some notable and hazardous exceptions, like failure-prone sliding doors. Imagine, they open when they shouldn't, won't close when they should, catch fingers and arms, get stuck open or closed, are noisy, and frequently require expensive servicing. Other potential problem areas are automatic transmissions, front brakes (premature wear and noise—see "Secret Warranties/Service Tips"), and trim and accessory items that come loose, break away, or malfunction. Phil Bailey, master mechanic and owner of Bailey's garage in Lachine, Quebec, recently sent me the following email alert:

You may be interested to know that Honda Odyssey transmissions appear to be almost as bad as Chrysler's! I now have 3 clients who have had transmissions replaced under warranty. In one case, a client has had his whole vehicle replaced 3 times. 1999, 2000, and now, a 2001. Looks like Honda rushed to market without their usual thoroughness....

As stated earlier, poor-quality body and trim items are commonplace. For example, the roof rack may fall off, "magic" seat may not fold flat when inserted into well, side windows and seats rattle, door seals come off, and loose front windshield gasket produces excessive wind noise.

Dealer servicing has come in for a great deal of criticism from *Lemon-Aid* readers. Owners complain that recall repairs take an eternity to perform due to parts shortages and dealers reluctant or unable to perform the required tasks. "Goodwill" refunds are also hard to come by because of Honda's failure to sufficiently empower dealers to take the initiative.

Model year changes: 1996—Isuzu markets the Odyssey as its own Oasis in the U.S. **1997**—Small improvements that include intermittent windshield wipers. **1998**—A new 3.0L V6 and 2.3L engine, a revised chassis, and a restyled grille and instrument panel make their debut. **1999**—A new, powerful engine and increased size make this Below Average–rated minivan an Above Average buy. Nevertheless, seats are still too firm, steering requires fully extended arms, power sliding doors operate slowly, and the cupholder under the radio is useless.

Safety summary/Recalls: All models: Cannot secure a child safety seat with the vehicle's seatbelts; too much play in the lapbelt. **1995**—Airbag failed to deploy. • Front two wheels separated from car while driving. • When vehicle is going over a hill, the cruise control has a tendency to overshoot the set speed by almost 10 km/h. • AC doesn't cool the vehicle sufficiently and it puts out a nasty odour. • Defroster can't clear up fogged windows. • Due to its design, the muffler can suddenly fly off while the vehicle is underway. • Far rear seatbelt retracted so tightly that it had to be cut to free the passenger. • Rear middle seatbelt slips and won't stay snug around the lap. **1996**—Airbags failed to deploy. • While backing out the vehicle, occupant turned AC on: vehicle shot forward with no brakes. • Cruise control failed while vehicle was going uphill. **1997**—Sudden acceleration upon brake application. • Minivan was put in Drive, and AC was turned on: vehicle suddenly accelerated, brakes failed, and the minivan hit a brick wall. • Both front airbags failed to deploy in a head-on collision. **1999**—Sudden, unintended acceleration due to stuck accelerator. • Fire erupted in the electrical harness. • Another fire erupted as vehicle was getting fuel. • Plastic gas tank cracks, leaks fuel. • Gasoline smell when transmission is put into

Reverse. • Side window exploded while driving. • Check Engine light comes on and vehicle loses all power. • Engine and electrical shutdown when coming to a stop. • When driving, all the instrument panel lights will suddenly go out (faulty multiplex controller suspected). • When parked on a hill, vehicle may roll backward; transmission doesn't hold vehicle when stopped at a light on a hill and foot is taken off accelerator or brake. • Complete loss of power steering due to a pinhole in the power steering return hose. • Poor power steering performance in cold weather. • Frequent reports of total brake failure. • ABS bangs when engages, but isn't very effective in stopping the vehicle. • Premature failure of the brake pads and master cylinder. • Brake fading after successive stops. • Many incidents of sudden tire tread separation (Firestone). • Power door locks lock and unlock on their own. • Sliding door is difficult to close and may open suddenly when passing over a pothole (in spite of recall repairs). • Many incidents where power sliding door stop didn't work, crushing fingers and arms. • Design of the gear shifter interferes with the radio controls. • Child unable to get out of seatbelt due to buckle lockup. • Faulty fuel gauge. • Inconvenient cell phone jack location. **Recalls: All models: 1997–98**—Faulty ball joints may cause sudden deceleration or loss of steering control. **1999**—Faulty sliding doors, wire harness, and resonator chamber.

Secret Warranties/Service Tips

All models/years—Most of Honda's TSBs allow for special warranty consideration on a "goodwill" basis by the company's District Service Manager or Zone Office, even after the warranty has expired or the vehicle has changed hands. **All models: 1995–97**—In a settlement with the U.S. Environmental Protection Agency, Honda paid fines totaling $17.1 million (U.S.) and extended its emissions warranty on 1.6 million 1995–97 models to 14 years/150,000 miles (see page 63). Canadian owners may wish to use this settlement as leverage for free repairs in Canada, or use the full terms of the settlement when visiting the U.S. One thing is certain: Neither Transport Canada nor Environment Canada are sufficiently enthused to render any assistance. • Rear wheel bearing noise can be silenced by replacing the hub bearing assembly and hub caps. • If the driver's seat makes a clicking noise, you may need to install a stop in the rear seat rail. **1997**—If the Tailgate Open indicator light stays on, you may need to replace the tailgate latch assembly. • Distorted sound from the front speakers can be corrected only by installing new speakers. **1997–98**—If the blower motor works only on high speed, try replacing the blower motor and resistor. **1998**—The squeaking sun visor only requires a bit of wool felt to keep the peace. **1999**—Insufficient EGR flow causing poor engine performance or a DTC PO401 code reading has prompted Honda to carry out a free service campaign whereby the company will replace at no charge, the rear intake manifold end plate and gasket, the PCV hose, and the intake manifold cover.• Excessive front brake noise will be silenced under a "goodwill" repair if you get Honda's permission first, says TSB #99013. This correction involves refinishing the front discs and installing new pads. • There's an incredibly large number of sliding door problems covered by a recall and a plethora of service bulletins that are simply too numerous to print here. Ask Honda politely for the bulletins or "goodwill" assistance. If refused, subpoena the documents through small claims court. Normally, ALLDATA would supply the data for $20 (U.S.), but Honda USA has enjoined the company from giving out bulletin information to its customers. Shameful! • Problems with the fuel tank pressure sensor are covered in TSB # 99-056 and could call for the installation of an inline orifice in the two-way valve vacuum hose. • AC knocking may require the installation of a new compressor clutch set. • Front windows that bind or are noisy when activated require that a mechanic inspect the window regulator guide rail for proper lubrication, and possibly replace the glass run channel and adjust the glass channels. • An inaccurate fuel gauge is likely caused by a faulty sending unit.

Odyssey Profile

	1996	1997	1998	1999
Cost Price ($)				
Base	28,795	28,995	29,800	30,600
Used Values ($)				
Base ↑	14,000	16,500	19,500	22,500
Base ↓	12,500	15,000	18,000	21,000
Extended Warranty	N	N	N	N
Secret Warranty	Y	Y	Y	Y
Reliability	⑤	⑤	⑤	⑤
Crash Safety	④	④	—	⑤

MAZDA

MPV

Rating: Average (1996–98); Below Average (1988–95). The MPV is a good performer hobbled by poor reliability and servicing, yet there are remarkably few safety-related complaints in NHTSA's database. The 1997–98 models have lots of potential, if they don't fall apart as they age. There was no '99 model. **Maintenance/Repair costs:** Higher than average, but any garage can repair these minivans. **Parts:** Limited supply and sometimes costly. There are plenty of reasonably priced 2- and 3-year-old models on the market that have just come off lease. Be wary of earlier high-mileage versions, though; they tend to deteriorate fairly rapidly after the first few years. Other minivans you may wish to consider: a late-model GM Trans Sport, Silhouette, or Venture, Honda Odyssey, Mercury Villager, Nissan Quest, or Toyota Sienna.

Strengths and weaknesses: Handling and overall highway performance put the MPV in the top third of the minivan pack, but the poor winter handling, below-average reliability of early models that are no longer under warranty, "take it or leave it" handling of warranty claims, mediocre servicing, and high fuel and parts costs make pre-1996 versions below-average buys when it comes to overall operating costs.

The 5-speed manual transmission shifts easily and has well-spaced gears, but it's relatively rare. The automatic performs fairly well but sometimes hesitates before going into gear at about 25 km/h and again at 50 km/h. Steering is crisp and predictable. Rear-drive setup makes for easy load-carrying and trailer-towing. The base 2.6L 16-valve 121-hp 4-cylinder engine is a dog, especially when hooked up to the automatic 4-speed transmission that robs it of what little power it has. The 3.0L 6-cylinder engine, on the other hand, delivers snappy acceleration with the front-drive, and impressive acceleration with the 4X4.

Overheating and head gasket failures are commonplace with the 4-banger, and the temperature gauge warns you only when it's too late. Some cases of chronic engine knocking in cold weather with the 3.0L have been fixed by installing tighter-fitting, Teflon-coated pistons. Valve lifter problems are also common with this engine. Winter driving is compromised by the MPV's light rear end and mediocre traction. Low ground clearance means that off-road excursions shouldn't be too adventurous.

Owners report that the electronic computer module (ECU), automatic transmission driveshaft, upper shock mounts, front 4X4 drive axles and lash adjusters, AC core, and radiator fail within the first three years. Cold temperatures tend to "fry" the automatic window motor, and the paint is easily chipped and flakes off early, especially around the hood, tailgate, and front fenders. Premature brake caliper and rotor wear, and excessive vibration/pulsation are chronic problem areas (repairs are needed about every 12,000 km). Premature paint peeling afflicting white-coloured MPVs is quite common.

Model year changes: 1995—Base engine has been upgraded to a 155-hp 3.0L V6. **1996**—Standard passenger airbag, four-wheel ABS, and four-door convenience. **1997**—Lots of sporty cladding, but nothing substantial is changed. **1998**—Carried over unchanged, until the redesigned 2000 model's launch in the spring of '99.

Technical service bulletins: All models: 1994—Rough idle on warm restart. • Tips for troubleshooting excessive engine noise. • Loose, rattling outer door handles. • Tips for troubleshooting premature automatic transmission planetary failures. • Soft shifts. • Gear slips under heavy throttle. • Brake pulsation repair tips. • Steering column squeaks. • Slightly off-centre steering column. **1995**—Brake pulsation repair. • Loose, rattling outer door handles. • Slightly off-centre steering wheel. • Tips for troubleshooting excessive engine noise. **1996–98**—Brake pulsation repair tips. • Front power window noise. • Wind noise around doors. • Steering wheel a bit off centre. • Water leak from sunroof.

Safety summary: All models: 1998—Lots of buffeting about by strong winds. • Airbags failed to deploy. • Rear anti-sway bar brackets snapped off from rear axle housing. • ABS brake failure. • Defective gas cap causes the false activation of the Check Engine light. **Recalls: All models: 1989**—Rear brake shoes may fail. **1989–91**—Takata seatbelt replacement. **1990–91**—Rear brakes may be too aggressive when braking at low speeds, causing the rear wheels to lock up with a possible loss of vehicle control. • The shoe linings on the rear brakes can change over time and increase friction, causing the rear-wheel ABS to activate prematurely.

Secret Warranties/Service Tips

All models/years—TSB #006-94 looks into all the causes and remedies for excessive brake vibrations, and TSB #11-14-95 gives an excellent diagnostic flow chart for troubleshooting excessive engine noise. • Serious paint peeling and delaminating will be fully covered for up to six years under a Mazda secret warranty, say owners. • Troubleshooting tips for correcting wind noise around doors. **All models: 1996–98**—Tips for correcting water leaks from the sliding sunroof. **1997–98**—Front power window noise can be silenced by installing a modified window regulator.

MPV Profile

	1992	1993	1994	1995	1996	1997	1998
Cost Price ($)							
Base 4X2	18,495	19,345	20,615	21,780	27,330	—	—
LX 4X2	18,895	23,745	24,975	26,720	30,900	27,845	25,199
Used Values ($)							

Base 4X2 ↑	5,500	6,000	7,500	9,500	11,500	—	—
Base 4X2 ↓	4,500	5,000	6,500	8,500	10,000	—	—
LX 4X2 ↑	6,000	7,000	8,500	10,500	12,500	14,500	16,500
LX 4X2 ↓	5,000	6,000	7,500	9,000	11,000	13,000	15,000
Extended Warranty	Y	Y	Y	Y	Y	N	N
Secret Warranty	N	N	Y	Y	Y	Y	Y
Reliability	②	②	②	②	③	③	③
Air conditioning	②	②	③	③	③	④	④
Auto. transmission	②	②	③	③	③	④	④
Body integrity	②	②	②	②	②	②	②
Braking system	①	①	②	②	②	③	③
Electrical system	①	①	②	②	②	②	③
Engines	②	②	②	③	③	④	④
Exhaust/Converter	②	③	③	④	④	⑤	⑤
Fuel system	③	③	④	④	④	⑤	⑤
Ignition system	③	③	④	④	④	⑤	⑤
Rust/Paint	②	②	③	③	③	③	④
Steering	②	③	③	④	⑤	⑤	⑤
Suspension	②	②	②	③	④	④	④
Crash Safety	—	—	④	④	④	④	—

Note: 4X4 models are worth about $1000 more than base models.

TOYOTA

Previa, Sienna

Rating: Previa: Above Average (1991–97); the Previa has high-priced reliability and mediocre road performance. **Sienna:** Above Average (1998–99). Ditch the original equipment Firestone tires, unless, paraphrasing Clint Eastwood, you feel "lucky." As with the Honda Odyssey, Sienna owners continue to report some serious safety-related failures including poor headlight illumination, brake malfunctions, and faulty sliding doors. This said, the number of Toyota complaints is far less than what one finds with Chrysler, Ford, and GM minivans. **Maintenance/Repair costs:** Higher than average, and only Toyota dealers can repair these minivans, particularly when it comes to troubleshooting the supercharged 2.4L engine and All Trac. **Parts:** Limited supply, but reasonably priced. Other minivans you may wish to consider: the GM Silhouette, Trans Sport, and Venture; Honda Odyssey; Mercury Villager; or Nissan Quest.

Strengths and weaknesses: The redesigned 1991 Previa's performance and reliability are so much improved over its LE predecessor that it almost seems like a different vehicle. Roomier and rendered more stable thanks to a longer wheelbase, equipped with a new 2.4L engine (supercharged as of the 1994 model year), and loaded with standard safety and convenience features, 1991–97 Previas are almost as driver-friendly as the Chrysler and Mazda competition. Still, they can't match Ford, GM, or Chrysler front-drive minivans for responsive handling and a comfortable ride, and Toyota's small engine is overworked and doesn't hesitate to tell you so.

Previa owners have learned to live with engine noise, poor fuel economy, premature front brake wear, excessive brake vibration and pulsation, electrical glitches, AC malfunctions, and fit and finish blemishes. Four-wheel drive models with automatic transmissions steal lots of power from the 4-cylinder powerplant, although they have fewer reliability problems than similar drivetrains found on competitors, especially Chrysler minivans.

Sienna

Toyota's Camry-based front-drive Sienna minivan replaced the Previa for the 1998 model year. It's built in the same high-quality Kentucky assembly plant as the Camry and comes with lots of safety and convenience features, including side airbags, anti-lock brakes, and a low-tire-pressure warning system.

Sienna abandons the Previa's futuristic look in favour of a more conservative Chevrolet Venture styling. It seats seven, offers a power sliding door (an additional door was added with the 1999 version) with optional remote controls, and has a V6 powerplant (an engine the Previa sorely needed). As with most minivans and vans, you can save about $1,000 by buying the Sienna's cargo version, but you won't get as many features.

Some of the Sienna's strong points: standard ABS and side airbags (LE, XLE); a smooth-running V6 engine and transmission that's a bit more refined and capable than what the Odyssey offers; a comfortable, stable ride; a fourth door; a quiet interior; easy entry/exit; and better-than-average fit and finish reliability. Its weak areas: V6 performance is compromised by AC and the automatic transmission powertrain; it lacks the trailer-towing brawn of rear-drive minivans; although the rear seats fold flat to accommodate the width of a 4' x 8' board, the tailgate won't close, plus the heavy seats are difficult to reinstall (a two-person job, and the centre seat barely fits through the door). There's also no traction control, fuel economy (premium fuel) isn't impressive, the low-mounted radio is hard to reach, and third-row seats lack a fore/aft adjustment to increase cargo space.

Reliability problems include engine failure due to sludge buildup, premature torque converter failures, persistent drifting, uneven and premature tire wear, premature front and rear brake wear, early replacement of the inner tie rod and steering rack, excessive vibration at 90 km/h, electrical shorts, brake noise and malfunctions, sliding door defects, and various other body glitches, including excessive creaks and rattles, and paint that's easily chipped.

Model year changes: 1992—A driver-side airbag, knee bolsters, a centre-mounted rear brake light, and optional ABS. **1993**—Carried over unchanged. **1994**—A standard passenger-side airbag, new ALLTrac model introduced, no more 5-speed manual transmission, new front bucket seats with adjustable head restraints, bumper, and spoiler. **1995**—DX models get a supercharged engine. **1996**—The super-charged engine is the only powerplant offered. **1997**—Extra sound-proofing. **1998**—Introduction of the Sienna; no more Previa. **1999**—An optional, passenger-side power sliding door and a remote keyless locking/unlocking device that doubles as an engine immobilizing anti-theft device.

Safety summary/Recalls: Previa: all years—Wind buffeting makes the Previa wander, and rear-seat head restraints block visibility. **1996**—Defective brake booster. • Brake master cylinder failure. • Multiple ABS failures. • Poor, noisy AC compressor performance. • Windshield wipers suddenly stopped working. • Middle right bench seat lapbelt is impossible to adjust due to its poor design. • Speed sensor failure. **Sienna: 1998**—Sudden acceleration, due to a defective throttle cable; vehicle hit a wall. • Brakes made a loud grinding noise, pedal went to the floor, and vehicle failed to stop. • Extremely loud groaning or grinding noise when braking. • When vehicle is turning left, steering wheel has to be manually returned to the straight-ahead position or vehicle will continue turning. • Many owners have complained the vehicle pulls sharply to one side or another when driving at moderate speeds. • Shape and design of the Sienna creates severe blind spots. • Headlights give poor illumination. • Windshields are distorted, exhibiting a "melted" image. • Rear door doesn't shut tightly. • Sliding door won't latch in cold weather. • Design of the inside sliding door lock release makes it difficult to operate, requiring excessive force to activate. • Poor visibility due to the tinted window design. • Headrests and third-row seats are loose and vibrate. • Shoulder belts in the middle row lock up instantly when first put on and stay locked up, binding the passenger. **1999**—Airbags failed to deploy. Many complaints that the steering wheel locks up when making a turn (left-hand turns, especially), won't return to centre without extreme effort, or simply stops responding. • Wheel lug nuts broke and allowed wheel to fall off. • Vehicle suddenly pulls to the right or left, especially when accelerating. • Window exploded at stoplight. • Many complaints of sudden tire tread separation (Firestone). • Severe vibration at cruising speeds. • Rear brake drums may overheat and warp. • Power sliding door doesn't latch properly and can be dangerous to children because it opens and closes unexpectedly and requires too much pressure to prevent closure. • Distracting dashboard reflection into the windshield. • Windshield distortion. • Faulty fuel cap causes the Check Engine light to come on. **Recalls: All models: 1991—1997**—Oil leakage will result in a sufficiently low oil supply to cause bearing damage to the front differential unit. This can lead to eventual seizure of the unit, increasing the risk of a crash. Dealers will install a modified air breather plug to prevent such oil loss.

Secret Warranties/Service Tips

All models/years—Owner feedback confirms that front brake pads and discs will be replaced under Toyota's "goodwill" policy if they wear out before 2 years/40,000 km. Improved disc brake pad kits are described in TSB #BR94-004. Brake pulsation/vibration, another generic Toyota problem, is fully addressed in TSB #BR94-002, "Cause and Repair of Vibration and Pulsation." **Previa: 1994–96**—Excessive brake vibration or pulsation can be corrected by installing upgraded front brake pads. **Sienna: 1998**—Upgraded brake pads and rotors should reduce brake groan and squeak noises. **1998–99**—To reduce sliding door creaks, the control junction materials have been upgraded. **1998–2000**—Outline of various diagnostic procedures and fixes to correct vehicle pulling to one side. • Power steering squeaks can be silenced by installing a countermeasure steering rack end under warranty. • Power steering "feel" can be improved by replacing the steering rack guide. • False activation of the security alarm can be fixed by modifying the hood latch switch. • Power window rattles can be corrected by installing a revised lower window frame mounting bracket. **1999–2000**—If the power sliding door is inoperative, or won't close properly, Toyota says the cable should be adjusted.

Previa, Sienna Profile

	1992	1993	1994	1995	1996	1997	1998	1999
Cost Price ($)								
Previa	20,778	21,448	24,748	28,578	35,908	36,998	—	—
Sienna CE 3d	—	—	—	—	—	—	25,628	25,760
Sienna CE 4d	—	—	—	—	—	—	26,808	26,940
Sienna LE 4d	—	—	—	—	—	—	29,558	29,980
Used Values ($)								
Previa ↑	6,000	7,500	9,000	11,500	14,500	16,500	—	—
Previa ↓	5,000	6,000	7,500	10,000	13,000	15,000	—	—
Sienna CE 3d ↑	—	—	—	—	—	—	17,500	20,000
Sienna CE 3d ↓	—	—	—	—	—	—	16,000	18,500
Sienna CE 4d ↑	—	—	—	—	—	—	18,500	21,000
Sienna CE 4d ↓	—	—	—	—	—	—	16,500	19,000
Sienna LE 4d ↑	—	—	—	—	—	—	20,500	22,500
Sienna LE 4d ↓	—	—	—	—	—	—	18,500	20,500
Extended Warranty	Y	Y	Y	Y	Y	Y	N	N
Secret Warranty	N	N	N	N	N	N	N	N
Reliability	③	④	⑤	⑤	⑤	⑤	⑤	⑤
Air conditioning	③	③	③	④	⑤	⑤	⑤	⑤
Auto. transmission	③	③	④	⑤	⑤	⑤	⑤	⑤
Body integrity	❷	④	⑤	④	④	③	③	④
Braking system	❷	❷	❷	❷	❷	③	③	④
Electrical system	③	③	③	❶	❶	❷	③	④
Engines	③	④	⑤	⑤	⑤	⑤	⑤	⑤
Exhaust/Converter	③	④	③	③	④	⑤	⑤	⑤
Fuel system	③	④	⑤	⑤	⑤	⑤	⑤	⑤
Ignition system	③	③	④	⑤	⑤	⑤	⑤	⑤
Rust/Paint	④	④	⑤	⑤	⑤	⑤	③	④
Steering	④	③	④	④	④	⑤	⑤	⑤
Suspension	③	③	④	④	④	⑤	⑤	⑤
Crash Safety	—	③	④	④	④	④	⑤	⑤
Side Impact	—	—	—	—	—	—	—	⑤

APPENDIX I
THIRTY YEARS OF "BEATERS,"
"ORPHANS," AND "CHICK MAGNETS"

Over the past thirty years, there have been many excellent cars built that can still be found, reasonably priced, on the used-car market. I've chosen a few of the ones I am most familiar with and which I see quite often in want ads or on the Internet. As I see the prices some of these older cars are fetching, I wish I had kept my first car, a 1959 Chevrolet Impala (available in the States for about $10,000 (U.S.), in good condition).

Beater psychology

It's funny—in Ontario and Quebec, you are what you drive. Owning a beater is seen by others as an admission that you're too poor or cheap to own a nicer vehicle. On the other hand, Maritimers and western Canadians who drive beaters are considered frugal and resourceful individuals. Consequently, there are fewer and fewer garages and parts suppliers in Ontario and Quebec that specialize in repairing older cars and scurrying around the country hunting for 10-year-old parts. But when you head west or east, you immediately notice the popularity of vehicles 10 to 20 years old and the surprisingly large number of independent garages that service them.

My take on this is that the Maritimes' traditionally distressed economy forces motorists to buy the least expensive vehicles and keep them for as long as they can, while western Canadians embrace beaters because of the kinder Prairie weather (from a corrosion standpoint) and family tradition. Families in Manitoba, Saskatchewan, and Alberta view their cars and trucks as appliances—not "chick magnets." (B.C. is altogether different, as is its wont.) Their pragmatic repair-or-recycle disposition and large rural families mean that an old but functional car or truck will be passed down through generations of the same family. Furthermore, western Canadians prefer cars and trucks with rear-wheel drive for winter driving.

As I said before, British Columbians are an automotive breed apart: they aren't forced to be frugal, but the wide availability of well-preserved used cars is too tempting to resist, even at prices that are outrageously inflated. Consequently, you'll find in B.C. lots of classic cars, convertibles, and European imports, along with plenty of garages to service them. Interestingly, B.C. is perhaps the only place where the sun hasn't set on the British automotive empire. (Quick, why do Brits drink warm beer? Because Lucas makes their refrigerators.)

It's getting pretty hard to find a vehicle 10 years old or more that's safe and reliable. Personally, I'd be reluctant to buy any decade-old vehicle anywhere east of Manitoba. Apart from salt being a real body killer, it's just too easy to fall prey to scam artists who cover up major mechanical or body problems resulting from accidents or environmental damage. As an alternative I'd look for an orphaned vehicle, recently axed only because its popularity waned (Mazda MX-3, for example) or because it didn't fit in the automaker's long-term plans (Nissan's Axxess minivan, for example).

Nevertheless, if an independent mechanic gives you the green light, and if you have the time, knowledge, and parts suppliers to do your own maintenance and repairs, you're in better shape. In this case, you might seriously consider a 10- to 20-year-old, beat-up-looking vehicle, or even a recently discontinued model (Ford's Escort, the Chrysler Colt, or Nissan's Axxess minivan, for example) that runs well (most of the time) and is reasonably priced. Look for one of the following recommended vehicles, avoid the non-recommended ones, and take your time. Insist upon an independent check-up, where you should pay close attention to the listed trouble areas.

If you have a bit more money to spend and want to take less of a risk, look up the recommended vehicles found at the beginning of each vehicle category in Part Three.

Recommended

Acura—The 5-cylinder **Vigor**, a spin-off of the Honda Accord sedan, sells for $7,000–$10,000. It went through only three model years (1992–94). Due to its original high cost and the absence of a more economical, smoother, and easier-to-repair 6-cylinder powerplant, most buyers chose the cheaper Accord instead. This compact has power to spare, handles well, and has an impressive reliability/durability record. On the other hand, owners report the following deficiencies: lots of engine, tire, and road noise intrude into the passenger compartment at highway speeds; the engine and transmission lack smoothness; and the brakes aren't easy to modulate. The suspension is firm but not harsh and rear leg room is limited. Vigors are also notoriously thirsty for premium fuel. Problem areas: excessive brake noise and premature brake wear, in addition to fit and finish deficiencies. The 1992 Vigor turned in below average crash-test scores.

Checker—The quintessential taxi that was last made in 1982, the **Checker** is the poor man's Bentley. Its rear-drive configuration, sturdy, off-the-shelf GM mechanicals, and thick body panels all add up to bulletproof reliability. Beware of corrosion along door rocker panels and wheelwells, and badly repaired collision damage.

Chrysler—**Dart**, **Valiant**, **Duster**, **Scamp**, **Diplomat**, **Caravelle**, **Newport**, rear-drive **New Yorker Fifth Avenue**, and **Gran Fury**. Problem areas: electrical system, suspension, brakes, body and frame rust, plus constant stalling when humidity is high.

If you can get past the two-tone paint job, Chrysler's rear-drive Fifth Avenue (shown above), Caravelle Salon, and Diplomat Salon are excellent buys. They have high performance, reliable powertrains, and lots of room. Weak spots: brakes, electrical shorts, and ignition glitches.

The **Caravelle**, **Diplomat**, and **New Yorker Fifth Avenue** are reasonably reliable and simple-to-repair throwbacks to a time when land yachts ruled the highways. Powered with 6- and 8-cylinder engines, they will practically run forever with minimal care. The fuel-efficient "slant 6" powerplant was too small for this type of car and was changed to a gas-guzzling but smooth and reliable V8 after 1983. Handling is vague and sloppy, though, and emergency braking is often accompanied by rear-wheel lockup. Still, what do you want for $1,500–$3,500 in a 1984–89 "retro rocket"?

Overall reliability is fairly good, and inexpensive parts are available anywhere. Problem areas are the carburetor, ignition, electrical system, brake, and suspension (premature idler-arm wear). It's a good idea to adjust the torsion bars frequently for better suspension performance. Doors, windshield pillars, the bottoms of both front and rear fenders, and the trunk lid rust through more quickly than average.

Chrysler's 1991–93 **2000GTX** is an above average buy that may cost $3,500–$5,500, depending upon the model year. It's a reliable Japanese-built sedan that was discontinued in 1994. It has a competitive price, modern styling, and high-performance options that put it on par with such benchmark cars as the Honda Accord and Toyota Camry. The base engine provides uninspiring yet adequate performance, but this car is distinguished by its high-performing optional powerplant— a 16-valve version that's smooth and powerful. The manual transmission and clutch are exceptionally smooth. Handling is acceptable in all situations. Excellent braking with anti-lock brakes, but mediocre without. The ride is firm but fairly comfortable on most roads, especially with the adjustable suspension. Interior room is generous for four people and you can carry a fifth passenger in a pinch (literally!). Front brakes need more attention than average. The 2000GTX hasn't been crash-tested.

The Chrysler **Stealth** is a serious, reasonably priced sports car that's as much go as show. Although 1995 was its last model year in Canada, it's still sold in the United States as the Mitsubishi 3000GT. Prices range from $5,500–$9,000 for the 1991–93 Base or ES model. A '95 high-performance R/T will go for about $15,000—not a bad price for an "orphan" sports car, eh?

These models were carried over unchanged until the '94 model year when they got a passenger airbag, slightly revised styling, projector-beam headlights (instead of the hidden lights used previously), and a 20-horsepower boost and six-speed transmission for the Turbo R/T version. Problem areas: engine, transmission, front brake, and electrical failures. The 1993 model excelled in crash tests, earning a five-star rating.

Ford—Maverick, Comet, Fairmont, Zephyr, Tracer, Mustang, Capri, Cougar, Thunderbird V6, Torino, Marquis, Grand Marquis, LTD, and **LTD Crown Victoria.** Problem areas: trunk, wheelwell, and rocker panel rusting; brakes; steering; and electrical system failures. The 1993 **Festiva** is marginally acceptable for city use as long as you check out the brakes, exhaust system, and body panels for rust.

General Motors—Chevette and **Acadian.** Problem areas: steering system defects, and brakes you have to stand on to stop. Rear-drive **Nova, Ventura, Skylark,** and **Phoenix.** Problem areas: undercarriage, steering system, and suspension rust-out. Front-drive **Nova** and **Spectrum; Camaro, Firebird, Malibu, LeMans, Century, Regal, Cutlass, Monte Carlo,** and **Grand Prix.** Problem areas: rear brake backing plate rust-out and steering failures; **Bel Air, Impala, Caprice, Laurentian, Catalina, Parisienne, LeSabre, Bonneville,** and **Delta 88.** Be wary of under-carriage, suspension component, and rear brake backing plate rust-out.

Mazda—For sports cars thrills, minus the bills, the 1992–96 **MX-3's** base 1.6L engine supplies plenty of power for most driving situations, plus, it's reasonably priced at $3,500–$7,000. When equipped with the optional 1.8L V6 powerplant (the smallest V6 on the market at the time) and high-performance options, the car transforms itself into a 130-hp pocket rocket. In fact, the MX-3 GS easily outperforms the Honda del Sol, Toyota Paseo, and Geo Storm on comfort and high performance acumen. It does fall a bit short of the Saturn SC due to its limited low-end torque, and fuel economy is disappointing. Reverse gear is sometimes hard to engage.

Brake and wheel bearing problems are commonplace. Most of the MX-3's parts are used on other Mazda cars, so their overall reliability should be outstanding. Crash safety ratings have been average.

Body assembly is also only average and rattles/squeaks are common. Owners have complained of paint defects and sheet metal that's too thin above the door handles (dents in the metal appear where you would ordinarily place your thumb when closing the door). Some owners report wind and water leaks around the doors and windows. Moderate engine noise increases dramatically above 100 km/h.

The key word for the 1988–95 **929** is understatement: the engine is unobtrusive, the exterior is anonymous, and the interior is far from flashy. In spite of its lack of pizzazz and imprecise power steering, the 929 will accelerate and handle curves as well as the best large European sedans and it has proven to be fairly reliable. For these advantages, you can expect to pay from $4,000–$8,000 for an '88 through '93 model. The '94s and '95s are priced in the $11,000–$15,000 range.

The car's main drawbacks are its limited interior room and trunk space. The driver's seat doesn't have enough rear travel for tall drivers, and head room is tight. Owners report some problems with premature disc brake wear, electrical glitches, exhaust system rust-out, electronic shock absorber durability (particularly with the 1989–91 models), and fit and finish deficiencies. The only real safety negative is the 929's consistently poor crash test scores since the '88 model was first tested.

Shocks are very expensive to replace. Manual transmission isn't offered, and the automatic's many settings can be confusing. Furthermore, the transmission's lockup feature frequently cuts in and out. The rear end sometimes wants to slide out a bit on slippery surfaces, and the front end bounces around on bumpy roads. The optional automatic adjusting suspension does little to improve the car's ride or handling.

Redesigned in 1992, the 929 got a more rounded body and a longer wheelbase that added to interior room while sacrificing trunk space. Despite these improvements, tall occupants will still feel cramped.

Selling for $3,000–$5,000 for a base 1988–91 model, the **RX-7** is an impressive performer with a ride that can be painful on bad roads, due primarily to the car's stiff suspension. The GSL and Turbo models are very well equipped and luxuriously finished. Except for some oil-burning problems, apex seal failures, and leaking engine O-rings, the RX-7 has served to dispel any doubts concerning the durability of rotary engines.

Nevertheless, careful maintenance is in order, since contaminated oil or overheating will easily damage the rotary engine. Clutches wear quickly if used hard. Disc brakes need frequent attention paid to the calipers and rotors. The MacPherson struts get soft more quickly than average. Fuel, exhaust system, and electrical glitches and AC malfunctions are also common. Be wary of leaky sunroofs. Radiators have a short life span. Rocker panels and body seams are prone to serious rusting. The underbody on older cars should also be inspected carefully for corrosion damage. Fuel economy has never been this car's strong suit and crash-test scores were below average.

For more info, check out the Mazda RX-7 Lemon Site on the Internet at *scuderiaciriani.com/rx7/lemon_site/sources.htm*. It's a treasure trove of maintenance tips, common defects, copies of service bulletins, and good specific buying and selling information.

Nissan—The **Micra,** a subcompact commuter car, was sold during 1985–91. It uses generic Nissan parts that are fairly reliable and not difficult to find, except for body panels that are more problematic. Electrical shorts, premature front-brake wear, and body rusting along the door rocker panels and wheelwells are the more common deficiencies.

The 1991–95 **Axxess** minivan is an excellent choice that's fairly reliable, easily serviced, and has posted respectable crash-safety ratings. You get carlike handling and ride comfort in a minivan that's about the size of the higher-priced Honda Odyssey. As with most minivans equipped with a full load and a small engine, acceleration isn't confidence inspiring on the highway; however, the Axxess is ideal for city-to-suburb commuting. What further sets the Axxess apart, however, is its reasonable price and better-than-average reliability. Prices have remained stable, $3,000–$7,500, for the top-of-the-line SE. You may have trouble finding one. But it's worth the wait.

Expect some electrical problems, premature wear of the front disc brakes, manual transmission malfunctions, and paint defects. Owners have also reported that the resonator (located just behind the muffler) fails around the 3-year mark and costs about $250 to replace. Windshield wipers are another rip-off. Nissan original equipment wipers are rare, aren't very durable, and they're way overpriced; use regular blades that are shorter, easier to find, more durable, and less costly.

Pulsar and **NX** models are good small-car buys ($1,500–$4,000, depending upon the year), as long as you pick the right years and stay away from failure-prone and expensive-to-repair turbo models. The **Pulsar** was replaced by the 1991 **NX**, a similar small car that also shares Sentra components. For 1983–86 models, overall reliability is poor to very poor. As with other discontinued Nissans, the 1987–93 models have shown remarkable performance improvement and are all the more attractive due to their depreciated prices. Crash test scores were below average for the 1990 and earlier models, while the 1991 and later versions scored quite well. All Pulsars built before 1991 are prone to premature wear on the front brake pads and discs and faulty air conditioners. From 1991 on, the only problems reported concern minor AC malfunctions, premature wearout of front brakes and suspension components, and exhaust systems that don't last very long (two years, tops). Complaints of premature rusting and paint peeling are legion for the 1983–90 models.

1990–92 **Stanzas** are roomy, reasonably priced ($2,500–$3,500), four-passenger compacts that offer peppy performance, responsive steering, nimble handling, and good fuel economy. Overall reliability has been fairly good during over the years. Except for some road noise, suspension thumps, starting difficulties, transmission malfunctions, and a biodegradable exhaust system, no major problems have been reported on 1988–92 Stanzas.

Owners complain of premature front brake wear and rust perforations, problems that are common for all years. Especially prone to rust perforation are wheel openings, the front edge of the hood, the rear hatch, and door bottoms. 1990 models produced below average crashworthiness scores, but the 1991 and 1992 models did better than average.

Nissan's answer to the Corvette, the 1989–96 **300ZX** has everything: high-performance capability, a heavy chassis, complicated electronics, and average depreciation resulting in a price range of $7,000–$21,000. Turbocharged 1990 and later models are much faster than previous versions and better overall buys. This weighty rear-drive offers a high degree of luxury equipment along with a potent 300-hp engine. Traction is poor on slippery surfaces, though, and the rear suspension hits hard when going over speed bumps. Crashworthiness scores have been average.

The complexity of all the bells and whistles on the 300ZX translates into a lot more problems than you'd experience with either a Mustang or a Camaro—two cars that have their own reliability problems, but are far easier and less costly to repair. The best example of this is the electrical system, long a source of recurring, hard-to-diagnose shorts. Fuel-injectors are a constant problem and lead to poor engine performance. The manual transmission has been failure-prone, clutches don't last long, front and rear brakes are noisy and wear out quickly, and the aluminum wheels are easily damaged by corrosion and road hazards. The exhaust system is practically biodegradable. The glitzy digital dash with three odometers and weird spongy/stiff variable shock absorbers are more gimmicky than practical. Body assembly is mediocre.

Subaru—Sold 1988–95, the **Justy** does everything reasonably well for an entry-level Subaru. Pairing smooth and nimble handling with precise and predictable steering, the 4X4 system is a boon for people who often need easy-to-engage extra traction and an automatic transmission. Price range is $1,500–$3,500.

The **Justy**'s reliability record has been about average from the 1991 model onwards. Some owners complain about poor engine idling and frequent cold-weather stalling, manual and automatic transmission malfunctions, premature exhaust system rust-out, catalytic converter failures, and paint peeling. With the exception of the CVT, servicing and repairs are made easy due to a very straightforward design.

Toyota—Consider any models from the late '80s and early '90s except the **LE Van**, which has a history of chronic brakes, chassis, and body rusting problems. Chassis rusting and V6 engine head gasket failures are common problems with the 1988–94 sport-utilities and pickups (Toyota will pay for the engine repairs up to eight years). **Celicas** are an especially fine buy, combining smooth engine performance and bulletproof reliability with sports cars thrills.

Selling for $3,000–$7,5 00, the 1987–93 **MR2** is a mid-engine, rear-drive, 4-cylinder sports car that's both reliable and fun to drive. On the downside, you have to put up with a cramped interior, quirky turbo handling, inflated insurance premiums, and undetermined crashworthiness.

The '91 model was redesigned to provide more interior room and additional comfort. Four-wheel disc brakes were standard and ABS was optional. More horsepower and torque was provided by a new 2.2L 130-hp 4-cylinder base engine. Handling was compromised by these changes and didn't improve until the '93 model upgraded the rear suspension.

Except for vague steering and some front-end instability, handling is practically flawless. The standard 16-valve 4-cylinder motor is smooth and adequate. The supercharged and turbocharged engines, though overpriced, produce more power than you would ever want to use. They also have a bit of turbo lag and require deft handling. The engine's placement behind the driver's seat also makes it inaccessible for most repairs and produces excessive noise and vibration, which make long trips very uncomfortable.

In order of frequency, the most common complaints on all MR2s are as follows: brake, transmission, electrical system, and body hardware (fit and finish) deficiencies.

The **Cressida** ages well and offers an excellent combination of dependable, no-surprise, rear-drive performance, comfort, and luxury. All this in the $3,000–$9,000 price range for an '85 to '92 model. There is little to find at fault when it comes to overall reliability, and the engine is a model of smooth power. Its only shortcomings: a bit less interior and trunk space than one would find with the Nissan Maxima or Acura Legend, inconvenient and confusing dash controls, and poor fuel economy.

The 1990–93 models are more crashworthy, reliable, and trouble-free than earlier versions, but they're also much more expensive. Two complaints continue to surface throughout the years: premature front brake wear and excessive brake pulsation/vibration. Toyota has issued a drawer full of bulletins to eliminate the problems, but they seem to reappear each year in some form or another. AC glitches and electrical short circuits are also commonplace. Exhaust system parts rust quickly.

From its humble beginnings as a rear-drive, stretched Celica in 1979, the **Supra** became Toyota's flagship sports car when it switched to front-drive in 1986 and took on its own unique personality—with the help of a powerful 3.0L DOHC V6 powerplant. Supra prices range from a low of $13,000 for a '90 model, up to $50,000 for a '97.

It's an attractively styled, high-performance sports car that had been quite reliable up until it caught the Corvette/Nissan 300ZX malady in 1993: cumulative add-ons that drove up the car's price and weight, and drove down its reliability. The 6-cylinder engines are smooth and powerful and handling is sure and precise—better than the Celica because of the independent rear suspension. Like most sports cars, the Supra has limited rear seating, fuel mileage is marginal around town, and insurance premiums are likely to be much higher than average. Additionally, crashworthiness has never been determined.

Early models (pre-'93) are more reasonably priced and are practically trouble free, except for some premature front brake wear and vibrations. On later models, owners report major turbocharger problems; frequent rear differential replacements; electrical short circuits; AC malfunctions; and premature brake, suspension, and exhaust system wear. The 3.0L engine is an oil-burner at times, and cornering is often accompanied by a rear-end growl. Seatbelt guides and the power antenna are failure prone. Body deficiencies are common.

Volvo—The 1989–93 **240 series** is an average at $3,500–$5,500. Problems with entry-level Volvos like the 240 mirror the quality control problems manifested by Saab, the other Swedish automaker, except for the fact that Volvo styling is more bland than bizarre. The 240 is a solid and spacious car. Unfortunately, it doesn't live up to Volvo's advertising as an automotive longevity wonder.

The V6 is an honest, though imperfect, engine. Avoid the turbocharged 4-cylinder engine and failure-prone air conditioning systems. Diesels suffer from cooling system breakdowns and leaky cylinder head gaskets. The brakes on all model years need frequent and expensive servicing, and exhaust systems are notorious for their short life span. The GL and GLE suffer from occasional electrical bugs.

Interestingly, when a '79 Volvo 240 was crash-tested, researchers concluded both the driver and passenger would have sustained severe head trauma. Nevertheless, the 240 had the lowest rate of driver deaths among popular passenger vehicles on U.S. roads during 1989–93, says an IIHS study. Furthermore, the 240 didn't record a single driver death during the five years of the study. 1992–93 models produced excellent NHTSA crashworthiness scores.

Volvo's **700 series** models (1986–92), selling for $3,500–$5,500, are more spacious, luxurious, and more complicated to service than the entry-level 240. The standard engine and transmission perform well, but aren't as refined as the 850s. The 700 series suffers from some brake, electrical, engine cooling, air conditioning, and body deficiencies that are best diagnosed and fixed by a Volvo-trained mechanic. Brakes tend to wear rapidly, and can require expensive servicing. Exhaust systems usually need replacing after a few years. The 1988 model performed poorly in crash tests, while the 1991–92 versions did quite well.

Not Recommended

American Motors—**Hornet**, **Gremlin**, **Concord**, **Spirit**, **Pacer**, and **Eagle 4X4**. Watch out for faulty engines, transmissions, brakes, and steering. Although these cars are—uh, interestingly styled—and notoriously unreliable, they can be easily fixed if you've got the right connection for parts.

Audi—**Fox**, **4000**, and **5000**. Likely trouble spots: engine, transmission, and fuel system failures, plus, a combination of *sudden* acceleration and *no* acceleration. These early Audis are unreliable, hard to diagnose, and complicated to maintain and repair.

Stay away from all models before the 1995 model year. This includes the **80, 90, 100, 200, 4000**, and **5000**. Again, likely problem areas are the engine, transmission, and fuel system, plus, a combination of sudden acceleration and poor acceleration. Fox models are particularly bad buys because of their anemic engine; atrocious handling; and failure-prone electrical, brake, and body parts. Nevertheless, overall crash-worthiness scores have been impressive, except for the Fox, which posted below average scores.

British Leyland—Austin Marina, MG, MGB, and **Triumph.** These attractively styled sedans and roadsters taught a generation of young men the fundamentals of car repair. Watch out for electrical system, engine, transmission, and clutch defects. Extensive and expensive chassis rusting is commonplace.

Chrysler—Charger, Horizon, and **Omni.** Built from 1978 to 1990 and priced from a few hundred to $1,000, these cars aren't a bargain by any stretch of the imagination. Expect serious reliability problems with the 2.2L engine, in addition to fuel, electrical, and ignition system failures that are difficult to diagnose and even harder to repair due to the poor quality of components and their scarcity. The power-steering rack develops leaks and the exhaust system rusts quickly. Other problems include rapid brake wear and unreliable electronic components. Air conditioners and turbochargers often malfunction and are expensive to troubleshoot and repair.

All models suffer from extensive surface rust, with perforations found around rear wheels and the rear hatch. Many owners also complain of severe underbody rusting that affects safety. All years have such poor body assembly that doors constantly stick shut (some owners have had to climb out the windows), locks fall off, handles detach, and water and air leaks are legion. Crashworthiness is also sub-par.

Although they don't cost much—$500–$1,000, depending on the year—steer clear of 1983–89 **Aries** or **Reliants**, Chrysler's first-generation K-cars. Uncomplicated mechanical components and a roomy interior made these cars attractive buys when new, but once in service they quickly deteriorate. Both cars use dirt-cheap, low-tech components that tend to break down frequently. They have also performed poorly in crash tests.

All cars have a problem with idle shake caused by the transverse-mounted 4-cylinder engine, as well as driveability problems, especially in cold or damp weather. The "gutless" 2.2L Chrysler-built 4-cylinder motor is a bit more reliable than the 2.6L Mitsubishi engine, which has a tendency to self-destruct. It also suffers from premature wear of the timing belt guide and piston ring, and leaky camshaft oil plugs. The 2.2L powerplant has multiple problems, the main ones being a weak cylinder head gasket, and timing belt failures. The turbocharged version often requires expensive repairs. The MAP sensor fails frequently and is costly to replace.

Carbureted engines are renowned for stalling and poor driveability. Exhaust systems, wheel bearings, and air conditioning components aren't durable. Water infiltration around the windshield and into the trunk is common. Serious corrosion generally starts along the trunk line and the edges of the rear wheelwells. Perforations tend to develop along the bottom door edges, around the windshield, and on the floor.

The 1985–89 **Lancer** and **LeBaron GTS** may only cost $1,000–$2,000, but they can cost you far more. In fact, they suffer from many of the same problems as the **Aries** and **Reliant** K-cars.

The **Aspen** and **Volaré**, second-generation K-cars selling for $1,000–$2,000, continue the poor-quality tradition with chronic engine, brakes, steering, and suspension failures and extensive chassis and front fender rusting. Parts are inexpensive and relatively easy to find. Crashworthiness is poor through 1984, and then is rated better than average thereafter.

Their 1989–95 replacements, the **Spirit, Lebaron,** and **Acclaim**, are third generation K-cars costing $2,000–$3,500. Although the interior will seat five comfortably and offers all the advantages of the hatchback design, road performance is merely passable with the standard engines and suspension.

Poor reliability causes maintenance costs to mount quickly. The manual transmission is balky and its clutch has a poor durability record. Turbo models are especially risky buys at all times. Head gaskets are prone to leaks, on all engines. Shock absorbers, MacPherson struts, and brakes wear out quickly. Front brake rotors are prone to rusting and warping. The electrical system is troublesome: the distributor pickup and computer modules malfunction constantly, causing stalling and hard starting (especially in wet weather). Air conditioning components have a short life span, and body hardware is fragile. Crash test scores are below average.

Cordoba and **Mirada** rear drives were failure-prone early '80s models that have absolutely no value to collectors and can be picked up for less than $500. They shared their chassis and poor quality components with the **Diplomat** and **LeBaron**. Likely problem areas: transmission, differential, carburetor, electrical system, brake, and body defects. The "lean-burn" computer was a disaster, characterized by poor engine performance and frequent, expensive replacements.

With '87 to '94 models selling for $1,500–$5,500, respectively, the **Duster**, (not to be confused with the Plymouth Valiant twin), **Shadow**, and **Sundance** aren't recommended because they still have many of the same generic mechanical and body weaknesses that Chrysler owners have suffered with throughout the years. Overall, the '94 version seems to be the best of a bad lot.

On early models, the turbocharged engine isn't very reliable and can be quite expensive to repair. The fuel-injection system can be temperamental and the MacPherson struts leak or wear out prematurely. Front brakes are particularly prone to rapid wear, and parking brake cables need frequent service. Convertible tops on the 1991 Shadow tend to leak profusely, and non-metallic paint chips easily.

Owners report that the cylinder head, oil-pan gasket, and rear crankshaft seal leak; the air conditioning compressor rarely lasts more than two years; windshield wiper fluid often freezes in hoses; and the power-steering assembly seldom lasts longer than five years. The upgraded 1992 41TE automatic transmission is still problematic: engine head gaskets often need replacing; oil leaks and oil pump failures are common; rear brakes are noisy; the heating, air conditioning, and ventilation systems often malfunction; electrical components (notably electronic modules) aren't durable; and excessive suspension vibrations are common. Body assembly is sloppy, paint discolours or peels prematurely, door mouldings fall off, and doors freeze shut.

As for crash safety: the '87 model performed poorly; however, the 1991–93 models posted above average scores.

Even though they sell at attractively low prices ($500 for an '86; $4,000 for a '93), the **Daytona, Laser, Pacifica, Shelby Z,** and **Turbo Z** will give you sports car thrills combined with wallet-busting bills. Without the failure-prone turbo-charged engine and sport suspension, these coupes provide mediocre handling and acceleration.

All engines are troublesome. If they're not maintained meticulously from the very beginning, the turbocharger seldom lasts longer than 75,000 km and its failure can cause serious damage to the engine and your wallet. Fuel system problems are common on all versions, requiring the frequent replacement of electronic computer modules. The manual transmission has a sloppy shift linkage and a heavy clutch that doesn't stand up to hard use. Models loaded with electrical accessories have a higher failure rate than stripped-down versions. Electronic instrument panels and other electrical items are temperamental. The body is particularly poorly assembled, and paint delamination and water and wind leaks are common. Five-star crash scores were earned by the 1989 through 1993 models.

Datsun/Nissan—210, 310, 510, 810, F-10, and **240Z.** Likely problem areas: electrical system glitches, poorly-performing brakes with sticking calipers and warped rotors, and extensive chassis, fuel tank, suspension and steering component rusting. The 240Z and its Z successors are actually attractive, well-built sports cars. Unfortunately, they draw rust like iron filings to a magnet and once afflicted, suspension and steering assemblies have nothing to which they can anchor. Many a buyer has been seduced by the style only to wake up with an irreparable, dangerously defective lemon. Most of these cars go for a few hundred dollars, however, the Z-cars may fetch $1,500–$5,000 depending upon their condition and the degree to which you're prepared to take a risk.

Eagle—Medallion, Monaco, and **Premier.** These bargain-priced French imports—$700–$900 for the **Medallion** and $1,200–$3,000 for the **Premier**—had a 1988–92 model run. Sold through Chrysler's Renault connection, they are two of the most failure-prone imports to ever hit our shores. Powertrain, fuel system, electrical system, AC, suspension, and brakes are the worst offenders. The '91 and '92 **Monaco** and **Premier** are covered by a 10-year ABS brake warranty set up through an agreement between Chrysler and NHTSA and honoured, so far, by Chrysler Canada.

Fiat—"Fix it, again, Tony." All Fiat models and years are known for temperamental fuel and electrical systems and biodegradable bodies; the **124/128** became the Yugo's gene pool. **Alfa Romeos** have similar problems.

Ford—**Cortina**, **Pinto**, **Festiva**, **Fiesta**, **Bobcat**, and **Mustang II**. Watch out for electrical system, engine, and chassis rusting; fire-prone **Pintos** and **Bobcats** are mobile Molotov cocktails.

The German import **Fiesta** and the **Festiva,** built in South Korea, are two small imports that only survived a few years in Canada. Parts are practically unobtainable for both vehicles. The 1978–80 **Fiesta** was a fairly well made, inexpensive small car that's now worth $300–$500. Highway driving isn't recommended due to its weak engine and brakes. The slightly larger and more refined 1988–92 **Festiva** is an $800–$1,500 subcompact that's two feet shorter than the Escort, and weighs about 1,700 lb. Acceleration is slow, but the manual transmission is precise and easy to use. The 1993 **Festiva** is only adequate for city use and with one passenger at best. Floorboards, body panels, and exhaust components quickly rust out; brakes and electrical components frequently need replacing; and the tall body and tiny tires make highway cruising a scream. Crash tests of an '89 **Festiva** showed the driver and passenger would sustain only minor injuries, however.

The 1994–97 Korean-built **Aspire's** size, engine, and drivetrain limitations restrict it to an urban environment as well, and its low quality control often restricts it to the driveway. Be wary of brake, electrical, and fuel system failures. Parts are also hard to find. This said, you can pick up an Aspire dirt-cheap—$3,000–$5,500. The engine lacks high-end torque, and the widely spaced gear ratios on the manual shifter rob it of much-needed mid-range power. It takes 13 seconds to reach 100 km/h—and an additional 4 seconds with the automatic gearbox, which is jerky when pushed. Air conditioning slows down the car even more. Steering is heavy and vague at high speeds. Unfortunately, the three-door version doesn't offer power steering. Expect excessive low-speed engine and road/tire noise at higher speeds. The car has consistently posted higher-than-average crash-test scores.

General Motors—**Vega**, **Astre**, **Monza**, and **Firenza**. Engine, transmission, fuel and electrical system, and brake failures are legendary. Interestingly, little body rusting. **Cadillac Cimarron** and **Allanté** have poor quality powertrain and body components that are expensive to replace; for all front-drives expect problems with the engine, automatic transmission, electronic modules, steering, brakes, and rust/paint peeling. **Citation, Skylark, Omega,** and **Phoenix.** Don't accept any of these cars—even as a gift. Biggest problem: dangerous, expensive-to-repair brakes: step on the brake pedal and the rear wheels lock up as you spin out of control. Other traps for the unwary: engine, brake, and electronic module failures, plus severe rust canker that destroys the unit body chassis.

The Pontiac **Fiero,** sold 1984–88, snares lots of unsuspecting first-time buyers through its attractive, sports-car styling, high-performance pretensions, and $700–$1,500 price. However, one quickly learns to both fear and hate the Fiero as it shows off its fiery disposition (several safety recalls) and "I'll start when I want to" character. Its main failings were the powertrain, fuel and electrical systems, and poor body construction.

Buick's **Reatta,** a luxury two-seater sold only 1988–91 (present value: $8,000–$11,000 for the convertible), has higher-than-average maintenance costs, although repairs aren't that dealer-dependent, except for the electronically controlled fuel system. The **Reatta** also has higher-than-average parts costs and body parts are tough to find. GM improved the quality somewhat with its 1991 models by upgrading the brakes and powertrain components, but then discontinued production.

The Geo **Storm** was GM's Japanese-made small car that only had two model years in Canada (1992–93). Owners report serious body hardware deficiencies (not paint or rust, however), in addition to brake, exhaust, electrical, and ignition problems. Prices vary between $3,000 and $4,000, depending on the model chosen.

Hyundai—Pony and **Stellar.** Two of the worst South Korean small cars ever imported into Canada. Their most serious problems involved electrical and fuel system failures causing fires, no-starts, stalling, and chronic engine hesitation. Stellars have irreparable suspension, steering, and brake deficiencies that make them dangerous to drive. These cars were shooting stars that captured lots of sales in the '80s during their first few years on the market—and then crashed once word got around that they were unsafe and unreliable.

The **Excel** is a low-tech and low-quality economy car that was orphaned in 1995. Resale prices are low ($500 for an '88; $2,500 for a '94), but these cars are no bargain in the long run. Although overall comfort and handling are passable, the engine is distinctly short on power and the carburetor provides uneven throttle response, especially when the car is cold, which results in difficult starts. Poor interior ventilation, with chronic window fogging and poor defrosting, is particularly irritating.

Likely problem areas are defective constant velocity joints, water pumps, oil-pan gaskets, oil pressure switches, front struts, and heat exchange under dash, as well as a leaking head gasket. Excels made after 1989 are noted for their noisy automatic transmissions and engines that fail to start when the weather turns cold or wet. Other problem areas include faulty radiator hoses, alternators, Hyundai radios, and wiper motors. Owners also complain of premature brake wear and temperamental carburetors, electrical problems, poor engine performance, and premature rusting due to poor-quality body parts and paint. Body construction is sloppy, giving rise to wind/water leaks, rattles, and breakage. Mufflers last a little over two years. During its 1988–94 model run, the Excel racked up poor crash-safety scores for the '88 and '89 models, but garnered above average scores in the following model years.

An Excel cross-dressing as a sports car, the 1991–95 **Scoupe** is essentially a cute coupe with an engine more suited to high gas mileage than hard driving. Plenty of interior room up front, but the roof is too angular; if you're short and have to pull the seat up, your head almost touches the roof. The rear interior room is inadequate. The Scoupe is fuel-efficient, has a good heating and ventilation system, and has posted above average crashworthiness scores.

Selling for $3,000–$5,500, this is far from a performance car, mainly due to the Excel's underpinnings and drivetrain. The 4-speed automatic transmission robs the base engine of much needed horsepower, making for poor acceleration on inclines and constant shifting between 2500 rpms and 3500 rpms when pushed. Suspension may be too firm for some. There's plenty of body roll in turns, and mediocre steering. Brakes are hard to modulate.

Body construction is sloppy, giving rise to wind/water leaks, rattles, and breakage. Lots of engine and road noise intrude into the interior. Owners also report frequent transmission glitches, electrical system shorts, and brake and wheel bearing problems.

Jaguar—All models were affected by chronic fuel and electrical system shutdowns (Lucas, the electrical system supplier, is called "The Prince of Darkness" by the British motoring press). Other problems: powertrain failures, lousy body construction, poor parts supply, and few mechanics who want to repair these machines. Overall quality control has improved since 1995 with Ford at the helm, but servicing is still spotty and prices are way too high.

Lada—Discontinued a few years ago, these cheap Russian imports ($500–$2,500 for 1990–97 models) incorporate a 20-year-old rear-drive design and use poor-quality body and mechanical components. They're noisy and trucklike on the road, and the dealer network is sparse, making parts hard to get.

Defective fuel and ignition systems (particularly the ignition control module) and a poorly designed electrical system are the most common problems. Frequent carburetor replacements, at $325 plus tax, are rendered necessary due to the butterfly shaft warping or corroding—the result of an inherently defective design. Front brakes need to be replaced often, and transmissions, engine head gaskets, and differentials aren't durable either. Rear window defogger wires corrode easily.

Ladas are poorly rustproofed and paint quality is bad, which translates into rapid surface rusting and sheet metal perforation. They've also never been crash-tested.

Lincoln—Versailles. Problem areas: brake, electrical and fuel systems, and suspension defects. Early front-wheel drive **Continentals** were particularly unreliable due to chronic transmission, computer module, electrical system, and fuel system glitches.

Passport/Isuzu—The **I-Mark, Stylus**, and **Optima** compacts were sold from 1988 until 1992 and can be bought for $1,500–$2,500, depending upon the year and model. Repair costs are higher than average due to the cars' mediocre reliability and the difficulty in finding parts at a reasonable cost. Be especially wary of transmission defects, front brake rotor warpage, and poor body construction. 1988–89 models garnered below average crash test scores, while the last three model years (1990–92) did quite well.

Renault—All models suffer from fuel and electrical system failures, poor quality CV joints and brakes, no parts, and few mechanics. The Renault 10, 12, 18, and Fuego were the worst of a bad lot. The Renault 5, the last model sold in North America wasn't as bad as its predecessors.

Saab—All models through 1995 have been beset by electrical fires, short circuits, hard-to-find parts, and few competent mechanics. Much improved after 1995.

Dacia, **Skoda, and Yugo**—Cheap, unreliable, Eastern European imports, a step below Lada. Reliability problems affect mostly the powertrain, brakes, electrical and fuel systems, and sloppy body construction.

Volkswagen—The original **Beetle** was cheap to own but deadly to drive. Its main deficiencies: poorly anchored, unsafe front seats; a heater that never worked (fortunately, we were too young and hot-blooded in those days to notice); fuel tank placement that was dangerous in collisions; and poorly-designed wheels and seat tracks. The **Camper** minivan was safer, but less reliable, with engine, transmission, fuel system, and heater failings. **Rabbit/Dasher** and **411/412** models are known for unreliable powertrain, electrical, cooling, and fuel systems; ineffective and poor quality brakes; hard-to-find parts; and non-existent servicing.

Sold 1987–93, the **Fox** now costs $1,500–$2,500. With its old design, it can't offer the mechanical or interior efficiency that newer small cars provide. Other failings are the absence of power steering and an automatic transmission. It's true that these cars are fun to drive, but they have a checkered reputation as far as reliability and durability are concerned. Furthermore, as time goes on, these cars become more troublesome and difficult to repair. Crashworthiness, as tested by NHTSA, is way below average.

Owners report common failures with engine timing belts, starter motors, the heating system, and brake cylinders. Other problem areas include electrical, engine cooling, and fuel systems. The manual transmission shift linkage needs frequent adjustment, and the front brakes and shocks, as on most VWs, need more frequent servicing than those of comparable makes.

VW's **Scirocco** is fun to drive, but risky to own. You'll like its nimble handling, strong and responsive engine, and tight steering. You'll like a lot less the car's chronic breakdowns, parts shortages, and poor crashworthiness. Electrical short circuits, chronic fuel supply problems, premature front brake wear, and fragile body parts are common owner complaints. Sold 1985–89, expect to pay $1,500–$2,500, depending upon the model year.

Selling for $5,000–$12,500, the 1990–95 **Corrado** is an attractive, mid-sized, two-door coupe with a comfortable interior for the driver and front passenger. It gives good all-round performance, with the accent on smooth acceleration, a firm but not harsh ride, and excellent handling with little body roll. So why is it not recommended? Poor reliability, hard-to-find parts, limited servicing outlets, and undetermined crashworthiness. The following systems can be particularly troublesome: heating, defrosting, brake, electrical, and fuel. Plus, both the engine and transmission are problematic.

Appendix II
Best Internet Gripe Sites

Websites come and go. Please email lemonaid@earthlink.net if you find
a site has closed down or moved. Also let me know if you have discovered a website that should be included in next year's *Lemon-Aid* guides.
Sites like Chrysler Defective Transmissions (*http://badtrans.webprovider.
com/home.htm*), Ford Suckz (*http://members.xoom.com/fordsuckz/
index.html*), and My VW Lemon (*http://www.myvwlemon.com*) can be easily copied if you wish to set up your own protest/gripe site.

Consumer Protection

Auto Extremist (*http://www.autoextremist.com/*) The bare-knuckled,
unvarnished, high-octane truth about the entire auto industry. This site
provides unusually comprehensive vehicle reviews, auto industry facts
and rumours, and acerbic comments.

Automobile Protection Association (*http://www.apa.ca/*) Phil Edmonston
and the Center for Auto Safety founded this non-profit national consumers association in Montreal in the late 60s. Since then, the group has
fought for safer vehicles and exposed many scams associated with new car
sales, leasing, and repairs. The Association fights for its members through
mediation and makes invoice prices for new vehicles available to non-
members for a $55 fee.

CBC *Marketplace* (*http://cbc.ca/consumers/market/files/cars/index.html*)
Marketplace, the CBC's premiere national consumer show, pulls no
punches in exposing scams and reporting on automaker mistakes. In
fact, its site has extensive links and in-depth reports on Chrysler paint
delamination, ABS brake failures, and a host of other automotive top-
ics that private broadcasters are afraid to touch. *Marketplace* is also useful for giving consumer groups national exposure in their battles with
automakers.

Center for Auto Safety (*http://www.autosafety.org*) Set up in 1970 to provide consumers a voice for auto safety and quality and to help lemon
owners fight back across the United States, the Center for Auto Safety
(CAS) was founded by Ralph Nader and Consumers Union. CAS collects complaints and provides a lawyer referral service to its members.

The Complaint Station (*http://www.thecomplaintstation.com/*) This site
provides a central location to file your complaints or research previous
complaints, which are grouped according to auto manufacturer, tire
company, or retailer.

Consumer Reports **and** ***Consumers Union*** (*http://consumerreports.org/*) It costs $3.95 a month to subscribe online, but CR's database is chock full of comparison tests and in-depth stories on products and services. It's also a great place to get replacement tire ratings. Be aware that some of the top-rated tires and other products either aren't sold in Canada or are sold under a different name. Another disappointment: your $3.95 subscription is *automatically* renewed each month, unless you specifically ask for it to be canceled.

Lemon-Aid (*http://lemonaidcars.com/*) The official website sponsored by the *Lemon-Aid* guides. Quick, easy, and free access to confidential service bulletins, owner complaints, recalls, and defect investigations. Includes a Secret Warranty Watch, paint delamination jurisprudence, and tips for making a successful claim.

Auto Safety

Airbag killer sites (*http://www.gov.on.ca/health/english/program/ pubhealth/phero/phero_199906.html* and *www.plescia.org/indexair.htm*) The above sites will give you anecdotal evidence of drivers and passengers who have been severely injured by airbags in low-speed collisions or who have loved ones that were killed. The last website is a recent Canadian study that concludes airbags are dangerous to women who wear seatbelts.

NHTSA (*http://www.nhtsa.dot.gov/cars/problems/*) Run by the Big Daddy of federal government auto safety regulators, National Highway Traffic Safety Administration, has a comprehensive database covering owner complaints, recall campaigns, defect investigations initiated by the department, and automaker service bulletin summaries that may not be found in the ALLDATA database. Best of all, this data is easily accessed by typing in your vehicle's year, make, and model

Insurance Institute for Highway Safety (*http://www.hwysafety.org/*) A dazzling site that's long on crash photos and graphs that show which vehicles are the most crashworthy.

The Safety Forum (*http://www.safetyforum.com*) This is an awesome kickbutt site that shines a light on corporate weasels who make unsafe products. It contains comprehensive news archives and links to useful sites, plus names of court-recognized experts on everything from unsafe tires and Chrysler minivan latches to dangerous van conversions.

Strategic Safety (*http://www.strategicsafety.com/mainindex.html*) The people who blew the whistle on dangerous Firestone Wilderness and ATX tires, this firm is founded by a former "Nader Raider" in partnership with a trial lawyer specializing in product liability cases. Strategic Safety provides research, investigation, analysis, and education on safety issues.

Transport Canada (*http://www.tc.gc.ca/roadsafety/Recalls/search_e.asp*)
Cybersurfers can access the recall database for 1970–2000 model vehicles, but, unlike NHTSA's website, owner complaints aren't listed, defect investigations aren't disclosed, and service bulletin summaries aren't provided. And you can't complain on-line. Buyers wishing to know if a vehicle can be imported into Canada from Europe or the States can get a list of admissible vehicles (those that conform to Canadian federal safety and pollution regulations) at *http://www.tc. gc.ca/roadsafety/rsimp_e.htm#US,* or by calling the Registrar of Imported Vehicles at 1-800-511-7755.

Trujillo vs. Volvo (*http://www.law.emory.edu/1circuit/mar98/97-1792.01a. html*) This lawsuit provides an interesting, though lengthy, dissertation on the safety hazards that airbags pose and why automakers are ultimately responsible for the injuries and deaths caused by their deployment.

Information/Mediation/Protest

BMW
The Unofficial BMW Lemon Site (*http://www.bmwlemon.com*)
Everything you wanted to know, or maybe didn't want to know, about factory-related defects affecting the 3 Series, 5 Series, and 7 Series, V8-equipped models. Plus a useful link to Dodge Dakota lemon sites (go figure).

Chrysler
Chrysler Paint Problems (*http://www.coymedia.com/lemon.shtml*)

Chrysler Peeling Paint Page (*http://peelingpaint.homestead.com/*) This is an incredibly comprehensive site that's gives you easy, step-by-step procedures to follow in order to get Chrysler to repaint your vehicle for free. This site *must* be your starting point in dealing with Chrysler for paint or any other problem.

Chrysler Products' Problem Web Page (*http://www.wam.umd.edu/~ gluckman/Chrysler/*) This page was designed to be a resource for Chrysler owners who have had problems in dealing with Chrysler, including issues with peeling paint, transmission failure, the Chrysler-installed Bendix-10 ABS, and other maladies.

Chrysler Owner Review Committee (*rar17@daimlerchrysler.com*) No, you won't read about Chrysler Canada's newest consumer complaint committee in your owner's manual or see it touted anywhere at your local dealership. Chrysler's Review Committee was set up in February 1998 by Robert Renaud (the email address above) in response to the bad publicity and threats of court action coming from Chrysler Lemon Owners Groups (CLOGs). These groups have succeeded in getting sizeable refunds for brake, transmission, and paint repairs. If you have had any of these problems and want "goodwill" repairs or a refund for repairs already carried out, go through Chrysler's regular customer relations hotline. If you're not satisfied by the response you get, phone Lou Spadotto, the National Service Manager, Parts, Service, and Engineering at tel.: 519-973-2300; fax: 519-561-7005.

Chrysler Transmissions An essential site for getting a refund for any Chrysler premature automatic transmission failure is *http://badtrans. webprovider.com/home.htm>http://badtrans.webprovider.com/home.htm.* A useful forum for Chrysler minivan owners with tranny failures is *http://www.aei.ca/%7egregoire/claude.html>http://www.aei.ca/ %7egregoire/claude.html.* Complaints in French accepted.

Chrysler 300M Lemon (*http://www.geocities.com/MotorCity/Flats/7501/*)

Chrysler-Plymouth-Dodge Central (*http://www.allpar.com/*) This is an excellent website that's jam-packed with historical information, tips on fixing common problems inexpensively, and advice on how to deal with Chrysler representatives and technical service managers.

CLOGs (Chrysler Lemon Owners' Groups) These protest groups, originally formed in British Columbia and New Brunswick, have been incredibly effective in getting fair treatment from Chrysler (see Chrysler Owner Review Committee, above). Currently the most active group seems to be CLOG Alberta. If you own a Chrysler vehicle with paint, automatic transmission, engine head gasket, ABS brake, or air conditioning problems, contact CLOG Alberta founder Chris Ekstrom. He's been helping Chrysler owners across the country through referrals to the company and "Lemon Parades" in front of Chrysler and Mercedes dealerships. Email Chris at clog_alberta@hotmail.com.

Defective Dodge Transmission Site (*http://badtrans.webprovider.com/ index.htm*)

Dodge Caravan Lemon (*http://www.geocities.com/Baja/Mesa/7135/*)

Dodge Dakota Lemon (*http://www.madisoncountydodge.com/*)

Dodge Dakota Lemon (*http://members.xoom.com/rhyder/Dodge_Dakota/ Lemon_/lemon_.html*)

Dodge Dakota Lemon (*http://www.watsonville.com/dakota*)

Dodge Durango Lemon (*http://www.tecinfo.com/~rsguy2/Durango.htm*)

Dodge Ram Lemon (*http://sites.netscape.com/bharrisgte/cybil*)

Neon Enthusiasts Page (*http://neons.org/index.html*) Good source for technical information and troubleshooting tips. Lots of service bulletins. Chrysler's engine headgasket service bulletin can be downloaded to reinforce your claim for a free engine repair on many of Chrysler's 4-cylinder engines (*http://neons.org/neontsb/TSB/09/090598.htm*).

Daewoo
Daewoo Complaints (*http://www.badcustomerservice.co.uk/press.htm*) This 2000 Galant owner set up this site after his new Daewoo burned up and the automaker wouldn't make good on its claim that it would replace the vehicle.

Ford
British Columbia Dead Ford Owners' Page (*http://modena. intergate.ca/personal/djk/*) Dead Ford is a play on the acronym F. O. R. D.: "Found on the Road, Dead." The site is a useful gathering place for Ford car, truck, sport-utility, minivan, and van owners who discuss common problems and solutions. Includes important links to other Ford protest sites.

Ford Contour/Mystique (*http://www.contour.org/FAQ/*) This website provides a comprehensive listing of common problems and fixes affecting the Ford Contour, Mercury Mystique, and European-sold Mondeo.

Ford Diesel Website (*http://www.Ford-diesel.com*) Everything from engine cavitation repairs, servicing tips, discounted parts, and lots of other diesel links are found on this independently-run site.

Ford Insider Info (*http://www.blueovalnews.com*) Set up by a Ford Mustang enthusiast living in the Detroit area, this website is the place to go for all the latest insider info on the company's activities.

Ford Paint Delamination/Peeling (*http://www.ihs2000.com/~peel*) Everything you should know about the cause and treatment of Ford paint delamination. Useful links to other sites and tips on dealing with Ford and GM paint problems.

Ford Suckz (*http://members.xoom.com/fordsuckz/index.html*) An excellent site set up by a Sable owner who succeeded in getting Ford to refund his engine repair costs. Lots of helpful links to other sites.

Ford Trucks "Suck" (*http://www.fordtruckssuck.com/*)

Ford Windstar Faulty Engine Head Gaskets (*http://home.att.net/ ~ccatanese/ford/*) This is the most comprehensive site relating to faulty engine gaskets on Ford's 3.8L and 4.2L engines. Plenty of technical help supported by internal service bulletins and extended warranties you can download. Many links to other helpful sites.

Taurus Transmission Victims (*http://members.aol.com/MKBradley/ index.html*) A great site for learning about Ford's biodegradable automatic transmissions (1991–99) from Continental Taurus, Sable, and Windstar owners. Expert mechanics give the why and how. Useful for small claims court technical explanations.

GM
GM Paint Delamination/Peeling Unfortunately, there's no longer a single website that relates to all the GM cars, trucks, minivans, and vans afflicted by this defect. Nevertheless, there are many sites where the problem is discussed for specific vehicles. Simply access Alta Vista or any other browser and type in "GM paint delamination," or "GM peeling paint."

GMC Safari Paint Delamination (*http://members.home.net/ssbassi/ index.htm*) A pictorial presentation of the paint delamination problem affecting this man's 1992 Safari minivan. Some useful links and owner feedback pages.

GM Saturn Exposed (*http://www.saturnexposed.com*) Go beyond the GM Saturn hype and learn why Saturn owners call their car "a different kind of headache." Plenty of owner summaries, service tips, and links to other Saturn gripe sites.

GM Suburban Lemons (*http://www.gmclemon.com*) Covers faulty brakes, verbal duels with callous GM reps, fuel leaks, corroded battery cables and short circuits. Lot of links to other gripe sites, copies of service bulletins relating to Suburban defects (brakes, especially), and summaries of complaints from other owners. (Incidentally, GM bought back this owner's Suburban, shortly after his website went up.)

GMAC Sucks (*http://www.gmacsucks.com*) An online complaint forum about GMAC and General Motors set up by a U.S. Army veteran whose vehicle was repossessed while he was stationed in Kosovo. Lots of links to other gripe sites as well as complaint summaries.

Kia
Do Not Buy a Kia (*http://members.tripod.com/aiki_joe/kia/index.html*) A wonderfully comprehensive site set up by a dissatisfied Kia Sephia owner. A compendium of Kia reviews and owner comments from diverse sources around the country.

Volkswagen
VW Lemon Page (*http://www.myvwlemon.com/ubb/Forum3/HTML/ 000002.html*)

Sport-Utilities/RVs

The Roadhog Info Trough (*http://www.suv.org*)

The RV Home Page (*http://www.rvhome.com*) An impressive website that offers an incredible amount of consumer information. Newsgroups, bulletin boards, maps, road and traffic conditions, new- and used-vehicle price guides, and technical advice are given in a slick, easy-to-download manner. There's also a link to the RV Consumer group—a non-profit association that publicizes and mediates owner complaints.

RV Links (*http://walden.mvp.net/~vdrex/links.htm*) Over 110 RV links from the obscure to the essential.

SUV On Line (*http://www.suv.com*) Everything you probably didn't want to know, about the joys and frustrations of sport-utility ownership. Over 75 bulletin boards containing owner comments. Lots of technical advice.

Information/Services

ALLDATA Service Bulletins (*http://www.alldata.com/consumer/TSB/yr.html*) Free summaries of automotive recalls and technical service bulletins are listed by year, make, model and engine option. NHTSA and, ALLDATA summaries are so short and cryptic, they're of limited usefulness. You can't see the contents of individual bulletins unless you purchase for about $20 U.S. a CD-ROM disc that holds all the bulletins that pertain to your vehicle. One caveat: BMW and Honda have refused to allow ALLDATA to distribute their service bulletins to customers.

The Auto Channel (*http://www.theautochannel.com/*) This website gives you comprehensive information useful in choosing a new or used vehicle, filing a claim for compensation, or linking up with other owners.

Automobile News Groups These news groups are compilations of email raves and gripes. They cover all makes and models and fall into four distinct areas: rec.autos.makers.chrysler (you can add any automaker's name at the end); rec.autos.tech; rec.autos.driving; and rec.autos.misc.

Autopedia (*http://autopedia.com/index.html*) An automotive encyclopedia, Autopedia offers a compendium of automotive-related information. Its legal section and lemon law listings by state are particularly helpful.

BBC TV's *Top Gear* **Car Reviews** (*http://www.topgear.beeb.com/*) Britain's automotive equivalent to CBC's Marketplace, *Top Gear* blows the whistle on the best and worst European-sold vehicles, auto products, and industry practices.

Canadian Driver (*http://www.canadiandriver.com/reviews/index.htm*) A well-written and up-to-date collection of articles and links to other sites that will appeal to drivers on both sides of the border.

Carfax (*http://www.carfax.com/*) If you suspect a used vehicle is a rebuilt wreck, use Carfax (tel.: 1-888-422-7329) to carry out a background check to see if the vehicle has been "scrapped," had flood damage, is stolen, or shows incorrect mileage on the odometer. There's a fee of $14.95 U.S. ($23.39 Cdn.) if the order is placed via the Internet. An initial, free search on the Internet will confirm whether or not your vehicle is listed in the database. A word of caution, though. If you are sure of the vehicle's history, don't be misled. I was told that the "database contains 6 important vehicle history records…. These 6 records confirm a clean history or reveal costly hidden problems…." I paid the fee and was given a list showing the six times my car was taken in for a mandatory emissions test.

Cartrackers (*http://www.cartrackers.com*) This is a large site that has a nice balance of the pro and cons of car ownership. Its technical resources are impressive and there are experts to advise you on everything from secret warranties to simple maintenance. Plenty of useful links, particularly the one to the Ford Explorer message board for SUV owners at *http://www.4x4central.com.*

The David Ingram Show (*http://www.mediaontap.com/aroundtheworld*) Vancouver-based financial consultant David Ingram produces an award-winning weekly TV show carried by Rogers Cable and the Internet. His show covers all the scams, from the political world to the auto industry. He's an excellent source of information for consumers and his show has far more influence than its viewing audience would suggest. I have appeared on his show several times and those interviews are archived on his site.

Kelley Blue Book Prices and Ratings (*http://www.kbb.com*) Providing over nine million free reports every month, the Kelley Blue Book site is an excellent price guide. It gives free new- and used-car pricing reports on its site. *http://www.edmunds*.com provides a similar service.

Phil Bailey's Auto World (*http://www2.cronomagic.com/pages/baileycar/index.htm*) I've known Phil Bailey for years. He's been advising Montreal motorists for several decades on local radio shows. His strong opinions about airbag dangers and the best and worst new and used cars are well supported. He owns his own garage and specializes in the diagnosis and repair of foreign cars, particularly British ones. He's also very knowledgeable about American and Japanese imports.

Women's Garage (*www.womensgarage.com*) Three Canadian mechanics with almost 100 years cumulative experience set up this site to advise motorists on the maintenance and repair of all motor vehicles.